W9-APS-336

СОДЕРЖАНИЕ

TABLES BY COUNTRY - TABLEAUX PAR PAYS - ТАБЛИЦЫ ПО СТРАНАМ

COUNTRY	PAYS	СТРАНЫ	Table - Tableau - Таблица							
			1	2	3	4	5	6	7	8
Albania	Albanie	Албания	19	24	33	-	-	-	73	78
Andorra	Andorre	Андорра	-	-	-	-	-	-	-	-
Armenia	Arménie	Армения	19	24	33	-	-	-	73	78
Austria	Autriche	Австрия	19	24	33	50	55	64	73	78
Azerbaijan	Azerbaïdjan	Азербайджан	19	24	34	50	55	64	73	78
Belarus	Bélarus	Беларусь	19	24	34	50	55	64	73	78
Belgium	Belgique	Бельгия	19	24	34	50	55	64	73	78
Bosnia and Herzegovina	Bosnie-Herzégovine	Босния и Герцеговина	19	25	35	-	55	64	73	78
Bulgaria	Bulgarie	Болгария	19	25	35	50	55	64	73	78
Canada	Canada	Канада	19	25	35	50	56	65	73	78
Croatia	Croatie	Хорватия	19	25	36	50	56	65	73	79
Cyprus	Chypre	Кипр	-	-	-	-	-	-	-	-
Czech Republic	République tchèque	Чешская Республика	19	25	36	50	56	65	73	79
Denmark	Danemark	Дания	19	25	36	50	56	-	73	79
Estonia	Estonie	Эстония	20	26	37	50	56	65	74	79
Finland	Finlande	Финляндия	20	26	37	50	56	65	74	79
France	France	Франция	20	26	37	50	57	65	74	79
Georgia	Géorgie	Грузия	20	26	38	51	57	66	74	79
Germany	Allemagne	Германия	20	26	38	51	57	66	74	79
Greece	Grèce	Греция	20	26	38	51	57	66	74	79
Hungary	Hongrie	Венгрия	20	27	39	51	57	66	74	80
Iceland	Islande	Исландия	-	-	-	-	-	-	-	-
Ireland	Irlande	Ирландия	20	27	39	51	57	66	74	80
Israel	Israël	Израиль	20	27	39	51	58	66	74	80
Italy	Italie	Италия	20	27	40	51	58	67	74	80
Kazakhstan	Kazakhstan	Казахстан	20	27	40	51	58	67	74	80
Kyrgyzstan	Kirghizistan	Кыргызстан	20	27	40	51	58	67	74	80
Latvia	Lettonie	Латвия	21	28	41	51	58	67	75	80
Liechtenstein	Liechtenstein	Лихтенштейн	-	-	-	-	-	-	-	-
Lithuania	Lituanie	Литва	21	28	41	51	58	67	75	80
Luxembourg	Luxembourg	Люксембург	21	28	41	51	59	67	75	80
Malta	Malte	Мальта	-	-	-	-	-	-	-	-
Monaco	Monaco	Монако	-	-	-	-	-	-	-	-
Netherlands	Pays-Bas	Нидерланды	21	28	42	52	59	68	75	81
Norway	Norvège	Норвегия	21	28	42	52	59	68	75	81
Poland	Pologne	Польша	21	28	42	52	59	68	75	81
Portugal	Portugal	Португалия	21	29	43	52	59	68	75	81
Republic of Moldova	République de Moldova	Республика Молдова	21	29	43	52	59	68	75	81
Romania	Roumanie	Румыния	21	29	43	52	60	68	75	81
Russian Federation	Fédération de Russie	Российская Федерация	21	29	44	52	60	69	75	81
San Marino	Saint-Marin	Сан-Марино	-	-	-	-	-	-	-	-
Slovakia	Slovaquie	Словакия	21	29	44	52	60	69	75	81
Slovenia	Slovénie	Словения	21	29	44	52	60	69	75	81
Spain	Espagne	Испания	22	30	45	52	60	69	76	82
Sweden	Suède	Швеция	22	30	45	52	60	69	76	82
Switzerland	Suisse	Швейцария	22	30	45	-	61	69	76	82
Tajikistan	Tadjikistan	Таджикистан	22	30	46	52	61	70	76	82
The former Yugoslav Republic of Macedonia	L'ex-République yougoslave de Macédoine	Бывшая Югославская Республика Македония	22	30	46	53	61	70	76	82
Turkey	Turquie	Турция	22	30	46	53	61	70	76	82
Turkmenistan	Turkménistan	Туркменистан	22	31	47	53	61	70	76	82
Ukraine	Ukraine	Украина	22	31	47	53	61	70	76	82
United Kingdom	Royaume-Uni	Соединенное Королевство	22	31	47	-	62	-	76	82
United States	Etats-Unis	Соединенные Штаты	22	31	48	-	62	70	76	83
Uzbekistan	Ouzbékistan	Узбекистан	22	31	48	53	62	71	76	83
Yugoslavia	Yougoslavie	Югославия	22	31	48	-	62	71	76	83

TABLES BY COUNTRY - TABLEAUX PAR PAYS - ТАБЛИЦЫ ПО СТРАНАМ

Table - Tableau - Таблица

9	10	10 (a)	10 (b)	10 (c)	11	11 (a)	11 (b)	12	13	14	15	16	17	18	19	20	21	22
87	94	-	-	-	130	-	-	153	-	169	175	-	-	-	215	223	-	-
-	-	-	-	-	-	-	-	-	-	-	-	-	-	-	-	-	-	-
87	94	-	-	118	-	-	-	153	-	-	-	-	-	-	-	-	-	-
87	94	104	110	118	130	138	144	153	162	169	176	205	210	211	215	-	231	-
87	94	-	110	-	-	-	-	153	-	-	-	-	-	-	215	223	-	-
87	94	-	110	-	-	-	-	153	-	169	-	-	-	-	-	-	-	-
87	94	104	110	118	130	138	-	153	162	169	177	205	-	-	215	223	231	237
87	-	-	-	-	-	-	-	-	-	-	-	-	-	-	-	-	-	-
87	95	-	110	-	130	138	144	154	162	169	178	205	210	211	215	223	231	237
87	95	-	-	-	-	-	-	154	-	-	-	205	-	-	-	223	-	237
88	95	104	110	119	130	138	144	154	162	169	179	205	-	211	215	223	231	237
88	95	104	111	-	130	138	-	-	-	-	-	-	-	-	-	223	-	237
88	95	104	111	119	-	-	-	154	162	170	180	205	-	-	216	-	231	-
88	95	104	111	119	131	-	-	154	162	-	-	-	-	-	216	223	-	237
88	96	-	111	120	131	-	-	154	-	170	181	206	-	-	-	223	-	-
88	96	105	111	120	131	138	145	155	163	170	182	206	-	-	-	224	231	238
88	96	105	111	120	131	139	145	155	163	170	183	206	-	-	216	224	232	238
88	96	-	112	-	-	-	-	155	-	-	-	-	-	-	-	224	-	-
88	96	105	112	121	131	139	145	155	163	170	184	206	210	211	216	224	232	238
89	96	-	-	-	131	-	146	155	-	-	-	-	-	-	-	224	232	-
89	97	105	112	121	132	139	146	155	163	170	185	206	210	211	216	-	232	-
89	97	105	112	121	132	139	146	-	163	-	-	-	-	-	-	224	-	238
89	97	105	112	122	132	139	-	156	163	-	-	-	-	-	-	224	-	238
89	97	-	-	-	132	-	-	156	164	-	-	-	-	-	-	224	-	-
89	97	106	112	-	132	139	-	156	164	171	186	206	-	-	216	224	-	-
89	97	106	113	122	-	-	-	156	-	171	187	207	-	-	217	-	-	-
-	98	-	113	122	-	-	-	156	-	171	188	207	-	-	-	-	232	-
89	98	106	113	123	132	140	147	156	164	171	189	-	-	-	217	224	232	238
-	-	-	-	-	-	-	-	-	-	-	-	-	-	-	-	-	-	-
89	98	106	113	123	133	140	-	157	-	171	190	207	-	-	217	225	-	238
90	98	-	113	123	133	-	-	157	-	171	191	207	-	-	-	-	233	-
90	98	106	113	124	133	140	147	-	164	-	-	-	-	-	-	225	-	239
-	-	-	-	-	-	-	-	-	-	-	-	-	-	-	-	-	-	-
90	98	-	114	124	133	140	147	157	164	172	192	207	-	-	217	225	233	239
90	99	106	114	-	133	140	148	157	-	-	-	-	-	-	217	225	-	-
90	99	-	114	-	133	140	148	157	164	172	193	207	-	-	217	225	233	239
90	99	107	-	124	134	-	-	157	165	-	-	-	-	-	-	225	233	239
90	99	107	114	125	134	141	148	158	165	172	194	208	-	211	-	-	233	-
90	99	-	-	-	134	-	-	158	165	172	195	208	210	211	218	225	233	239
90	99	-	114	-	134	141	-	158	165	172	196	208	-	-	218	225	234	239
-	-	-	-	-	-	-	-	-	-	-	-	-	-	-	-	-	-	-
91	100	-	114	-	134	-	-	158	165	172	197	208	210	211	218	-	234	-
91	100	107	115	125	134	141	149	158	165	-	-	-	-	-	-	225	234	240
91	100	107	115	125	135	141	149	158	166	-	-	-	-	-	218	226	234	-
91	100	107	115	126	135	141	149	159	166	-	-	-	-	-	-	226	234	240
91	100	107	115	126	135	141	-	159	-	173	198	208	-	-	218	-	234	-
91	100	-	115	-	-	-	-	159	-	-	-	-	-	-	-	-	-	-
91	101	108	115	-	135	-	-	159	166	-	-	-	-	-	-	-	-	-
91	101	-	-	126	135	-	150	159	-	-	-	-	-	-	218	226	-	-
91	-	-	-	-	-	-	-	-	-	173	199	208	-	-	219	226	-	240
92	101	-	116	-	135	-	-	159	-	173	200	209	210	211	219	226	235	-
92	101	-	116	127	136	142	150	160	166	173	201	209	-	-	219	226	-	-
92	101	-	-	127	136	-	-	160	166	173	202	209	-	-	219	226	235	-
92	-	-	-	-	-	-	-	-	-	-	-	-	-	-	-	-	-	-
92	101	-	-	-	-	-	-	160	166	173	203	209	210	211	219	226	-	-

EXPLANATORY NOTES

Introduction

The **Annual Bulletin of Transport Statistics for Europe and North America**, published by the United Nations Economic Commission for Europe (UN/ECE), provides basic data on transport activity in the ECE Region (List of ECE member countries on the following page). Data in this publication covers transport activity; transport equipment and transport infrastructure by mode (rail, road, inland waterway, maritime, intermodal and oil pipeline). General information on population, energy consumption in transport and on road traffic accidents are also provided.

This publication , as well as the Bulletin on Statistics of Road Traffic Accidents in Europe and North America[1], are produced under the auspices of the UN/ECE Inland Transport Committee. Its subsidiary body, the Working Party on Transport Statistics, administers the annual collection of data from ECE member countries and, at the same time, aims to harmonize transport statistics at the international level.

Sources

The statistics appearing in this Bulletin are collected by means of a Common Questionnaire, developed jointly by UN/ECE, Eurostat and the European Conference of Ministers of Transport (ECMT). Data are submitted by Central Statistical Offices and other official national and international sources.

Comparability of data

Terminology used in this publication is defined in the Annex which corresponds to the Glossary for Transport Statistics (second edition, ECE/TRANS/NONE/98/8). Where individual series differ fundamentally from the agreed definitions and/or the coverage is incomplete, this is indicated in footnotes.

Time period

The statistics are presented in the form of time series. Figures are given for 1999, 1998 and for 1990 (base year).

Units of measurement

The units of measurement are indicated in each table. Unless otherwise stated, they are metric.

Rounding

Where necessary, each figure has been rounded to the nearest final digit. For this reason, there may occur in some series a slight discrepancy between the sum of the constituent items and the totals shown.

Revisions

In general, the data for the last year should be considered provisional; those for previous years final.

---

[1] Statistics of Road Traffic Accidents in Europe and North America, 2001 edition; (UN Sales No. E/F/R.01.II.E.13).

Symbols and abbreviations employed

*	=	Secretariat estimate.
.	=	Not applicable.
:	=	Not available.
-	=	Magnitude zero.
0	=	Magnitude not zero, but less than half of unit employed.
km	=	Kilometre.
kg	=	Kilogramme.
t, tonne	=	Metric tonne
tkm	=	Tonne-kilometre.
kW	=	Kilowatt.
TJ	=	Terajoule = 10^{12} joules.

UN/ECE member countries and nomenclature

As of January 1995, the Economic Commission for Europe had the following 55 member countries: Albania, Andorra, Armenia, Austria, Azerbaijan, Belarus, Belgium, Bosnia and Herzegovina, Bulgaria, Canada, Croatia, Cyprus, Czech Republic, Denmark, Estonia, Finland, France, Georgia, Germany, Greece, Hungary, Iceland, Ireland, Israel, Italy, Kazakhstan, Kyrgyzstan, Latvia, Liechtenstein, Lithuania, Luxembourg, Malta, Monaco, Netherlands, Norway, Poland, Portugal, Republic of Moldova, Romania, Russian Federation, San Marino, Slovakia, Slovenia, Spain, Sweden, Switzerland, Tajikistan, The former Yugoslav Republic of Macedonia, Turkey, Turkmenistan, Ukraine, United Kingdom, United States of America, Uzbekistan and Yugoslavia.

Unless otherwise indicated, data provided for Yugoslavia refer to the Federal Republic of Yugoslavia (Serbia and Montenegro).

Data inquiries

The Annual Bulletin for Transport Statistics is continuously reviewed, for possible revisions to its format or content and comments or suggestions for changes are thus encouraged. Please address your inquiries or comments to:

Transport Division
UN/ECE
Palais des Nations
CH-1211 Geneva 10
Switzerland

Telephone:	(+41-22) 917 1313
Telefax:	(+41-22) 917 0039
E-mail:	stat.trans@unece.org

NOTES EXPLICATIVES

Introduction

Le **Bulletin annuel de statistiques des transports pour l'Europe et l'Amérique du Nord**, publié par la Commission économique des Nations Unies pour l'Europe (CEE/ONU), fournit des données de base sur l'activité du secteur des transports dans la région de la CEE (voir la liste des pays membres de la CEE à la page suivante). Les données figurant dans cet ouvrage portent sur l'activité du secteur des transports, le matériel de transport et l'infrasructure des transports selon le mode (Chemins de fer, routes, voies navigables intérieures, transports maritimes, transports intermodaux et oléoducs). On y trouve également des informations générales sur la population , la consommation d'énergie dans les transports et les accidents de la circulation routière.

Le présent bulletin, ainsi que le bulletin intitulé Statistiques des accidents de la circulation routière en Europe et en Amérique du Nord [1], sont élaborés sous les auspices du Comité des transports intérieurs de la CEE/ONU. L'organe subsidiaire du Comité, le Groupe de travail des statistiques des transports, gère la collecte annuelle des données auprès des pays membres de la CEE et s'efforce parallèlement d'harmoniser les statistiques des transports au niveau international.

Sources

Les statistiques publiées dans le présent bulletin sont rassenblées au moyen d'un questionnaire commun élaboré conjointement par la CEE/ONU, Eurostat et la Conférence européenne des Ministres des transports (CEMT). Les données émanent des services statistiques nationaux et d'autres sources nationales et internationales officielles.

Comparabilité des données

Les termes employés dans le présent bulletin sont définis dans l'annexe, laquelle correspond au Glossaire des statistiques de transport (deuxième édition, ECE/TRANS/NONE/98/8). Lorsqu'une série s'écarte trop des définitions convenues ou que les données sont incomplètes, ces divergences sont signalées dans des notes.

Période couverte

Les statistiques sont présentées sous forme de séries chronologiques. Les chiffres se rapportent aux années 1999, 1998 et à l'année 1990, qui constitue l'année de référence.

Unités de mesure

Les unités de mesure sont indiquées dans chaque tableau. Sauf indication contraire, il s'agit d'unités métriques.

Arrondissement des chiffres

Chaque fois qu'on l'a jugé nécessaire, les chiffres ont été arrondis à l'unité du dernier chiffre significatif. Il peut donc y avoir, pour certaines séries, une légère différence entre la somme des éléments constituants et le total indiqué.

---

[1] Statistiques des accidents de la circulation routière en Europe et en Amérique du Nord, édition 2001; (numéro de vente : E/F/R.01.II.E.13).

Révisions

En général, les données relatives à la dernière année doivent être considérées comme provisoires tandis que celles des années précédentes peuvent être considérées comme définitives.

Signes et abréviations conventionnels

*	= Estimation du secrétariat.
.	= Ne s'applique pas.
...	= Aucune donnée disponible.
-	= Résultat rigoureusement nul.
0	= Résultat inférieur à la moitié de la dernière unité retenue.
km	= Kilomètre.
kg	= Kilogramme.
t, tonne	= Tonne métrique.
tkm	= Tonne-kilomètre.
kW	= Kilowatt.
TJ	= Térajoule = 10^{12} joules.

Pays membres de la CEE/ONU et nomenclature

Depuis janvier 1995, la Commission économique pour l'Europe comprenait les 55 pays membres suivants : Albanie, Allemagne, Andorre, Arménie, Autriche, Azerbaïdjan, Bélarus, Belgique, Bosnie-Herzégovine, Bulgarie, Canada, Chypre, Croatie, Danemark, Espagne, Estonie, Etats-Unis, Ex-République yougoslave de Macédoine, Fédération de Russie, Finlande, France, Géorgie, Grèce, Hongrie, Irlande, Islande, Israël, Italie, Kazakhstan, Kirghizistan, Lettonie, Liechtenstein, Lituanie, Luxembourg, Malte, Monaco, Norvège, Ouzbékistan, Pays-Bas, Pologne, Portugal, République de Moldova, République tchèque, Roumanie, Royaume-Uni, Saint-Marin, Slovaquie, Slovénie, Suède, Suisse, Tadjikistan, Turquie, Turkménistan, Ukraine et Yougoslavie.

Sauf indication contraire, les données fournies pour la Yougoslavie se rapportent à la République fédérative de Yougoslavie (Serbie et Montenegro).

Demandes de renseignements

Le bulletin annuel de statistiques des transports est examiné de façon suivie, aux fins de modifications éventuelles de sa présentation ou de son contenu; les commentaires et suggestions concernant des changements à apporter sont par conséquent les bienvenus. Pour tout commentaire ou demande de renseignements, s'adresser au service suivant :

Division des transport
CEE/ONU
Palais des Nations, CH-1211 Genève 10
Suisse

Téléphone:	(41-22) 917 1313
Téléfax:	(41-22) 917 00 39
Courrier électronique:	stat.trans@unece.org

ПОЯСНИТЕЛЬНЫЕ ПРИМЕЧАНИЯ

Введение

Ежегодный бюллетень европейской и североамериканской статистики транспорта, публикуемый Европейской экономической комиссией Организации Объединенных Наций (ЕЭК ООН), содержит базисные данные о транспортной деятельности в регионе ЕЭК (перечень стран - членов ЕЭК см. на следующей стр.). Содержащиеся в этой публикации данные охватывают транспортную деятельность; транспортное оборудование и транспортную инфраструктуру в разбивке по видам транспорта (железнодорожный, автомобильный, внутренний водный, морской транспорт, интермодальные перевозки и нефтепроводный транспорт). Представлена также общая информация о населении, потреблении энергии на транспорте и дорожно-транспортных происшествиях.

Настоящая публикация, а также Бюллетень статистики дорожно-транспортных происшествий в Европе и Северной Америке [1] издаются под эгидой Комитета по внутреннему транспорту ЕЭК ООН. Вопросами ежегодного сбора данных о странах - членах ЕЭК занимается его вспомогательный орган - Рабочая группа по статистике транспорта, которая в то же время стремится согласовать транспортную статистику на международном уровне

Источники

Сбор статистических данных, указанных в настоящем Бюллетене, осуществляется с помощью Общего вопросника, разработанного совместно ЕЭК ООН, Евростатом и ЕКМТ. Данные представляются центральными статистическими управлениями и другими официальными национальными и международными источниками.

Сопоставимость данных

Терминология, используемая в настоящей публикации, определена в приложении и соответствует Глоссарию по статистике транспорта (второе издание, ECE/TRANS/NONE/98/8). В тех случаях, когда отдельные ряды существенно отличаются от согласованных определений и/или охват неполный, это указывается в сносках.

Отчетный период

Статистические данные представляются в виде временны́х рядов. Цифры указываются за 1999, 1998 и 1990 годы (базовый год).

Единицы измерения

Единицы измерения приводятся в каждой таблице. Если не указано иное, речь идет о метрических единицах.

Округление

При необходимости каждая цифра округляется до ближайшего разряда. Поэтому в некоторых рядах данных могут иметь место небольшие расхождения между суммой данных по отдельным статьям и приведенными итогами.

---

[1] Статистика дорожно-транспортных происшествий в Европе и Северной Америке, издание 2001 года (публикация ООН, в продаже под № E/F/R.01.II.E.1).

Пересмотр данных

Как правило, данные за последний год следует считать предварительными, а данные за предыдущие годы - окончательными.

Условные обозначения и сокращения

*	= Оценка секретариата
.	= Не применимо
:	= Данные отсутствуют
-	= Нулевая величина
0	= Величина не нулевая, но меньше половины применяемой единицы измерения.
км	= Километр.
кт	= Килограмм.
т, тонна	= Метрическая тонна.
ткм	= Тонно-километр.
кВт	= Киловатт.
Тлж	= Тераджоуль (10^{12} джоулям).

Страны-члены и номенклатура ООН/ЕЭК

По состоянию на июль 1995 гола в состав Европейской экономической комиссии входили следующие 55 стран-членов: Австрия, Азербайджан, Албания, Андорра, Армения, Беларусь, Бельгия, Болгария, Босния и Герцеговина, Бывшая Югославская Республика Македония, Венгрия, Германия, Греция, Грузия, Дания, Израиль, Ирландия, Исландия, Испания, Италия, Казахстан, Канада, Кипр, Кыргызстан, Латвия, Литва, Лихтенштейн, Люксембург, Мальта, Монако, Нидерланды, Норвегия, Польша, Португалия, Республика Молдова, Российская Федерация, Румыния, Сан-Марино, Словакия, Словения, Соединенное Королевство, Соединенные Штаты Америки, Таджикистан, Туркменистан, Турция, Узбекистан, Украина, Финляндия, Франция, Хорватия, Чешская Республика, Швейцария, Швеция, Эстония, Югославия.

Если не указано иное, данные по Югославии за период до 1 января 1992 года относятся к Социалистической Федеративной Республике Югославии, которая состояла из шести республик, в то время как данные по Югославии за период после этой даты относятся к Союзной Республике Югославия, которая состоит из двух республик (Сербия и Черногория).

Запросы в отношении данных

ООН/ЕЭК с одобрением встретит любые замечания и предложения в отношении ее статистических бюллетеней. Все замечания или запросы должны направляться по следующему адресу :

Transport Division
UN/ECE
Palais des Nations
Switzerland
Телефон: (41-22)-917 1313
Телефакс: (41-22) 917 00 39
Электронная Почта: stat.trans@unece.org

A. Population and area of country
A. Population et superficie du pays
A. Численность населения и площадъ страны

Country	Population (1 000)			Area	Inhabitants per
	1980	1998	1999	km^2	km^2 1999
Albania	2 670	3 354	3 401	28 748	118
Andorra	...	60	66	468	141
Armenia	3 090	3 798	3 800	29 800	128
Austria	7 550	8 083	8 121	83 858	97
Azerbaijan	6 150	7 953	8 149	86 600	94
Belarus	9 630	10 179	9 990	207 600	48
Belgium	9 843	10 214	10 230	30 528	335
Bosnia and Herzegovina	...	3 800	3 850	51 197	75
Bulgaria	8 877	8 230	8 210	110 994	74
Canada	24 040	30 300	30 490	9 970 610	3
Croatia	4 590	4 501	4 381	56 542	77
Cyprus	630	663	667	9 251	72
Czech Republic	10 330	10 290	10 267	78 866	130
Denmark	5 122	5 314	5 349	43 094	124
Estonia	1 470	1 457	1 366	45 227	30
Finland	4 780	5 160	5 181	338 145	15
France	53 880	58 967	59 040	551 500	107
Georgia	5 060	5 445	4 946	69 700	71
Germany	78 000	82 037	82 163	357 022	230
Greece	9 587	10 516	10 522	131 957	80
Hungary	10 710	10 068	10 043	93 030	108
Iceland	230	274	280	103 000	3
Ireland	3 400	3 745	3 787	70 273	54
Israel	3 922	6 041	6 369	21 056	302
Italy	56 430	57 623	57 844	301 318	192
Kazakhstan	15 000	14 958	14 930	2 724 900	5
Kyrgyzstan	3 640	4 699	4 908	199 900	25
Latvia	2 510	2 439	2 366	64 589	37
Liechtenstein	25	31	0	160	0
Lithuania	3 420	3 702	3 693	65 300	57
Luxembourg	365	429	430	2 586	166
Malta	320	379	390	316	1 234
Monaco	...	30	32	2	16 000
Netherlands	14 140	15 760	15 810	41 526	381
Norway	4 090	4 432	44 910	323 758	139
Poland	35 580	38 667	38 644	312 685	124
Portugal	9 770	9 474	9 490	91 982	103
Republic of Moldova	4 100	3 651	3 644	33 851	108
Romania	22 200	22 503	22 430	238 391	94
Russian Federation	140 500	146 328	144 819	17 075 400	8
San Marino	...	30	30	61	492
Slovakia	4 980	5 393	5 400	49 036	110
Slovenia	1 901	1 978	1 990	20 273	98
Spain	37 540	39 277	39 420	505 992	78
Sweden	8 310	8 854	8 883	449 964	20
Switzerland	6 320	7 124	7 209	41 285	175
Tajikistan	3 970	6 188	6 240	143 100	44
The former Yugoslav Republic of Macedonia	1 890	2 008	2 031	25 713	79
Turkey	44 470	64 790	64 340	774 815	83
Turkmenistan	2 800	4 993	4 640	491 200	9
Ukraine	50 600	49 851	49 037	603 700	81
United Kingdom	56 330	59 340	58 058	242 900	239
United States	227 760	270 299	274 634	9 363 520	29
Uzbekistan	15 900	24 231	23 950	448 900	53
Yugoslavia	9 842	10 600	10 630	102 173	104

B. Consumption of energy in the transport sector
B. Consommation d'énergie dans le secteur du transport
B. Потребление энергии в транспортном секторе

Country	Total (TJ) 1999	of which in %					% share in total final energy consumption	
		Air	Road	Rail	IWT*	Pipeline	1980	1999
Albania	8 749	-	100.0	-	-	-	20.9	29.1
Armenia	2 428	37.9	43.1	0.0	...	...	...	6.0
Austria	273 346	8.6	84.8	3.4	...	3.1	23.2	27.0
Azerbaijan	26 707	25.7	49.5	-	...	...	...	9.8
Belarus	101 050	-	76.1	17.3	0.0	5.3	...	13.2
Belgium	411 484	16.4	79.0	1.9	2.7	-	17.1	23.8
Bosnia and Herzegovina	17 372	10.6	63.6	...	...	...	...	20.7
Bulgaria	86 525	6.1	85.5	4.2	0.1	4.0	...	21.3
Canada	2 264 207	10.0	73.2	3.5	2.8	10.4	28.2	29.1
Croatia	65 595	5.8	87.1	3.1	1.9	-	...	25.5
Cyprus	35 665	33.0	66.8	...	...	...	43.6	50.5
Czech Republic	172 463	4.6	87.6	5.1	-	0.7	...	16.6
Denmark	209 719	18.4	76.6	2.2	2.4	-	23.9	32.0
Estonia	20 135	4.8	82.5	10.2	1.0	-	...	19.1
Finland	190 463	11.6	83.1	2.0	2.9	0.4	15.6	18.0
France	2 167 929	13.0	82.9	2.2	1.5	-	22.8	30.5
Georgia	30 349	8.4	87.6	...	...	...	...	13.6
Germany	2 858 619	10.6	85.9	2.9	0.5	-	18.4	28.5
Greece	318 973	17.5	70.3	0.7	11.4	-	35.8	40.1
Hungary	139 394	6.6	87.7	6.0	-	-	12.5	19.5
Iceland	14 232	38.2	58.8	-	2.9		...	15.8
Ireland	157 812	14.6	80.9	3.2	1.1	-	27.0	35.6
Israel	161 914	16.2	83.8	-	-	-	...	31.7
Italy	1 774 864	8.7	88.7	1.3	0.5	0.1	24.0	32.2
Kazakhstan	103 352	13.7	58.2	...	...	...	...	12.4
Kyrgyzstan	12 391	13.5	83.1	...	...	...	...	15.4
Latvia	29 679	4.4	82.7	9.6	1.4	0.7	...	21.4
Lithuania	50 316	2.3	90.8	6.1	0.2	0.2	15.4	25.7
Luxembourg	73 674	19.3	78.4	1.1	-	-	...	51.3
Malta	14 400	52.6	47.4	-	-	-	...	60.2
Netherlands	591 063	24.9	69.0	1.2	4.8	-	16.9	24.4
Norway	214 323	15.4	64.5	1.2	16.6	-	19.3	25.2
Poland	452 088	2.5	91.9	5.3	0.2	0.2	7.5	17.5
Portugal	259 113	12.4	85.5	1.3	0.6	-	31.2	34.8
Republic of Moldova	8 665	6.3	59.9	5.8	-	23.2	...	10.7
Romania	135 166	4.4	77.6	9.1	6.7	0.8	4.6	13.6
Russian Federation	3 449 850	10.8	41.9	5.3	1.2	39.0	...	20.1
Slovakia	62 371	1.3	93.3	5.4	-	-	...	11.5
Slovenia	56 051	1.6	96.4	1.9	-	-	...	28.9
Spain	1 366 729	13.4	79.2	2.1	5.0	-	32.1	39.3
Sweden	341 159	12.0	83.2	3.1	1.7	-	17.2	23.0
Switzerland	289 253	23.3	73.2	3.3	0.1	-	25.3	32.3
Tajikistan	45 083	0.5	99.0	...	...	...	...	36.4
The former Yugoslav Republic of Macedonia	17 037	10.8	87.7	...	...	...	...	24.1
Turkey	496 878	10.3	85.5	2.1	1.8	0.3	20.6	22.8
Turkmenistan	21 683	0.0	97.9	...	...	...	...	6.1
Ukraine	287 076	10.7	51.3	31.4	-	2.5	...	7.8
United Kingdom	2 158 720	20.6	75.1	2.3	2.0	-	24.8	32.3
United States	25 169 581	14.0	80.9	1.6	0.5	2.8	31.7	40.8
Uzbekistan	165 473	8.0	53.3	3.5	-	34.5	...	10.7
Yugoslavia	67 562	11.9	87.1	...	...	...	...	18.9

* IWT - Inland waterway transport

Sources: Energy balances of OECD and Non-OECD countries 1998-1999, OECD 2001 Edition (IEA Statistics).

C. Road traffic accidents involving personal injury
C. Accidents de la circulation routière ayant entrainé des lésions corporelles
C. Дорожно-транспортные происшествия, повлекшие за собой телесные увечья

Country	Number of accidents			Persons killed per 10 000 inhabitants				Persons injured per 10 000 inhabitants			
	1980	1990	1999	1980	1990	1998	1999	1980	1990	1998	1999
Albania	...	...	468	...	...	0.92	0.81	...	...	1.01	1.13
Andorra	...	...	96	...	...		0.76	...	...		22.19
Armenia	...	...	1 031	...	...	0.83	0.60	...	...	3.40	3.35
Austria	46 214	46 338	42 348	2.31	1.80	1.19	1.33	82.95	78.46	63.19	67.68
Azerbaijan	...	3 176	1 996	...	1.78	0.75	0.68	...	5.00	2.88	2.84
Belarus	...	9 311	6 709	...	2.21	1.81	1.77	...	9.07	6.78	6.70
Belgium	60 758	62 446	51 601	2.43	1.98	1.47	1.37	83.56	86.44	69.28	69.55
Bosnia and Herzegovina	...	...	...	...	...	...	...	...	...	...	...
Bulgaria	...	6 478	7 586	...	1.81	1.22	1.28	...	7.87	9.70	11.08
Canada	184 302	182 294	150 919	2.27	1.49	0.97	0.96	109.39	98.80	...	...
Croatia	15 053	14 471	12 958	3.49	2.85	1.44	1.51	32.13	41.42	40.25	41.32
Cyprus	2 851	3 172	2 500	1.35	1.72	1.67	1.69	63.51	72.08	59.04	55.67
Czech Republic	18 326	21 910	26 918	1.23	1.25	1.32	1.42	23.19	27.15	34.24	33.81
Denmark	12 334	9 155	7 605	1.35	1.23	0.94	0.96	29.42	20.70	17.27	17.56
Estonia	2 441	2 099	1 472	2.06	2.78	1.95	1.70	12.08	15.15	13.66	12.37
Finland	6 790	10 175	6 997	1.15	1.30	0.78	0.83	17.66	25.57	17.63	17.47
France	241 049	162 573	124 524	2.30	1.81	1.43	1.36	61.91	39.81	28.58	28.38
Georgia	...	...	1 782	...	...	0.86	1.09	...	...	3.95	4.39
Germany	379 235	340 043	395 689	1.67	1.00	0.95	0.95	63.92	56.47	60.62	63.43
Greece	18 233	19 609	24 231	1.27	1.68	2.12	2.03	26.39	26.50	31.78	30.71
Hungary	18 994	27 801	18 923	1.52	2.35	1.36	1.30	22.25	35.80	26.22	24.56
Iceland	522	583	1 064	1.09	0.94	0.99	0.75	29.83	33.52	51.06	54.04
Ireland	5 683	6 067	7 807	1.66	1.36	1.22	1.09	25.01	26.89	34.11	31.63
Israel	12 716	17 496	22 798	1.12	0.89	0.91	0.75	44.97	56.50	80.68	70.70
Italy	163 770	161 782	219 032	1.51	1.15	1.02	1.15	39.50	38.33	50.99	54.75
Kazakhstan	...	...	11 568	...	...	1.48	1.43	...	...	9.29	9.12
Kyrgyzstan	...	...	2 666	...	...	1.24	1.19	...	...	7.35	6.73
Latvia	4 717	4 325	4 442	2.60	3.28	2.57	2.55	15.51	17.66	18.93	19.93
Lithuania	...	5 135	6 356	...	2.50	2.24	2.03	...	14.70	20.71	20.84
Luxembourg	1 577	1 216	1 062	2.72	1.85	1.33	1.35	63.42	46.25	35.37	35.05
Malta	...	...	...	0.61	0.11	0.42	0.31	24.73	13.35	22.11	29.08
Netherlands	49 396	44 892	...	1.41	0.92	0.68	...	...	9.13	...	...
Norway	7 848	8 801	8 361	0.89	0.78	0.79	0.07	25.06	28.03	27.35	2.55
Poland	40 373	50 532	55 106	1.69	1.92	1.83	1.74	13.00	15.61	20.06	17.71
Portugal	...	45 110	47 966	2.32	2.34	1.97	1.84	42.07	63.97	70.30	68.84
Republic of Moldova	...	6 049	2 669	...	...	1.35	1.09	...	...	9.91	8.49
Romania	4 817	9 708	7 846	0.85	1.63	1.23	1.12	1.77	7.25	3.21	2.94
Russian Federation	...	...	159 823	...	...	1.98	2.05	...	...	12.56	12.58
San Marino	...	...	8 578								
Slovakia	...	8 236	8 578	...	0.68	1.52	1.20	...	20.07	23.92	...
Slovenia	6 941	5 177	6 929	2.94	2.59	1.56	1.68	...	...	37.27	45.12
Spain	67 803	101 507	97 811	1.34	1.79	1.52	1.46	28.68	39.99	35.99	36.25
Sweden	15 231	16 975	15 834	1.02	0.90	0.60	0.65	23.16	26.28	24.12	24.73
Switzerland	25 649	23 834	23 434	1.95	1.43	0.84	0.81	50.59	43.86	39.01	40.96
Tajikistan	...	...	1 474	...	...	0.63	0.67	...	...	2.61	27.68
The former Yugoslav Republic of Macedonia	...	...	2 188	...	...	0.93	1.06	...	...	15.04	14.69
Turkey	...	55 771	72 068	0.93	1.11	0.76	0.89	5.40	15.53	17.68	19.45
Turkmenistan	...	...	1 764	...	...	...	...	...	...	...	...
Ukraine	37 630	50 908	34 554	1.46	1.85	1.11	1.07	...	10.31	8.06	7.81
United Kingdom	257 282	265 600	242 610	1.11	0.94	0.60	0.61	58.54	60.37	56.46	56.87
United States	2 298 000	2 163 000	2 091 000	2.26	1.79	1.53	1.52	125.71	129.56	118.09	117.83
Uzbekistan	...	17 892	...	...	1.38	...	...	...	...	...	...
Yugoslavia	...	...	...	...	...	...	...	...	...	...	...

RAILWAY TRANSPORT

TRANSPORT FERROVIAIRE

ЖЕЛЕЗНЫЕ ДОРОГИ

RAILWAY TRANSPORT- TRANSPORT FERROVIAIRE
ЖЕЛЕЗНЫЕ ДОРОГИ

1. Employment in principal railway enterprise(s)

1. Emplois dans les entreprise(s) ferroviaire(s) principale(s)

1. Занятость в основном(ых) железнодорожном(ых) предприятии(ях)

Item	Description
1	**Principal railway enterprise(s) - (number)**
2	**Employment in principal railway enterprise(s) - (number)**
	by gender
2.11	- Female
2.12	- Male
	by type of employment
2.21	- General administration
2.22	- Railway operations
2.23	- Other

Rubrique	Description
1	**Entreprise(s) ferroviaire(s) principale(s) - (nombre)**
2	**Emplois dans les entreprise(s) ferroviaire(s) principale(s) - (nombre)**
	par genre
2.11	- Femme
2.12	- Homme
	par type d'emploi
2.21	- Administration générale
2.22	- Exploitation ferroviaire
2.23	- Autre

Статья	Описание
1	**Основное железнодорожное предприятие (основные железнодорожные предприятия) - (число)**
2	**Занятость в основном(ых) железнодорожном(ых) предприятии(ях)**
	по полу
2.11	- Женский
2.12	- Мужской
	по виду занятости
2.21	- Общая администрация
2.22	- Железнодорожные операции
2.23	- Прочие

RAILWAY TRANSPORT- TRANSPORT FERROVIAIRE
ЖЕЛЕЗНЫЕ ДОРОГИ

1. Employment in principal railway enterprise(s)
1. Emplois dans les entreprise(s) ferroviaire(s) principale(s)
1. Занятость в основном(ых) железнодорожном(ых) предприятии(ях)

Unit: number - Unité: nombre - Единица: число

		Albania Albanie Албания			Armenia Arménie Армения			Austria Autriche Австрия		
		1990	1998	1999	1990	1998	1999	1990	1998	1999
1	Railway enterprise(s)	...	1	1	...	1	1	1	1	...
2	Total number of employees	...	3 149	2 926	...	1 350	1 350	66 929	53 495	51 791
	by gender									
2.11	- Female	...	209	190	...	385	385	...	...	...
2.12	- Male	...	2 940	2 736	...	965	965	...	...	...
	by type of employment									
2.21	- General administration	...	...	...	...	524	524	...	1 246	1 195
2.22	- Railway operations	...	...	...	...	...	...	...	50 060	50 596
2.23	- Other	...	...	...	...	...	...	...	2 189	2 126

		Azerbaijan Azerbaïdjan Азербайджан			Belarus Bélarus Беларусь			Belgium Belgique Бельгия		
		1990	1998	1999	1990	1998	1999	1990	1998	1999
1	Railway enterprise(s)	...	1	...	...	1	...	1	1	1
2	Total number of employees	...	35 285	...	88 135	80 462	...	45 205	40 469	41 537
	by gender									
2.11	- Female	...	...	...	...	...	...	...	2 225	2 545
2.12	- Male	...	...	...	...	...	...	...	38 244	38 992
	by type of employment									
2.21	- General administration	...	714	...	...	1 478	...	...	...	...
2.22	- Railway operations	...	24 606	...	...	68 235	...	...	...	...
2.23	- Other	...	9 965	...	...	10 749	...	...	...	...

		Bosnia-Herzegovina Bosnie-Herzégovine Босния и Герцеговина			Bulgaria Bulgarie Болгария			Canada Canada Канада		
		1990	1998	1999	1990	1998	1999	1990	1998	1999
1	Railway enterprise(s)	...	1	1	1	1	1	...	3	...
2	Total number of employees	...	3 864	3 867	64 082	42 720	...	...	45 230	...
	by gender									
2.11	- Female	...	...	...	...	...	...	...	...	...
2.12	- Male	...	...	...	...	...	...	...	...	...
	by type of employment									
2.21	- General administration	...	...	...	...	999	...	...	7 834	...
2.22	- Railway operations	...	...	...	...	40 499	...	...	37 396	...
2.23	- Other	...	...	...	...	1 222	...	...	-	...

		Croatia Croatie Хорватия			Czech Republic République tchèque Чешская Республика			Denmark Danemark Дания		
		1990	1998	1999	1990	1998	1999	1990	1998	1999
1	Railway enterprise(s)	...	1	1	...	5	6	1	3	...
2	Total number of employees	39 456	20 688	19 468	...	93 261	90 479	21 197	10 922	...
	by gender									
2.11	- Female	...	...	2 769	...	29 288	28 493	...	2 512	...
2.12	- Male	...	...	16 699	...	63 973	60 906	...	8 410*	...
	by type of employment									
2.21	- General administration	4 289	1 669	1 713	...	4 450	4 172	1 611	330	...
2.22	- Railway operations	29 115	14 097	17 121	...	86 982	84 928	18 921	9 537	...
2.23	- Other	6 052	4 922	634	...	1 829	1 379	665	1 055	...

RAILWAY TRANSPORT- TRANSPORT FERROVIAIRE
ЖЕЛЕЗНЫЕ ДОРОГИ

1. Employment in principal railway enterprise(s)
1. Emplois dans les entreprise(s) ferroviaire(s) principale(s)
1. Занятость в основном(ых) железнодорожном(ых) предприятии(ях)

Unit: number - Unité: nombre - Единица: число

		Estonia Estonie Эстония			Finland Finlande Финляндия			France France Франция		
		1990	1998	1999	1990	1998	1999	1990	1998	1999
1	Railway enterprise(s)	...	1	...	1	1	1	1	1	1
2	Total number of employees	...	6 405	...	19 165	13 613	12 973	202 081	173 422	174 068
	by gender									
2.11	- Female	...	...	...	...	1 866	1 819	...	...	...
2.12	- Male	...	...	...	...	11 747	11 154	...	...	...
	by type of employment									
2.21	- General administration	...	276	...	...	924	1 025	18 080	10 666	10 270
2.22	- Railway operations	...	5 766	...	...	12 591	11 847	175 136	157 894	158 800
2.23	- Other	...	363	...	...	98	101	8 865	4 862	4 998

		Georgia Georgie Грузия			Germany Allemagne Германия			Greece Grèce Греция		
		1990	1998	1999	1990	1998	1999	1990	1998	1999
1	Railway enterprise(s)	...	1	...	...	1	1	1	1	...
2	Total number of employees	...	16 495	...	...	209 602	244 851	13 324	10 874	...
	by gender									
2.11	- Female	...	...	...	...	33 327	45 297	...	...	...
2.12	- Male	...	...	...	...	176 275	199 554	...	...	...
	by type of employment									
2.21	- General administration	...	730	...	...	21 429	22 890	1 298	1 391	...
2.22	- Railway operations	...	14 654	...	...	181 629	167 678	...	9 463	...
2.23	- Other	...	1 111	...	...	6 544	54 283	...	20	...

		Hungary Hongrie Венгрия			Ireland Irlande Ирландия			Israel Israël Израиль		
		1990	1998	1999	1990	1998	1999	1990	1998	1999
1	Railway enterprise(s)	2	2	2	1	1	1	1	1	1
2	Total number of employees	129 067	59 678	58 598	11 799	...	...	...	1 212	1 349
	by gender									
2.11	- Female	...	...	...	...	...	...	...	...	...
2.12	- Male	...	...	...	...	...	...	...	...	...
	by type of employment									
2.21	- General administration	...	1 479	1 563	...	...	...	...	...	...
2.22	- Railway operations	...	50 647	49 093	...	...	...	...	...	...
2.23	- Other	...	7 552	7 942	...	...	...	...	...	...

		Italy Italie Италия			Kazakhstan Kazakhstan Казахстан			Kyrgyzstan Kirghizistan Кыргызстан		
		1990	1998	1999	1990	1998	1999	1990	1998	1999
1	Railway enterprise(s)	1	1	...	...	1	...	1	1	1
2	Total number of employees	200 405	115 437	112 018	...	147 244	...	5 174	5 940	4 902
	by gender									
2.11	- Female	...	10 020	10 201	...	...	...	1 780	1 927	1 596
2.12	- Male	...	105 417	101 817	...	...	...	3 394	4 013	3 306
	by type of employment									
2.21	- General administration	...	14 872	14 372	...	3 268	...	...	...	...
2.22	- Railway operations	...	100 565	97 646	...	141 770	...	...	...	...
2.23	- Other	...	-	-	...	2 206	...	...	...	...

RAILWAY TRANSPORT- TRANSPORT FERROVIAIRE
ЖЕЛЕЗНЫЕ ДОРОГИ

1. Employment in principal railway enterprise(s)
1. Emplois dans les entreprise(s) ferroviaire(s) principale(s)
1. Занятость в основном(ых) железнодорожном(ых) предприятии(ях)

Unit: number - Unité: nombre - Единица: число

		Latvia Lettonie Латвия			Lithuania Lituanie Литва			Luxembourg Luxembourg Люксембург		
		1990	1998	1999	1990	1998	1999	1990	1998	1999
1	Railway enterprise(s)	1	1	1	1	1	1	1	1	...
2	Total number of employees	23 736	17 792	15 905	18 788	16 921	16 718	3 571	3 050	...
	by gender									
2.11	- Female	...	6 269	5 439	...	...	...	117	...	...
2.12	- Male	...	11 523	10 466	...	...	...	3 454	...	...
	by type of employment									
2.21	- General administration	...	1 309	1 211	...	370	357	...	214	...
2.22	- Railway operations	...	14 227	12 755	...	14 866	14 171	...	2 560	...
2.23	- Other	...	2 256	1 939	...	1 685	2 190	...	276	...

		Netherlands Pays-Bas Нидерланды			Norway Norvège Норвегия			Poland Pologne Польша		
		1990	1998	1999	1990	1998	1999	1990	1998	1999
1	Railway enterprise(s)	1	2	...	...	1	1	...	1	1
2	Total number of employees	26 165	26 286	...	13 576	6 713	6 261	336 614	211 542	194 264
	by gender									
2.11	- Female	...	...	...	...	1 416	1 376	...	62 985	56 699
2.12	- Male	...	...	...	...	5 297	4 885	...	148 557	137 565
	by type of employment									
2.21	- General administration	...	...	...	...	1 447	...	...	6 482	5 561
2.22	- Railway operations	...	...	...	...	4 684	...	...	200 308	184 733
2.23	- Other	...	...	...	...	582	...	...	4 752	3 970

		Portugal Portugal Португалия			Republic of Moldova République de Moldova Республика Молдова			Romania Roumanie Румыния		
		1990	1998	1999	1990	1998	1999	1990	1998	1999
1	Railway enterprise(s)	1	2	2	...	1	1	1	6	6
2	Total number of employees	22 110	13 021	12 832	...	20 608	13 626	247 659	104 940	102 235
	by gender									
2.11	- Female	...	2 152	2 164	...	6 795	4 001	...	23 571	23 079
2.12	- Male	...	10 869	10 668	...	13 813	9 625	...	81 369	79 156
	by type of employment									
2.21	- General administration	...	3 226	3 066	...	...	...	...	3 434	3 486
2.22	- Railway operations	...	9 782	9 762	...	12 221	9 173	...	90 949	90 298
2.23	- Other	...	13	4	...	...	...	...	10 557	8 451

		Russian Federation Fédération de Russie Российская Федерация			Slovakia Slovaquie Словакия			Slovenia Slovénie Словения		
		1990	1998	1999	1990	1998	1999	1990	1998	1999
1	Railway enterprise(s)	...	1	...	...	1	1	1	1	1
2	Total number of employees	...	1 274 104	1 236 740	...	49 435	48 913	21 295	9 088	8 973
	by gender									
2.11	- Female	...	458 677	460 318	...	...	13 118	...	1 290	1 278
2.12	- Male	...	815 427	776 422	...	...	35 795	...	7 798	7 695
	by type of employment									
2.21	- General administration	...	14 825	15 047	...	1 592	449	...	807	...
2.22	- Railway operations	...	1 073 642	1 053 454	...	44 389	45 310	...	8 079	...
2.23	- Other	...	185 637	168 239	...	3 454	3 154	...	263	...

RAILWAY TRANSPORT- TRANSPORT FERROVIAIRE
ЖЕЛЕЗНЫЕ ДОРОГИ

1. Employment in principal railway enterprise(s)
1. Emplois dans les entreprise(s) ferroviaire(s) principale(s)
1. Занятость в основном(ых) железнодорожном(ых) предприятии(ях)

Unit: number - Unité: nombre - Единица: число

		Spain Espagne Испания			Sweden Suède Швеция			Switzerland Suisse Швейцария		
		1990	1998	1999	1990	1998	1999	1990	1998	1999
1	Railway enterprise(s)	1	1	1	1	1	1	1	1	...
2	Total number of employees	49 724	35 451	34 537	20 552	11 134	10 461	37 200	30 862	...
	by gender									
2.11	- Female	...	...	...	...	2 756	2 634	...	...	...
2.12	- Male	...	...	...	...	8 378	7 827	...	...	...
	by type of employment									
2.21	- General administration	...	2 098	2 063	1 933	1 787	1 701	...	2 202	...
2.22	- Railway operations	...	33 353	32 474	17 765	8 670	8 104	...	28 238	...
2.23	- Other	...	-	-	854	677	656	...	422	...

		Tajikistan Tadjikistan Таджикистан			The FYR of Macedonia [1]			Turkey Turquie Турция		
		1990	1998	1999	1990	1998	1999	1990	1998	1999
1	Railway enterprise(s)	...	1	1	...	1	1	1	1	...
2	Total number of employees	...	5 618	5 730	...	4 302	4 199	49 285	41 819	...
	by gender									
2.11	- Female	...	...	...	...	553	549	...	...	...
2.12	- Male	...	...	...	...	3 749	3 650	...	...	...
	by type of employment									
2.21	- General administration	...	681	685	...	470	473	...	2 402	...
2.22	- Railway operations	...	4 294	4 307	...	3 832	3 726	...	29 151	...
2.23	- Other	...	643	738	...	-	-	...	10 266	...

		Turkmenistan Turkménistan Туркменистан			Ukraine Ukraine Украина			United Kingdom Royaume-Uni Соединенное Королевство		
		1990	1998	1999	1990	1998	1999	1990	1998	1999
1	Railway enterprise(s)	...	1	...	1	1	1	...	...	...
2	Total number of employees	...	18 535	...	445 000	380 660	373 071	126 800	...	...
	by gender									
2.11	- Female	...	...	...	...	...	...	...	...	...
2.12	- Male	...	...	...	...	...	...	...	...	...
	by type of employment									
2.21	- General administration	...	245	...	...	705	756	...	...	...
2.22	- Railway operations	...	15 402	...	...	318 723	311 872	...	...	...
2.23	- Other	...	2 888	...	...	61 232	60 443	...	...	...

		United States Etats-Unis [2] Соединенные Штаты			Uzbekistan Ouzbékistan Узбекистан			Yugoslavia Yugoslavie Югославия		
		1990	1998	1999	1990	1998	1999	1990	1998	1999
1	Railway enterprise(s)	...	559	555	...	1	...	...	2	2
2	Total number of employees	...	178 222	177 557	...	68 596	...	46 904	36 303	35 469
	by gender									
2.11	- Female	...	...	...	...	...	...	...	5 965	5 886
2.12	- Male	...	...	...	...	...	...	...	30 338	29 583
	by type of employment									
2.21	- General administration	...	30 414	30 335	...	633	...	...	6 968	4 069
2.22	- Railway operations	...	147 808	147 222	...	32 613	...	...	29 335	31 400
2.23	- Other	...	-	-	...	35 350	...	...	-	-

1- The former Yugoslav Republic of Macedonia.
2- Class 1 railways.

1- L'ex-République yougoslave de Macédoine
2- Chemins de fer de 1ère classe.

1- Бывшая Югославская Республика Македония
2- Железные дороги первого класса.

RAILWAY TRANSPORT- TRANSPORT FERROVIAIRE
ЖЕЛЕЗНЫЕ ДОРОГИ

2. Networks at 31 December
2. Réseau au 31 décembre
2. Сети на 31 декабря

Item	Description	Rubrique	Description
1	**Total length of lines operated - (km)**	**1**	**Longueur totale des lignes exploitées - (km)**
	by type of track		*par nombre de voies*
1.11	- Single track	1.11	- à deux voies ou plus
1.12	- Double track or more	1.12	- à voie unique
	by track gauge		*par écartement des voies*
1.21	- Standard gauge	1.21	- écartement large
1.22	- Large gauge	1.22	- écartement standard
1.23	- Narrow gauge	1.23	- écartement étroit
	by nature of traffic		*par nature de trafic*
1.31	- Passenger only	1.31	- voyageurs seulement
1.32	- Freight only	1.32	- marchandises seulement
1.33	- Passenger and freight	1.33	- voyageurs et marchandises
2	**Length of electrified lines operated - (km)**	**2**	**Longueur des lignes électrifiées exploitées - (km)**
	by type of track		*par nombre de voies*
2.11	- Single track	2.11	- à deux voies ou plus
2.12	- Double track or more	2.12	- à voie unique
	by track gauge		*par écartement des voies*
2.21	- Standard gauge	2.21	- écartement large
2.22	- Large gauge	2.22	- écartement standard
2.23	- Narrow gauge	2.23	- écartement étroit
	by nature of traffic		*par nature de trafic*
2.31	- Passenger only	2.31	- voyageurs seulement
2.32	- Freight only	2.32	- marchandises seulement
2.33	- Passenger and freight	2.33	- voyageurs et marchandises

Статья	Описание
1	**Общая протяженность эксплуатируемых линий - (км)**
	по числу путей
1.11	- Однопутные
1.12	- Двухпутные или более
	по ширине колеи
1.21	- Нормальная колея
1.22	- Широкая колея
1.23	- Узкая колея
	по типу перевозок
1.31	- Только пассажирские
1.32	- Только грузовыеlу
1.33	- Только грузовые
2	**Протяженность эксплуатируемых электрифицированных линий - (км)**
	по числу путей
2.11	- Однопутные
2.12	- Двухпутные или более
	по ширине колеи
2.21	- Нормальная колея
2.22	- Широкая колея
2.23	- Узкая колея
	по типу перевозок
2.31	- Только пассажирские
2.32	- Только грузовыеlу
2.33	- Только грузовые

RAILWAY TRANSPORT- TRANSPORT FERROVIAIRE
ЖЕЛЕЗНЫЕ ДОРОГИ

2. Networks at 31 December
2. Réseau au 31 décembre
2. Сети на 31 декабря

Unit : km - Unité : km - Единица - км

		Albania Albanie Албания			Armenia Arménie Армения			Austria Autriche Австрия		
		1990	1998	1999	1990	1998	1999	1990	1998	1999
1	**Total length of lines**	674	394	394	836	796	843	5 624	5 643	5 740
	by type of track									
1.11	- Single track	674	394	394	...	789	836	...	3 876	3 973
1.12	- Double track or more	-	-	-	...	7	7	...	1 767	1 767
	by track gauge									
1.21	- Standard gauge	674	394	394	-	-	-	...	5 345	5 442
1.22	- Large gauge	-	-	-	836	796	843	-	-	-
1.23	- Narrow gauge	-	-	-	-	-	-	...	298	298
	by nature of traffic									
1.31	- Passenger only	-	-	-	-	-	-	...	...	...
1.32	- Freight only	...	70	70	-	-	-	...	...	...
1.33	- Passenger and freight	...	324	324	836	796	843	...	...	...
2	**Length of electrified lines**	-	-	-	820	779	779	3 246	3 427	3 456
	by type of track									
2.11	- Single track	-	-	-	...	772	772	...	1 660	1 689
2.12	- Double track or more	-	-	-	...	7	7	...	1 767	1 767
	by track gauge									
2.21	- Standard gauge	-	-	-	-	-	-	...	3 343	3 372
2.22	- Large gauge	-	-	-	820	779	779	...	-	-
2.23	- Narrow gauge	-	-	-	-	-	-	...	84	84
	by nature of traffic									
2.31	- Passenger only	-	-	-	-	-	-	...	...	...
2.32	- Freight only	-	-	-	-	-	-	...	...	...
2.33	- Passenger and freight	-	-	-	820	779	779	...	...	...

		Azerbaijan Azerbaïdjan Азербайджан			Belarus Bélarus Беларусь			Belgium Belgique Бельгия		
		1990	1998	1999	1990	1998	1999	1990	1998	1999
1	**Total length of lines**	2 080	2 117	2 116	5 569	5 531	5 523	3 479	3 470	3 472
	by type of track									
1.11	- Single track	...	1 286	1 313	4 679	3 913	3 863	1 076	843	845
1.12	- Double track or more	...	831	803	890	1 618	1 660	2 403	2 627	2 627
	by track gauge									
1.21	- Standard gauge	-	-	-	...	20	29	3 479	3 470	3 472
1.22	- Large gauge	2 080	2 117	2 116	...	5 511	5 494	-	-	-
1.23	- Narrow gauge	-	-	-	-	-	-	-	-	-
	by nature of traffic									
1.31	- Passenger only	...	169	...	-	-	-	...	...	...
1.32	- Freight only	-	-	-	-	-	-	680	...	...
1.33	- Passenger and freight	...	1 948	...	5 569	5 531	5 523	...	...	...
2	**Length of electrified lines**	...	1 271	1 270	890	876	876	2 293	2 643	2 701
	by type of track									
2.11	- Single track	...	454	467	-	47	56	162	306	345
2.12	- Double track or more	...	817	803	890	829	820	2 131	2 337	2 356
	by track gauge									
2.21	- Standard gauge	-	-	-	...	20	29	2 293	2 643	2 701
2.22	- Large gauge	...	1 271	1 270	...	856	847	-	-	-
2.23	- Narrow gauge	-	-	-	-	-	-	-	-	-
	by nature of traffic									
2.31	- Passenger only	...	169	...	-	-	-	...	...	...
2.32	- Freight only	-	-	-	-	-	-	122	...	...
2.33	- Passenger and freight	...	1 102	...	890	876	876	...	...	...

2. Networks at 31 December
2. Réseau au 31 décembre
2. Сети на 31 декабря

Unit : km - Unité : km - Единица - км

		Bosnia-Herzegovina Bosnie-Herzégovine Босния и Герцеговина			Bulgaria Bulgarie Болгария			Canada Canada Канада		
		1990	1998	1999	1990	1998	1999	1990	1998	1999
1	**Total length of lines**	**944**	**607**	**608**	**4 299**	**4 290**	**4 290**	**...**	**73 360**	**...**
	by type of track									
1.11	- Single track	...	...	...	3 339	3 325	3 325	...	...	...
1.12	- Double track or more	...	...	...	960	965	965	...	...	...
	by track gauge									
1.21	- Standard gauge	944	607	607	4 054	4 045	4 045	...	...	...
1.22	- Large gauge	-	-	-	-	-	-	...	...	...
1.23	- Narrow gauge	-	-	-	245	245	245	...	...	...
	by nature of traffic									
1.31	- Passenger only	-	-	-	-	-	-	...	...	...
1.32	- Freight only	-	-	-	-	-	-	...	...	...
1.33	- Passenger and freight	944	607	607	4 299	4 290	4 290	...	...	...
2	**Length of electrified lines**	**751**	**439**	**439**	**2 640**	**2 708**	**2 708**	**...**	**...**	**...**
	by type of track									
2.11	- Single track	...	...	...	1 680	1 743	1 743	...	...	...
2.12	- Double track or more	...	...	...	960	965	965	...	...	...
	by track gauge									
2.21	- Standard gauge	751	439	439	2 640	2 708	2 708	...	...	...
2.22	- Large gauge	-	-	-	-	-	-	...	...	...
2.23	- Narrow gauge	-	-	-	-	-	-	...	...	...
	by nature of traffic									
2.31	- Passenger only	-	-	-	-	-	-	...	...	...
2.32	- Freight only	-	-	-	-	-	-	...	...	...
2.33	- Passenger and freight	751	439	439	2 640	2 708	2 708	...	...	...

		Croatia Croatie Хорватия			Czech Republic République tchèque Чешская Республика			Denmark Danemark Дания		
		1990	1998	1999	1990	1998	1999	1990	1998	1999
1	**Total length of lines**	**2 444**	**2 726**	**2 726**	**9 451**	**9 430**	**9 444**	**2 344**	**2 264**	**2 324**
	by type of track									
1.11	- Single track	2 194	2 478	2 478	7 510	7 489	7 515	1 417	1 371	1 430
1.12	- Double track or more	250	248	248	1 941	1 941	1 929	927	893	894
	by track gauge									
1.21	- Standard gauge	2 444	2 726	2 726	...	9 336	9 342	2 344	2 264	2 324
1.22	- Large gauge	-	-	-	...	-	-	-	-	-
1.23	- Narrow gauge	-	-	-	...	94	102	-	-	-
	by nature of traffic									
1.31	- Passenger only	-	-	-	-	41	427	51	120	...
1.32	- Freight only	-	-	-	-	37	185	365	228	...
1.33	- Passenger and freight	2 444	2 726	2 726	9 451	9 352	8 832	1 928	1 916	...
2	**Length of electrified lines**	**844**	**983**	**983**	**2 579**	**2 859**	**2 843**	**230**	**617**	**613**
	by type of track									
2.11	- Single track	600	739	739	...	1 134	1 130	1	100	100
2.12	- Double track or more	244	244	244	...	1 725	1 713	229	517	513
	by track gauge									
2.21	- Standard gauge	844	983	983	2 579	2 859	2 843	230	617	613
2.22	- Large gauge	-	-	-	-	-	-	-	-	-
2.23	- Narrow gauge	-	-	-	-	-	-	-	-	-
	by nature of traffic									
2.31	- Passenger only	-	-	-	-	-	3	...	120	...
2.32	- Freight only	-	-	-	-	-	103	...	-	...
2.33	- Passenger and freight	844	983	983	2 579	2 859	2 737	...	497	...

25

RAILWAY TRANSPORT- TRANSPORT FERROVIAIRE
ЖЕЛЕЗНЫЕ ДОРОГИ

2. Networks at 31 December
2. Réseau au 31 décembre
2. Сети на 31 декабря

Unit : km - Unité : km - Единица - км

		Estonia Estonie Эстония			Finland Finlande Финляндия			France France Франция		
		1990	1998	1999	1990	1998	1999	1990	1998	1999
1	**Total length of lines**	**1 026**	**968**	**968**	**5 873**	**5 867**	**5 836**	**34 070**	**31 770**	**31 735**
	by type of track									
1.11	- Single track	928	863	863	5 392	5 360	5 329	18 284	15 831	15 794
1.12	- Double track or more	98	105	105	481	507	507	15 786	15 939	15 941
	by track gauge									
1.21	- Standard gauge	-	-	-	-	-	-	34 062	31 603	31 566
1.22	- Large gauge	1 026	966	968	5 873	5 867	5 836	-	-	-
1.23	- Narrow gauge	-	-	-	-	-	-	198	167	169
	by nature of traffic									
1.31	- Passenger only	3	3	3	-	-	-	974	2 327	2 189
1.32	- Freight only	30	86	86	1 538	1 889	1 858	10 353	7 675	7 654
1.33	- Passenger and freight	993	879	879	4 335	3 978	3 978	22 933	21 768	21 892
2	**Length of electrified lines**	**132**	**132**	**132**	**1 663**	**2 197**	**2 234**	**12 609**	**14 153**	**14 206**
	by type of track									
2.11	- Single track	64	64	64	1 222	1 690	1 727	1 786	1 891	1 898
2.12	- Double track or more	68	68	68	441	507	507	10 726	12 262	12 308
	by track gauge									
2.21	- Standard gauge	-	-	-	-	-	-	12 415	14 054	14 105
2.22	- Large gauge	132	132	132	1 663	2 197	2 234	-	-	-
2.23	- Narrow gauge	-	-	-	-	-	-	97	99	101
	by nature of traffic									
2.31	- Passenger only	3	3	3	-	-	-	874	1 538	1 335
2.32	- Freight only	-	-	-	59	106	106	774	604	613
2.33	- Passenger and freight	128	128	129	1 604	2 091	2 128	10 864	12 011	12 258

		Georgia Georgie Грузия			Germany Allemagne Германия			Greece Grèce Греция		
		1990	1998	1999	1990	1998	1999	1990	1998	1999
1	**Total length of lines**	**1 600**	**1 576**	**1 545**	**...**	**38 126**	**37 525**	**2 484**	**2 299**	**2 299**
	by type of track									
1.11	- Single track	...	1 291	1 257	...	20 696	19 970	2 239	1 978	1 978
1.12	- Double track or more	...	285	288	...	17 430	17 555	245	321	321
	by track gauge									
1.21	- Standard gauge	...	-	-	...	38 078	37 476	1 592	1 565	1 565
1.22	- Large gauge	...	1 539	1 508	...	-	-	-	-	-
1.23	- Narrow gauge	...	37	37	...	48	49	892	734	734
	by nature of traffic									
1.31	- Passenger only	...	-	-	...	1 711	1 764	-	-	-
1.32	- Freight only	...	-	-	...	5 239	4 802	-	-	-
1.33	- Passenger and freight	...	1 576	1 545	...	31 176	30 959	2 484	2 299	2 299
2	**Length of electrified lines**	**...**	**1 576**	**1 545**	**...**	**18 857**	**18 934**			
	by type of track									
2.11	- Single track	...	1 291	1 257	...	4 147	4 094	-	-	-
2.12	- Double track or more	...	285	288	...	14 710	14 840	-	-	-
	by track gauge									
2.21	- Standard gauge	...	-	-	...	18 857	18 934	-	-	-
2.22	- Large gauge	...	1 539	1 508	...	-	-	-	-	-
2.23	- Narrow gauge	...	37	37	...	-	-	-	-	-
	by nature of traffic									
2.31	- Passenger only	...	-	-	...	1 483	1 536	-	-	-
2.32	- Freight only	...	-	-	...	1 905	1 901	-	-	-
2.33	- Passenger and freight	...	1 576	1 545	...	15 469	15 497	-	-	-

RAILWAY TRANSPORT- TRANSPORT FERROVIAIRE
ЖЕЛЕЗНЫЕ ДОРОГИ

2. Networks at 31 December
2. Réseau au 31 décembre
2. Сети на 31 декабря

Unit : km - Unité : km - Единица - км

		Hungary Hongrie Венгрия			Ireland Irlande Ирландия			Israel Israël Израиль		
		1990	1998	1999	1990	1998	1999	1990	1998	1999
1	**Total length of lines**	**7 772**	**7 642**	**7 652**	**1 944**	**1 909**	**1 919**	**574**	**666**	**663**
	by type of track									
1.11	- Single track	6 536	6 349	6 359	1 424	1 419	1 419	...	411	416
1.12	- Double track or more	1 236	1 293	1 293	520	490	500	...	255	247
	by track gauge									
1.21	- Standard gauge	7 511	7 393	7 403	...	-	-	574	666	663
1.22	- Large gauge	35	37	37	...	1 909	1 919	-	-	-
1.23	- Narrow gauge	226	212	212	...	-	-	-	-	-
	by nature of traffic									
1.31	- Passenger only	-	12	12	-	6	6	-	-	-
1.32	- Freight only	220	240	240	291	246	246	-	249	249
1.33	- Passenger and freight	7 552	7 390	7 400	1 653	1 657	1 667	574	417	414
2	**Length of electrified lines**	**2 249**	**2 594**	**2 620**	**37**	**37**	**47**	**-**	**-**	**-**
	by type of track									
2.11	- Single track	1 134	1 355	1 381	-	-	-	-	-	-
2.12	- Double track or more	1 115	1 239	1 239	37	37	47	-	-	-
	by track gauge									
2.21	- Standard gauge	2 249	2 594	2 620	...	-	-	-	-	-
2.22	- Large gauge	-	-	-	...	37	47	-	-	-
2.23	- Narrow gauge	-	-	-	...	-	-	-	-	-
	by nature of traffic									
2.31	- Passenger only	-	-	-	-	-	-	-	-	-
2.32	- Freight only	...	41	41	-	-	-	-	-	-
2.33	- Passenger and freight	...	2 553	2 579	37	37	47	-	-	-

		Italy Italie Италия			Kazakhstan Kazakhstan Казахстан			Kyrgyzstan Kirghizistan Кыргызстан		
		1990	1998	1999	1990	1998	1999	1990	1998	1999
1	**Total length of lines**	**16 086**	**16 080**	**16 108**	**14 500**	**13 642**	**13 604**	**400**	**417**	**417**
	by type of track									
1.11	- Single track	...	9 945	9 935	...	8 567	8 638	400	417	417
1.12	- Double track or more	...	6 135	6 173	...	5 076	4 966	-	-	-
	by track gauge									
1.21	- Standard gauge	16 086	16 080	16 108	...	...	128	-	-	-
1.22	- Large gauge	-	-	-	...	...	13 476	400	417	417
1.23	- Narrow gauge	-	-	-	...	...	-	-	-	-
	by nature of traffic									
1.31	- Passenger only	...	-	-	...	-	-	-	-	-
1.32	- Freight only	...	-	-	...	-	-	-	-	-
1.33	- Passenger and freight	...	16 080	16 108	...	...	...	400	417	417
2	**Length of electrified lines**	**9 512**	**10 488**	**10 688**	**...**	**3 703**	**3 664**	**-**	**-**	**-**
	by type of track									
2.11	- Single track	...	4 394	4 549	...	207	225	-	-	-
2.12	- Double track or more	...	6 094	6 139	...	3 497	3 439	-	-	-
	by track gauge									
2.21	- Standard gauge	9 512	10 488	10 688	...	-	-	-	-	-
2.22	- Large gauge	-	-	-	...	3 703	3 664	-	-	-
2.23	- Narrow gauge	-	-	-	...	-	-	-	-	-
	by nature of traffic									
2.31	- Passenger only	...	-	-	...	-	-	-	-	-
2.32	- Freight only	...	-	-	...	-	-	-	-	-
2.33	- Passenger and freight	...	10 488	10 688	...	3 703	3 664	-	-	-

RAILWAY TRANSPORT- TRANSPORT FERROVIAIRE
ЖЕЛЕЗНЫЕ ДОРОГИ

2. Networks at 31 December
2. Réseau au 31 décembre
2. Сети на 31 декабря

Unit : km - Unité : km - Единица - км

		Latvia Lettonie Латвия			Lithuania Lituanie Литва			Luxembourg Luxembourg Люксембург		
		1990	1998	1999	1990	1998	1999	1990	1998	1999
1	**Total length of lines**	**2 397**	**2 413**	**2 413**	**2 007**	**1 998**	**1 905**	**271**	**274**	**274**
	by type of track									
1.11	- Single track	2 093	2 110	2 110	...	1 433	1 340	125	134	134
1.12	- Double track or more	304	303	303	...	565	565	146	140	140
	by track gauge									
1.21	- Standard gauge	-	-	-	...	22	22	271	274	274
1.22	- Large gauge	2 364	2 380	2 380	...	1 807	1 807	-	-	-
1.23	- Narrow gauge	33	33	33	...	169	76	-	-	-
	by nature of traffic									
1.31	- Passenger only	-	51	51	-	-	-	-	-	-
1.32	- Freight only	-	211	215	-	-	-	39	38	38
1.33	- Passenger and freight	2 397	2 151	2 147	2 007	1 998	1 905	232	236	236
2	**Length of electrified lines**	**271**	**270**	**258**	**122**	**122**	**122**	**197**	**261**	**261**
	by type of track									
2.11	- Single track	55	54	54	-	5	5	74	121	121
2.12	- Double track or more	216	216	204	...	117	117	123	140	140
	by track gauge									
2.21	- Standard gauge	-	-	-	-	-	-	197	261	261
2.22	- Large gauge	271	270	258	122	122	122	-	-	-
2.23	- Narrow gauge	-	-	-	-	-	-	-	-	-
	by nature of traffic									
2.31	- Passenger only	-	-	-	-	-	-	-	-	-
2.32	- Freight only	-	-	-	-	-	-	26	25	25
2.33	- Passenger and freight	271	270	258	122	122	122	171	236	236

		Netherlands Pays-Bas Нидерланды			Norway Norvège Норвегия			Poland Pologne Польша		
		1990	1998	1999	1990	1998	1999	1990	1998	1999
1	**Total length of lines**	**2 780**	**2 808**	**2 808**	**4 044**	**4 006**	**4 179**	**26 228**	**23 210**	**22 891**
	by type of track									
1.11	- Single track	1 006	848	848	3 945	3 875	3 994	17 235	14 337	13 993
1.12	- Double track or more	1 774	1 960	1 960	99	131	185	8 993	8 873	8 898
	by track gauge									
1.21	- Standard gauge	2 780	2 808	2 808	4 044	4 006	4 179	...	21 491	21 347
1.22	- Large gauge	-	-	-	-	-	-	...	622	559
1.23	- Narrow gauge	-	-	-	-	-	-	2 235	1 097	985
	by nature of traffic									
1.31	- Passenger only	...	...	...	-	-	...	-	-	-
1.32	- Freight only	239	...	...	...	...	...	-	-	-
1.33	- Passenger and freight	...	...	...	...	...	...	26 228	23 210	22 891
2	**Length of electrified lines**	**1 939**	**2 061**	**2 061**	**2 426**	**2 456**	**2 519**	**11 387**	**11 614**	**11 967**
	by type of track									
2.11	- Single track	241	184	184	2 327	2 325	2 334	3 561	3 668	3 956
2.12	- Double track or more	1 698	1 877	1 877	99	131	185	7 826	7 946	8 011
	by track gauge									
2.21	- Standard gauge	1 939	2 061	2 061	2 426	2 456	2 519	...	11 598	11 952
2.22	- Large gauge	-	-	-	-	-	-	...	16	15
2.23	- Narrow gauge	-	-	-	-	-	-	-	-	-
	by nature of traffic									
2.31	- Passenger only	...	...	...	-	-	-	-	-	-
2.32	- Freight only	...	...	...	-	-	-	-	-	-
2.33	- Passenger and freight	...	...	...	2 426	2 456	2 519	11 387	11 614	11 967

RAILWAY TRANSPORT- TRANSPORT FERROVIAIRE
ЖЕЛЕЗНЫЕ ДОРОГИ

2. Networks at 31 December
2. Réseau au 31 décembre
2. Сети на 31 декабря

Unit : km - Unité : km - Единица - км

		Portugal Portugal Португалия			Republic of Moldova République de Moldova Республика Молдова			Romania Roumanie Румыния		
		1990	1998	1999	1990	1998	1999	1990	1998	1999
1	**Total length of lines**	3 127	2 794	2 814	1 150	1 220	1 140	11 348	11 010	10 981
	by type of track									
1.11	- Single track	...	2 329	2 317	...	1 010	961	8 399	8 045	8 016
1.12	- Double track or more	...	465	497	...	210	179	2 949	2 965	2 965
	by track gauge									
1.21	- Standard gauge	...	-	-	...	26	14	10 876	10 895	10 924
1.22	- Large gauge	...	2 580	2 599	...	1 194	1 126	45	57	57
1.23	- Narrow gauge	...	214	215	...	-	-	427	58	-
	by nature of traffic									
1.31	- Passenger only	...	261	343	...	-	-	-	-	-
1.32	- Freight only	...	186	193	...	-	-	-	-	-
1.33	- Passenger and freight	...	2 347	2 278	...	1 220	1 140	11 348	11 010	10 981
2	**Length of electrified lines**	457	873	901	-	-	-	3 680	3 929	3 942
	by type of track									
2.11	- Single track	54	442	438	-	-	-	...	1 620	1 633
2.12	- Double track or more	403	431	463	-	-	-	...	2 309	2 309
	by track gauge									
2.21	- Standard gauge	-	-	-	-	-	-	3 680	3 929	3 942
2.22	- Large gauge	...	873	901	-	-	-	-	-	-
2.23	- Narrow gauge	...	-	-	-	-	-	-	-	-
	by nature of traffic									
2.31	- Passenger only	26	41	59	-	-	-	-	-	-
2.32	- Freight only	-	11	35	-	-	-	-	-	-
2.33	- Passenger and freight	436	821	807	-	-	-	3 680	3 929	3 942

		Russian Federation Fédération de Russie Российская Федерация			Slovakia Slovaquie Словакия			Slovenia Slovénie Словения		
		1990	1998	1999	1990	1998	1999	1990	1998	1999
1	**Total length of lines**	87 200	86 151	86 031	3 660	3 665	3 665	1 196	1 201	1 206
	by type of track									
1.11	- Single track	...	49 662	49 692	2 649	2 646	2 646	864	870	876
1.12	- Double track or more	...	36 489	36 339	1 011	1 019	1 019	332	331	330
	by track gauge									
1.21	- Standard gauge	...	-	-	3 507	3 509	3 509	1 196	1 201	1 206
1.22	- Large gauge	...	85 112	85 021	102	106	106	-	-	-
1.23	- Narrow gauge	...	1 039	1 010	51	50	50	-	-	-
	by nature of traffic									
1.31	- Passenger only	...	-	-	-	50	50	...	2	2
1.32	- Freight only	...	-	-	-	106	106	...	106	106
1.33	- Passenger and freight	...	86 151	86 031	3 660	3 509	3 509	...	1 093	1 098
2	**Length of electrified lines**	...	39 836	40 293	1 330	1 535	1 535	499	499	504
	by type of track									
2.11	- Single track	...	9 774	9 909	...	624	624	167	168	174
2.12	- Double track or more	...	30 062	30 384	...	911	911	332	331	330
	by track gauge									
2.21	- Standard gauge	...	-	-	...	1 394	1 394	499	499	504
2.22	- Large gauge	...	39 836	40 293	...	95	95	-	-	-
2.23	- Narrow gauge	...	-	-	...	46	46	-	-	-
	by nature of traffic									
2.31	- Passenger only	...	-	-	-	46	46	...	-	-
2.32	- Freight only	...	-	-	-	95	95	...	10	10
2.33	- Passenger and freight	...	39 836	40 293	1 330	1 394	1 394	...	489	494

RAILWAY TRANSPORT- TRANSPORT FERROVIAIRE
ЖЕЛЕЗНЫЕ ДОРОГИ

2. Networks at 31 December
2. Réseau au 31 décembre
2. Сети на 31 декабря

Unit : km - Unité : km - Единица - км

		Spain Espagne Испания			Sweden Suède Швеция			Switzerland Suisse Швейцария		
		1990	1998	1999	1990	1998	1999	1990	1998	1999
1	**Total length of lines**	**12 560**	**12 303**	**12 319**	**10 801**	**9 855**	**9 884**	**2 982**	**2 910**	**2 902**
	by type of track									
1.11	- Single track	9 857	8 898	8 905	9 610	8 336	8 343	1 464	...	...
1.12	- Double track or more	2 703	3 405	3 414	1 191	1 519	1 541	1 518	...	...
	by track gauge									
1.21	- Standard gauge	...	481	481	10 801	9 855	9 884	...	2 836	2 828
1.22	- Large gauge	...	11 803	11 819	-	-	-	-	-	-
1.23	- Narrow gauge	...	19	19	-	-	-	...	74	74
	by nature of traffic									
1.31	- Passenger only	...	1 685	1 561	-	...	...	...	...	...
1.32	- Freight only	1 407	716	708	1 730	...	...	66	...	100
1.33	- Passenger and freight	...	9 902	10 050	9 071	...	...	...	...	...
2	**Length of electrified lines**	**6 416**	**6 950**	**6 959**	**6 995**	**7 360**	**7 372**	**2 969**	**2 902**	**2 894**
	by type of track									
2.11	- Single track	3 232	3 566	3 566	5 804	5 841	5 831	1 451	...	...
2.12	- Double track or more	3 184	3 384	3 393	1 191	1 519	1 541	1 518	...	...
	by track gauge									
2.21	- Standard gauge	...	481	481	6 995	7 360	7 372	...	2 828	2 820
2.22	- Large gauge	...	6 450	6 459	-	-	-	-	-	-
2.23	- Narrow gauge	...	19	19	-	-	-	...	74	74
	by nature of traffic									
2.31	- Passenger only	...	981	1 007	-	...	...	...	...	...
2.32	- Freight only	...	265	258	-	...	...	...	...	...
2.33	- Passenger and freight	...	5 704	5 694	6 995	...	...	...	...	...

		Tajikistan Tadjikistan Таджикистан			The FYR of Macedonia [1]			Turkey Turquie Турция		
		1990	1998	1999	1990	1998	1999	1990	1998	1999
1	**Total length of lines**	**500**	**547**	**547**	**696**	**699**	**699**	**8 429**	**8 607**	**8 682**
	by type of track									
1.11	- Single track	...	485	485	696	699	699	8 163	8 240	8 257
1.12	- Double track or more	...	62	62	-	-	-	266	367	425
	by track gauge									
1.21	- Standard gauge	...	-	-	696	699	699	8 429	8 607	8 682
1.22	- Large gauge	...	547	547	-	-	-	-	-	-
1.23	- Narrow gauge	...	-	-	-	-	-	-	-	-
	by nature of traffic									
1.31	- Passenger only	...	-	-	-	-	-	-	-	-
1.32	- Freight only	...	-	-	-	-	-	-	-	-
1.33	- Passenger and freight	...	547	547	696	699	699	8 429	8 607	8 682
2	**Length of electrified lines**	**...**	**-**	**-**	**233**	**233**	**233**	**603**	**1 706**	**1 763**
	by type of track									
2.11	- Single track	...	-	-	233	233	233	414	1 478	1 479
2.12	- Double track or more	...	-	-	-	-	-	189	228	284
	by track gauge									
2.21	- Standard gauge	...	-	-	233	233	233	603	1 706	1 763
2.22	- Large gauge	...	-	-	-	-	-	-	-	-
2.23	- Narrow gauge	...	-	-	-	-	-	-	-	-
	by nature of traffic									
2.31	- Passenger only	...	-	-	-	-	-	-	-	-
2.32	- Freight only	...	-	-	-	-	-	-	-	-
2.33	- Passenger and freight	...	-	-	233	233	233	603	1 706	1 763

1- The former Yugoslav Republic of Macedonia

1- L'ex-République yougoslave de Macédoine

1- Бывшая Югославская Республика Македония

RAILWAY TRANSPORT- TRANSPORT FERROVIAIRE
ЖЕЛЕЗНЫЕ ДОРОГИ

2. Networks at 31 December
2. Réseau au 31 décembre
2. Сети на 31 декабря

Unit : km - Unité : km - Единица - км

		Turkmenistan Turkménistan Туркменистан			Ukraine Ukraine Украина			United Kingdom Royaume-Uni Соединенное Королевство		
		1990	1998	1999	1990	1998	1999	1990	1998	1999
1	**Total length of lines**	**2 100**	**2 393**	**2 446**	**22 799**	**22 510**	**22 473**	**...**	**16 994**	**16 984**
	by type of track	...								
1.11	- Single track	...	2 365	2 417	...	15 086	15 114	...	...	...
1.12	- Double track or more	...	28	29	...	7 424	7 359	...	...	...
	by track gauge									
1.21	- Standard gauge	...	-	-	...	49	48	...	16 659	16 649
1.22	- Large gauge	...	2 393	2 446	...	21 951	21 972	...	335	335
1.23	- Narrow gauge	...	-	-	...	510	453	...	-	-
	by nature of traffic									
1.31	- Passenger only	...	-	-		-	-	...	333	333
1.32	- Freight only	...	-	-		-	-	...	1 621	1 611
1.33	- Passenger and freight	...	2 393	2 446	22 799	22 510	22 473	...	15 040	15 040
2	**Length of electrified lines**	**-**	**-**	**-**	**8 113**	**8 927**	**9 104**	**...**	**5 166**	**5 166**
	by type of track									
2.11	- Single track	-	-	-	...	2 902	4 423	...	...	...
2.12	- Double track or more	-	-	-	...	6 025	4 681	...	...	...
	by track gauge									
2.21	- Standard gauge	-	-	-	-	-	-	...	5 166	5 166
2.22	- Large gauge	-	-	-	8 113	8 927	9 104	...	-	-
2.23	- Narrow gauge	-	-	-	-	-	-	...	-	-
	by nature of traffic									
2.31	- Passenger only	-	-	-	-	-	-	...	...	...
2.32	- Freight only	-	-	-	-	-	-	...	...	...
2.33	- Passenger and freight	-	-	-	8 113	8 927	9 104	...	...	...

		United States Etats-Unis Соединенные Штаты			Uzbekistan Ouzbékistan Узбекистан			Yugoslavia Yugoslavie Югославия		
		1990	1998	1999	1990	1998	1999	1990	1998	1999
1	**Total length of lines**	**192 732**	**161 817**	**159 983**	**3 500**	**3 641**	**3 645**	**3 959**	**4 058**	**4 058**
	by type of track									
1.11	- Single track	...	...	...	...	3 241	3 227	3 682	3 782	3 782
1.12	- Double track or more	...	...	...	...	400	418	277	276	276
	by track gauge									
1.21	- Standard gauge	...	...	...	...	-	-	3 959	4 058	4 058
1.22	- Large gauge	...	...	...	...	3 641	3 645	-	-	-
1.23	- Narrow gauge	...	...	...	...	...	...	-	-	-
	by nature of traffic									
1.31	- Passenger only	...	...	...	...	-	-			
1.32	- Freight only	154 108	...	...	...	-	-	-	-	-
1.33	- Passenger and freight	...	...	...	...	3 641	3 645	3 959	4 058	4 058
2	**Length of electrified lines**	**1 667**	**...**	**...**	**...**	**587**	**619**	**1 342**	**1 364**	**1 364**
	by type of track									
2.11	- Single track	...	...	...	...	187	219	...	1 093	1 093
2.12	- Double track or more	1 233	...	...	...	400	400	...	271	271
	by track gauge									
2.21	- Standard gauge	...	...	...	...	-	-	1 342	1 364	1 364
2.22	- Large gauge	...	...	...	...	587	619	-	-	-
2.23	- Narrow gauge	...	...	...	...	-	-	-	-	-
	by nature of traffic									
2.31	- Passenger only	...	...	...	...	-	-	-	-	-
2.32	- Freight only	...	...	...	...	-	-	-	-	-
2.33	- Passenger and freight	...	...	...	...	587	619	1 342	1 364	1 364

1- Class 1 railways including AMTRAK.

1- Chemins de fer de 1ère classe y compris l'AMTRAK.

1- Железные дороги 1-ого класса, включая данные по AMTRAK.

RAILWAY TRANSPORT- TRANSPORT FERROVIAIRE
ЖЕЛЕЗНЫЕ ДОРОГИ

3. Mobile equipment at 31 December

3. Equipement mobile au 31 décembre

3. Подвижной состав на 31 декабря

Item Rubrique Статья	Description	Description	Описание
1.1	**Locomotives (number)**	**Locomotives (nombre)**	**Локомотивы (число)**
1.11	- Electric locomotives	- Locomotives électriques	- Электровозы
1.12	- Diesel locomotives	- Locomotives Diesel	- Тепловозы
1.13	- Steam locomotives	- Locomotives à vapeur	- Паровозы
1.2	**Locomotives - power (1000 kW)**	**Locomotives - puissance (1000 kW)**	**Локомотивы (1000 кВт)**
1.21	- Electric locomotives	- Locomotives électriques	- Электровозы
1.22	- Diesel locomotives	- Locomotives Diesel	- Тепловозы
1.23	- Steam locomotives	- Locomotives à vapeur	- Паровозы
2.1	**Railcars (number)**	**Automotrices (nombre)**	**Автомотрисы (число)**
2.11	- Electric railcars	- Automotrices électriques	- Электромотрисы
2.12	- Diesel railcars	- Automotrices Diesel	- Дизельные автомотрисы
2.2	**Railcars - power (1000 kW)**	**Automotrices - puissance (1000 kW)**	**Автомотрисы (1000 кВт)**
2.21	- Electric railcars	- Automotrices électriques	- Электромотрисы
2.22	- Diesel railcars	- Automotrices Diesel	- Дизельные автомотрисы
3.1	**Passenger carriages (number)**	**Voitures de voyageurs (nombre)**	**Пассажирские вагоны (число)**
3.11	- Coaches	- voitures	- Пассажирские вагоны
3.12	- Passenger railcars and railcar trailers	- Automotrices de voyageurs et remorques d'automotrices	- Пассажирские автомотрисы
3.2	**Number of seats and berths (1000)**	**Nombre de places assises et couchées (1000)**	**Число сидячих и спальных мест (1000)**
3.21	- Coaches	- voitures	- Пассажирские вагоны
3.22	- Passenger railcars and railcar trailers	- Automotrices de voyageurs et remorques d'automotrices	- Пассажирские автомотрисы
4	**Vans (number)**	**Fourgons (nombre)**	**Багажные вагоны (число)**
5	**Wagons (number)**	**Wagons (nombre)**	**Вагоны (число)**
5.10	- Covered wagons	- Wagons couverts	- Крытые вагоны
5.20	- High-sided wagons	- Wagons-tombereaux	- Полувагоны
5.30	- Flat wagons	- Wagons plat	- Вагоны-платформы
5.40	- Other wagons	- Autres wagons	- Прочие вагоны
5.1	**Principal Railway Enterprise(s) Wagons**	**Wagons de(s) l'entreprise(s) ferroviaire(s) principale(s)**	**Товарные вагоны, принадлежащие основ ным железнодорожным предприятиям**
5.11	- Covered wagons	- Wagons couverts	- Крытые вагоны
5.21	- High-sided wagons	- Wagons-tombereaux	- Полувагоны
5.31	- Flat wagons	- Wagons plat	- Вагоны-платформы
5.41	- Other wagons	- Autres wagons	- Прочие вагоны
6	**Wagons (capacity in 10^3 tonnes)**	**Wagons (capacité en 10^3 tonnes)**	**Вагоны (емкость в 10^3 т)**
6.10	- Covered wagons	- Wagons couverts	- Крытые вагоны
6.20	- High-sided wagons	- Wagons-tombereaux	- Полувагоны
6.30	- Flat wagons	- Wagons plat	- Вагоны-платформы
6.40	- Other wagons	- Autres wagons	- Прочие вагоны
6.1	**Principal Railway Enterprise(s) Wagons**	**Wagons de(s) l'entreprise(s) ferroviaire(s) principale(s)**	**Товарные вагоны, принадлежащие основ ным железнодорожным предприятиям**
6.11	- Covered wagons	- Wagons couverts	- Крытые вагоны
6.21	- High-sided wagons	- Wagons-tombereaux	- Полувагоны
6.31	- Flat wagons	- Wagons plat	- Вагоны-платформы
6.41	- Other wagons	- Autres wagons	- Прочие вагоны

RAILWAY TRANSPORT- TRANSPORT FERROVIAIRE
ЖЕЛЕЗНЫЕ ДОРОГИ

3. Mobile equipment at 31 December
3. Equipement mobile au 31 décembre
3. Подвижной состав на 31 декабря

		Albania Albanie Албания			Armenia Arménie Армения			Austria Autriche Австрия		
		1990	1998	1999	1990	1998	1999	1990	1998	1999
1.1	**Locomotives (number)**	...	68	68	...	59	...	1 232	...	1 181
1.11	- Electric	...	-	-	...	46	...	725	...	714
1.12	- Diesel	...	68	68	...	11	...	489	525	448
1.13	- Steam	...	-	-	...	-	...	18	40	19
1.2	**Locomotives (1000 kW)**	...	94	94	...	...	...	2 557	...	...
1.21	- Electric	...	-	-	...	...	...	2 285	...	...
1.22	- Diesel	...	94	94	...	...	...	268	...	...
1.23	- Steam	...	-	-	...	...	...	4	...	...
2.1	**Railcars (number)**	...	-	-	...	28	...	321	...	888
2.11	- Electric	...	-	-	...	28	...	225	...	759
2.12	- Diesel	...	-	-	...	-	...	96	163	129
2.2	**Railcars (1000 kW)**	...	-		...	...	...	318	...	...
2.21	- Electric	...	-	-	...	...	...	285	...	...
2.22	- Diesel	...	-	-	...	...	...	33	...	...
3.1	**Passenger carriages (number)**	...	79	99	...	134	...	3 461	3 583	3 571
3.11	- Coaches	...	79	99	...	134	...	...	2 669	2 670
3.12	- Railcars and railcar trailers	...	-	-	...	-	...	...	914	901
3.2	**Seats and berths (1000)**	...	5	6	...	...	...	...	235	237
3.21	- Coaches	...	5	6	...	...	...	...	...	...
3.22	- Railcars and railcar trailers	...	-	-	...	...	...	...	...	...
4	**Vans (number)**	...	13	13	...	...	...	...	144	137
5	**Total wagons (number)**	...	1 648	840	...	...	...	34 330	19 316	18 741
5.10	- Covered	...	...	146	...	...	...	...	9 240	8 282
5.20	- High-sided	...	...	255	...	...	...	...	2 978	2 929
5.30	- Flat	...	...	287	...	...	...	...	6 318	6 137
5.40	- Other wagons	...	...	152	...	...	...	...	780	1 393
5.1	**Principal Railway Enterprise(s)**	...	1 648	840	...	...	...	...	18 683	18 180
5.11	- Covered	...	...	146	...	...	...	11 675	9 099	8 153
5.21	- High-sided	...	...	255	...	...	...	5 690	2 862	2 820
5.31	- Flat	...	...	287	...	...	...	...	6 069	5 957
5.41	- Other wagons	...	...	152	...	...	...	6 183	653	1 250
6	**Total wagons (1000 tonnes)**	...	64.0	35.0	...	...	...	1 250.0	...	...
6.10	- Covered	...	...	5.0	...	...	...	...	...	...
6.20	- High-sided	...	...	9.0	...	...	...	...	...	...
6.30	- Flat	...	...	14.0	...	...	...	...	...	...
6.40	- Other wagons	...	...	7.0	...	...	...	...	...	...
6.1	**Principal Railway Enterprise(s)**	...	64.0	35.0	...	...	...	...	...	...
6.11	- Covered	...	...	5.0	...	...	...	...	...	...
6.21	- High-sided	...	...	9.0	...	...	...	...	...	...
6.31	- Flat	...	...	14.0	...	...	...	...	...	...
6.41	- Other wagons	...	...	7.0	...	...	...	...	...	...

RAILWAY TRANSPORT- TRANSPORT FERROVIAIRE
ЖЕЛЕЗНЫЕ ДОРОГИ

3. Mobile equipment at 31 December
3. Equipement mobile au 31 décembre
3. Подвижной состав на 31 декабря

		Azerbaijan Azerbaïdjan Азербайджан			Belarus Bélarus Беларусь			Belgium Belgique Бельгия		
		1990	1998	1999	1990	1998	1999	1990	1998	1999
1.1	**Locomotives (number)**	809	576	573	...	...	...	1 040	943	939
1.11	- Electric	...	238	235	...	...	...	381	372	383
1.12	- Diesel	...	279	279	...	...	...	659	571	556
1.13	- Steam	...	59	59	...	...	...	-	-	-
1.2	**Locomotives (1000 kW)**	...	...	...	...	...	...	1 508	1 511	1 607
1.21	- Electric	...	...	...	...	...	...	1 062	1 041	1 149
1.22	- Diesel	...	...	...	...	...	...	446	470	458
1.23	- Steam	...	...	...	...	...	...	-	-	-
2.1	**Railcars (number)**	...	77	78	...	...	...	687	665	682
2.11	- Electric	...	76	76	...	...	...	663	648	665
2.12	- Diesel	...	1	2	...	...	...	24	17	17
2.2	**Railcars (1000 kW)**	...	...	...	...	...	...	549	707	741
2.21	- Electric	...	...	...	...	...	...	544	703	737
2.22	- Diesel	...	...	...	...	...	...	5	4	4
3.1	**Passenger carriages (number)**	...	1 020	871	...	...	...	3 271	3 398	3 468
3.11	- Coaches	931	866	715	...	...	...	1 826	1 681	1 683
3.12	- Railcars and railcar trailers	...	154	156	...	...	...	1 445	1 717	1 785
3.2	**Seats and berths (1000)**	...	32	31	...	...	...	292	291	295
3.21	- Coaches	...	...	...	...	...	...	168	152	152
3.22	- Railcars and railcar trailers	...	...	...	...	...	...	124	139	143
4	**Vans (number)**	...	46	37	...	...	...	42	29	29
5	**Total wagons (number)**	30 875	26 058	...	45 604	...	...	30 566	18 575	18 688
5.10	- Covered	...	...	...	...	...	...	...	2 350	2 286
5.20	- High-sided	...	...	...	...	...	...	...	3 903	3 395
5.30	- Flat	...	...	...	...	...	...	...	11 011	11 037
5.40	- Other wagons	...	...	...	...	...	...	...	1 847	1 970
5.1	**Principal Railway Enterprise(s)**	...	25 872	...	...	...	...	27 345	12 947	12 986
5.11	- Covered	...	8 853	...	...	...	...	7 500	1 559	1 630
5.21	- High-sided	...	5 145	5 676	...	...	...	8 001	2 947	2 843
5.31	- Flat	...	4 656	4 707	...	...	...	11 167	8 397	8 467
5.41	- Other wagons	...	7 218	5 735	...	...	...	677	44	46
6	**Total wagons (1000 tonnes)**	...	1 657.3	1 749.5	...	...	...	1 358.0	1 017.0	1 028.0
6.10	- Covered	...	...	...	...	...	...	...	84.0	91.0
6.20	- High-sided	...	...	...	...	...	...	...	212.0	205.0
6.30	- Flat	...	...	...	...	...	...	...	618.0	618.0
6.40	- Other wagons	...	...	...	...	...	...	...	103.0	114.0
6.1	**Principal Railway Enterprise(s)**	...	1 643.7	1 644.4	...	...	...	1 180.0	664.0	667.0
6.11	- Covered	...	540.7	582.7	...	...	...	246.0	57.0	57.0
6.21	- High-sided	...	341.1	383.5	...	...	...	350.0	158.0	150.0
6.31	- Flat	...	309.4	309.5	...	...	...	554.0	447.0	458.0
6.41	- Other wagons	...	452.5	368.8	...	...	...	30.0	2.0	2.0

RAILWAY TRANSPORT- TRANSPORT FERROVIAIRE
ЖЕЛЕЗНЫЕ ДОРОГИ

3. Mobile equipment at 31 December
3. Equipement mobile au 31 décembre
3. Подвижной состав на 31 декабря

		Bosnia-Herzegovina Bosnie-Herzégovine Босния и Герцеговина			Bulgaria Bulgarie Болгария			Canada Canada Канада		
		1990	1998	1999	1990	1998	1999	1990	1998	1999
1.1	**Locomotives (number)**	...	...	131	1 111	715	714	...	3 180	...
1.11	- Electric	...	...	51	365	305	304	...	38	...
1.12	- Diesel	...	...	80	637	410	410	...	3 142	...
1.13	- Steam	...	...	-	109	-	-	...	-	...
1.2	**Locomotives (1000 kW)**	...	...	...	2 078	1 445	1 445	...	...	...
1.21	- Electric	...	...	...	1 187	969	968	...	...	...
1.22	- Diesel	...	...	...	722	476	477	...	...	...
1.23	- Steam	...	...	...	169	-	-	...	-	...
2.1	**Railcars (number)**	...	...	15	94	84	82	...	...	...
2.11	- Electric	...	...	15	83	80	78	...	...	...
2.12	- Diesel	...	...	-	11	4	4	...	...	...
2.2	**Railcars (1000 kW)**	...	...	...	145	108	105	...	...	...
2.21	- Electric	...	...	...	139	106	103	...	...	...
2.22	- Diesel	...	...	...	6	2	2	...	...	...
3.1	**Passenger carriages (number)**	...	17	177	2 026	1 793	1 757	...	430	...
3.11	- Coaches	...	...	165	1 932	1 709	1 675	...		...
3.12	- Railcars and railcar trailers	...	...	12	94	84	82	...		...
3.2	**Seats and berths (1000)**	...	...	10	...	143	141	...	...	...
3.21	- Coaches	...	...	...	125	117	115	...	...	...
3.22	- Railcars and railcar trailers	...	...	...	...	26	26	...	...	...
4	**Vans (number)**	...	...	6	105	98	97	...	...	...
5	**Total wagons (number)**	...	...	3 184	40 918	26 266	25 637	...	105 676	...
5.10	- Covered	...	...	...	8 487	3 630	3 354	...	25 993	...
5.20	- High-sided	...	...	...	15 056	7 636	7 554	...	52 976	...
5.30	- Flat	...	...	...	5 963	5 357	5 249	...	22 872	...
5.40	- Other wagons	...	...	...	11 412	9 643	9 480	...	3 835	...
5.1	**Principal Railway Enterprise(s)**	...	644	3 039	40 918	26 266	25 695	...	92 719	...
5.11	- Covered	...	...	1 672	8 487	3 630	3 354	...	22 845	...
5.21	- High-sided	...	...	841	15 056	7 636	7 554	...	49 076	...
5.31	- Flat	...	...	284	5 963	5 357	5 249	...	17 682	...
5.41	- Other wagons	...	...	242	11 412	9 643	9 480	...	3 116	...
6	**Total wagons (1000 tonnes)**	...	...	...	2 075.8	1 483.0	1 455.0	...	...	...
6.10	- Covered	...	...	...	302.3	155.0	146.0	...	...	...
6.20	- High-sided	...	...	...	786.5	454.0	450.0	...	...	...
6.30	- Flat	...	...	...	340.3	312.0	306.0	...	...	...
6.40	- Other wagons	...	...	...	646.7	562.0	553.0	...	...	...
6.1	**Principal Railway Enterprise(s)**	...	...	...	2 075.8	1 483.0	1 455.0	...	...	...
6.11	- Covered	...	...	51.4	302.3	155.0	146.0	...	...	...
6.21	- High-sided	...	...	...	786.5	454.0	450.0	...	...	...
6.31	- Flat	...	...	...	340.3	312.0	306.0	...	...	...
6.41	- Other wagons	...	...	...	646.7	562.0	553.0	...	...	...

RAILWAY TRANSPORT- TRANSPORT FERROVIAIRE
ЖЕЛЕЗНЫЕ ДОРОГИ

3. Mobile equipment at 31 December
3. Equipement mobile au 31 décembre
3. Подвижной состав на 31 декабря

		Croatia Croatie Хорватия			Czech Republic République tchèque Чешская Республика			Denmark Danemark Дания		
		1990	1998	1999	1990	1998	1999	1990	1998	1999
1.1	**Locomotives (number)**	**448**	**430**	**389**	...	**2 923**	**2 851**	**328**	**208**	...
1.11	- Electric	138	140	136	...	1 073	1 051	10	22	...
1.12	- Diesel	306	288	251	...	1 831	1 780	318	186	...
1.13	- Steam	4	2	2	...	19	20	-	-	...
1.2	**Locomotives (1000 kW)**	**469**	**760**	**688**	...	**4 066**	**3 977**	**367**	**321**	...
1.21	- Electric	1	516	505	...	2 390	2 339	40	88	...
1.22	- Diesel	450	243	182	...	1 661	1 623	327	233	...
1.23	- Steam	318	1	1	...	15	15	-	-	...
2.1	**Railcars (number)**	**279**	**110**	**91**	...	**972**	**983**	**546**	**481**	...
2.11	- Electric	...	29	25	...	166	166	299	96	...
2.12	- Diesel	...	81	66	...	806	817	247	385	...
2.2	**Railcars (1000 kW)**	...	**69**	**55**	...	**230**	**230**	**240**	**233**	...
2.21	- Electric	...	37	31	...	32	32	178	85	...
2.22	- Diesel	...	32	24	...	198	198	62	148	...
3.1	**Passenger carriages (number)**	**1 052**	**777**	**720**	...	**5 778**	**5 607**	**1 533**	**1 518**	...
3.11	- Coaches	...	526	521	...	3 514	3 338	660	286	...
3.12	- Railcars and railcar trailers	...	251	199	...	2 264	2 269	873	1 232	...
3.2	**Seats and berths (1000)**	**76**	**49**	**45**	...	**381**	**375**	**97**	**53**	...
3.21	- Coaches	57	32	31	...	247	235	...	20	...
3.22	- Railcars and railcar trailers	19	17	14	...	134	140	...	33	...
4	**Vans (number)**	...	**57**	**57**	...	**568**	**606**	**15**	**1**	...
5	**Total wagons (number)**	**13 730**	**10 302**	**10 270**	...	**71 678**	**67 110**	**4 261**	**3 108**	**2 450**
5.10	- Covered	...	4 927	4 917	...	...	...	2 677	1 408	...
5.20	- High-sided	...	3 535	3 518	...	...	...	251	119	...
5.30	- Flat	...	896	894	...	...	...	1 254	1 432	...
5.40	- Other wagons	...	944	941	...	...	...	79	-	...
5.1	**Principal Railway Enterprise(s)**	**13 730**	**10 302**	**10 270**	...	**61 090**	**56 289**	**3 890**	**2 869**	**2 259**
5.11	- Covered	...	4 927	4 917	...	14 734	12 794	...	...	...
5.21	- High-sided	...	3 535	3 518	...	34 736	32 978	...	...	...
5.31	- Flat	...	896	894	...	6 992	6 790	...	...	...
5.41	- Other wagons	...	944	941	...	4 628	3 727	...	...	...
6	**Total wagons (1000 tonnes)**	**575.9**	**480.0**	**483.0**	...	**3 339.0**	**3 174.0**	**148.0**	**106.0**	...
6.10	- Covered	...	221.0	223.0	...	...	...	...	39.0	...
6.20	- High-sided	...	177.0	178.0	...	...	...	...	5.0	...
6.30	- Flat	...	42.0	42.0	...	...	...	...	62.0	...
6.40	- Other wagons	...	40.0	40.0	...	...	...	...	-	...
6.1	**Principal Railway Enterprise(s)**	**575.9**	**480.0**	**483.0**	...	**2 810.0**	**2 636.0**	...	**98.0**	...
6.11	- Covered	...	221.0	223.0	...	575.0	514.0	...	...	...
6.21	- High-sided	...	177.0	178.0	...	1 629.0	1 568.0	...	...	...
6.31	- Flat	...	42.0	42.0	...	367.0	362.0	...	...	...
6.41	- Other wagons	...	40.0	40.0	...	239.0	192.0	...	...	...

RAILWAY TRANSPORT- TRANSPORT FERROVIAIRE
ЖЕЛЕЗНЫЕ ДОРОГИ

3. Mobile equipment at 31 December
3. Equipement mobile au 31 décembre
3. Подвижной состав на 31 декабря

		Estonia Estonie Эстония			Finland Finlande Финляндия			France France Франция		
		1990	1998	1999	1990	1998	1999	1990	1998	1999
1.1	**Locomotives (number)**	...	**113**	**119**	**682**	**640**	**639**	**5 654**	**5 125**	**5 006**
1.11	- Electric	...	-	-	110	129	130	2 298	2 126	2 024
1.12	- Diesel	...	111	117	572	511	509	3 356	2 999	2 982
1.13	- Steam	...	2	2	-	-	-	-	-	-
1.2	**Locomotives (1000 kW)**	...	...	...	**747**	**814**	**817**	**9 555**	...	...
1.21	- Electric	...	...	...	341	455	461	7 590	...	...
1.22	- Diesel	...	...	...	406	359	356	1 965	...	...
1.23	- Steam	...	...	...	-	-	-	-	...	...
2.1	**Railcars (number)**	...	**83**	**76**	**100**	**102**	**102**	**1 768**	**2 078**	**2 123**
2.11	- Electric	...	41	36	100	102	102	1 013	1 337	1 387
2.12	- Diesel	...	42	40	-	-	-	755	741	736
2.2	**Railcars (1000 kW)**	...	...	...	**74**	**82**	**82**	**2 877**	...	...
2.21	- Electric	...	...	...	74	82	82	2 527	...	...
2.22	- Diesel	...	...	...	-	-	-	350	...	...
3.1	**Passenger carriages (number)**	...	**328**	...	**965**	**968**	**994**	**15 798**	**15 830**	**15 764**
3.11	- Coaches	...	132	...	765	756	782	9 720	7 723	7 493
3.12	- Railcars and railcar trailers	...	196	...	200	212	212	6 078	8 107	8 271
3.2	**Seats and berths (1000)**	...	**23**	...	**66**	**63**	**65**	...	**1 274**	**1 279**
3.21	- Coaches	...	...	...	47	44	46	...	...	...
3.22	- Railcars and railcar trailers	...	...	...	19	19	19	...	...	...
4	**Vans (number)**	...	**7**	...	**36**	**35**	**35**	**551**	**236**	**236**
5	**Total wagons (number)**	...	**6 810**	**6 340**	**15 395**	**13 095**	**13 002**	**162 049**	**117 221**	**112 868**
5.10	- Covered	...	...	...	5 201	5 203	5 192	38 739	17 613	...
5.20	- High-sided	...	...	...	2 080	982	948	26 289	15 621	...
5.30	- Flat	...	...	...	7 329	5 878	5 833	58 336	53 282	...
5.40	- Other wagons	...	...	...	785	1 032	1 029	38 685	30 705	...
5.1	**Principal Railway Enterprise(s)**	...	**5 114**	**4 567**	**14 972**	**12 737**	**12 647**	**89 146**	**51 344**	**48 330**
5.11	- Covered	...	708	1 058	...	5 103	5 092	32 689	12 845	11 489
5.21	- High-sided	...	1 613	1 571	...	982	948	17 877	8 469	7 734
5.31	- Flat	...	440	581	...	5 874	5 829	37 873	29 755	28 819
5.41	- Other wagons	...	2 353	1 357	...	778	778	707	275	288
6	**Total wagons (1000 tonnes)**	...	**446.4**	**421.0**	**590.1**	**552.0**	**552.0**	**7 224.0**	**5 630.0**	**5 489.0**
6.10	- Covered	...	...	...	147.1	187.0	190.0	1 538.0	774.0	...
6.20	- High-sided	...	...	...	86.4	50.0	49.0	1 244.0	758.0	...
6.30	- Flat	...	...	...	313.0	263.0	261.0	2 544.0	2 440.0	...
6.40	- Other wagons	...	...	...	43.6	52.0	52.0	1 898.0	1 658.0	...
6.1	**Principal Railway Enterprise(s)**	...	**340.7**	**303.7**	**571.9**	**537.0**	**537.0**	**3 917.0**	**2 503.0**	**2 395.0**
6.11	- Covered	...	46.0	68.8	...	181.0	184.0	1 254.0	543.0	496.0
6.21	- High-sided	...	108.9	106.0	...	50.0	49.0	814.0	430.0	406.0
6.31	- Flat	...	29.3	38.6	...	263.0	261.0	1 822.0	1 517.0	1 479.0
6.41	- Other wagons	...	156.5	90.2	...	43.0	43.0	27.0	13.0	14.0

RAILWAY TRANSPORT- TRANSPORT FERROVIAIRE
ЖЕЛЕЗНЫЕ ДОРОГИ

3. Mobile equipment at 31 December
3. Equipement mobile au 31 décembre
3. Подвижной состав на 31 декабря

		Georgia Georgie Грузия			Germany Allemagne Германия			Greece Grèce Греция		
		1990	1998	1999	1990	1998	1999	1990	1998	1999
1.1	**Locomotives (number)**	...	421	407	...	7 897	7 449	233	356	...
1.11	- Electric	...	240	228	...	3 773	3 709	-	6	...
1.12	- Diesel	...	177	175	...	4 071	3 722	233	260	...
1.13	- Steam	...	4	4	...	53	18	-	90	...
1.2	**Locomotives (1000 kW)**	...	...	...	...	18 719	18 506	340	...	...
1.21	- Electric	...	...	...	...	15 183	15 078	-	-	...
1.22	- Diesel	...	...	...	...	3 536	3 428	340	...	...
1.23	- Steam	...	...	...	...	-	-	-	-	...
2.1	**Railcars (number)**	...	99	90	...	2 733	5 544	168	345	...
2.11	- Electric	...	99	90	...	1 772	3 748	-	-	...
2.12	- Diesel	...	-	-	...	961	1 796	168	345	...
2.2	**Railcars (1000 kW)**	...	...	...	...	...	...	101	...	...
2.21	- Electric	...	...	...	...	...	...	-	-	...
2.22	- Diesel	...	-	-	...	...	...	101	...	...
3.1	**Passenger carriages (number)**	...	1 296	1 161	...	19 488	19 586	810	624	...
3.11	- Coaches	...	1 101	986	...	14 287	14 192	512	279	...
3.12	- Railcars and railcar trailers	...	195	175	...	5 201	5 394	298	345	...
3.2	**Seats and berths (1000)**	...	128	118	...	1 418	1 412	52	17	...
3.21	- Coaches	...	...	...	...	1 055	1 035	...	...	...
3.22	- Railcars and railcar trailers	...	...	...	...	364	377	...	...	...
4	**Vans (number)**	...	52	29	...	311	167	168	35	...
5	**Total wagons (number)**	...	17 491	17 488	...	197 720	187 946	10 967	2 669	...
5.10	- Covered	...	...	...	...	46 370	42 193	7 928	1 098	...
5.20	- High-sided	...	...	...	...	46 544	43 484	1 731	522	...
5.30	- Flat	...	...	...	...	59 872	59 703	928	359	...
5.40	- Other wagons	...	...	...	...	44 934	42 566	380	690	...
5.1	**Principal Railway Enterprise(s)**	...	16 682	16 678	...	136 663	129 159	10 967	2 669	...
5.11	- Covered	...	4 694	4 701	...	36 847	32 498	7 928	1 098	...
5.21	- High-sided	...	5 227	5 184	...	43 831	40 961	1 731	522	...
5.31	- Flat	...	1 800	1 826	...	54 067	53 843	928	359	...
5.41	- Other wagons	...	4 961	4 967	...	1 918	1 857	380	690	...
6	**Total wagons (1000 tonnes)**	...	1 223.5	1 223.1	...	...	...	261.0	110.8	...
6.10	- Covered	...	...	...	...	...	...	177.0	31.8	...
6.20	- High-sided	...	...	...	...	...	...	47.0	27.9	...
6.30	- Flat	...	...	...	...	...	...	26.0	16.1	...
6.40	- Other wagons	...	...	...	...	...	...	11.0	35.0	...
6.1	**Principal Railway Enterprise(s)**	...	1 171.3	1 171.0	...	5 978.4	5 249.0	261.0	110.8	...
6.11	- Covered	...	347.6	348.1	...	1 153.2	987.0	177.0	31.8	...
6.21	- High-sided	...	359.7	356.7	...	2 087.1	1 813.0	47.0	27.9	...
6.31	- Flat	...	116.8	118.5	...	2 682.2	2 397.0	26.0	16.1	...
6.41	- Other wagons	...	347.3	347.7	...	55.9	53.0	11.0	35.0	...

RAILWAY TRANSPORT- TRANSPORT FERROVIAIRE
ЖЕЛЕЗНЫЕ ДОРОГИ

3. Mobile equipment at 31 December
3. Equipement mobile au 31 décembre
3. Подвижной состав на 31 декабря

		Hungary Hongrie Венгрия			Ireland Irlande Ирландия			Israel Israël Израиль		
		1990	1998	1999	1990	1998	1999	1990	1998	1999
1.1	**Locomotives (number)**	**1 617**	**1 207**	**1 161**	**126**	**110**	**110**	**52**	**53**	**53**
1.11	- Electric	503	485	481	-	-	-	-	-	-
1.12	- Diesel	1 087	708	665	116	110	110	52	53	53
1.13	- Steam	27	14	15	10	-	-	-	-	-
1.2	**Locomotives (1000 kW)**	**1 981**	**1 608**	**1 587**	...	**141**	**141**	...	**84**	**84**
1.21	- Electric	1 098	1 056	1 048	-	-	-	-	-	-
1.22	- Diesel	869	545	533	116	141	141	...	84	84
1.23	- Steam	14	7	6	...	-	-	-	-	-
2.1	**Railcars (number)**	**282**	**333**	**340**	**40**	**57**	**82**	...	**24**	**24**
2.11	- Electric	-	24	24	40	40	40	-	-	-
2.12	- Diesel	282	309	316	-	17	42	...	24	24
2.2	**Railcars (1000 kW)**	**81**	**102**	**100**	...	**25**	**32**	...	**24**	**24**
2.21	- Electric	-	36	36	...	21	21	-	-	-
2.22	- Diesel	81	66	64	-	4	11	...	24	24
3.1	**Passenger carriages (number)**	**4 454**	**3 498**	**3 476**	**333**	**347**	**373**	**73**	**179**	**180**
3.11	- Coaches	4 172	...	2 839	253	250	251	...	107	108
3.12	- Railcars and railcar trailers	282	...	637	80	97	122	...	72	72
3.2	**Seats and berths (1000)**	**286**	**234**	**215**	**22**	**22**	**24**	**6**	**12**	**12**
3.21	- Coaches	...	230	211	...	16	...	...	8	8
3.22	- Railcars and railcar trailers	...	4	4	...	6	...	...	4	4
4	**Vans (number)**	...	**76**	**76**	**65**	**50**	**49**	-	-	-
5	**Total wagons (number)**	...	**26 614**	**24 496**	**1 887**	**1 819**	**1 819**	**1 400**	**1 280**	**1 298**
5.10	- Covered	...	...	4 065	...	922	912	...	-	-
5.20	- High-sided	...	...	10 332	...	-	-	...	-	85
5.30	- Flat	...	...	3 109	...	897	907	...	444	423
5.40	- Other wagons	...	...	6 990	...	-	-	...	836	790
5.1	**Principal Railway Enterprise(s)**	**63 237**	**23 962**	**22 055**	**1 834**	**1 772**	**1 772**	...	**786**	**814**
5.11	- Covered	22 917	4 904	3 995	...	900	890	...	-	-
5.21	- High-sided	24 801	10 152	9 994	...	-	-	...	-	85
5.31	- Flat	8 787	3 366	3 046	...	872	882	...	394	373
5.41	- Other wagons	6 732	5 540	5 020	...	-	-	...	392	356
6	**Total wagons (1000 tonnes)**	...	**1 115.0**	**1 075.0**	**49.4**	**48.0**	**49.0**	**71.6**	**76.5**	**74.1**
6.10	- Covered	...	...	133.0	...	...	...	...	-	-
6.20	- High-sided	...	...	493.0	...	-	-	...	-	3.6
6.30	- Flat	...	...	123.0	...	...	...	...	26.7	26.5
6.40	- Other wagons	...	...	326.0	...	-	-	...	49.8	44.0
6.1	**Principal Railway Enterprise(s)**	**2 263.0**	**1 014.0**	**972.0**	**48.5**	...	...	...	**45.5**	**44.6**
6.11	- Covered	718.0	159.0	129.0	...	...	...	...	-	-
6.21	- High-sided	921.0	458.0	480.0	...	-	-	...	-	3.6
6.31	- Flat	324.0	130.0	120.0	...	...	...	...	23.2	23.0
6.41	- Other wagons	300.0	267.0	243.0	...	-	-	...	22.3	18.0

RAILWAY TRANSPORT- TRANSPORT FERROVIAIRE
ЖЕЛЕЗНЫЕ ДОРОГИ

3. Mobile equipment at 31 December

3. Equipement mobile au 31 décembre

3. Подвижной состав на 31 декабря

		Italy Italie Италия			Kazakhstan Kazakhstan Казахстан			Kyrgyzstan Kirghizistan Кыргызстан		
		1990	1998	1999	1990	1998	1999	1990	1998	1999
1.1	**Locomotives (number)**	**3 146**	**3 144**	**3 195**	...	**2 294**	...	...	**59**	...
1.11	- Electric	1 978	1 956	2 007	...	631	...	...	-	...
1.12	- Diesel	1 168	1 165	1 165	...	1 569	...	...	53	...
1.13	- Steam	26	23	23	...	94	...	...	6	...
1.2	**Locomotives (1000 kW)**	...	**7 312**	**7 598**	...	**8 468**	...	...	...	...
1.21	- Electric	...	6 693	6 979	...	3 571	...	...	-	...
1.22	- Diesel	...	601	601	...	4 759	...	...	...	...
1.23	- Steam	...	18	18	...	138	...	...	...	...
2.1	**Railcars (number)**	**1 646**	**1 368**	**1 428**	...	**171**	...	...	-	-
2.11	- Electric	662	550	610	...	72	...	...	-	...
2.12	- Diesel	984	818	818	...	99	...	...	-	...
2.2	**Railcars (1000 kW)**	...	**689**	**767**	...	...	...	...	-	-
2.21	- Electric	...	506	584	...	...	...	...	-	-
2.22	- Diesel	...	183	183	...	...	...	...	-	-
3.1	**Passenger carriages (number)**	**14 025**	**12 827**	**12 580**	...	**2 374**	...	...	**414**	...
3.11	- Coaches	...	9 989	9 620	...	2 229	...	...	414	...
3.12	- Railcars and railcar trailers	...	2 838	2 960	...	145	...	...	-	...
3.2	**Seats and berths (1000)**	**1 075**	**923**	**913**	...	...	...	...	...	...
3.21	- Coaches	...	730	705	...	87	...	...	...	...
3.22	- Railcars and railcar trailers	...	193	208	...	...	...	...	...	...
4	**Vans (number)**	...	**1 420**	**1 362**	...	**81**	...	...	**19**	**17**
5	**Total wagons (number)**	**99 728**	**76 696**	**75 798**	...	**99 995**	...	...	**2 940**	...
5.10	- Covered	...	...	...	...	...	...	...	...	...
5.20	- High-sided	...	...	...	...	...	...	...	...	...
5.30	- Flat	...	...	...	...	...	...	...	...	...
5.40	- Other wagons	...	...	...	...	...	...	...	...	...
5.1	**Principal Railway Enterprise(s)**	...	**67 930**	**67 795**	...	**89 865**	...	...	**2 412**	...
5.11	- Covered	...	28 715	28 733	...	14 893	...	...	620	...
5.21	- High-sided	...	16 222	16 081	...	33 987	...	...	641	...
5.31	- Flat	...	22 713	22 701	...	11 948	...	...	443	...
5.41	- Other wagons	...	280	280	...	29 037	...	...	708	...
6	**Total wagons (1000 tonnes)**	**3 515.6**	**3 166.2**	**3 140.7**	...	**6 558.5**	...	...	**191.6**	...
6.10	- Covered	...	...	...	...	...	...	...	...	...
6.20	- High-sided	...	...	...	...	...	...	...	...	...
6.30	- Flat	...	...	...	...	...	...	...	...	...
6.40	- Other wagons	...	...	...	...	...	...	...	...	...
6.1	**Principal Railway Enterprise(s)**	...	**2 889.0**	**2 885.4**	...	**5 900.0**	...	...	**157.2**	...
6.11	- Covered	...	974.5	975.7	...	982.9	...	...	40.3	...
6.21	- High-sided	...	677.6	673.4	...	2 311.1	...	...	41.7	...
6.31	- Flat	...	1 221.8	1 221.3	...	776.6	...	...	29.2	...
6.41	- Other wagons	...	15.1	15.1	...	1 829.3	...	...	46.0	...

RAILWAY TRANSPORT- TRANSPORT FERROVIAIRE
ЖЕЛЕЗНЫЕ ДОРОГИ

3. Mobile equipment at 31 December
3. Equipement mobile au 31 décembre
3. Подвижной состав на 31 декабря

		Latvia Lettonie Латвия			Lithuania Lituanie Литва			Luxembourg Luxembourg Люксембург		
		1990	1998	1999	1990	1998	1999	1990	1998	1999
1.1	**Locomotives (number)**	484	288	270	...	298	286	80	79	...
1.11	- Electric	2	-	-	...	-	-	19	56	...
1.12	- Diesel	372	273	261	...	282	270	61	23	...
1.13	- Steam	100	15	9	...	16	16	-	-	...
1.2	**Locomotives (1000 kW)**	861	459	431	...	532	516	98	...	...
1.21	- Electric	3	-	-	...	-	-	49	...	...
1.22	- Diesel	...	437	418	...	508	492	49	...	...
1.23	- Steam	...	22	13	...	24	24	-	-	...
2.1	**Railcars (number)**	265	200	192	...	69	65	19	34	...
2.11	- Electric	201	147	141	...	16	16	13	32	...
2.12	- Diesel	64	53	51	...	53	49	6	2	...
2.2	**Railcars (1000 kW)**	206	155	149	...	96	92	13	37	...
2.21	- Electric	161	118	113	...	38	38	11	36	...
2.22	- Diesel	45	37	36	...	58	54	2	1	...
3.1	**Passenger carriages (number)**	1 244	768	715	...	589	572	116	146	...
3.11	- Coaches	...	300	266	...	258	258	76	74	...
3.12	- Railcars and railcar trailers	...	468	449	...	331	314	40	72	...
3.2	**Seats and berths (1000)**	90	60	56	...	45	43	10	12	...
3.21	- Coaches	...	12	11	...	11	11	...	...	...
3.22	- Railcars and railcar trailers	...	47	42	...	34	32	...	...	...
4	**Vans (number)**	18	6	6	...	4	4	...	8	...
5	**Total wagons (number)**	11 085	10 296	9 307	...	13 596	13 567	2 647	2 388	...
5.10	- Covered	1 966	1 885	1 800	...	2 484	2 466	555	...	...
5.20	- High-sided	1 889	1 747	1 503	...	2 192	2 354	583	...	...
5.30	- Flat	1 006	1 114	946	...	1 505	1 546	1 501	...	...
5.40	- Other wagons	6 224	5 550	5 058	...	7 415	7 201	8	...	...
5.1	**Principal Railway Enterprise(s)**	11 085	8 332	7 878	...	10 434	10 465	2 515	2 201	...
5.11	- Covered	1 966	1 858	1 799	...	2 480	2 462	549	234	...
5.21	- High-sided	1 889	1 566	1 477	...	1 979	1 961	464	380	...
5.31	- Flat	1 006	997	941	...	1 348	1 346	1 501	1 587	...
5.41	- Other wagons	6 224	3 911	3 661	...	4 627	4 696	1	-	...
6	**Total wagons (1000 tonnes)**	719.5	674.0	607.0	...	882.0	945.0	110.3	113.5	...
6.10	- Covered	128.7	116.0	111.0	...	149.0	148.0	15.4	...	...
6.20	- High-sided	130.1	123.0	104.0	...	153.0	162.0	23.2	...	...
6.30	- Flat	67.6	75.0	63.0	...	97.0	98.0	70.7	...	...
6.40	- Other wagons	393.1	360.0	329.0	...	483.0	437.0	1.0	...	...
6.1	**Principal Railway Enterprise(s)**	719.5	549.0	516.0	...	647.0	650.0	102.1	103.2	...
6.11	- Covered	128.7	114.0	110.0	...	149.0	148.0	15.2	7.7	...
6.21	- High-sided	130.1	111.0	102.0	...	137.0	135.0	16.2	17.0	...
6.31	- Flat	67.6	67.0	63.0	...	84.0	85.0	70.7	78.5	...
6.41	- Other wagons	393.1	257.0	241.0	...	277.0	282.0	0.0	-	...

41

RAILWAY TRANSPORT- TRANSPORT FERROVIAIRE
ЖЕЛЕЗНЫЕ ДОРОГИ

3. Mobile equipment at 31 December
3. Equipement mobile au 31 décembre
3. Подвижной состав на 31 декабря

		Netherlands Pays-Bas Нидерланды			Norway Norvège Норвегия			Poland Pologne Польша		
		1990	1998	1999	1990	1998	1999	1990	1998	1999
1.1	**Locomotives (number)**	522	330	...	326	197	185	4 076	4 568	4 148
1.11	- Electric	146	147	...	149	92	92	1 705	1 940	1 796
1.12	- Diesel	376	183	...	177	105	93	2 268	2 548	2 275
1.13	- Steam	-	-	...	-	-	-	103	80	77
1.2	**Locomotives (1000 kW)**	619	...	...	536	516	491	...	7 728	7 067
1.21	- Electric	452	...	...	444	409	409	...	5 524	5 136
1.22	- Diesel	167	...	...	92	107	82	...	2 146	1 875
1.23	- Steam	-	-	...	-	-	-	...	58	56
2.1	**Railcars (number)**	722	...	...	160	133	145	1 407	1 303	1 279
2.11	- Electric	604	...	...	131	118	130	1 368	1 257	1 235
2.12	- Diesel	118	...	...	29	15	15	39	46	44
2.2	**Railcars (1000 kW)**	566	...	...	116	122	133	...	777	764
2.21	- Electric	508	...	...	102	111	122	...	769	756
2.22	- Diesel	58	...	...	14	11	11	...	8	8
3.1	**Passenger carriages (number)**	2 622	2 723	...	905	801	849	7 698	10 264	10 069
3.11	- Coaches	575	767	...	522	439	440	...	6 402	6 279
3.12	- Railcars and railcar trailers	2 047	1 956	...	383	362	409	...	3 862	3 790
3.2	**Seats and berths (1000)**	154	199	...	55	61	64	...	721	703
3.21	- Coaches	...	...	...	26	40	40	...	449	439
3.22	- Railcars and railcar trailers	...	...	...	30	21	24	...	272	264
4	**Vans (number)**	-	...	...	33	20	20	...	127	127
5	**Total wagons (number)**	6 496	4 560	...	5 819	2 974	2 766	89 940	137 037	...
5.10	- Covered	...	...	...	2 038	701	638	12 981	...	...
5.20	- High-sided	...	...	...	135	69	62	51 522	...	...
5.30	- Flat	...	...	...	3 449	1 973	1 841	12 334	...	...
5.40	- Other wagons	...	...	...	197	231	225	13 103	...	...
5.1	**Principal Railway Enterprise(s)**	5 021	3 320	...	5 492	2 735	2 527	...	101 113	96 026
5.11	- Covered	2 222	...	...	...	691	628	...	16 191	13 258
5.21	- High-sided	789	...	...	...	69	62	67 037	65 211	
5.31	- Flat	1 803	...	...	...	1 931	1 799	...	15 101	14 454
5.41	- Other wagons	207	...	...	...	44	38	...	2 784	3 103
6	**Total wagons (1000 tonnes)**	240.8	...	...	177.0	112.0	96.0	...	7 419.8	...
6.10	- Covered	...	...	...	57.0	23.0	19.0	...	...	...
6.20	- High-sided	...	...	...	4.0	4.0	3.0	...	...	...
6.30	- Flat	...	...	...	110.0	77.0	67.0	...	...	...
6.40	- Other wagons	...	...	...	6.0	8.0	7.0	...	...	...
6.1	**Principal Railway Enterprise(s)**	165.4	...	...	165.0	104.0	88.0	...	5 465.6	4 714.0
6.11	- Covered	62.4	...	...	...	22.0	18.0	...	692.0	487.0
6.21	- High-sided	35.6	...	...	...	4.0	3.0	...	3 819.4	3 478.0
6.31	- Flat	61.5	...	...	...	76.0	66.0	...	829.6	635.0
6.41	- Other wagons	5.9	...	...	...	2.0	1.0	...	124.6	114.0

42

RAILWAY TRANSPORT- TRANSPORT FERROVIAIRE
ЖЕЛЕЗНЫЕ ДОРОГИ

3. Mobile equipment at 31 December
3. Equipement mobile au 31 décembre
3. Подвижной состав на 31 декабря

		Portugal Portugal Португалия			Republic of Moldova République de Moldova Республика Молдова			Romania Roumanie Румыния		
		1990	1998	1999	1990	1998	1999	1990	1998	1999
1.1	Locomotives (number)	320	251	249	...	191	177	4 364	3 442	3 362
1.11	- Electric	54	82	81	-	-	-	1 079	1 084	1 054
1.12	- Diesel	266	169	168	...	191	177	2 290	2 259	2 241
1.13	- Steam	-	-	-	-	-	-	995	99	67
1.2	Locomotives (1000 kW)	344	464	463	...	622	578	...	...	...
1.21	- Electric	128	290	290	-	-	-	...	...	...
1.22	- Diesel	216	174	173	...	622	578	...	...	...
1.23	- Steam	-	-	-	-	-		...	...	...
2.1	Railcars (number)	228	330	354	...	34	31	141	126	117
2.11	- Electric	107	204	229	...	-	-	6	8	8
2.12	- Diesel	121	126	125	...	34	31	135	118	109
2.2	Railcars (1000 kW)	159	347	416	...	36	33	29	...	...
2.21	- Electric	118	304	372	...	-	-	11	...	...
2.22	- Diesel	41	43	44	...	36	33	18	...	...
3.1	Passenger carriages (number)	1 033	1 406	1 446	...	592	583	6 352	6 437	6 428
3.11	- Coaches	525	480	444	...	454	454	...	6 019	5 580
3.12	- Railcars and railcar trailers	508	926	1 002	...	138	129	...	418	848
3.2	Seats and berths (1000)	85	107	104	...	33	33	466	456	442
3.21	- Coaches	...	...	...	...	19	19	...	445	433
3.22	- Railcars and railcar trailers	...	...	...	...	14	14	...	11	8
4	Vans (number)	90	31	56	...	4	7	...	329	305
5	Total wagons (number)	5 821	4 642	4 539	...	13 573	12 264	166 086	154 740	141 673
5.10	- Covered	2 237	1 517	1 521	...	3 108	2 928	...	...	...
5.20	- High-sided	882	720	722	...	2 388	2 096	...	...	...
5.30	- Flat	1 019	1 375	1 377	...	1 042	958	...	...	...
5.40	- Other wagons	1 683	1 030	919	...	7 035	6 282	...	...	...
5.1	Principal Railway Enterprise(s)	5 678	4 411	4 308	...	12 233	11 010	...	137 086	129 819
5.11	- Covered	...	1 467	1 471	...	3 104	2 926	...	34 860	33 102
5.21	- High-sided	...	720	722	...	2 388	2 096	...	55 480	50 865
5.31	- Flat	...	1 375	1 377	...	968	893	...	20 783	15 655
5.41	- Other wagons	...	849	738	...	5 773	5 095	...	25 963	30 197
6	Total wagons (1000 tonnes)	167.8	173.0	170.0	...	954.0	887.0	7 549.6	6 941.9	...
6.10	- Covered	57.8	45.0	45.0	...	225.0	222.0	...	...	...
6.20	- High-sided	32.0	31.0	31.0	...	186.0	165.0	...	...	...
6.30	- Flat	35.5	58.0	58.0	...	81.0	61.0	...	...	...
6.40	- Other wagons	42.5	39.0	36.0	...	462.0	439.0	...	...	...
6.1	Principal Railway Enterprise(s)	161.7	161.0	158.0	...	850.0	789.0	...	6 238.8	5 947.0
6.11	- Covered	...	43.0	43.0	...	225.0	222.0	...	1 275.0	1 211.0
6.21	- High-sided	...	31.0	31.0	...	186.0	165.0	...	3 029.4	2 799.0
6.31	- Flat	...	58.0	58.0	...	75.0	57.0	...	905.4	881.0
6.41	- Other wagons	...	29.0	26.0	...	364.0	345.0	...	1 029.0	1 056.0

RAILWAY TRANSPORT- TRANSPORT FERROVIAIRE
ЖЕЛЕЗНЫЕ ДОРОГИ

3. Mobile equipment at 31 December
3. Equipement mobile au 31 décembre
3. Подвижной состав на 31 декабря

		Russian Federation Fédération de Russie Российская Федерация			Slovakia Slovaquie Словакия			Slovenia Slovénie Словения		
		1990	1998	1999	1990	1998	1999	1990	1998	1999
1.1	**Locomotives (number)**	...	10 483	...	...	1 257	1 248	236	210	187
1.11	- Electric	...	4 526	...	...	564	564	99	95	88
1.12	- Diesel	...	5 929	...	...	693	684	134	110	94
1.13	- Steam	...	28	...	...	-	-	3	5	5
1.2	**Locomotives (1000 kW)**	...	...	...	...	2 531	2 362	...	338	310
1.21	- Electric	...	...	...	...	1 880	1 720	...	225	211
1.22	- Diesel	...	...	...	...	651	642	...	109	95
1.23	- Steam	...	...	...	...	-	-	...	4	4
2.1	**Railcars (number)**	...	7 752	...	...	370	383	122	113	110
2.11	- Electric	...	7 352	...	...	73	73	32	30	29
2.12	- Diesel	...	400	...	...	297	310	90	83	81
2.2	**Railcars (1000 kW)**	...	...	...	...	131	132	...	60	58
2.21	- Electric	...	...	...	...	57	54	...	31	30
2.22	- Diesel	...	...	...	...	74	78	...	29	28
3.1	**Passenger carriages (number)**	...	43 032	...	...	2 524	2 462	606	467	457
3.11	- Coaches	...	27 547	...	...	1 734	1 711	...	194	191
3.12	- Railcars and railcar trailers	...	15 485	...	...	790	751	...	273	266
3.2	**Seats and berths (1000)**	...	1 038	...	...	119	117	...	28	27
3.21	- Coaches	...	...	...	...	95	93	...	10	10
3.22	- Railcars and railcar trailers	...	...	...	...	24	24	...	18	17
4	**Vans (number)**	...	777	...	...	...	220	...	8	8
5	**Total wagons (number)**	...	...	...	...	35 632	25 241	8 692	7 052	6 377
5.10	- Covered	...	...	...	...	...	6 788	2 945	2 900	2 548
5.20	- High-sided	...	...	...	...	...	10 832	4 774	2 566	2 254
5.30	- Flat	...	...	...	...	...	998	...	1 185	1 175
5.40	- Other wagons	...	...	...	...	...	6 623	...	401	400
5.1	**Principal Railway Enterprise(s)**	...	592 102	...	...	31 022	21 815	...	6 764	6 089
5.11	- Covered	...	101 023	...	...	8 766	6 186	...	2 880	2 528
5.21	- High-sided	...	266 924	...	...	14 764	9 652	...	2 526	2 214
5.31	- Flat	...	85 845	...	...	4 346	475	...	1 073	1 063
5.41	- Other wagons	...	138 310	...	...	3 146	5 502	...	285	284
6	**Total wagons (1000 tonnes)**	...	...	...	...	1 705.7	...	381.8	328.0	307.0
6.10	- Covered	...	...	...	...	...	...	...	118.0	109.0
6.20	- High-sided	...	...	...	...	...	...	...	130.0	119.0
6.30	- Flat	...	...	...	...	...	...	...	58.0	57.0
6.40	- Other wagons	...	...	...	...	...	...	...	22.0	22.0
6.1	**Principal Railway Enterprise(s)**	...	...	...	...	1 456.6	...	...	313.0	292.0
6.11	- Covered	...	6 719.1	...	...	298.6	...	...	117.0	108.0
6.21	- High-sided	...	18 142.8	...	...	730.8	...	...	128.0	117.0
6.31	- Flat	...	5 769.6	...	...	261.0	...	...	52.0	51.0
6.41	- Other wagons	...	...	...	...	166.2	...	...	16.0	16.0

RAILWAY TRANSPORT- TRANSPORT FERROVIAIRE
ЖЕЛЕЗНЫЕ ДОРОГИ

3. Mobile equipment at 31 December
3. Equipement mobile au 31 décembre
3. Подвижной состав на 31 декабря

		Spain Espagne Испания			Sweden Suède Швеция			Switzerland Suisse Швейцария		
		1990	1998	1999	1990	1998	1999	1990	1998	1999
1.1	Locomotives (number)	1 287	935	928	1 015	613	607	1 435	1 380	...
1.11	- Electric	593	452	449	629	376	372	1 158	1 105	...
1.12	- Diesel	694	483	479	386	237	235	277	275	...
1.13	- Steam	-	-	-	-	-	-	-	-	...
1.2	Locomotives (1000 kW)	2 517	2 217	2 206	2 133	1 498	1 492	3 297	...	...
1.21	- Electric	1 756	1 684	1 677	1 862	1 305	1 302	3 202	...	...
1.22	- Diesel	761	533	529	271	193	190	95	...	...
1.23	- Steam	-	-	-	-	-	-	-	-	...
2.1	Railcars (number)	785	765	790	289	341	322	252	247	...
2.11	- Electric	635	618	641	189	281	270	252	247	...
2.12	- Diesel	150	147	149	100	60	52	-	-	...
2.2	Railcars (1000 kW)	763	1 411	1 458	249	459	448	429	...	...
2.21	- Electric	665	1 287	1 336	210	423	414	429	...	...
2.22	- Diesel	98	124	122	39	36	34	-	-	...
3.1	Passenger carriages (number)	3 907	3 813	3 829	1 698	1 571	1 512	4 124	3 561	...
3.11	- Coaches	1 864	1 381	1 345	1 214	721	695	3 804	3 324	...
3.12	- Railcars and railcar trailers	2 043	2 432	2 484	484	850	817	320	237	...
3.2	Seats and berths (1000)	216	264	267	104	96	93	286	294	...
3.21	- Coaches	55	36	39	73	38	36	...	...	...
3.22	- Railcars and railcar trailers	161	228	228	31	59	57	...	...	...
4	Vans (number)	545	167	163	198	126	136	421	253	...
5	Total wagons (number)	31 484	26 502	26 126	25 516	17 215	17 977	26 936	19 951	...
5.10	- Covered	...	4 227	4 124	8 315	5 495	5 448	...	...	...
5.20	- High-sided	...	4 817	4 601	830	439	520	...	...	...
5.30	- Flat	...	8 479	8 369	13 698	9 974	10 714	...	...	...
5.40	- Other wagons	...	8 979	9 032	2 673	1 307	1 295	...	...	...
5.1	Principal Railway Enterprise(s)	23 785	18 892	18 424	22 408	11 502	11 168	20 156	13 577	...
5.11	- Covered	...	4 227	4 124	...	3 919	3 878	10 932	5 665	...
5.21	- High-sided	...	4 817	4 601	...	424	505	4 289	3 153	...
5.31	- Flat	...	8 479	8 369	...	7 047	6 730	3 778	3 861	...
5.41	- Other wagons	...	1 369	1 330	...	112	55	1 157	898	...
6	Total wagons (1000 tonnes)	1 281.0	1 173.4	1 155.0	839.0	621.0	666.0	964.0	...	...
6.10	- Covered	...	165.6	161.0	239.0	179.0	178.0	...	...	...
6.20	- High-sided	...	218.3	206.0	28.0	17.0	22.0	...	...	...
6.30	- Flat	...	103.4	394.0	415.0	375.0	417.0	...	...	...
6.40	- Other wagons	...	386.2	394.0	157.0	50.0	49.0	...	...	...
6.1	Principal Railway Enterprise(s)	970.0	837.9	810.0	720.0	374.0	370.0	667.0	...	...
6.11	- Covered	...	165.6	161.0	...	117.0	116.0	292.0	146.5	...
6.21	- High-sided	...	218.3	206.0	...	16.0	21.0	169.0	122.7	...
6.31	- Flat	...	103.4	394.0	...	236.0	230.0	163.0	159.0	...
6.41	- Other wagons	...	50.6	49.0	...	5.0	3.0	44.0	29.8	...

RAILWAY TRANSPORT- TRANSPORT FERROVIAIRE
ЖЕЛЕЗНЫЕ ДОРОГИ

3. Mobile equipment at 31 December
3. Equipement mobile au 31 décembre
3. Подвижной состав на 31 декабря

		Tajikistan Tadjikistan Таджикистан			The FYR of Macedonia [1]			Turkey Turquie Турция		
		1990	1998	1999	1990	1998	1999	1990	1998	1999
1.1	**Locomotives (number)**	...	58	57	67	81	81	769	704	...
1.11	- Electric	...	-	-	13	13	13	33	68	...
1.12	- Diesel	...	58	57	54	68	68	678	586	...
1.13	- Steam	...	-	-	-	-	-	58	50	...
1.2	**Locomotives (1000 kW)**	...	111	156	112	116	116	1 124	...	...
1.21	- Electric	...	-	-	56	56	56	99	...	...
1.22	- Diesel	...	111	156	56	60	60	952	...	...
1.23	- Steam	...	-	-	-	-	-	73	...	...
2.1	**Railcars (number)**	-	-	-	25	21	21	122	150	...
2.11	- Electric	-	-	-	4	4	4	88	93	...
2.12	- Diesel	-	-	-	21	17	17	34	57	...
2.2	**Railcars (1000 kW)**	-	-	-	...	12	12	98	...	...
2.21	- Electric	-	-	-	...	5	5	91	...	...
2.22	- Diesel	-	-	-	...	7	7	7	...	...
3.1	**Passenger carriages (number)**	...	315	281	175	169	169	1 049	1 424	...
3.11	- Coaches	...	315	281	...	103	103	...	1 046	...
3.12	- Railcars and railcar trailers	-	-	-	...	66	66	...	378	...
3.2	**Seats and berths (1000)**	...	13	12	9	9	9	69	93	...
3.21	- Coaches	...	13	12	...	6	6	...	...	...
3.22	- Railcars and railcar trailers	...	-	-	...	4	4	...	...	...
4	**Vans (number)**	...	7	15	...	-	-	340	389	...
5	**Total wagons (number)**	...	2 749	2 762	2 430	2 431	2 431	21 888	17 815	...
5.10	- Covered	...	568	572	...	846	846	...	...	...
5.20	- High-sided	...	567	575	...	1 129	1 129	...	...	...
5.30	- Flat	...	285	284	...	197	197	...	...	...
5.40	- Other wagons	...	1 329	1 331	...	259	259	...	...	...
5.1	**Principal Railway Enterprise(s)**	...	2 193	2 206	...	2 431	2 431	20 542	16 989	...
5.11	- Covered	...	497	501	...	846	846	6 841	4 502	...
5.21	- High-sided	...	567	575	...	1 129	1 129	9 048	8 265	...
5.31	- Flat	...	285	284	...	197	197	4 223	3 919	...
5.41	- Other wagons	...	844	846	...	259	259	340	303	...
6	**Total wagons (1000 tonnes)**	...	165.8	166.6	113.9	77.0	77.0	765.1	688.8	...
6.10	- Covered	...	28.4	28.6	...	5.0	5.0	...	...	...
6.20	- High-sided	...	39.7	40.3	...	49.0	49.0	...	...	...
6.30	- Flat	...	19.1	19.0	...	9.0	9.0	...	...	...
6.40	- Other wagons	...	78.6	78.7	...	14.0	14.0	...	...	...
6.1	**Principal Railway Enterprise(s)**	...	133.1	133.9	...	77.0	77.0	702.6	647.2	...
6.11	- Covered	...	24.8	25.0	...	5.0	5.0	177.8	122.2	...
6.21	- High-sided	...	39.7	40.3	...	49.0	49.0	368.5	373.2	...
6.31	- Flat	...	19.1	19.0	...	9.0	9.0	144.0	137.9	...
6.41	- Other wagons	...	49.5	49.6	...	14.0	14.0	12.2	13.8	...

1- The former Yugoslav Republic of Macedonia

1- L'ex-République yougoslave de Macédoine

1- Бывшая Югославская Республика Македония

RAILWAY TRANSPORT- TRANSPORT FERROVIAIRE
ЖЕЛЕЗНЫЕ ДОРОГИ

3. Mobile equipment at 31 December
3. Equipement mobile au 31 décembre
3. Подвижной состав на 31 декабря

		Turkmenistan Turkménistan Туркменистан			Ukraine Ukraine Украина			United Kingdom Royaume-Uni Соединенное Королевство		
		1990	1998	1999	1990	1998	1999	1990	1998	1999
1.1	**Locomotives (number)**	...	**320**	**325**	...	**5 107**	**4 828**	**2 242**	...	...
1.11	- Electric	-	-	-	...	1 848	1 811	278	...	...
1.12	- Diesel	...	320	325	...	3 020	2 848	1 964	...	...
1.13	- Steam	-	-	-	...	239	169	-	...	...
1.2	**Locomotives (1000 kW)**	...	...	...	...	**15 243**	**14 735**	**2 838**	...	...
1.21	- Electric	-	-	-	...	8 912	8 749	278	...	...
1.22	- Diesel	...	...	...	...	6 123	5 841	2 560	...	...
1.23	- Steam	-	-	-	...	208	145	-	...	...
2.1	**Railcars (number)**	...	-	-	...	**1 882**	**1 842**	**4 316**	...	...
2.11	- Electric	-	-	-	...	1 475	1 467	2 535	...	...
2.12	- Diesel	...	-	-	...	407	375	1 781	...	...
2.2	**Railcars (1000 kW)**	...	-	-	...	...	...	**1 845**	...	...
2.21	- Electric	-	-	-	...	...	...	1 447	...	...
2.22	- Diesel	...	-	-	...	...	...	398	...	...
3.1	**Passenger carriages (number)**	...	**338**	**333**	...	**9 594**	**9 159**	**12 564**	...	...
3.11	- Coaches	...	338	333	...	9 283	8 859	3 128	...	...
3.12	- Railcars and railcar trailers	...	-	-	...	311	300	9 436	...	...
3.2	**Seats and berths (1000)**	...	**13**	**14**	...	**370**	**360**	**856**	...	...
3.21	- Coaches	...	13	14	...	...	...	...	...	...
3.22	- Railcars and railcar trailers	...	-	-	...	...	...	...	...	...
4	**Vans (number)**	...	**10**	**11**	...	**233**	**203**	**1 609**	...	...
5	**Total wagons (number)**	...	**13 899**	**13 904**	...	**241 134**	**230 326**	**20 763**	...	...
5.10	- Covered	...	...	...	...	...	...	1 957	...	...
5.20	- High-sided	...	...	...	...	...	...	13 522	...	...
5.30	- Flat	...	...	...	...	...	...	5 225	...	...
5.40	- Other wagons	...	...	...	...	...	...	59	...	...
5.1	**Principal Railway Enterprise(s)**	...	**11 517**	**11 522**	...	**185 914**	**185 738**	**13 640**	...	...
5.11	- Covered	...	2 356	2 341	...	20 136	20 930	...	...	...
5.21	- High-sided	...	1 801	1 794	...	84 161	84 745	...	...	...
5.31	- Flat	...	2 845	2 859	...	15 952	16 240	...	...	...
5.41	- Other wagons	...	4 515	4 528	...	65 665	63 823	...	...	...
6	**Total wagons (1000 tonnes)**	...	**886.8**	**884.0**	...	...	...	**773.9**	...	...
6.10	- Covered	...	...	...	...	...	...	...	...	...
6.20	- High-sided	...	...	...	...	...	...	...	...	...
6.30	- Flat	...	...	...	...	...	...	...	...	...
6.40	- Other wagons	...	...	...	...	...	...	...	...	...
6.1	**Principal Railway Enterprise(s)**	...	**732.0**	**729.2**	...	**11 982.5**	**11 592.8**	**594.6**	...	...
6.11	- Covered	...	160.2	158.0	...	1 338.5	1 338.0	...	...	...
6.21	- High-sided	...	117.1	114.8	...	5 702.7	5 685.2	...	...	...
6.31	- Flat	...	162.2	163.0	...	1 088.8	1 069.7	...	...	...
6.41	- Other wagons	...	292.5	293.4	...	3 852.5	3 499.9	...	...	...

RAILWAY TRANSPORT- TRANSPORT FERROVIAIRE
ЖЕЛЕЗНЫЕ ДОРОГИ

3. Mobile equipment at 31 December
3. Equipement mobile au 31 décembre
3. Подвижной состав на 31 декабря

		United States Etats-Unis [1] Соединенные Штаты			Uzbekistan Ouzbékistan Узбекистан			Yugoslavia Yugoslavie Югославия		
		1990	1998	1999	1990	1998	1999	1990	1998	1999
1.1	**Locomotives (number)**	18 835	20 261	20 256	...	317	792	518	482	465
1.11	- Electric	-	-	-	...	26	76	...	189	187
1.12	- Diesel	18 835	20 261	20 256	...	291	703	...	293	278
1.13	- Steam	-	-	-	...	-	13	...	-	-
1.2	**Locomotives (1000 kW)**	37 431	...	...	...	...	...	1 147	1 143	1 122
1.21	- Electric	-	-	-	...	...	...	...	848	839
1.22	- Diesel	37 431	...	...	...	...	...	...	295	283
1.23	- Steam	-	-	-	...	-	-	...	-	-
2.1	**Railcars (number)**	1 212 261	1 315 667	1 368 836	...	28	42	...	143	117
2.11	- Electric	...	...	...	...	28	42	...	49	49
2.12	- Diesel	...	...	...	...	-	-	...	94	68
2.2	**Railcars (1000 kW)**	...	...	...	...	...	...	...	85	82
2.21	- Electric	...	...	...	...	...	...	...	66	66
2.22	- Diesel	...	...	...	...	-	-	...	18	15
3.1	**Passenger carriages (number)**	6 223	2 307	...	...	1 162	1 119	1 362	1 166	1 008
3.11	- Coaches	...	...	...	...	1 162	1 119	...	772	683
3.12	- Railcars and railcar trailers	...	...	...	...	-	-	...	394	325
3.2	**Seats and berths (1000)**	532	...	...	...	53	51	85	75	58
3.21	- Coaches	...	...	...	...	53	51	...	46	34
3.22	- Railcars and railcar trailers	...	...	...	...	-	-	...	28	24
4	**Vans (number)**	...	...	...	...	18	16	...	49	32
5	**Total wagons (number)**	762 429	...	...	...	14 608	30 979	17 542	18 131	16 534
5.10	- Covered	204 473	...	...	...	3 659	8 027	...	8 878	7 997
5.20	- High-sided	98 745	...	...	...	3 010	6 541	...	7 431	6 767
5.30	- Flat	87 584	...	...	...	1 425	3 823	...	1 267	1 215
5.40	- Other wagons	371 627	...	...	...	6 514	12 588	...	555	555
5.1	**Principal Railway Enterprise(s)**	312 597	...	...	...	14 608	30 979	17 542	17 327	16 480
5.11	- Covered	...	...	...	...	3 659	8 027	...	8 074	7 943
5.21	- High-sided	...	...	...	...	3 010	6 541	...	7 431	6 767
5.31	- Flat	...	...	...	...	1 425	3 823	...	1 267	1 215
5.41	- Other wagons	...	...	...	...	6 514	12 588	...	555	555
6	**Total wagons (1000 tonnes)**	...	...	...	...	938.9	2 059.5	716.0	757.2	713.5
6.10	- Covered	...	...	...	...	248.5	545.8	...	353.9	333.3
6.20	- High-sided	...	...	...	...	213.0	452.1	...	319.4	298.7
6.30	- Flat	...	...	...	...	95.2	312.4	...	55.5	53.1
6.40	- Other wagons	...	...	...	...	382.2	749.2	...	28.4	28.4
6.1	**Principal Railway Enterprise(s)**	...	...	...	...	938.9	2 059.5	716.0	740.2	710.9
6.11	- Covered	...	...	...	...	248.5	545.8	...	336.9	330.7
6.21	- High-sided	...	...	...	...	213.0	452.1	...	319.4	298.7
6.31	- Flat	...	...	...	...	95.2	312.4	...	55.5	53.1
6.41	- Other wagons	...	...	...	...	382.2	749.2	...	28.4	28.4

1- Class 1 railways including AMTRAK.

1- Chemins de fer de 1ère classe y compris l'AMTRAK.

1- Железные дороги 1-ого класса, включая данные по AMTRAK.

RAILWAY TRANSPORT- TRANSPORT FERROVIAIRE
ЖЕЛЕЗНЫЕ ДОРОГИ

4. Tractive vehicle movements

4. Mouvements de véhicules moteurs

4. Передвижение тягового транспортного средства

Item	Description
1	**Tractive vehicle movements** - (1000 tractive vehicle-kilometres)
	by type of motor vehicle and source of power
1.1	- Electric locomotives
1.2	- Diesel locomotives
1.3	- Steam locomotives
1.4	- Electric railcars
1.5	- Diesel railcars

Rubrique	Description
1	**Mouvements de véhicules moteurs** - (1000 véhicules moteurs-kilomètres)
	par type de véhicule moteur et mode de propulsion
1.1	- Locomotives électriques
1.2	- Locomotives diesel
1.3	- Locomotives à vapeur
1.4	- Automotrices électriques
1.5	- Automotrices diesel

Статья	Описание
1	**Передвижение тягового транспортного средства** - (1000 тяговое транспортное средство-км)
	по типу транспортного средства и источнику тяги
1.1	- Электровозы
1.2	- Тепловозы
1.3	- Паровозы
1.4	- Электрические автомотрисы
1.5	- Дизельные автомотрисы

RAILWAY TRANSPORT- TRANSPORT FERROVIAIRE
ЖЕЛЕЗНЫЕ ДОРОГИ

4. Tractive vehicle movements
4. Mouvements de véhicules moteurs
4. Передвижение тягового транспортного средства

(1000 tractive vehicle-km)

		Austria Autriche Австрия			Azerbaijan Azerbaïdjan Азербайджан			Belarus Bélarus Беларусь		
		1990	1998	1999	1990	1998	1999	1990	1998	1999
1	Total tractive vehicle movements	...	164 443	...	...	19 088	...	...	116 066	...
1.1	- Electric locomotives	...	102 875	...	...	10 121	...	...	13 231	...
1.2	- Diesel locomotives	...	15 513	...	...	3 687	...	...	44 410	...
1.3	- Steam locomotives	...	21	...	...	-	...	...	0	...
1.4	- Electric railcars	...	32 800	...	...	5 279	...	...	38 858	...
1.5	- Diesel railcars	...	13 234	...	...	-	...	...	19 489	...

		Belgium Belgique Бельгия			Bulgaria Bulgarie Болгария			Canada Canada Канада		
		1990	1998	1999	1990	1998	1999	1990	1998	1999
1	Total tractive vehicle movements	...	145 405	149 750	...	44 195	44 002	...	332 882	...
1.1	- Electric locomotives	...	40 914	39 275	...	31 890	32 268	...	604	...
1.2	- Diesel locomotives	...	18 670	17 914	...	12 305	11 734	...	332 278	...
1.3	- Steam locomotives	...	-	-	...	...	...	...	-	...
1.4	- Electric railcars	...	84 583	91 312	...	-	-	...	...	...
1.5	- Diesel railcars	...	1 238	1 249	...	-	-	...	...	...

		Croatia Croatie Хорватия			Czech Republic République tchèque Чешская Республика			Denmark Danemark Дания		
		1990	1998	1999	1990	1998	1999	1990	1998	1999
1	Total tractive vehicle movements	...	22 679	21 773	...	190 096	188 615	82 177	91 377	...
1.1	- Electric locomotives	...	8 900	8 727	...	75 688	74 457	1 890	4 693	...
1.2	- Diesel locomotives	...	7 153	6 565	...	50 641	47 532	24 529	10 504	...
1.3	- Steam locomotives	...	-	-	...	22	27	-	-	...
1.4	- Electric railcars	...	1 946	2 017	...	16 519	16 765	37 250	34 826	...
1.5	- Diesel railcars	...	4 680	4 464	...	47 226	49 834	18 508	41 354	...

		Estonia Estonie Эстония			Finland Finlande Финляндия			France France Франция		
		1990	1998	1999	1990	1998	1999	1990	1998	1999
1	Total tractive vehicle movements	...	12 700	...	...	63 966	65 473	650 445	659 076	678 855
1.1	- Electric locomotives	...	-	...	...	26 709	27 662	324 068	306 886	306 503
1.2	- Diesel locomotives	...	6 764	...	...	26 525	27 062	117 477	81 028	82 178
1.3	- Steam locomotives	...	-	...	...	-	-	-	-	-
1.4	- Electric railcars	...	2 276	...	...	10 732	10 749	134 079	212 178	228 385
1.5	- Diesel railcars	...	3 660	...	...	-	-	74 821	58 984	61 789

RAILWAY TRANSPORT- TRANSPORT FERROVIAIRE
ЖЕЛЕЗНЫЕ ДОРОГИ

4. Tractive vehicle movements

4. Mouvements de véhicules moteurs

4. Передвижение тягового транспортного средства

(1000 tractive vehicle-km)

		Georgia Georgie Грузия			Germany Allemagne Германия			Greece Grèce Греция		
		1990	1998	1999	1990	1998	1999	1990	1998	1999
1	Total tractive vehicle movements	...	9 639	...	...	1 092 141	...	...	18 198	...
1.1	- Electric locomotives	...	7 253	...	...	527 456	...	-	-	...
1.2	- Diesel locomotives	...	1 197	...	...	152 344	...	...	6 475	...
1.3	- Steam locomotives	...	-	...	...	45	...	-	-	...
1.4	- Electric railcars	...	1 189	...	...	327 316	...	-	-	...
1.5	- Diesel railcars	...	-	...	...	84 980	...	...	11 723	...

		Hungary Hongrie Венгрия			Ireland Irlande Ирландия			Israel Israël Израиль		
		1990	1998	1999	1990	1998	1999	1990	1998	1999
1	Total tractive vehicle movements	...	111 111	109 829	...	...	...	...	5 730	7 552
1.1	- Electric locomotives	...	58 323	58 153	...	-	1	...	-	-
1.2	- Diesel locomotives	...	24 690	22 241	...	...	...	...	3 298	3 712
1.3	- Steam locomotives	...	25	21	...	-	1	...	-	-
1.4	- Electric railcars	...	1 967	2 299	...	...	...	...	-	-
1.5	- Diesel railcars	...	26 106	27 115	...	...	...	...	2 433	3 840

		Italy Italie Италия			Kazakhstan Kazakhstan Казахстан			Kyrgyzstan Kirghizistan Кыргызстан		
		1990	1998	1999	1990	1998	1999	1990	1998	1999
1	Total tractive vehicle movements	...	404 743	397 140	...	121 331	...	...	923	...
1.1	- Electric locomotives	...	258 154	247 221	...	53 220	...	-	-	-
1.2	- Diesel locomotives	...	20 156	19 134	...	66 679	...	...	923	...
1.3	- Steam locomotives	...	21	20	...	-	...	...	-	-
1.4	- Electric railcars	...	63 399	67 510	...	1 383	...	-	-	-
1.5	- Diesel railcars	...	63 013	63 255	...	49	...	-	-	-

		Latvia Lettonie Латвия			Lithuania Lituanie Литва			Luxembourg Luxembourg Люксембург		
		1990	1998	1999	1990	1998	1999	1990	1998	1999
1	Total tractive vehicle movements	...	31 202	28 180	...	19 926	18 710	...	8 906	...
1.1	- Electric locomotives	...	-	-	...	-	-	...	2 268	...
1.2	- Diesel locomotives	...	13 540	12 089	...	14 275	13 458	...	1 843	...
1.3	- Steam locomotives	...	7	4	...	-	-	...	-	...
1.4	- Electric railcars	...	12 082	10 973	...	1 054	943	...	4 502	...
1.5	- Diesel railcars	...	5 573	5 114	...	4 597	4 309	...	293	...

RAILWAY TRANSPORT- TRANSPORT FERROVIAIRE
ЖЕЛЕЗНЫЕ ДОРОГИ

4. Tractive vehicle movements

4. Mouvements de véhicules moteurs

4. Передвижение тягового транспортного средства

(1000 tractive vehicle-km)

		Netherlands Pays-Bas Нидерланды			Norway Norvège Норвегия			Poland Pologne Польша		
		1990	1998	1999	1990	1998	1999	1990	1998	1999
1	Total tractive vehicle movements	165 732	...	...	...	41 715	38 993	...	407 667	395 876
1.1	- Electric locomotives	26 373	...	...	...	16 341	13 512	...	192 182	186 729
1.2	- Diesel locomotives	6 554	...	...	...	6 618	5 779	...	84 534	79 003
1.3	- Steam locomotives	-	...	...	-	-	-	...	375	334
1.4	- Electric railcars	117 200	...	...	...	16 654	16 573	...	129 423	128 721
1.5	- Diesel railcars	15 605	...	...	...	2 102	3 129	...	1 153	1 089

		Portugal Portugal Португалия			Republic of Moldova République de Moldova Республика Молдова			Romania Roumanie Румыния		
		1990	1998	1999	1990	1998	1999	1990	1998	1999
1	Total tractive vehicle movements	...	56 897	...	...	8 136	5 696	...	137 660	78 467
1.1	- Electric locomotives	...	...	...	-	-	-	...	83 620	42 142
1.2	- Diesel locomotives	...	...	...	...	6 442	4 345	...	54 040	36 424
1.3	- Steam locomotives	...	-	-	-	-	-	...	-	-
1.4	- Electric railcars	...	...	...	-	-	-	...	-	-
1.5	- Diesel railcars	...	...	...	...	1 694	1 351	...	2 200	1 547

		Russian Federation Fédération de Russie Российская Федерация			Slovakia Slovaquie Словакия			Slovenia Slovénie Словения		
		1990	1998	1999	1990	1998	1999	1990	1998	1999
1	Total tractive vehicle movements	...	1 306 904	1 423 845	...	79 287	...	...	20 387	20 351
1.1	- Electric locomotives	...	801 768	...	...	35 632	...	...	9 404	9 297
1.2	- Diesel locomotives	...	504 763	...	...	23 755	...	...	2 872	2 794
1.3	- Steam locomotives	...	373	-	...	-	-	...	12	13
1.4	- Electric railcars	...	...	...	...	5 272	...	...	3 348	3 507
1.5	- Diesel railcars	...	...	...	...	14 628	...	...	4 751	4 740

		Spain Espagne Испания			Sweden Suède Швеция			Tajikistan Tadjikistan Таджикистан		
		1990	1998	1999	1990	1998	1999	1990	1998	1999
1	Total tractive vehicle movements	...	197 753	199 641	125 600	127 747	129 853	...	1 291	1 257
1.1	- Electric locomotives	...	62 131	62 170	87 351	66 153	66 809	...	-	-
1.2	- Diesel locomotives	...	22 813	23 185	5 477	3 611	4 111	...	1 291	1 257
1.3	- Steam locomotives	...	-	-	-	-	-	...	-	-
1.4	- Electric railcars	...	93 948	96 200	23 435	49 447	51 274	...	-	-
1.5	- Diesel railcars	...	18 861	18 086	9 337	8 536	7 659	...	-	-

RAILWAY TRANSPORT- TRANSPORT FERROVIAIRE
ЖЕЛЕЗНЫЕ ДОРОГИ

4. Tractive vehicle movements

4. Mouvements de véhicules moteurs

4. Передвижение тягового транспортного средства

(1000 tractive vehicle-km)

		The FYR of Macedonia [1]			Turkey Turquie Турция			Turkmenistan Turkménistan Туркменистан		
		1990	1998	1999	1990	1998	1999	1990	1998	1999
1	**Total tractive vehicle movements**	...	**2 742**	**3 008**	...	**62 568**	...	...	**11 886**	...
1.1	- Electric locomotives	...	1 180	1 098	...	8 541	...	-	-	...
1.2	- Diesel locomotives	...	1 161	1 403	...	37 826	...	...	11 886	...
1.3	- Steam locomotives	...	-	-	...	5	...	...	-	...
1.4	- Electric railcars	...	370	442	...	9 745	...	-	-	...
1.5	- Diesel railcars	...	31	65	...	6 451	...	...	-	...

		Ukraine Ukraine Украина			Uzbekistan Ouzbékistan Узбекистан					
		1990	1998	1999	1990	1998	1999			
1	**Total tractive vehicle movements**	...	**458 332**	...	...	**615 529**	...			
1.1	- Electric locomotives	...	161 938	...	...	178 397	...			
1.2	- Diesel locomotives	...	108 712	...	...	429 850	...			
1.3	- Steam locomotives	...	129	...	...	-	...			
1.4	- Electric railcars	...	165 203	...	...	7 282	...			
1.5	- Diesel railcars	...	22 350	...	...	-	...			

1- The former Yugoslav Republic of Macedonia

1- L'ex-République yougoslave de Macédoine

1- Бывшая Югославская Республика Македония

RAILWAY TRANSPORT- TRANSPORT FERROVIAIRE
ЖЕЛЕЗНЫЕ ДОРОГИ

5. Train movements
5. Parcours des trains
5. Движение поездов

Item	Description	Rubrique	Description
1	**Train movements - Total** (1000 train-kilometres) *by type of motor vehicle and source of power*	1	**Parcours des trains - Total** (1000 de train-kilomètres) *par type de véhicule moteur et mode de propulsion*
1.10	- Electric locomotives	1.10	- Locomotives électriques
1.20	- Diesel locomotives	1.20	- Locomotives diesel
1.30	- Steam locomotives	1.30	- Locomotives à vapeur
1.40	- Electric railcars	1.40	- Automotrices électriques
1.50	- Diesel railcars	1.50	- Automotrices diesel
1.1	**Passenger train movements** *by type of motor vehicle and source of power*	1.1	**Parcours des trains de voyageurs** *par type de véhicule moteur et mode de propulsion*
1.11	- Electric locomotives	1.11	- Locomotives électriques
1.21	- Diesel locomotives	1.21	- Locomotives diesel
1.31	- Steam locomotives	1.31	- Locomotives à vapeur
1.41	- Electric railcars	1.41	- Automotrices électriques
1.51	- Diesel railcars	1.51	- Automotrices diesel
1.2	**Goods train movements** *by type of motor vehicle and source of power*	1.2	**Parcours des trains de marchandises** *par type de véhicule moteur et mode de propulsion*
1.12	- Electric locomotives	1.12	- Locomotives électriques
1.22	- Diesel locomotives	1.22	- Locomotives diesel
1.32	- Steam locomotives	1.32	- Locomotives à vapeur
1.42	- Electric railcars	1.42	- Automotrices électriques
1.52	- Diesel railcars	1.52	- Automotrices diesel
1.3	**Other train movements**	1.3	**Parcours des autres trains**

Статья	Описание
1	**Движение поездов - Всего** (1000 Поездо-километры) *по типу транспортного средства и по типу тяги*
1.10	- Электровозы
1.20	- Тепловозы
1.30	- Паровозы
1.40	- Электрические автомотрисы
1.50	- Дизельные автомотрисы
1.1	**Движение пассажирских поездов** *по типу транспортного средства и по типу тяги*
1.11	- Электровозы
1.21	- Тепловозы
1.31	- Паровозы
1.41	- Электрические автомотрисы
1.51	- Дизельные автомотрисы
1.2	**Движение грузовых поездов** *по типу транспортного средства и по типу тяги*
1.12	- Электровозы
1.22	- Тепловозы
1.32	- Паровозы
1.42	- Электрические автомотрисы
1.52	- Дизельные автомотрисы
1.3	**Движение других поездов**

RAILWAY TRANSPORT- TRANSPORT FERROVIAIRE
ЖЕЛЕЗНЫЕ ДОРОГИ

5. Train movements
5. Parcours des trains
5. Движение поездов

(1000 train-kilometres)

		Austria Autriche Австрия			Azerbaijan Azerbaïdjan Азербайджан			Belarus Bélarus Беларусь		
		1990	1998	1999	1990	1998	1999	1990	1998	1999
1	Total train movements	115 218	140 025	...	...	11 355	...	...	59 595	...
1.10	- Electric locomotives	...	90 371	...	...	7 823	...	...	12 247	...
1.20	- Diesel locomotives	...	13 094	...	...	791	...	...	29 652	...
1.30	- Steam locomotives	...	20	...	...	-	...	...	-	...
1.40	- Electric railcars	...	25 938	...	...	2 740	...	...	7 948	...
1.50	- Diesel railcars	...	10 602	...	...	-	...	...	9 748	...
1.1	Passenger train movements	75 460	92 800	...	...	6 134	...	...	38 947	...
1.11	- Electric locomotives	...	50 695	...	...	3 100	...	...	7 464	...
1.21	- Diesel locomotives	...	5 553	...	...	418	...	...	13 918	...
1.31	- Steam locomotives	...	20	...	...	-	...	...	-	...
1.41	- Electric railcars	...	25 934	...	...	2 616	...	...	7 885	...
1.51	- Diesel railcars	...	10 598	...	...	-	...	...	9 680	...
1.2	Goods train movements	39 758	47 225	...	...	4 627	...	...	18 626	...
1.12	- Electric locomotives	...	39 676	...	...	4 375	...	...	4 685	...
1.22	- Diesel locomotives	...	7 541	...	...	252	...	...	13 941	...
1.32	- Steam locomotives	...	-	...	...	-	...	...	-	...
1.42	- Electric railcars	...	4	...	...	-	...	...	-	...
1.52	- Diesel railcars	...	4	...	...	-	...	...	-	...
1.3	Other train movements	-	-	...	...	594	...	...	2 022	...

		Belgium Belgique Бельгия			Bosnia-Herzegovina Bosnie-Herzégovine Босния и Герцеговина			Bulgaria Bulgarie Болгария		
		1990	1998	1999	1990	1998	1999	1990	1998	1999
1	Total train movements	92 110	94 193	95 702	...	2 837	...	58 792	42 702	42 418
1.10	- Electric locomotives	...	30 932	29 503	...	...	...	...	27 769	28 518
1.20	- Diesel locomotives	...	9 977	9 680	...	...	...	...	7 927	7 580
1.30	- Steam locomotives	...	-	-	...	...	...	...	-	...
1.40	- Electric railcars	...	52 252	55 472	...	...	...	...	6 999	6 312
1.50	- Diesel railcars	...	1 032	1 047	...	...	...	...	7	8
1.1	Passenger train movements	70 695	74 804	76 844	...	409	...	35 262	29 816	30 104
1.11	- Electric locomotives	...	18 255	16 875	...	...	...	...	17 555	18 665
1.21	- Diesel locomotives	...	4 254	4 350	...	...	...	...	5 255	5 119
1.31	- Steam locomotives	...	-	-	...	...	...	...	-	...
1.41	- Electric railcars	...	51 268	54 575	...	...	...	...	6 999	6 312
1.51	- Diesel railcars	...	1 027	1 044	...	...	...	...	7	8
1.2	Goods train movements	21 415	18 431	17 976	...	2 428	...	23 530	12 590	11 867
1.12	- Electric locomotives	...	12 549	12 474	...	...	...	...	10 070	9 563
1.22	- Diesel locomotives	...	5 210	4 912	...	...	...	...	2 520	2 304
1.32	- Steam locomotives	...	...	...	...	...	...	...	...	...
1.42	- Electric railcars	...	672	590	...	...	...	...	-	...
1.52	- Diesel railcars	...	-	-	...	...	...	...	...	...
1.3	Other train movements	-	958	882	...	-	...	...	296	447

RAILWAY TRANSPORT- TRANSPORT FERROVIAIRE
ЖЕЛЕЗНЫЕ ДОРОГИ

5. Train movements
5. Parcours des trains
5. Движение поездов

(1000 train-kilometres)

		Canada Canada Канада			Croatia Croatie Хорватия			Czech Republic République tchèque Чешская Республика		
		1990	1998	1999	1990	1998	1999	1990	1998	1999
1	Total train movements	...	129 145	...	...	27 207	25 642	...	137 251	136 868
1.10	- Electric locomotives	...	...	...	...	9 626	9 469	...	65 285	64 560
1.20	- Diesel locomotives	...	...	...	...	10 813	9 470	...	25 695	23 219
1.30	- Steam locomotives	...	...	...	...	-	-	...	19	21
1.40	- Electric railcars	...	...	...	...	1 980	2 055	...	6 498	6 540
1.50	- Diesel railcars	...	...	...	...	4 788	4 648	...	39 754	42 528
1.1	Passenger train movements	...	11 181	...	...	17 177	16 522	...	93 298	95 710
1.11	- Electric locomotives	...	...	...	...	6 203	6 218	...	33 352	34 637
1.21	- Diesel locomotives	...	...	...	...	4 348	3 823	...	13 784	12 075
1.31	- Steam locomotives	...	...	...	...	-	-	...	15	20
1.41	- Electric railcars	...	...	...	...	1 946	2 017	...	6 498	6 540
1.51	- Diesel railcars	...	...	...	...	4 680	4 464	...	39 649	42 438
1.2	Goods train movements	...	117 150	...	...	5 502	5 251	74 943	43 875	41 157
1.12	- Electric locomotives	...	...	...	...	2 697	2 509	...	31 930	29 923
1.22	- Diesel locomotives	...	...	...	...	2 805	2 742	...	11 839	11 143
1.32	- Steam locomotives	...	...	...	...	-	-	...	2	1
1.42	- Electric railcars	...	...	...	...	-	-	...	-	-
1.52	- Diesel railcars	...	...	...	...	-	-	...	104	90
1.3	Other train movements	...	813	...	...	4 528	3 869	...	78	1

		Denmark Danemark Дания			Estonia Estonie Эстония			Finland Finlande Финляндия		
		1990	1998	1999	1990	1998	1999	1990	1998	1999
1	Total train movements	52 160	62 815	60 808	...	8 464	...	41 038	44 481	44 305
1.10	- Electric locomotives	...	4 285	...	...	-	...	...	22 959	23 368
1.20	- Diesel locomotives	...	9 930	...	...	4 725	...	...	13 858	13 344
1.30	- Steam locomotives	...	-	...	...	-	...	-	-	-
1.40	- Electric railcars	...	21 530	...	...	1 134	...	...	7 664	7 593
1.50	- Diesel railcars	...	27 070	...	...	2 605	...	-	-	-
1.1	Passenger train movements	45 230	54 405	54 975	...	4 160	...	24 238	27 105	27 061
1.11	- Electric locomotives	...	935	...	...	-	...	...	13 571	13 886
1.21	- Diesel locomotives	...	5 765	...	...	498	...	...	5 870	5 582
1.31	- Steam locomotives	...	-	...	...	-	...	-	-	-
1.41	- Electric railcars	...	21 375	...	...	1 108	...	...	7 664	7 593
1.51	- Diesel railcars	...	26 330	...	...	2 554	...	-	-	-
1.2	Goods train movements	6 930	6 735	5 833	6 400	4 118	...	16 800	17 376	17 244
1.12	- Electric locomotives	...	3 101	...	...	-	...	...	9 388	9 482
1.22	- Diesel locomotives	...	3 633	...	...	4 118	...	...	7 988	7 762
1.32	- Steam locomotives	...	-	...	...	-	...	...	-	-
1.42	- Electric railcars	...	-	...	...	-	...	...	-	-
1.52	- Diesel railcars	...	1	...	...	-	...	...	-	-
1.3	Other train movements	-	1 675	-	...	186	...	-	-	-

RAILWAY TRANSPORT- TRANSPORT FERROVIAIRE
ЖЕЛЕЗНЫЕ ДОРОГИ

5. Train movements
5. Parcours des trains
5. Движение поездов

(1000 train-kilometres)

		France France Франция			Georgia Georgie Грузия			Germany Allemagne Германия		
		1990	1998	1999	1990	1998	1999	1990	1998	1999
1	Total train movements	487 670	507 194	520 735	...	5 960	...	...	872 398	941 718
1.10	- Electric locomotives	277 197	261 382	261 168	...	4 708	...	...	544 835	606 565
1.20	- Diesel locomotives	60 659	44 249	45 485	...	63	...	...	142 763	150 647
1.30	- Steam locomotives	-	-	-	...	-	...	...	309	251
1.40	- Electric railcars	92 560	155 667	165 684	...	1 189	...	...	82 849	76 506
1.50	- Diesel railcars	57 254	45 896	48 398	...	-	...	...	101 642	107 749
1.1	Passenger train movements	318 414	348 415	362 527	...	3 131	...	...	683 935	726 937
1.11	- Electric locomotives	139 619	125 829	125 585	...	1 897	...	...	389 247	437 559
1.21	- Diesel locomotives	31 044	24 282	26 180	...	45	...	...	110 418	107 136
1.31	- Steam locomotives	-	-	-	...	-	...	...	214	-
1.41	- Electric railcars	91 223	152 673	162 678	...	1 189	...	...	82 849	76 493
1.51	- Diesel railcars	56 528	45 631	48 084	...	-	...	...	101 207	105 749
1.2	Goods train movements	163 586	154 077	154 768	...	2 743	...	...	187 997	204 506
1.12	- Electric locomotives	136 073	135 132	135 196	...	2 727	...	...	155 551	168 803
1.22	- Diesel locomotives	26 673	17 881	18 491	...	16	...	...	32 016	35 226
1.32	- Steam locomotives	-	-	-	...	-	...	...	95	251
1.42	- Electric railcars	440	1 064	1 081	...	-	...	...	-	-
1.52	- Diesel railcars	400	-	-	...	-	...	...	335	226
1.3	Other train movements	5 670	4 702	3 440	...	86	...	...	466	10 275

		Greece Grèce Греция			Hungary Hongrie Венгрия			Ireland Irlande Ирландия		
		1990	1998	1999	1990	1998	1999	1990	1998	1999
1	Total train movements	...	16 669	...	104 672	103 009	102 988	14 237	15 466	15 199
1.10	- Electric locomotives	-	-	...	...	56 107	...	...	-	-
1.20	- Diesel locomotives	...	6 642	...	...	21 027	...	...	12 393	12 069
1.30	- Steam locomotives	-	-	...	...	27	12	...	-	-
1.40	- Electric railcars	-	-	...	...	1 966	...	...	1 889	1 936
1.50	- Diesel railcars	...	10 027	...	...	23 882	...	...	1 184	1 194
1.1	Passenger train movements	...	15 262	...	68 771	70 467	71 324	9 868	11 291	11 132
1.11	- Electric locomotives	-	-	...	...	34 290	...	...	-	-
1.21	- Diesel locomotives	...	5 235	...	...	11 960	...	...	8 218	8 002
1.31	- Steam locomotives	-	-	...	...	15	12	...	-	-
1.41	- Electric railcars	-	-	...	...	1 966	...	...	1 889	1 936
1.51	- Diesel railcars	...	10 027	...	...	22 236	...	...	1 184	1 194
1.2	Goods train movements	...	1 315	...	35 901	17 667	16 870	4 369	4 175	4 067
1.12	- Electric locomotives	-	-	...	...	12 643	...	...	-	-
1.22	- Diesel locomotives	...	1 315	...	...	4 987	...	...	4 175	4 067
1.32	- Steam locomotives	-	-	...	...	-	...	...	-	-
1.42	- Electric railcars	-	-	...	...	-	...	...	-	-
1.52	- Diesel railcars	-	-	...	...	37	...	...	-	-
1.3	Other train movements	...	92	...	-	14 875	14 794	-	-	-

RAILWAY TRANSPORT- TRANSPORT FERROVIAIRE
ЖЕЛЕЗНЫЕ ДОРОГИ

5. Train movements
5. Parcours des trains
5. Движение поездов

(1000 train-kilometres)

		Israel Israël Израиль			Italy Italie Италия			Kazakhstan Kazakhstan Казахстан		
		1990	1998	1999	1990	1998	1999	1990	1998	1999
1	Total train movements	...	3 561	4 674	302 226	341 299	329 883	...	97 387	...
1.10	- Electric locomotives	...	-	-	...	242 275	230 467	...	42 166	...
1.20	- Diesel locomotives	...	2 451	2 970	...	18 987	18 077	...	52 119	...
1.30	- Steam locomotives	...	...	...	...	15	16	...	-	...
1.40	- Electric railcars	...	-	-	...	41 789	42 944	...	1 383	...
1.50	- Diesel railcars	...	1 110	1 704	...	38 233	38 379	...	49	...
1.1	Passenger train movements	...	2 139	3 227	235 647	253 858	249 287	...	41 818	...
1.11	- Electric locomotives	...	-	-	...	164 646	158 588	...	15 437	...
1.21	- Diesel locomotives	...	1 029	1 523	...	14 410	14 038	...	23 132	...
1.31	- Steam locomotives	...	-	-	...	7	12	...	-	...
1.41	- Electric railcars	...	-	-	...	38 948	40 757	...	1 383	...
1.51	- Diesel railcars	...	1 110	1 704	...	35 847	35 892	...	49	...
1.2	Goods train movements	...	1 422	1 447	66 579	66 459	58 026	...	55 569	...
1.12	- Electric locomotives	...	-	-	...	63 579	55 695	...	26 729	...
1.22	- Diesel locomotives	...	1 422	1 447	...	2 830	2 280	...	28 987	...
1.32	- Steam locomotives	...	-	-	...	-	1	...	-	...
1.42	- Electric railcars	...	-	-	...	13	9	...	-	...
1.52	- Diesel railcars	...	-	-	...	36	41	...	-	...
1.3	Other train movements	...	-	-	-	20 982	22 570	...	-	...

		Kyrgyzstan Kirghizistan Кыргызстан			Latvia Lettonie Латвия			Lithuania Lituanie Литва		
		1990	1998	1999	1990	1998	1999	1990	1998	1999
1	Total train movements	...	...	...	29 082	19 910	18 241	...	15 482	14 627
1.10	- Electric locomotives	-	-	-	...	-	-	...	-	-
1.20	- Diesel locomotives	...	...	...	...	11 172	10 049	...	9 831	9 375
1.30	- Steam locomotives	...	-	-	...	-	-	...	-	-
1.40	- Electric railcars	-	-	-	...	4 583	4 402	...	1 054	943
1.50	- Diesel railcars	-	-	-	...	4 155	3 790	...	4 597	4 309
1.1	Passenger train movements	...	...	...	14 920	10 795	9 884	...	8 226	7 730
1.11	- Electric locomotives	-	-	-	...	-	-	...	-	-
1.21	- Diesel locomotives	...	...	...	...	2 057	1 692	...	2 656	2 536
1.31	- Steam locomotives	...	-	-	...	-	-	...	-	-
1.41	- Electric railcars	-	-	-	...	4 583	4 402	...	1 053	941
1.51	- Diesel railcars	-	-	-	...	4 155	3 790	...	4 517	4 253
1.2	Goods train movements	...	443	...	14 162	9 115	8 357	...	6 914	6 598
1.12	- Electric locomotives	-	-	-	...	-	-	...	-	-
1.22	- Diesel locomotives	...	443	...	...	9 115	8 357	...	6 914	6 598
1.32	- Steam locomotives	...	-	-	...	-	-	...	-	-
1.42	- Electric railcars	-	-	-	...	-	-	...	-	-
1.52	- Diesel railcars	-	-	-	...	-	-	...	-	-
1.3	Other train movements	...	-	-	-	-	-	...	342	299

RAILWAY TRANSPORT- TRANSPORT FERROVIAIRE
ЖЕЛЕЗНЫЕ ДОРОГИ

5. Train movements
5. Parcours des trains
5. Движение поездов

(1000 train-kilometres)

		Luxembourg Luxembourg Люксембург			Netherlands Pays-Bas Нидерланды			Norway Norvège Норвегия		
		1990	1998	1999	1990	1998	1999	1990	1998	1999
1	**Total train movements**	4 903	7 308	...	117 314	121 658	...	36 705	37 417	35 765
1.10	- Electric locomotives	...	1 754	...	24 833	...	...	18 432	15 446	13 297
1.20	- Diesel locomotives	...	1 011	...	2 627	...	...	5 825	4 911	4 497
1.30	- Steam locomotives	-	-	...	-	1	...	-	-	-
1.40	- Electric railcars	...	4 251	...	76 494	...	...	10 462	14 998	14 924
1.50	- Diesel railcars	...	292	...	13 360	...	...	1 986	2 062	3 047
1.1	**Passenger train movements**	3 363	6 219	...	105 742	117 300	...	25 296	27 604	27 609
1.11	- Electric locomotives	...	1 201	...	...	...	...	...	8 026	7 386
1.21	- Diesel locomotives	...	475	...	...	...	...	...	2 518	2 252
1.31	- Steam locomotives	-	-	...	-	-	...	-	-	-
1.41	- Electric railcars	...	4 251	...	...	...	...	10 462	14 998	14 924
1.51	- Diesel railcars	...	292	...	...	...	...	1 986	2 062	3 047
1.2	**Goods train movements**	1 540	1 089	...	11 572	4 358	...	11 409	9 685	8 156
1.12	- Electric locomotives	...	553	...	...	...	...	...	7 420	5 911
1.22	- Diesel locomotives	...	536	...	...	...	...	...	2 265	2 245
1.32	- Steam locomotives	-	-	...	-	-	...	-	-	-
1.42	- Electric railcars	-	-	...	...	...	...	-	-	-
1.52	- Diesel railcars	-	-	...	...	...	...	-	-	-
1.3	**Other train movements**	-	-	...	-	-	...	-	128	-

		Poland Pologne Польша			Portugal Portugal Португалия			Republic of Moldova République de Moldova Республика Молдова		
		1990	1998	1999	1990	1998	1999	1990	1998	1999
1	**Total train movements**	360 223	284 182	279 317	...	45 961	39 164	...	5 339	3 794
1.10	- Electric locomotives	...	168 603	164 822	...	...	...	-	-	-
1.20	- Diesel locomotives	...	46 087	44 169	...	...	...	...	3 645	2 443
1.30	- Steam locomotives	...	315	272	...	-	-	-	-	-
1.40	- Electric railcars	...	68 045	69 001	...	...	...	-	-	-
1.50	- Diesel railcars	...	1 132	1 053	...	...	...	...	1 694	1 351
1.1	**Passenger train movements**	234 547	171 833	175 696	27 400	...	31 603	...	3 673	2 926
1.11	- Electric locomotives	...	77 510	80 541	...	...	...	-	-	-
1.21	- Diesel locomotives	...	29 453	29 560	...	...	...	...	2 022	1 578
1.31	- Steam locomotives	...	218	199	...	-	-	-	-	-
1.41	- Electric railcars	...	63 555	64 387	...	...	...	-	-	-
1.51	- Diesel railcars	...	1 097	1 009	...	...	...	...	1 651	1 348
1.2	**Goods train movements**	125 676	100 725	92 188	6 300	...	7 561	...	1 666	868
1.12	- Electric locomotives	...	87 093	80 205	...	...	...	-	-	-
1.22	- Diesel locomotives	...	13 539	11 912	...	...	...	...	1 623	865
1.32	- Steam locomotives	...	93	71	...	-	-	-	-	-
1.42	- Electric railcars	...	-	-	...	...	...	-	-	-
1.52	- Diesel railcars	...	-	-	...	-	-	...	43	3
1.3	**Other train movements**	-	11 624	11 433	...	...	...	-	-	-

RAILWAY TRANSPORT- TRANSPORT FERROVIAIRE
ЖЕЛЕЗНЫЕ ДОРОГИ

5. Train movements
5. Parcours des trains
5. Движение поездов

(1000 train-kilometres)

		Romania Roumanie Румыния			Russian Federation Fédération de Russie Российская Федерация			Slovakia Slovaquie Словакия		
		1990	1998	1999	1990	1998	1999	1990	1998	1999
1	Total train movements	150 406	109 160	97 676	...	1 103 882	1 193 360	...	59 169	56 212
1.10	- Electric locomotives	...	...	...	...	648 567	...	...	33 256	...
1.20	- Diesel locomotives	...	...	...	...	282 056	...	...	11 820	...
1.30	- Steam locomotives	...	-	...	...	-	-	...	-	...
1.40	- Electric railcars	...	-	...	...	162 899	164 273	...	2 720	...
1.50	- Diesel railcars	...	...	...	...	10 358	10 446	...	11 373	...
1.1	Passenger train movements	86 764	75 941	70 042	...	500 135	498 199	...	37 107	36 606
1.11	- Electric locomotives	...	43 040	39 875	...	229 864	228 406	...	17 684	...
1.21	- Diesel locomotives	...	31 067	28 416	...	103 178	101 763	...	5 330	...
1.31	- Steam locomotives	...	-	3	...	-	-	...	-	-
1.41	- Electric railcars	...	-	-	...	157 217	158 103	...	2 720	...
1.51	- Diesel railcars	...	1 834	1 748	...	9 876	9 927	...	11 373	...
1.2	Goods train movements	63 642	32 761	27 399	...	541 924	627 927	...	22 062	19 391
1.12	- Electric locomotives	...	22 977	18 476	...	391 794	467 904	...	15 572	...
1.22	- Diesel locomotives	...	9 784	8 923	...	150 130	160 023	...	6 490	...
1.32	- Steam locomotives	...	-	-	...	-	-	...	-	-
1.42	- Electric railcars	...	-	-	...	-	-	...	-	-
1.52	- Diesel railcars	...	-	-	...	-	-	...	-	-
1.3	Other train movements	-	458	235	...	61 823	67 234	...	-	215

		Slovenia Slovénie Словения			Spain Espagne Испания			Sweden Suède Швеция		
		1990	1998	1999	1990	1998	1999	1990	1998	1999
1	Total train movements	22 968	18 071	18 131	168 906	173 061	175 543	99 634	101 814	103 827
1.10	- Electric locomotives	...	8 387	8 317	...	61 272	60 638	...	54 977	56 055
1.20	- Diesel locomotives	...	1 575	1 554	...	16 490	17 402	...	2 661	3 050
1.30	- Steam locomotives	...	10	12	...	-	-	-	-	-
1.40	- Electric railcars	...	3 348	3 508	...	77 987	80 448	...	36 475	37 764
1.50	- Diesel railcars	...	4 751	4 740	...	17 312	17 055	...	7 701	6 958
1.1	Passenger train movements	12 258	10 598	10 511	120 278	125 816	128 190	58 751	65 641	67 092
1.11	- Electric locomotives	...	2 760	2 602	...	23 500	22 697	...	22 580	23 533
1.21	- Diesel locomotives	...	151	144	...	7 016	8 238	...	1	6
1.31	- Steam locomotives	...	9	10	...	-	-	-	-	-
1.41	- Electric railcars	...	3 229	3 401	...	77 987	80 200	...	35 409	36 715
1.51	- Diesel railcars	...	4 449	4 354	...	17 312	17 055	...	7 651	6 838
1.2	Goods train movements	10 710	7 473	7 620	48 268	40 218	40 086	39 808	34 064	34 474
1.12	- Electric locomotives	...	5 627	5 715	...	33 394	31 839	...	31 411	31 468
1.22	- Diesel locomotives	...	1 424	1 410	...	6 824	8 247	...	2 653	3 006
1.32	- Steam locomotives	...	1	2	...	-	-	-	-	-
1.42	- Electric railcars	...	119	107	...	-	-	-	-	-
1.52	- Diesel railcars	...	302	386	...	-	-	-	-	-
1.3	Other train movements	-	-	-	360	7 027	7 267	1 075	2 109	2 261

RAILWAY TRANSPORT- TRANSPORT FERROVIAIRE
ЖЕЛЕЗНЫЕ ДОРОГИ

5. Train movements
5. Parcours des trains
5. Движение поездов

(1000 train-kilometres)

		Switzerland Suisse Швейцария			Tajikistan Tadjikistan Таджикистан			The FYR of Macedonia [1]		
		1990	1998	1999	1990	1998	1999	1990	1998	1999
1	Total train movements	121 809	123 487	...	...	1 598	1 234	...	2 751	2 769
1.10	- Electric locomotives	...	...	...	...	-	-	...	1 178	975
1.20	- Diesel locomotives	...	...	...	...	1 598	1 234	...	1 184	1 300
1.30	- Steam locomotives	...	-	...	...	-	-	...	-	-
1.40	- Electric railcars	...	...	...	...	-	-	...	361	437
1.50	- Diesel railcars	...	-	...	...	-	-	...	28	57
1.1	Passenger train movements	94 660	...	...	...	648	345	...	1 902	2 038
1.11	- Electric locomotives	...	...	...	...	-	-	...	478	358
1.21	- Diesel locomotives	...	-	...	...	648	345	...	1 035	1 186
1.31	- Steam locomotives	...	...	...	...	-	-	...	-	-
1.41	- Electric railcars	...	...	...	...	-	-	...	361	437
1.51	- Diesel railcars	...	...	...	...	-	-	...	28	57
1.2	Goods train movements	27 149	...	...	...	926	874	...	849	731
1.12	- Electric locomotives	...	...	...	...	-	-	...	700	617
1.22	- Diesel locomotives	...	...	...	...	926	874	...	149	114
1.32	- Steam locomotives	...	-	...	...	-	-	...	-	-
1.42	- Electric railcars	...	-	...	...	-	-	...	-	-
1.52	- Diesel railcars	...	-	...	...	-	-	...	-	-
1.3	Other train movements	-	-	...	...	24	15	-	-	-

		Turkey Turquie Турция			Turkmenistan Turkménistan Туркменистан			Ukraine Ukraine Украина		
		1990	1998	1999	1990	1998	1999	1990	1998	1999
1	Total train movements	...	44 295	...	...	10 545	...	...	236 940	232 694
1.10	- Electric locomotives	...	8 059	...	-	-	...	...	133 285	132 076
1.20	- Diesel locomotives	...	28 281	...	...	10 545	...	...	53 953	50 655
1.30	- Steam locomotives	...	1	...	...	-	...	...	4	3
1.40	- Electric railcars	...	4 617	...	-	-	...	...	37 975	38 556
1.50	- Diesel railcars	...	3 337	...	...	-	...	...	11 723	11 404
1.1	Passenger train movements	26 300	26 721	...	...	4 282	...	132 800	143 535	141 131
1.11	- Electric locomotives	...	6 297	...	-	-	...	...	61 011	60 805
1.21	- Diesel locomotives	...	12 469	...	...	4 282	...	...	33 728	31 365
1.31	- Steam locomotives	...	1	...	...	-	...	...	3	2
1.41	- Electric railcars	...	4 617	...	-	-	...	...	37 203	37 727
1.51	- Diesel railcars	...	3 337	...	...	-	...	...	11 590	11 232
1.2	Goods train movements	17 883	17 178	...	...	5 414	...	...	83 496	81 321
1.12	- Electric locomotives	...	1 752	...	-	-	...	...	68 468	67 443
1.22	- Diesel locomotives	...	15 426	...	...	5 414	...	...	15 028	13 878
1.32	- Steam locomotives	...	...	...	...	-	...	...	-	-
1.42	- Electric railcars	...	-	...	...	-	...	...	-	-
1.52	- Diesel railcars	...	-	...	...	-	...	...	-	-
1.3	Other train movements	...	396	...	...	849	...	...	9 909	10 242

1- The former Yugoslav Republic of Macedonia

1- L'ex-République yougoslave de Macédoine

1- Бывшая Югославская Республика Македония

RAILWAY TRANSPORT- TRANSPORT FERROVIAIRE
ЖЕЛЕЗНЫЕ ДОРОГИ

5. Train movements
5. Parcours des trains
5. Движение поездов

(1000 train-kilometres)

		United Kingdom Royaume-Uni Соединенное Королевство			United States Etats-Unis 1) Соединенные Штаты			Uzbekistan Ouzbékistan Узбекистан		
		1990	1998	1999	1990	1998	1999	1990	1998	1999
1	Total train movements	...	...	...	10 266 900	817 167	843 955	...	18 045	...
1.10	- Electric locomotives	...	...	...	...	...	...	...	4 029	...
1.20	- Diesel locomotives	...	...	...	...	...	...	...	12 964	...
1.30	- Steam locomotives	...	...	...	...	...	...	...	-	...
1.40	- Electric railcars	...	...	...	...	...	...	...	1 052	...
1.50	- Diesel railcars	...	...	...	...	...	...	...	-	...
1.1	Passenger train movements	375 600	...	...	9 656 000	52 977	54 834	...	8 493	...
1.11	- Electric locomotives	...	...	...	...	...	...	...	831	...
1.21	- Diesel locomotives	...	...	...	...	...	...	...	6 610	...
1.31	- Steam locomotives	...	...	...	...	...	...	...	-	...
1.41	- Electric railcars	...	...	...	...	...	...	...	1 052	...
1.51	- Diesel railcars	...	...	...	...	...	...	...	-	...
1.2	Goods train movements	61 800	...	...	610 900	764 190	789 121	...	9 552	...
1.12	- Electric locomotives	...	...	...	...	-	-	...	3 198	...
1.22	- Diesel locomotives	...	...	...	...	764 190	789 121	...	6 354	...
1.32	- Steam locomotives	...	...	...	...	-	-	...	-	...
1.42	- Electric railcars	...	...	...	...	-	-	...	-	...
1.52	- Diesel railcars	...	...	...	...	-	-	...	-	...
1.3	Other train movements	...	...	...	-	-	-	...	-	...

		Yugoslavia Yugoslavie Югославия								
		1990	1998	1999						
1	Total train movements	...	28 729	19 573						
1.10	- Electric locomotives	...	12 367	8 770						
1.20	- Diesel locomotives	...	5 895	3 019						
1.30	- Steam locomotives	...	4	2						
1.40	- Electric railcars	...	7 638	5 487						
1.50	- Diesel railcars	...	2 825	2 295						
1.1	Passenger train movements	...	23 498	16 682						
1.11	- Electric locomotives	...	8 699	6 877						
1.21	- Diesel locomotives	...	4 332	2 021						
1.31	- Steam locomotives	...	4	2						
1.41	- Electric railcars	...	7 638	5 487						
1.51	- Diesel railcars	...	2 825	2 295						
1.2	Goods train movements	...	5 231	2 891						
1.12	- Electric locomotives	...	3 668	1 893						
1.22	- Diesel locomotives	...	1 563	998						
1.32	- Steam locomotives	...	-	-						
1.42	- Electric railcars	...	-	-						
1.52	- Diesel railcars	...	-	-						
1.3	Other train movements	...	-	-						

1- Class 1 railways. 1- Chemins de fer de 1ère classe. 1- Железные дороги первого класса.

RAILWAY TRANSPORT- TRANSPORT FERROVIAIRE
ЖЕЛЕЗНЫЕ ДОРОГИ

6. Hauled vehicles movements of trains
6. Mouvements de véhicules remorqués par les trains
6. Движение буксируемых траспортных средств

Item	Description	Rubrique	Description
1	**Hauled vehicle movements - Total** (million gross tonne-kilometres) *by type of motor vehicle and source of power*	1	**Mouvements de véhicules remorqués - Total** (millions de tonnes-kilomètres brutes) *par type de véhicule moteur et mode de propulsion*
1.10	- Electric locomotives	1.10	- Locomotives électriques
1.20	- Diesel locomotives	1.20	- Locomotives diesel
1.30	- Steam locomotives	1.30	- Locomotives à vapeur
1.40	- Electric railcars	1.40	- Automotrices électriques
1.50	- Diesel railcars	1.50	- Automotrices diesel
1.1	**Hauled passenger vehicles movements in passenger (and mixed) trains** *by type of motor vehicle and source of power*	1.1	**Mouvements de véhicules de voyageurs remorqués dans les trains de voyageurs (et mixtes)** *par type de véhicule moteur et mode de propulsion*
1.11	- Electric locomotives	1.11	- Locomotives électriques
1.21	- Diesel locomotives	1.21	- Locomotives diesel
1.31	- Steam locomotives	1.31	- Locomotives à vapeur
1.41	- Electric railcars	1.41	- Automotrices électriques
1.51	- Diesel railcars	1.51	- Automotrices diesel
1.2	**Hauled goods vehicles movements in goods (and mixed) trains** *by type of motor vehicle and source of power*	1.2	**Mouvements de véhicules de marchandises remorqués dans les trains de marchandises (et mixtes)** *par type de véhicule moteur et mode de propulsion*
1.12	- Electric locomotives	1.12	- Locomotives électriques
1.22	- Diesel locomotives	1.22	- Locomotives diesel
1.32	- Steam locomotives	1.32	- Locomotives à vapeur
1.42	- Electric railcars	1.42	- Automotrices électriques
1.52	- Diesel railcars	1.52	- Automotrices diesel
1.3	**Hauled vehicle movements in other trains**	1.3	**Mouvements de véhicules remorqués dans les autres trains**

Статья	Описание
1	**Движение буксируемых транспортных средств - Всего** (млн. ткм. брутто) *по типу транспортного средства и по типу тяги*
1.10	- Электровозы
1.20	- Тепловозы
1.30	- Паровозы
1.40	- Электрические автомотрисы
1.50	- Дизельные автомотрисы
1.1	**Движение пассажирских буксируемых транспортных средств в составе пассажирских (и смешанных) поездов** *по типу транспортного средства и по типу тяги*
1.11	- Электровозы
1.21	- Тепловозы
1.31	- Паровозы
1.41	- Электрические автомотрисы
1.51	- Дизельные автомотрисы
1.2	**Движение грузовых буксируемых транспортных средств в составе пассажирских (и смешанных) поездов** *по типу транспортного средства и по типу тяги*
1.12	- Электровозы
1.22	- Тепловозы
1.32	- Паровозы
1.42	- Электрические автомотрисы
1.52	- Дизельные автомотрисы
1.3	**Движение буксируемых транспортных средств в составе других поездов**

RAILWAY TRANSPORT- TRANSPORT FERROVIAIRE
ЖЕЛЕЗНЫЕ ДОРОГИ

6. Hauled vehicles movements of trains
6. Mouvements de véhicules remorqués par les trains
6. Движение буксируемых траспортных средств

(million gross-tonne-km)

		Austria Autriche Австрия			Azerbaijan Azerbaïdjan Азербайджан			Belarus Bélarus Беларусь		
		1990	1998	1999	1990	1998	1999	1990	1998	1999
1	Total hauled vehicles movements	...	57 183	57 188	...	12 297	...	...	80 417	...
1.10	- Electric locomotives	...	45 323	...	...	11 162	...	...	19 545	...
1.20	- Diesel locomotives	...	5 738	...	...	517	...	...	52 801	...
1.30	- Steam locomotives	...	1	...	...	-	...	...	-	...
1.40	- Electric railcars	...	5 553	...	...	618	...	...	4 695	...
1.50	- Diesel railcars	...	568	...	...	-	...	...	3 376	...
1.1	In passenger (and mixed) trains	...	22 077	21 404	...	2 742	...	...	22 721	...
1.11	- Electric locomotives	...	15 270	...	...	1 920	...	...	5 967	...
1.21	- Diesel locomotives	...	687	...	...	232	...	...	8 733	...
1.31	- Steam locomotives	...	1	...	...	-	...	...	-	...
1.41	- Electric railcars	...	5 551	...	...	590	...	...	4 665	...
1.51	- Diesel railcars	...	568	...	...	-	...	...	3 356	...
1.2	In goods (and mixed) trains	...	35 098	...	...	9 423	...	...	56 942	...
1.12	- Electric locomotives	...	30 053	...	...	9 174	...	...	13 526	...
1.22	- Diesel locomotives	...	5 043	...	...	249	...	...	43 416	...
1.32	- Steam locomotives	...	-	...	...	-	...	...	-	...
1.42	- Electric railcars	...	2	...	...	-	...	...	-	...
1.52	- Diesel railcars	...	-	...	...	-	...	...	-	...
1.3	In other trains	-	8	...	...	132	...	...	754	...

		Belgium Belgique Бельгия			Bosnia-Herzegovina Bosnie-Herzégovine Босния и Герцеговина			Bulgaria Bulgarie Болгария		
		1990	1998	1999	1990	1998	1999	1990	1998	1999
1	Total hauled vehicles movements	...	40 832	41 569	...	208	...	28 660	20 812	18 919
1.10	- Electric locomotives	...	20 211	19 577	...	...	...	...	16 415	15 023
1.20	- Diesel locomotives	...	6 036	5 900	...	...	...	...	2 656	2 344
1.30	- Steam locomotives	...	-	-	...	...	-	...	...	...
1.40	- Electric railcars	...	14 519	16 026	...	...	...	...	1 740	1 551
1.50	- Diesel railcars	...	66	66	...	...	...	...	1	1
1.1	In passenger (and mixed) trains	...	21 708	22 627	...	51	...	...	9 538	8 844
1.11	- Electric locomotives	...	6 907	6 223	...	...	...	...	6 514	6 174
1.21	- Diesel locomotives	...	819	860	...	...	...	...	1 283	1 118
1.31	- Steam locomotives	...	-	-	...	...	...	...	-	...
1.41	- Electric railcars	...	13 919	15 481	...	...	...	...	1 740	1 551
1.51	- Diesel railcars	...	63	63	...	...	...	...	-	1
1.2	In goods (and mixed) trains	...	18 355	18 227	...	157	...	28 660	11 191	9 904
1.12	- Electric locomotives	...	13 256	13 300	...	...	...	23 558	9 381	8 701
1.22	- Diesel locomotives	...	5 031	4 866	...	...	...	5 101	1 360	1 203
1.32	- Steam locomotives	...	-	-	...	...	...	-	-	-
1.42	- Electric railcars	...	68	61	...	...	...	-	-	-
1.52	- Diesel railcars	...	-	-	...	...	...	-	-	-
1.3	In other trains	...	769	715	...	-	...	...	83	170

64

RAILWAY TRANSPORT- TRANSPORT FERROVIAIRE
ЖЕЛЕЗНЫЕ ДОРОГИ

6. Hauled vehicles movements of trains
6. Mouvements de véhicules remorqués par les trains
6. Движение буксируемых траспортных средств

(million gross-tonne-km)

		Canada Canada Канада			Croatia Croatie Хорватия			Czech Republic République tchèque Чешская Республика		
		1990	1998	1999	1990	1998	1999	1990	1998	1999
1	Total hauled vehicles movements	...	559	...	...	6 750	6 308	...	58 625	64 223
1.10	- Electric locomotives	...	...	...	...	3 659	3 419	...	45 480	41 785
1.20	- Diesel locomotives	...	...	...	...	2 421	2 214	...	8 646	7 857
1.30	- Steam locomotives	...	...	...	...	-	-	...	3	3
1.40	- Electric railcars	...	...	...	...	350	363	...	2 020	1 989
1.50	- Diesel railcars	...	...	...	...	320	312	...	2 476	12 589
1.1	In passenger (and mixed) trains	...	6	...	...	2 778	2 685	...	17 474	27 253
1.11	- Electric locomotives	...	...	...	...	1 301	1 314	...	10 429	10 507
1.21	- Diesel locomotives	...	...	...	...	806	696	...	2 550	2 173
1.31	- Steam locomotives	...	...	...	...	-	-	...	3	3
1.41	- Electric railcars	...	...	...	...	350	363	...	2 020	1 989
1.51	- Diesel railcars	...	...	...	...	321	312	...	2 472	12 581
1.2	In goods (and mixed) trains	...	553	...	...	3 972	3 623	82 990	41 135	36 970
1.12	- Electric locomotives	...	...	...	...	2 358	2 105	...	35 051	31 278
1.22	- Diesel locomotives	...	...	...	...	1 614	1 518	...	6 080	5 684
1.32	- Steam locomotives	...	...	...	...	-	-	...	-	-
1.42	- Electric railcars	...	...	...	...	-	-	...	-	-
1.52	- Diesel railcars	...	...	...	...	-	-	...	4	8
1.3	In other trains	...	-	...	-	-	-	...	16	-

		Estonia Estonie Эстония			Finland Finlande Финляндия			France France Франция		
		1990	1998	1999	1990	1998	1999	1990	1998	1999
1	Total hauled vehicles movements	14 427	11 606	...	17 003	29 286	29 016	250 542	270 034	275 968
1.10	- Electric locomotives	...	-	...	...	17 750	17 882	175 857	169 321	169 431
1.20	- Diesel locomotives	...	10 730	...	7 821	10 408	10 015	29 562	21 293	21 926
1.30	- Steam locomotives	...	-	...	-	-	-	-	-	-
1.40	- Electric railcars	...	261	...	...	1 128	1 119	37 768	74 729	79 505
1.50	- Diesel railcars	...	615	...	-	-	-	7 355	4 691	5 106
1.1	In passenger (and mixed) trains	...	1 130	...	...	8 255	8 339	112 999	129 796	134 862
1.11	- Electric locomotives	...	-	...	...	5 594	5 704	58 536	45 072	44 977
1.21	- Diesel locomotives	...	267	...	...	1 539	1 516	9 868	6 546	6 543
1.31	- Steam locomotives	...	-	...	-	-	-	-	-	-
1.41	- Electric railcars	...	256	...	...	1 122	1 119	37 298	73 511	78 267
1.51	- Diesel railcars	...	607	...	-	-	-	7 297	4 667	5 075
1.2	In goods (and mixed) trains	...	10 391	...	...	21 031	20 677	135 111	139 300	140 171
1.12	- Electric locomotives	...	-	...	...	12 156	12 178	116 214	124 187	124 392
1.22	- Diesel locomotives	...	10 391	...	...	8 869	8 499	18 678	14 654	15 306
1.32	- Steam locomotives	...	-	...	-	-	-	-	-	-
1.42	- Electric railcars	...	-	...	-	6	-	189	459	473
1.52	- Diesel railcars	...	-	...	-	-	-	30	-	-
1.3	In other trains	...	85	...	-	-	-	2 432	938	935

65

RAILWAY TRANSPORT- TRANSPORT FERROVIAIRE
ЖЕЛЕЗНЫЕ ДОРОГИ

6. Hauled vehicles movements of trains
6. Mouvements de véhicules remorqués par les trains
6. Движение буксируемых траспортных средств

(million gross-tonne-km)

		Georgia Georgie Грузия			Germany Allemagne Германия			Greece Grèce Греция		
		1990	1998	1999	1990	1998	1999	1990	1998	1999
1	Total hauled vehicles movements	...	6 308	...	...	334 006	359 344	...	3 656	...
1.10	- Electric locomotives	...	6 288	...	...	243 520	280 992	-	-	...
1.20	- Diesel locomotives	...	20	...	...	41 922	46 542	...	1 965	...
1.30	- Steam locomotives	...	-	...	...	141	393	-	-	...
1.40	- Electric railcars	...	-	...	...	40 094	23 130	-	-	...
1.50	- Diesel railcars	...	-	...	...	8 329	8 287	...	1 691	...
1.1	In passenger (and mixed) trains	...	1 155	...	...	164 990	171 794	...	3 071	...
1.11	- Electric locomotives	...	1 149	...	...	99 645	124 333	-	...	...
1.21	- Diesel locomotives	...	6	...	...	17 035	16 353	...	1 380	...
1.31	- Steam locomotives	...	-	...	...	17	-	-	-	...
1.41	- Electric railcars	...	-	...	...	40 094	23 129	-	-	...
1.51	- Diesel railcars	...	-	...	...	8 199	7 979	...	1 691	...
1.2	In goods (and mixed) trains	...	5 138	...	...	168 915	186 361	...	563	...
1.12	- Electric locomotives	...	5 124	...	...	143 868	156 655	-	-	...
1.22	- Diesel locomotives	...	14	...	...	24 804	29 211	...	563	...
1.32	- Steam locomotives	...	-	...	...	123	393	-	-	...
1.42	- Electric railcars	...	-	...	...	-	-	-	-	...
1.52	- Diesel railcars	...	-	...	...	120	102	-	-	...
1.3	In other trains	...	15	...	...	101	1 189	...	22	...

		Hungary Hongrie Венгрия			Ireland Irlande Ирландия			Israel Israël Израиль		
		1990	1998	1999	1990	1998	1999	1990	1998	1999
1	Total hauled vehicles movements	55 132	31 411	30 809	1 245	5 727	...	...	2 611	2 995
1.10	- Electric locomotives	...	23 958	23 907	...	-	...	...	-	-
1.20	- Diesel locomotives	...	5 356	4 692	...	5 415	...	...	2 284	2 605
1.30	- Steam locomotives	...	3	3	...	-	...	...	-	-
1.40	- Electric railcars	...	391	461	...	213	...	...	-	-
1.50	- Diesel railcars	...	1 703	1 746	...	99	...	...	327	390
1.1	In passenger (and mixed) trains	17 933	13 598	15 241	...	3 132	...	...	810	905
1.11	- Electric locomotives	...	9 428	10 923	...	-	...	...	-	-
1.21	- Diesel locomotives	...	2 148	2 109	...	2 820	...	...	483	515
1.31	- Steam locomotives	...	2	3	...	-	...	...	-	-
1.41	- Electric railcars	...	391	461	...	213	...	...	-	-
1.51	- Diesel railcars	...	1 629	1 745	...	99	...	...	327	390
1.2	In goods (and mixed) trains	37 168	15 956	15 568	...	2 595	...	...	1 801	2 090
1.12	- Electric locomotives	...	13 061	12 984	...	-	...	...	-	-
1.22	- Diesel locomotives	...	2 892	2 583	...	2 595	...	...	1 801	2 090
1.32	- Steam locomotives	...	-	-	...	-	...	...	-	-
1.42	- Electric railcars	...	-	-	...	-	...	...	-	-
1.52	- Diesel railcars	...	3	1	...	-	...	...	-	-
1.3	In other trains	32	15	-	...	-	...	...	-	-

RAILWAY TRANSPORT- TRANSPORT FERROVIAIRE
ЖЕЛЕЗНЫЕ ДОРОГИ

6. Hauled vehicles movements of trains
6. Mouvements de véhicules remorqués par les trains
6. Движение буксируемых траспортных средств

(million gross-tonne-km)

		Italy Italie Италия			Kazakhstan Kazakhstan Казахстан			Kyrgyzstan Kirghizistan Кыргызстан		
		1990	1998	1999	1990	1998	1999	1990	1998	1999
1	Total hauled vehicles movements	...	108 796	99 964	...	209 093	...	...	...	...
1.10	- Electric locomotives	...	103 437	95 338	...	109 134	...	-	-	-
1.20	- Diesel locomotives	...	3 991	3 538	...	99 470	...	...	...	...
1.30	- Steam locomotives	...	1	4	...	-	...	...	-	-
1.40	- Electric railcars	...	1 164	881	...	471	...	-	-	-
1.50	- Diesel railcars	...	203	203	...	18	...	-	-	-
1.1	In passenger (and mixed) trains	...	65 456	60 938	...	31 523	...	...	...	...
1.11	- Electric locomotives	...	61 391	57 278	...	12 932	...	-	-	-
1.21	- Diesel locomotives	...	2 805	2 641	...	18 102	...	...	...	...
1.31	- Steam locomotives	...	1	3	...	-	...	...	-	-
1.41	- Electric railcars	...	1 093	844	...	471	...	-	-	-
1.51	- Diesel railcars	...	166	172	...	18	...	-	-	-
1.2	In goods (and mixed) trains	...	40 451	36 701	...	177 570	...	...	811	...
1.12	- Electric locomotives	...	39 453	35 957	...	96 202	...	...	-	...
1.22	- Diesel locomotives	...	992	736	...	81 368	...	...	811	...
1.32	- Steam locomotives	...	-	-	...	-	...	...	-	...
1.42	- Electric railcars	...	3	2	...	-	...	...	-	...
1.52	- Diesel railcars	...	3	6	...	-	...	...	-	...
1.3	In other trains	...	2 889	2 325	...	-	...	...	-	-

		Latvia Lettonie Латвия			Lithuania Lituanie Литва			Luxembourg Luxembourg Люксембург		
		1990	1998	1999	1990	1998	1999	1990	1998	1999
1	Total hauled vehicles movements	35 046	26 977	25 122	...	19 067	17 861	1 394	2 513	...
1.10	- Electric locomotives	...	-	-	...	-	-	...	786	...
1.20	- Diesel locomotives	...	24 586	22 977	...	17 455	16 488	...	1 148	...
1.30	- Steam locomotives	...	-	-	...	-	-	...	-	...
1.40	- Electric railcars	...	1 398	1 271	...	352	241	...	560	...
1.50	- Diesel railcars	...	993	874	...	1 260	1 132	...	19	...
1.1	In passenger (and mixed) trains	...	3 229	2 808	...	2 886	2 554	...	912	...
1.11	- Electric locomotives	...	-	-	...	-	-	...	236	...
1.21	- Diesel locomotives	...	838	663	...	1 294	1 196	...	97	...
1.31	- Steam locomotives	...	-	...	...	-	-	...	-	...
1.41	- Electric railcars	...	1 398	1 271	...	352	240	...	560	...
1.51	- Diesel railcars	...	993	874	...	1 240	1 118	...	19	...
1.2	In goods (and mixed) trains	...	23 748	22 314	...	16 055	15 208	1 394	1 601	...
1.12	- Electric locomotives	...	-	-	...	-	-	548	550	...
1.22	- Diesel locomotives	...	23 748	22 314	...	16 055	15 208	846	1 051	...
1.32	- Steam locomotives	...	-	-	...	-	-	-	-	...
1.42	- Electric railcars	...	-	-	...	-	-	-	-	...
1.52	- Diesel railcars	...	-	-	...	-	-	-	-	...
1.3	In other trains	...	-	-	...	126	99	...	-	...

RAILWAY TRANSPORT- TRANSPORT FERROVIAIRE
ЖЕЛЕЗНЫЕ ДОРОГИ

6. Hauled vehicles movements of trains
6. Mouvements de véhicules remorqués par les trains
6. Движение буксируемых траспортных средств

(million gross-tonne-km)

		Netherlands Pays-Bas Нидерланды			Norway Norvège Норвегия			Poland Pologne Польша		
		1990	1998	1999	1990	1998	1999	1990	1998	1999
1	Total hauled vehicles movements	...	...	...	...	12 351	13 415	171 563	180 687	169 872
1.10	- Electric locomotives	...	...	...	...	7 511	7 378	...	147 221	137 946
1.20	- Diesel locomotives	...	...	...	...	2 412	3 139	...	15 979	14 497
1.30	- Steam locomotives	...	...	...	-	-	-	...	89	59
1.40	- Electric railcars	...	...	...	...	2 163	2 708	...	17 331	17 312
1.50	- Diesel railcars	...	...	...	...	265	190	...	67	58
1.1	In passenger (and mixed) trains	...	...	...	...	6 180	7 425	...	50 336	50 840
1.11	- Electric locomotives	...	...	...	...	2 884	2 864	...	28 552	29 151
1.21	- Diesel locomotives	...	...	...	...	868	1 663	...	5 275	5 260
1.31	- Steam locomotives	...	...	...	-	-	-	...	34	31
1.41	- Electric railcars	...	...	...	...	2 163	2 708	...	16 410	16 343
1.51	- Diesel railcars	...	...	...	...	265	190	...	65	55
1.2	In goods (and mixed) trains	7 499	...	...	...	6 171	5 990	...	127 854	116 637
1.12	- Electric locomotives	...	...	...	...	4 627	4 514	...	117 716	107 889
1.22	- Diesel locomotives	...	...	...	...	1 544	1 476	...	10 083	8 720
1.32	- Steam locomotives	...	...	...	-	-	-	...	55	28
1.42	- Electric railcars	...	...	...	-	-	-	...	-	-
1.52	- Diesel railcars	...	...	...	-	-	-	...	-	-
1.3	In other trains	-	...	...	-	-	-	...	2 497	2 395

		Portugal Portugal Португалия			Republic of Moldova République de Moldova Республика Молдова			Romania Roumanie Румыния		
		1990	1998	1999	1990	1998	1999	1990	1998	1999
1	Total hauled vehicles movements	...	12 179	11 975	14 423	6 669	3 602	98 799	70 036	...
1.10	- Electric locomotives	...	...	...	-	-	-	...	...	...
1.20	- Diesel locomotives	...	...	...	...	5 908	3 101	...	...	...
1.30	- Steam locomotives	...	-	-	...	-	-	...	-	...
1.40	- Electric railcars	...	...	...	...	-	-	...	-	...
1.50	- Diesel railcars	...	...	...	...	761	501	...	...	...
1.1	In passenger (and mixed) trains	...	...	7 483	...	1 968	1 397	...	27 028	...
1.11	- Electric locomotives	...	...	...	-	-	-	...	17 357	...
1.21	- Diesel locomotives	...	...	...	...	1 231	896	...	9 561	...
1.31	- Steam locomotives	...	-	-	...	-	-	...	-	...
1.41	- Electric railcars	...	...	...	...	-	-	...	-	...
1.51	- Diesel railcars	...	...	...	...	737	501	...	110	...
1.2	In goods (and mixed) trains	...	...	...	...	4 701	2 205	...	42 911	...
1.12	- Electric locomotives	...	...	...	-	-	-	...	29 339	...
1.22	- Diesel locomotives	...	...	...	...	4 677	2 205	...	13 572	...
1.32	- Steam locomotives	...	-	-	-	-	-	...	-	...
1.42	- Electric railcars	...	-	-	-	-	-	...	-	...
1.52	- Diesel railcars	...	-	-	...	24	-	...	-	...
1.3	In other trains	...	...	...	-	-	-	...	97	80

RAILWAY TRANSPORT- TRANSPORT FERROVIAIRE
ЖЕЛЕЗНЫЕ ДОРОГИ

6. Hauled vehicles movements of trains
6. Mouvements de véhicules remorqués par les trains
6. Движение буксируемых траспортных средств

(million gross-tonne-km)

		Russian Federation Fédération de Russie Российская Федерация			Slovakia Slovaquie Словакия			Slovenia Slovénie Словения		
		1990	1998	1999	1990	1998	1999	1990	1998	1999
1	Total hauled vehicles movements	...	2 141 872	2 468 310	56 852	33 577	29 041	11 190	7 155	7 326
1.10	- Electric locomotives	...	1 543 534	1 831 215	41 373	...	...	...	5 375	5 473
1.20	- Diesel locomotives	...	508 015	546 370	13 747	...	...	...	806	844
1.30	- Steam locomotives	...	-	-	-	-	-	...	2	2
1.40	- Electric railcars	...	87 446	87 776	677	...	...	...	616	654
1.50	- Diesel railcars	...	2 877	2 949	1 055	...	...	...	356	353
1.1	In passenger (and mixed) trains	...	326 827	337 412	11 144	8 672	8 511	2 687	1 695	1 691
1.11	- Electric locomotives	...	178 773	187 278	6 948	...	...	...	731	694
1.21	- Diesel locomotives	...	59 957	61 848	2 280	...	...	...	28	30
1.31	- Steam locomotives	...	-	-	-	-	-	...	2	2
1.41	- Electric railcars	...	85 288	85 407	810	...	...	...	598	638
1.51	- Diesel railcars	...	2 809	2 879	1 106	...	...	...	336	327
1.2	In goods (and mixed) trains	...	1 789 721	2 104 216	45 523	24 905	20 530	8 503	5 460	5 593
1.12	- Electric locomotives	...	1 352 148	1 631 627	33 671	...	...	...	4 644	4 779
1.22	- Diesel locomotives	...	437 573	472 589	11 852	...	...	...	778	814
1.32	- Steam locomotives	...	-	-	-	-	-	...	-	-
1.42	- Electric railcars	...	-	-	-	-	-	...	18	16
1.52	- Diesel railcars	...	-	-	-	-	-	...	20	26
1.3	In other trains	...	25 324	26 682	185	-	-	-	-	-

		Spain Espagne Испания			Sweden Suède Швеция			Switzerland Suisse Швейцария		
		1990	1998	1999	1990	1998	1999	1990	1998	1999
1	Total hauled vehicles movements	27 034	62 978	61 620	48 157	44 402	45 498	...	54 536	...
1.10	- Electric locomotives	...	35 118	33 629	43 755	35 375	35 918	...	...	...
1.20	- Diesel locomotives	...	7 729	7 881	1 928	1 286	1 444	...	...	...
1.30	- Steam locomotives	...	-	-	-	-	-	...	-	...
1.40	- Electric railcars	...	17 726	18 199	2 059	7 113	7 539	...	...	...
1.50	- Diesel railcars	...	2 406	1 911	415	628	597	...	-	...
1.1	In passenger (and mixed) trains	...	31 034	30 229	...	13 849	14 567	...	...	...
1.11	- Electric locomotives	...	8 914	7 981	...	6 314	6 630	...	...	...
1.21	- Diesel locomotives	...	2 082	2 234	...	-	1	...	...	...
1.31	- Steam locomotives	...	-	-	...	-	-	...	...	...
1.41	- Electric railcars	...	17 654	18 103	...	6 911	7 347	...	...	...
1.51	- Diesel railcars	...	2 384	1 911	...	624	589	...	...	...
1.2	In goods (and mixed) trains	...	31 139	30 728	...	30 130	29 851	...	...	...
1.12	- Electric locomotives	...	26 108	25 582	...	28 850	28 420	...	...	...
1.22	- Diesel locomotives	...	5 031	5 146	...	1 280	1 431	...	...	...
1.32	- Steam locomotives	...	-	-	...	-	-	...	...	...
1.42	- Electric railcars	...	-	-	...	-	-	...	...	...
1.52	- Diesel railcars	...	-	-	...	-	-	...	...	...
1.3	In other trains	...	805	663	...	423	1 080	...	...	...

RAILWAY TRANSPORT- TRANSPORT FERROVIAIRE
ЖЕЛЕЗНЫЕ ДОРОГИ

6. Hauled vehicles movements of trains
6. Mouvements de véhicules remorqués par les trains
6. Движение буксируемых траспортных средств

(million gross-tonne-km)

		Tajikistan Tadjikistan Таджикистан			The FYR of Macedonia [1]			Turkey Turquie Турция		
		1990	1998	1999	1990	1998	1999	1990	1998	1999
1	Total hauled vehicles movements	...	3 113	2 519	2 217	1 143	1 032	15 689	23 710	...
1.10	- Electric locomotives	...	-	-	...	777	642	...	3 663	...
1.20	- Diesel locomotives	...	3 113	2 519	...	272	275	...	18 173	...
1.30	- Steam locomotives	...	-		...	-	-	...	1	...
1.40	- Electric railcars	...	-	-	...	93	112	...	1 481	...
1.50	- Diesel railcars	...	-	-	...	1	3	...	392	...
1.1	In passenger (and mixed) trains	...	550	287	733	433	397	...	6 740	...
1.11	- Electric locomotives	...	-		...	140	69	...	1 867	...
1.21	- Diesel locomotives	...	550	287	...	199	213	...	3 000	...
1.31	- Steam locomotives	...	-		...	-	-	...	-	...
1.41	- Electric railcars	...	-		...	93	112	...	1 481	...
1.51	- Diesel railcars	...	-		...	1	3	...	392	...
1.2	In goods (and mixed) trains	...	2 552	2 224	1 483	710	635	15 689	16 819	...
1.12	- Electric locomotives	...	-		...	637	573	...	1 794	...
1.22	- Diesel locomotives	...	2 552	2 224	...	73	62	...	15 025	...
1.32	- Steam locomotives	...	-		...	-	-	...	-	...
1.42	- Electric railcars	...	-	-	...	-	-	...	-	...
1.52	- Diesel railcars	...	-	-	...	-	-	...	-	...
1.3	In other trains	...	11	8	-	-	-	...	151	...

		Turkmenistan Turkménistan Туркменистан			Ukraine Ukraine Украина			United States Etats-Unis [2] Соединенные Штаты		
		1990	1998	1999	1990	1998	1999	1990	1998	1999
1	Total hauled vehicles movements	...	17 740	...	868 000	360 332	350 930	...	3 830 397	3 989 352
1.10	- Electric locomotives	-	-	...	...	275 294	271 482	...	...	...
1.20	- Diesel locomotives	...	17 740	...	...	62 163	56 255	...	...	...
1.30	- Steam locomotives	...	-	...	...	3	2	...	...	...
1.40	- Electric railcars	-	-	...	...	19 343	19 852	...	...	...
1.50	- Diesel railcars	...	-	...	...	3 529	3 339	...	...	...
1.1	In passenger (and mixed) trains	...	3 145	...	...	90 106	...	...	...	...
1.11	- Electric locomotives	-	-	...	...	48 722	...	...	...	...
1.21	- Diesel locomotives	...	3 145	...	...	18 850	...	...	...	...
1.31	- Steam locomotives	...	-	...	...	2	...	...	...	...
1.41	- Electric railcars	-	-	...	...	19 025	...	...	...	...
1.51	- Diesel railcars	...	-	...	...	3 507	...	...	...	...
1.2	In goods (and mixed) trains	...	14 035	...	...	265 140	...	...	3 830 397	3 989 352
1.12	- Electric locomotives	-	-	...	...	224 400	...	...	...	...
1.22	- Diesel locomotives	...	14 035	...	...	40 739	...	...	...	...
1.32	- Steam locomotives	...	-	...	...	1	...	...	...	...
1.42	- Electric railcars	-	-	...	...	-	...	...	...	...
1.52	- Diesel railcars	...	-	...	...	-	...	...	...	...
1.3	In other trains	...	560	...	...	5 086	...	...	...	...

1- The former Yugoslav Republic of Macedonia

2- Class 1 railways.

1- L'ex-République yougoslave de Macédoine

2- Chemins de fer de 1ère classe.

1- Бывшая Югославская Республика Македония

2- Железные дороги первого класса.

RAILWAY TRANSPORT- TRANSPORT FERROVIAIRE
ЖЕЛЕЗНЫЕ ДОРОГИ

6. Hauled vehicles movements of trains
6. Mouvements de véhicules remorqués par les trains
6. Движение буксируемых траспортных средств

(million gross-tonne-km)

		Uzbekistan Ouzbékistan Узбекистан			Yugoslavia Yugoslavie Югославия					
		1990	1998	1999	1990	1998	1999			
1	**Total hauled vehicles movements**	...	**34 201**	...	**21 188**	**9 147**	**5 394**			
1.10	- Electric locomotives	...	10 642	...	...	6 214	3 433			
1.20	- Diesel locomotives	...	23 114	...	...	1 887	1 178			
1.30	- Steam locomotives	...	-	...	...	-	-			
1.40	- Electric railcars	...	445	...	...	951	702			
1.50	- Diesel railcars	...	-	...	...	95	81			
1.1	**In passenger (and mixed) trains**	...	**5 720**	...	**7 095**	**4 356**	**2 863**			
1.11	- Electric locomotives	...	726	...	...	2 644	1 736			
1.21	- Diesel locomotives	...	4 549	...	...	666	344			
1.31	- Steam locomotives	...	-	...	...	-	-			
1.41	- Electric railcars	...	445	...	...	951	702			
1.51	- Diesel railcars	...	-	...	...	95	81			
1.2	**In goods (and mixed) trains**	...	**28 481**	...	**14 093**	**4 791**	**2 531**			
1.12	- Electric locomotives	...	9 916	...	...	3 570	1 697			
1.22	- Diesel locomotives	...	18 565	...	...	1 221	834			
1.32	- Steam locomotives	...	-	...	...	-	-			
1.42	- Electric railcars	...	-	...	...	-	-			
1.52	- Diesel railcars	...	-	...	...	-	-			
1.3	**In other trains**	...	-	...	...	-	-			

RAILWAY TRANSPORT- TRANSPORT FERROVIAIRE
ЖЕЛЕЗНЫЕ ДОРОГИ

7. Passenger transport
7. Transport de voyageurs
7. Пассажирские перевозки

Item	Description
1	**Number of passengers** - (1000)
	by type of transport
1.10	- National rail transport
1.11	- International rail transport
2	**Number of passenger kilometres** - (million passenger-kilometre)
2.11	*by type of transport*
2.21	- National rail transport
2.22	- International rail transport

Rubrique	Description
1	**Nombre de voyageurs** - (1000)
	par type de transport
1.10	- Transport ferroviaire national
1.11	- Transport ferroviaire international
2	**Nombre de voyageurs-kilomètres** - (millions voyageur-kilomètre)
2.11	*par type de transport*
2.21	- Transport ferroviaire national
2.22	- Transport ferroviaire international

Статья	Описание
1	**Число пассажиров** - (1000)
	по типу транспорта
1.10	- Национальные железнодорожные перевозки
1.11	- Международные железнодорожные перевозки
2	**Количество пассажиро-километров** - (мил. Пассажиро-киломер)
2.11	*по типу транспорта*
2.21	- Национальные железнодорожные перевозки
2.22	- Международные железнодорожные перевозки

RAILWAY TRANSPORT- TRANSPORT FERROVIAIRE
ЖЕЛЕЗНЫЕ ДОРОГИ

7. Passenger transport
7. Transport de voyageurs
7. Пассажирские перевозки

		Albania Albanie Албания			Armenia Arménie Армения			Austria Autriche Австрия		
		1990	1998	1999	1990	1998	1999	1990	1998	1999
1	Number of passengers (1000)	11 908	2 269	2 270	20 000	1 612	1 323	168 385	179 465	181 715
1.10	- National transport	...	2 269	2 270	...	1 525	1 302	158 872	172 354	175 007
1.11	- International transport	...	...	...	...	87	21	9 513	7 111	6 708
2	Passenger - kilometres (million)	779	116	121	1 796	52	46	8 575	7 971	7 997
2.10	- National transport	...	116	121	...	44	41	6 652	6 912	6 958
2.11	- International transport	...	-	-	...	9	5	1 923	1 059	1 039

		Azerbaijan Azerbaïdjan Азербайджан			Belarus Bélarus Беларусь			Belgium Belgique Бельгия		
		1990	1998	1999	1990	1998	1999	1990	1998	1999
1	Number of passengers (1000)	15 504	4 287	...	147 207	151 022	...	142 372	145 857	147 291
1.10	- National transport	...	...	...	...	144 320	...	133 628	133 923	134 819
1.11	- International transport	...	...	...	...	6 702	...	8 744	11 934	12 472
2	Passenger - kilometres (million)	1 827	533	...	16 852	13 268	...	6 539	7 097	7 354
2.10	- National transport	...	...	...	...	11 184	...	5 592	5 830	6 033
2.11	- International transport	...	...	...	...	2 084	...	948	1 267	1 321

		Bosnia-Herzegovina Bosnie-Herzégovine Босния и Герцеговина			Bulgaria Bulgarie Болгария			Canada Canada Канада		
		1990	1998	1999	1990	1998	1999	1990	1998	1999
1	Number of passengers (1000)	...	176	183	102 399	64 260	53 112	...	3 980	...
1.10	- National transport	...	...	...	...	63 911	52 894	...	...	...
1.11	- International transport	...	...	...	...	349	218	...	...	...
2	Passenger - kilometres (million)	...	4	40	7 793	4 740	3 819	...	1 458	...
2.10	- National transport	...	...	...	...	4 674	3 767	...	...	...
2.11	- International transport	...	...	...	...	66	52	...	...	...

		Croatia Croatie Хорватия			Czech Republic République tchèque Чешская Республика			Denmark Danemark Дания		
		1990	1998	1999	1990	1998	1999	1990	1998	1999
1	Number of passengers (1000)	40 248	28 470	29 472	289 573	182 944	177 046	145 385	149 191	149 300
1.10	- National transport	38 965	27 783	28 813	...	180 013	174 424	143 660	147 974	...
1.11	- International transport	1 283	687	659	...	2 931	2 622	1 725	1 217	...
2	Passenger - kilometres (million)	3 429	1 092	1 137	13 313	7 018	6 957	4 851	5 369	5 113
2.10	- National transport	3 137	1 048	1 091	...	6 379	6 364	4 577	5 186	...
2.11	- International transport	292	44	46	...	639	593	274	183	...

RAILWAY TRANSPORT- TRANSPORT FERROVIAIRE
ЖЕЛЕЗНЫЕ ДОРОГИ

7. Passenger transport
7. Transport de voyageurs
7. Пассажирские перевозки

		Estonia Estonie Эстония			Finland Finlande Финляндия			France France Франция		
		1990	1998	1999	1990	1998	1999	1990	1998	1999
1	Number of passengers (1000)	23 100	6 716	...	45 998	51 370	53 209	842 546	812 177	850 154
1.10	- National transport	...	...	...	45 727	51 155	53 032	...	786 123	823 503
1.11	- International transport	...	...	...	271	215	177	...	26 054	26 651
2	Passenger - kilometres (million)	1 510	236	...	3 331	3 377	3 415	63 691	64 186	66 298
2.10	- National transport	...	188	...	3 254	3 314	3 364	...	55 733	57 447
2.11	- International transport	...	48	...	77	63	51	...	8 453	8 851

		Georgia Georgie Грузия			Germany Allemagne Германия			Greece Grèce Греция		
		1990	1998	1999	1990	1998	1999	1990	1998	1999
1	Number of passengers (1000)	...	2 318	...	...	1 332 000	1 678 382	12 067	11 677	...
1.10	- National transport	...	...	...	...	1 321 090	1 668 993	11 166	11 509	...
1.11	- International transport	...	...	...	...	10 910	9 389	901	168	...
2	Passenger - kilometres (million)	...	397	...	...	59 184	72 822	1 978	1 552	...
2.10	- National transport	...	...	...	...	55 819	69 444	1 692	1 524	...
2.11	- International transport	...	...	...	...	3 365	3 378	286	28	...

		Hungary Hongrie Венгрия			Ireland Irlande Ирландия			Israel Israël Израиль		
		1990	1998	1999	1990	1998	1999	1990	1998	1999
1	Number of passengers (1000)	210 581	156 973	156 847	25 010	32 146	32 765	2 524	6 382	8 785
1.10	- National transport	203 181	154 867	155 149	...	...	...	2 524	6 382	8 785
1.11	- International transport	7 400	2 106	1 698	...	...	...	-	-	-
2	Passenger - kilometres (million)	11 403	8 884	9 514	1 226	1 421	1 458	170	383	529
2.10	- National transport	...	8 453	9 219	...	...	...	170	383	529
2.11	- International transport	...	431	295	...	...	...	-	-	-

		Italy Italie Италия			Kazakhstan Kazakhstan Казахстан			Kyrgyzstan Kirghizistan Кыргызстан		
		1990	1998	1999	1990	1998	1999	1990	1998	1999
1	Number of passengers (1000)	429 400	425 881	431 502	...	21 600	...	1 439	635	445
1.10	- National transport	416 400	...	...	...	...	...	1 439	635	445
1.11	- International transport	13 000			...	...	...	-	-	-
2	Passenger - kilometres (million)	45 512	41 392	40 971	...	10 668	...	205	59	31
2.10	- National transport	40 512	36 940	37 005	...	...	...	205	59	31
2.11	- International transport	5 000	4 452	3 966	...	...	...	-	-	-

RAILWAY TRANSPORT- TRANSPORT FERROVIAIRE
ЖЕЛЕЗНЫЕ ДОРОГИ

7. Passenger transport
7. Transport de voyageurs
7. Пассажирские перевозки

		Latvia Lettonie Латвия			Lithuania Lituanie Литва			Luxembourg Luxembourg Люксембург		
		1990	1998	1999	1990	1998	1999	1990	1998	1999
1	Number of passengers (1000)	144 500	30 100	24 862	43 400	12 194	11 527	10 044	11 735	...
1.10	- National transport	...	29 190	24 122	...	10 536	10 044	8 895	...	...
1.11	- International transport	...	910	740	...	1 658	1 483	1 149	...	...
2	Passenger - kilometres (million)	5 366	1 059	984	3 640	800	745	208	300	...
2.10	- National transport	...	876	831	...	533	501	169	...	...
2.11	- International transport	...	183	153	...	267	244	39	...	...

		Netherlands Pays-Bas Нидерланды			Norway Norvège Норвегия			Poland Pologne Польша		
		1990	1998	1999	1990	1998	1999	1990	1998	1999
1	Number of passengers (1000)	255 656	321 000	...	34 485	46 972	50 019	789 922	324 467	324 719
1.10	- National transport	249 038	...	...	34 186	46 856	49 899	780 028	321 729	321 567
1.11	- International transport	6 618	...	...	299	116	120	9 894	2 738	3 152
2	Passenger - kilometres (million)	11 060	14 879	...	2 404	2 590	2 674	50 373	20 553	21 518
2.10	- National transport	10 432	...	...	2 011	2 540	2 624	46 839	19 920	20 834
2.11	- International transport	628	...	...	93	50	50	3 534	633	684

		Portugal Portugal Португалия			Republic of Moldova République de Moldova Республика Молдова			Romania Roumanie Румыния		
		1990	1998	1999	1990	1998	1999	1990	1998	1999
1	Number of passengers (1000)	225 882	177 965	167 525	20 000	9 412	5 410	407 931	146 800	129 339
1.10	- National transport	225 340	177 323	166 998	...	...	...	404 280	146 199	128 706
1.11	- International transport	542	642	537	...	...	...	3 651	601	633
2	Passenger - kilometres (million)	5 664	4 602	4 380	1 626	656	343	30 582	13 422	12 304
2.10	- National transport	5 560	4 521	4 141	...	...	...	29 418	12 763	12 141
2.11	- International transport	104	81	239	...	...	...	1 164	114	163

		Russian Federation Fédération de Russie Российская Федерация			Slovakia Slovaquie Словакия			Slovenia Slovénie Словения		
		1990	1998	1999	1990	1998	1999	1990	1998	1999
1	Number of passengers (1000)	3 143 000	1 471 306	1 337 509	119 262	70 008	69 431	21 096	13 907	13 766
1.10	- National transport	...	...	...	116 647	66 714	67 295	19 427	12 971	12 987
1.11	- International transport	...	764	526	2 615	3 294	2 136	1 669	936	769
2	Passenger - kilometres (million)	274 400	152 932	141 042	6 381	3 092	2 968	1 429	645	623
2.10	- National transport	...	...	...	5 347	2 844	2 795	1 166	520	523
2.11	- International transport	...	773	460	1 034	248	173	263	125	100

RAILWAY TRANSPORT- TRANSPORT FERROVIAIRE
ЖЕЛЕЗНЫЕ ДОРОГИ

7. Passenger transport
7. Transport de voyageurs
7. Пассажирские перевозки

		Spain Espagne Испания			Sweden Suède Швеция			Switzerland Suisse Швейцария		
		1990	1998	1999	1990	1998	1999	1990	1998	1999
1	Number of passengers (1000)	274 350	402 170	418 904	82 785	110 949	114 917	264 043	266 090	...
1.10	- National transport	...	401 231	417 954	81 489	...	...	255 848	261 303	...
1.11	- International transport	...	939	950	1 296	...	...	8 195	4 787	...
2	Passenger - kilometres (million)	15 476	17 478	18 143	6 225	6 997	7 434	11 061	12 485	...
2.10	- National transport	...	16 671	17 338	...	...	...	9 574	11 798	...
2.11	- International transport	...	807	805	...	...	...	1 487	687	...

		Tajikistan Tadjikistan Таджикистан			The FYR of Macedonia [1]			Turkey Turquie Турция		
		1990	1998	1999	1990	1998	1999	1990	1998	1999
1	Number of passengers (1000)	...	719	639	5 055	1 715	1 662	139 089	109 774	...
1.10	- National transport	...	513	530	...	1 697	1 654	138 974	109 556	...
1.11	- International transport	...	196	109	...	18	8	115	218	...
2	Passenger - kilometres (million)	...	121	61	355	150	150	6 410	6 160	...
2.10	- National transport	...	...	...	...	148	149	6 375	6 099	...
2.11	- International transport	...	...	...	...	2	1	35	61	...

		Turkmenistan Turkménistan Туркменистан			Ukraine Ukraine Украина			United Kingdom Royaume-Uni Соединенное Королевство		
		1990	1998	1999	1990	1998	1999	1990	1998	1999
1	Number of passengers (1000)	...	3 049	...	657 000	553 724	536 196	792 382	...	...
1.10	- National transport	...	2 112	...	...	...	...	762 382	896 837	951 575
1.11	- International transport	...	937	...	...	...	...	-	...	...
2	Passenger - kilometres (million)	...	571	...	76 038	49 938	47 600	33 191	...	...
2.10	- National transport	...	372	...	...	...	...	...	36 460	38 757
2.11	- International transport	...	199	...	...	...	...	...	...	...

		United States Etats-Unis [2] Соединенные Штаты			Uzbekistan Ouzbékistan Узбекистан			Yugoslavia Yugoslavie Югославия		
		1990	1998	1999	1990	1998	1999	1990	1998	1999
1	Number of passengers (1000)	...	21 247	21 500	...	17 390	...	...	14 045	9 902
1.10	- National transport	...	...	...	...	...	...	...	13 307	9 306
1.11	- International transport	...	...	...	...	...	...	...	738	596
2	Passenger - kilometres (million)	...	8 534	8 576	...	2 189	...	...	1 622	860
2.10	- National transport	...	...	...	...	...	...	...	1 460	790
2.11	- International transport	...	...	...	...	...	...	...	162	70

1- The former Yugoslav Republic of Macedonia
2- Including AMTRAK.

1- L'ex-République yougoslave de Macédoine
2- Y compris l'AMTRAK.

1- Бывшая Югославская Республика Македония
2- Включая данные по AMTRAK.

RAILWAY TRANSPORT- TRANSPORT FERROVIAIRE
ЖЕЛЕЗНЫЕ ДОРОГИ

8. Goods transport (excluding empty privately-owned wagons)

8. Transports de marchandises (non compris les wagons de particulier à vide)

8. Грузовые перевозки (кроме порожних вагонов, принадлежащих частным владельцам)

Item	Description
1	**Goods transported by rail - (1000 tonnes)**
1.1	- National transport
1.2	- International - loaded (goods having left the country by rail other than goods in transit)
1.3	- International - unloaded (goods having entered the country by rail other than goods in transit)
1.4	- Goods in transit by rail
2	**Tonne-kilometre of goods transported by rail - (million tonne-kilometres)**
2.1	- National transport
2.2	- International - loaded (goods having left the country by rail other than goods in transit)
2.3	- International - unloaded (goods having entered the country by rail other than goods in transit)
2.4	- Goods in transit by rail

Rubrique	Description
1	**Marchandises transportées par chemin de fer - (1000 tonnes)**
1.1	- Transport national
1.2	- Transport international - chargements (marchandises sorties du pays par rail autres que les marchandises en transit)
1.3	- Transport international - déchargements (marchandises entrées dans le pays par rail autres que les marchandises en transit)
1.4	- Marchandises en transit par rail
2	**Tonnes-kilomètres transportées par chemin de fer - (million tonnes-kilomètres)**
2.1	- Transport national
1.2	- Transport international - chargements (marchandises sorties du pays par rail autres que les marchandises en transit)
1.3	- Transport international - déchargements (marchandises entrées dans le pays par rail autres que les marchandises en transit)
2.4	- Marchandises en transit par rail

Статья	Описание
1	**Перевезенные грузы (1000 тонн)**
1.1	- Национальный транспорт
1.2	- Международный транспорт - погруженный (грузы, вывозимые из страны железнодорожным транспортом, в отличие от транзитных грузов)
1.3	- Международный транспорт - выгруженный (грузы, ввезенные в страну железнодорожным транспортом, в отличие от транзитных грузов)
1.4	- Сквозные транзитные грузы, перевозимые железнодорожным транспортом от начала до конца
2	**Перевезенные грузы (в млн. тонн-км)**
2.1	- Национальный транспорт
1.2	- Международный транспорт - погруженный (грузы, вывозимые из страны железнодорожным транспортом, в отличие от транзитных грузов)
1.3	- Международный транспорт - выгруженный (грузы, ввезенные в страну железнодорожным транспортом, в отличие от транзитных грузов)
2.4	- Сквозные транзитные грузы, перевозимые железнодорожным транспортом от начала до конца

RAILWAY TRANSPORT- TRANSPORT FERROVIAIRE
ЖЕЛЕЗНЫЕ ДОРОГИ

8. Goods transport (excluding empty privately-owned wagons)
8. Transports de marchandises (non compris les wagons de particulier à vide)
8. Грузовые перевозки (кроме порожних вагонов, принадлежащих частным владельцам)

		Albania Albanie Албания			Armenia Arménie Армения			Austria Autriche Австрия		
		1990	1998	1999	1990	1998	1999	1990	1998	1999
1	**Tonnes carried (1000 tonnes)**	**8 048**	**305**	**361**	**15 000**	**1 763**	**1 390**	**60 209**	**72 637**	**74 114**
1.1	- National	...	305	361	...	443	408	...	17 378	18 911
1.2	- International - loaded	...	-	-	...	274	177	...	16 013	15 719
1.3	- International - unloaded	...	-	-	...	1 046	805	...	25 182	25 506
1.4	- Transit	...	-	-	...	-	-	...	14 064	13 978
2	**Tonne - kilometres (millions)**	**584**	**25**	**27**	...	**419**	**323**	...	**14 715**	**15 039**
2.1	- National	...	25	27	...	150	95	...	3 100	3 520
2.2	- International - loaded	...	-	-	...	53	41	...	3 398	3 281
2.3	- International - unloaded	...	-	-	...	215	188	...	4 627	4 786
2.4	- Transit	...	-	-	...	-	-	...	3 590	3 452

		Azerbaijan Azerbaïdjan Азербайджан			Belarus Bélarus Беларусь			Belgium Belgique Бельгия		
		1990	1998	1999	1990	1998	1999	1990	1998	1999
1	**Tonnes carried (1000 tonnes)**	**32 688**	**10 597**	...	...	**87 903**	...	**67 126**	**60 694**	**59 149**
1.1	- National	...	...	...	...	35 492	...	30 227	24 488	23 696
1.2	- International - loaded	...	...	...	...	16 138	...	19 953	19 928	20 111
1.3	- International - unloaded	...	...	...	...	8 946	...	12 175	13 353	13 280
1.4	- Transit	...	...	...	...	27 327	...	4 771	2 925	2 062
2	**Tonne - kilometres (millions)**	**37 288**	**4 613**	...	**75 430**	**30 373**	...	**8 354**	**7 600**	**7 392**
2.1	- National	...	...	...	...	10 173	...	2 631	2 168	2 040
2.2	- International - loaded	...	...	...	...	5 813	...	4 971	2 985	3 032
2.3	- International - unloaded	...	...	...	...	2 660	...	(a)	1 933	1 946
2.4	- Transit	...	...	...	...	11 727	...	752	514	374

		Bosnia-Herzegovina Bosnie-Herzégovine Босния и Герцеговина			Bulgaria Bulgarie Болгария			Canada Canada Канада		
		1990	1998	1999	1990	1998	1999	1990	1998	1999
1	**Tonnes carried (1000 tonnes)**	...	**2 605**	...	**63 253**	**24 461**	**21 090**	...	**281 426**	...
1.1	- National	...	...	...	...	21 751	18 635	...	259 521	...
1.2	- International - loaded	...	...	...	...	1 522	1 089	...	65 243	...
1.3	- International - unloaded	...	...	...	...	733	738	...	17 176	...
1.4	- Transit	...	...	...	546	455	628	...	4 729	...
2	**Tonne - kilometres (millions)**	...	**73**	...	**14 132**	**6 152**	**5 297**	...	**299 508**	...
2.1	- National	...	...	...	...	5 306	4 484	...	...	...
2.2	- International - loaded	...	...	...	...	468	322	...	...	...
2.3	- International - unloaded	...	...	...	...	198	185	...	...	...
2.4	- Transit	...	...	...	...	180	306	...	...	...

(a) Including under previous item.   (a) Compris sous la rubrique précédente.   (a) Включено в переыдущий показатель.

RAILWAY TRANSPORT- TRANSPORT FERROVIAIRE
ЖЕЛЕЗНЫЕ ДОРОГИ

8. Goods transport (excluding empty privately-owned wagons)
8. Transports de marchandises (non compris les wagons de particulier à vide)
8. Грузовые перевозки (кроме порожних вагонов, принадлежащих частным владельцам)

		Croatia Croatie Хорватия			Czech Republic République tchèque Чешская Республика			Denmark Danemark Дания		
		1990	1998	1999	1990	1998	1999	1990	1998	1999
1	**Tonnes carried (1000 tonnes)**	**35 796**	**12 643**	**11 491**	**170 450**	**104 788**	**90 735**	**7 297**	**7 988**	**7 455**
1.1	- National	21 500	3 803	3 416	...	51 075	43 229	2 535	2 653	2 332
1.2	- International - loaded	4 100	1 581	1 495	...	25 415	24 661	1 173	...	...
1.3	- International - unloaded	4 000	1 810	1 577	...	22 053	17 627	1 869	...	...
1.4	- Transit	6 200	5 449	5 003	...	6 245	5 218	1 721	1 941	1 996
2	**Tonne - kilometres (millions)**	**6 535**	**2 001**	**1 849**	**41 150**	**18 709**	**16 713**	**1 570**	**2 058**	**1 938**
2.1	- National	3 944	685	613	...	8 195	7 117	570	609	...
2.2	- International - loaded	857	326	320	...	6 114	5 796	589	...	...
2.3	- International - unloaded	681	410	361	...	2 725	2 333	(a)	...	...
2.4	- Transit	1 053	580	555	...	1 675	1 467	411	657	676

		Estonia Estonie Эстония			Finland Finlande Финляндия			France France Франция		
		1990	1998	1999	1990	1998	1999	1990	1998	1999
1	**Tonnes carried (1000 tonnes)**	**30 200**	**31 940**	**...**	**34 562**	**40 740**	**39 979**	**134 276**	**136 653**	**136 835**
1.1	- National	...	...	...	14 465	23 613	23 212	...	90 549	90 168
1.2	- International - loaded	...	...	...	8 087	1 059	1 107	23 210	18 585	19 020
1.3	- International - unloaded	...	...	...	6 239	13 120	12 851	20 360	16 915	17 376
1.4	- Transit	...	...	...	5 771	2 948	2 809	...	10 604	10 271
2	**Tonne - kilometres (millions)**	**6 977**	**5 788**	**7 020**	**8 357**	**9 885**	**9 753**	**50 670**	**53 959**	**53 438**
2.1	- National	...	446	545	4 268	6 313	6 380	29 980	32 715	32 386
2.2	- International - loaded	...	...	...	...	333	331	8 810	7 783	7 890
2.3	- International - unloaded	...	...	...	...	2 661	2 557	6 170	6 229	6 266
2.4	- Transit	...	...	...	1 210	578	485	5 710	7 232	6 896

		Georgia Georgie Грузия			Germany Allemagne Германия			Greece Grèce Греция		
		1990	1998	1999	1990	1998	1999	1990	1998	1999
1	**Tonnes carried (1000 tonnes)**	**28 300**	**8 495**	**...**	**...**	**288 665**	**276 710**	**3 710**	**2 128**	**...**
1.1	- National	...	...	...	...	195 484	186 370	922	...	...
1.2	- International - loaded	...	...	...	...	39 585	37 407	1 866	...	...
1.3	- International - unloaded	...	...	...	...	44 087	43 973	814	...	...
1.4	- Transit	...	...	...	...	9 508	8 960	108	...	...
2	**Tonne - kilometres (millions)**	**...**	**2 574**	**...**	**...**	**73 273**	**70 948**	**647**	**310**	**...**
2.1	- National	...	...	...	...	36 116	35 066	223	...	...
2.2	- International - loaded	...	...	...	...	15 474	14 839	369	...	...
2.3	- International - unloaded	...	...	...	...	14 299	13 983	(a)	...	...
2.4	- Transit	...	...	...	...	7 384	7 060	55	...	...

(a) Including under previous item.   (a) Compris sous la rubrique précédente.   (a) Включено в переыдущий показатель.

RAILWAY TRANSPORT- TRANSPORT FERROVIAIRE
ЖЕЛЕЗНЫЕ ДОРОГИ

8. Goods transport (excluding empty privately-owned wagons)
8. Transports de marchandises (non compris les wagons de particulier à vide)
8. Грузовые перевозки (кроме порожних вагонов, принадлежащих частным владельцам)

		Hungary Hongrie Венгрия			Ireland Irlande Ирландия			Israel Israël Израиль		
		1990	1998	1999	1990	1998	1999	1990	1998	1999
1	Tonnes carried (1000 tonnes)	87 722	53 123	49 210	3 278	2 780	...	7 219	9 155	9 936
1.1	- National	47 397	19 980	18 314	3 278	2 780	2 780	7 219	9 155	9 936
1.2	- International - loaded	11 509	12 837	10 979	-	-	-	-	-	-
1.3	- International - unloaded	16 712	15 197	15 164	-	-	-	-	-	-
1.4	- Transit	12 104	5 109	4 753	-	-	-	-	-	-
2	Tonne - kilometres (millions)	16 781	8 148	7 728	589	466	...	1 048	1 049	1 128
2.1	- National	6 587	2 340	2 313	589	466	...	1 048	1 049	1 128
2.2	- International - loaded	2 697	1 920	1 600	-	-	...	-	-	-
2.3	- International - unloaded	3 729	2 547	2 501	-	-	...	-	-	-
2.4	- Transit	3 768	1 341	1 314	-	-	...	-	-	-

		Italy Italie Италия			Kazakhstan Kazakhstan Казахстан			Kyrgyzstan Kirghizistan Кыргызстан		
		1990	1998	1999	1990	1998	1999	1990	1998	1999
1	Tonnes carried (1000 tonnes)	59 180	75 825	73 955	345 000	170 106	...	8 000	1 445	1 079
1.1	- National	21 206	30 187	29 401	...	69 552	...	8 000	1 445	1 079
1.2	- International - loaded	10 481	14 007	13 691	...	62 888	...	-	-	-
1.3	- International - unloaded	27 492	31 594	30 825	...	20 519	...	-	-	-
1.4	- Transit	182	37	38	...	17 147	...	-	-	-
2	Tonne - kilometres (millions)	19 259	22 454	21 549	406 963	103 045	...	2 620	466	354
2.1	- National	9 089	11 344	10 997	...	...	...	2 620	466	354
2.2	- International - loaded	10 170	3 331	3 144	...	...	...	-	-	-
2.3	- International - unloaded	(a)	7 765	7 389	...	...	...	-	-	-
2.4	- Transit	114	14	19	...	...	...	-	-	-

		Latvia Lettonie Латвия			Lithuania Lituanie Литва			Luxembourg Luxembourg Люксембург		
		1990	1998	1999	1990	1998	1999	1990	1998	1999
1	Tonnes carried (1000 tonnes)	84 111	37 857	33 208	66 487	30 912	28 347	17 586	16 561	...
1.1	- National	8 000	2 432	1 938	...	5 977	4 595	2 626	...	...
1.2	- International - loaded	10 000	2 555	1 663	...	6 210	4 359	3 682	...	...
1.3	- International - unloaded	27 000	4 643	3 577	...	4 977	4 316	6 692	...	...
1.4	- Transit	39 000	28 227	26 030	...	13 748	15 077	4 386	6 713	...
2	Tonne - kilometres (millions)	18 538	12 995	12 210	...	8 265	7 849	709	625	...
2.1	- National	...	454	381	...	1 370	1 091	112	...	...
2.2	- International - loaded	...	493	369	...	1 248	762	425	...	...
2.3	- International - unloaded	...	1 122	938	...	933	779	(a)	...	...
2.4	- Transit	...	10 926	10 522	...	4 714	5 217	172	...	...

(a) Including under previous item.　　　　(a) Compris sous la rubrique précédente.　　　　(a) Включено в переыдущий показатель.

RAILWAY TRANSPORT- TRANSPORT FERROVIAIRE
ЖЕЛЕЗНЫЕ ДОРОГИ

8. Goods transport (excluding empty privately-owned wagons)
8. Transports de marchandises (non compris les wagons de particulier à vide)
8. Грузовые перевозки (кроме порожних вагонов, принадлежащих частным владельцам)

		Netherlands Pays-Bas Нидерланды			Norway Norvège Норвегия			Poland Pologne Польша		
		1990	1998	1999	1990	1998	1999	1990	1998	1999
1	Tonnes carried (1000 tonnes)	18 386	24 700	...	21 546	7 548	8 299	281 658	202 851	185 130
1.1	- National	4 974	...	...	20 232	5 802	6 427	232 633	151 203	143 499
1.2	- International - loaded	7 851	...	...	...	...	...	23 691	23 703	17 409
1.3	- International - unloaded	5 365	...	...	...	...	...	17 519	22 549	19 854
1.4	- Transit	197	...	...	...	...	...	7 815	5 396	4 368
2	Tonne - kilometres (millions)	3 068	3 778	...	...	2 421	2 456	83 530	60 937	55 076
2.1	- National	1 019	...	...	2 173	1 934	1 961	...	44 589	42 390
2.2	- International - loaded	1 149	...	...	...	...	...	...	6 697	4 684
2.3	- International - unloaded	887	...	...	...	...	...	...	6 500	5 364
2.4	- Transit	12	...	...	...	...	...	...	3 151	2 638

		Portugal Portugal Португалия			Republic of Moldova République de Moldova Республика Молдова			Romania Roumanie Румыния		
		1990	1998	1999	1990	1998	1999	1990	1998	1999
1	Tonnes carried (1000 tonnes)	5 940	8 966	9 265	65 400	11 090	6 612	218 828	76 512	62 941
1.1	- National	5 432	7 723	8 289	...	1 002	627	...	60 140	49 222
1.2	- International - loaded	236	290	259	...	1 910	1 904	...	6 836	7 048
1.3	- International - unloaded	272	953	717	...	2 613	1 976	...	8 919	5 691
1.4	- Transit	-	-	-	...	5 565	2 105	1 982	617	980
2	Tonne - kilometres (millions)	1 444	2 048	2 179	15 007	2 652	1 232	57 253	17 676	14 679
2.1	- National	1 286	1 638	1 861	...	179	83	...	13 477	10 214
2.2	- International - loaded	...	92	80	...	221	253	...	1 912	1 981
2.3	- International - unloaded	...	318	238	...	349	248	...	1 959	1 814
2.4	- Transit	-	-	-	...	1 903	648	...	328	670

		Russian Federation Fédération de Russie Российская Федерация			Slovakia Slovaquie Словакия			Slovenia Slovénie Словения		
		1990	1998	1999	1990	1998	1999	1990	1998	1999
1	Tonnes carried (1000 tonnes)	2 140 100	834 756	947 395	117 237	56 569	49 115	22 445	13 151	13 028
1.1	- National	...	...	...	...	14 930	12 377	8 594	1 358	1 543
1.2	- International - loaded	...	...	...	...	13 524	13 398	4 093	1 187	1 242
1.3	- International - unloaded	...	...	...	...	16 634	16 642	3 920	3 775	3 775
1.4	- Transit	...	...	...	...	11 481	6 698	5 838	6 810	6 444
2	Tonne - kilometres (millions)	2 523 000	1 019 547	1 204 547	23 176	11 753	9 859	4 209	2 632	2 571
2.1	- National	...	...	...	...	3 097	...	...	168	185
2.2	- International - loaded	...	...	...	...	...	...	...	175	166
2.3	- International - unloaded	...	...	...	...	...	...	...	526	526
2.4	- Transit	...	...	...	...	...	...	...	1 763	1 694

RAILWAY TRANSPORT- TRANSPORT FERROVIAIRE
ЖЕЛЕЗНЫЕ ДОРОГИ

8. Goods transport (excluding empty privately-owned wagons)
8. Transports de marchandises (non compris les wagons de particulier à vide)
8. Грузовые перевозки (кроме порожних вагонов, принадлежащих частным владельцам)

		Spain Espagne Испания			Sweden Suède Швеция			Switzerland Suisse Швейцария		
		1990	1998	1999	1990	1998	1999	1990	1998	1999
1	Tonnes carried (1000 tonnes)	25 717	25 653	25 330	52 991	27 792	27 811	51 810	49 720	...
1.1	- National	22 685	20 059	20 611	29 846	19 382	19 379	24 003	18 948	...
1.2	- International - loaded	1 278	2 887	2 300	18 930	5 190	5 264	4 295	4 135	...
1.3	- International - unloaded	1 754	2 422	2 363	4 068	2 843	2 779	8 755	7 919	...
1.4	- Transit	72	285	56	147	377	389	14 184	18 718	...
2	Tonne - kilometres (millions)	10 142	11 316	11 465	18 441	14 254	14 399	8 958	8 738	...
2.1	- National	8 748	9 114	9 492	10 275	9 223	9 270	2 781	...	...
2.2	- International - loaded	1 394	1 175	1 030	5 791	3 475	3 563	926	...	...
2.3	- International - unloaded	(a)	973	903	2 248	1 328	1 316	...	...	...
2.4	- Transit	(a)	54	40	127	229	250	4 110	...	...

		Tajikistan Tadjikistan Таджикистан			The FYR of Macedonia [1]			Turkey Turquie Турция		
		1990	1998	1999	1990	1998	1999	1990	1998	1999
1	Tonnes carried (1000 tonnes)	...	2 512	3 008	6 499	2 694	2 166	...	15 607	...
1.1	- National	...	...	...	...	159	177	...	14 160	...
1.2	- International - loaded	...	1 881	839	...	463	346	...	300	...
1.3	- International - unloaded	...	...	2 169	...	1 800	1 529	...	1 147	...
1.4	- Transit	...	...	...	...	272	114	...	-	...
2	Tonne - kilometres (millions)	...	1 458	1 282	769	408	380	...	8 376	...
2.1	- National	...	...	...	...	13	15	...	7 973	...
2.2	- International - loaded	...	...	...	...	58	65	...	135	...
2.3	- International - unloaded	...	...	...	...	272	272	...	252	...
2.4	- Transit	...	...	...	...	65	28	...	16	...

		Turkmenistan Turkménistan Туркменистан			Ukraine Ukraine Украина			United Kingdom Royaume-Uni Соединенное Королевство		
		1990	1998	1999	1990	1998	1999	1990	1998	1999
1	Tonnes carried (1000 tonnes)	28 100	15 981	...	974 300	335 052	...	139 163	102 136	102 809
1.1	- National	...	8 007	...	...	...	...	138 323	...	...
1.2	- International - loaded	...	829	...	...	...	...	327	...	...
1.3	- International - unloaded	...	1 059	...	...	...	...	513	...	...
1.4	- Transit	...	6 086	...	...	...	...	-	...	...
2	Tonne - kilometres (millions)	...	7 701	...	474 000	158 693	...	16 278	17 369	18 409
2.1	- National	...	4 339	...	...	...	...	16 078	...	...
2.2	- International - loaded	...	575	...	...	...	...	200	...	...
2.3	- International - unloaded	...	412	...	...	...	...	(a)	...	...
2.4	- Transit	...	2 375	...	...	...	...	-	...	...

(a) Including under previous item.   (a) Compris sous la rubrique précédente.   (a) Включено в переыдущий показатель.

1- The former Yugoslav Republic of Macedonia   1- L'ex-République yougoslave deMacédoine   1- Бывшая Югославская Республика Македония

RAILWAY TRANSPORT- TRANSPORT FERROVIAIRE
ЖЕЛЕЗНЫЕ ДОРОГИ

8. Goods transport (excluding empty privately-owned wagons)
8. Transports de marchandises (non compris les wagons de particulier à vide)
8. Грузовые перевозки (кроме порожних вагонов, принадлежащих частным владельцам)

		United States Etats-Unis [1] Соединенные Штаты			Uzbekistan Ouzbékistan Узбекистан			Yugoslavia Yugoslavie Югославия		
		1990	1998	1999	1990	1998	1999	1990	1998	1999
1	**Tonnes carried (1000 tonnes)**	...	...	...	82 900	54 480	...	...	12 213	6 083
1.1	- National	...	1 495 636	1 557 948	...	...	...	...	8 363	4 473
1.2	- International - loaded	1 293 100	...	...	...	...	...	...	666	279
1.3	- International - unloaded	32 900	...	...	...	...	...	...	1 889	866
1.4	- Transit	...	...	...	...	...	...	...	1 295	465
2	**Tonne - kilometres (millions)**	1 509 592	...	...	...	15 672	...	...	2 793	1 267
2.1	- National	...	2 010 946	2 092 957	...	...	...	...	1 555	778
2.2	- International - loaded	...	...	...	...	...	...	...	155	62
2.3	- International - unloaded	...	...	...	...	...	...	...	445	183
2.4	- Transit	...	...	...	...	...	...	...	638	244

(a) Including under previous item.

(a) Compris sous la rubrique précédente.

(a) Включено в переыдущий показатель.

1- Class 1 railways.

1- Chemins de fer de 1ère classe.

1- Железные дороги первого класса.

ROAD TRANSPORT

TRANSPORT ROUTIER

АВТОМОБИЛЬНЫЕ ДОРОГИ

ROAD TRANSPORT - TRANSPORT ROUTIER
АВТОМОБИЛЬНЫЕ ДОРОГИ

9. Road infrastructure at 31 December

9. Infrastructure routière au 31 décembre

9. Дорожная инфраструктура на 31 декабря

Item	Description
1	**Total length of roads in kilometres**
1.1	**Motorways**
1.2	**Other roads**
1.21	- State roads
1.22	- Provincial roads
1.23	- Local roads
2	**Length of international "E" network in kilometres**

Rubrique	Description
1	**Longueur totale des routes en kilomètres**
1.1	**Autoroutes**
1.2	**Autres routes**
1.21	- Routes d'état
1.22	- Routes provinciales
1.23	- Routes communales
2	**Longueur du réseau international "E" en kilomètres**

Статья	Описание
1	**Общая протяженность дорог в километрах**
1.1	**Автомагистрали**
1.2	**Другие дороги**
1.21	- Государственные дороги
1.22	- Областные дороги
1.23	- Дороги местного значения
2	**Дороги категории "E" в километрах**

ROAD TRANSPORT - TRANSPORT ROUTIER
АВТОМОБИЛЬНЫЕ ДОРОГИ

9. Road infrastructure at 31 December
9. Infrastructure routière au 31 décembre
9. Дорожная инфраструктура на 31 декабря

Unit : km - Unité : km - Единица - км

		Albania Albanie Албания			Armenia Arménie Армения			Austria Autriche Австрия		
		1990	1998	1999	1990	1998	1999	1990	1998	1999
1	**Total length of roads**	17 450	18 000	18 000	7 690	7 527	7 527	...	106 361	106 022
1.1	**Motorways**	-	-	-	-	-	-	1 445	1 613	1 634
1.2	**Other roads**	17 450	18 000	18 000	7 690	7 527	7 527	...	104 748	104 388
1.21	- State roads	7 450	3 220	3 220	3 320	3 361	3 361	10 433	10 276	10 260
1.22	- Provincial roads	10 000	4 300	4 300	4 370	4 167	4 167	23 474	23 472	23 075
1.23	- Local roads	(a)	10 480	10 480	(a)	(a)	(a)	...	71 000	71 053
2	**"E" roads**	...	679	679	...	151	151	2 320	2 250	2 250

		Azerbaijan Azerbaïdjan Азербайджан			Belarus Bélarus Беларусь			Belgium Belgique Бельгия		
		1990	1998	1999	1990	1998	1999	1990	1998	1999
1	**Total length of roads**	26 800	24 981	...	48 902	63 355	...	140 241	146 482	147 121
1.1	**Motorways**	-	-	...	-	-	...	1 666	1 691	1 702
1.2	**Other roads**	26 800	24 981	30 587	48 902	63 355	...	138 575	144 791	145 419
1.21	- State roads	...	...	8 418	...	15 462	...	13 115	12 542	12 550
1.22	- Provincial roads	...	...	17 930	...	47 893	...	1 360	1 349	1 349
1.23	- Local roads	...	...	4 239	...	(a)	...	124 100	130 900	131 520
2	**"E" roads**	...	...	...	...	...	...	1 419	1 818	1 818

		Bosnia-Herzegovina Bosnie-Herzégovine Босния и Герцеговина			Bulgaria Bulgarie Болгария			Canada Canada Канада		
		1990	1998	1999	1990	1998	1999	1990	1998	1999
1	**Total length of roads**	21 188	...	...	36 922	36 759	37 612	825 743	...	...
1.1	**Motorways**	-	-	...	273	319	324	14 985	...	...
1.2	**Other roads**	21 188	...	...	36 649	36 440	37 288	810 758	...	...
1.21	- State roads	...	...	...	2 933	3 080	36 964	132 246	...	...
1.22	- Provincial roads	...	...	...	3 798	10 060	...	134 297	...	...
1.23	- Local roads	...	...	...	29 918	23 300	...	544 215	...	...
2	**"E" roads**	...	...	...	...	...	...	-	-	...

(a) Included under item 1.22.   (a) Compris sous la rubrique 1.22.   (a) Включено в статью 1.22.

ROAD TRANSPORT - TRANSPORT ROUTIER
АВТОМОБИЛЬНЫЕ ДОРОГИ

9. Road infrastructure at 31 December
9. Infrastructure routière au 31 décembre
9. Дорожная инфраструктура на 31 декабря

Unit : km - Unité : km - Единица - км

		Croatia Croatie Хорватия			Cyprus Chypre Кипр			Czech Republic République tchèque Чешская Республика		
		1990	1998	1999	1990	1998	1999	1990	1998	1999
1	Total length of roads	32 796	27 840	28 009	9 043	11 024	11 585	...	127 694	127 732
1.1	Motorways	291	330	382	-	204	216	357	499	499
1.2	Other roads	32 505	27 510	27 627	9 043	10 820	11 369	...	127 195	127 233
1.21	- State roads	4 838	7 048	7 041	...	5 163	5 628	55 535	54 895	54 933
1.22	- Provincial roads	10 085	10 193	10 403	...	2 502	2 520	...	-	-
1.23	- Local roads	17 582	10 269	10 183	...	3 155	3 221	...	72 300*	...
2	"E" roads	2 090	2 154	2 100	...	-	-	...	2 655	2 655

		Denmark Danemark Дания			Estonia Estonie Эстония			Finland Finlande Финляндия		
		1990	1998	1999	1990	1998	1999	1990	1998	1999
1	Total length of roads	70 922	71 462	71 591	...	49 480	49 480	77 080	77 894	77 900
1.1	Motorways	653	873	892	41	75	75	225	473	512
1.2	Other roads	70 269	70 589	70 699	...	49 405	49 405	76 855	77 421	77 388
1.21	- State roads	3 908	758	749	14 781	3 823	3 823	11 266	...	...
1.22	- Provincial roads	7 102	9 949	9 955	...	12 532	12 532	30 072	...	...
1.23	- Local roads	59 259	59 882	59 995	...	33 050	33 050	35 517	...	...
2	"E" roads	...	935	927	...	...	...	...	3 657	3 662

		France France Франция			Georgia Georgie Грузия			Germany Allemagne Германия		
		1990	1998	1999	1990	1998	1999	1990	1998	1999
1	Total length of roads	808 098	980 367	984 348	21 600	20 215	...	...	649 088	649 158
1.1	Motorways	6 824	9 303	9 626	-	-	...	10 854	11 427	11 515
1.2	Other roads	801 274	971 064	974 722	21 600	20 215	...	...	637 661	637 643
1.21	- State roads	28 274	26 584	25 722	...	...	...	42 554	41 386	41 321
1.22	- Provincial roads	352 000	358 580	359 090	...	...	...	173 053	177 852	177 899
1.23	- Local roads	421 000	585 900	589 910	...	...	...	...	418 423	418 423
2	"E" roads	...	...	...	...	...	...	...	10 417	...

ROAD TRANSPORT - TRANSPORT ROUTIER
АВТОМОБИЛЬНЫЕ ДОРОГИ

9. Road infrastructure at 31 December
9. Infrastructure routière au 31 décembre
9. Дорожная инфраструктура на 31 декабря

Unit : km - Unité : km - Единица - км

		Greece Grèce Греция			Hungary Hongrie Венгрия			Iceland Islande Исландия		
		1990	1998	1999	1990	1998	1999	1990	1998	1999
1	Total length of roads	38 312	...	...	29 741	30 245	...	12 480	12 689	12 682
1.1	Motorways	-	...	...	267	448	448	-	-	-
1.2	Other roads	38 312	...	...	29 474	29 797	...	12 480	12 689	12 682
1.21	- State roads	9 100	...	...	6 469	6 537	...	8 256	4 306	4 305
1.22	- Provincial roads	29 212	...	...	23 005	23 260	...	3 124	3 907	3 898
1.23	- Local roads	-	...	...	(a)	(a)	...	1 100	4 476	4 479
2	"E" roads	...	...	...	...	2 001	2 058	-	-	-

		Ireland Irlande Ирландия			Israel Israël Израиль			Italy Italie Италия		
		1990	1998	1999	1990	1998	1999	1990	1998	1999
1	Total length of roads	92 289	95 835	...	13 199	15 965	16 115	821 185	...	...
1.1	Motorways	26	103	103	56	56	56	6 185	6 478	6 478
1.2	Other roads	92 263	95 732	...	13 143	15 909	16 059	815 000	...	...
1.21	- State roads	5 253	5 432	5 429	4 036	5 139	5 204	44 742	42 977	43 319
1.22	- Provincial roads	10 566	11 690	...	(a)	(a)	(a)	111 011	115 125	115 222
1.23	- Local roads	76 444	78 610	...	9 107	10 770	10 855	660 000	...	...
2	"E" roads	...	794	823	-	-	...	5 837	...	...

		Kazakhstan Kazakhstan Казахстан			Latvia Lettonie Латвия			Lithuania Lituanie Литва		
		1990	1998	1999	1990	1998	1999	1990	1998	1999
1	Total length of roads	86 428	119 390	113 686	59 541	57 818	57 961	53 291	72 459	73 650
1.1	Motorways	-	-	-	-	-	-	421	417	417
1.2	Other roads	86 428	119 390	113 686	59 541	57 818	57 961	52 870	72 042	73 233
1.21	- State roads	...	18 884	18 885	20 600	20 329	20 318	20 904	20 747	20 854
1.22	- Provincial roads	...	66 302	66 284	(b)	32 365	32 481	27 409	45 987	46 828
1.23	- Local roads	...	34 204	28 517	38 941	5 124	5 162	4 557	5 308	5 551
2	"E" roads	...	...	...	-	202	202	-	...	...

(a) Included under item 1.22.   (a) Compris sous la rubrique 1.22.   (a) Включено в статью 1.22.

(b) Included under item 1.23.   (b) Compris sous la rubrique 1.23.   (b) Включено в статью 1.23.

ROAD TRANSPORT - TRANSPORT ROUTIER
АВТОМОБИЛЬНЫЕ ДОРОГИ

9. Road infrastructure at 31 December

9. Infrastructure routière au 31 décembre

9. Дорожная инфраструктура на 31 декабря

Unit : km - Unité : km - Единица - км

		Luxembourg Luxembourg Люксембург			Malta Malte Мальта			Netherlands Pays-Bas Нидерланды		
		1990	1998	1999	1990	1998	1999	1990	1998	1999
1	Total length of roads	5 091	5 179	5 179	1 593	1 971	2 154	103 845	...	...
1.1	Motorways	78	115	115	-	-	-	2 092	...	...
1.2	Other roads	5 013	5 064	5 064	1 593	1 971	2 154	101 753	...	...
1.21	- State roads	869	837	837	...	157	264	1 956	...	...
1.22	- Provincial roads	1 828	1 911	1 911	...	1 167	1 890	7 082	...	...
1.23	- Local roads	2 316	2 316	2 316	...	647	...	92 715	...	...
2	"E" roads	...	...	...	-	-	-	...	...	...

		Norway Norvège Норвегия			Poland Pologne Польша			Portugal Portugal Португалия		
		1990	1998	1999	1990	1998	1999	1990	1998	1999
1	Total length of roads	89 332	91 311	91 469	363 116	381 046	371 729	61 538	...	...
1.1	Motorways	395	570	589	257	268	268	316	1 252	1 441
1.2	Other roads	88 937	90 741	90 880	362 859	380 778	371 461	61 222	...	...
1.21	- State roads	26 236	26 611	26 705	45 280	45 409	17 852	9 198	10 156	14 099
1.22	- Provincial roads	26 974	27 108	27 213	128 854	128 544	156 258	34 617	4 805	4 528
1.23	- Local roads	35 727	37 022	36 962	188 725	206 825	197 351	17 407	...	...
2	"E" roads	...	6 273	6 284	...	5 570	5 570	...	2 296	2 260

		Republic of Moldova République de Moldova Республика Молдова			Romania Roumanie Румыния			Russian Federation Fédération de Russie Российская Федерация		
		1990	1998	1999	1990	1998	1999	1990	1998	1999
1	Total length of roads	14 100	12 652	...	72 816	73 260	73 435	...	517 376	525 210
1.1	Motorways	-	-	...	113	113	113	...	29 204	29 300
1.2	Other roads	14 100	12 652	12 657	72 703	73 147	73 322	...	488 172	495 910
1.21	- State roads	5 000	2 814	2 813	14 570	14 570	14 572	...	16 622	16 622
1.22	- Provincial roads	5 300	6 588	6 588	26 967	27 713	28 128	...	471 550	479 288
1.23	- Local roads	3 800	3 250	3 256	31 166	30 864	30 622	...	...	...
2	"E" roads	...	94	94	...	4 672	4 670	...	16 690	16 690

ROAD TRANSPORT - TRANSPORT ROUTIER
АВТОМОБИЛЬНЫЕ ДОРОГИ

9. Road infrastructure at 31 December

9. Infrastructure routière au 31 décembre

9. Дорожная инфраструктура на 31 декабря

Unit : km - Unité : km - Единица - км

		Slovakia Slovaquie Словакия			Slovenia Slovénie Словения			Spain Espagne Испания		
		1990	1998	1999	1990	1998	1999	1990	1998	1999
1	Total length of roads	17 937	17 711	17 734	39 552	37 364	38 260	161 369	163 273	163 769
1.1	Motorways	192	288	295	228	369	399	5 126	8 269	8 893
1.2	Other roads	17 745	17 423	17 439	39 324	36 995	37 861	156 243	155 004	154 876
1.21	- State roads	3 061	3 223	3 220	4 752	5 797	5 855	20 701	17 132	17 195
1.22	- Provincial roads	3 856	3 773	3 826	9 572	13 533	13 874	71 063	69 373	69 521
1.23	- Local roads	10 828	10 427	10 393	25 000	17 665	18 132	64 479	68 499	68 160
2	"E" roads	...	1 583	1 570	631	610	619	...	...	...

		Sweden Suède Швеция			Switzerland Suisse Швейцария			Tajikistan Tadjikistan Таджикистан		
		1990	1998	1999	1990	1998	1999	1990	1998	1999
1	Total length of roads	133 558	138 032	139 056	70 970	71 211	...	12 897	13 615	13 612
1.1	Motorways	939	1 439	1 484	1 495	1 638	...	-	-	-
1.2	Other roads	132 619	136 593	137 572	69 475	69 573	-	12 897	13 615	13 612
1.21	- State roads	13 166	14 651	14 692	18 278	18 176	...	3 671	4 732	4 732
1.22	- Provincial roads	83 753	83 442	83 357	51 197	51 397	...	9 226	8 883	8 880
1.23	- Local roads	35 700	38 500	39 523	(a)	(a)	...	(a)	(a)	(a)
2	"E" roads	4 410	4 873	4 901	1 390	...	...	...	...	...

		The FYR of Macedonia [1]			Turkey Turquie Турция			Turkmenistan Turkménistan Туркменистан		
		1990	1998	1999	1990	1998	1999	1990	1998	1999
1	Total length of roads	10 591	11 513	12 165	59 409	379 059	...	...	13 597	...
1.1	Motorways	83	144	144	281	1 726	...	...	-	...
1.2	Other roads	10 508	11 369	12 021	59 128	377 333	...	...	13 597	...
1.21	- State roads	862	765	765	31 149	31 345	...	...	6 463	...
1.22	- Provincial roads	2 822	3 461	3 461	27 979	26 540	...	...	7 134	...
1.23	- Local roads	6 824	7 143	7 795	...	319 448	...	...	(a)	...
2	"E" roads	565	584	584	5 460	...	...	...	...	...

(a) Included under item 1.22.

(a) Compris sous la rubrique 1.22.

(a) Включено в статью 1.22.

1. The former Yugoslav Republic of Macedonia.

1. L'ex-République yougoslave de Macédoine.

1. Бывшая Югославская Республика Македония.

ROAD TRANSPORT - TRANSPORT ROUTIER
АВТОМОБИЛЬНЫЕ ДОРОГИ

9. Road infrastructure at 31 December

9. Infrastructure routière au 31 décembre

9. Дорожная инфраструктура на 31 декабря

Unit : km - Unité : km - Единица - км

		Ukraine Ukraine Украина			United Kingdom Royaume-Uni Соединенное Королевство			United States Etats-Unis Соединенные Штаты		
		1990	1998	1999	1990	1998	1999	1990	1998	1999
1	Total length of roads	167 804	176 310	176 310	382 115	396 081	...	6 244 498	6 285 242	6 302 846
1.1	Motorways	1 647	1 770	1 770	3 181	3 421	3 358	61 654	88 892	89 206
1.2	Other roads	166 157	174 540	174 540	378 934	392 660	...	6 182 844	6 196 350	6 213 640
1.21	- State roads	29 231	19 077	19 077	12 674	12 230	...	...	...	...
1.22	- Provincial roads	22 585	155 463	155 604	35 149	38 272	...	...	...	...
1.23	- Local roads	114 341	(a)	(a)	331 111	342 158	...	...	...	...
2	"E" roads	...	7 764	7 773	...	3 753	...	-	-	-

		Uzbekistan Ouzbékistan Узбекистан			Yugoslavia Yugoslavie Югославия					
		1990	1998	1999	1990	1998	1999			
1	Total length of roads	42 700	43 463	...	46 019	50 497	44 870			
1.1	Motorways	...	-	...	374	374	374			
1.2	Other roads	...	43 463	...	45 645	50 123	44 496			
1.21	- State roads	...	3 237	...	...	5 848	5 241			
1.22	- Provincial roads	...	18 767	...	...	12 650	11 351			
1.23	- Local roads	...	21 459	...	...	31 625	27 904			
2	"E" roads	...	...	...	...	2 602	2 602			

(a) Included under item 1.22.   (a) Compris sous la rubrique 1.22.   (a) Включено в статью 1.22.

ROAD TRANSPORT - TRANSPORT ROUTIER
АВТОМОБИЛЬНЫЕ ДОРОГИ

10. Road vehicle fleet in the country at 31 December - By vehicle category
10. Parc automobile du pays au 31 décembre - Par catégories de véhicules
10. Парк автодорожных транспортных средств страны по состоянию на 31 декабря
- по категории транспортного средства

Item	Description	Rubrique	Description
1	**Passenger vehicles (number)**	1	**Véhicules routiers pour le transport des voyageurs (nombre)**
1.1	Mopeds	1.1	Cyclomoteurs
1.2	Motorcycles	1.2	Motocycles
1.3	Passenger cars	1.3	Voitures particulières
1.4	Motor coaches, buses and trolley buses	1.4	Autocars, autobus et trolleybus
1.5	Trams	1.5	Tramways
2	**Goods road vehicles (number)**	2	**Véhicules routiers pour le transport des marchandises (nombre)**
2.1	Lorries	2.1	Camions
2.2	Road tractors	2.2	Tracteurs routiers
2.3	Semi-trailers	2.3	Semi-remorques
2.4	Trailers	2.4	Remorques
3	**Load capacity of goods road vehicles (1000 tonnes)**	3	**Charge utile des véhicules routiers pour le transport des marchandises (1000 tonnes)**
3.1	Lorries	3.1	Camions
3.2	Semi-trailers	3.2	Semi-remorques
3.3	Trailers	3.3	Remorques

Статья	Описание
1	**Пассажирские автодорожные транспортные средства (число)**
1.1	Мопеды
1.2	Мотоциклы
1.3	Пассажирские автомобили
1.4	Автобусы дальнего следования, городские автобусы и троллейбусы
1.5	Трамваи
2	**Грузовые автодорожные транспортные средства (число)**
2.1	Грузовые автомобили
2.2	Дорожные тягачи
2.3	Полуприцепы
2.4	Прицепы
3	**Грузовые автодорожные транспортные средства грузоподъемностью (1000 тонн)**
3.1	Грузовые автомобили
3.2	Полуприцепы
3.3	Прицепы

ROAD TRANSPORT - TRANSPORT ROUTIER
АВТОМОБИЛЬНЫЕ ДОРОГИ

10. Road vehicle fleet in the country at 31 December - By vehicle category
10. Parc automobile du pays au 31 décembre - Par catégories de véhicules
10. Парк автодорожных транспортных средств страны по состоянию на 31 декабря
- по категории транспортного средства

		Albania Albanie Албания			Armenia Arménie Армения			Austria Autriche Австрия		
		1990	1998	1999	1990	1998	1999	1990	1998	1999
1	**Passenger vehicles (Number)**									
1.1	Mopeds	...	...	...	...	...	...	430 022	363 000	360 000
1.2	Motorcycles	...	4 109	4 061	...	...	...	105 177	238 000	263 000
1.3	Passenger cars	...	90 766	99 220	...	...	...	2 991 284	3 887 174	4 010 000
1.4	Motor coaches, buses, etc.	...	9 227	10 316	...	...	...	9 402	9 675	9 834
1.5	Trams	...	-	-	...	87	77	...	...	...
2	**Goods road vehicles (Number)**									
2.1	Lorries	...	34 378	37 880	...	...	...	252 504	309 630	318 757
2.2	Road tractors	...	2 731	3 018	...	...	...	...	15 705	17 015
2.3	Semi-trailers	...	...	...	...	1 102	1 539	(a)	20 317	22 206
2.4	Trailers	...	3 990	4 245	...	1 638	1 323	296 240	445 959	517 788
3	**Load capacity of goods road vehicles (1000 t)**									
3.1	Lorries	...	...	...	...	...	...	563.8	...	...
3.2	Semi-trailers	...	...	...	...	11.4	14.1	(b)	...	...
3.3	Trailers	...	...	...	...	8.8	6.0	807.9	...	...

		Azerbaijan Azerbaïdjan Азербайджан			Belarus Bélarus Беларусь			Belgium Belgique Бельгия		
		1990	1998	1999	1990	1998	1999	1990	1998	1999
1	**Passenger vehicles (Number)**									
1.1	Mopeds	...	...	...	...	...	...	...	...	...
1.2	Motorcycles	...	9 271	9 269	...	566 080	...	139 174	241 110	260 567
1.3	Passenger cars	260 200	281 320	311 600	604 500	1 279 208	...	3 864 159	4 491 734	4 583 615
1.4	Motor coaches, buses, etc.	...	...	...	...	...	...	15 644	18 175	18 562
1.5	Trams	...	...	...	...	357	...	...	...	...
2	**Goods road vehicles (Number)**									
2.1	Lorries	99 507	77 800	69 700	34 353	61 334	...	343 241	484 179	514 226
2.2	Road tractors	...	...	...	24 447	...	...	37 138	46 410	48 666
2.3	Semi-trailers	...	...	...	...	...	...	...	64 317	68 080
2.4	Trailers	...	...	...	...	...	...	...	91 107	94 926
3	**Load capacity of goods road vehicles (1000 t)**									
3.1	Lorries	...	...	...	...	...	...	806.3	924.5	942.5
3.2	Semi-trailers	...	...	...	...	...	...	...	1 673.7	1 748.9
3.3	Trailers	...	...	...	...	...	...	...	253.5	257.4

ROAD TRANSPORT - TRANSPORT ROUTIER
АВТОМОБИЛЬНЫЕ ДОРОГИ

10. Road vehicle fleet in the country at 31 December - By vehicle category
10. Parc automobile du pays au 31 décembre - Par catégories de véhicules
10. Парк автодорожных транспортных средств страны по состоянию на 31 декабря
- по категории транспортного средства

		Bulgaria Bulgarie Болгария			Canada Canada Канада			Croatia Croatie Хорватия		
		1990	1998	1999	1990	1998	1999	1990	1998	1999
1	Passenger vehicles (Number)									
1.1	Mopeds	281 270	281 749	284	28 000	19 822	...	...	31 581	38 000
1.2	Motorcycles	225 533	233 952	235	331 000	313 680	...	17 520	18 957	20 000
1.3	Passenger cars	1 317 437	1 809 350	1 908	12 622 000	13 887 270	...	795 410	1 000 052	1 059 000
1.4	Motor coaches, buses, etc.	34 599	42 264	5 104	...	68 307	...	5 836	4 814	4 715
1.5	Trams	444	366	355	...	...	...	...	449	446
2	Goods road vehicles (Number)									
2.1	Lorries	...	220 948	2 016	3 867 000	3 625 818	...	56 823	110 360	112 675
2.2	Road tractors	...	21 320	1 017	(c)	(c)	...	...	5 408	5 492
2.3	Semi-trailers	...	...	1 126	...	3 873 766	...	...	7 939	8 210
2.4	Trailers	...	...	925	...	(d)	...	...	13 921	14 682
3	Load capacity of goods road vehicles (1000 t)									
3.1	Lorries	...	...	20.0	...	...	...	...	339.0	339.0
3.2	Semi-trailers	...	...	23.0	...	...	...	...	147.0	151.0
3.3	Trailers	...	...	8.0	...	...	...	...	114.0	116.0

		Cyprus Chypre Кипр			Czech Republic République tchèque Чешская Республика			Denmark Danemark Дания		
		1990	1998	1999	1990	1998	1999	1990	1998	1999
1	Passenger vehicles (Number)									
1.1	Mopeds	36 466	32 419	32 097	...	519 818	454 055	119 928	48 107	57 707
1.2	Motorcycles	14 487	11 918	12 659	...	407 256	345 590	44 111	64 013	69 231
1.3	Passenger cars	178 602	249 225	256 989	3 043 316	3 492 961	3 439 745	1 590 345	1 817 147	1 843 254
1.4	Motor coaches, buses, etc.	2 308	2 754	2 835	20 474	20 668	19 702	8 109	13 911	13 909
1.5	Trams	-	-	-	...	1 982	1 899	...	...	...
2	Goods road vehicles (Number)									
2.1	Lorries	74 018	108 091	110 114	202 929	260 276	268 259	286 613	347 136	362 002
2.2	Road tractors	...	1 203	1 011	...	20 035	21 151	6 628	10 497	11 256
2.3	Semi-trailers	...	1 595	1 802	...	20 283	21 483	14 798	23 211	23 594
2.4	Trailers	...	190	247	...	83 645	93 207	302 923	473 357	502 616
3	Load capacity of goods road vehicles (1000 t)									
3.1	Lorries	...	...	...	...	831.4	801.8	527.0	629.0	646.0
3.2	Semi-trailers	...	...	...	...	491.7	529.6	380.0	652.0	668.0
3.3	Trailers	...	...	...	...	373.4	366.4	238.0	348.0	366.0

ROAD TRANSPORT - TRANSPORT ROUTIER
АВТОМОБИЛЬНЫЕ ДОРОГИ

10. Road vehicle fleet in the country at 31 December - By vehicle category
10. Parc automobile du pays au 31 décembre - Par catégories de véhicules
10. Парк автодорожных транспортных средств страны по состоянию на 31 декабря
- по категории транспортного средства

		Estonia Estonie Эстония			Finland Finlande [1) Финляндия			France France Франция		
		1990	1998	1999	1990	1998	1999	1990	1998	1999
1	**Passenger vehicles (Number)**									
1.1	Mopeds	...	...	...	109 000	99 820	103 000	2 300 000	1 482 000	1 461 000
1.2	Motorcycles	105 700	6 100	6 700	59 716	72 704	80 178	813 000	839 000	912 000
1.3	Passenger cars	241 664	450 954	458 700	1 938 856	2 021 116	2 082 580	23 550 000	26 809 000	27 480 000
1.4	Motor coaches, buses, etc.	7 900	6 448	6 338	9 327	9 040	9 487	73 700	84 961	85 668
1.5	Trams	132	130	...	112	104	104	...	...	...
2	**Goods road vehicles (Number)**									
2.1	Lorries	67 700	80 617	81 030	261 495	280 610	293 707	3 567 767	4 984 586	5 074 835
2.2	Road tractors	...	...	...	(c)	5 253	5 209	166 809	184 359	190 916
2.3	Semi-trailers	7 976	35 785	36 950	6 291	12 474	12 656	138 024	260 602	269 224
2.4	Trailers	8 542	...	...	338 724	464 806	486 949	26 960	50 268	51 108
3	**Load capacity of goods road vehicles (1000 t)**									
3.1	Lorries	...	...	...	717.0	747.0	772.0	4 415.0	6 568.0	6 628.0
3.2	Semi-trailers	93.0	...	...	95.0	224.0	226.0	3 325.0	6 654.0	6 902.0
3.3	Trailers	45.0	...	...	515.0	639.0	668.0	351.0	626.0	680.0

		Georgia Georgie Грузия			Germany Allemagne Германия			Greece Grèce Греция		
		1990	1998	1999	1990	1998	1999	1990	1998	1999
1	**Passenger vehicles (Number)**									
1.1	Mopeds	...	...	...	...	1 747 000	1 743 000	...	1 505 424	...
1.2	Motorcycles	...	7 637	...	...	2 925 843	3 177 000	256 594	633 765	...
1.3	Passenger cars	...	260 437	...	...	41 673 787	42 324 000	1 735 523	2 675 676	...
1.4	Motor coaches, buses, etc.	13 982	...	...	...	83 285	84 687	21 430	26 320	...
1.5	Trams	...	...	...	...	5 335	5 159	...	...	...
2	**Goods road vehicles (Number)**									
2.1	Lorries	84 863	56 169	...	...	2 370 599	2 465 535	743 176	978 688	...
2.2	Road tractors	...	...	...	...	140 516	153 527	409	8 669	...
2.3	Semi-trailers	...	...	...	...	179 766	193 580	4 573	...	...
2.4	Trailers	...	...	...	...	3 191 543	3 308 892	4 846	...	...
3	**Load capacity of goods road vehicles (1000 t)**									
3.1	Lorries	...	...	...	...	6 068.0	6 215.0	...	...	...
3.2	Semi-trailers	...	...	...	...	4 435.0	4 834.0	...	...	...
3.3	Trailers	...	...	...	...	5 013.0	5 193.0	...	...	...

For notes see end of table.   Voir notes à la fin du tableau.   См. примечания в конце таблицы.

ROAD TRANSPORT - TRANSPORT ROUTIER
АВТОМОБИЛЬНЫЕ ДОРОГИ

10. Road vehicle fleet in the country at 31 December - By vehicle category
10. Parc automobile du pays au 31 décembre - Par catégories de véhicules
10. Парк автодорожных транспортных средств страны по состоянию на 31 декабря
- по категории транспортного средства

		Hungary Hongrie Венгрия			Iceland Islande Исландия			Ireland Irlande Ирландия		
		1990	1998	1999	1990	1998	1999	1990	1998	1999
1	**Passenger vehicles (Number)**									
1.1	Mopeds	...	...	...	422	527	...	10 000	...	...
1.2	Motorcycles	168 817	97 073	87 573	1 113	1 379	...	22 744	24 398	26 700
1.3	Passenger cars	1 944 553	2 218 124	2 256 000	119 731	140 372	151 000	797 713	1 196 900	1 269 200
1.4	Motor coaches, buses, etc.	26 438	18 795	17 988	1 328	1 544	1 621	4 047	6 104	6 564
1.5	Trams	1 122	900	969	-	-	-	-	-	-
2	**Goods road vehicles (Number)**									
2.1	Lorries	208 302	295 048	308 944	13 122	15 905	17 115	143 166	170 866	188 814
2.2	Road tractors	38 397	24 591	23 559	...	645	692	...	...	...
2.3	Semi-trailers	...	9 206	10 868	775	1 119	1 213	70 744	...	...
2.4	Trailers	...	80 565	83 983	1 113	3 756	3 930	...	...	...
3	**Load capacity of goods road vehicles (1000 t)**									
3.1	Lorries	...	679.0	683.0	...	50.6	53.0	...	...	...
3.2	Semi-trailers	...	186.0	230.0	...	28.9	30.0	...	...	...
3.3	Trailers	...	345.0	401.0	...	10.5	11.0	...	...	...

		Israel Israël [2] Израиль			Italy Italie Италия			Kazakhstan Kazakhstan Казахстан		
		1990	1998	1999	1990	1998	1999	1990	1998	1999
1	**Passenger vehicles (Number)**									
1.1	Mopeds	15 899	35 238	35 130	3 028 834	4 000 000	...	...	532	1 470
1.2	Motorcycles	22 177	39 773	40 513	2 974 671	2 759 000	2 975 651	...	194 831	154 380
1.3	Passenger cars	811 720	1 297 965	1 341 339	27 415 828	31 573 000	32 038 291	809 700	971 170	987 724
1.4	Motor coaches, buses, etc.	8 886	14 986	16 805	77 731	85 799	85 762	55 011	29 547	26 146
1.5	Trams	-	-	-	...	...	-	...	248	247
2	**Goods road vehicles (Number)**									
2.1	Lorries	154 211	282 904	292 107	2 348 992	3 171 494	3 221 335	...	128 133	106 331
2.2	Road tractors	2 511	3 913	3 863	67 780	102 526	106 726	...	6 907	5 862
2.3	Semi-trailers	5 248	6 869	6 921	670 116	142 943	149 176	...	9 352	7 755
2.4	Trailers	5 638	23 928	25 564	...	671 993	650 394	...	20 743	16 131
3	**Load capacity of goods road vehicles (1000 t)**									
3.1	Lorries	...	...	...	...	...	...	...	743.0	646.6
3.2	Semi-trailers	...	...	...	...	...	...	...	120.7	101.8
3.3	Trailers	...	...	...	...	...	...	...	158.9	122.9

For notes see end of table.   Voir notes à la fin du tableau.   См. примечания в конце таблицы.

ROAD TRANSPORT - TRANSPORT ROUTIER
АВТОМОБИЛЬНЫЕ ДОРОГИ

10. Road vehicle fleet in the country at 31 December - By vehicle category
10. Parc automobile du pays au 31 décembre - Par catégories de véhicules
10. Парк автодорожных транспортных средств страны по состоянию на 31 декабря
- по категории транспортного средства

		Kyrgyzstan Kirghizistan Кыргызстан			Latvia Lettonie Латвия			Lithuania Lituanie Литва		
		1990	1998	1999	1990	1998	1999	1990	1998	1999
1	Passenger vehicles (Number)									
1.1	Mopeds	...	...	...	...	...	...	...	...	...
1.2	Motorcycles	...	22 539	19 555	...	19 409	20 057	192 123	19 266	20 000
1.3	Passenger cars	194 592	187 734	187 322	331 837	482 670	525 572	492 978	980 910	1 089 000
1.4	Motor coaches, buses, etc.	...	...	...	12 138	11 829	11 870	15 707	15 679	16 090
1.5	Trams	-	-	-	...	339	336	-	-	-
2	Goods road vehicles (Number)									
2.1	Lorries	...	...	...	53 692	74 954	80 112	83 035	89 866	86 824
2.2	Road tractors	...	...	...	6 273	9 988	10 108	7 752	9 588	9 752
2.3	Semi-trailers	5 987	3 732	3 643	8 656	3 232	4 433	11 474	9 252	9 256
2.4	Trailers	7 387	13 100	13 533	10 571	48 336	49 612	11 836	6 255	6 365
3	Load capacity of goods road vehicles (1000 t)									
3.1	Lorries	...	...	...	236.0	222.0	242.0	...	368.0	368.0
3.2	Semi-trailers	...	39.5	34.9	102.0	...	...	...	159.0	168.0
3.3	Trailers	...	65.0	69.9	62.0	...	...	...	47.0	47.0

		Luxembourg Luxembourg Люксембург			Malta Malte [3) Мальта			Netherlands Pays-Bas Нидерланды		
		1990	1998	1999	1990	1998	1999	1990	1998	1999
1	Passenger vehicles (Number)									
1.1	Mopeds	...	...	...	...	(e)	(e)	458 000	529 000	...
1.2	Motorcycles	3 930	9 946	10 810	7 685	14 847	11 870	159 000	392 459	...
1.3	Passenger cars	191 588	253 406	263 475	109 131	191 440	182 642	5 205 000	6 119 581	...
1.4	Motor coaches, buses, etc.	760	945	984	978	1 117	729	11 628	11 006	...
1.5	Trams	...	...	...	-	-	-	...	...	...
2	Goods road vehicles (Number)									
2.1	Lorries	12 078	18 025	19 226	21 870	48 403	42 687	491 000	710 169	...
2.2	Road tractors	6 697	9 870	3 327	(c)	(c)	17	35 208	52 647	...
2.3	Semi-trailers	...	...	...	...	403	407	...	...	...
2.4	Trailers	...	...	...	...	...	...	...	...	...
3	Load capacity of goods road vehicles (1000 t)									
3.1	Lorries	...	...	...	...	...	...	...	...	...
3.2	Semi-trailers	...	...	...	...	...	...	...	...	...
3.3	Trailers	...	...	...	...	...	...	...	...	...

For note see end of table.　　　　Voir note à la fin du tableau.　　　　См. примечания в конце таблицы.

98

ROAD TRANSPORT - TRANSPORT ROUTIER
АВТОМОБИЛЬНЫЕ ДОРОГИ

10. Road vehicle fleet in the country at 31 December - By vehicle category
10. Parc automobile du pays au 31 décembre - Par catégories de véhicules
10. Парк автодорожных транспортных средств страны по состоянию на 31 декабря
- по категории транспортного средства

		Norway Norvège Норвегия			Poland Pologne Польша			Portugal Portugal Португалия		
		1990	1998	1999	1990	1998	1999	1990	1998	1999
1	Passenger vehicles (Number)									
1.1	Mopeds	137 585	113 868	115 000	...	743 611	637 000	...	...	...
1.2	Motorcycles	30 369	70 479	78 000	1 356 553	819 902	804 000	134 594	301 000	324 000
1.3	Passenger cars	1 613 037	1 786 404	1 814 000	5 260 646	8 890 763	9 283 000	2 552 336	4 587 000	4 932 000
1.4	Motor coaches, buses, etc.	21 222	36 218	37 039	92 403	80 827	78 958	12 099	17 513	18 556
1.5	Trams	...	...	...	...	3 876	3 771	...	72	84
2	Goods road vehicles (Number)									
2.1	Lorries	304 327	389 696	...	1 010 143	1 484 575	1 597 874	508 520	1 436 098	1 540 631
2.2	Road tractors	3 604	5 133	5 265	35 934	78 239	85 013	11 481	38 751	44 258
2.3	Semi-trailers	4 009	6 390	6 692	43 092	88 283	96 807	21 315	316 956	332 577
2.4	Trailers	358 626	651 742	672 253	566 816	653 622	608 156	154 779	...	...
3	Load capacity of goods road vehicles (1000 t)									
3.1	Lorries	...	...	...	...	3 618.0	3 571.0	1 291.0	...	...
3.2	Semi-trailers	...	...	...	...	1 558.0	1 741.0	393.0	...	...
3.3	Trailers	...	...	...	...	2 564.0	2 373.0	...	...	...

		Republic of Moldova République de Moldova Республика Молдова			Romania Roumanie Румыния			Russian Federation Fédération de Russie Российская Федерация		
		1990	1998	1999	1990	1998	1999	1990	1998	1999
1	Passenger vehicles (Number)									
1.1	Mopeds	...	...	...	206 202	204 000	204 000	...	...	...
1.2	Motorcycles	...	116 000	97 000	105 444	121 335	122 000	...	7 165 929	6 329 000
1.3	Passenger cars	208 984	222 769	232 000	1 292 283	2 822 254	2 980 000	8 964 000	18 819 558	19 718 000
1.4	Motor coaches, buses, etc.	11 910	12 917	13 582	29 108	46 508	48 250	473 300	639 732	645 396
1.5	Trams	...	-	-	2 374	2 202	...	14 800	12 400	12 300
2	Goods road vehicles (Number)									
2.1	Lorries	76 909	57 404	52 430	...	380 312	410 159	2 660 200	3 108 231	3 196 177
2.2	Road tractors	...	3 705	3 359	...	26 552	28 721	...	...	...
2.3	Semi-trailers	...	5 225	4 772	...	160 681	170 614	...	236 612	230 657
2.4	Trailers	...	5 391	4 461	...	...	...	...	1 423 315	1 455 205
3	Load capacity of goods road vehicles (1000 t)									
3.1	Lorries	...	219.0	189.0	...	...	...	...	...	...
3.2	Semi-trailers	...	66.0	61.0	...	...	...	...	...	...
3.3	Trailers	...	32.0	27.0	...	...	...	...	...	...

ROAD TRANSPORT - TRANSPORT ROUTIER
АВТОМОБИЛЬНЫЕ ДОРОГИ

10. Road vehicle fleet in the country at 31 December - By vehicle category
10. Parc automobile du pays au 31 décembre - Par catégories de véhicules
10. Парк автодорожных транспортных средств страны по состоянию на 31 декабря
- по категории транспортного средства

		Slovakia Slovaquie Словакия			Slovenia Slovénie Словения			Spain Espagne Испания		
		1990	1998	1999	1990	1998	1999	1990	1998	1999
1	Passenger vehicles (Number)									
1.1	Mopeds	...	...	...	...	...	...	...	...	...
1.2	Motorcycles	286 250	100 891	44 000	15 842	9 213	9 978	1 073 400	1 361 000	1 404 000
1.3	Passenger cars	875 550	1 196 109	1 236 000	578 268	814 000	849 000	11 995 640	16 050 057	16 847 000
1.4	Motor coaches, buses, etc.	14 301	11 515	11 335	3 077	2 327	2 319	45 767	51 805	53 540
1.5	Trams	...	373	371	-	-	-	...	...	...
2	Goods road vehicles (Number)									
2.1	Lorries	145 531	154 771	157 651	30 767	45 769	47 888	2 332 928	3 393 446	3 604 972
2.2	Road tractors	...	1 721	...	...	3 912	4 077	68 157	116 305	130 216
2.3	Semi-trailers	...	4 246	3 666	...	4 511	4 801	88 979	147 698	161 329
2.4	Trailers	...	186 995	...	23 277	20 878	22 979	16 634	53 186	59 757
3	Load capacity of goods road vehicles (1000 t)									
3.1	Lorries	...	...	...	...	...	...	...	...	...
3.2	Semi-trailers	...	...	...	...	111.6	120.4	...	...	...
3.3	Trailers	...	...	...	...	77.8	82.4	...	...	...

		Sweden Suède Швеция			Switzerland Suisse [4] Швейцария			Tajikistan Tadjikistan Таджикистан		
		1990	1998	1999	1990	1998	1999	1990	1998	1999
1	Passenger vehicles (Number)									
1.1	Mopeds	...	...	...	464 609	283 722	...	...	5 735	5 484
1.2	Motorcycles	41 100	101 003	120 000	299 264	435 042	464 357	...	47 538	40 133
1.3	Passenger cars	3 600 518	3 790 695	3 890 000	2 985 399	3 383 273	3 467 275	...	154 283	148 825
1.4	Motor coaches, buses, etc.	14 595	14 924	14 869	31 293	39 012	39 692	...	9 777	9 242
1.5	Trams	...	...	...	662	...	...	-	-	-
2	Goods road vehicles (Number)									
2.1	Lorries	309 520	331 810	347 805	246 194	259 871	266 074	...	61 745	53 275
2.2	Road tractors	3 975	6 163	6 488	5 942	7 509	...	...	2 676	2 165
2.3	Semi-trailers	8 788	15 383	16 148	7 759	10 238	...	...	545	602
2.4	Trailers	422 131	486 512	499 248	85 110	129 631	...	...	3 362	2 907
3	Load capacity of goods road vehicles (1000 t)									
3.1	Lorries	891.4	823.0	843.0	633.0	644.0	...	...	...	...
3.2	Semi-trailers	229.7	441.0	470.0	93.9	147.0	...	...	...	...
3.3	Trailers	918.6	814.0	829.0	219.0	265.0	...	...	...	...

For notes see end of table.   Voir notes à la fin du tableau.   См. примечания в конце таблицы.

ROAD TRANSPORT - TRANSPORT ROUTIER
АВТОМОБИЛЬНЫЕ ДОРОГИ

10. Road vehicle fleet in the country at 31 December - By vehicle category

10. Parc automobile du pays au 31 décembre - Par catégories de véhicules

10. Парк автодорожных транспортных средств страны по состоянию на 31 декабря - по категории транспортного средства

		The FYR of Macedonia [5]			Turkey Turquie Турция			Ukraine Ukraine Украина		
		1990	1998	1999	1990	1998	1999	1990	1998	1999
1	**Passenger vehicles (Number)**									
1.1	Mopeds	...	...	...	(e)	(e)	...	...	...	...
1.2	Motorcycles	1 868	3 566	4 000	531 941	940 935	...	...	2 472 145	...
1.3	Passenger cars	230 774	288 678	290 000	1 649 879	3 838 288	...	3 362 697	5 127 323	...
1.4	Motor coaches, buses, etc.	2 320	2 478	2 479	188 099	319 856	...	...	...	...
1.5	Trams	...	-	-	...	...	...	...	3 570	...
2	**Goods road vehicles (Number)**									
2.1	Lorries	15 489	20 075	20 011	520 760	997 167	...	...	...	...
2.2	Road tractors	2 332	3 365	3 459	...	36 601	...	...	...	...
2.3	Semi-trailers	5 737	5 774	5 588	...	...	...	...	...	...
2.4	Trailers	(d)	(d)	(d)	...	...	...	...	...	...
3	**Load capacity of goods road vehicles (1000 t)**									
3.1	Lorries	...	...	...	...	...	...	...	...	...
3.2	Semi-trailers	...	...	...	...	...	...	...	...	...
3.3	Trailers	...	...	...	...	...	...	...	...	...

		United Kingdom Royaume-Uni [6] Соединенное Королевство			United States Etats-Unis Соединенные Штаты			Yugoslavia Yugoslavie Югославия		
		1990	1998	1999	1990	1998	1999	1990	1998	1999
1	**Passenger vehicles (Number)**									
1.1	Mopeds	279 000	90 000	100 000	(e)	(e)	(e)	...	...	...
1.2	Motorcycles	712 000	710 000	770 000	4 222 987	3 879 450	4 152 433	43 000	...	...
1.3	Passenger cars	21 485 000	23 886 000	24 594 000	181 975000	203 168743	207 788420	1 406 000	...	...
1.4	Motor coaches, buses, etc.	157 000	166 000	173 000	626 987	715 540	728 777	13 100	...	...
1.5	Trams	...	...	...	...	1 205	...	...	186	206
2	**Goods road vehicles (Number)**									
2.1	Lorries	2 330 200	2 644 000	2 802 000	16 008 545	7 732 270	7 791 426	93 000	...	...
2.2	Road tractors	106 000	...	...	1 338 149	1 500 546	1 533 771	...	...	...
2.3	Semi-trailers	230 500	...	...	3 606 169	4 405 222	4 560 664	...	...	...
2.4	Trailers	422 131	...	...	...	19 943 753	20 746 608	...	...	...
3	**Load capacity of goods road vehicles (1000 t)**									
3.1	Lorries	...	...	...	28 567.0	...	...	...	...	...
3.2	Semi-trailers	...	...	...	70 891.0	...	...	...	...	...
3.3	Trailers	...	...	...	...	...	...	...	...	...

For notes see end of table.   Voir notes à la fin du tableau.   См. примечания в конце таблицы.

ROAD TRANSPORT - TRANSPORT ROUTIER
АВТОМОБИЛЬНЫЕ ДОРОГИ

NOTES TO TABLE 10 - NOTES DU TABLEAU 10 - ПРИМЕЧАНИЯ К ТАБЛИЦЕ 10

General notes - Notes générales - Общие примечания

(a) Included under item 2.4.

(b) Included under item 3.3.

(c) Included under item 2.1.

(d) Included under item 2.3.

(e) Included under item 1.2.

(a) Compris sous la rubrique 2.4.

(b) Compris sous la rubrique 3.3.

(c) Compris sous la rubrique 2.1.

(d) Compris sous la rubrique 2.3.

(e) Compris sous la rubrique 1.2.

(a) Включено в статью 2.4.

(b) Включено в статью 3.3.

(c) Включено в статью 2.1.

(d) Включено в статью 2.3.

(e) Включено в статью 1.2.

Country notes - Notes relatives aux pays - Примечания к данным, представляемым странами

1- Excluding mopeds and goods road vehicles registered in Aland (items 1.1, 2 and 3). Trams in Helsinki/Helsingfors only (item 1.5).

1- Non compris les cyclomoteurs et les véhicules routiers pour le transport des marchandises immatriculés à Aland (rubriques 1.1,2 et 3). Seul les tramways d'Helsinki/Helsinfors sont comptabilisés (rubrique 1.5).

1- За исключением мопедов и грузовых автодорожных средств, зарегистрированных на Аландских островах (пп. 1.1, 2 и 3). Трамваи только в Хельсинки/ Хельсингфорсе (пункт 1.5).

2- Lorries include special vehicles.

2- Les camions incluent les véhicules spéciaux.

2- Грузовые автомобили, включая специальные транспортные спедства.

3- Lorries include agricultural tractors and special vehicles.

3- Les camions incluent les tracteurs agricoles et les véhicules spéciaux.

3- Грузовые автомобили, включая сельскохозяйственные тракторы и специальные транспортные спедства.

4- Excluding trolley buses (item 1.4).

4- Non compris les trolleybus (rubrique 1.4).

4- За исключением троллейбусов (пункт 1.4).

5- The former Yugoslav Republic of Macedonia.

5- L'ex-République yougoslave de Macédoine.

5- Бывшая Югославская Республика Македония.

6- Data for road tractors, semi-trailers and trailers refer to Great Britain only.

6- Les données pour les tracteurs routiers, les semi-remorques et les remorques se réferent à la Grande Bretagne.

6- Данные по дорожным тракторам, полутракторам и трейлерам относятся только к Великобритании.

ROAD TRANSPORT - TRANSPORT ROUTIER
АВТОМОБИЛЬНЫЕ ДОРОГИ

10 (a). Road vehicle fleet in the country at 31 December - By age group
10 (a). Parc automobile du pays au 31 décembre - Par groupe d'âge
10 (a). Парк автодорожных транспортных средств страны по состоянию на 31 декабря - по возрасту

Item	Description	Rubrique	Description
1	**Passenger cars**	**1**	**Voitures particulières**
	Of which:		*Dont:*
1.1	≤ 2 years	1.1	≤ 2 ans
1.2	2 ≥ 5 years	1.2	2 ≥ 5 ans
1.3	5 ≥ 10 years	1.3	5 ≥ 10 ans
1.4	> 10 years	1.4	> 10 ans
2	**Motor coaches, Buses and trolley buses**	**2**	**Autocars, autobus et trolleybus**
	Of which:		*Dont:*
2.1	≤ 2 years	2.1	≤ 2 ans
2.2	2 ≥ 5 years	2.2	2 ≥ 5 ans
2.3	5 ≥ 10 years	2.3	5 ≥ 10 ans
2.4	> 10 years	2.4	> 10 ans
3	**Lorries**	**2**	**Camions**
	Of which:		*Dont:*
3.1	≤ 2 years	2.1	≤ 2 ans
3.2	2 ≥ 5 years	2.2	2 ≥ 5 ans
3.3	5 ≥ 10 years	2.3	5 ≥ 10 ans
3.4	> 10 years	2.4	> 10 ans
4	**Road tractors**	**3**	**Tracteurs routiers**
	Of which:		*Dont:*
4.1	≤ 2 years	3.1	≤ 2 ans
4.2	2 ≥ 5 years	2.3	2 ≥ 5 ans
4.3	5 ≥ 10 years	3.2	5 ≥ 10 ans
4.4	> 10 years	3.3	> 10 ans

Статья	Описание
1	**Пассажирские автомобили**
	В том числе:
1.1	< 2 года
1.2	2 i 5 лет
1.3	5 i 10 лет
1.4	> 10 лет
2	**Автобусы дальнего следования, городские автобусы и троллейбусы**
	В том числе:
2.1	< 2 года
2.2	2 i 5 лет
2.3	5 i 10 лет
2.4	> 10 лет
3	**Грузовые автомобили**
	В том числе:
3.1	< 2 года
3.2	2 i 5 лет
3.3	5 i 10 лет
3.4	> 10 лет
4	**Дорожные тягачи**
	В том числе:
4.1	< 2 года
4.2	2 i 5 лет
4.3	5 i 10 лет
4.4	> 10 лет

ROAD TRANSPORT - TRANSPORT ROUTIER
АВТОМОБИЛЬНЫЕ ДОРОГИ

10 (a). Road vehicle fleet in the country at 31 December - By age group
10 (a). Parc automobile du pays au 31 décembre - Par groupe d'âge
10 (a). Парк автодорожных транспортных средств страны по состоянию на 31 декабря - по возрасту

(Number - Nombre - Число)

		Austria Autriche Австрия			Belgium Belgique [1,2] Бельгия			Croatia Croatie [1] Хорватия		
		1990	1998	1999	1990	1998	1999	1990	1998	1999
1	**Passenger cars**	2 991 284	3 887 174	4 010 000	3 864 159	4 491 734	4 583 615	795 410	1 000 052	1 059 000
	Of which:									
1.1	≤ 2 years	...	536 536	574 000	708 304	658 000	733 000	...	134 000	166 000
1.2	2 ≥ 5 years	...	821 335	819 000	1 148 452	1 013 000	1 019 000	...	64 000	84 000
1.3	5 ≥ 10 years	...	1 329 050	1 323 000	1 358 218	1 633 000	1 579 000	...	389 000	345 000
1.4	> 10 years	...	1 200 253	1 294 000	649 185	1 187 000	1 253 000	...	413 000	464 000
2	**Motor coaches, Buses, etc.**	9 402	9 675	9 834	15 644	18 175	18 562	5 836	4 814	4 715
	Of which:									
2.1	≤ 2 years	...	1 038	1 294	1 451	1 425	1 583	...	257	275
2.2	2 ≥ 5 years	...	1 640	1 628	2 183	2 420	2 329	...	374	317
2.3	5 ≥ 10 years	...	2 693	2 687	3 952	4 155	4 202	...	1 341	1 112
2.4	> 10 years	...	4 304	4 225	8 058	6 588	6 559	...	2 842	3 011
3	**Lorries**	252 504	309 630	318 757	343 241	484 179	514 226	56 823	110 360	112 675
	Of which:									
3.1	≤ 2 years	...	54 116	55 970	58 237	74 889	85 401	...	15 249	11 645
3.2	2 ≥ 5 years	...	67 773	70 619	85 787	91 498	102 708	...	11 415	12 594
3.3	5 ≥ 10 years	...	96 325	96 684	95 026	140 450	133 857	...	32 200	24 283
3.4	> 10 years	...	91 416	95 484	104 191	146 285	155 067	...	51 496	64 153
4	**Road tractors**	...	15 705	17 015	37 138	46 410	48 666	...	5 408	5 492
	Of which:									
4.1	≤ 2 years	...	5 645	6 751	7 434	8 243	9 437	...	473	503
4.2	2 ≥ 5 years	...	4 372	4 780	9 238	10 921	12 439	...	690	690
4.3	5 ≥ 10 years	...	3 945	3 680	7 599	10 421	9 027	...	2 009	1 840
4.4	> 10 years	...	1 743	1 804	12 867	12 757	13 152	...	2 236	2 409

		Cyprus Chypre Кипр			Czech Republic République tchèque [3] Чешская Республика			Denmark Danemark [1] Дания		
		1990	1998	1999	1990	1998	1999	1990	1998	1999
1	**Passenger cars**	178 602	249 225	256 989	3 043 316	3 492 961	3 439 745	1 590 345	1 817 147	1 843 254
	Of which:									
1.1	≤ 2 years	...	14 120	13 583	...	272 759	239 334	157 413	445 000	446 000
1.2	2 ≥ 5 years	...	53 633	46 082	...	378 467	461 789	367 262	338 000	394 000
1.3	5 ≥ 10 years	...	86 398	95 282	...	727 460	720 696	532 672	395 000	390 000
1.4	> 10 years	...	95 074	102 042	...	2 114 275	2 017 926	532 998	640 000	613 000
2	**Motor coaches, Buses, etc.**	2 308	2 754	2 835	20 474	20 668	19 702	8 109	13 911	13 909
	Of which:									
2.1	≤ 2 years	...	232	268	...	1 316	1 370	...	2 436	2 313
2.2	2 ≥ 5 years	...	501	468	...	2 002	2 145	...	3 611	2 427
2.3	5 ≥ 10 years	...	767	741	...	6 275	4 460	...	4 257	5 686
2.4	> 10 years	...	1 254	1 358	...	10 367	11 006	...	3 607	3 483
3	**Lorries**	74 018	108 091	110 114	202 929	260 276	268 259	286 613	347 136	362 002
	Of which:									
3.1	≤ 2 years	...	12 692	12 723	...	36 482	30 289	...	93 091	98 890
3.2	2 ≥ 5 years	...	21 965	21 577	...	57 952	68 249	...	67 666	75 499
3.3	5 ≥ 10 years	...	37 275	35 559	...	55 175	59 973	...	87 238	88 377
3.4	> 10 years	...	36 159	40 255	...	110 667	109 748	...	99 141	99 236
4	**Road tractors**	...	1 203	1 011	...	20 035	21 151	6 628	10 497	11 256
	Of which:									
4.1	≤ 2 years	...	...	...	...	2 988	3 405	...	5 287	5 559
4.2	2 ≥ 5 years	...	...	...	...	3 421	4 090	...	2 729	3 481
4.3	5 ≥ 10 years	...	...	...	...	7 246	6 640	...	1 798	1 531
4.4	> 10 years	...	...	...	...	6 380	7 016	...	683	685

For note see end of table.   Voir note à la fin du tableau.   См. примечания в конце таблицы.

ROAD TRANSPORT - TRANSPORT ROUTIER
АВТОМОБИЛЬНЫЕ ДОРОГИ

10 (a). Road vehicle fleet in the country at 31 December - By age group
10 (a). Parc automobile du pays au 31 décembre - Par groupe d'âge
10 (a). Парк автодорожных транспортных средств страны по состоянию на 31 декабря - по возрасту

(Number - Nombre - Число)

		Finland Finlande [4] Финляндия			France France Франция			Germany Allemagne [1] Германия		
		1990	1998	1999	1990	1998	1999	1990	1998	1999
1	**Passenger cars**	1 938 856	2 021 116	2 082 580	23 550 000	26 809 000	27 480 000	...	41 673 787	42 324 000
	Of which:									
1.1	≤ 2 years	...	231 000	263 000	...	3 746 000	4 155 000	...	5 484 000	5 775 000
1.2	2 ≥ 5 years	...	247 000	284 000	...	6 319 000	5 761 000	...	9 807 000	10 134 000
1.3	5 ≥ 10 years	...	522 000	421 000	...	9 665 000	9 224 000	...	15 377 000	15 499 000
1.4	> 10 years	...	1 008 000	1 101 000	...	7 079 000	8 340 000	...	11 007 000	10 916 000
2	**Motor coaches, Buses, etc.**	9 327	9 040	9 487	73 700	84 961	85 668	...	83 285	84 687
	Of which:									
2.1	≤ 2 years	...	982	1 055	...	8 802	10 160	...	8 286	8 934
2.2	2 ≥ 5 years	...	1 099	1 292	...	11 764	12 162	...	17 026	16 327
2.3	5 ≥ 10 years	...	1 915	1 710	...	20 660	20 226	...	21 369	29 363
2.4	> 10 years	...	5 008	5 392	...	43 735	43 120	...	36 604	30 063
3	**Lorries**	261 495	280 610	293 707	3 567 767	4 984 586	5 074 835	...	2 370 599	2 465 535
	Of which:									
3.1	≤ 2 years	...	35 090	38 686	...	702 773	774 253	...	406 731	452 667
3.2	2 ≥ 5 years	...	28 599	39 264	...	958 182	973 774	...	591 179	590 291
3.3	5 ≥ 10 years	...	88 853	62 292	...	1 739 425	1 619 170	...	842 374	873 997
3.4	> 10 years	...	125 069	150 346	...	1 584 206	1 707 638	...	530 315	548 580
4	**Road tractors**	...	5 253	5 209	166 809	184 359	190 916	...	140 516	153 527
	Of which:									
4.1	≤ 2 years	...	1 387	1 023	...	46 527	54 484	...	...	...
4.2	2 ≥ 5 years	...	1 087	1 339	...	58 382	62 738	...	...	...
4.3	5 ≥ 10 years	...	1 618	1 461	...	79 450	73 694	...	...	...
4.4	> 10 years	...	1 161	1 386	...	-	-	...	...	...

		Hungary Hongrie [3] Венгрия			Iceland Islande Исландия			Ireland Irlande Ирландия		
		1990	1998	1999	1990	1998	1999	1990	1998	1999
1	**Passenger cars**	1 944 553	2 218 124	2 256 000	119 731	140 372	151 000	797 713	1 196 900	1 269 200
	Of which:									
1.1	≤ 2 years	...	176 032	229 000	...	34 702	43 000	...	260 900	297 200
1.2	2 ≥ 5 years	...	231 473	224 000	...	18 077	20 000	...	279 300	329 400
1.3	5 ≥ 10 years	...	484 269	450 000	...	43 817	36 000	...	428 600	416 900
1.4	> 10 years	...	1 326 350	1 353 000	...	43 776	52 000	...	228 100	225 700
2	**Motor coaches, Buses, etc.**	26 438	18 795	17 988	1 328	1 544	1 621	4 047	6 104	6 564
	Of which:									
2.1	≤ 2 years	...	1 019	1 286	...	270	315	...	...	...
2.2	2 ≥ 5 years	...	1 482	1 428	...	157	154	...	...	...
2.3	5 ≥ 10 years	...	3 659	2 736	...	435	390	...	...	...
2.4	> 10 years	...	12 372	12 283	...	682	762	...	...	...
3	**Lorries**	208 302	295 048	308 944	13 122	15 905	17 115	143 166	170 866	188 814
	Of which:									
3.1	≤ 2 years	...	42 433	52 243	...	3 389	4 297	...	42 479	51 747
3.2	2 ≥ 5 years	...	46 681	46 280	...	1 506	1 723	...	41 769	49 044
3.3	5 ≥ 10 years	...	72 777	71 998	...	5 002	4 647	...	61 210	58 926
3.4	> 10 years	...	133 157	138 423	...	6 008	6 448	...	25 408	29 097
4	**Road tractors**	38 397	24 591	23 559	...	645	692	...	...	...
	Of which:									
4.1	≤ 2 years	...	2 769	3 348	...	137	152	...	...	...
4.2	2 ≥ 5 years	...	3 436	3 558	...	39	63	...	...	...
4.3	5 ≥ 10 years	...	6 897	6 365	...	180	145	...	...	...
4.4	> 10 years	...	11 489	10 288	...	289	332	...	...	...

For note see end of table.   **Voir note à la fin du tableau.**   **См. примечания в конце таблицы.**

ROAD TRANSPORT - TRANSPORT ROUTIER
АВТОМОБИЛЬНЫЕ ДОРОГИ

10 (a). Road vehicle fleet in the country at 31 December - By age group
10 (a). Parc automobile du pays au 31 décembre - Par groupe d'âge
10 (a). Парк автодорожных транспортных средств страны по состоянию на 31 декабря - по возрасту

(Number - Nombre - Число)

		Italy Italie Италия			Kazakhstan Kazakhstan Казахстан			Latvia Lettonie Латвия		
		1990	1998	1999	1990	1998	1999	1990	1998	1999
1	**Passenger cars**	27 415 828	31 573 000	32 038 291	809 700	971 170	987 724	331 837	482 670	525 572
	Of which:									
1.1	≤ 2 years	...	4 866 000	4 695 924	...	...	...	...	9 961	12 000
1.2	2 ≥ 5 years	...	...	...	...	...	...	...	9 850	11 000
1.3	5 ≥ 10 years	...	...	...	...	...	...	...	59 731	53 000
1.4	> 10 years	...	...	11 924 867	...	...	...	...	403 128	450 000
2	**Motor coaches, Buses, etc.**	77 731	85 799	85 762	55 011	29 547	26 146	12 138	11 829	11 870
	Of which:									
2.1	≤ 2 years	...	...	9 008	...	1 753	1 512	...	433	596
2.2	2 ≥ 5 years	...	...	...	...	...	...	...	422	496
2.3	5 ≥ 10 years	...	...	...	...	17 287	13 006	...	3 579	2 668
2.4	> 10 years	...	...	52 229	...	10 507	...	...	7 395	8 110
3	**Lorries**	2 348 992	3 171 494	3 221 335	...	128 133	106 331	53 692	74 954	80 112
	Of which:									
3.1	≤ 2 years	...	...	378 482	...	3 486	2 362	...	2 311	3 795
3.2	2 ≥ 5 years	...	...	...	...	...	...	...	1 623	2 118
3.3	5 ≥ 10 years	...	...	...	...	77 210	55 137	...	17 292	13 569
3.4	> 10 years	...	...	1 627 073	...	47 437	48 832	...	53 728	60 630
4	**Road tractors**	67 780	102 526	106 726	...	6 907	5 862	6 273	9 988	10 108
	Of which:									
4.1	≤ 2 years	...	...	18 770	...	...	...	...	643	605
4.2	2 ≥ 5 years	...	...	...	...	...	...	...	837	648
4.3	5 ≥ 10 years	...	...	...	...	...	...	...	3 298	2 928
4.4	> 10 years	...	...	40 877	...	...	...	...	5 210	5 927

		Lithuania Lituanie Литва			Malta Malte [5] Мальта			Norway Norvège [1] Норвегия		
		1990	1998	1999	1990	1998	1999	1990	1998	1999
1	**Passenger cars**	492 978	980 910	1 089 000	109 131	191 440	182 642	1 613 037	1 786 404	1 814 000
	Of which:									
1.1	≤ 2 years	...	7 000	9 000	...	16 664	19 653	...	242 000	218 000
1.2	2 ≥ 5 years	...	10 000	11 000	...	34 866	34 243	...	306 000	350 000
1.3	5 ≥ 10 years	...	128 000	114 000	...	48 084	48 471	...	396 000	456 000
1.4	> 10 years	...	835 000	955 000	...	91 826	80 275	...	842 000	790 000
2	**Motor coaches, Buses, etc.**	15 707	15 679	16 090	978	1 117	729	21 222	36 218	37 039
	Of which:									
2.1	≤ 2 years	...	475	438	...	25	7	...	5 567	4 912
2.2	2 ≥ 5 years	...	523	609	...	67	46	...	9 327	9 586
2.3	5 ≥ 10 years	...	3 993	3 178	...	92	40	...	11 500	13 368
2.4	> 10 years	...	10 688	11 865	...	933	636	...	9 824	9 173
3	**Lorries**	83 035	89 866	86 824	21 870	48 403	42 687	304 327	389 696	...
	Of which:									
3.1	≤ 2 years	...	1 941	1 288	...	2 597	2 145	...	...	...
3.2	2 ≥ 5 years	...	1 833	1 264	...	5 418	5 483	...	...	...
3.3	5 ≥ 10 years	...	22 083	14 550	...	12 768	12 171	...	...	...
3.4	> 10 years	...	64 009	69 722	...	27 620	22 888	...	...	...
4	**Road tractors**	7 752	9 588	9 752	(a)	(a)	17	3 604	5 133	5 265
	Of which:									
4.1	≤ 2 years	...	566	437	(a)	(a)	5	...	...	...
4.2	2 ≥ 5 years	...	805	761	(a)	(a)	2	...	...	...
4.3	5 ≥ 10 years	...	3 896	3 401	(a)	(a)	5	...	...	...
4.4	> 10 years	...	4 321	5 153	(a)	(a)	5	...	...	...

For note see end of table.   Voir note à la fin du tableau.   См. примечания в конце таблицы.

10 (a). Road vehicle fleet in the country at 31 December - By age group
10 (a). Parc automobile du pays au 31 décembre - Par groupe d'âge
10 (a). Парк автодорожных транспортных средств страны по состоянию на 31 декабря - по возрасту

(Number - Nombre - Число)

		Portugal Portugal Португалия			Republic of Moldova République de Moldova Республика Молдова			Slovenia Slovénie Словения		
		1990	1998	1999	1990	1998	1999	1990	1998	1999
1	**Passenger cars**	2 552 336	4 587 000	4 932 000	208 984	222 769	232 000	578 268	814 000	849 000
	Of which:									
1.1	≤ 2 years	...	585 000	659 000	...	...	...	...	191 000	206 000
1.2	2 ≥ 5 years	...	707 000	741 000	...	...	...	...	182 000	185 000
1.3	5 ≥ 10 years	...	1 143 000	1 189 000	...	...	...	...	275 000	286 000
1.4	> 10 years	...	2 152 000	2 343 000	...	...	...	...	166 000	172 000
2	**Motor coaches, Buses, etc.**	12 099	17 513	18 556	11 910	12 917	13 582	3 077	2 327	2 319
	Of which:									
2.1	≤ 2 years	...	1 819	2 107	...	...	...	...	330	408
2.2	2 ≥ 5 years	...	2 127	2 183	...	...	...	...	309	266
2.3	5 ≥ 10 years	...	2 523	2 676	...	...	...	...	734	646
2.4	> 10 years	...	11 044	11 590	...	4 145	4 243	...	954	999
3	**Lorries**	508 520	1 436 098	1 540 631	76 909	57 404	52 430	30 767	45 769	47 888
	Of which:									
3.1	≤ 2 years	...	190 305	207 515	...	...	...	...	10 105	10 759
3.2	2 ≥ 5 years	...	234 318	215 145	...	...	...	...	9 800	10 847
3.3	5 ≥ 10 years	...	368 881	407 967	...	...	...	...	11 703	11 597
3.4	> 10 years	...	642 594	710 004	...	25 761	24 031	...	14 161	14 685
4	**Road tractors**	11 481	38 751	44 258	...	3 705	3 359	...	3 912	4 077
	Of which:									
4.1	≤ 2 years	...	8 010	9 881	...	...	...	...	671	810
4.2	2 ≥ 5 years	...	5 620	7 998	...	...	...	...	882	970
4.3	5 ≥ 10 years	...	9 169	8 806	...	...	...	...	1 032	1 041
4.4	> 10 years	...	15 952	17 573	...	...	...	...	1 327	1 256

		Spain Espagne [1] Испания			Sweden Suède [1] Швеция			Switzerland Suisse [1,3] Швейцария		
		1990	1998	1999	1990	1998	1999	1990	1998	1999
1	**Passenger cars**	11 995 640	16 050 057	16 847 000	3 600 518	3 790 695	3 890 000	2 985 399	3 383 273	3 467 275
	Of which:									
1.1	≤ 2 years	...	2 359 000	2 734 000	...	540 000	580 000	618 523	529 000	...
1.2	2 ≥ 5 years	...	2 718 000	2 863 000	...	501 000	571 000	844 118	752 000	...
1.3	5 ≥ 10 years	...	4 682 000	4 467 000	...	923 000	849 000	1 072 805	1 226 000	...
1.4	> 10 years	...	6 291 000	6 783 000	...	1 826 000	1 890 000	449 953	875 000	...
2	**Motor coaches, Buses, etc.**	45 767	51 805	53 540	14 595	14 924	14 869	31 293	39 012	39 692
	Of which:									
2.1	≤ 2 years	...	7 006	7 504	...	2 284	2 518	4 830	...	...
2.2	2 ≥ 5 years	...	7 219	8 708	...	2 637	2 934	6 227	...	...
2.3	5 ≥ 10 years	...	13 531	11 379	...	4 393	3 779	9 017	...	...
2.4	> 10 years	...	24 049	25 949	...	5 610	5 638	11 219	...	...
3	**Lorries**	2 332 928	3 393 446	3 604 972	309 520	331 810	347 805	246 194	259 871	266 074
	Of which:									
3.1	≤ 2 years	...	501 323	579 725	...	56 968	...	49 339	34 955	...
3.2	2 ≥ 5 years	...	540 660	602 463	...	43 104	53 955	67 280	47 614	...
3.3	5 ≥ 10 years	...	1 098 870	1 007 185	...	99 290	67 237	79 352	86 203	...
3.4	> 10 years	...	1 252 593	1 415 599	...	132 448	159 097	50 223	91 099	...
4	**Road tractors**	68 157	116 305	130 216	3 975	6 163	6 488	5 942	7 509	...
	Of which:									
4.1	≤ 2 years	...	27 303	33 172	...	1 397	...	1 354	1 421	...
4.2	2 ≥ 5 years	...	23 373	30 570	...	1 709	1 228	1 548	1 844	...
4.3	5 ≥ 10 years	...	32 817	27 224	...	1 496	1 862	1 710	2 342	...
4.4	> 10 years	...	32 812	39 250	...	1 561	1 803	1 330	1 902	...

For note see end of table.   Voir note à la fin du tableau.   См. примечания в конце таблицы.

107

ROAD TRANSPORT - TRANSPORT ROUTIER
АВТОМОБИЛЬНЫЕ ДОРОГИ

10 (a). Road vehicle fleet in the country at 31 December - By age group
10 (a). Parc automobile du pays au 31 décembre - Par groupe d'âge
10 (a). Парк автодорожных транспортных средств страны по состоянию на 31 декабря - по возрасту

(Number - Nombre - Число)

		The FYR of Macedonia [6]								
		1990	1998	1999						
1	**Passenger cars**	230 774	288 678	290 000						
	Of which:									
1.1	≤ 2 years	...	14 000	15 000						
1.2	2 ≥ 5 years	...	34 000	32 000						
1.3	5 ≥ 10 years	...	43 000	41 000						
1.4	> 10 years	...	198 000	202 000						
2	**Motor coaches, Buses, etc.**	2 320	2 478	2 479						
	Of which:									
2.1	≤ 2 years	...	98	88						
2.2	2 ≥ 5 years	...	70	115						
2.3	5 ≥ 10 years	...	410	319						
2.4	> 10 years	...	1 900	1 957						
3	**Lorries**	15 489	20 075	20 011						
	Of which:									
3.1	≤ 2 years	...	891	847						
3.2	2 ≥ 5 years	...	1 689	1 646						
3.3	5 ≥ 10 years	...	3 438	3 235						
3.4	> 10 years	...	14 057	14 283						
4	**Road tractors**	2 332	3 365	3 459						
	Of which:									
4.1	≤ 2 years	...	26	69						
4.2	2 ≥ 5 years	...	214	243						
4.3	5 ≥ 10 years	...	1 546	1 106						
4.4	> 10 years	...	1 579	2 041						

NOTES TO TABLE 10(a) - NOTES DU TABLEAU 10(a) - ПРИМЕЧАНИЯ К ТАБЛИЦЕ 10(a)

General notes - Notes générales - Общие примечания

(a) Included under item 3.

(a) Compris sous la rubrique 3.

(a) Включено в статью 3.

Country notes - Notes relatives aux pays - Примечания к данным, представляемым странами

1- Due to rounding off, total for passenger cars might slightly differ from the number indicated in table 10.

1- En raison des arrondissements, le total des voitures particulières peut être légèrement différent de celui indiqué dans le tableau 10.

1- В связи с округлением, итоги по пассажирским автомобилям могут несколько отличаться от данных, приведенных в таблице 10.

2- Excluding vehicles for which technical characteristics are unknown (items 2, 3 and 4).

2- Non compris les véhicules dont les données techniques manquent (rubriques 2, 3 et 4).

2- За исключением дорожно-транспортных средств, технические характеристики которы: неизвестны (пп. 2, 3 и 4).

3- Excluding trolley buses (item 2).

3- Non compris les trolleybus (rubrique 2).

3- За исключением троллейбусов (пункт 2).

4- Excluding vehicles registered in Aland.

4- Non compris les véhicules immatriculés à Aland.

4- За исключением дорожно-транспортных средств, зарегистрированных на Аландских островах.

5- Lorries include agricultural tractors and special vehicles.

5- Les camions incluent les tracteurs agricoles et les véhicules spéciaux.

5- Грузовые автомобили, включая сельскохозяйственные тракторы и специальные транспортные спедства.

6- The former Yugoslav Republic of Macedonia.

6- L'ex-République yougoslave de Macédoine.

6- Бывшая Югославская Республика Македония.

ROAD TRANSPORT - TRANSPORT ROUTIER
АВТОМОБИЛЬНЫЕ ДОРОГИ

10 (b). Road vehicle fleet in the country at 31 December - By fuel type
10 (b). Parc automobile du pays au 31 décembre - Par type de combustible utilisé
10 (b). Парк автодорожных транспортных средств страны по состоянию на 31 декабря - по типу двигателя

Item	Description	Rubrique	Description
1	**Passenger cars**	1	**Voitures particulières**
	Of which:		*Dont:*
1.1	- Petrol	1.1	- Essence
1.2	- Diesel	1.2	- Diesel
1.3	- Electricity	1.3	- Électricité
1.4	- Other sources	1.4	- Autres sources
2	**Motor coaches, Buses and Trolleybuses**	2	**Autocars, autobus et trolleybus**
	Of which:		*Dont:*
2.1	- Petrol	2.1	- Essence
2.2	- Diesel	2.2	- Diesel
2.3	- Electricity	2.3	- Électricité
2.4	- Other sources	2.4	- Autres sources
3	**Lorries**	3	**Camions**
	Of which:		*Dont:*
3.1	- Petrol	3.1	- Essence
3.2	- Diesel	3.2	- Diesel
3.3	- Other sources	3.3	- Autres sources

Статья	Описание
1	**Пассажирские автомобили**
	В том числе:
1.1	- бензиновый
1.2	- дизельный
1.3	- электрический
1.4	- прочие
2	**Автобусы дальнего следования, городские автобусы и троллейбусы**
	В том числе:
2.1	- бензиновый
2.2	- дизельный
2.3	-электрический
2.4	- прочие
3	**Грузовые автомобили**
	В том числе:
3.1	- бензиновый
3.2	- дизельный
3.3	- прочие

ROAD TRANSPORT - TRANSPORT ROUTIER
АВТОМОБИЛЬНЫЕ ДОРОГИ

10 (b). Road vehicle fleet in the country at 31 December - By fuel type
10 (b). Parc automobile du pays au 31 décembre - Par type de combustible utilisé
10 (b). Парк автодорожных транспортных средств страны по состоянию на 31 декабря - по типу двигателя

(Number - Nombre - Число)

		Austria Autriche Австрия			Azerbaijan Azerbaïdjan Азербайджан			Belarus Bélarus Беларусь		
		1990	1998	1999	1990	1998	1999	1990	1998	1999
1	Passenger cars	2 991 284	3 887 174	4 010 000	260 200	281 320	311 600	604 500	1 279 208	...
	Of which:									
1.1	- Petrol	...	2 680 035	2 658 000	257 968	...	...	...	...	...
1.2	- Diesel	...	1 206 970	1 351 000	1 875	...	...	...	...	...
1.3	- Electricity	...	169	166	-	...	...	...	...	...
1.4	- Other sources	...	-	834	357	...	...	...	...	...
2	Motor coaches, Buses and Trolleybuses	9 402	9 675	9 834	...	...	...	...	...	...
	Of which:									
2.1	- Petrol	...	14	17	...	...	...	...	...	...
2.2	- Diesel	...	9 544	9 703	...	...	...	...	...	...
2.3	- Electricity	...	117	114	...	234	...	...	1 776	...
2.4	- Other sources	...	-	-	...	...	...	...	...	...
3	Lorries	...	...	...	...	...	...	...	...	...
	Of which:									
3.1	- Petrol	...	42 416	39 224	78 140	...	...	...	...	...
3.2	- Diesel	...	267 183	279 502	20 480	...	...	...	...	...
3.3	- Other sources	...	...	...	...	...	...	...	...	...

		Belgium Belgique [1] Бельгия			Bulgaria Bulgarie Болгария			Croatia Croatie [1] Хорватия		
		1990	1998	1999	1990	1998	1999	1990	1998	1999
1	Passenger cars	3 864 159	4 491 734	4 583 615	1 317 437	1 809 350	1 908	795 410	1 000 052	1 059 000
	Of which:									
1.1	- Petrol	2 744 249	2 783 825	2 768 698	...	...	...	...	809 000	850 000
1.2	- Diesel	1 014 905	1 643 392	1 748 956	...	...	...	...	191 000	209 000
1.3	- Electricity	23	47	71	...	...	...	...	-	-
1.4	- Other sources	104 982	64 470	65 890	...	...	...	...	52	-
2	Motor coaches, Buses and Trolleybuses	15 644	18 175	18 562	34 599	42 264	5 104	5 836	4 814	4 715
	Of which:									
2.1	- Petrol	797	244	235	...	...	...	...	42	41
2.2	- Diesel	14 754	17 730	18 165	...	...	...	...	4 772	4 674
2.3	- Electricity	-	2	2	836	777	750	...	-	-
1.4	- Other sources	93	199	160	...	...	...	...	-	-
3	Lorries	343 241	484 179	514 226	...	220 948	2 016	56 823	110 360	112 675
	Of which:									
3.1	- Petrol	92 127	70 250	66 360	...	...	...	...	15 319	15 099
3.2	- Diesel	240 196	399 240	431 984	...	...	...	...	95 041	97 576
1.4	- Other sources	10 918	14 689	15 882	...	...	...	...	-	-

For note see end of table.   Voir note à la fin du tableau.   См. примечания в конце таблицы.

110

ROAD TRANSPORT - TRANSPORT ROUTIER
АВТОМОБИЛЬНЫЕ ДОРОГИ

10 (b). Road vehicle fleet in the country at 31 December - By fuel type
10 (b). Parc automobile du pays au 31 décembre - Par type de combustible utilisé
10 (b). Парк автодорожных транспортных средств страны по состоянию на 31 декабря - по типу двигателя

(Number - Nombre - Число)

		Cyprus Chypre Кипр			Czech Republic République tchèque Чешская Республика			Denmark Danemark Дания		
		1990	1998	1999	1990	1998	1999	1990	1998	1999
1	Passenger cars	178 602	249 225	256 989	3 043 316	3 492 961	3 439 745	1 590 345	1 817 147	1 843 254
	Of which:									
1.1	- Petrol	167 204	222 987	228 253	2 833 720	3 189 084	3 091 432	1 509 927	1 733 602	1 750 178
1.2	- Diesel	11 398	26 238	28 736	200 813	295 526	340 631	77 442	83 240	92 810
1.3	- Electricity	-	-	-	11	13	11	-	229	...
1.4	- Other sources	-	-	-	8 772	8 338	7 671	2 976	76	...
2	Motor coaches, Buses and Trolleybuses	2 308	2 754	2 835	20 474	20 668	19 702	8 109	13 911	13 909
	Of which:									
2.1	- Petrol	191	154	154	287	278	237	62	1 604	1 609
2.2	- Diesel	2 117	2 600	2 681	19 326	19 564	18 656	8 043	12 122	12 038
2.3	- Electricity	-	-	-	718	708	721	-	-	-
1.4	- Other sources	-	-	-	143	118	88	4	185	262
3	Lorries	74 018	108 091	110 114	202 929	260 276	268 259	286 613	347 136	362 002
	Of which:									
3.1	- Petrol	15 086	10 384	9 450	34 658	45 027	47 422	87 357	99 045	102 198
3.2	- Diesel	58 932	97 707	100 664	163 645	211 290	217 548	196 435	247 872	259 615
1.4	- Other sources	-	-	-	4 626	3 959	3 289	2 821	219	189

		Estonia Estonie Эстония			Finland Finlande [2] Финляндия			France France Франция		
		1990	1998	1999	1990	1998	1999	1990	1998	1999
1	Passenger cars	241 664	450 954	458 700	1 938 856	2 021 116	2 082 580	23 550 000	26 809 000	27 480 000
	Of which:									
1.1	- Petrol	...	...	...	1 771 325	1 829 000	1 872 000	19 775 000	...	18 099 000
1.2	- Diesel	...	...	...	154 951	179 000	196 000	3 775 000	8 609 000	9 261 000
1.3	- Electricity	...	...	...	5	-	-	-	...	2 000
1.4	- Other sources	...	...	...	12 575	13 116	14 580	-	...	118 000
2	Motor coaches, Buses and Trolleybuses	7 900	6 448	6 338	9 327	9 040	9 487	73 700	84 961	85 668
	Of which:									
2.1	- Petrol	...	...	...	16	24	23	...	1 743	1 462
2.2	- Diesel	...	...	...	9 271	8 958	9 389	...	82 845	83 602
2.3	- Electricity	211	142	142	-	-	-	...	373	604
1.4	- Other sources	...	...	...	40	58	75	...	-	-
3	Lorries	67 700	80 617	81 030	261 495	280 610	293 707	3 567 767	4 984 586	5 074 835
	Of which:									
3.1	- Petrol	...	...	...	61 125	46 975	45 132	1 502 242	1 037 928	904 812
3.2	- Diesel	...	...	...	200 354	230 482	245 271	2 050 944	3 927 689	4 145 254
1.4	- Other sources	...	...	...	16	3 153	3 304	14 581	18 969	24 769

For note see end of table.   Voir note à la fin du tableau.   См. примечания в конце таблицы.

ROAD TRANSPORT - TRANSPORT ROUTIER
АВТОМОБИЛЬНЫЕ ДОРОГИ

10 (b). Road vehicle fleet in the country at 31 December - By fuel type
10 (b). Parc automobile du pays au 31 décembre - Par type de combustible utilisé
10 (b). Парк автодорожных транспортных средств страны по состоянию на 31 декабря - по типу двигателя

(Number - Nombre - Число)

		Georgia Georgie Грузия			Germany Allemagne [1] Германия			Hungary Hongrie Венгрия		
		1990	1998	1999	1990	1998	1999	1990	1998	1999
1	**Passenger cars**	...	260 437	...	...	41 673 787	42 324 000	1 944 553	2 218 124	2 256 000
	Of which:									
1.1	- Petrol	...	...	...	...	36 181 000	36 668 000	1 929 944	2 009 717	2 036 000
1.2	- Diesel	...	...	...	...	5 487 000	5 633 000	14 609	205 450	216 000
1.3	- Electricity	...	...	...	...	3 000	3 000	-	584	1 081
1.4	- Other sources	...	...	...	...	2 787	20 000	-	2 373	2 919
2	**Motor coaches, Buses and Trolleybuses**	13 982	...	...	...	83 285	84 687	26 438	18 795	17 988
	Of which:									
2.1	- Petrol	10 368	...	...	...	446	376	10 557	3 377	2 598
2.2	- Diesel	2 089	...	...	...	82 356	83 749	15 564	15 137	15 085
2.3	- Electricity	463	...	...	...	114	115	317	263	255
1.4	- Other sources	1 062	...	...	...	369	447	-	18	50
3	**Lorries**	84 863	56 169	...	...	2 370 599	2 465 535	208 302	295 048	308 944
	Of which:									
3.1	- Petrol	63 798	...	...	...	304 788	296 163	107 620	91 814	89 442
3.2	- Diesel	16 770	...	...	...	2 063 481	2 166 672	100 682	202 533	218 728
1.4	- Other sources	4 295	...	...	...	2 330	2 700	-	701	774

		Iceland Islande Исландия			Ireland Irlande Ирландия			Italy Italie Италия		
		1990	1998	1999	1990	1998	1999	1990	1998	1999
1	**Passenger cars**	119 731	140 372	151 000	797 713	1 196 900	1 269 200	27 415 828	31 573 000	32 038 291
	Of which:									
1.1	- Petrol	...	129 204	137 000	...	1 028 100	1 095 500	...	26 268 000	26 386 617
1.2	- Diesel	...	11 162	14 000	...	167 900	173 000	...	3 748 000	4 132 262
1.3	- Electricity	-	6	-	...	-	-	...	1 556 000	548
1.4	- Other sources	...	-	-	...	900	700	...	1 000	1 518 864
2	**Motor coaches, Buses and Trolleybuses**	1 328	1 544	1 621	4 047	6 104	6 564	77 731	85 799	85 762
	Of which:									
2.1	- Petrol	...	183	178	...	170	141	...	1 462	1 203
2.2	- Diesel	...	1 361	1 443	...	5 918	6 406	...	84 207	84 052
2.3	- Electricity	-	-	-	...	-	-	...	130	-
1.4	- Other sources	...	-	-	...	16	17	...	(a)	507
3	**Lorries**	13 122	15 905	17 115	143 166	170 866	188 814	2 348 992	3 171 494	3 221 335
	Of which:									
3.1	- Petrol	5 894	7 564	7 873	...	6 348	5 244	...	386 413	361 784
3.2	- Diesel	7 228	8 340	9 240	...	164 388	183 478	...	2 771 691	2 830 834
1.4	- Other sources	-	1	2	...	130	92	...	13 390	28 717

For note see end of table.   Voir note à la fin du tableau.   См. примечания в конце таблицы.

112

ROAD TRANSPORT - TRANSPORT ROUTIER
АВТОМОБИЛЬНЫЕ ДОРОГИ

10 (b). Road vehicle fleet in the country at 31 December - By fuel type

10 (b). Parc automobile du pays au 31 décembre - Par type de combustible utilisé

10 (b). Парк автодорожных транспортных средств страны по состоянию на 31 декабря - по типу двигателя

(Number - Nombre - Число)

		Kazakhstan Kazakhstan Казахстан			Kyrgyzstan Kirghizistan Кыргызстан			Latvia Lettonie Латвия		
		1990	1998	1999	1990	1998	1999	1990	1998	1999
1	Passenger cars	809 700	971 170	987 724	194 592	187 734	187 322	331 837	482 670	525 572
	Of which:									
1.1	- Petrol	...	...	...	...	...	...	325 300	449 000	485 000
1.2	- Diesel	...	...	...	...	...	...	6 400	34 000	41 000
1.3	- Electricity	...	...	...	...	...	...	-	-	-
1.4	- Other sources	...	...	...	...	...	...	137	- 330	- 428
2	Motor coaches, Buses and Trolleybuses	55 011	29 547	26 146	...	...	...	12 138	11 829	11 870
	Of which:									
2.1	- Petrol	...	24 559	21 353	...	...	...	...	8 023	7 644
2.2	- Diesel	...	4 091	3 929	...	...	...	...	3 447	3 877
2.3	- Electricity	825	599	537	287	232	232	416	321	314
1.4	- Other sources	...	298	327	...	...	...	...	38	35
3	Lorries	...	128 133	106 331	...	...	...	53 692	74 954	80 112
	Of which:									
3.1	- Petrol	...	87 669	71 230	...	...	...	...	51 775	52 396
3.2	- Diesel	...	37 606	33 218	...	...	...	...	22 690	27 245
1.4	- Other sources	...	2 858	1 883	...	...	...	...	489	471

		Lithuania Lituanie Литва			Luxembourg Luxembourg Люксембург			Malta Malte [3] Мальта		
		1990	1998	1999	1990	1998	1999	1990	1998	1999
1	Passenger cars	492 978	980 910	1 089 000	191 588	253 406	263 475	109 131	191 440	182 642
	Of which:									
1.1	- Petrol	...	...	...	...	...	194 215	...	162 989	152 048
1.2	- Diesel	...	...	...	...	...	68 958	...	28 451	30 594
1.3	- Electricity	...	...	...	...	...	3	...	-	-
1.4	- Other sources	...	...	...	...	...	299	...	-	-
2	Motor coaches, Buses and Trolleybuses	15 707	15 679	16 090	760	945	984	978	1 117	729
	Of which:									
2.1	- Petrol	...	...	...	...	...	...	-	-	-
2.2	- Diesel	...	...	...	...	...	964	978	1 117	729
2.3	- Electricity	550	523	500	...	...	...	-	-	-
1.4	- Other sources	...	...	...	...	...	...	-	-	-
3	Lorries	83 035	89 866	86 824	12 078	18 025	19 226	21 870	48 403	42 687
	Of which:									
3.1	- Petrol	...	...	...	...	...	2 897	...	5 330	3 879
3.2	- Diesel	...	...	...	...	...	16 292	...	43 073	38 808
1.4	- Other sources	...	...	...	...	...	37	...	-	-

For note see end of table.   Voir note à la fin du tableau.   См. примечания в конце таблицы.

113

10 (b). Road vehicle fleet in the country at 31 December - By fuel type
10 (b). Parc automobile du pays au 31 décembre - Par type de combustible utilisé
10 (b). Парк автодорожных транспортных средств страны по состоянию на 31 декабря - по типу двигателя

(Number - Nombre - Число)

		Netherlands Pays-Bas [1] Нидерланды			Norway Norvège [1] Норвегия			Poland Pologne [1] Польша		
		1990	1998	1999	1990	1998	1999	1990	1998	1999
1	Passenger cars	5 205 000	6 119 581	...	1 613 037	1 786 404	1 814 000	5 260 646	8 890 763	9 283 000
	Of which:									
1.1	- Petrol	4 058 000	5 051 000	...	1 564 326	1 673 000	1 691 000	...	8 048 000	8 380 000
1.2	- Diesel	548 000	718 000	...	48 711	113 000	123 000	...	814 000	749 000
1.3	- Electricity	-	-	...	-	-	-	...	29 000	154 000
1.4	- Other sources	599 000	350 581	...	-	404	-	...	- 237	-
2	Motor coaches, Buses and Trolleybuses	11 628	11 006	...	21 222	36 218	37 039	92 403	80 827	78 958
	Of which:									
2.1	- Petrol	37	17	...	4 714	4 451	4 168	...	7 881	7 944
2.2	- Diesel	11 518	10 779	...	16 508	31 767	32 871	...	71 862	69 086
2.3	- Electricity	-	-	...	-	-	-	...	236	241
1.4	- Other sources	73	210	...	-	-	-	...	848	1 687
3	Lorries	491 000	710 169	...	304 327	389 696	...	1 010 143	1 484 575	1 597 874
	Of which:									
3.1	- Petrol	...	93 525	...	...	...	...	...	546 392	610 244
3.2	- Diesel	...	594 717	...	...	...	...	...	640 659	672 218
1.4	- Other sources	...	21 927	...	...	...	...	...	297 524	315 412

		Republic of Moldova République de Moldova Республика Молдова			Russian Federation Fédération de Russie Российская Федерация			Slovakia Slovaquie Словакия		
		1990	1998	1999	1990	1998	1999	1990	1998	1999
1	Passenger cars	208 984	222 769	232 000	8 964 000	18 819 558	19 718 000	875 550	1 196 109	1 236 000
	Of which:									
1.1	- Petrol	...	...	...	8 947 700	...	...	...	...	...
1.2	- Diesel	...	...	...	16 300	...	...	...	...	...
1.3	- Electricity	...	...	...	...	...	...	...	...	...
1.4	- Other sources	...	...	...	...	...	...	...	...	...
2	Motor coaches, Buses and Trolleybuses	11 910	12 917	13 582	473 300	639 732	645 396	14 301	11 515	11 335
	Of which:									
2.1	- Petrol	9 641	5 757	4 355	...	...	...	...	...	...
2.2	- Diesel	1 534	1 609	1 589	...	...	...	...	...	...
2.3	- Electricity	605	410	403	28 600	12 257	...	...	222	234
1.4	- Other sources	130	5 141	7 235	...	...	...	...	...	...
3	Lorries	76 909	57 404	52 430	2 660 200	3 108 231	3 196 177	145 531	154 771	157 651
	Of which:									
3.1	- Petrol	60 888	30 846	25 040	...	...	...	...	...	...
3.2	- Diesel	12 952	10 193	9 285	...	...	...	...	...	...
1.4	- Other sources	3 069	16 365	18 105	...	...	...	...	...	...

For note see end of table.	Voir note à la fin du tableau.	См. примечания в конце таблицы.

114

ROAD TRANSPORT - TRANSPORT ROUTIER
АВТОМОБИЛЬНЫЕ ДОРОГИ

10 (b). Road vehicle fleet in the country at 31 December - By fuel type
10 (b). Parc automobile du pays au 31 décembre - Par type de combustible utilisé
10 (b). Парк автодорожных транспортных средств страны по состоянию на 31 декабря - по типу двигателя

(Number - Nombre - Число)

		Slovenia Slovénie Словения			Spain Espagne Испания			Sweden Suède [1] Швеция		
		1990	1998	1999	1990	1998	1999	1990	1998	1999
1	Passenger cars	578 268	814 000	849 000	11 995 640	16 050 057	16 847 000	3 600 518	3 790 695	3 890 000
	Of which:									
1.1	- Petrol	...	735 000	763 000	10 774 894	12 681 210	12 803 000	3 494 345	3 629 000	3 710 000
1.2	- Diesel	...	78 000	85 000	1 220 746	3 368 847	4 044 000	104 672	161 000	179 000
1.3	- Electricity	...	-	-	-	-	-	1 501	1 000	1 000
1.4	- Other sources	...	1 000	1 000	-	-	-	-	- 305	-
2	Motor coaches, Buses and Trolleybuses	3 077	2 327	2 319	45 767	51 805	53 540	14 595	14 924	14 869
	Of which:									
2.1	- Petrol	...	34	36	934	934	930	888	739	650
2.2	- Diesel	...	2 286	2 274	44 833	50 871	52 610	13 632	13 524	13 481
2.3	- Electricity	...	-	-	-	-	-	75	661	738
1.4	- Other sources	...	7	9	-	-	-	(a)	(a)	(a)
3	Lorries	30 767	45 769	47 888	2 332 928	3 393 446	3 604 972	309 520	331 810	347 805
	Of which:									
3.1	- Petrol	...	6 932	7 070	842 860	878 138	858 454	195 171	189 393	186 498
3.2	- Diesel	...	38 519	40 395	1 490 068	2 515 308	2 746 518	114 059	141 893	160 918
1.4	- Other sources	...	318	423	-	-	-	290	524	389

		Switzerland Suisse [4] Швейцария			Tajikistan Tadjikistan Таджикистан			The FYR of Macedonia [5]		
		1990	1998	1999	1990	1998	1999	1990	1998	1999
1	Passenger cars	2 985 399	3 383 273	3 467 275	...	154 283	148 825	230 774	288 678	290 000
	Of which:									
1.1	- Petrol	2 905 764	3 269 384	...	...	...	...	225 004	277 000	276 000
1.2	- Diesel	79 129	112 720	...	...	...	...	4 393	10 000	12 000
1.3	- Electricity	...	1 169	...	...	...	...	-	-	-
1.4	- Other sources	...	-	...	...	...	...	1 377	1 678	2 000
2	Motor coaches, Buses and Trolleybuses	31 293	39 012	39 692	...	9 777	9 242	2 320	2 478	2 479
	Of which:									
2.1	- Petrol	18 411	...	...	...	...	...	413	464	468
2.2	- Diesel	12 747	...	...	...	...	...	1 852	1 961	1 953
2.3	- Electricity	-	...	...	...	170	147	-	-	-
1.4	- Other sources	135	...	...	...	...	...	55	53	58
3	Lorries	246 194	259 871	266 074	...	61 745	53 275	15 489	20 075	20 011
	Of which:									
3.1	- Petrol	152 544	147 992	...	...	...	...	3 266	5 661	5 802
3.2	- Diesel	93 584	111 491	...	...	...	...	11 949	14 126	13 911
1.4	- Other sources	66	388	...	...	...	...	274	288	298

For note see end of table.	Voir note à la fin du tableau.	См. примечания в конце таблицы.

115

ROAD TRANSPORT - TRANSPORT ROUTIER
АВТОМОБИЛЬНЫЕ ДОРОГИ

10 (b). Road vehicle fleet in the country at 31 December - By fuel type
10 (b). Parc automobile du pays au 31 décembre - Par type de combustible utilisé
10 (b). Парк автодорожных транспортных средств страны по состоянию на 31 декабря - по типу двигателя

(Number - Nombre - Число)

		Ukraine Ukraine Украина			United Kingdom Royaume-Uni [6] Соединенное Королевство					
		1990	1998	1999	1990	1998	1999			
1	**Passenger cars**	3 362 697	5 127 323	...	21 485 000	23 886 000	24 594 000			
	Of which:									
1.1	- Petrol	...	...	...	...	20 591 000	21 031 000			
1.2	- Diesel	...	...	...	...	2 693 000	2 929 000			
1.3	- Electricity	...	...	...	...	-	-			
1.4	- Other sources	...	...	...	...	602 000	634 000			
2	**Motor coaches, Buses and Trolleybuses**	...	...	...	157 000	166 000	173 000			
	Of which:									
2.1	- Petrol	...	...	...	...	36 000	33 000			
2.2	- Diesel	...	...	...	...	125 000	140 000			
2.3	- Electricity	...	5 623	...	...	-	-			
1.4	- Other sources	...	...	...	...	5 000	-			
3	**Lorries**	...	...	...	2 330 200	2 644 000	2 802 000			
	Of which:									
3.1	- Petrol	...	...	...	...	708 000	631 000			
3.2	- Diesel	...	...	...	...	1 936 000	2 088 000			
1.4	- Other sources	...	...	...	...	-	83 000			

NOTES TO TABLE 10(b) - NOTES DU TABLEAU 10(b) - ПРИМЕЧАНИЯ К ТАБЛИЦЕ 10(b)

General notes - Notes générales - Общие примечания

(a) Included under item 2.3.

(a) Compris sous la rubrique 2.3.

(a) Включено в статью 2.3.

Country notes - Notes relatives aux pays - Примечания к данным, представляемым странами

1- Due to rounding off, total for passenger cars might slightly differ from the number indicated in table 10.

1- En raison des arrondissements, le total des voitures particulières peut être légèrement différent de celui indiqué dans le tableau 10.

1- В связи с округлением, итоги по пассажирским автомобилям могут несколько отличаться от данных, приведенных в таблице 10.

2- Excluding vehicles registered in Aland.

2- Non compris les véhicules immatriculés à Aland.

2- За исключением дорожно-транспортных средств, зарегистрированных на Аландских островах.

3- Road tractors are included with lorries.

3- Les tracteurs routiers sont comptabilisés avec les camions.

3- Дорожные тягачи включены в раздел грузовых автомобилей.

4- Excluding trolley buses (item 2).

4- Non compris les trolleybus (rubrique 2).

4- За исключением троллейбусов (статья 2).

5- The former Yugoslav Republic of Macedonia.

5- L'ex-République yougoslave de Macédoine.

5- Бывшая Югославская Республика Македония.

6- Data refer to Great Britain.

6- Les données se réfèrent à la Grande Bretagne.

6- Данные относятся к Великобритании.

ROAD TRANSPORT - TRANSPORT ROUTIER
АВТОМОБИЛЬНЫЕ ДОРОГИ

10 (c). Goods road transport equipment at 31 December - By load capacity

10 (c). Vehicules routiers pour le transport des marchandises au 31 décembre - Par classe de charge utile

10 (c). Транспортное оборудование на 31 декабря - по грузоподъемности

Item Rubrique Статья	Description	Description	Описание
	Goods road vehicles registered in the country (number)	**Véhicules routiers immatriculés dans le pays (nombre)**	**Автодорожные транспортные средства, зарегистрированные в стране (количество)**
1	**Lorries**	**Camions**	**Грузовые автомобили**
1.1	- Up to 999 kg	- Jusqu'à 999 kg	- До 999 кг
1.2	- 1 000 kg - 1 499 kg	- 1 000 kg - 1 499 kg	- 1 000 кг - 1 499 кг
1.3	- 1 500kg - 2 999 kg	- 1 500kg - 2 999 kg	- 1 500 кг - 2 999 кг
1.4	- 3 000 kg - 4 999 kg	- 3 000 kg - 4 999 kg	- 3 000 кг - 4 999 кг
1.5	- 5 000 kg - 6 999 kg	- 5 000 kg - 6 999 kg	- 5 000 кг - 6 999 кг
1.6	- 7 000 kg - 9 999 kg	- 7 000 kg - 9 999 kg	- 7 000 кг - 9 999 кг
1.7	- 10 000 kg - 14 999 kg	- 10 000 kg - 14 999 kg	- 10 000 кг - 14 999 кг
1.8	- 15 000 kg and more	- 15 000 kg et plus	- 15 000 кг и более
3	**Semi-trailers**	**Semi-remorques**	**Полуприцепы**
3.1	- Up to 4 999 kg	- Jusqu'à 4 999 kg	- До 4 999 кг
3.2	- 5 000 kg - 9 999 kg	- 5 000 kg - 9 999 kg	- 5 000 кг - 9 999 кг
3.0	- 10 000 kg - 14 999 kg	- 10 000 kg - 14 999 kg	- 10 000 кг - 14 999 кг
3.3	- 15 000 kg - 19 999 kg	- 15 000 kg - 19 999 kg	- 15 000 кг - 19 999 кг
3.4	- 20 000 kg and more	- 20 000 kg et plus	- 20 000 кг и более
4	**Trailers**	**Remorques**	**Прицепы**
4.1	- Up to 4 999 kg	- Jusqu'à 4 999 kg	- До 4 999 кг
4.2	- 5 000 kg - 9 999 kg	- 5 000 kg - 9 999 kg	- 5 000 кг - 9 999 кг
4.3	- 10 000 kg - 14 999 kg	- 10 000 kg - 14 999 kg	- 10 000 кг - 14 999 кг
4.4	- 15 000 kg and more	- 15 000 kg et plus	- 15 000 кг и более
	Load capacity of goods road vehicles registered in the country (1000 tonnes)	**Charge utile des véhicules routiers immatriculés dans le pays (1000 tonnes)**	**Грузоподъемность автотранспортных средств, зарегистрированных в стране (1000 тонн)**
6	**Lorries**	**Camions**	**Грузовые автомобили**
6.1	- Up to 999 kg	- Jusqu'à 999 kg	- До 999 кг
6.2	- 1 000 kg - 1 499 kg	- 1 000 kg - 1 499 kg	- 1 000 кг - 1 499 кг
6.3	- 1 500kg - 2 999 kg	- 1 500kg - 2 999 kg	- 1 500 кг - 2 999 кг
6.4	- 3 000 kg - 4 999 kg	- 3 000 kg - 4 999 kg	- 3 000 кг - 4 999 кг
6.5	- 5 000 kg - 6 999 kg	- 5 000 kg - 6 999 kg	- 5 000 кг - 6 999 кг
6.6	- 7 000 kg - 9 999 kg	- 7 000 kg - 9 999 kg	- 7 000 кг - 9 999 кг
6.7	- 10 000 kg - 14 999 kg	- 10 000 kg - 14 999 kg	- 10 000 кг - 14 999 кг
6.8	- 15 000 kg and more	- 15 000 kg et plus	- 15 000 кг и более
7	**Semi-trailers**	**Semi-remorques**	**Полуприцепы**
7.1	- Up to 4 999 kg	- Jusqu'à 4 999 kg	- До 4 999 кг
7.2	- 5 000 kg - 9 999 kg	- 5 000 kg - 9 999 kg	- 5 000 кг - 9 999 кг
7.3	- 10 000 kg - 14 999 kg	- 10 000 kg - 14 999 kg	- 10 000 кг - 14 999 кг
7.4	- 15 000 kg - 19 999 kg	- 15 000 kg - 19 999 kg	- 15 000 кг - 19 999 кг
7.5	- 20 000 kg and more	- 20 000 kg et plus	- 20 000 кг и более
8	**Trailers**	**Remorques**	**Прицепы**
8.1	- Up to 4 999 kg	- Jusqu'à 4 999 kg	- До 4 999 кг
8.2	- 5 000 kg - 9 999 kg	- 5 000 kg - 9 999 kg	- 5 000 кг - 9 999 кг
8.3	- 10 000 kg - 14 999 kg	- 10 000 kg - 14 999 kg	- 10 000 кг - 14 999 кг
8.4	- 15 000 kg and more	- 15 000 kg et plus	- 15 000 кг и более

ROAD TRANSPORT - TRANSPORT ROUTIER
АВТОМОБИЛЬНЫЕ ДОРОГИ

10 (c). Goods road transport equipment at 31 December - By load capacity
10 (c). Vehicules routiers pour le transport des marchandises au 31 décembre - Par classe de charge utile
10 (c). Транспортное оборудование на 31 декабря - по грузоподъемности

		Armenia Arménie Армения			Austria Autriche Австрия			Belgium Belgique [1] Бельгия		
		1990	1998	1999	1990	1998	1999	1990	1998	1999
		Number - Nombre - Число								
1	**Lorries**	...	...	...	252 504	309 630	318 757	343 241	484 179	514 226
1.1	Up to 999 kg	...	...	...	176 116	182 832	190 733	...	231 676	253 394
1.2	1 000 kg - 1 499 kg	...	...	...	...	50 945	53 211	...	94 188	93 881
1.3	1 500kg - 2 999 kg	...	...	...	35 356	21 173	20 914	...	41 162	38 706
1.4	3 000 kg - 4 999 kg	...	...	...	...	12 027	11 458	...	22 020	21 506
1.5	5 000 kg - 6 999 kg	...	...	...	13 564	10 537	9 915	...	15 250	15 135
1.6	7 000 kg - 9 999 kg	...	...	...	20 118	17 138	16 404	...	18 433	18 006
1.7	10 000 kg - 14 999 kg	...	...	...	7 313	12 043	12 537	...	17 651	17 850
1.8	15 000 kg and more	...	...	...	37	2 935	3 585	...	5 692	5 663
3	**Semi-trailers**	...	1 102	1 539	(a)	20 317	22 206	...	64 317	68 080
3.1	Up to 4 999 kg	...	...	...	(a)	...	...	...	951	939
3.2	5 000 - 9 999 kg	...	...	...	(a)	...	...	...	673	656
3.3	10 000 - 14 999 kg	...	...	...	(a)	...	...	...	1 557	1 524
3.4	15 000 - 19 999 kg	...	995	1 420	(a)	...	...	...	1 427	1 404
3.5	20 000 kg and more	...	107	119	(a)	...	...	...	55 296	57 547
4	**Trailers**	...	1 638	1 323	296 240	445 959	517 788	...	91 107	94 926
4.1	Up to 4 999 kg	...	1 240	946	247 777	385 740	...	...	74 584	77 355
4.2	5 000 - 9 999 kg	...	358	336	28 283	18 691	...	...	1 538	1 523
4.3	10 000 - 14 999 kg	...	(b)	(b)	(b)	13 853	...	...	3 669	3 629
4.4	15 000 kg and more	...	40	41	20 180	27 675	...	...	5 594	5 552
		1000 tonnes - 1000 тонн								
5	**Lorries**	...	...	...	563.8	...	...	806.3	924.5	942.5
5.1	Up to 999 kg	...	...	...	135.8	...	...	...	76.3	103.6
5.2	1 000 kg - 1 499 kg	...	...	...	...	...	...	...	115.2	114.7
5.3	1 500kg - 2 999 kg	...	...	...	103.3	...	...	...	81.9	77.3
5.4	3 000 kg - 4 999 kg	...	...	...	...	...	...	...	86.0	84.1
5.5	5 000 kg - 6 999 kg	...	...	...	80.2	...	...	...	90.7	89.9
5.6	7 000 kg - 9 999 kg	...	...	...	161.9	...	...	...	156.7	153.2
5.7	10 000 kg - 14 999 kg	...	...	...	82.0	...	...	...	218.7	221.7
5.8	15 000 kg and more	...	...	...	0.6	...	...	...	99.0	98.0
6	**Semi-trailers**	...	11.4	14.1	(a)	...	...	...	1 673.7	1 748.9
6.1	Up to 4 999 kg	...	...	...	(a)	...	...	...	1.3	1.3
6.2	5 000 - 9 999 kg	...	...	...	(a)	...	...	...	5.4	5.2
6.3	10 000 - 14 999 kg	...	...	...	(a)	...	...	...	19.4	19.1
6.4	15 000 - 19 999 kg	...	...	...	(a)	...	...	...	24.9	24.5
6.5	20 000 kg and more	...	...	...	(a)	...	...	...	1 623.4	1 699.6
7	**Trailers**	...	8.8	6.0	807.9	...	...	...	253.5	257.4
7.1	Up to 4 999 kg	...	...	...	155.1	...	...	...	84.9	90.0
7.2	5 000 - 9 999 kg	...	...	...	236.3	...	...	...	11.4	11.3
7.3	10 000 - 14 999 kg	...	...	...	(c)	...	...	...	48.3	47.7
7.4	15 000 kg and more	...	...	...	416.5	...	...	...	108.9	108.3

For note see end of table.   Voir note à la fin du tableau.   См. примечания в конце таблицы.

118

ROAD TRANSPORT - TRANSPORT ROUTIER
АВТОМОБИЛЬНЫЕ ДОРОГИ

10 (c). Goods road transport equipment at 31 December - By load capacity
10 (c). Vehicules routiers pour le transport des marchandises au 31 décembre - Par classe de charge utile
10 (c). Транспортное оборудование на 31 декабря - по грузоподъемности

		Croatia Croatie Хорватия			Czech Republic République tchèque Чешская Республика			Denmark Danemark Дания		
		1990	1998	1999	1990	1998	1999	1990	1998	1999
		Number - Nombre - Число								
1	**Lorries**	**56 823**	**110 360**	**112 675**	**202 929**	**260 276**	**268 259**	**286 613**	**347 136**	**362 002**
1.1	Up to 999 kg	...	37 341	38 628	...	76 569	86 390	226 454	148 493	163 173
1.2	1 000 kg - 1 499 kg	...	28 179	29 192	...	36 011	41 534	(d)	161 583	161 752
1.3	1 500kg - 2 999 kg	...	17 126	17 573	...	55 055	53 959	33 867	5 135	5 102
1.4	3 000 kg - 4 999 kg	...	7 092	7 090	...	35 910	34 380	(e)	5 248	5 215
1.5	5 000 kg - 6 999 kg	...	5 742	5 464	...	7 979	6 651	6 756	5 507	5 308
1.6	7 000 kg - 9 999 kg	...	6 892	6 747	...	33 183	30 372	9 091	8 139	8 058
1.7	10 000 kg - 14 999 kg	...	5 121	5 111	...	15 014	14 549	9 940	10 076	9 988
1.8	15 000 kg and more	...	2 867	2 870	...	334	424	505	2 955	3 406
3	**Semi-trailers**	...	**7 939**	**8 210**	...	**20 283**	**21 483**	**14 798**	**23 211**	**23 594**
3.1	Up to 4 999 kg	...	2 133	2 281	...	346	343	...	177	177
3.2	5 000 - 9 999 kg	...	231	230	...	189	211	...	158	148
3.3	10 000 - 14 999 kg	...	140	137	...	762	682	...	325	382
3.4	15 000 - 19 999 kg	...	147	141	...	653	584	...	378	445
3.5	20 000 kg and more	...	5 288	5 421	...	18 315	19 663	13 434	22 173	22 442
4	**Trailers**	...	**13 921**	**14 682**	...	**83 645**	**93 207**	**302 923**	**473 357**	**502 616**
4.1	Up to 4 999 kg	...	6 454	7 027	...	55 578	66 452	291 486	461 338	490 443
4.2	5 000 - 9 999 kg	...	2 265	2 457	...	7 374	6 935	3 834	2 798	2 702
4.3	10 000 - 14 999 kg	...	2 792	2 850	...	14 987	14 361	(b)	4 624	4 707
4.4	15 000 kg and more	...	2 410	2 348	...	5 674	5 459	7 603	4 597	4 764
		1000 tonnes - 1000 тонн								
5	**Lorries**	...	**339.0**	**339.0**	...	**831.4**	**801.8**	**527.0**	**629.0**	**646.0**
5.1	Up to 999 kg	...	26.0	27.0	...	47.6	54.9	204.0	104.0	114.0
5.2	1 000 kg - 1 499 kg	...	23.0	24.0	...	43.1	50.0	(f)	213.0	214.0
5.3	1 500kg - 2 999 kg	...	34.0	35.0	...	117.7	114.4	75.0	12.0	12.0
5.4	3 000 kg - 4 999 kg	...	27.0	27.0	...	124.7	118.9	(g)	21.0	21.0
5.5	5 000 kg - 6 999 kg	...	34.0	32.0	...	45.1	37.8	40.0	33.0	32.0
5.6	7 000 kg - 9 999 kg	...	57.0	56.0	...	279.3	255.5	76.0	69.0	68.0
5.7	10 000 kg - 14 999 kg	...	63.0	64.0	...	168.0	162.8	123.0	127.0	127.0
5.8	15 000 kg and more	...	75.0	74.0	...	5.9	7.4	9.0	50.0	58.0
6	**Semi-trailers**	...	**147.0**	**151.0**	...	**491.7**	**529.6**	**380.0**	**652.0**	**668.0**
6.1	Up to 4 999 kg	...	5.0	5.0	...	0.8	0.8	...	1.0	1.0
6.2	5 000 - 9 999 kg	...	1.0	1.0	...	1.3	1.5	...	1.0	1.0
6.3	10 000 - 14 999 kg	...	2.0	2.0	...	9.8	8.7	...	4.0	5.0
6.4	15 000 - 19 999 kg	...	3.0	3.0	...	11.5	10.2	...	7.0	8.0
6.5	20 000 kg and more	...	136.0	140.0	...	468.3	508.4	360.0	639.0	654.0
7	**Trailers**	...	**114.0**	**116.0**	...	**373.4**	**366.4**	**238.0**	**348.0**	**366.0**
7.1	Up to 4 999 kg	...	15.0	17.0	...	45.2	51.8	109.0	188.0	203.0
7.2	5 000 - 9 999 kg	...	15.0	16.0	...	45.0	42.4	74.0	21.0	20.0
7.3	10 000 - 14 999 kg	...	34.0	35.0	...	174.0	167.2	(h)	60.0	61.0
7.4	15 000 kg and more	...	49.0	48.0	...	109.2	105.0	55.0	79.0	82.0

For note see end of table.   Voir note à la fin du tableau.   См. примечания в конце таблицы.

119

10 (c). Goods road transport equipment at 31 December - By load capacity
10 (c). Vehicules routiers pour le transport des marchandises au 31 décembre - Par classe de charge utile
10 (c). Транспортное оборудование на 31 декабря - по грузоподъемности

		Estonia / Estonie / Эстония			Finland / Finlande [2] / Финляндия			France / France / Франция		
		1990	1998	1999	1990	1998	1999	1990	1998	1999
		Number - Nombre - Число								
1	**Lorries**	**67 700**	**80 617**	**81 030**	**261 495**	**280 610**	**293 707**	**3 567 767**	**4 984 586**	**5 074 835**
1.1	Up to 999 kg	...	...	...	204 258	98 492	112 532	2 347 450	3 455 416	3 546 239
1.2	1 000 kg - 1 499 kg	...	...	...	(d)	124 386	122 289	676 481	851 511	855 693
1.3	1 500kg - 2 999 kg	...	...	...	15 250	9 473	9 740	308 187	358 828	354 949
1.4	3 000 kg - 4 999 kg	...	...	...	(e)	5 276	5 440	60 601	63 957	61 155
1.5	5 000 kg - 6 999 kg	...	...	...	6 265	4 771	4 812	45 318	62 156	62 627
1.6	7 000 kg - 9 999 kg	...	...	...	10 004	7 665	7 627	65 842	91 150	91 796
1.7	10 000 kg - 14 999 kg	...	...	...	19 922	16 753	17 069	55 922	69 790	71 023
1.8	15 000 kg and more	...	...	...	5 796	10 751	10 968	7 966	31 778	31 353
3	**Semi-trailers**	**7 976**	**35 785**	**36 950**	**6 291**	**12 474**	**12 656**	**138 024**	**260 602**	**269 224**
3.1	Up to 4 999 kg	...	...	...	...	57	59	822	1 318	1 282
3.2	5 000 - 9 999 kg	...	...	...	...	161	164	1 392	2 612	2 482
3.3	10 000 - 14 999 kg	...	...	...	...	1 307	1 350	6 736	9 837	8 915
3.4	15 000 - 19 999 kg	...	...	...	...	10 227	10 326	6 193	12 517	12 453
3.5	20 000 kg and more	1 103	...	...	381	717	706	122 881	234 318	244 092
4	**Trailers**	**8 542**	**...**	**...**	**338 724**	**464 806**	**486 949**	**26 960**	**50 268**	**51 108**
4.1	Up to 4 999 kg	4 124	...	...	320 453	446 896	466 212	2 387	3 468	3 216
4.2	5 000 - 9 999 kg	...	...	...	...	155	168	6 543	12 708	12 914
4.3	10 000 - 14 999 kg	...	...	...	...	1 398	1 347	9 669	16 774	17 016
4.4	15 000 kg and more	173	...	...	14 889	16 283	16 889	8 361	17 318	17 962
		1000 tonnes - 1000 тонн								
5	**Lorries**	**...**	**...**	**...**	**717.0**	**747.0**	**772.0**	**4 415.0**	**6 568.0**	**6 628.0**
5.1	Up to 999 kg	...	...	...	199.0	71.0	83.0	1 174.0	2 108.0	2 163.0
5.2	1 000 kg - 1 499 kg	...	...	...	(f)	141.0	140.0	860.0	1 056.0	1 061.0
5.3	1 500kg - 2 999 kg	...	...	...	42.0	19.0	20.0	532.0	599.0	593.0
5.4	3 000 kg - 4 999 kg	...	...	...	(g)	21.0	22.0	248.0	264.0	253.0
5.5	5 000 kg - 6 999 kg	...	...	...	38.0	29.0	29.0	269.0	370.0	373.0
5.6	7 000 kg - 9 999 kg	...	...	...	83.0	64.0	64.0	559.0	783.0	789.0
5.7	10 000 kg - 14 999 kg	...	...	...	252.0	217.0	223.0	649.0	854.0	869.0
5.8	15 000 kg and more	...	...	...	103.0	185.0	189.0	124.0	534.0	527.0
6	**Semi-trailers**	**93.0**	**...**	**...**	**95.0**	**224.0**	**226.0**	**3 325.0**	**6 654.0**	**6 902.0**
6.1	Up to 4 999 kg	...	...	...	...	0.0	0.0	2.0	4.0	3.0
6.2	5 000 - 9 999 kg	...	...	...	...	1.0	1.0	11.0	20.0	19.0
6.3	10 000 - 14 999 kg	...	...	...	...	18.0	19.0	89.0	122.0	111.0
6.4	15 000 - 19 999 kg	...	...	...	...	184.0	186.0	126.0	228.0	227.0
6.5	20 000 kg and more	...	...	...	11.0	21.0	19.0	3 097.0	6 280.0	6 542.0
7	**Trailers**	**45.0**	**...**	**...**	**515.0**	**639.0**	**668.0**	**351.0**	**626.0**	**680.0**
7.1	Up to 4 999 kg	...	...	...	158.0	234.0	246.0	9.0	9.0	11.0
7.2	5 000 - 9 999 kg	...	...	...	...	1.0	1.0	48.0	95.0	109.0
7.3	10 000 - 14 999 kg	...	...	...	...	19.0	18.0	128.0	210.0	222.0
7.4	15 000 kg and more	...	...	...	311.0	385.0	401.0	166.0	312.0	338.0

For note see end of table.   Voir note à la fin du tableau.   См. примечания в конце таблицы.

ROAD TRANSPORT - TRANSPORT ROUTIER
АВТОМОБИЛЬНЫЕ ДОРОГИ

10 (c). Goods road transport equipment at 31 December - By load capacity
10 (c). Vehicules routiers pour le transport des marchandises au 31 décembre - Par classe de charge utile
10 (c). Транспортное оборудование на 31 декабря - по грузоподъемности

		Germany Allemagne [3] Германия			Hungary Hongrie Венгрия			Iceland Islande Исландия		
		1990	1998	1999	1990	1998	1999	1990	1998	1999
		Number - Nombre - Число								
1	**Lorries**	...	2 370 599	2 465 535	208 302	295 048	308 944	13 122	15 905	17 115
1.1	Up to 999 kg	...	1 177 617	1 240 802	...	95 861	100 267	4 749	7 229	7 912
1.2	1 000 kg - 1 499 kg	...	350 095	376 107	...	95 049	104 447	...	3 497	3 799
1.3	1 500kg - 2 999 kg	...	339 714	351 310	...	30 676	34 267	3 846	1 208	1 293
1.4	3 000 kg - 4 999 kg	...	174 276	167 664	...	35 149	32 428	908	922	963
1.5	5 000 kg - 6 999 kg	...	61 094	59 646	...	20 117	19 452	446	393	401
1.6	7 000 kg - 9 999 kg	...	121 322	118 747	...	10 765	10 508	1 215	969	980
1.7	10 000 kg - 14 999 kg	...	85 288	82 866	...	6 812	6 945	1 286	1 077	1 096
1.8	15 000 kg and more	...	61 193	68 393	...	619	630	672	610	671
3	**Semi-trailers**	...	179 766	193 580	...	9 206	10 868	775	1 119	1 213
3.1	Up to 4 999 kg	...	3 761	...	...	526	689	...	11	19
3.2	5 000 - 9 999 kg	...	5 600	...	...	1 009	1 042	...	9	10
3.3	10 000 - 14 999 kg	...	11 770	11 615	...	626	618	...	33	34
3.4	15 000 - 19 999 kg	...	5 498	5 406	...	452	472	...	127	126
3.5	20 000 kg and more	...	153 137	167 367	...	6 593	8 047	...	939	1 024
4	**Trailers**	...	3 191 543	3 308 892	...	80 565	83 983	1 113	3 756	3 930
4.1	Up to 4 999 kg	...	2 861 758*	3 065 448*	...	47 898	48 230	...	3 202	3 341
4.2	5 000 - 9 999 kg	...	73 063	71 703	...	24 271	23 922	...	303	308
4.3	10 000 - 14 999 kg	...	125 667	132 276	...	4 605	5 517	...	169	186
4.4	15 000 kg and more	...	131 055	39 465	...	3 791	6 314	...	82	95
		1000 tonnes - 1000 тонн								
5	**Lorries**	...	6 068.0	6 215.0	...	679.0	683.0	...	50.6	53.0
5.1	Up to 999 kg	...	864.0	917.0	...	67.0	70.0	...	4.8	5.0
5.2	1 000 kg - 1 499 kg	...	407.0	441.0	...	107.0	120.0	...	4.1	4.0
5.3	1 500kg - 2 999 kg	...	766.0	791.0	...	60.0	65.0	...	2.4	3.0
5.4	3 000 kg - 4 999 kg	...	631.0	606.0	...	147.0	134.0	...	3.7	4.0
5.5	5 000 kg - 6 999 kg	...	364.0	356.0	...	115.0	110.0	...	2.3	2.0
5.6	7 000 kg - 9 999 kg	...	1 027.0	1 007.0	...	90.0	89.0	...	8.3	8.0
5.7	10 000 kg - 14 999 kg	...	1 040.0	1 012.0	...	82.0	81.0	...	13.6	14.0
5.8	15 000 kg and more	...	969.0	1 085.0	...	11.0	14.0	...	11.3	13.0
6	**Semi-trailers**	...	4 435.0	4 834.0	...	186.0	230.0	...	28.9	30.0
6.1	Up to 4 999 kg	...	7.0	7.0	...	1.0	1.0	...	0.0	-
6.2	5 000 - 9 999 kg	...	44.0	42.0	...	8.0	8.0	...	0.1	-
6.3	10 000 - 14 999 kg	...	145.0	143.0	...	7.0	7.0	...	0.4	-
6.4	15 000 - 19 999 kg	...	101.0	99.0	...	8.0	8.0	...	2.3	2.0
6.5	20 000 kg and more	...	4 138.0	4 543.0	...	162.0	206.0	...	26.0	28.0
7	**Trailers**	...	5 013.0	5 193.0	...	345.0	401.0	...	10.5	11.0
7.1	Up to 4 999 kg	...	2 094*	2 204*	...	49.0	46.0	...	4.8	5.0
7.2	5 000 - 9 999 kg	...	529.0	521.0	...	151.0	151.0	...	2.0	2.0
7.3	10 000 - 14 999 kg	...	1 636.0	1 733.0	...	55.0	65.0	...	2.1	2.0
7.4	15 000 kg and more	...	754.0	735.0	...	90.0	139.0	...	1.6	2.0

For note see end of table.　　　　Voir note à la fin du tableau.　　　　См. примечания в конце таблицы.

121

ROAD TRANSPORT - TRANSPORT ROUTIER
АВТОМОБИЛЬНЫЕ ДОРОГИ

10 (c). Goods road transport equipment at 31 December - By load capacity

10 (c). Vehicules routiers pour le transport des marchandises au 31 décembre - Par classe de charge utile

10 (c). Транспортное оборудование на 31 декабря - по грузоподъемности

		Ireland Irlande Ирландия			Kazakhstan Kazakhstan Казахстан			Kyrgyzstan Kirghizistan Кыргызстан		
		1990	1998	1999	1990	1998	1999	1990	1998	1999
		Number - Nombre - Число								
1	**Lorries**	143 166	170 866	188 814	...	128 133	106 331	...	...	...
1.1	Up to 999 kg	...	26 777	25 350	...	9 276	8 134	...	...	...
1.2	1 000 kg - 1 499 kg	...	63 973	70 201	...	(d)	(d)	...	...	...
1.3	1 500kg - 2 999 kg	...	...	...	...	59 276	46 583	...	...	...
1.4	3 000 kg - 4 999 kg	...	...	...	...	(e)	(e)	...	...	...
1.5	5 000 kg - 6 999 kg	...	...	...	...	23 915	20 427	...	...	...
1.6	7 000 kg - 9 999 kg	...	...	...	...	17 506	14 843	...	...	...
1.7	10 000 kg - 14 999 kg	...	10 263	13 197	...	15 046	13 049	...	...	...
1.8	15 000 kg and more	...	...	...	...	3 114	3 295	...	...	...
3	**Semi-trailers**	70 744	...	...	...	9 352	7 755	5 987	3 732	3 643
3.1	Up to 4 999 kg	...	...	...	...	...	...	...	...	...
3.2	5 000 - 9 999 kg	...	...	...	...	...	...	...	...	...
3.3	10 000 - 14 999 kg	...	...	...	...	...	...	...	...	...
3.4	15 000 - 19 999 kg	...	...	...	...	...	...	...	3 511	3 457
3.5	20 000 kg and more	...	...	...	...	1 121	1 098	...	221	186
4	**Trailers**	...	...	...	...	20 743	16 131	7 387	13 100	13 533
4.1	Up to 4 999 kg	...	...	...	...	3 219	2 340	...	846	751
4.2	5 000 - 9 999 kg	...	...	...	...	12 931	9 851	...	12 200	12 734
4.3	10 000 - 14 999 kg	...	...	...	...	4 309	3 688	...	(b)	(b)
4.4	15 000 kg and more	...	...	...	...	284	252	...	54	48
		1000 tonnes - 1000 тонн								
5	**Lorries**	...	...	...	...	743.0	646.6	...	...	...
5.1	Up to 999 kg	...	...	...	...	...	...	...	...	...
5.2	1 000 kg - 1 499 kg	...	...	...	...	...	...	...	...	...
5.3	1 500kg - 2 999 kg	...	...	...	...	...	...	...	...	...
5.4	3 000 kg - 4 999 kg	...	...	...	...	...	...	...	...	...
5.5	5 000 kg - 6 999 kg	...	...	...	...	...	...	...	...	...
5.6	7 000 kg - 9 999 kg	...	...	...	...	...	...	...	...	...
5.7	10 000 kg - 14 999 kg	...	...	...	...	...	...	...	...	...
5.8	15 000 kg and more	...	...	...	...	...	...	...	...	...
6	**Semi-trailers**	...	...	...	...	120.7	101.8	...	39.5	34.9
6.1	Up to 4 999 kg	...	...	...	...	...	...	...	...	...
6.2	5 000 - 9 999 kg	...	...	...	...	...	...	...	...	...
6.3	10 000 - 14 999 kg	...	...	...	...	...	...	...	...	...
6.4	15 000 - 19 999 kg	...	...	...	...	...	...	...	...	...
6.5	20 000 kg and more	...	...	...	...	...	...	...	...	...
7	**Trailers**	...	...	...	...	158.9	122.9	...	65.0	69.9
7.1	Up to 4 999 kg	...	...	...	...	...	...	...	...	...
7.2	5 000 - 9 999 kg	...	...	...	...	...	...	...	...	...
7.3	10 000 - 14 999 kg	...	...	...	...	...	...	...	...	...
7.4	15 000 kg and more	...	...	...	...	...	...	...	...	...

For note see end of table.   Voir note à la fin du tableau.   См. примечания в конце таблицы.

ROAD TRANSPORT - TRANSPORT ROUTIER
АВТОМОБИЛЬНЫЕ ДОРОГИ

10 (c). Goods road transport equipment at 31 December - By load capacity

10 (c). Vehicules routiers pour le transport des marchandises au 31 décembre - Par classe de charge utile

10 (c). Транспортное оборудование на 31 декабря - по грузоподъемности

		Latvia Lettonie Латвия			Lithuania Lituanie Литва			Luxembourg Luxembourg Люксембург		
		1990	1998	1999	1990	1998	1999	1990	1998	1999
		Number - Nombre - Число								
1	**Lorries**	**53 692**	**74 954**	**80 112**	**83 035**	**89 866**	**86 824**	**12 078**	**18 025**	**19 226**
1.1	Up to 999 kg	...	11 974	13 948	...	21 568	14 358	3 780	...	2 185
1.2	1 000 kg - 1 499 kg	...	6 403	7 760	...	(d)	8 238	3 032	...	4 031
1.3	1 500kg - 2 999 kg	...	10 035	11 109	...	40 440	13 520	1 631	...	8 199
1.4	3 000 kg - 4 999 kg	...	14 295	14 784	...	(e)	24 011	616	...	850
1.5	5 000 kg - 6 999 kg	...	7 524	7 722	...	10 424	9 503	604	...	800
1.6	7 000 kg - 9 999 kg	...	4 540	4 842	...	9 975	9 588	809	...	1 492
1.7	10 000 kg - 14 999 kg	...	2 957	3 371	...	5 662	6 035	1 606	...	1 669
1.8	15 000 kg and more	...	512	614	...	1 797	1 571	...	...	...
3	**Semi-trailers**	**8 656**	**3 232**	**4 433**	**11 474**	**9 252**	**9 256**	**...**	**...**	**...**
3.1	Up to 4 999 kg	...	...	...	...	...	139	...	...	...
3.2	5 000 - 9 999 kg	...	...	...	...	...	1 492	...	...	...
3.3	10 000 - 14 999 kg	...	...	...	...	...	1 960	...	...	...
3.4	15 000 - 19 999 kg	...	...	...	...	...	697	...	...	...
3.5	20 000 kg and more	1 226	...	...	...	4 438	4 968	...	...	...
4	**Trailers**	**10 571**	**48 336**	**49 612**	**11 836**	**6 255**	**6 365**	**...**	**...**	**...**
4.1	Up to 4 999 kg	3 456	...	...	...	1 581	1 661	...	...	...
4.2	5 000 - 9 999 kg	...	...	...	...	4 239	3 537	...	...	...
4.3	10 000 - 14 999 kg	...	...	...	...	(b)	808	...	...	...
4.4	15 000 kg and more	193	...	...	...	435	359	...	...	...
		1000 tonnes - 1000 тонн								
5	**Lorries**	**236.0**	**222.0**	**242.0**	**...**	**368.0**	**368.0**	**...**	**...**	**...**
5.1	Up to 999 kg	...	10.0	11.0	...	17.0	9.0	...	...	...
5.2	1 000 kg - 1 499 kg	...	7.0	9.0	...	(f)	10.0	...	...	...
5.3	1 500kg - 2 999 kg	...	23.0	25.0	...	129.0	29.0	...	...	...
5.4	3 000 kg - 4 999 kg	...	58.0	59.0	...	(g)	91.0	...	...	...
5.5	5 000 kg - 6 999 kg	...	44.0	48.0	...	55.0	52.0	...	...	...
5.6	7 000 kg - 9 999 kg	...	37.0	39.0	...	76.0	77.0	...	...	...
5.7	10 000 kg - 14 999 kg	...	33.0	38.0	...	58.0	66.0	...	...	...
5.8	15 000 kg and more	...	10.0	13.0	...	33.0	33.0	...	...	...
6	**Semi-trailers**	**102.0**	**...**	**...**	**...**	**159.0**	**168.0**	**...**	**...**	**...**
6.1	Up to 4 999 kg	...	...	...	...	...	1.0	...	...	...
6.2	5 000 - 9 999 kg	...	...	...	...	...	11.0	...	...	...
6.3	10 000 - 14 999 kg	...	...	...	...	...	24.0	...	...	...
6.4	15 000 - 19 999 kg	...	...	...	...	...	12.0	...	...	...
6.5	20 000 kg and more	...	...	...	...	106.0	120.0	...	...	...
7	**Trailers**	**62.0**	**...**	**...**	**...**	**47.0**	**47.0**	**...**	**...**	**...**
7.1	Up to 4 999 kg	...	...	...	...	5.0	5.0	...	...	...
7.2	5 000 - 9 999 kg	...	...	...	...	32.0	24.0	...	...	...
7.3	10 000 - 14 999 kg	...	...	...	...	(h)	9.0	...	...	...
7.4	15 000 kg and more	...	...	...	...	10.0	9.0	...	...	...

For note see end of table.   Voir note à la fin du tableau.   См. примечания в конце таблицы.

123

ROAD TRANSPORT - TRANSPORT ROUTIER
АВТОМОБИЛЬНЫЕ ДОРОГИ

10 (c). Goods road transport equipment at 31 December - By load capacity
10 (c). Vehicules routiers pour le transport des marchandises au 31 décembre - Par classe de charge utile
10 (c). Транспортное оборудование на 31 декабря - по грузоподъемности

		Malta Malte [4] Мальта			Netherlands Pays-Bas Нидерланды			Portugal Portugal Португалия		
		1990	1998	1999	1990	1998	1999	1990	1998	1999
		Number - Nombre - Число								
1	**Lorries**	21 870	48 403	42 687	491 000	710 169	...	508 520	1 436 098	1 540 631
1.1	Up to 999 kg	...	...	...	...	...	...	323 413	...	...
1.2	1 000 kg - 1 499 kg	...	...	...	...	...	...	(d)	...	...
1.3	1 500kg - 2 999 kg	...	...	...	...	...	...	108 862	...	...
1.4	3 000 kg - 4 999 kg	...	...	...	...	10 646	...	(e)	...	...
1.5	5 000 kg - 6 999 kg	...	...	...	...	9 375	...	24 887	...	...
1.6	7 000 kg - 9 999 kg	...	...	...	...	20 679	...	30 300	...	...
1.7	10 000 kg - 14 999 kg	...	...	...	...	17 758	...	21 058	...	...
1.8	15 000 kg and more	...	...	...	...	11 533	...	(i)	...	...
3	**Semi-trailers**	...	403	407	...	...	...	21 315	316 956	332 577
3.1	Up to 4 999 kg	...	-	-	...	...	...	...	...	...
3.2	5 000 - 9 999 kg	...	-	-	...	...	...	...	...	...
3.3	10 000 - 14 999 kg	...	-	-	...	...	...	...	...	...
3.4	15 000 - 19 999 kg	...	-	-	...	...	...	...	...	...
3.5	20 000 kg and more	...	403	407	...	...	...	...	...	...
4	**Trailers**	...	...	...	...	...	...	154 779	...	...
4.1	Up to 4 999 kg	...	...	...	...	...	...	...	...	...
4.2	5 000 - 9 999 kg	...	...	...	...	...	...	...	...	...
4.3	10 000 - 14 999 kg	...	...	...	...	...	...	...	...	...
4.4	15 000 kg and more	...	...	...	...	...	...	...	...	...
		1000 tonnes - 1000 тонн								
5	**Lorries**	...	...	...	...	...	...	1 291.0	...	...
5.1	Up to 999 kg	...	...	...	...	...	...	331.0	...	...
5.2	1 000 kg - 1 499 kg	...	...	...	...	...	...	(f)	...	...
5.3	1 500kg - 2 999 kg	...	...	...	...	...	...	285.0	...	...
5.4	3 000 kg - 4 999 kg	...	...	...	...	...	...	(g)	...	...
5.5	5 000 kg - 6 999 kg	...	...	...	...	...	...	149.0	...	...
5.6	7 000 kg - 9 999 kg	...	...	...	...	...	...	249.0	...	...
5.7	10 000 kg - 14 999 kg	...	...	...	...	...	...	277.0	...	...
5.8	15 000 kg and more	...	...	...	...	...	...	(j)	...	...
6	**Semi-trailers**	...	...	...	...	...	...	393.0	...	...
6.1	Up to 4 999 kg	...	...	...	...	...	...	...	...	...
6.2	5 000 - 9 999 kg	...	...	...	...	...	...	...	...	...
6.3	10 000 - 14 999 kg	...	...	...	...	...	...	...	...	...
6.4	15 000 - 19 999 kg	...	...	...	...	...	...	...	...	...
6.5	20 000 kg and more	...	...	...	...	...	...	...	...	...
7	**Trailers**	...	...	...	...	...	...	...	...	...
7.1	Up to 4 999 kg	...	...	...	...	...	...	...	...	...
7.2	5 000 - 9 999 kg	...	...	...	...	...	...	...	...	...
7.3	10 000 - 14 999 kg	...	...	...	...	...	...	...	...	...
7.4	15 000 kg and more	...	...	...	...	...	...	...	...	...

For note see end of table.   Voir note à la fin du tableau.   См. примечания в конце таблицы.

124

ROAD TRANSPORT - TRANSPORT ROUTIER
АВТОМОБИЛЬНЫЕ ДОРОГИ

10 (c). Goods road transport equipment at 31 December - By load capacity

10 (c). Véhicules routiers pour le transport des marchandises au 31 décembre - Par classe de charge utile

10 (c). Транспортное оборудование на 31 декабря - по грузоподъемности

		Republic of Moldova République de Moldova Республика Молдова			Slovenia Slovénie Словения			Spain Espagne Испания		
		1990	1998	1999	1990	1998	1999	1990	1998	1999
		Number - Nombre - Число								
1	**Lorries**	76 909	57 404	52 430	30 767	45 769	47 888	2 332 928	3 393 446	3 604 972
1.1	Up to 999 kg	...	3 116	2 702	...	13 532	14 084	...	2 489 076	2 662 100
1.2	1 000 kg - 1 499 kg	...	648	581	...	9 470	9 927	...	461 096	481 863
1.3	1 500kg - 2 999 kg	...	7 202	5 967	...	8 114	8 955	...	168 004	175 716
1.4	3 000 kg - 4 999 kg	...	15 451	12 285	...	3 484	3 546	...	78 048	80 899
1.5	5 000 kg - 6 999 kg	...	7 999	6 764	...	3 473	3 257	...	35 921	37 624
1.6	7 000 kg - 9 999 kg	...	3 253	2 883	...	3 053	3 078	...	55 722	58 556
1.7	10 000 kg - 14 999 kg	...	4 213	3 775	...	3 497	3 695	...	105 579	108 214
1.8	15 000 kg and more	...	897	951	...	1 146	1 346	...	(i)	(i)
3	**Semi-trailers**	...	5 225	4 772	...	4 511	4 801	88 979	147 698	161 329
3.1	Up to 4 999 kg	...	148	125	...	62	68	...	6 634	6 892
3.2	5 000 - 9 999 kg	...	1 047	959	...	117	121	...	1 051	1 066
3.3	10 000 - 14 999 kg	...	3 129	2 753	...	121	128	...	...	...
3.4	15 000 - 19 999 kg	...	251	228	...	42	39	...	...	...
3.5	20 000 kg and more	...	650	707	...	4 169	4 445	...	...	...
4	**Trailers**	...	5 391	4 461	23 277	20 878	22 979	16 634	53 186	59 757
4.1	Up to 4 999 kg	...	1 334	961	...	16 022	17 960	...	39 279	45 359
4.2	5 000 - 9 999 kg	...	3 723	3 196	...	2 066	2 146	...	4 684	3 914
4.3	10 000 - 14 999 kg	...	271	240	...	1 677	1 786	...	9 223	10 484
4.4	15 000 kg and more	...	63	64	...	1 113	1 087	...	(c)	...
		1000 tonnes - 1000 тонн								
5	**Lorries**	...	219.0	189.0	...	...	...	...	...	...
5.1	Up to 999 kg	...	2.0	2.0	...	...	...	...	...	...
5.2	1 000 kg - 1 499 kg	...	1.0	1.0	...	9.5	9.9	...	...	...
5.3	1 500kg - 2 999 kg	...	17.0	14.0	...	10.7	11.5	...	...	...
5.4	3 000 kg - 4 999 kg	...	61.0	48.0	...	11.8	11.8	...	...	...
5.5	5 000 kg - 6 999 kg	...	44.0	37.0	...	19.1	17.9	...	...	...
5.6	7 000 kg - 9 999 kg	...	26.0	23.0	...	24.3	24.6	...	...	...
5.7	10 000 kg - 14 999 kg	...	49.0	44.0	...	42.7	45.5	...	...	...
5.8	15 000 kg and more	...	19.0	20.0	...	21.4	24.5	...	...	...
6	**Semi-trailers**	...	66.0	61.0	...	111.6	120.4	...	...	...
6.1	Up to 4 999 kg	...	0.0	0.0	...	0.1	0.1	...	...	...
6.2	5 000 - 9 999 kg	...	8.0	7.0	...	0.8	0.9	...	...	...
6.3	10 000 - 14 999 kg	...	39.0	34.0	...	1.4	1.5	...	...	...
6.4	15 000 - 19 999 kg	...	4.0	4.0	...	0.7	0.7	...	...	...
6.5	20 000 kg and more	...	15.0	16.0	...	108.5	117.2	...	...	...
7	**Trailers**	...	32.0	27.0	...	77.8	82.4	...	...	...
7.1	Up to 4 999 kg	...	5.0	3.0	...	23.8	27.1	...	...	...
7.2	5 000 - 9 999 kg	...	23.0	20.0	...	12.7	13.1	...	...	...
7.3	10 000 - 14 999 kg	...	3.0	3.0	...	20.5	21.8	...	...	...
7.4	15 000 kg and more	...	1.0	1.0	...	20.7	20.4	...	...	...

For note see end of table.   Voir note à la fin du tableau.   См. примечания в конце таблицы.

10 (c). Goods road transport equipment at 31 December - By load capacity
10 (c). Vehicules routiers pour le transport des marchandises au 31 décembre - Par classe de charge utile
10 (c). Транспортное оборудование на 31 декабря - по грузоподъемности

		Sweden Suède Швеция			Switzerland Suisse Швейцария			Turkey Turquie Турция		
		1990	1998	1999	1990	1998	1999	1990	1998	1999
		Number - Nombre - Число								
1	**Lorries**	**309 520**	**331 810**	**347 805**	**246 194**	**259 871**	**266 074**	**520 760**	**997 167**	**...**
1.1	Up to 999 kg	154 710	197 137	212 816	49 118	68 818	...	218 544	...	...
1.2	1 000 kg - 1 499 kg	69 247	65 306	64 899	109 081	115 558	...	(d)	...	...
1.3	1 500kg - 2 999 kg	20 278	14 713	14 187	42 006	33 875	...	45 628	...	...
1.4	3 000 kg - 4 999 kg	9 593	7 437	7 470	4 053	3 311	...	134 037	...	...
1.5	5 000 kg - 6 999 kg	7 512	6 280	6 312	12 397	7 363	...	(k)	...	...
1.6	7 000 kg - 9 999 kg	16 192	11 370	11 479	18 286	17 322	...	21 568	...	...
1.7	10 000 kg - 14 999 kg	24 923	20 117	20 390	8 060	8 678	...	100 983	...	...
1.8	15 000 kg and more	7 065	9 450	10 252	3 193	4 946	...		...	...
3	**Semi-trailers**	**8 788**	**15 383**	**16 148**	**7 759**	**10 238**	**...**	**...**	**...**	**...**
3.1	Up to 4 999 kg	41	228	115	2 031	2 215	...	...	...	...
3.2	5 000 - 9 999 kg	125	170	172	381	316	...	...	...	...
3.3	10 000 - 14 999 kg	351	373	381	2 136	2 275	...	...	...	...
3.4	15 000 - 19 999 kg	504	376	383	2 744	3 557	...	...	...	...
3.5	20 000 kg and more	7 767	14 236	15 097	467	1 875	...	...	...	...
4	**Trailers**	**422 131**	**486 512**	**499 248**	**85 110**	**129 631**	**...**	**...**	**...**	**...**
4.1	Up to 4 999 kg	398 701	463 787	476 083	68 274	114 904	...	...	...	...
4.2	5 000 - 9 999 kg	3 012	1 923	1 867	15 057	9 649	...	...	...	...
4.3	10 000 - 14 999 kg	4 060	3 284	3 421	560	3 632	...	...	...	...
4.4	15 000 kg and more	16 358	17 518	17 877	1 219	1 446	...	...	...	...
		1000 tonnes - 1000 тонн								
5	**Lorries**	**891.4**	**823.0**	**843.0**	**633.0**	**644.0**	**...**	**...**	**...**	**...**
5.1	Up to 999 kg	189.1	133.0	142.0	36.0	50.0	...	...	...	...
5.2	1 000 kg - 1 499 kg	...	77.0	76.0	131.0	140.0	...	...	...	...
5.3	1 500kg - 2 999 kg	77.5	29.0	28.0	73.0	58.0	...	...	...	...
5.4	3 000 kg - 4 999 kg	...	30.0	30.0	17.0	13.0	...	...	...	...
5.5	5 000 kg - 6 999 kg	45.3	38.0	38.0	76.0	45.0	...	...	...	...
5.6	7 000 kg - 9 999 kg	135.5	95.0	92.0	142.0	143.0	...	...	...	...
5.7	10 000 kg - 14 999 kg	326.9	265.0	267.0	108.0	115.0	...	...	...	...
5.8	15 000 kg and more	117.1	156.0	170.0	50.0	80.0	...	...	...	...
6	**Semi-trailers**	**229.7**	**441.0**	**470.0**	**93.9**	**147.0**	**...**	**...**	**...**	**...**
6.1	Up to 4 999 kg	0.1	0.0	0.0	5.0	6.0	...	...	...	...
6.2	5 000 - 9 999 kg	-	1.0	1.0	3.0	3.0	...	...	...	...
6.3	10 000 - 14 999 kg	5.6	5.0	5.0	29.0	31.0	...	...	...	...
6.4	15 000 - 19 999 kg	9.0	6.0	7.0	45.0	59.0	...	...	...	...
6.5	20 000 kg and more	215.0	428.0	456.0	12.0	48.0	...	...	...	...
7	**Trailers**	**918.6**	**814.0**	**829.0**	**219.0**	**265.0**	**...**	**...**	**...**	**...**
7.1	Up to 4 999 kg	252.0	343.0	353.0	60.0	108.0	...	...	...	...
7.2	5 000 - 9 999 kg	82.0	14.0	12.0	119.0	76.0	...	...	...	...
7.3	10 000 - 14 999 kg	...	43.0	39.0	7.0	48.0	...	...	...	...
7.4	15 000 kg and more	584.6	413.0	426.0	33.0	33.0	...	...	...	...

For note see end of table.   Voir note à la fin du tableau.   См. примечания в конце таблицы.

10 (c). Goods road transport equipment at 31 December - By load capacity

10 (c). Vehicules routiers pour le transport des marchandises au 31 décembre - Par classe de charge utile

10 (c). Транспортное оборудование на 31 декабря - по грузоподъемности

		United Kingdom Royaume-Uni [5] Соединенное Королевство			United States Etats-Unis Соединенные Штаты					
		1990	1998	1999	1990	1998	1999			
		Number - Nombre - Число								
1	Lorries	2 330 200	2 644 000	2 802 000	16 008 545	7 732 270	7 791 426			
1.1	Up to 999 kg	...	2 289 000	...	12 911 654	...	...			
1.2	1 000 kg - 1 499 kg	...	156 000	...	(d)	...	...			
1.3	1 500kg - 2 999 kg	...	15 000	...	1 342 900	...	...			
1.4	3 000 kg - 4 999 kg	...	21 000	...	(e)	...	...			
1.5	5 000 kg - 6 999 kg	...	69 000	...	592 507	...	...			
1.6	7 000 kg - 9 999 kg	...	6 000	...	647 763	...	...			
1.7	10 000 kg - 14 999 kg	...	25 000	...	312 996	...	...			
1.8	15 000 kg and more	...	19 000	...	200 726	...	...			
3	Semi-trailers	230 500	...	...	3 606 169	4 405 222	4 560 664			
3.1	Up to 4 999 kg	...	...	...	...	...	...			
3.2	5 000 - 9 999 kg	...	...	...	...	...	...			
3.3	10 000 - 14 999 kg	...	...	...	...	...	...			
3.4	15 000 - 19 999 kg	...	...	...	...	...	...			
3.5	20 000 kg and more	...	...	...	...	...	...			
4	Trailers	422 131	...	...	...	19 943 753	20 746 608			
4.1	Up to 4 999 kg	...	...	...	...	...	...			
4.2	5 000 - 9 999 kg	...	...	...	...	...	...			
4.3	10 000 - 14 999 kg	...	...	...	...	...	...			
4.4	15 000 kg and more	...	...	...	...	...	...			
		1000 tonnes - 1000 тонн								
5	Lorries	...	...	...	28 567.0	...	...			
5.1	Up to 999 kg	...	...	...	7 529.0	...	...			
5.2	1 000 kg - 1 499 kg	...	...	...	(f)	...	...			
5.3	1 500kg - 2 999 kg	...	...	...	4 215.0	...	...			
5.4	3 000 kg - 4 999 kg	...	...	...	(g)	...	...			
5.5	5 000 kg - 6 999 kg	...	...	...	3 581.0	...	...			
5.6	7 000 kg - 9 999 kg	...	...	...	5 320.0	...	...			
5.7	10 000 kg - 14 999 kg	...	...	...	3 887.0	...	...			
5.8	15 000 kg and more	...	...	...	4 036.0	...	...			
6	Semi-trailers	...	...	...	70 891.0	...	...			
6.1	Up to 4 999 kg	...	...	...	...	...	...			
6.2	5 000 - 9 999 kg	...	...	...	...	...	...			
6.3	10 000 - 14 999 kg	...	...	...	...	...	...			
6.4	15 000 - 19 999 kg	...	...	...	...	...	...			
6.5	20 000 kg and more	...	...	...	...	...	...			
7	Trailers	...	...	...	...	...	...			
7.1	Up to 4 999 kg	...	...	...	...	...	...			
7.2	5 000 - 9 999 kg	...	...	...	...	...	...			
7.3	10 000 - 14 999 kg	...	...	...	...	...	...			
7.4	15 000 kg and more	...	...	...	...	...	...			

ROAD TRANSPORT - TRANSPORT ROUTIER
АВТОМОБИЛЬНЫЕ ДОРОГИ

NOTES TO TABLE 10 (c) - NOTES DU TABLEAU 10 (c) - ПРИМЕЧАНИЯ К ТАБЛИЦЕ 10 (c)

General notes - Notes générales - Общие примечания

(a) Included under item 4.	(a) Compris sous la rubrique 4.	(a) Включено в статью 4.
(b) Included under item 4.2.	(b) Compris sous la rubrique 4.2.	(b) Включено в статью 4.2.
(c) Included under item 7.3.	(c) Compris sous la rubrique 7.3.	(c) Включено в статью 7.3.
(d) Included under item 1.1.	(d) Compris sous la rubrique 1.1.	(d) Включено в статью 1.1.
(e) Included under item 1.3.	(e) Compris sous la rubrique 1.3.	(e) Включено в статью 1.3.
(f) Included under item 5.1.	(f) Compris sous la rubrique 5.1.	(f) Включено в статью 5.1.
(g) Included under item 5.3.	(g) Compris sous la rubrique 5.3.	(g) Включено в статью 5.3.
(h) Included under item 7.2.	(h) Compris sous la rubrique 7.2.	(h) Включено в статью 7.2.
(i) Included under item 1.7.	(i) Compris sous la rubrique 1.7.	(i) Включено в статью 1.7.
(j) Included under item 5.7.	(j) Compris sous la rubrique 5.7.	(j) Включено в статью 5.7.
(k) Included under item 1.4.	(k) Compris sous la rubrique 1.4.	(k) Включено в статью 1.4.

Country notes - Notes relatives aux pays - Примечания к данным, представляемым странами

1- Excluding vehicles for which technical informations are unknown.

2- Excluding vehicles registered in Aland.

3- The breakdown by load capacity differs from the norm used as follows:
Lorries:
   Items 1.7/5.7: 10 000 kg - 13 999 kg
   Items 1.8/5.8: 14 000 kg and more
Semi-trailers:
   Items 3.3/6.3: 10 000 kg - 15 999 kg
   Items 3.4/6.4: 16 000 kg - 19 999 kg
Trailers:
   Items 4.3/7.3: 10 000 kg - 15 999 kg
   Items 4.4/7.4: 16 000 kg and more

4- Lorries include agricultural tractors and special vehicles.

5- Data for semi-trailers and trailers refer to Great Britain only.

1- Non compris les véhicules dont les données . techniques manquent.

2- Non compris les véhicules immatriculés à Aland.

3- La répartition par classe de charge utile diffère du standard utilisé comme suit:
Camions:
   Rubriques 1.7/5.7: 10 000 kg - 13 999 kg
   Rubriques 1.8/5.8: 14 000 kg et plus
Semi-remorques:
   Rubriques 3.3/6.3: 10 000 kg - 15 999 kg
   Rubriques 3.4/6.4: 16 000 kg - 19 999 kg
Remorques:
   Rubriques 4.3/7.3: 10 000 kg - 15 999 kg
   Rubriques 4.4/7.4: 16 000 kg et plus

4- Les camions incluent les tracteurs agricoles et les véhicules spéciaux.

5- Les données pour les semi-remorques et les remorques se réferent à la Grande Bretagne.

1- За исключением дорожно-транспортных средств, технические характеристики которых неизвестны.

2- За исключением дорожно-транспортных средств, зарегистрированных на Аландских островах.

3- Разбивка по грузоподъемности отличается от используемых норм следующим образом:
Грузовые автомобили:
   Статья 1.7/5.7: 10 000 кг - 13 999 кг
   Статья 1.8/5.8: 14 000 кг и более
Полуприцепы:
   Статья 3.3/6.3: 10 000 кг - 15 999 кг
   Статья 3.4/6.4: 16 000 кг - 19 999 кг
Прицепы:
   Статья 4.3/7.3: 10 000 кг - 15 999 кг
   Статья 4.4/7.4: 16 000 кг и более

4- Грузовые автомобили, включая сельскохозяйственные тракторы и специальные транспортные спедства.

5- Данные по полутракторам и трейлерам относятся только к великобритании.

ROAD TRANSPORT - TRANSPORT ROUTIER
АВТОМОБИЛЬНЫЕ ДОРОГИ

11. New road vehicle registrations during the year - By vehicle category
11. Nouvelles immatriculations de véhicules routiers durant l'année - Par catégories de véhicules
11. Парк новых дорожно-транспортных средств, зарегистрированных на конец года - по виду транспорта

Item	Description	Rubrique	Description
1	**Passenger vehicles (Number)**	**1**	**Véhicules routiers pour le transport des voyageurs (Nombre)**
1.1	Mopeds	1.1	Cyclomoteurs
1.2	Motorcycles	1.2	Motocycles
1.3	Passenger cars	1.3	Voitures particulières
1.4	Motor coaches, Buses and Trolleybuses	1.4	Autocars, autobus et trolleybus
2	**Goods road vehicles (Number)**	**2**	**Véhicules routiers pour le transport des marchandises (Nombre)**
2.1	Lorries	2.1	Camions
2.2	Road tractors	2.2	Tracteurs routiers
2.3	Semi-trailers	2.3	Semi-remorques
2.4	Trailers	2.4	Remorques
3	**Load capacity of goods road vehicles (1000 tonnes)**	**3**	**Charge utile des véhicules routiers pour le transport des marchandises (1000 tonnes)**
3.1	Lorries	3.1	Camions
3.2	Semi-trailers	3.2	Semi-remorques
3.3	Trailers	3.3	Remorques

Статья	Описание
1	**Пассажирские автодорожные транспортные средства (число)**
1.1	Мопеды
1.2	Мотоциклы
1.3	Пассажирские автомобили
1.4	Автобусы дальнего следования, городские автобусы и троллейбусы
2	**Грузовые автодорожные транспортные средства (число)**
2.1	Грузовые автомобили
2.2	Дорожные тягачи
2.3	Полуприцепы
2.4	Прицепы
3	**Грузоподъемность грузовых автодорожных транспортных средств (1000 тонн)**
3.1	Грузовые автомобили
3.2	Полуприцепы
3.3	Прицепы

ROAD TRANSPORT - TRANSPORT ROUTIER
АВТОМОБИЛЬНЫЕ ДОРОГИ

11. New road vehicle registrations during the year - By vehicle category
11. Nouvelles immatriculations de véhicules routiers durant l'année - Par catégories de véhicules
11. Парк новых дорожно-транспортных средств, зарегистрированных на конец года - по виду транспорта

		Albania Albanie Албания			Austria Autriche Австрия			Belgium Belgique Бельгия		
		1990	1998	1999	1990	1998	1999	1990	1998	1999
1	**Passenger vehicles (Number)**									
1.1	Mopeds	...	...	...	9 729	(a)	(a)	(a)	(a)	(a)
1.2	Motorcycles	...	...	...	9 155	45 566	49 881	9 276	21 267	27 539
1.3	Passenger cars	20 854	...	...	288 636	295 865	314 182	498 698	463 724	504 203
1.4	Motor coaches, Buses, etc.	675	...	...	574	510	799	862	1 023	963
2	**Goods road vehicles (Number)**									
2.1	Lorries	4 912	...	...	26 795	28 956	29 837	41 262	51 664	60 269
2.2	Road tractors	...	...	...	...	3 874	4 282	4 295	5 472	5 776
2.3	Semi-trailers	...	...	...	...	2 816	3 189	4 484	5 092	5 946
2.4	Trailers	...	...	...	19 719	21 850	21 973	3 559	6 920	6 670
3	**Load capacity of goods road vehicles (1000t)**									
3.1	Lorries	...	...	...	...	...	...	...	...	...
3.2	Semi-trailers	...	...	...	...	...	...	...	...	...
3.3	Trailers	...	...	...	...	...	...	...	...	...

		Bulgaria Bulgarie Болгария			Croatia Croatie Хорватия			Cyprus Chypre Кипр		
		1990	1998	1999	1990	1998	1999	1990	1998	1999
1	**Passenger vehicles (Number)**									
1.1	Mopeds	3 283	(a)	(a)	...	...	...	7 118	...	...
1.2	Motorcycles	6 057	2 403	1 127	...	2 124	1 866	1 228	1 918	2 150
1.3	Passenger cars	46 433	70 797	103 459	...	85 893	89 846	19 532	24 856	20 133
1.4	Motor coaches, Buses, etc.	2 369	857	229	...	247	192	263	142	145
2	**Goods road vehicles (Number)**									
2.1	Lorries	15 105	8 551	1	...	7 720	5 864	9 806	7 301	6 639
2.2	Road tractors	680	861	...	...	452	368	...	121	113
2.3	Semi-trailers	...	...	6	...	654	501	...	256	218
2.4	Trailers	...	...	1	...	2 033	1 204	...	51	48
3	**Load capacity of goods road vehicles (1000t)**									
3.1	Lorries	...	...	-	...	20.0	14.0	...	...	...
3.2	Semi-trailers	...	...	-	...	12.0	9.0	...	...	...
3.3	Trailers	...	...	-	...	10.0	7.0	...	...	...

For note see end of table.　　　　Voir note à la fin du tableau.　　　　См. примечания в конце таблицы.

130

ROAD TRANSPORT - TRANSPORT ROUTIER
АВТОМОБИЛЬНЫЕ ДОРОГИ

11. New road vehicle registrations during the year - By vehicle category
11. Nouvelles immatriculations de véhicules routiers durant l'année - Par catégories de véhicules
11. Парк новых дорожно-транспортных средств, зарегистрированных на конец года - по виду транспорта

		Denmark Danemark Дания			Estonia Estonie Эстония			Finland Finlande [1] Финляндия		
		1990	1998	1999	1990	1998	1999	1990	1998	1999
1	Passenger vehicles (Number)									
1.1	Mopeds	(a)	(a)	(a)	...	...	...	...	...	...
1.2	Motorcycles	1 677	3 372	4 198	...	86	82	5 096	3 810	5 781
1.3	Passenger cars	80 837	162 683	144 054	...	8 400	6 864	139 041	126 386	137 017
1.4	Motor coaches, Buses, etc.	786	888	748	...	40	69	452	520	544
2	Goods road vehicles (Number)	...	...	...	...	...	...	...	...	...
2.1	Lorries	22 593	34 497	37 095	...	2 178	1 413	29 172	19 109	19 504
2.2	Road tractors	3 779	2 240	2 126	...	367	399	...	504	324
2.3	Semi-trailers	...	3 875	2 562	...	...	...	345	2 229	569
2.4	Trailers	17 171	33 089	32 945	...	...	...	25 181	22 628	24 488
3	Load capacity of goods road vehicles (1000t)	...	...	...	...	...	...	...	...	...
3.1	Lorries	...	...	...	...	...	...	71.0	54.0	53.0
3.2	Semi-trailers	...	...	...	...	...	...	6.0	42.0	11.0
3.3	Trailers	...	...	...	...	...	...	49.0	38.0	38.0

		France France Франция			Germany Allemagne Германия			Greece Grèce Греция		
		1990	1998	1999	1990	1998	1999	1990	1998	1999
1	Passenger vehicles (Number)									
1.1	Mopeds	...	...	...	...	...	...	(a)	(a)	...
1.2	Motorcycles	125 225	173 289	193 817	...	289 982	282 462	21 556	64 284	...
1.3	Passenger cars	2 309 130	1 943 553	2 148 423	...	3 735 987	3 802 176	132 487	181 883	266 988
1.4	Motor coaches, Buses, etc.	4 210	4 851	5 316	...	5 802	6 321	936	932	...
2	Goods road vehicles (Number)									
2.1	Lorries	420 618	367 392	399 889	...	237 184	258 215	42 561	...	...
2.2	Road tractors	22 154	26 340	28 300	...	24 972	28 457	...	...	...
2.3	Semi-trailers	19 481	18 794	20 651	...	21 752	23 460	861	...	...
2.4	Trailers	3 445	2 807	3 350	...	160 159	174 141	539	...	...
3	Load capacity of goods road vehicles (1000t)									
3.1	Lorries	499.0	439.0	498.0	...	563.0	649.0	73.1	...	...
3.2	Semi-trailers	476.0	492.0	542.0	...	584.0	636.0	19.9	...	...
3.3	Trailers	48.0	35.0	37.0	...	319.0	359.0	10.3	...	...

For note see end of table.   Voir note à la fin du tableau.   См. примечания в конце таблицы.

131

ROAD TRANSPORT - TRANSPORT ROUTIER
АВТОМОБИЛЬНЫЕ ДОРОГИ

11. New road vehicle registrations during the year - By vehicle category
11. Nouvelles immatriculations de véhicules routiers durant l'année - Par catégories de véhicules
11. Парк новых дорожно-транспортных средств, зарегистрированных на конец года - по виду транспорта

		Hungary Hongrie Венгрия			Iceland Islande Исландия			Ireland Irlande Ирландия		
		1990	1998	1999	1990	1998	1999	1990	1998	1999
1	**Passenger vehicles (Number)**									
1.1	Mopeds	...	1 887	1 875	(a)	(a)	(a)	...	...	...
1.2	Motorcycles	...	920	1 752	113	146	...	2 684	3 117	4 955
1.3	Passenger cars	143 073	101 328	126 085	6 836	15 064	17 007	83 420	138 538	170 322
1.4	Motor coaches, Buses, etc.	...	498	777	106	118	118	299	389	686
2	**Goods road vehicles (Number)**									
2.1	Lorries	...	25 087	27 270	...	1 472	1 797	23 979	23 811	30 066
2.2	Road tractors	...	1 595	2 371	...	72	51	38	37	...
2.3	Semi-trailers	...	806	1 098	44	89	96	...	...	...
2.4	Trailers	...	1 229	1 625	378	182	183	...	...	...
3	**Load capacity of goods road vehicles (1000t)**									
3.1	Lorries	...	34.0	37.0	...	3.9	4.0	...	...	...
3.2	Semi-trailers	...	21.0	29.0	...	2.8	3.0	...	...	...
3.3	Trailers	...	6.0	7.0	...	1.0	1.0	...	...	...

		Israel Israël [2] Израиль			Italy Italie Италия			Latvia Lettonie Латвия		
		1990	1998	1999	1990	1998	1999	1990	1998	1999
1	**Passenger vehicles (Number)**									
1.1	Mopeds	3 014*	...	...	...	...	...	...	...	...
1.2	Motorcycles	2 735	5 444	4 249	114 233	234 298	346 903	...	392	509
1.3	Passenger cars	64 041	111 810	112 508	2 395 909	2 437 718	2 312 455	...	57 363	45 861
1.4	Motor coaches, Buses, etc.	614	990	1 714	4 185	4 348	4 680	...	655	783
2	**Goods road vehicles (Number)**									
2.1	Lorries	13 684	28 800	28 396	...	194 767	196 769	...	4 768	6 298
2.2	Road tractors	198	234	237	...	7 479	10 935	...	1 133	401
2.3	Semi-trailers	848	286	315	...	9 461	11 269	...	893	572
2.4	Trailers	(c)	3 607	3 393	...	15 902	16 782	...	1 731	1 652
3	**Load capacity of goods road vehicles (1000t)**									
3.1	Lorries	...	...	...	...	...	...	...	15.0	22.0
3.2	Semi-trailers	...	...	...	...	...	...	...	...	...
3.3	Trailers	...	...	...	...	...	...	...	...	...

For note see end of table.   **Voir note à la fin du tableau.**   **См. примечания в конце таблицы.**

ROAD TRANSPORT - TRANSPORT ROUTIER
АВТОМОБИЛЬНЫЕ ДОРОГИ

11. New road vehicle registrations during the year - By vehicle category

11. Nouvelles immatriculations de véhicules routiers durant l'année - Par catégories de véhicules

11. Парк новых дорожно-транспортных средств, зарегистрированных на конец года - по виду транспорта

		Lithuania Lituanie Литва			Luxembourg Luxembourg Люксембург			Malta Malte [3] Мальта		
		1990	1998	1999	1990	1998	1999	1990	1998	1999
1	**Passenger vehicles (Number)**									
1.1	Mopeds	...	...	...	...	...	...	...	(a)	(a)
1.2	Motorcycles	...	332	211	750	...	...	231	681	985
1.3	Passenger cars	...	147 105	142 069	38 648	39 534	...	8 218	10 750	13 341
1.4	Motor coaches, Buses, etc.	...	1 076	521	61	107	...	...	49	5
2	**Goods road vehicles (Number)**									
2.1	Lorries	...	12 050	7 214	1 986	2 171	...	1 435	2 769	2 176
2.2	Road tractors	...	1 250	518	346	578	...	(d)	(d)	1
2.3	Semi-trailers	...	971	517	...	...	...	...	59	63
2.4	Trailers	...	832	410	...	...	...	...	...	...
3	**Load capacity of goods road vehicles (1000t)**									
3.1	Lorries	...	...	...	...	...	...	...	...	...
3.2	Semi-trailers	...	...	...	...	...	...	...	...	...
3.3	Trailers	...	...	...	...	...	...	...	...	...

		Netherlands Pays-Bas Нидерланды			Norway Norvège Норвегия			Poland Pologne Польша		
		1990	1998	1999	1990	1998	1999	1990	1998	1999
1	**Passenger vehicles (Number)**									
1.1	Mopeds	...	...	...	7 222	3 977	...	...	...	...
1.2	Motorcycles	15 519	14 602	...	732	11 320	10 030	31 354	5 488	6 237
1.3	Passenger cars	502 671	543 110	...	63 668	141 090	123 843	358 055	557 783	599 250
1.4	Motor coaches, Buses, etc.	1 121	...	...	1 751	2 774	2 222	4 195	2 259	2 512
2	**Goods road vehicles (Number)**									
2.1	Lorries	61 597	101 543	...	21 951	6 217	5 007	58 741	103 933	140 063
2.2	Road tractors	5 500	...	...	142	811	545	2 271	10 347	7 912
2.3	Semi-trailers	6 576	...	...	138	778	510	...	10 037	8 203
2.4	Trailers	15 232	...	...	9 184	23 122	25 633	...	15 472	10 201
3	**Load capacity of goods road vehicles (1000t)**									
3.1	Lorries	...	...	...	...	...	...	...	195.0	209.0
3.2	Semi-trailers	...	...	...	...	...	...	...	223.0	192.0
3.3	Trailers	...	...	...	...	...	...	...	70.0	39.0

For note see end of table.   Voir note à la fin du tableau.   См. примечания в конце таблицы.

ROAD TRANSPORT - TRANSPORT ROUTIER
АВТОМОБИЛЬНЫЕ ДОРОГИ

11. New road vehicle registrations during the year - By vehicle category

11. Nouvelles immatriculations de véhicules routiers durant l'année - Par catégories de véhicules

11. Парк новых дорожно-транспортных средств, зарегистрированных на конец года - по виду транспорта

		Portugal Portugal Португалия			Republic of Moldova République de Moldova Республика Молдова			Romania Roumanie Румыния		
		1990	1998	1999	1990	1998	1999	1990	1998	1999
1	Passenger vehicles (Number)									
1.1	Mopeds	...	...	...	...	...	...	...	...	...
1.2	Motorcycles	7 311	29 413	22 927	...	...	...	...	80	21
1.3	Passenger cars	212 348	323 981	351 575	...	255	229	...	105 986	90 047
1.4	Motor coaches, Buses, etc.	645	1 263	1 206	...	131	25	...	476	185
2	Goods road vehicles (Number)									
2.1	Lorries	...	104 326	106 395	...	225	105	...	23 798	19 081
2.2	Road tractors	...	4 499	5 507	...	75	9	...	998	441
2.3	Semi-trailers	...	14 051	15 621	...	79	23	...	4 746	2 972
2.4	Trailers	...	...	...	...	13	5	...	...	...
3	Load capacity of goods road vehicles (1000t)									
3.1	Lorries	...	...	...	...	3.0	1.0	...	...	...
3.2	Semi-trailers	...	...	...	...	2.0	0.0	...	...	...
3.3	Trailers	...	...	...	...	0.0	0.0	...	...	...

		Russian Federation Fédération de Russie Российская Федерация			Slovakia Slovaquie Словакия			Slovenia Slovénie Словения		
		1990	1998	1999	1990	1998	1999	1990	1998	1999
1	Passenger vehicles (Number)									
1.1	Mopeds	...	...	...	...	...	...	...	...	...
1.2	Motorcycles	...	...	...	...	10 894	1 914	827	1 236	1 590
1.3	Passenger cars	525 688	1 187 932	...	...	76 007	58 152	...	71 022	81 869
1.4	Motor coaches, Buses, etc.	...	4 834	...	...	319	139	...	147	152
2	Goods road vehicles (Number)									
2.1	Lorries	...	...	...	...	9 044	7 146	...	3 572	4 289
2.2	Road tractors	...	...	...	...	...	...	...	283	339
2.3	Semi-trailers	...	...	...	...	...	...	...	433	361
2.4	Trailers	...	...	...	...	8 180	6 966	...	904	1 168
3	Load capacity of goods road vehicles (1000t)									
3.1	Lorries	...	...	...	...	...	...	...	...	...
3.2	Semi-trailers	...	...	...	...	...	...	...	11.0	9.4
3.3	Trailers	...	...	...	...	...	...	...	3.2	4.8

For note see end of table.   Voir note à la fin du tableau.   См. примечания в конце таблицы.

ROAD TRANSPORT - TRANSPORT ROUTIER
АВТОМОБИЛЬНЫЕ ДОРОГИ

11. New road vehicle registrations during the year - By vehicle category

11. Nouvelles immatriculations de véhicules routiers durant l'année - Par catégories de véhicules

11. Парк новых дорожно-транспортных средств, зарегистрированных на конец года - по виду транспорта

		Spain Espagne Испания			Sweden Suède Швеция			Switzerland Suisse Швейцария		
		1990	1998	1999	1990	1998	1999	1990	1998	1999
1	**Passenger vehicles (Number)**									
1.1	Mopeds	(a)	(a)	(a)	(a)	(a)	(a)	...	...	...
1.2	Motorcycles	118 525	1 627 899	1 913 162	7 761	13 106	15 752	33 918	43 614	48 335
1.3	Passenger cars	1 007 014	1 282 970	1 502 531	235 192	286 671	335 632	322 974	295 165	314 691
1.4	Motor coaches, Buses, etc.	2 829	3 657	3 877	1 136	1 081	12 820	2 596	...	...
2	**Goods road vehicles (Number)**									
2.1	Lorries	255 984	267 650	316 926	33 741	30 628	34 144	25 504	20 734	...
2.2	Road tractors	8 894	14 952	18 389	415	777	1 025	777	890	...
2.3	Semi-trailers	...	13 458	14 823	982	2 040	1 311	681	654	...
2.4	Trailers	...	6 000	6 828	25 041	21 217	21 276	7 607	9 817	...
3	**Load capacity of goods road vehicles (1000t)**									
3.1	Lorries	...	...	...	95.9	74.0	97.0	...	...	...
3.2	Semi-trailers	...	...	...	28.6	64.0	40.0	...	...	...
3.3	Trailers	...	...	...	91.2	106.0	86.0	...	...	...

		The FYR of Macedonia [4]			Turkey Turquie Турция			Ukraine Ukraine Украина		
		1990	1998	1999	1990	1998	1999	1990	1998	1999
1	**Passenger vehicles (Number)**									
1.1	Mopeds	...	...	...	...	...	...	...	...	...
1.2	Motorcycles	240	880	834	59 383	...	...	...	...	...
1.3	Passenger cars	13 809	8 676	9 840	218 059	271 843	...	...	12 020	...
1.4	Motor coaches, Buses, etc.	113	93	54	13 424	22 599	...	...	...	...
2	**Goods road vehicles (Number)**									
2.1	Lorries	869	746	611	33 860	116 156	...	...	...	...
2.2	Road tractors	129	82	184	756	...	...	...	...	...
2.3	Semi-trailers	...	134	193	...	...	...	...	...	...
2.4	Trailers	...	...	...	...	...	...	...	...	...
3	**Load capacity of goods road vehicles (1000t)**									
3.1	Lorries	...	...	...	...	...	...	...	...	...
3.2	Semi-trailers	...	...	...	...	...	...	...	...	...
3.3	Trailers	...	...	...	...	...	...	...	...	...

For note see end of table.   Voir note à la fin du tableau.   См. примечания в конце таблицы.

ROAD TRANSPORT - TRANSPORT ROUTIER
АВТОМОБИЛЬНЫЕ ДОРОГИ

11. New road vehicle registrations during the year - By vehicle category

11. Nouvelles immatriculations de véhicules routiers durant l'année - Par catégories de véhicules

11. Парк новых дорожно-транспортных средств, зарегистрированных на конец года - по виду транспорта

		United Kingdom Royaume-Uni [5] Соединенное Королевство			United States Etats-Unis Соединенные Штаты					
		1990	1998	1999	1990	1998	1999			
1	**Passenger vehicles (Number)**									
1.1	Mopeds	...	...	...	...	...	...			
1.2	Motorcycles	78 454	148 138	...	303 000	432 000	...			
1.3	Passenger cars	2 077 078	2 362 589	2 315 170	9 103 204	8 139 000	...			
1.4	Motor coaches, Buses, etc.	5 401	14 242	14 219	...	33 965	...			
2	**Goods road vehicles (Number)**									
2.1	Lorries	...	285 940	...	4 798 515	6 407 702	...			
2.2	Road tractors	...	17 018	...	...	...	...			
2.3	Semi-trailers	...	...	...	...	...	...			
2.4	Trailers	...	...	...	...	...	...			
3	**Load capacity of goods road vehicles (1000t)**									
3.1	Lorries	...	...	...	...	...	...			
3.2	Semi-trailers	...	...	...	...	...	...			
3.3	Trailers	...	...	...	...	...	...			

NOTES TO TABLE 11 - NOTES DU TABLEAU 11 - ПРИМЕЧАНИЯ К ТАБЛИЦЕ 11

General notes - Notes générales - Общие примечания

(a) Included under item 1.2.
(b) Included under item 2.4.
(c) Included under item 2.3.
(d) Included under item 2.1.

(a) Compris sous la rubrique 1.2.
(b) Compris sous la rubrique 2.4.
(c) Compris sous la rubrique 2.3.
(d) Compris sous la rubrique 2.1.

(a) Включено в статью 1.2.
(b) Включено в статью 2.4.
(c) Включено в статью 2.3.
(d) Включено в статью 2.1.

Country notes - Notes relatives aux pays - Примечания к данным, представляемым странами

1- Excluding road tractors, semi-trailers and trailers registered in Aland.

2- Lorries include special vehicles.

3- Lorries include agricultural tractors and special vehicles.

4- The former Yugoslav Republic of Macedonia.

5- Data refer to Great Britain.

1- Non compris les tracteurs routiers, les semi-remorques et les remorques immatriculés à Aland.

2- Les Camions incluent les véhicules spéciaux.

3- Les Camions incluent les tracteurs agricoles et les véhicules spéciaux.

4- L'ex-République yougoslave de Macédoine.

5- Les données se réfèrent à la Grande Bretagne.

1- За исключением дорожные тягачи полуприцепы и прицепы, зарегистрированных на Аландских островах.

2- Грузовые автомобили, включая специальные транспортные средства.

3- Грузовые автомобили, включая сельскохозяйственные тракторы и специальные транспортные средства.

4- Бывшая Югославская Республика Македония.

5- Данные относятся к Великобритании.

ROAD TRANSPORT - TRANSPORT ROUTIER
АВТОМОБИЛЬНЫЕ ДОРОГИ

11 (a). New road vehicle registrations during the year - By fuel type

11 (a). Nouvelles immatriculations de véhicules routiers durant l'année - Par type de combustible utilisé

11 (a). Парк новых дорожно-транспортных средств, зарегистрированных на конец года - по типу двигателя

Item	Description	Rubrique	Description
1	**Passenger cars**	**1**	**Voitures particulières**
	Of which:		*Dont:*
1.1	- Petrol	1.1	- Essence
1.2	- Diesel	1.2	- Diesel
1.3	- Electricity	1.3	- Électricité
1.4	- Other sources	1.4	- Autres sources
2	**Motor coaches, Buses and Trolleybuses**	**2**	**Autocars, autobus et trolleybus**
	Of which:		*Dont:*
2.1	- Petrol	2.1	- Essence
2.2	- Diesel	2.2	- Diesel
2.3	- Electricity	2.3	- Électricité
2.4	- Other sources	2.4	- Autres sources
3	**Lorries**	**3**	**Camions**
	Of which:		*Dont:*
3.1	- Petrol	3.1	- Essence
3.2	- Diesel	3.2	- Diesel
3.3	- Other sources	3.3	- Autres sources

Статья	Описание
1	**Пассажирские автомобили**
	В том числе:
1.1	- бензиновый
1.2	- дизельный
1.3	- электрический
1.4	- прочие
2	**Автобусы дальнего следования, городские автобусы и троллейбусы**
	В том числе:
2.1	- бензиновый
2.2	- дизельный
2.3	-электрический
2.4	- прочие
3	**Грузовые автомобили**
	В том числе:
3.1	- бензиновый
3.2	- дизельный
3.3	- прочие

ROAD TRANSPORT - TRANSPORT ROUTIER
АВТОМОБИЛЬНЫЕ ДОРОГИ

11 (a). New road vehicle registrations during the year - By fuel type

11 (a). Nouvelles immatriculations de véhicules routiers durant l'année - Par type de combustible utilisé

11 (a). Парк новых дорожно-транспортных средств, зарегистрированных на конец года - по типу двигателя

(number - nombre - Число)

		Austria Autriche Австрия			Belgium Belgique Бельгия			Bulgaria Bulgarie Болгария		
		1990	1998	1999	1990	1998	1999	1990	1998	1999
1	**Passenger cars**	**288 636**	**295 865**	**314 951**	**498 698**	**463 724**	**504 203**	**46 433**	**70 797**	**103 459**
	Of which:									
1.1	- Petrol	...	134 556	133 951	...	...	...	...	...	...
1.2	- Diesel	...	161 297	180 228	210 369	243 185	273 898	...	...	...
1.3	- Electricity	...	12	3	...	...	...	...	...	...
1.4	- Other sources	...	-	769	...	...	...	...	...	...
2	**Motor coaches, Buses and Trolleybuses**	**574**	**510**	**799**	**862**	**1 023**	**963**	**2 369**	**857**	**229**
	Of which:									
2.1	- Petrol	...	...	-	7	...	...	...	...	...
2.2	- Diesel	...	...	799	855	...	...	...	...	...
2.3	- Electricity	...	...	-	-	...	...	...	...	3
2.4	- Other sources	...	...	-	-	...	...	...	...	...
3	**Lorries**	**26 795**	**28 956**	**29 837**	**41 262**	**51 664**	**60 269**	**15 105**	**8 551**	**1**
	Of which:									
3.1	- Petrol	...	...	507	...	...	...	...	...	...
3.2	- Diesel	...	...	28 616	...	...	...	...	...	...
3.3	- Other sources	...	...	2	...	...	...	...	...	...

		Croatia Croatie Хорватия			Cyprus Chypre Кипр			Finland Finlande [1] Финляндия		
		1990	1998	1999	1990	1998	1999	1990	1998	1999
1	**Passenger cars**	...	**85 893**	**89 846**	**19 532**	**24 856**	**20 133**	**139 041**	**126 386**	**137 017**
	Of which:									
1.1	- Petrol	...	70 245	70 136	17 874	19 692	16 476	131 830	106 025	114 295
1.2	- Diesel	...	15 648	19 710	1 658	5 164	3 657	7 211	19 725	22 025
1.3	- Electricity	...	-	-	-	-	-	-	-	3
1.4	- Other sources	...	-	-	-	-	-	-	636	694
2	**Motor coaches, Buses and Trolleybuses**	...	**247**	**192**	**263**	**142**	**145**	**452**	**520**	**544**
	Of which:									
2.1	- Petrol	...	2	-	37	-	-	...	-	-
2.2	- Diesel	...	245	192	226	142	145	...	504	529
2.3	- Electricity	...	-	-	-	-	-	...	-	-
2.4	- Other sources	...	-	-	-	-	-	...	16	15
3	**Lorries**	...	**7 720**	**5 864**	**9 806**	**7 301**	**6 639**	**29 172**	**19 109**	**19 504**
	Of which:									
3.1	- Petrol	...	825	503	738	124	67	7 846	863	596
3.2	- Diesel	...	6 895	5 361	9 068	7 177	6 572	21 326	18 104	18 751
3.3	- Other sources	...	-	-	-	-	-	-	25	21

For note see end of table.   Voir note en fin de tableau.   См. примечания в конце таблицы.

138

ROAD TRANSPORT - TRANSPORT ROUTIER
АВТОМОБИЛЬНЫЕ ДОРОГИ

11 (a). New road vehicle registrations during the year - By fuel type

11 (a). Nouvelles immatriculations de véhicules routiers durant l'année - Par type de combustible utilisé

11 (a). Парк новых дорожно-транспортных средств, зарегистрированных на конец года - по типу двигателя

(number - nombre - Число)

		France France Франция			Germany Allemagne Германия			Hungary Hongrie Венгрия		
		1990	1998	1999	1990	1998	1999	1990	1998	1999
1	**Passenger cars**	**2 309 130**	**1 943 553**	**2 148 423**	...	**3 735 987**	**3 802 176**	**143 073**	**101 328**	**126 085**
	Of which:									
1.1	- Petrol	1 546 938	1 138 628	1 185 187	...	3 077 600	2 948 556	...	97 566	121 391
1.2	- Diesel	762 064	780 983	947 489	...	657 480	852 849	...	3 753	4 686
1.3	- Electricity	-	505	529	...	210	121	...	...	1
1.4	- Other sources	128	23 437	15 218	...	697	650	...	...	7
2	**Motor coaches, Buses and Trolleybuses**	**4 210**	**4 851**	**5 316**	...	**5 802**	**6 321**	...	**498**	**777**
	Of which:									
2.1	- Petrol	64	5	1	...	2	2	...	8	6
2.2	- Diesel	4 143	4 737	5 071	...	5 680	6 246	...	489	745
2.3	- Electricity	3	-	8	...	-	-	...	-	-
2.4	- Other sources	-	109	236	...	120	73	...	1	26
3	**Lorries**	**420 618**	**367 392**	**399 889**	...	**237 184**	**258 215**	...	**25 087**	**27 270**
	Of which:									
3.1	- Petrol	79 727	22 319	19 139	...	15 811	15 599	...	4 000	3 702
3.2	- Diesel	340 700	341 538	376 089	...	...	242 127	...	21 066	23 552
3.3	- Other sources	191	3 535	4 661	...	...	489	...	21	16

		Iceland Islande Исландия			Ireland Irlande Ирландия			Italy Italie Италия		
		1990	1998	1999	1990	1998	1999	1990	1998	1999
1	**Passenger cars**	**6 836**	**15 064**	**17 007**	**83 420**	**138 538**	**170 322**	**2 395 909**	**2 437 718**	**2 312 455**
	Of which:									
1.1	- Petrol	...	12 751	14 248	...	121 210	151 219	...	...	...
1.2	- Diesel	...	2 309	2 759	...	17 326	19 103	...	...	...
1.3	- Electricity	...	4	-	...	-	-	...	...	...
1.4	- Other sources	...	-	-	...	2	-	...	...	...
2	**Motor coaches, Buses and Trolleybuses**	**106**	**118**	**118**	**299**	**389**	**686**	**4 185**	**4 348**	**4 680**
	Of which:									
2.1	- Petrol	...	7	10	...	-	-	...	3	...
2.2	- Diesel	...	111	108	...	389	686	...	4 302	...
2.3	- Electricity	...	-	-	...	-	-	...	43	...
2.4	- Other sources	...	-	-	...	-	-	...	(a)	...
3	**Lorries**	...	**1 472**	**1 797**	**23 979**	**23 811**	**30 066**	...	**194 767**	**196 769**
	Of which:									
3.1	- Petrol	...	678	768	...	190	150	...	23 086	...
3.2	- Diesel	...	793	1 029	...	23 621	29 916	...	159 787	...
3.3	- Other sources	...	1	-	...	-	-	...	11 894	...

For note see end of table.	Voir note en fin de tableau.	См. примечания в конце таблицы.

ROAD TRANSPORT - TRANSPORT ROUTIER
АВТОМОБИЛЬНЫЕ ДОРОГИ

11 (a). New road vehicle registrations during the year - By fuel type

11 (a). Nouvelles immatriculations de véhicules routiers durant l'année - Par type de combustible utilisé

11 (a). Парк новых дорожно-транспортных средств, зарегистрированных на конец года - по типу двигателя

(number - nombre - Число)

		Latvia / Lettonie / Латвия			Lithuania / Lituanie / Литва			Malta / Malte [2] / Мальта		
		1990	1998	1999	1990	1998	1999	1990	1998	1999
1	Passenger cars	...	57 363	45 861	...	147 105	142 069	8 218	10 750	13 341
	Of which:									
1.1	- Petrol	...	48 195	39 196	...	...	...	...	7 948	9 369
1.2	- Diesel	...	9 165	6 648	...	...	...	...	2 792	3 972
1.3	- Electricity	...	-	-	...	...	...	...	10	-
1.4	- Other sources	...	3	17	...	...	...	...	-	-
2	Motor coaches, Buses and Trolleybuses	...	655	783	...	1 076	521	...	49	5
	Of which:									
2.1	- Petrol	...	84	242	...	...	...	...	-	-
2.2	- Diesel	...	536	537	...	...	...	...	49	5
2.3	- Electricity	...	35	2	...	10	15	...	-	-
2.4	- Other sources	...	-	2	...	...	...	...	-	-
3	Lorries	...	4 768	6 298	...	12 050	7 214	1 435	2 769	2 176
	Of which:									
3.1	- Petrol	...	1 041	1 798	...	...	...	...	-	54
3.2	- Diesel	...	3 724	4 490	...	...	...	...	2 769	2 122
3.3	- Other sources	...	3	10	...	...	...	...	-	-

		Netherlands / Pays-Bas / Нидерланды			Norway / Norvège / Норвегия			Poland / Pologne / Польша		
		1990	1998	1999	1990	1998	1999	1990	1998	1999
1	Passenger cars	502 671	543 110	...	63 668	141 090	123 843	358 055	557 783	599 250
	Of which:									
1.1	- Petrol	...	432 059	...	61 240	129 163	111 526	...	517 726	540 256
1.2	- Diesel	...	110 318	...	2 428	11 927	12 317	...	34 404	44 440
1.3	- Electricity	...	-	...	-	-	-	...	5 653	14 554
1.4	- Other sources	...	733	...	-	-	-	...	-	-
2	Motor coaches, Buses and Trolleybuses	1 121	...	...	1 751	2 774	2 222	4 195	2 259	2 512
	Of which:									
2.1	- Petrol	...	...	...	393	297	102	...	99	186
2.2	- Diesel	...	...	...	1 358	2 477	2 120	...	2 093	2 213
2.3	- Electricity	...	...	...	-	-	-	...	67	113
2.4	- Other sources	...	...	...	-	-	-	...	-	-
3	Lorries	61 597	101 543	...	21 951	6 217	5 007	58 741	103 933	140 063
	Of which:									
3.1	- Petrol	...	...	...	9 282	...	...	...	47 751	76 960
3.2	- Diesel	...	...	...	12 669	...	...	...	55 382	61 574
3.3	- Other sources	...	...	...	-	...	...	...	800	1 529

For note see end of table.   Voir note en fin de tableau.   См. примечания в конце таблицы.

ROAD TRANSPORT - TRANSPORT ROUTIER
АВТОМОБИЛЬНЫЕ ДОРОГИ

11 (a). New road vehicle registrations during the year - By fuel type

11 (a). Nouvelles immatriculations de véhicules routiers durant l'année - Par type de combustible utilisé

11 (a). Парк новых дорожно-транспортных средств, зарегистрированных на конец года - по типу двигателя

(number - nombre - Число)

		Republic of Moldova République de Moldova Республика Молдова			Russian Federation Fédération de Russie Российская Федерация			Slovenia Slovénie Словения		
		1990	1998	1999	1990	1998	1999	1990	1998	1999
1	**Passenger cars**	...	**255**	**229**	**525 688**	**1 187 932**	...	...	**71 022**	**81 869**
	Of which:									
1.1	- Petrol	...	226	188	...	...	...	...	64 721	73 437
1.2	- Diesel	...	8	5	...	...	...	...	6 167	8 134
1.3	- Electricity	...	-	-	...	...	...	...	-	-
1.4	- Other sources	...	21	36	...	...	...	...	134	298
2	**Motor coaches, Buses and Trolleybuses**	...	**131**	**25**	...	**4 834**	...	...	**147**	**152**
	Of which:									
2.1	- Petrol	...	30	21	...	...	...	...	2	2
2.2	- Diesel	...	89	4	...	...	...	...	145	148
2.3	- Electricity	...	-	-	...	162	...	...	-	-
2.4	- Other sources	...	12	-	...	...	...	...	-	2
3	**Lorries**	...	**225**	**105**	...	...	...	...	**3 572**	**4 289**
	Of which:									
3.1	- Petrol	...	110	66	...	...	...	...	542	726
3.2	- Diesel	...	113	30	...	...	...	...	2 959	3 454
3.3	- Other sources	...	2	9	...	...	...	...	71	109

		Spain Espagne Испания			Sweden Suède Швеция			Switzerland Suisse Швейцария		
		1990	1998	1999	1990	1998	1999	1990	1998	1999
1	**Passenger cars**	**1 007 014**	**1 282 970**	**1 502 531**	**235 192**	**286 671**	**335 632**	**322 974**	**295 165**	**314 691**
	Of which:									
1.1	- Petrol	874 668	662 798	735 779	233 546	246 082	305 313	314 281	278 426	...
1.2	- Diesel	132 346	620 172	766 752	1 640	40 499	30 264	8 479	16 632	...
1.3	- Electricity	-	-	-	6	90	55	-	57	...
1.4	- Other sources	-	-	-	(a)	(a)	(a)	214	50	...
2	**Motor coaches, Buses and Trolleybuses**	**2 829**	**3 657**	**3 877**	**1 136**	**1 081**	**12 820**	**2 596**	...	...
	Of which:									
2.1	- Petrol	...	-	-	...	...	...	787	...	...
2.2	- Diesel	...	3 657	3 877	923	978	1 149	1 794	...	...
2.3	- Electricity	...	-	-	...	...	...	-	...	...
2.4	- Other sources	...	-	-	...	...	...	15	...	...
3	**Lorries**	**255 984**	**267 650**	**316 926**	**33 741**	**30 628**	**34 144**	**25 504**	**20 734**	...
	Of which:									
3.1	- Petrol	...	21 217	23 168	...	...	...	...	...	...
3.2	- Diesel	...	246 433	293 758	...	24 429	25 717	...	...	...
3.3	- Other sources	...	-	-	...	...	...	...	...	...

For note see end of table.   Voir note en fin de tableau.   См. примечания в конце таблицы.

141

ROAD TRANSPORT - TRANSPORT ROUTIER
АВТОМОБИЛЬНЫЕ ДОРОГИ

11 (a). New road vehicle registrations during the year - By fuel type

11 (a). Nouvelles immatriculations de véhicules routiers durant l'année - Par type de combustible utilisé

11 (a). Парк новых дорожно-транспортных средств, зарегистрированных на конец года - по типу двигателя

(number - nombre - Число)

		United Kingdom Royaume-Uni [3] Соединенное Королевство								
		1990	1998	1999						
1	**Passenger cars**	2 077 078	2 362 589	2 315 170						
	Of which:									
1.1	- Petrol	...	1 918 663	1 940 731						
1.2	- Diesel	...	339 395	312 751						
1.3	- Electricity	...	41	...						
1.4	- Other sources	...	104 490	...						
2	**Motor coaches, Buses and Trolleybuses**	5 401	14 242	14 219						
	Of which:									
2.1	- Petrol	...	666	614						
2.2	- Diesel	...	13 074	13 213						
2.3	- Electricity	...	10	...						
2.4	- Other sources	...	492	...						
3	**Lorries**	...	285 940	...						
	Of which:									
3.1	- Petrol	...	...	...						
3.2	- Diesel	...	...	...						
3.3	- Other sources	...	...	...						

NOTES TO TABLE 11(a) - NOTES DU TABLEAU 11(a) - ПРИМЕЧАНИЯ К ТАБЛИЦЕ 11(a)

General notes - Notes générales - Общие примечания

(a) Included under item 1.3.

(a) Compris sous la rubrique 1.3.

(a) Включено в статью 1.3.

Country notes - Notes relatives aux pays - Примечания к данным, представляемым странами

1- Excluding vehicles registered in Aland.

1- Non compris les véhicules immatriculés à Aland.

1- За исключением дорожно-транспортных средств, зарегистрированных на Аландских островах.

2- Lorries include agricultural tractors and special vehicles.

2- Les camions incluent les tracteurs agricoles et les véhicules spéciaux.

2- Грузовые автомобили, включая сельскохозяйственные тракторы и специальные транспортные спедства.

3- Data refer to Great Britain.

3- Les données se réfèrent à la Grande Bretagne.

3- Данные относятся к Великобритании.

ROAD TRANSPORT - TRANSPORT ROUTIER
АВТОМОБИЛЬНЫЕ ДОРОГИ

11(b). New goods road vehicles registered during the year - By load capacity

11(b). Nouveaux véhicules routiers pour le transport de marchandises immatriculés durant l'année - Par classe de charge utile

11(b). Новые грузовые автодорожные транспортные средства, зарегистрированные на конец года по грузоподъемности

Item Rubrique Статья	Description	Description	Описание
	New goods road vehicles registered during the year (number)	**Nouveaux véhicules routiers immatriculés durant l'année (nombre)**	**Автодорожные транспортные средства, зарегистрированные в стране (количество)**
1	**Lorries**	**Camions**	**Грузовые автомобили**
1.1	- Up to 999 kg	- Jusqu'à 999 kg	- До 999 кг
1.2	- 1 000 kg - 1 499 kg	- 1 000 kg - 1 499 kg	- 1 000 кг - 1 499 кг
1.3	- 1 500kg - 2 999 kg	- 1 500kg - 2 999 kg	- 1 500 кг - 2 999 кг
1.4	- 3 000 kg - 4 999 kg	- 3 000 kg - 4 999 kg	- 3 000 кг - 4 999 кг
1.5	- 5 000 kg - 6 999 kg	- 5 000 kg - 6 999 kg	- 5 000 кг - 6 999 кг
1.6	- 7 000 kg - 9 999 kg	- 7 000 kg - 9 999 kg	- 7 000 кг - 9 999 кг
1.7	- 10 000 kg - 14 999 kg	- 10 000 kg - 14 999 kg	- 10 000 кг - 14 999 кг
1.8	- 15 000 kg and more	- 15 000 kg et plus	- 15 000 кг и более
3	**Semi-trailers**	**Semi-remorques**	**Полуприцепы**
3.1	- Up to 4 999 kg	- Jusqu'à 4 999 kg	- До 4 999 кг
3.2	- 5 000 kg - 9 999 kg	- 5 000 kg - 9 999 kg	- 5 000 кг - 9 999 кг
3.0	- 10 000 kg - 14 999 kg	- 10 000 kg - 14 999 kg	- 10 000 кг - 14 999 кг
3.3	- 15 000 kg - 19 999 kg	- 15 000 kg - 19 999 kg	- 15 000 кг - 19 999 кг
3.4	- 20 000 kg and more	- 20 000 kg et plus	- 20 000 кг и более
4	**Trailers**	**Remorques**	**Прицепы**
4.1	- Up to 4 999 kg	- Jusqu'à 4 999 kg	- До 4 999 кг
4.2	- 5 000 kg - 9 999 kg	- 5 000 kg - 9 999 kg	- 5 000 кг - 9 999 кг
4.3	- 10 000 kg - 14 999 kg	- 10 000 kg - 14 999 kg	- 10 000 кг - 14 999 кг
4.4	- 15 000 kg and more	- 15 000 kg et plus	- 15 000 кг и более
	Load capacity of new goods road vehicles registered during the year (1000 tonnes)	**Charge utile des nouveaux véhicules routiers immatriculés durant l'année (1000 tonnes)**	**Грузоподъемность автотранспортных средств, зарегистрированных в стране (1000 тонн)**
5	**Lorries**	**Camions**	**Грузовые автомобили**
5.1	- Up to 999 kg	- Jusqu'à 999 kg	- До 999 кг
5.2	- 1 000 kg - 1 499 kg	- 1 000 kg - 1 499 kg	- 1 000 кг - 1 499 кг
5.3	- 1 500kg - 2 999 kg	- 1 500kg - 2 999 kg	- 1 500 кг - 2 999 кг
5.4	- 3 000 kg - 4 999 kg	- 3 000 kg - 4 999 kg	- 3 000 кг - 4 999 кг
5.5	- 5 000 kg - 6 999 kg	- 5 000 kg - 6 999 kg	- 5 000 кг - 6 999 кг
5.6	- 7 000 kg - 9 999 kg	- 7 000 kg - 9 999 kg	- 7 000 кг - 9 999 кг
5.7	- 10 000 kg - 14 999 kg	- 10 000 kg - 14 999 kg	- 10 000 кг - 14 999 кг
5.8	- 15 000 kg and more	- 15 000 kg et plus	- 15 000 кг и более
6	**Semi-trailers**	**Semi-remorques**	**Полуприцепы**
6.1	- Up to 4 999 kg	- Jusqu'à 4 999 kg	- До 4 999 кг
6.2	- 5 000 kg - 9 999 kg	- 5 000 kg - 9 999 kg	- 5 000 кг - 9 999 кг
6.3	- 10 000 kg - 14 999 kg	- 10 000 kg - 14 999 kg	- 10 000 кг - 14 999 кг
6.4	- 15 000 kg - 19 999 kg	- 15 000 kg - 19 999 kg	- 15 000 кг - 19 999 кг
6.5	- 20 000 kg and more	- 20 000 kg et plus	- 20 000 кг и более
7	**Trailers**	**Remorques**	**Прицепы**
7.1	- Up to 4 999 kg	- Jusqu'à 4 999 kg	- До 4 999 кг
7.2	- 5 000 kg - 9 999 kg	- 5 000 kg - 9 999 kg	- 5 000 кг - 9 999 кг
7.3	- 10 000 kg - 14 999 kg	- 10 000 kg - 14 999 kg	- 10 000 кг - 14 999 кг
7.4	- 15 000 kg and more	- 15 000 kg et plus	- 15 000 кг и более

ROAD TRANSPORT - TRANSPORT ROUTIER
АВТОМОБИЛЬНЫЕ ДОРОГИ

11(b). New goods road vehicles registered during the year - By load capacity

11(b). Nouveaux véhicules routiers pour le transport de marchandises immatriculés durant l'année - Par classe de charge utile

11(b). Новые грузовые автодорожные транспортные средства, зарегистрированные на конец года по грузоподъемности

		Austria Autriche Австрия			Bulgaria Bulgarie Болгария			Croatia Croatie Хорватия		
		1990	1998	1999	1990	1998	1999	1990	1998	1999
		Number - Nombre - Число								
1	**Lorries**	**26 795**	**28 956**	**29 837**	**15 105**	**8 551**	**1**	**...**	**7 720**	**5 864**
1.1	Up to 999 kg	20 227	19 340	19 068	...	...	...	...	3 176	2 378
1.2	1 000 kg - 1 499 kg	...	4 860	5 120	...	...	...	...	2 007	1 601
1.3	1 500kg - 2 999 kg	2 818	1 184	1 187	...	...	...	...	1 249	1 046
1.4	3 000 kg - 4 999 kg	...	363	327	...	...	1	...	349	250
1.5	5 000 kg - 6 999 kg	1 080	395	407	...	...	...	...	181	97
1.6	7 000 kg - 9 999 kg	1 727	849	818	...	...	...	...	305	182
1.7	10 000 kg - 14 999 kg	940	1 151	1 223	...	...	...	...	287	216
1.8	15 000 kg and more	3	814	930	...	...	...	...	166	94
3	**Semi-trailers**	**...**	**2 816**	**3 189**	**...**	**...**	**6**	**...**	**654**	**501**
3.1	Up to 4 999 kg	...	9	1	...	...	...	...	203	166
3.2	5 000 - 9 999 kg	...	8	4	...	...	...	...	19	6
3.3	10 000 - 14 999 kg	...	...	...	...	...	...	...	6	7
3.4	15 000 - 19 999 kg	...	...	...	...	...	...	...	8	3
3.5	20 000 kg and more	...	...	...	...	...	6	...	418	319
4	**Trailers**	**19 719**	**21 850**	**21 973**	**...**	**...**	**1**	**...**	**2 033**	**1 204**
4.1	Up to 4 999 kg	16 704	19 764	19 955	...	...	...	...	1 395	733
4.2	5 000 - 9 999 kg	1 283	644	632	...	...	...	...	389	270
4.3	10 000 - 14 999 kg	(a)	1 442	1 386	...	...	1	...	157	140
4.4	15 000 kg and more	1 732	...	...	...	...	...	...	92	61
		1000 tonnes - 1000 тонн								
5	**Lorries**	**...**	**...**	**...**	**...**	**...**	**-**	**...**	**20.0**	**14.0**
5.1	Up to 999 kg	...	...	...	...	...	...	...	2.0	2.0
5.2	1 000 kg - 1 499 kg	...	...	...	...	...	...	...	2.0	1.0
5.3	1 500kg - 2 999 kg	...	...	...	...	...	...	...	2.0	2.0
5.4	3 000 kg - 4 999 kg	...	...	...	...	...	...	...	1.0	1.0
5.5	5 000 kg - 6 999 kg	...	...	...	...	...	...	...	1.0	1.0
5.6	7 000 kg - 9 999 kg	...	...	...	...	...	...	...	3.0	1.0
5.7	10 000 kg - 14 999 kg	...	...	...	...	...	...	...	4.0	3.0
5.8	15 000 kg and more	...	...	...	...	...	...	...	5.0	3.0
6	**Semi-trailers**	**...**	**...**	**...**	**...**	**...**	**-**	**...**	**12.0**	**9.0**
6.1	Up to 4 999 kg	...	...	...	...	...	...	...	1.0	-
6.2	5 000 - 9 999 kg	...	...	...	...	...	...	...	-	-
6.3	10 000 - 14 999 kg	...	...	...	...	...	...	...	-	-
6.4	15 000 - 19 999 kg	...	...	...	...	...	...	...	-	-
6.5	20 000 kg and more	...	...	...	...	...	-	...	11.0	9.0
7	**Trailers**	**...**	**...**	**...**	**...**	**...**	**-**	**...**	**10.0**	**7.0**
7.1	Up to 4 999 kg	...	...	...	...	...	...	...	4.0	2.0
7.2	5 000 - 9 999 kg	...	...	...	...	...	...	...	2.0	2.0
7.3	10 000 - 14 999 kg	...	...	...	...	...	-	...	2.0	2.0
7.4	15 000 kg and more	...	...	...	...	...	...	...	2.0	1.0

For note see end of table.   Voir note à la fin du tableau.   См. примечания в конце таблицы.

144

ROAD TRANSPORT - TRANSPORT ROUTIER
АВТОМОБИЛЬНЫЕ ДОРОГИ

11(b). New goods road vehicles registered during the year - By load capacity

11(b). Nouveaux véhicules routiers pour le transport de marchandises immatriculés durant l'année - Par classe de charge utile

11(b). Новые грузовые автодорожные транспортные средства, зарегистрированные на конец года по грузоподъемности

		Finland Finlande [1] Финляндия			France France Франция			Germany Allemagne Германия		
		1990	1998	1999	1990	1998	1999	1990	1998	1999
		Number - Nombre - Число								
1	**Lorries**	**29 172**	**19 109**	**19 504**	**420 618**	**367 392**	**399 889**	...	**237 184**	**258 215**
1.1	Up to 999 kg	24 619	9 157	9 197	288 083	267 947	292 163	...	122 332	129 619
1.2	1 000 kg - 1 499 kg	...	6 164	6 695	80 244	58 731	60 463	...	46 675	50 578
1.3	1 500kg - 2 999 kg	1 128	498	456	26 560	21 380	22 729	...	33 236	38 396
1.4	3 000 kg - 4 999 kg	...	248	281	5 968	3 214	3 472	...	7 962	7 776
1.5	5 000 kg - 6 999 kg	354	191	210	4 560	4 287	4 896	...	4 370	2 449
1.6	7 000 kg - 9 999 kg	602	355	354	7 510	5 862	7 160	...	7 505	8 016
1.7	10 000 kg - 14 999 kg	1 281	1 469	1 268	6 611	4 766	6 216	...	15 104	2 817
1.8	15 000 kg and more	1 188	910	887	1 082	1 205	1 527	...	(b)	18 564
3	**Semi-trailers**	**345**	**2 229**	**569**	**19 481**	**18 794**	**20 651**	...	**21 752**	**23 460**
3.1	Up to 4 999 kg	...	2	-	81	88	42	...	169	...
3.2	5 000 - 9 999 kg	...	4	2	134	59	115	...	100	...
3.3	10 000 - 14 999 kg	...	22	14	651	242	205	...	558	...
3.4	15 000 - 19 999 kg	...	2 155	530	758	554	574	...	265	...
3.5	20 000 kg and more	15	46	19	17 857	17 851	19 715	...	20 660	...
4	**Trailers**	**25 181**	**22 628**	**24 488**	**3 445**	**2 807**	**3 350**	...	**160 159**	**174 141**
4.1	Up to 4 999 kg	23 764	21 619	23 502	194	295	415	...	145 545	157 460
4.2	5 000 - 9 999 kg	...	23	10	878	547	733	...	3 598	4 036
4.3	10 000 - 14 999 kg	...	42	20	1 148	896	978	...	8 140	12 625
4.4	15 000 kg and more	1 380	944	956	1 225	1 069	1 224	...	2 876	(c)
		1000 tonnes - 1000 тонн								
5	**Lorries**	**71.0**	**54.0**	**53.0**	**499.0**	**439.0**	**498.0**	...	**563.0**	**649.0**
5.1	Up to 999 kg	23.0	7.0	8.0	144.0	164.0	178.0	...	93.0	99.0
5.2	1 000 kg - 1 499 kg	...	7.0	7.0	104.0	73.0	75.0	...	57.0	63.0
5.3	1 500kg - 2 999 kg	3.0	1.0	1.0	41.0	35.0	38.0	...	74.0	84.0
5.4	3 000 kg - 4 999 kg	...	1.0	1.0	24.0	13.0	14.0	...	28.0	28.0
5.5	5 000 kg - 6 999 kg	2.0	1.0	1.0	27.0	26.0	29.0	...	26.0	14.0
5.6	7 000 kg - 9 999 kg	5.0	3.0	3.0	64.0	50.0	62.0	...	64.0	61.0
5.7	10 000 kg - 14 999 kg	17.0	19.0	17.0	78.0	58.0	76.0	...	221.0	300.0
5.8	15 000 kg and more	21.0	16.0	15.0	17.0	20.0	26.0	...	...	...
6	**Semi-trailers**	**6.0**	**42.0**	**11.0**	**476.0**	**492.0**	**542.0**	...	**584.0**	**636.0**
6.1	Up to 4 999 kg	...	0.0	0.0	-	0.0	-	...	6.0	...
6.2	5 000 - 9 999 kg	...	0.0	0.0	1.0	0.0	1.0	...	1.0	...
6.3	10 000 - 14 999 kg	...	0.0	0.0	8.0	3.0	3.0	...	7.0	...
6.4	15 000 - 19 999 kg	...	39.0	10.0	17.0	10.0	10.0	...	5.0	...
6.5	20 000 kg and more	-	2.0	1.0	450.0	479.0	528.0	...	572.0	...
7	**Trailers**	**49.0**	**38.0**	**38.0**	**48.0**	**35.0**	**37.0**	...	**319.0**	**359.0**
7.1	Up to 4 999 kg	14.0	13.0	14.0	1.0	1.0	1.0	...	133.0	145.0
7.2	5 000 - 9 999 kg	-	0.0	0.0	7.0	4.0	4.0	...	26.0	31.0
7.3	10 000 - 14 999 kg	-	1.0	0.0	15.0	11.0	12.0	...	110.0	183.0
7.4	15 000 kg and more	35.0	24.0	24.0	25.0	19.0	20.0	...	50.0	(d)

For note see end of table.　　　　Voir note à la fin du tableau.　　　　См. примечания в конце таблицы.

145

ROAD TRANSPORT - TRANSPORT ROUTIER
АВТОМОБИЛЬНЫЕ ДОРОГИ

11(b). New goods road vehicles registered during the year - By load capacity

11(b). Nouveaux véhicules routiers pour le transport de marchandises immatriculés durant l'année - Par classe de charge utile

11(b). Новые грузовые автодорожные транспортные средства, зарегистрированные на конец года по грузоподъемности

		Greece Grèce Греция			Hungary Hongrie Венгрия			Iceland Islande Исландия		
		1990	1998	1999	1990	1998	1999	1990	1998	1999
		Number - Nombre - Число								
1	**Lorries**	**42 561**	...	...	...	**25 087**	**27 270**	...	**1 472**	**1 797**
1.1	Up to 999 kg	36 348	...	...	...	8 831	9 528	...	807	1 055
1.2	1 000 kg - 1 499 kg	...	...	...	...	10 558	11 902	...	303	415
1.3	1 500kg - 2 999 kg	3 192	...	...	...	4 084	4 187	...	127	109
1.4	3 000 kg - 4 999 kg	...	...	...	...	1 112	1 027	...	41	55
1.5	5 000 kg - 6 999 kg	575	...	...	...	137	195	...	23	16
1.6	7 000 kg - 9 999 kg	896	...	...	...	95	83	...	44	36
1.7	10 000 kg - 14 999 kg	905	...	...	...	195	250	...	57	43
1.8	15 000 kg and more	645	...	...	...	75	98	...	70	68
3	**Semi-trailers**	**861**	...	...	...	**806**	**1 098**	**44**	**89**	**96**
3.1	Up to 4 999 kg	...	...	...	...	14	5	...	1	7
3.2	5 000 - 9 999 kg	...	...	...	...	74	1	...	-	1
3.3	10 000 - 14 999 kg	...	...	...	...	4	3	...	-	1
3.4	15 000 - 19 999 kg	...	...	...	...	6	6	...	5	-
3.5	20 000 kg and more	...	...	...	...	708	1 083	...	83	87
4	**Trailers**	**539**	...	...	...	**1 229**	**1 625**	**378**	**182**	**183**
4.1	Up to 4 999 kg	11	...	...	...	908	1 243	...	132	145
4.2	5 000 - 9 999 kg	23	...	...	...	38	77	...	12	7
4.3	10 000 - 14 999 kg	...	...	...	...	65	137	...	20	17
4.4	15 000 kg and more	505	...	...	...	218	176	...	18	14
		1000 tonnes - 1000 тонн								
5	**Lorries**	**73.1**	...	...	...	**34.0**	**37.0**	...	**3.9**	**4.0**
5.1	Up to 999 kg	29.5	...	...	...	6.0	7.0	...	0.5	-
5.2	1 000 kg - 1 499 kg	...	...	...	...	13.0	14.0	...	0.4	-
5.3	1 500kg - 2 999 kg	9.6	...	...	...	7.0	7.0	...	0.3	-
5.4	3 000 kg - 4 999 kg	...	...	...	...	3.0	3.0	...	0.2	-
5.5	5 000 kg - 6 999 kg	3.7	...	...	...	1.0	1.0	...	0.1	-
5.6	7 000 kg - 9 999 kg	7.0	...	...	...	2.0	2.0	...	0.4	-
5.7	10 000 kg - 14 999 kg	11.1	...	...	...	1.0	2.0	...	0.7	1.0
5.8	15 000 kg and more	12.2	...	...	...	1.0	1.0	...	1.4	1.0
6	**Semi-trailers**	**19.9**	...	...	...	**21.0**	**29.0**	...	**2.8**	**3.0**
6.1	Up to 4 999 kg	...	...	...	...	0.0	0.0	...	0.0	-
6.2	5 000 - 9 999 kg	...	...	...	...	0.0	0.0	...	-	-
6.3	10 000 - 14 999 kg	...	...	...	...	0.0	0.0	...	-	-
6.4	15 000 - 19 999 kg	...	...	...	...	0.0	0.0	...	0.1	-
6.5	20 000 kg and more	...	...	...	...	21.0	29.0	...	2.7	2.0
7	**Trailers**	**10.3**	...	...	...	**6.0**	**7.0**	...	**1.0**	**1.0**
7.1	Up to 4 999 kg	0.0	...	...	...	1.0	1.0	...	0.2	-
7.2	5 000 - 9 999 kg	0.2	...	...	...	0.0	1.0	...	0.1	-
7.3	10 000 - 14 999 kg	...	...	...	...	1.0	1.0	...	0.2	-
7.4	15 000 kg and more	10.1	...	...	...	4.0	4.0	...	0.4	-

For note see end of table.   Voir note à la fin du tableau.   См. примечания в конце таблицы.

11(b). New goods road vehicles registered during the year - By load capacity

11(b). Nouveaux véhicules routiers pour le transport de marchandises immatriculés durant l'année - Par classe de charge utile

11(b). Новые грузовые автодорожные транспортные средства, зарегистрированные на конец года по грузоподъемности

		Latvia Lettonie Латвия			Malta Malte [2] Мальта			Netherlands Pays-Bas Нидерланды		
		1990	1998	1999	1990	1998	1999	1990	1998	1999
		Number - Nombre - Число								
1	**Lorries**	...	**4 768**	**6 298**	**1 435**	**2 769**	**2 176**	**61 597**	**101 543**	...
1.1	Up to 999 kg	...	...	1 695	...	...	...	...	...	...
1.2	1 000 kg - 1 499 kg	...	1 078	1 295	...	...	...	...	...	...
1.3	1 500kg - 2 999 kg	...	829	1 538	...	...	...	...	...	...
1.4	3 000 kg - 4 999 kg	...	264	480	...	...	...	...	...	...
1.5	5 000 kg - 6 999 kg	...	186	177	...	...	...	...	...	...
1.6	7 000 kg - 9 999 kg	...	236	363	...	...	...	...	...	...
1.7	10 000 kg - 14 999 kg	...	263	584	...	...	...	...	...	...
1.8	15 000 kg and more	...	144	166	...	...	...	...	...	...
3	**Semi-trailers**	...	893	572	...	**59**	**63**	**6 576**	...	...
3.1	Up to 4 999 kg	...	...	...	...	-	-	...	...	...
3.2	5 000 - 9 999 kg	...	...	...	...	-	-	...	...	...
3.3	10 000 - 14 999 kg	...	...	...	...	-	...	...	...	...
3.4	15 000 - 19 999 kg	...	...	...	...	-	-	...	...	...
3.5	20 000 kg and more	...	...	...	...	59	63	...	...	...
4	**Trailers**	...	**1 731**	**1 652**	...	...	...	**15 232**	...	...
4.1	Up to 4 999 kg	...	...	...	...	...	...	13 518	...	...
4.2	5 000 - 9 999 kg	...	...	...	...	...	...	913	...	...
4.3	10 000 - 14 999 kg	...	...	...	...	...	...	...	...	...
4.4	15 000 kg and more	...	...	...	...	...	...	801	...	...
		1000 tonnes - 1000 тонн								
5	**Lorries**	...	**15.0**	**22.0**	...	...	...	...	...	...
5.1	Up to 999 kg	...	1.0	1.0	...	...	...	...	...	...
5.2	1 000 kg - 1 499 kg	...	1.0	2.0	...	...	...	...	...	...
5.3	1 500kg - 2 999 kg	...	2.0	3.0	...	...	...	...	...	...
5.4	3 000 kg - 4 999 kg	...	1.0	2.0	...	...	...	...	...	...
5.5	5 000 kg - 6 999 kg	...	1.0	1.0	...	...	...	...	...	...
5.6	7 000 kg - 9 999 kg	...	2.0	3.0	...	...	...	...	...	...
5.7	10 000 kg - 14 999 kg	...	4.0	7.0	...	...	...	...	...	...
5.8	15 000 kg and more	...	3.0	3.0	...	...	...	...	...	...
6	**Semi-trailers**	...	...	...	...	...	...	...	...	...
6.1	Up to 4 999 kg	...	...	...	...	...	...	...	...	...
6.2	5 000 - 9 999 kg	...	...	...	...	...	...	...	...	...
6.3	10 000 - 14 999 kg	...	...	...	...	...	...	...	...	...
6.4	15 000 - 19 999 kg	...	...	...	...	...	...	...	...	...
6.5	20 000 kg and more	...	...	...	...	...	...	...	...	...
7	**Trailers**	...	...	...	...	...	...	...	...	...
7.1	Up to 4 999 kg	...	...	...	...	...	...	...	...	...
7.2	5 000 - 9 999 kg	...	...	...	...	...	...	...	...	...
7.3	10 000 - 14 999 kg	...	...	...	...	...	...	...	...	...
7.4	15 000 kg and more	...	...	...	...	...	...	...	...	...

For note see end of table.   Voir note à la fin du tableau.   См. примечания в конце таблицы.

ROAD TRANSPORT - TRANSPORT ROUTIER
АВТОМОБИЛЬНЫЕ ДОРОГИ

11(b). New goods road vehicles registered during the year - By load capacity

11(b). Nouveaux véhicules routiers pour le transport de marchandises immatriculés durant l'année - Par classe de charge utile

11(b). Новые грузовые автодорожные транспортные средства, зарегистрированные на конец года по грузоподъемности

		Norway Norvège Норвегия			Poland Pologne Польша			Republic of Moldova République de Moldova Республика Молдова		
		1990	1998	1999	1990	1998	1999	1990	1998	1999
		Number - Nombre - Число								
1	**Lorries**	21 951	6 217	5 007	58 741	103 933	140 063	...	225	105
1.1	Up to 999 kg	...	...	...	...	...	...	...	25	24
1.2	1 000 kg - 1 499 kg	...	...	...	...	...	...	...	5	12
1.3	1 500kg - 2 999 kg	...	...	...	...	...	...	...	28	14
1.4	3 000 kg - 4 999 kg	...	...	...	...	...	...	...	50	17
1.5	5 000 kg - 6 999 kg	...	...	...	...	...	...	...	25	12
1.6	7 000 kg - 9 999 kg	...	...	...	...	...	...	...	5	7
1.7	10 000 kg - 14 999 kg	...	...	...	...	...	...	...	15	8
1.8	15 000 kg and more	...	...	...	...	...	...	...	72	11
3	**Semi-trailers**	138	778	510	...	10 037	8 203	...	79	23
3.1	Up to 4 999 kg	...	...	...	...	...	...	...	1	-
3.2	5 000 - 9 999 kg	...	...	...	...	...	...	...	2	-
3.3	10 000 - 14 999 kg	...	...	...	...	...	...	...	4	9
3.4	15 000 - 19 999 kg	...	...	...	...	...	...	...	1	7
3.5	20 000 kg and more	...	...	...	...	...	...	...	71	7
4	**Trailers**	9 184	23 122	25 633	...	15 472	10 201	...	13	5
4.1	Up to 4 999 kg	8 066	...	...	...	...	...	...	1	-
4.2	5 000 - 9 999 kg	858	...	...	...	...	...	...	11	2
4.3	10 000 - 14 999 kg	...	...	...	...	...	...	...	1	3
4.4	15 000 kg and more	260	...	...	...	...	...	...	-	-
		1000 tonnes - 1000 тонн								
5	**Lorries**	...	...	...	...	195.0	209.0	...	3.0	1.0
5.1	Up to 999 kg	...	...	...	...	...	...	...	0.0	0.0
5.2	1 000 kg - 1 499 kg	...	...	...	...	...	...	...	0.0	0.0
5.3	1 500kg - 2 999 kg	...	...	...	...	...	...	...	0.0	0.0
5.4	3 000 kg - 4 999 kg	...	...	...	...	...	...	...	0.0	0.0
5.5	5 000 kg - 6 999 kg	...	...	...	...	...	...	...	0.0	0.0
5.6	7 000 kg - 9 999 kg	...	...	...	...	...	...	...	0.0	0.0
5.7	10 000 kg - 14 999 kg	...	...	...	...	...	...	...	0.0	0.0
5.8	15 000 kg and more	...	...	...	...	...	...	...	2.0	0.0
6	**Semi-trailers**	...	...	...	...	223.0	192.0	...	2.0	0.0
6.1	Up to 4 999 kg	...	...	...	...	...	...	...	0.0	-
6.2	5 000 - 9 999 kg	...	...	...	...	...	...	...	0.0	-
6.3	10 000 - 14 999 kg	...	...	...	...	...	...	...	0.0	0.0
6.4	15 000 - 19 999 kg	...	...	...	...	...	...	...	0.0	0.0
6.5	20 000 kg and more	...	...	...	...	...	...	...	0.0	0.0
7	**Trailers**	...	...	...	...	70.0	39.0	...	0.0	0.0
7.1	Up to 4 999 kg	...	...	...	...	...	...	...	0.0	0.0
7.2	5 000 - 9 999 kg	...	...	...	...	...	...	...	0.0	0.0
7.3	10 000 - 14 999 kg	...	...	...	...	...	...	...	0.0	0.0
7.4	15 000 kg and more	...	...	...	...	...	...	...	0.0	0.0

For note see end of table.　　　　Voir note à la fin du tableau.　　　　См. примечания в конце таблицы.

ROAD TRANSPORT - TRANSPORT ROUTIER
АВТОМОБИЛЬНЫЕ ДОРОГИ

11(b). New goods road vehicles registered during the year - By load capacity

11(b). Nouveaux véhicules routiers pour le transport de marchandises immatriculés durant l'année - Par classe de charge utile

11(b). Новые грузовые автодорожные транспортные средства, зарегистрированные на конец года по грузоподъемности

		Slovenia Slovénie Словения			Spain Espagne Испания			Sweden Suède Швеция		
		1990	1998	1999	1990	1998	1999	1990	1998	1999
Number - Nombre - Число										
1	**Lorries**	...	3 572	4 289	255 984	267 650	316 926	33 741	30 628	34 144
1.1	Up to 999 kg	...	1 073	1 266	...	210 002	...	26 318	22 488	24 692
1.2	1 000 kg - 1 499 kg	...	707	849	...	42 899	...	...	3 973	4 017
1.3	1 500kg - 2 999 kg	...	1 085	1 284	...	...	...	2 165	557	507
1.4	3 000 kg - 4 999 kg	...	219	255	...	4 422	...	...	325	384
1.5	5 000 kg - 6 999 kg	...	84	101	...	2 064	...	506	324	402
1.6	7 000 kg - 9 999 kg	...	114	154	...	3 473	...	806	583	805
1.7	10 000 kg - 14 999 kg	...	220	237	...	4 790	...	2 203	1 534	1 916
1.8	15 000 kg and more	...	70	143	...	...	...	1 743	880	1 421
3	**Semi-trailers**	...	433	361	...	13 458	14 823	982	2 040	1 311
3.1	Up to 4 999 kg	...	6	5	...	...	...	11	9	22
3.2	5 000 - 9 999 kg	...	5	4	...	...	...	12	15	22
3.3	10 000 - 14 999 kg	...	22	17	...	...	...	3	...	...
3.4	15 000 - 19 999 kg	...	2	2	...	12 851	14 206	7	14	9
3.5	20 000 kg and more	...	398	333	...	...	...	949	1 992	1 246
4	**Trailers**	...	904	1 168	...	6 000	6 828	25 041	21 217	21 276
4.1	Up to 4 999 kg	...	667	837	...	...	...	21 920	19 799	18 507
4.2	5 000 - 9 999 kg	...	73	111	...	...	...	85	56	315
4.3	10 000 - 14 999 kg	...	142	183	...	979	...	324	189	...
4.4	15 000 kg and more	...	22	37	...	...	...	2 712	3 301	2 454
1000 tonnes - 1000 тонн										
5	**Lorries**	...	...	...	...	...	...	95.9	74.0	97.0
5.1	Up to 999 kg	...	...	...	...	...	...	22.2	19.0	21.0
5.2	1 000 kg - 1 499 kg	...	0.7	0.8	...	...	...	...	...	...
5.3	1 500kg - 2 999 kg	...	1.2	1.3	...	...	...	3.0	1.0	1.0
5.4	3 000 kg - 4 999 kg	...	0.7	0.8	...	...	...	2.4	1.0	2.0
5.5	5 000 kg - 6 999 kg	...	0.5	0.6	...	...	...	3.0	2.0	2.0
5.6	7 000 kg - 9 999 kg	...	0.9	1.3	...	...	...	6.8	5.0	7.0
5.7	10 000 kg - 14 999 kg	...	2.7	3.0	...	...	...	29.1	25.0	31.0
5.8	15 000 kg and more	...	1.2	3.9	...	...	...	29.4	20.0	33.0
6	**Semi-trailers**	...	11.0	9.4	...	...	...	28.6	64.0	40.0
6.1	Up to 4 999 kg	...	0.0	0.0	...	...	...	0.0	0.0	0.0
6.2	5 000 - 9 999 kg	...	0.0	0.0	...	...	...	0.1	0.0	0.0
6.3	10 000 - 14 999 kg	...	0.2	0.2	...	...	...	0.0	0.0	0.0
6.4	15 000 - 19 999 kg	...	0.0	0.0	...	...	...	0.1	0.0	0.0
6.5	20 000 kg and more	...	10.6	9.1	...	...	...	28.3	64.0	40.0
7	**Trailers**	...	3.2	4.8	...	...	...	91.2	106.0	86.0
7.1	Up to 4 999 kg	...	0.7	1.1	...	...	...	15.5	11.0	18.0
7.2	5 000 - 9 999 kg	...	0.4	0.7	...	...	...	0.7	3.0	4.0
7.3	10 000 - 14 999 kg	...	1.6	2.3	...	...	...	4.4	...	...
7.4	15 000 kg and more	...	0.4	0.7	...	...	...	70.7	92.0	70.0

For note see end of table.　　　　Voir note à la fin du tableau.　　　　См. примечания в конце таблицы.

ROAD TRANSPORT - TRANSPORT ROUTIER
АВТОМОБИЛЬНЫЕ ДОРОГИ

11(b). New goods road vehicles registered during the year - By load capacity

11(b). Nouveaux véhicules routiers pour le transport de marchandises immatriculés durant l'année - Par classe de charge utile

11(b). Новые грузовые автодорожные транспортные средства, зарегистрированные на конец года по грузоподъемности

		Turkey Turquie Турция			United Kingdom Royaume-Uni [3] Соединенное Королевство					
		1990	1998	1999	1990	1998	1999			
		Number - Nombre - Число								
1	**Lorries**	**33 860**	**116 156**	...	...	**285 940**	...			
1.1	Up to 999 kg	14 834	...	...	...	240 368	...			
1.2	1 000 kg - 1 499 kg	...	...	...	...	16 491	...			
1.3	1 500kg - 2 999 kg	...	...	...	...	1 022	...			
1.4	3 000 kg - 4 999 kg	...	...	...	...	1 447	...			
1.5	5 000 kg - 6 999 kg	...	...	...	...	6 508	...			
1.6	7 000 kg - 9 999 kg	92	...	...	...	937	...			
1.7	10 000 kg - 14 999 kg	11 221	...	...	...	2 829	...			
1.8	15 000 kg and more	...	...	...	...	2 104	...			
3	**Semi-trailers**	...	...	...	...	...	...			
3.1	Up to 4 999 kg	...	...	...	...	...	...			
3.2	5 000 - 9 999 kg	...	...	...	...	...	...			
3.3	10 000 - 14 999 kg	...	...	...	...	...	...			
3.4	15 000 - 19 999 kg	...	...	...	...	...	...			
3.5	20 000 kg and more	...	...	...	...	...	...			
4	**Trailers**	...	...	...	...	...	...			
4.1	Up to 4 999 kg	...	...	...	...	...	...			
4.2	5 000 - 9 999 kg	...	...	...	...	...	...			
4.3	10 000 - 14 999 kg	...	...	...	...	...	...			
4.4	15 000 kg and more	...	...	...	...	...	...			
		1000 tonnes - 1000 тонн								
5	**Lorries**	...	...	...	...	...	...			
5.1	Up to 999 kg	...	...	...	...	...	...			
5.2	1 000 kg - 1 499 kg	...	...	...	...	...	...			
5.3	1 500kg - 2 999 kg	...	...	...	...	...	...			
5.4	3 000 kg - 4 999 kg	...	...	...	...	...	...			
5.5	5 000 kg - 6 999 kg	...	...	...	...	...	...			
5.6	7 000 kg - 9 999 kg	...	...	...	...	...	...			
5.7	10 000 kg - 14 999 kg	...	...	...	...	...	...			
5.8	15 000 kg and more	...	...	...	...	...	...			
6	**Semi-trailers**	...	...	...	...	...	...			
6.1	Up to 4 999 kg	...	...	...	...	...	...			
6.2	5 000 - 9 999 kg	...	...	...	...	...	...			
6.3	10 000 - 14 999 kg	...	...	...	...	...	...			
6.4	15 000 - 19 999 kg	...	...	...	...	...	...			
6.5	20 000 kg and more	...	...	...	...	...	...			
7	**Trailers**	...	...	...	...	...	...			
7.1	Up to 4 999 kg	...	...	...	...	...	...			
7.2	5 000 - 9 999 kg	...	...	...	...	...	...			
7.3	10 000 - 14 999 kg	...	...	...	...	...	...			
7.4	15 000 kg and more	...	...	...	...	...	...			

For note see end of table.   Voir note à la fin du tableau.   См. примечания в конце таблицы.

ROAD TRANSPORT - TRANSPORT ROUTIER
АВТОМОБИЛЬНЫЕ ДОРОГИ

NOTES TO TABLE 11 (b) - NOTES DU TABLEAU 11 (b) - ПРИМЕЧАНИЯ К ТАБЛИЦЕ 11 (b)

General notes - Notes générales - Общие примечания

(a) Included under item 4.2.

(b) Included under item 1.7.

(c) Included under item 4.3.

(d) Included under item 7.3.

(a) Compris sous la rubrique 4.2.

(b) Compris sous la rubrique 1.7.

(c) Compris sous la rubrique 4.3.

(d) Compris sous la rubrique 7.3.

(a) Включено в статью 4.2.

(b) Включено в статью 1.7.

(c) Включено в статью 4.3.

(d) Включено в статью 7.3.

Country notes - Notes relatives aux pays - Примечания к данным, представляемым странами

1- Excluding vehicles registered in Aland.

2- Lorries include agricultural tractors and special vehicles.

3- Data refer to Great Britain.

1- Non compris les véhicules immatriculés à Aland.

2- Les camions incluent les tracteurs agricoles et les véhicules spéciaux.

3- Les données se réferent à la Grande Bretagne.

1- За исключением дорожно-транспортных средств, зарегистрированных на Аландских островах.

2- Грузовые автомобили, включая сельскохозяйственные тракторы и специапьные транспортные спедства.

3- Данные относятся к Великобритании.

ROAD TRANSPORT - TRANSPORT ROUTIER
АВТОМОБИЛЬНЫЕ ДОРОГИ

12. Road traffic indicators (Passenger and good vehicles)
12. Indicateurs du trafic routier (véhicules routiers pour le transport des voyageurs et des marchandises)
12. Указатели дорожного движения (пассажирские и грузовые автомобили)

Item	Description	Rubrique	Description
1	**Motor vehicles movement on national territory (million vehicle-kilometres)**	1	**Mouvements de véhicules automobiles sur le territoire national (millions de véhicules-kilomètres)**
1.1	- Motorcycles	1.1	- Motocycles
1.2	- Passenger cars	1.2	- Voitures particulières
1.3	- Motor coaches, Buses and Trolleybuses	1.3	- Autobus, autocars et trolleybus
1.4	- Lorries and road tractors	1.4	- Camions et tracteurs routiers
2	**Passenger transport on national territory (million passenger-kilometres)**	2	**Transport de voyageurs sur le territoire national (millions de voyageurs-kilomètres)**
2.1	- Motorcycles	2.1	- Motocycles
2.2	- Passenger cars	2.2	- Voitures particulières
2.3	- Motor coaches, Buses and Trolleybuses	2.3	- Autobus, autocars et trolleybus
3	**Goods carried in million tonnes**	3	**Marchandises transportées en millions de tonnes**
3.1	- National transport	3.1	- Transport national
3.2	- International transport - loaded	3.2	- Transport international - chargements
3.3	- International transport - unloaded	3.3	- Transport international - déchargements
3.4	- Cross trade road transport	3.4	- Transport routier international effectué par des tiers
3.5	- Road cabotage transport	3.5	- Cabotage routier
4	**Goods carried in million tonnes-kilometres**	4	**Marchandises transportées (millions de tonnes-kilomètres)**
4.1	- National transport	4.1	- Transport national
4.2	- International transport - loaded	4.2	- Transport international - chargements
4.3	- International transport - unloaded	4.3	- Transport international - déchargements
4.4	- Cross trade road transport	4.4	- Transport routier international effectué par des tiers
4.5	- Road cabotage transport	4.5	- Cabotage routier

Статья	Описание
1	**Дорожное движение по национальной территории - транспортное средство-км (млн.)**
1.1	- Мотоциклы
1.2	- Легковые автомобили
1.3	- Автобусы дальнего следования, городские автобусы и троллейбусы
1.4	- Грузовые автомобили и дорожные тягачи
2	**Пассажирские перевозки по национальной территории - пассажиро-км (млн.)**
2.1	- Мотоциклы
2.2	- Легковые автомобили
2.3	- Автобусы дальнего следования, городские автобусы и троллейбусы
3	**Перевезенные грузы в млн. тонн**
3.1	- Национальные перевозки
3.2	- Международные перевозки - загрузка в стране
3.3	- Международные перевозки - разгрузка в стране
3.4	- Автодорожная перевозка, осуществляемая третьей стороной
3.5	- Автодорожная каботажная перевозка
4	**Перевезенные грузы в млн. тонн-км**
4.1	- Национальные перевозки
4.2	- Международные перевозки - загрузка в стране
4.3	- Международные перевозки - разгрузка в стране
4.4	- Автодорожная перевозка, осуществляемая третьей стороной
4.5	- Автодорожная каботажная перевозка

ROAD TRANSPORT - TRANSPORT ROUTIER
АВТОМОБИЛЬНЫЕ ДОРОГИ

12. Road traffic indicators (Passenger and good vehicles)
12. Indicateurs du trafic routier (véhicules routiers pour le transport des voyageurs et des marchandises)
12. Указатели дорожного движения (пассажирские и грузовые автомобили)

(Millions - Миллионы)

		Albania Albanie Албания			Armenia Arménie Армения			Austria Autriche Австрия		
		1990	1998	1999	1990	1998	1999	1990	1998	1999
1	**Vehicle-kilometres**	...	...	...	...	242.4	178.0	...	...	...
1.1	- Motorcycles	...	...	...	...	...	...			
1.2	- Passenger cars	...	...	...	...	75.9	58.5	...	...	...
1.3	- Motor coaches, Buses, etc.	...	...	...	...	91.8	56.1	...	...	...
1.4	- Lorries and road tractors	...	...	...	...	74.7	63.4	...	...	...
2	**Passenger-kilometres**	...	...	...	...	1 952.8	1 597.2	63 822.0	...	...
2.1	- Motorcycles				...	...	...	121.0	...	...
2.2	- Passenger cars	...			...	2.1	1.8	63 701.0		
2.3	- Motor coaches, Buses, etc.	893.7			...	1 950.7	1 595.4	13 990.0	...	...
3	**Tonne of goods carried**	7.715	...	...	...	20.930	19.868	...	260.255	274.023
3.1	- National	...	...	...	...	...	...	...	229.088	240.272
3.2	- International - loaded	...	...	...	...	...	...	...	12.904	13.978
3.3	- International - unloaded	...	...	...	...	...	...	...	12.905	13.438
3.4	- Cross trade transport	...	...	...	...	...	...	...	3.474	4.033
3.5	- Road cabotage transport	...	...	...	...	...	...	...	1.884	2.302
4	**Tonne-km of goods carried**	368.6	...	...	...	219.0	223.6	5 287.0	16 118.0	16 827.0
4.1	- National	...	...	...	...	...	...	...	11 715.0	12 117.0
4.2	- International - loaded	...	...	...	...	...	...	...	1 972.0	2 131.0
4.3	- International - unloaded	...	...	...	...	...	...	...	1 904.0	1 984.0
4.4	- Cross trade transport	...	...	...	...	...	...	...	527.0	596.0
4.5	- Road cabotage transport	...	...	...	...	...	...	...	-	-

		Azerbaijan Azerbaïdjan Азербайджан			Belarus Bélarus Беларусь			Belgium Belgique Бельгия		
		1990	1998	1999	1990	1998	1999	1990	1998	1999
1	**Vehicle-kilometres**	...	...	...	...	...	...	70 275.6	86 065.4	...
1.1	- Motorcycles	...	...	...	...	...	...	352.9	1 063.5	...
1.1	- Passenger cars	...	...	...	...	...	...	59 887.4	72 415.1	74 911.2
1.2	- Motor coaches, Buses, etc.	...	...	...	...	...	...	570.6	681.9	...
1.3	- Lorries and road tractors	...	...	...	...	...	...	9 464.7	11 904.9	...
2	**Passenger-kilometres**	7 819.0	...	...	...	...	...	100 996.3	117 525.9	-
2.1	- Motorcycles	...	...	...	...	...	...	352.9	1 063.8	...
2.2	- Passenger cars	782.0	108.0	...	...	...	...	89 232.2	102 829.5	104 875.7
2.3	- Motor coaches, Buses, etc.	7 037.0	5 127.0	...	...	...	...	11 411.2	13 632.6	...
3	**Tonne of goods carried**	153.000	16.300	...	...	80.200	...	329.483	342.234	...
3.1	- National	...	...	...	...	...	...	276.870	283.952	...
3.2	- International - loaded	...	...	...	...	...	...	32.322	34.359	...
3.3	- International - unloaded	...	...	...	...	...	...	20.285	23.923	...
3.4	- Cross trade transport	...	...	...	...	...	...	...	...	...
3.5	- Road cabotage transport	...	...	...	...	...	...	...	...	...
4	**Tonne-km of goods carried**	3 287.0	706.0	...	...	3 126.0	...	32 049.0	37 355.0	...
4.1	- National	...	...	...	...	...	...	12 616.0	17 123.0	...
4.2	- International - loaded	...	...	...	...	...	...	11 328.0	12 018.0	...
4.3	- International - unloaded	...	...	...	...	...	...	8 105.0	8 215.0	...
4.4	- Cross trade transport	...	...	...	...	...	...	...	...	...
4.5	- Road cabotage transport	...	...	...	...	...	...	...	...	...

ROAD TRANSPORT - TRANSPORT ROUTIER
АВТОМОБИЛЬНЫЕ ДОРОГИ

12. Road traffic indicators (Passenger and good vehicles)
12. Indicateurs du trafic routier (véhicules routiers pour le transport des voyageurs et des marchandises)
12. Указатели дорожного движения (пассажирские и грузовые автомобили)

(Millions - Миллионы)

		Bulgaria / Bulgarie / Болгария			Canada / Canada / Канада			Croatia / Croatie / Хорватия		
		1990	1998	1999	1990	1998	1999	1990	1998	1999
1	Vehicle-kilometres	...	...	...	...	...	...	...	...	...
1.1	- Motorcycles	...	...	...	...	...	...	...	...	...
1.2	- Passenger cars	...	...	...	...	...	...	...	...	...
1.3	- Motor coaches, Buses, etc.	...	...	...	...	...	...	...	...	...
1.4	- Lorries and road tractors	...	...	...	...	...	...	...	...	...
2	Passenger-kilometres	...	...	8 186.0	...	...	...	...	...	...
2.1	- Motorcycles	...	...	...	...	...	...	...	...	...
2.2	- Passenger cars	...	...	...	...	...	...	...	...	...
2.3	- Motor coaches, Buses, etc.	25 955.0	...	8 186.0	...	...	...	...	3 964.0	3 355.0
3	Tonne of goods carried	295.870	...	15.467	...	233.931	...	12.764	32.564	36.126
3.1	- National	...	...	12.024	...	177.829	...	...	31.140	34.510
3.2	- International - loaded	...	...	1.814	...	34.284	...	...	0.698	0.771
3.3	- International - unloaded	...	...	1.138	...	21.818	...	...	0.659	0.734
3.4	- Cross trade transport	...	...	...	...	-	...	...	0.067	0.111
3.5	- Road cabotage transport	...	...	491.000	...	-	...	...	-	-
4	Tonne-km of goods carried	9 821.0	...	5 282.0	...	138 090.0	...	2 603.0	2 589.6	2 424.0
4.1	- National	...	...	168.0	...	76 693.0	...	...	1 813.0	1 607.0
4.2	- International - loaded	...	...	2 230.0	...	35 567.0	...	...	349.0	385.0
4.3	- International - unloaded	...	...	1 785.0	...	25 830.0	...	...	355.0	349.0
4.4	- Cross trade transport	...	...	...	...	-	...	...	72.6	83.0
4.5	- Road cabotage transport	...	...	1 099.0	...	-	...	...	-	-

		Czech Republic / République tchèque / Чешская Республика			Denmark / Danemark / Дания			Estonia / Estonie / Эстония		
		1990	1998	1999	1990	1998	1999	1990	1998	1999
1	Vehicle-kilometres	...	...	...	...	...	...	...	...	...
1.1	- Motorcycles	...	...	...	...	...	...	...	...	...
1.1	- Passenger cars	...	...	...	...	...	...	...	...	...
1.2	- Motor coaches, Buses, etc.	...	...	...	...	...	...	...	...	...
1.3	- Lorries and road tractors	...	...	...	...	...	...	...	...	...
2	Passenger-kilometres	...	70 261.0	71 671.0	...	78 635.0	80 554.0	...	...	...
2.1	- Motorcycles	...	...	...	369.0	517.0	563.0	...	...	...
2.2	- Passenger cars	...	60 800.0	62 250.0	53 600.0	56 688.0	58 662.0	...	...	...
2.3	- Motor coaches, Buses, etc.	...	9 461.0	9 421.0	9 314.0	11 135.0	11 173.0	...	...	...
3	Tonne of goods carried	...	470.888	448.300	205.047	204.251	216.298	78.200	12.200	12.000
3.1	- National	...	443.370	416.720	194.452	190.432	199.992	...	9.500	9.300
3.2	- International - loaded	...	13.414	16.751	5.857	6.949	8.364	...	...	...
3.3	- International - unloaded	...	8.417	13.444	4.721	6.192	7.182	...	...	...
3.4	- Cross trade transport	...	5.687	1.385	...	0.434	0.476	...	...	...
3.5	- Road cabotage transport	...	-	-	...	0.244	0.284	...	...	...
4	Tonne-km of goods carried	...	33 911.0	36 964.0	11 914.0	21 372.0	23 240.0	2 097.0	3 791.0	3 975.0
4.1	- National	...	17 931.0	16 930.0	9 352.0	10 108.0	10 426.0	...	538.0	734.0
4.2	- International - loaded	...	7 240.0	10 161.0	2 841.0	5 668.0	6 484.0	...	...	...
4.3	- International - unloaded	...	6 078.0	8 451.0	2 305.0	5 128.0	5 792.0	...	...	...
4.4	- Cross trade transport	...	2 662.0	1 421.0	...	390.0	436.0	...	...	...
4.5	- Road cabotage transport	...	-	-	...	78.0	102.0	...	...	...

154

12. Road traffic indicators (Passenger and good vehicles)
12. Indicateurs du trafic routier (véhicules routiers pour le transport des voyageurs et des marchandises)
12. Указатели дорожного движения (пассажирские и грузовые автомобили)

(Millions - Миллионы)

		Finland Finlande Финляндия			France France Франция			Georgia Georgie Грузия		
		1990	1998	1999	1990	1998	1999	1990	1998	1999
1	Vehicle-kilometres	40 550.0	44 850.0	...	...	...	...	...	...	...
1.1	- Motorcycles	800.0	900.0	...	...	...	...	...	...	...
1.2	- Passenger cars	33 430.0	38 450.0	...	...	...	...	...	...	...
1.3	- Motor coaches, Buses, etc.	680.0	540.0	...	...	...	...	...	...	...
1.4	- Lorries and road tractors	5 640.0	5 810.0	...	...	...	...	...	...	...
2	Passenger-kilometres	56 100.0	62 000.0	63 400.0	...	...	...	...	...	...
2.1	- Motorcycles	800.0	900.0	900.0	...	...	...	...	...	...
2.2	- Passenger cars	46 800.0	53 300.0	54 900.0	585 600.0	678 600.0	699 600.0	...	...	...
2.3	- Motor coaches, Buses, etc.	8 500.0	7 800.0	7 600.0	41 300.0	42 700.0	40 700.0	...	...	...
3	Tonne of goods carried	...	406.275	...	1 706.341	1 784.342	1 894.272	...	15.000	...
3.1	- National	...	400.131	410.847	1 647.000	1 702.457	1 811.849	...	...	...
3.2	- International - loaded	...	3.287	...	29.000	40.422	40.407	...	...	...
3.3	- International - unloaded	...	2.622	...	30.000	37.623	36.978	...	...	...
3.4	- Cross trade transport	...	0.073	...	0.105	1.366	1.307	...	...	...
3.5	- Road cabotage transport	...	0.162	...	0.236	2.474	3.731	...	...	...
4	Tonne-km of goods carried	...	30 243.0	...	137 900.0	168 785.0	183 447.0	...	...	...
4.1	- National	25 400.0	25 611.0	25 575.0	118 200.0	145 458.0	158 863.0	...	...	...
4.2	- International - loaded	...	2 974.0	...	10 000.0	11 091.0	11 809.0	...	...	...
4.3	- International - unloaded	...	1 541.0	...	8 800.0	10 446.0	10 899.0	...	...	...
4.4	- Cross trade transport	...	74.0	...	-	1 234.0	1 118.0	...	...	...
4.5	- Road cabotage transport	...	43.0	...	-	556.0	758.0	...	...	...

		Germany Allemagne Германия			Greece Grèce Греция			Hungary Hongrie Венгрия		
		1990	1998	1999	1990	1998	1999	1990	1998	1999
1	Vehicle-kilometres	...	627 482.0	...	...	...	...	...	...	...
1.1	- Motorcycles	...	11 400.0	...	...	...	...	...	...	...
1.1	- Passenger cars	...	528 000.0	...	...	...	...	...	...	...
1.2	- Motor coaches, Buses, etc.	...	3 700.0	...	...	...	...	...	...	...
1.3	- Lorries and road tractors	...	69 500.0	...	...	...	...	...	...	...
2	Passenger-kilometres	...	...	...	...	...	...	...	...	...
2.1	- Motorcycles	...	...	...	...	...	...	...	...	...
2.2	- Passenger cars	...	...	...	...	...	...	...	46 500.0	46 550.0
2.3	- Motor coaches, Buses, etc.	...	...	...	...	...	...	...	17 377.0	17 179.0
3	Tonne of goods carried	...	2 968.023	3 181.363	...	...	...	569.750	258.392	263.003
3.1	- National	...	2 880.689	3 083.583	...	...	...	...	252.514	257.407
3.2	- International - loaded	...	41.966	47.250	...	...	...	...	3.298	3.140
3.3	- International - unloaded	...	36.468	39.005	...	...	...	...	2.221	2.221
3.4	- Cross trade transport	...	6.986	4.770	...	...	...	...	0.359	0.235
3.5	- Road cabotage transport	...	4.914	6.756	...	...	...	...	-	-
4	Tonne-km of goods carried	...	257 447.0	278 470.0	12 490.0	...	...	15 179.3	18 674.0	18 599.0
4.1	- National	...	210 402.0	226 892.0	...	...	...	...	11 744.0	12 014.0
4.2	- International - loaded	...	22 607.0	24 474.0	...	...	...	...	3 793.0	3 594.0
4.3	- International - unloaded	...	19 566.0	21 217.0	...	...	...	...	2 640.0	2 618.0
4.4	- Cross trade transport	...	3 855.0	4 355.0	...	...	...	...	497.0	374.0
4.5	- Road cabotage transport	...	1 016.0	1 533.0	...	...	...	...	-	-

ROAD TRANSPORT - TRANSPORT ROUTIER
АВТОМОБИЛЬНЫЕ ДОРОГИ

12. Road traffic indicators (Passenger and good vehicles)
12. Indicateurs du trafic routier (véhicules routiers pour le transport des voyageurs et des marchandises)
12. Указатели дорожного движения (пассажирские и грузовые автомобили)

(Millions - Миллионы)

		Ireland Irlande Ирландия			Israel Israël Израиль			Italy Italie Италия		
		1990	1998	1999	1990	1998	1999	1990	1998	1999
1	Vehicle-kilometres	24 446.0	...	...	...	...	...	...	...	...
1.1	- Motorcycles	241.0	...	...	...	...	...	...	...	...
1.2	- Passenger cars	19 271.0	...	...	...	...	...	...	...	...
1.3	- Motor coaches, Buses, etc.	257.0	...	...	...	...	...	...	...	...
1.4	- Lorries and road tractors	4 677.0	...	...	...	...	...	...	...	...
2	Passenger-kilometres	...	...	...	...	...	...	596 708.0	...	...
2.1	- Motorcycles	...	...	...	...	...	...	24 000.0	...	...
2.2	- Passenger cars	...	...	...	...	...	...	522 593.0	...	...
2.3	- Motor coaches, Buses, etc.	...	...	...	...	...	...	50 115.0	...	...
3	Tonne of goods carried	81.061	...	...	126.300	...	...	911.767	1 230.288	...
3.1	- National	78.955	...	...	...	...	...	889.065	1 197.630	...
3.2	- International - loaded	1.050	...	...	...	...	...	13.361	16.203	...
3.3	- International - unloaded	1.057	...	...	...	...	...	9.317	14.789	...
3.4	- Cross trade transport	...	...	...	...	...	...	...	-	...
3.5	- Road cabotage transport	...	...	...	...	...	...	...	1.666	...
4	Tonne-km of goods carried	4 394.0	...	...	4 370.0	...	...	177 900.0	191 482.0	...
4.1	- National	3 877.0	...	...	...	...	...	115 785.0	...	...
4.2	- International - loaded	515.0	...	...	...	...	...	10 519.0	...	...
4.3	- International - unloaded	492.0	...	...	...	...	...	9 977.0	...	...
4.4	- Cross trade transport	...	...	...	...	...	...	...	...	...
4.5	- Road cabotage transport	...	...	...	...	...	...	...	...	...

		Kazakhstan Kazakhstan Казахстан			Kyrgyzstan Kirghizistan Кыргызстан			Latvia Lettonie Латвия		
		1990	1998	1999	1990	1998	1999	1990	1998	1999
1	Vehicle-kilometres	...	...	...	...	...	...	...	...	...
1.1	- Motorcycles	...	...	...	...	...	...	...	...	...
1.1	- Passenger cars	...	...	...	...	...	...	...	...	...
1.2	- Motor coaches, Buses, etc.	...	...	...	...	...	...	...	...	...
1.3	- Lorries and road tractors	...	...	...	...	...	...	...	...	...
2	Passenger-kilometres	...	...	...	5 500.6	3 914.1	4 112.1	...	...	...
2.1	- Motorcycles	...	...	...	...	...	...	...	...	...
2.2	- Passenger cars	...	118.0	61.0	245.4	52.4	34.1	...	...	...
2.3	- Motor coaches, Buses, etc.	...	6 445.0	4 837.0	5 255.2	3 861.7	4 078.0	7 224.0	2 451.0	2 892.0
3	Tonne of goods carried	...	...	...	329.900	34.179	35.023	206.210	33.765	33.401
3.1	- National	2 235.816	471.157	423.467	329.900	34.179	35.023	...	32.060	31.718
3.2	- International - loaded	...	...	...	...	...	...	...	0.981	0.860
3.3	- International - unloaded	...	...	...	...	...	...	...	0.432	0.561
3.4	- Cross trade transport	...	...	...	...	...	...	...	0.292	0.262
3.5	- Road cabotage transport	...	...	...	...	...	...	...	...	...
4	Tonne-km of goods carried	...	...	...	5 626.9	1 014.7	1 125.0	5 853.0	4 108.0	4 161.0
4.1	- National	44 775.0	4 637.3	4 506.3	5 626.9	1 014.7	1 125.0	...	1 498.0	1 590.0
4.2	- International - loaded	...	...	...	...	...	...	...	1 306.0	1 242.0
4.3	- International - unloaded	...	...	...	...	...	...	...	561.0	709.0
4.4	- Cross trade transport	...	...	...	...	...	...	...	743.0	620.0
4.5	- Road cabotage transport	...	...	...	...	...	...	...	...	...

ROAD TRANSPORT - TRANSPORT ROUTIER
АВТОМОБИЛЬНЫЕ ДОРОГИ

12. Road traffic indicators (Passenger and good vehicles)

12. Indicateurs du trafic routier (véhicules routiers pour le transport des voyageurs et des marchandises)

12. Указатели дорожного движения (пассажирские и грузовые автомобили)

(Millions - Миллионы)

		Lithuania Lituanie Литва			Luxembourg Luxembourg Люксембург			Netherlands Pays-Bas Нидерланды		
		1990	1998	1999	1990	1998	1999	1990	1998	1999
1	Vehicle-kilometres	...	...	...	...	...	...	96 816.0	...	...
1.1	- Motorcycles	...	...	...	...	...	...	2 450.0	...	...
1.2	- Passenger cars	...	...	...	...	...	...	80 041.0	...	...
1.3	- Motor coaches, Buses, etc.	...	...	...	...	...	...	621.0	...	...
1.4	- Lorries and road tractors	...	...	...	...	...	...	13 704.0	...	...
2	Passenger-kilometres	...	...	...	...	...	...	136 025.0	157 130.0	...
2.1	- Motorcycles	...	...	...	...	...	...	1 000.0	1 735.0	...
2.2	- Passenger cars	...	...	...	...	...	...	126 600.0	142 140.0	...
2.3	- Motor coaches, Buses, etc.	7 889.0	2 964.0	...	...	...	...	8 425.0	13 255.0	...
3	Tonne of goods carried	308.200	54.631	45 651.000	...	...	...	460.738	...	...
3.1	- National	...	50.105	41.449	19.598	...	...	386.940	...	...
3.2	- International - loaded	...	1.534	1.670	...	...	...	38.942	...	...
3.3	- International - unloaded	...	1.756	1.572	...	...	...	34.856	...	...
3.4	- Cross trade transport	...	1.174	0.914	...	...	...	-	...	...
3.5	- Road cabotage transport	...	0.062	0.046	7.281	...	...	-	...	...
4	Tonne-km of goods carried	7 336.0	5 611.0	7 740.0	3 178.0	...	...	54 989.0	...	...
4.1	- National	...	1 742.0	1 614.0	420.2	...	...	22 581.0	...	...
4.2	- International - loaded	...	1 231.0	2 314.0	...	...	...	15 469.0	...	...
4.3	- International - unloaded	...	1 274.0	1 812.0	...	...	...	11 536.0	...	...
4.4	- Cross trade transport	...	1 345.0	1 984.0	...	...	...	5 360.0	...	...
4.5	- Road cabotage transport	...	19.0	16.0	2 752.8	...	...	43.0	...	...

		Norway Norvège Норвегия			Poland Pologne Польша			Portugal Portugal Португалия		
		1990	1998	1999	1990	1998	1999	1990	1998	1999
1	Vehicle-kilometres	...	...	...	...	...	...	...	...	...
1.1	- Motorcycles	...	...	...	...	...	...	...	...	...
1.1	- Passenger cars	...	...	...	...	...	...	...	...	...
1.2	- Motor coaches, Buses, etc.	...	...	...	...	...	...	...	...	...
1.3	- Lorries and road tractors	...	...	...	...	...	...	...	...	...
2	Passenger-kilometres	43 171.0	52 925.0	53 141.0	...	...	...	...	...	...
2.1	- Motorcycles	705.0	924.0	1 000.0	...	...	...	...	...	...
2.2	- Passenger cars	42 466.0	45 780.0	45 785.0	...	...	...	...	...	...
2.3	- Motor coaches, Buses, etc.	3 890.0	4 248.0	4 248.0	46 599.0	34 035.0	33 250.0	...	11 419.0	11 481.0
3	Tonne of goods carried	...	246.015	243.717	1 292.358	1 077.295	1 068.388	241.115	271.760	280.302
3.1	- National	...	242.100	240.746	...	1 054.235	1 043.679	237.946	262.752	269.754
3.2	- International - loaded	...	1.951	1.826	...	12.535	13.865	1.654	4.090	4.671
3.3	- International - unloaded	...	1.863	2.007	...	9.537	10.379	1.515	4.269	5.217
3.4	- Cross trade transport	...	0.062	0.074	...	0.558	0.364	-	0.381	0.419
3.5	- Road cabotage transport	...	0.040	0.064	...	0.430	0.101	-	0.268	0.238
4	Tonne-km of goods carried	...	15 346.0	12 486.0	40 293.0	69 543.0	70 452.0	16 129.0	25 567.0	26 950.0
4.1	- National	...	12 343.0	9 312.0	...	46 846.0	47 199.0	10 978.0	14 695.0	15 220.0
4.2	- International - loaded	...	1 604.0	1 693.0	...	11 708.0	12 326.0	2 665.0	5 136.0	5 283.0
4.3	- International - unloaded	...	1 318.0	1 380.0	...	9 887.0	10 267.0	2 486.0	5 052.0	5 653.0
4.4	- Cross trade transport	...	74.0	77.0	...	932.0	596.0	-	402.0	694.0
4.5	- Road cabotage transport	...	7.0	24.0	...	170.0	64.0	-	282.0	99.0

ROAD TRANSPORT - TRANSPORT ROUTIER
АВТОМОБИЛЬНЫЕ ДОРОГИ

12. Road traffic indicators (Passenger and good vehicles)
12. Indicateurs du trafic routier (véhicules routiers pour le transport des voyageurs et des marchandises)
12. Указатели дорожного движения (пассажирские и грузовые автомобили)

(Millions - Миллионы)

		Republic of Moldova République de Moldova Республика Молдова			Romania Roumanie Румыния			Russian Federation Fédération de Russie Российская Федерация		
		1990	1998	1999	1990	1998	1999	1990	1998	1999
1	Vehicle-kilometres	...	...	...	...	...	...	...	...	...
1.1	- Motorcycles	...	...	...	...	...	...	...	...	...
1.2	- Passenger cars	...	...	...	...	...	...	...	...	...
1.3	- Motor coaches, Buses, etc.	...	...	...	...	...	...	...	...	...
1.4	- Lorries and road tractors	...	...	...	...	...	...	...	...	...
2	Passenger-kilometres	...	2 042.0	2 074.0	...	18 569.0	15 903.0	...	...	...
2.1	- Motorcycles	...	...	...	...	...	...	...	...	...
2.2	- Passenger cars	...	6.0	5.0	...	...	...	...	...	...
2.3	- Motor coaches, Buses, etc.	...	2 036.0	2 069.0	...	10 643.0	8 848.0	...	199 505.2	200 465.0
3	Tonne of goods carried	262.800	26.529	20.137	1 934.362	313.701	278.986	2 941.000	969.940	...
3.1	- National	...	24.681	18.985	...	310.280	276.494	...	...	...
3.2	- International - loaded	...	...	...	...	1.664	1.220	...	1.649	...
3.3	- International - unloaded	...	...	...	...	1.529	1.017	...	...	...
3.4	- Cross trade transport	...	...	...	...	0.228	0.255	...	...	...
3.5	- Road cabotage transport	...	...	...	...	-	-	...	...	...
4	Tonne-km of goods carried	6 305.0	940.0	952.0	28 993.0	15 785.0	13 456.0	68 000.0	21 000.0	...
4.1	- National	...	587.0	502.0	...	10 526.0	9 728.0	...	...	...
4.2	- International - loaded	...	...	...	...	2 545.0	1 930.0	...	1 659.9	...
4.3	- International - unloaded	...	...	...	...	2 367.0	1 676.0	...	(a)	...
4.4	- Cross trade transport	...	...	...	...	346.0	123.0	...	...	...
4.5	- Road cabotage transport	...	...	...	...	...	...	...	...	...

		Slovakia Slovaquie Словакия			Slovenia Slovénie Словения			Spain Espagne Испания		
		1990	1998	1999	1990	1998	1999	1990	1998	1999
1	Vehicle-kilometres	...	...	...	...	8 576.8	9 082.0	...	...	...
1.1	- Motorcycles	...	...	...	...	42.7	41.0	...	...	...
1.1	- Passenger cars	...	...	...	4 749.0	7 576.7	8 021.0	...	...	...
1.2	- Motor coaches, Buses, etc.	...	...	...	131.0	95.0	101.0	...	...	...
1.3	- Lorries and road tractors	...	...	...	740.0	862.4	919.0	...	...	...
2	Passenger-kilometres	...	...	...	...	...	...	...	...	...
2.1	- Motorcycles	...	...	...	...	...	...	...	...	...
2.2	- Passenger cars	...	...	...	...	...	...	...	...	...
2.3	- Motor coaches, Buses, etc.	...	14 153.0	13 284.0	...	1 947.0	1 840.0	...	...	...
3	Tonne of goods carried	...	185.659	151.294	70.586	80.274	87.310	987.138	719.335	827.059
3.1	- National	...	...	...	...	...	...	973.709	690.807	793.911
3.2	- International - loaded	...	...	...	...	...	...	7.208	14.417	16.412
3.3	- International - unloaded	...	...	...	...	...	...	6.221	13.106	15.401
3.4	- Cross trade transport	...	...	...	...	...	...	...	0.666	0.598
3.5	- Road cabotage transport	...	...	...	...	...	...	...	0.339	0.737
4	Tonne-km of goods carried	...	17 879.0	18 516.0	4 887.0	3 374.0	3 440.0	109 533.0	125 268.0	134 259.0
4.1	- National	...	...	...	...	...	...	97 262.0	91 330.0	98 146.0
4.2	- International - loaded	...	...	...	...	...	...	6 462.0	18 272.0	19 425.0
4.3	- International - unloaded	...	...	...	...	...	...	5 809.0	14 542.0	15 621.0
4.4	- Cross trade transport	...	...	...	...	...	...	...	1 001.0	795.0
4.5	- Road cabotage transport	...	...	...	...	...	...	...	123.0	272.0

(a) Included under previous item.　　　(a) Compris sous la rubrique précédente.　　　(a) Включено в предыдущий показатель.

12. Road traffic indicators (Passenger and good vehicles)
12. Indicateurs du trafic routier (véhicules routiers pour le transport des voyageurs et des marchandises)
12. Указатели дорожного движения (пассажирские и грузовые автомобили)

(Millions - Миллионы)

		Sweden / Suède / Швеция			Switzerland / Suisse / Швейцария			Tajikistan / Tadjikistan / Таджикистан		
		1990	1998	1999	1990	1998	1999	1990	1998	1999
1	Vehicle-kilometres	...	67 401.0	69 558.0	...	...	...	...	1 092.2	1 576.5
1.1	- Motorcycles	...	613.0	669.0	1 211.0	...	1 643.0	...	-	-
1.2	- Passenger cars	59 400.0	57 009.0	58 583.0	42 649.0	...	46 336.0	...	115.0	195.6
1.3	- Motor coaches, Buses, etc.	...	1 130.0	1 153.0	...	...	...	...	275.3	168.9
1.4	- Lorries and road tractors	...	8 649.0	9 153.0	...	5 811.0	...	...	701.9	1 212.0
2	Passenger-kilometres	95 900.0	...	...	...	...	...	...	904.0	851.7
2.1	- Motorcycles	1 200.0	...	...	1 393.0	...	...	...	-	-
2.2	- Passenger cars	85 600.0	...	...	73 271.0	...	...	...	47.9	28.8
2.3	- Motor coaches, Buses, etc.	8 600.0	...	...	...	...	...	...	856.1	822.9
3	Tonne of goods carried	...	317.622	310.221	...	...	...	...	...	...
3.1	- National	...	313.188	305.878	...	...	...	...	3.802	2.815
3.2	- International - loaded	...	2.487	2.583	...	...	...	...	...	...
3.3	- International - unloaded	...	1.846	1.656	...	...	...	...	...	...
3.4	- Cross trade transport	...	0.056	0.058	...	...	...	...	...	...
3.5	- Road cabotage transport	...	0.045	0.046	...	...	...	...	...	...
4	Tonne-km of goods carried	...	33 285.0	33 175.0	...	...	...	...	...	...
4.1	- National	26 519.0	30 369.0	30 491.0	...	...	...	...	50.0	48.0
4.2	- International - loaded	...	1 565.0	1 485.0	...	...	...	...	...	...
4.3	- International - unloaded	...	1 265.0	1 126.0	...	...	...	...	...	...
4.4	- Cross trade transport	...	60.0	54.0	...	...	...	...	...	...
4.5	- Road cabotage transport	...	26.0	19.0	...	...	...	...	...	...

		The FYR of Macedonia [1]			Turkey / Turquie / Турция			Ukraine / Ukraine / Украина		
		1990	1998	1999	1990	1998	1999	1990	1998	1999
1	Vehicle-kilometres	...	...	...	27 041.0	...	...	...	...	...
1.1	- Motorcycles	...	...	...	...	...	...	...	...	...
1.1	- Passenger cars	...	...	...	...	...	...	...	...	...
1.2	- Motor coaches, Buses, etc.	...	...	...	...	...	...	...	...	...
1.3	- Lorries and road tractors	...	...	...	...	...	...	...	...	...
2	Passenger-kilometres	1 492.0	...	...	134 991.0	...	...	...	...	...
2.1	- Motorcycles	...	...	...	16 428.0	...	...	...	...	...
2.2	- Passenger cars	...	...	...	34 325.0	...	...	88 368.0	...	...
2.3	- Motor coaches, Buses, etc.	...	753.0	796.0	84 238.0	...	...	110 247.0	...	...
3	Tonne of goods carried	8.036	1.895	2.327	...	...	...	4 897.000	1 081.000	...
3.1	- National	7.327	1.176	1.290	...	...	...	...	...	...
3.2	- International - loaded	0.223	0.224	0.352	...	...	...	...	...	...
3.3	- International - unloaded	0.356	0.397	0.596	...	...	...	...	...	...
3.4	- Cross trade transport	0.130	0.098	0.089	...	...	...	...	...	...
3.5	- Road cabotage transport	-	...	...	...	...	...	...	...	...
4	Tonne-km of goods carried	2 189.0	894.0	839.0	65 710.0	152 210.0	...	79 700.0	18 300.0	...
4.1	- National	1 774.0	435.0	354.0	...	...	...	...	...	...
4.2	- International - loaded	176.0	167.0	182.0	...	...	...	...	...	...
4.3	- International - unloaded	123.0	220.0	224.0	...	...	...	...	...	...
4.4	- Cross trade transport	116.0	72.0	79.0	...	...	...	...	...	...
4.5	- Road cabotage transport	-	...	...	...	...	...	...	...	...

1- The former Yugoslav Republic of Macedonia.

1- L'ex-République yougoslave de Macédoine.

1- Бывшая Югославская Республика Македония.

ROAD TRANSPORT - TRANSPORT ROUTIER
АВТОМОБИЛЬНЫЕ ДОРОГИ

12. Road traffic indicators (Passenger and good vehicles)

12. Indicateurs du trafic routier (véhicules routiers pour le transport des voyageurs et des marchandises)

12. Указатели дорожного движения (пассажирские и грузовые автомобили)

(Millions - Миллионы)

		United Kingdom Royaume-Uni Соединенное Королевство			United States Etats-Unis Соединенные Штаты			Yugoslavia Yugoslavie Югославия		
		1990	1998	1999	1990	1998	1999	1990	1998	1999
1	**Vehicle-kilometres**	**407 570.0**	**459 441.0**	**467 000.0**	...	...	...	...	...	...
1.1	- Motorcycles	6 400.0	3 950.0	4 600.0	...	...	...	...	...	...
1.2	- Passenger cars	330 740.0	418 389.0	...	...	...	...	...	...	...
1.3	- Motor coaches, Buses, etc.	4 690.0	5 009.0	5 009.0	...	...	...	...	...	...
1.4	- Lorries and road tractors	65 740.0	32 092.0	...	...	...	...	...	...	...
2	**Passenger-kilometres**	**608 100.0**	...	...	**5 062 172.0**	**6 471 044.9**	...	...	...	...
2.1	- Motorcycles	6 100.0	...	...	19 687.0	18 159.0	...	...	...	...
2.2	- Passenger cars	556 000.0	...	...	4 847 363.0	6 214 231.0	...	...	...	...
2.3	- Motor coaches, Buses, etc.	46 000.0	...	...	195 122.0	238 655.0	...	...	...	...
3	**Tonne of goods carried**	**1 696.380**	**1 695.583**	**1 637.536**	...	...	...	...	**81.829**	**77.171**
3.1	- National	1 687.000	1 679.434	1 621.143	...	3 586.207	...	...	81.646	77.013
3.2	- International - loaded	4.624	7.482	7.517	...	...	...	...	0.090	0.077
3.3	- International - unloaded	4.756	8.023	8.384	...	...	...	...	0.048	0.046
3.4	- Cross trade transport	...	0.474	0.359	...	...	...	...	0.045	0.035
3.5	- Road cabotage transport	...	0.170	0.133	...	...	...	...	-	-
4	**Tonne-km of goods carried**	**138 451.0**	**172 004.0**	**169 298.0**	...	...	...	...	**3 095.0**	**2 316.0**
4.1	- National	127 803.0	155 431.0	152 922.0	...	1 499 494.5	...	...	2 983.0	2 198.0
4.2	- International - loaded	5 411.0	8 058.0	7 967.0	...	...	...	...	59.0	61.0
4.3	- International - unloaded	5 237.0	8 064.0	8 077.0	...	...	...	...	34.0	32.0
4.4	- Cross trade transport	...	403.0	291.0	...	...	...	...	19.0	25.0
4.5	- Road cabotage transport	...	48.0	41.0	...	...	...	...	-	-

ROAD TRANSPORT - TRANSPORT ROUTIER
АВТОМОБИЛЬНЫЕ ДОРОГИ

13. Goods road vehicles operated for hire or reward

13. Véhicules routiers pour le transport des marchandises opérant pour le compte d'autrui

13. Грузовые автодорожные транспортные средства, осуществляющие перевозки за плату или вознаграждеие

Item	Description	Rubrique	Description
1	**Number of goods road vehicles operated for hire or reward**	**1**	**Nombre de véhicules routiers pour le transport des marchandises opérant pour le compte d'autrui**
1.1	- Lorries *% over total*	1.1	- Camions *% par rapport au total*
1.2	- Road tractors *% over total*	1.2	- Tracteurs routiers *% par rapport au total*
1.3	- Semi trailers *% over total*	1.3	- Semi-remorques *% par rapport au total*
1.4	- Trailers *% over total*	1.4	- Remorques *% par rapport au total*
2	**Load capacity of road vehicles operated for hire or rewards (1000 tonnes)**	**2**	**Charge utile des véhicules routiers pour le transport des marchandises opérant pour le compte d'autrui (1000 tonnes)**
2.1	- Lorries *% over total*	2.1	- Camions *% par rapport au total*
2.2	- Semi trailers *% over total*	2.2	- Semi-remorques *% par rapport au total*
2.3	- Trailers *% over total*	2.3	- Remorques *% par rapport au total*
3	**Goods carried by road vehicle operated for hire or reward**	**3**	**Transport de marchandises par les véhicules routiers opérant pour le compte d'autrui**
3.1	- In tonnes (1000) *% over total*	3.1	- En tonnes (1000) *% par rapport au total*
3.2	- In tonne-kilometres (million) *% over total*	3.2	- En tonnes-kilomètres (millions) *% par rapport au total*

Статья	Описание
1	**Грузовые автодорожные транспортные средства, осуществляющие перевозки за плату или вознаграждеие (число)**
1.1	- Грузовые автомобили *в % к общему итогу*
1.2	- Дорожные тягачи *в % к общему итогу*
1.3	- Полуприцепы *в % к общему итогу*
1.4	- Прицепы *в % к общему итогу*
2	**Перевозки за плату или вознаграждение (1000 тонн)**
2.1	- Грузовые автомобили *в % к общему итогу*
2.2	- Полуприцепы *в % к общему итогу*
2.3	- Прицепы *в % к общему итогу*
3	**Товары, перевезенные грузовыми автодорожными транспортными средствами за плату или вознаграждение**
3.1	- в тыс. Тонн *в % к общему итогу*
3.2	- в млн тн/км *в % к общему итогу*

ROAD TRANSPORT - TRANSPORT ROUTIER
АВТОМОБИЛЬНЫЕ ДОРОГИ

13. Goods road vehicles operated for hire or reward

13. Véhicules routiers pour le transport des marchandises opérant pour le compte d'autrui

13. Грузовые автодорожные транспортные средства, осуществляющие перевозки за плату или вознаграждеие

		Austria Autriche [1] Австрия			Belgium Belgique Бельгия			Bulgaria Bulgarie Болгария		
		1990	1998	1999	1990	1998	1999	1990	1998	1999
1	**Goods vehicles (number)**									
1.1	- Lorries	21 011	23 758	24 898	14 236	24 209	...	37 140	...	2 016
	% over total	*8.32*	*7.67*	*7.81*	*4.15*	*5.00*	...	...	...	*100.00*
1.2	- Road tractors	...	11 501	*12 729*	...	...	...	...	...	1 017
	% over total	...	*73.23*	*74.81*	...	...	...	...	...	*100.00*
1.3	- Semi trailers	...	...	...	...	33 123	...	...	...	1 126
	% over total	...	...	...	...	*51.50*	...	...	...	*100.00*
1.4	- Trailers	20 697	24 851	...	...	7 289	...	...	...	925
	% over total	*6.99*	*5.57*	...	...	*8.00*	...	...	...	*100.00*
2	**Load capacity (1000 tonnes)**									
2.1	- Lorries	...	...	...	112.9	110.9	...	...	...	20
	% over total	...	...	...	*14.00*	*12.00*	...	...	...	*100.00*
2.2	- Semi trailers	...	...	...	...	889.6	...	...	...	23
	% over total	...	...	...	...	*53.15*	...	...	...	*100.00*
2.3	- Trailers	...	...	...	...	65.9	...	...	...	8
	% over total	...	...	...	...	*26.00*	...	...	...	*100.00*
3	**Goods carried**									
3.1	- In 1000 tonnes	...	135 902.0	147 056.0	167 941.0	221 423.0	...	...	...	15 467.0
	% over total	...	*52.22*	*53.67*	*50.97*	*64.70*	...	...	...	*100.00*
3.2	- In million tkm	3 464.0	10 493.0	11 146.0	...	29 087.0	...	...	...	5 282.0
	% over total	*65.52*	*65.10*	*66.24*	...	*77.87*	...	...	...	*100.00*

		Croatia Croatie Хорватия			Czech Republic République tchèque Чешская Республика			Denmark Danemark Дания		
		1990	1998	1999	1990	1998	1999	1990	1998	1999
1	**Goods vehicles (number)**									
1.1	- Lorries	...	...	...	...	73 646	83 160	...	...	...
	% over total	...	...	...	...	*28.30*	*31.00*	...	...	...
1.2	- Road tractors	...	...	...	...	15 873	16 773	...	9 409	10 118
	% over total	...	...	...	...	*79.23*	*79.30*	...	*89.64*	*89.89*
1.3	- Semi trailers	...	...	...	...	16 509	17 100	...	...	...
	% over total	...	...	...	...	*81.39*	*79.60*	...	...	...
1.4	- Trailers	...	...	...	...	48 673	49 213	...	...	...
	% over total	...	...	...	...	*58.19*	*52.80*	...	...	...
2	**Load capacity (1000 tonnes)**									
2.1	- Lorries	...	...	...	...	319.3	248.6	...	...	...
	% over total	...	...	...	...	*38.41*	*31.00*	...	...	...
2.2	- Semi trailers	...	...	...	...	400.3	421.6	...	...	...
	% over total	...	...	...	...	*81.40*	*79.60*	...	...	...
2.3	- Trailers	...	...	...	...	217.3	193.5	...	...	...
	% over total	...	...	...	...	*58.19*	*52.80*	...	...	...
3	**Goods carried**									
3.1	- In 1000 tonnes	...	5 689.0	5 221.0	...	201 933.0	207 763.0	145 667.0	155 418.0	151 863.0
	% over total	...	*17.47*	*14.45*	...	*42.88*	*46.34*	*71.04*	*76.09*	*70.21*
3.2	- In million tkm	...	1 150.9	1 093.0	...	24 489.0	26 039.0	11 586.0	19 085.0	21 105.0
	% over total	...	*44.44*	*45.09*	...	*72.22*	*70.44*	*97.25*	*89.30*	*90.81*

1- Semi-trailers and trailers are included under a single item.

1- Les semi-remorques et les remorques sont groupées sous une seule catégorie.

1- Полуприцепы и прицепы включаются в одну статью.

ROAD TRANSPORT - TRANSPORT ROUTIER
АВТОМОБИЛЬНЫЕ ДОРОГИ

13. Goods road vehicles operated for hire or reward
13. Véhicules routiers pour le transport des marchandises opérant pour le compte d'autrui
13. Грузовые автодорожные транспортные средства, осуществляющие перевозки за плату или вознаграждеие.

		Finland Finlande [1) Финляндия			France France Франция			Germany Allemagne Германия		
		1990	1998	1999	1990	1998	1999	1990	1998	1999
1	**Goods vehicles (number)**									
1.1	- Lorries	28 276	31 192	32 128	...	161 302	173 216	...	...	...
	% over total	*10.81*	*11.12*	*10.94*	...	*3.24*	*3.41*	...	...	...
1.2	- Road tractors	...	4 612	*4 547*	...	108 416	113 759	...	...	...
	% over total	...	*87.80*	*87.29*	...	*58.81*	*59.59*	...	...	...
1.3	- Semi trailers	...	4 363	4 408	...	139 640	145 969	...	...	...
	% over total	...	*34.98*	*34.83*	...	*53.58*	*54.22*	...	...	...
1.4	- Trailers	...	10 581	10 745	...	16 913	17 661	...	...	...
	% over total	...	*2.28*	*2.21*	...	*33.65*	*34.56*	...	...	...
2	**Load capacity (1000 tonnes)**									
2.1	- Lorries	...	345.0	354.0	...	213.0	226.0	...	...	...
	% over total	...	*46.18*	*45.85*	...	*3.24*	*3.41*	...	...	...
2.2	- Semi trailers	...	79.0	79.0	...	3 566.0	3 742.0	...	...	...
	% over total	...	*35.27*	*34.96*	...	*53.59*	*54.22*	...	...	...
2.3	- Trailers	...	223.0	229.0	...	211.0	235.0	...	...	...
	% over total	...	*34.90*	*34.28*	...	*33.71*	*34.56*	...	...	...
3	**Goods carried**									
3.1	- In 1000 tonnes	...	282 302.0	289 768.0	...	1 041 649.0	1 153 657.0	...	1 513 047.0	1 612 028.0
	% over total	...	*69.49*	*70.53*	...	*58.38*	*60.90*	...	*50.98*	*50.67*
3.2	- In million tkm	...	27 576.0	22 832.0	...	137 306.0	152 225.0	...	185 065.0	200 135.0
	% over total	...	*91.18*	*89.27*	...	*81.35*	*82.98*	...	*71.88*	*71.87*

		Hungary Hongrie Венгрия			Iceland Islande Исландия			Ireland Irlande Ирландия		
		1990	1998	1999	1990	1998	1999	1990	1998	1999
1	**Goods vehicles (number)**									
1.1	- Lorries	...	...	...	...	...	9 803	...	9 381	13 994
	% over total	...	...	...	...	...	*57.28*	...	*5.49*	*7.41*
1.2	- Road tractors	...	...	...	...	...	495	...	...	...
	% over total	...	...	...	...	...	*71.53*	...	...	...
1.3	- Semi trailers	...	...	...	...	...	918	...	...	...
	% over total	...	...	...	...	...	*75.68*	...	...	...
1.4	- Trailers	...	...	...	...	...	1 186	...	...	...
	% over total	...	...	...	...	...	*30.18*	...	...	...
2	**Load capacity (1000 tonnes)**									
2.1	- Lorries	...	...	...	...	...	34.0	...	...	...
	% over total	...	...	...	...	...	*64.15*	...	...	...
2.2	- Semi trailers	...	...	...	...	...	24.0	...	...	...
	% over total	...	...	...	...	...	*80.00*	...	...	...
2.3	- Trailers	...	...	...	...	...	5.0	...	...	...
	% over total	...	...	...	...	...	*45.45*	...	...	...
3	**Goods carried**									
3.1	- In 1000 tonnes	...	152 735.0	161 785.0	...	...	...	34 635.0	...	...
	% over total	...	*59.11*	*61.51*	...	...	...	*42.73*	...	...
3.2	- In million tkm	...	14 177.0	14 518.0	...	...	...	3 126.0	...	...
	% over total	...	*75.92*	*78.06*	...	...	...	*71.14*	...	...

1- Excluding vehicles registered in Aland.

1- Non compris les véhicules immatriculés à Aland.

1- За исключением дорожно-транспортных средств, зарегистрированных на Аландских островах.

13. Goods road vehicles operated for hire or reward

13. Véhicules routiers pour le transport des marchandises opérant pour le compte d'autrui

13. Грузовые автодорожные транспортные средства, осуществляющие перевозки за плату или вознаграждеие

		Israel Israël Израиль			Italy Italie Италия			Latvia Lettonie Латвия		
		1990	1998	1999	1990	1998	1999	1990	1998	1999
1	**Goods vehicles (number)**									
1.1	- Lorries	...	...	...	...	...	...	...	...	...
	% over total	...	...	...	...	...	...	...	...	...
1.2	- Road tractors	...	...	...	...	...	...	...	...	...
	% over total	...	...	...	...	...	...	...	...	...
1.3	- Semi trailers	...	...	...	...	...	...	...	...	...
	% over total	...	...	...	...	...	...	...	...	...
1.4	- Trailers	...	...	...	...	...	...	...	...	...
	% over total	...	...	...	...	...	...	...	...	...
2	**Load capacity (1000 tonnes)**									
2.1	- Lorries	...	...	...	...	...	...	...	...	...
	% over total	...	...	...	...	...	...	...	...	...
2.2	- Semi trailers	...	...	...	...	...	...	...	...	...
	% over total	...	...	...	...	...	...	...	...	...
2.3	- Trailers	...	...	...	...	...	...	...	...	...
	% over total	...	...	...	...	...	...	...	...	...
3	**Goods carried**									
3.1	- In 1000 tonnes	93 200.0	...	...	500 604.0	845 654.0	...	...	11 159.0	13 567.0
	% over total	*73.79*	...	...	*54.90*	*68.74*	...	...	*33.05*	*40.62*
3.2	- In million tkm	3 356.0	...	...	113 592.0	164 043.0	...	...	2 864.0	3 119.0
	% over total	*76.80*	...	...	*63.85*	*85.67*	...	...	*69.72*	*74.96*

		Malta Malte Мальта			Netherlands Pays-Bas Нидерланды			Poland Pologne Польша		
		1990	1998	1999	1990	1998	1999	1990	1998	1999
1	**Goods vehicles (number)**									
1.1	- Lorries	...	...	...	55 650	...	...	...	...	...
	% over total	...	...	...	*11.33*	...	...	...	...	...
1.2	- Road tractors	...	...	...	...	...	...	...	...	...
	% over total	...	...	...	...	...	...	...	...	...
1.3	- Semi trailers	...	403	407	...	...	...	...	...	...
	% over total	...	*100.00*	*100.00*	...	...	...	...	...	...
1.4	- Trailers	...	...	...	...	...	...	...	...	...
	% over total	...	...	...	...	...	...	...	...	...
2	**Load capacity (1000 tonnes)**									
2.1	- Lorries	...	...	...	...	...	...	...	...	...
	% over total	...	...	...	...	...	...	...	...	...
2.2	- Semi trailers	...	...	...	...	...	...	...	...	...
	% over total	...	...	...	...	...	...	...	...	...
2.3	- Trailers	...	...	...	...	...	...	...	...	...
	% over total	...	...	...	...	...	...	...	...	...
3	**Goods carried**									
3.1	- In 1000 tonnes	...	...	...	312 861.0	...	...	347 108.0	372 905.0	372 326.0
	% over total	...	...	...	*67.90*	...	...	*26.86*	*34.61*	*34.85*
3.2	- In million tkm	...	...	...	43 414.0	...	...	19 131.0	43 551.0	45 046.0
	% over total	...	...	...	*78.95*	...	...	*47.48*	*62.62*	*63.94*

ROAD TRANSPORT - TRANSPORT ROUTIER
АВТОМОБИЛЬНЫЕ ДОРОГИ

13. Goods road vehicles operated for hire or reward

13. Véhicules routiers pour le transport des marchandises opérant pour le compte d'autrui

13. Грузовые автодорожные транспортные средства, осуществляющие перевозки за плату или вознаграждеие

		Portugal Portugal Португалия			Republic of Moldova République de Moldova Республика Молдова			Romania Roumanie Румыния		
		1990	1998	1999	1990	1998	1999	1990	1998	1999
1	**Goods vehicles (number)**									
1.1	- Lorries	18 106	...	...	...	...	...	...	...	...
	% over total	*3.56*	...	...	...	...	...	...	...	...
1.2	- Road tractors	...	...	...	...	...	...	...	...	...
	% over total	...	...	...	...	...	...	...	...	...
1.3	- Semi trailers	...	...	...	...	...	...	...	...	...
	% over total	...	...	...	...	...	...	...	...	...
1.4	- Trailers	...	...	...	...	...	...	...	...	...
	% over total	...	...	...	...	...	...	...	...	...
2	**Load capacity (1000 tonnes)**									
2.1	- Lorries	...	...	...	...	...	...	...	...	...
	% over total	...	...	...	...	...	...	...	...	...
2.2	- Semi trailers	...	...	...	...	...	...	...	...	...
	% over total	...	...	...	...	...	...	...	...	...
2.3	- Trailers	...	...	...	...	...	...	...	...	...
	% over total	...	...	...	...	...	...	...	...	...
3	**Goods carried**									
3.1	- In 1000 tonnes	54 576.0	95 577.0	99 436.0	...	5 472.0	3 681.0	...	88 964.0	78 615.0
	% over total	*22.63*	*35.17*	*35.47*	...	*20.63*	*18.28*	...	*28.36*	*28.18*
3.2	- In million tkm	8 678.0	17 855.0	18 650.0	...	402.0	512.0	...	7 031.0	5 363.0
	% over total	*53.80*	*69.84*	*69.20*	...	*42.77*	*53.78*	...	*44.54*	*39.86*

		Russian Federation Fédération de Russie Российская Федерация			Slovakia Slovaquie Словакия			Slovenia Slovénie Словения		
		1990	1998	1999	1990	1998	1999	1990	1998	1999
1	**Goods vehicles (number)**									
1.1	- Lorries	...	...	...	...	...	...	...	...	...
	% over total	...	...	...	...	...	...	...	...	...
1.2	- Road tractors	...	...	...	...	...	...	...	...	...
	% over total	...	...	...	...	...	...	...	...	...
1.3	- Semi trailers	...	...	...	...	...	...	...	...	...
	% over total	...	...	...	...	...	...	...	...	...
1.4	- Trailers	...	...	...	...	...	...	...	...	...
	% over total	...	...	...	...	...	...	...	...	...
2	**Load capacity (1000 tonnes)**									
2.1	- Lorries	...	...	...	...	...	...	...	...	...
	% over total	...	...	...	...	...	...	...	...	...
2.2	- Semi trailers	...	...	...	...	...	...	...	...	...
	% over total	...	...	...	...	...	...	...	...	...
2.3	- Trailers	...	...	...	...	...	...	...	...	...
	% over total	...	...	...	...	...	...	...	...	...
3	**Goods carried**									
3.1	- In 1000 tonnes	...	969 940.0	...	83 571.0	62 890.0	54 327.0	11 268.0	4 239.0	4 025.0
	% over total	...	*100.00*	...	...	*33.87*	*35.91*	*15.96*	*5.28*	*4.61*
3.2	- In million tkm	...	29 384.0	...	4 180.0	6 986.0	11 107.0	3 440.0	1 903.0	1 874.0
	% over total	...	*139.92*	...	...	*39.07*	*59.99*	*70.39*	*56.40*	*54.48*

ROAD TRANSPORT - TRANSPORT ROUTIER
АВТОМОБИЛЬНЫЕ ДОРОГИ

13. Goods road vehicles operated for hire or reward
13. Véhicules routiers pour le transport des marchandises opérant pour le compte d'autrui
13. Грузовые автодорожные транспортные средства, осуществляющие перевозки за плату или вознаграждеие

		Spain Espagne Испания			Sweden Suède Швеция			The FYR of Macedonia [1]		
		1990	1998	1999	1990	1998	1999	1990	1998	1999
1	**Goods vehicles (number)**									
1.1	- Lorries	...	...	...	43 685	43 009	43 716	...	...	...
	% over total	...	...	...	*14.11*	*12.96*	*12.57*	...	...	...
1.2	- Road tractors	...	...	...	...	5 512	5 642	...	...	...
	% over total	...	...	...	...	*89.44*	*86.96*	...	...	...
1.3	- Semi trailers	...	...	...	...	-	-	...	...	...
	% over total	...	...	...	...	-	-	...	...	...
1.4	- Trailers	...	...	...	...	620	-	...	...	...
	% over total	...	...	...	...	*0.13*	*#VALUE!*	...	...	...
2	**Load capacity (1000 tonnes)**									
2.1	- Lorries	...	...	...	...	486.0	413.0	...	...	...
	% over total	...	...	...	...	*59.05*	*48.99*	...	...	...
2.2	- Semi trailers	...	...	...	...	-	-	...	...	...
	% over total	...	...	...	...	-	-	...	...	...
2.3	- Trailers	...	...	...	...	1.0	-	...	...	...
	% over total	...	...	...	...	*0.12*	-	...	...	...
3	**Goods carried**									
3.1	- In 1000 tonnes	673 831.0	551 556.0	618 204.0	...	278 595.0	272 139.0	...	1 895.0	2 327.0
	% over total	*68.26*	*76.68*	*74.75*	...	*87.71*	*87.72*	...	*100.00*	*100.00*
3.2	- In million tkm	91 795.0	113 359.0	120 114.0	...	30 417.0	30 316.0	...	894.0	839.0
	% over total	*83.81*	*90.49*	*89.46*	...	*91.38*	*91.38*	...	*100.00*	*100.00*

		United Kingdom Royaume-Uni Соединенное Королевство			United States Etats-Unis Соединенные Штаты			Yugoslavia Yugoslavie Югославия		
		1990	1998	1999	1990	1998	1999	1990	1998	1999
1	**Goods vehicles (number)**									
1.1	- Lorries	...	...	...	...	...	...	...	...	...
	% over total	...	...	...	...	...	...	...	...	...
1.2	- Road tractors	...	...	...	...	...	...	...	...	...
	% over total	...	...	...	...	...	...	...	...	...
1.3	- Semi trailers	...	...	...	1 189 000	...	...	...	...	...
	% over total	...	...	...	*32.97*	...	...	...	...	...
1.4	- Trailers	...	...	...	...	...	...	...	...	...
	% over total	...	...	...	...	...	...	...	...	...
2	**Load capacity (1000 tonnes)**									
2.1	- Lorries	...	...	...	...	...	...	...	...	...
	% over total	...	...	...	...	...	...	...	...	...
2.2	- Semi trailers	...	...	...	...	...	...	...	...	...
	% over total	...	...	...	...	...	...	...	...	...
2.3	- Trailers	...	...	...	...	...	...	...	...	...
	% over total	...	...	...	...	...	...	...	...	...
3	**Goods carried**									
3.1	- In 1000 tonnes	1 004 006.0	1 078 961.0	1 029 060.0	...	...	...	...	6 027.0	4 279.0
	% over total	*59.19*	*63.63*	*62.84*	...	...	...	...	*7.37*	*5.54*
3.2	- In million tkm	106 319.0	132 321.0	128 571.0	...	...	...	...	945.0	632.0
	% over total	*76.79*	*76.93*	*75.94*	...	...	...	...	*30.53*	*27.29*

1- The former Yugoslav Republic of Macedonia.

1- L'ex-République yougoslave de Macédoine.

1- Бывшая Югославская Республика Македония.

INLAND WATERWAYS

VOIES NAVIGABLES INTERIEURES

ВНУТРЕННИЕ ВОДНЫЕ ПУТИ

INLAND WATERWAYS - VOIES NAVIGABLES INTERIEURES
ВНУТРЕННИЕ ВОДНЫЕ ПУТИ

14. Navigable inland waterway regularly used for transport at 31 December

14. Voies navigables intérieures régulièrement utilisées pour les transports au 31 décembre

14. Судоходные внутренние водные пути, регулярно используемые для перевозок, на 31 декабря

Item Rubrique Статья	Description	Description	Описание
1	**Total navigable inland waterways (kilometres)**	**Total des voies navigables intérieures (kilomètres)**	**Судоходные внутренние водные пути (километры)**
1.1	**Canals**	**Canaux**	**Каналы**
	By carrying capacity of vessels	*Par classe d'accessibilité des bateaux*	*По грузоподъемности судов*
1.11	- Up to 249 tonnes	- Jusqu'à 249 tonnes	- До 249 тонн
1.12	- 250 - 399 tonnes	- 250 - 399 tonnes	- 250 - 399 тонн
1.13	- 400 - 649 tonnes	- 400 - 649 tonnes	- 400 - 649 тонн
1.14	- 650 - 999 tonnes	- 650 - 999 tonnes	- 650 - 999 тонн
1.15	- 1000 - 1499 tonnes	- 1000 - 1499 tonnes	- 1000 - 1499 тонн
1.16	- 1500 - 2999 tonnes	- 1500 - 2999 tonnes	- 1500 - 2999 тонн
1.17	- 3000 tonnes and over	- 3000 tonnes et plus	- 3000 тонн и более
1.2	**Navigables rivers and lakes**	**Fleuves, rivières et lacs navigables**	**Судоходные реки и озера**
	By carrying capacity of vessels	*Par classe d'accessibilité des bateaux*	*По грузоподъемности судов*
1.21	- Up to 249 tonnes	- Jusqu'à 249 tonnes	- До 249 тонн
1.22	- 250 - 399 tonnes	- 250 - 399 tonnes	- 250 - 399 тонн
1.23	- 400 - 649 tonnes	- 400 - 649 tonnes	- 400 - 649 тонн
1.24	- 650 - 999 tonnes	- 650 - 999 tonnes	- 650 - 999 тонн
1.25	- 1000 - 1499 tonnes	- 1000 - 1499 tonnes	- 1000 - 1499 тонн
1.26	- 1500 - 2999 tonnes	- 1500 - 2999 tonnes	- 1500 - 2999 тонн
1.27	- 3000 tonnes and over	- 3000 tonnes et plus	- 3000 тонн и более

INLAND WATERWAYS - VOIES NAVIGABLES INTERIEURES
ВНУТРЕННИЕ ВОДНЫЕ ПУТИ

14. Navigable inland waterway regularly used for transport at 31 December
14. Voies navigables intérieures régulièrement utilisées pour les transports au 31 décembre
14. Судоходные внутренние водные пути, регулярно используемые для перевозок, на 31 декабря

Unit : km - Unité : km - Единица - км

		Albania Albanie Албания			Austria Autriche Австрия			Belarus Bélarus Беларусь		
		1990	1998	1999	1990	1998	1999	1990	1998	1999
1	Total navigable waterways	...	74	74	351	351	351	2 872	1 757	...
1.1	Canals	...	-	-	-	-	-	...	...	...
	By carrying capacity of vessels									
1.11	- Up to 249 tonnes	...	-	-	-	-	-	...	...	...
1.12	- 250 - 399 tonnes	...	-	-	-	-	-	...	...	...
1.13	- 400 - 649 tonnes	...	-	-	-	-	-	...	...	...
1.14	- 650 - 999 tonnes	...	-	-	-	-	-	...	...	...
1.15	- 1000 - 1499 tonnes	...	-	-	-	-	-	...	...	...
1.16	- 1500 - 2999 tonnes	...	-	-	-	-	-	...	...	...
1.17	- 3000 tonnes and over	...	-	-	-	-	-	...	...	...
1.2	Navigables rivers & lakes	...	74	74	351	351	351	...	...	...
	By carrying capacity of vessels									
1.21	- Up to 249 tonnes	...	-	-	-	-	-	...	...	...
1.22	- 250 - 399 tonnes	...	74	74	-	-	-	...	...	...
1.23	- 400 - 649 tonnes	...	-	-	-	-	-	...	...	...
1.24	- 650 - 999 tonnes	...	-	-	-	-	-	...	...	...
1.25	- 1000 - 1499 tonnes	...	-	-	-	-	-	...	...	...
1.26	- 1500 - 2999 tonnes	...	-	-	351	-	-	...	...	...
1.27	- 3000 tonnes and over	...	-	-	-	351	351	...	...	...

		Belgium Belgique Бельгия			Bulgaria Bulgarie Болгария			Croatia Croatie Хорватия		
		1990	1998	1999	1990	1998	1999	1990	1998	1999
1	Total navigable waterways	1 513	...	...	470	470	470	933	933	933
1.1	Canals	860	...	...	-	-	...	-	-	-
	By carrying capacity of vessels									
1.11	- Up to 249 tonnes	-	...	...	-	-	...	-	-	-
1.12	- 250 - 399 tonnes	150	...	...	-	-	...	-	-	-
1.13	- 400 - 649 tonnes	245	...	...	-	-	...	-	-	-
1.14	- 650 - 999 tonnes	-	...	...	-	-	...	-	-	-
1.15	- 1000 - 1499 tonnes	217	...	...	-	-	...	-	-	-
1.16	- 1500 - 2999 tonnes	48	...	...	-	-	...	-	-	-
1.17	- 3000 tonnes and over	200	...	...	-	-	...	-	-	-
1.2	Navigables rivers & lakes	653	...	...	470	470	470	933	933	933
	By carrying capacity of vessels									
1.21	- Up to 249 tonnes	8	...	...	...	...	...	-	-	-
1.22	- 250 - 399 tonnes	194	...	...	...	...	...	146	146	146
1.23	- 400 - 649 tonnes	80	...	...	...	...	...	199	199	199
1.24	- 650 - 999 tonnes	-	...	...	...	...	...	437	437	437
1.25	- 1000 - 1499 tonnes	213	...	...	...	...	...	14	14	14
1.26	- 1500 - 2999 tonnes	80	...	...	...	...	...	-	-	-
1.27	- 3000 tonnes and over	78	...	...	...	...	...	138	138	138

INLAND WATERWAYS - VOIES NAVIGABLES INTERIEURES
ВНУТРЕННИЕ ВОДНЫЕ ПУТИ

14. Navigable inland waterway regularly used for transport at 31 December

14. Voies navigables intérieures régulièrement utilisées pour les transports au 31 décembre

14. Судоходные внутренние водные пути, регулярно используемые для перевозок, на 31 декабря

Unit : km - Unité : km - Единица - км

		Czech Republic République tchèque Чешская Республика			Estonia Estonie Эстония			Finland Finlande Финляндия		
		1990	1998	1999	1990	1998	1999	1990	1998	1999
1	**Total navigable waterways**	...	664	664	520	520	520	6 237	6 245	6 245
1.1	**Canals**	...	39	39	-	-	-	77	125	125
	By carrying capacity of vessels									
1.11	- Up to 249 tonnes	...	...	...	-	-	-	9	9	9
1.12	- 250 - 399 tonnes	...	...	...	-	-	-	-	-	-
1.13	- 400 - 649 tonnes	...	...	...	-	-	-	-	-	-
1.14	- 650 - 999 tonnes	...	...	...	-	-	-	16	16	16
1.15	- 1000 - 1499 tonnes	...	...	...	-	-	-	-	-	-
1.16	- 1500 - 2999 tonnes	...	...	...	-	-	-	52	100	100
1.17	- 3000 tonnes and over	...	...	...	-	-	-	-	-	-
1.2	**Navigables rivers & lakes**	...	625	625	520	520	520	6 160	6 120	6 120
	By carrying capacity of vessels									
1.21	- Up to 249 tonnes	...	...	...	520	520	520	2 500	2 500	2 500
1.22	- 250 - 399 tonnes	...	...	...	-	-	-	-	-	-
1.23	- 400 - 649 tonnes	...	...	...	-	-	-	-	-	-
1.24	- 650 - 999 tonnes	...	...	...	-	-	-	2 890	2 845	2 845
1.25	- 1000 - 1499 tonnes	...	...	...	-	-	-	-	-	-
1.26	- 1500 - 2999 tonnes	...	...	...	-	-	-	770	775	775
1.27	- 3000 tonnes and over	...	...	...	-	-	-			

		France France Франция			Germany Allemagne Германия			Hungary Hongrie Венгрия		
		1990	1998	1999	1990	1998	1999	1990	1998	1999
1	**Total navigable waterways**	6 197	5 732	5 576	...	6 740	6 754	1 373	1 373	1 373
1.1	**Canals**	3 732	3 980	3 985	...	...	1 234	80	80	80
	By carrying capacity of vessels									
1.11	- Up to 249 tonnes	185	-	34	...	...	2	...	...	...
1.12	- 250 - 399 tonnes	2 940	3 046	3 096	...	...	22	...	...	...
1.13	- 400 - 649 tonnes	-	70	85	...	...	88	...	...	...
1.14	- 650 - 999 tonnes	204	310	217	...	...	112	...	...	...
1.15	- 1000 - 1499 tonnes	17	32	36	...	...	569	...	...	...
1.16	- 1500 - 2999 tonnes	31	21	21	...	...	424	...	...	...
1.17	- 3000 tonnes and over	355	501	496	...	...	109	...	...	...
1.2	**Navigables rivers & lakes**	2 465	1 752	1 591	...	...	4 782	1 293	1 293	1 293
	By carrying capacity of vessels									
1.21	- Up to 249 tonnes	37	-	-	...	...	106	...	...	...
1.22	- 250 - 399 tonnes	691	355	342	...	...	768	...	...	...
1.23	- 400 - 649 tonnes	213	161	113	...	...	125	...	...	...
1.24	- 650 - 999 tonnes	118	103	18	...	...	138	...	...	...
1.25	- 1000 - 1499 tonnes	19	-	-	...	...	1 088	...	...	...
1.26	- 1500 - 2999 tonnes	243	245	245	...	...	1 798	...	...	...
1.27	- 3000 tonnes and over	1 144	888	873	...	...	894	...	...	...

INLAND WATERWAYS - VOIES NAVIGABLES INTERIEURES
ВНУТРЕННИЕ ВОДНЫЕ ПУТИ

14. Navigable inland waterway regularly used for transport at 31 December
14. Voies navigables intérieures régulièrement utilisées pour les transports au 31 décembre
14. Судоходные внутренние водные пути, регулярно используемые для перевозок, на 31 декабря

Unit : km - Unité : km - Единица - км

		Italy Italie Италия			Kazakhstan Kazakhstan Казахстан			Kyrgyzstan Kirghizistan Кыргызстан		
		1990	1998	1999	1990	1998	1999	1990	1998	1999
1	Total navigable waterways	...	1 477	1 477	4 002	3 903	4 288	576	466	466
1.1	Canals	...	420	420	-	-	-	-	-	-
	By carrying capacity of vessels									
1.11	- Up to 249 tonnes	...	...	...	-	-	-	-	-	-
1.12	- 250 - 399 tonnes	...	...	...	-	-	-	-	-	-
1.13	- 400 - 649 tonnes	...	...	...	-	-	-	-	-	-
1.14	- 650 - 999 tonnes	...	...	...	-	-	-	-	-	-
1.15	- 1000 - 1499 tonnes	...	...	...	-	-	-	-	-	-
1.16	- 1500 - 2999 tonnes	...	...	...	-	-	-	-	-	-
1.17	- 3000 tonnes and over	...	...	...	-	-	-	-	-	-
1.2	Navigables rivers & lakes	...	1 057	1 057	4 002	3 903	4 288	576	466	466
	By carrying capacity of vessels									
1.21	- Up to 249 tonnes	...	...	...	...	1 212	1 212	...	...	...
1.22	- 250 - 399 tonnes	...	...	...	...	56	56	...	...	...
1.23	- 400 - 649 tonnes	...	...	...	...	2 536	2 469	...	...	...
1.24	- 650 - 999 tonnes	...	...	...	...	2 255	2 429	...	...	...
1.25	- 1000 - 1499 tonnes	...	...	...	...	1 132	1 132	...	...	...
1.26	- 1500 - 2999 tonnes	...	...	...	...	932	632	...	...	...
1.27	- 3000 tonnes and over	...	...	...	...	-	-	...	...	...

		Latvia Lettonie Латвия			Lithuania Lituanie Литва			Luxembourg Luxembourg Люксембург		
		1990	1998	1999	1990	1998	1999	1990	1998	1999
1	Total navigable waterways	347	-	-	369	369	369	37	37	...
1.1	Canals	-	-	-	-	-	-	-	-	...
	By carrying capacity of vessels									
1.11	- Up to 249 tonnes	-	-	-	-	-	-	-	-	...
1.12	- 250 - 399 tonnes	-	-	-	-	-	-	-	-	...
1.13	- 400 - 649 tonnes	-	-	-	-	-	-	-	-	...
1.14	- 650 - 999 tonnes	-	-	-	-	-	-	-	-	...
1.15	- 1000 - 1499 tonnes	-	-	-	-	-	-	-	-	...
1.16	- 1500 - 2999 tonnes	-	-	-	-	-	-	-	-	...
1.17	- 3000 tonnes and over	-	-	-	-	-	-	-	-	...
1.2	Navigables rivers & lakes	347	-	-	369	370	370	37	37	...
	By carrying capacity of vessels									
1.21	- Up to 249 tonnes	...	-	-	...	...	...	-	-	...
1.22	- 250 - 399 tonnes	...	-	-	...	...	...	-	-	...
1.23	- 400 - 649 tonnes	...	-	-	...	...	...	-	-	...
1.24	- 650 - 999 tonnes	...	-	-	...	...	...	-	-	...
1.25	- 1000 - 1499 tonnes	...	-	-	...	...	...	-	-	...
1.26	- 1500 - 2999 tonnes	...	-	-	...	...	...	37	37	...
1.27	- 3000 tonnes and over	...	-	-	...	...	...	-	-	...

INLAND WATERWAYS - VOIES NAVIGABLES INTERIEURES
ВНУТРЕННИЕ ВОДНЫЕ ПУТИ

14. Navigable inland waterway regularly used for transport at 31 December

14. Voies navigables intérieures régulièrement utilisées pour les transports au 31 décembre

14. Судоходные внутренние водные пути, регулярно используемые для перевозок, на 31 декабря

Unit : km - Unité : km - Единица - км

		Netherlands Pays-Bas Нидерланды			Poland Pologne Польша			Republic of Moldova République de Moldova Республика Молдова		
		1990	1998	1999	1990	1998	1999	1990	1998	1999
1	Total navigable waterways	5 046	5 046	...	3 997	3 812	3 813	...	40	40
1.1	Canals	3 745	3 745	...	379	334	334	-	-	-
	By carrying capacity of vessels									
1.11	- Up to 249 tonnes	1 157	1 157	...	...	...	...	-	-	-
1.12	- 250 - 399 tonnes	406	406	...	...	...	...	-	-	-
1.13	- 400 - 649 tonnes	846	846	...	...	...	...	-	-	-
1.14	- 650 - 999 tonnes	168	168	...	...	...	...	-	-	-
1.15	- 1000 - 1499 tonnes	543	543	...	...	...	...	-	-	-
1.16	- 1500 - 2999 tonnes	423	423	...	...	...	...	-	-	-
1.17	- 3000 tonnes and over	202	202	...	...	...	...	-	-	-
1.2	Navigables rivers & lakes	1 301	1 301	...	3 618	3 478	3 479	...	40	40
	By carrying capacity of vessels									
1.21	- Up to 249 tonnes	-	-	...	...	...	...	...	40	40
1.22	- 250 - 399 tonnes	1	1	...	...	...	...	...	-	-
1.23	- 400 - 649 tonnes	25	25	...	...	...	...	...	-	-
1.24	- 650 - 999 tonnes	45	45	...	...	...	...	...	-	-
1.25	- 1000 - 1499 tonnes	54	54	...	...	...	...	...	-	-
1.26	- 1500 - 2999 tonnes	713	713	...	...	...	...	...	-	-
1.27	- 3000 tonnes and over	463	463	...	...	...	...	...	-	-

		Romania Roumanie Румыния			Russian Federation Fédération de Russie Российская Федерация			Slovakia Slovaquie Словакия		
		1990	1998	1999	1990	1998	1999	1990	1998	1999
1	Total navigable waterways	1 782	1 779	1 779	103 000	89 089	84 605	2 379	172	172
1.1	Canals	132	132	132	...	15 376	12 583	...	39	39
	By carrying capacity of vessels									
1.11	- Up to 249 tonnes	-	-	-	...	...	...	...	-	-
1.12	- 250 - 399 tonnes	-	-	-	...	...	...	...	-	-
1.13	- 400 - 649 tonnes	40	40	40	...	...	...	...	-	-
1.14	- 650 - 999 tonnes	-	-	-	...	...	...	...	-	-
1.15	- 1000 - 1499 tonnes	-	-	-	...	...	...	...	-	-
1.16	- 1500 - 2999 tonnes	27	27	27	...	...	...	...	-	-
1.17	- 3000 tonnes and over	65	65	65	...	...	...	...	39	39
1.2	Navigables rivers & lakes	1 650	1 647	1 647	...	73 713	72 022	...	134	134
	By carrying capacity of vessels									
1.21	- Up to 249 tonnes	...	-	-	...	...	...	...	-	-
1.22	- 250 - 399 tonnes	...	-	-	...	...	...	...	-	-
1.23	- 400 - 649 tonnes	...	53	53	...	...	...	...	-	-
1.24	- 650 - 999 tonnes	...	274	274	...	...	...	...	-	-
1.25	- 1000 - 1499 tonnes	...	819	819	...	...	...	...	-	-
1.26	- 1500 - 2999 tonnes	...	233	233	...	...	...	...	134	134
1.27	- 3000 tonnes and over	...	268	268	...	...	...	...	-	-

INLAND WATERWAYS - VOIES NAVIGABLES INTERIEURES
ВНУТРЕННИЕ ВОДНЫЕ ПУТИ

14. Navigable inland waterway regularly used for transport at 31 December
14. Voies navigables intérieures régulièrement utilisées pour les transports au 31 décembre
14. Судоходные внутренние водные пути, регулярно используемые для перевозок, на 31 декабря

Unit : km - Unité : km - Единица - км

		Switzerland / Suisse / Швейцария			Turkmenistan / Turkménistan / Туркменистан			Ukraine / Ukraine / Украина		
		1990	1998	1999	1990	1998	1999	1990	1998	1999
1	Total navigable waterways	21	21	...	...	387	...	4 004	3 000	...
1.1	Canals	-	-	...	...	387	...	2 196	...	...
	By carrying capacity of vessels									
1.11	- Up to 249 tonnes	-	-	...	...	-	...	...	...	...
1.12	- 250 - 399 tonnes	-	-	...	...	-	...	...	...	...
1.13	- 400 - 649 tonnes	-	-	...	...	387	...	...	...	...
1.14	- 650 - 999 tonnes	-	-	...	...		...	...	...	...
1.15	- 1000 - 1499 tonnes	-	-	...	...		...	...	...	...
1.16	- 1500 - 2999 tonnes	-	-	...	...		...	...	...	...
1.17	- 3000 tonnes and over	-	-	...	...		...	...	...	...
1.2	Navigables rivers & lakes	21	21	...	...	-	...	1 808	...	...
	By carrying capacity of vessels									
1.21	- Up to 249 tonnes	-	-	...	...	-	...	...	...	...
1.22	- 250 - 399 tonnes	-	-	...	...	-	...	...	...	...
1.23	- 400 - 649 tonnes	-	-	...	...	-	...	...	...	...
1.24	- 650 - 999 tonnes	-	-	...	...	-	...	...	...	...
1.25	- 1000 - 1499 tonnes	6	-	...	...	-	...	...	...	...
1.26	- 1500 - 2999 tonnes	-	-	...	...	-	...	...	...	...
1.27	- 3000 tonnes and over	15	21	...	...	-	...	...	...	...

		United Kingdom / Royaume-Uni / Соединенное Королевство			United States / Etats-Unis / Соединенные Штаты			Yugoslavia / Yugoslavie / Югославия		
		1990	1998	1999	1990	1998	1999	1990	1998	1999
1	Total navigable waterways	1 631	1 153	1 153	41 484	41 843	...	...	1 419	1 419
1.1	Canals	369	191	191	...	...	...	...	342	342
	By carrying capacity of vessels									
1.11	- Up to 249 tonnes	77	...	...	...	...	...	...	21	21
1.12	- 250 - 399 tonnes	82	...	...	...	...	...	...	-	-
1.13	- 400 - 649 tonnes	152	...	...	...	...	...	...	321	321
1.14	- 650 - 999 tonnes	-	...	...	...	...	...	...	-	-
1.15	- 1000 - 1499 tonnes	58	...	...	...	...	...	...	-	-
1.16	- 1500 - 2999 tonnes	-	...	...	...	...	...	...	-	-
1.17	- 3000 tonnes and over	-	...	...	...	...	...	...	-	-
1.2	Navigables rivers & lakes	1 262	963	964	...	...	...	...	1 077	1 077
	By carrying capacity of vessels									
1.21	- Up to 249 tonnes	144	...	...	...	...	...	...	-	-
1.22	- 250 - 399 tonnes	149	...	...	...	...	...	...	-	-
1.23	- 400 - 649 tonnes	135	...	...	...	...	...	...	84	84
1.24	- 650 - 999 tonnes	145	...	...	...	...	...	...	-	-
1.25	- 1000 - 1499 tonnes	689	...	...	...	...	...	...	405	405
1.26	- 1500 - 2999 tonnes	-	...	...	...	...	...	...	-	-

INLAND WATERWAYS - VOIES NAVIGABLES INTERIEURES
ВНУТРЕННИЕ ВОДНЫЕ ПУТИ

15. Inland waterway vessels in service at end of year, by carrying capacity and year of construction

15. Bateaux pour voies navigables intérieures en service à la fin de l'année, selon la capacité de charge et l'année de construction

15. Суда для внутренних водных путей, находящиеся в эксплуатации на конец года, по грузоподъемности грузоподъемности и году выпуска

Item Rubrique Статья	**Number** **Carrying capacity (1000 t.)** **Power (1000 kW)** Description	**Nombre** **Capacité de charge (1000 t.)** **Puissance (1000 kW)** Description	**Число** **Грузоподъемность (1000 тонн)** **Мощность (1000 кВт)** Описание
1	**Self-propelled vessels**	**Automoteurs**	**Самоходные суда**
	- By carrying capacity	*- Par classe de capacité*	*- По грузоподъемности*
1.11	- Up to 249 tonnes	- Jusqu'à 249 tonnes	- До 249 тонн
1.12	- 250 - 399 tonnes	- 250 - 399 tonnes	- 250 - 399 тонн
1.13	- 400 - 649 tonnes	- 400 - 649 tonnes	- 400 - 649 тонн
1.14	- 650 - 999 tonnes	- 650 - 999 tonnes	- 650 - 999 тонн
1.15	- 1000 - 1499 tonnes	- 1000 - 1499 tonnes	- 1000 - 1499 тонн
1.16	- 1500 - 2999 tonnes	- 1500 - 2999 tonnes	- 1500 - 2999 тонн
1.17	- 3000 tonnes and over	- 3000 tonnes et plus	- 3000 тонн и более
	- By year of construction	*- Par année de construction*	*- По году выпуска*
1.21	- Up to 1949	- Jusqu'à 1949	- До 1949 года
1.22	- 1950 - 1969	- 1950 - 1969	- 1950 - 1969
1.23	- 1970 - 1979	- 1970 - 1979	- 1970 - 1979
1.24	- 1980 - 1989	- 1980 - 1989	- 1980 - 1989
1.25	- 1990 and over	- 1990 et plus	- 1990 и далее
2	**Dumb and pushed vessels**	**Chalands et barges**	**Несамоходные и толкаемые суда**
	- By carrying capacity	*- Par classe de capacité*	*- По грузоподъемности*
2.11	- Up to 249 tonnes	- Jusqu'à 249 tonnes	- До 249 тонн
2.12	- 250 - 399 tonnes	- 250 - 399 tonnes	- 250 - 399 тонн
2.13	- 400 - 649 tonnes	- 400 - 649 tonnes	- 400 - 649 тонн
2.14	- 650 - 999 tonnes	- 650 - 999 tonnes	- 650 - 999 тонн
2.15	- 1000 - 1499 tonnes	- 1000 - 1499 tonnes	- 1000 - 1499 тонн
2.16	- 1500 - 2999 tonnes	- 1500 - 2999 tonnes	- 1500 - 2999 тонн
2.17	- 3000 tonnes and over	- 3000 tonnes et plus	- 3000 тонн и более
	- By year of construction	*- Par année de construction*	*- По году выпуска*
2.21	- Up to 1949	- Jusqu'à 1949	- До 1949 года
2.22	- 1950 - 1969	- 1950 - 1969	- 1950 - 1969
2.23	- 1970 - 1979	- 1970 - 1979	- 1970 - 1979
2.24	- 1980 - 1989	- 1980 - 1989	- 1980 - 1989
2.25	- 1990 and over	- 1990 et plus	- 1990 и далее
3	**Tugs and pushers**	**Remorques et pousseurs**	**Буксиры и толкачи**
	- By year of construction	*- Par année de construction*	*- По году выпуска*
3.21	- Up to 1949	- Jusqu'à 1949	- До 1949 года
3.22	- 1950 - 1969	- 1950 - 1969	- 1950 - 1969
3.23	- 1970 - 1979	- 1970 - 1979	- 1970 - 1979
3.24	- 1980 - 1989	- 1980 - 1989	- 1980 - 1989
3.25	- 1990 and over	- 1990 et plus	- 1990 и далее

INLAND WATERWAYS - VOIES NAVIGABLES INTERIEURES
ВНУТРЕННИЕ ВОДНЫЕ ПУТИ

15. Inland waterway vessels in service at end of year, by carrying capacity and year of construction

15. Bateaux pour voies navigables intérieures en service à la fin de l'année, selon la capacité de charge et l'année de construction

15. Суда для внутренних водных путей, находящиеся в эксплуатации на конец года, по грузоподъемности грузоподъемности и году выпуска

		Albania - Albanie - Албания								
		Number Nombre Число			Carrying capacity (1000 t.) Capacité de charge (1000 t.) Грузоподъемность (1000 тонн)			Power (1000 kW) Puissance (1000 kW) Мощность (1000 кВт)		
		1990	1998	1999	1990	1998	1999	1990	1998	1999
1	**Self-propelled vessels**	...	9	9	...	1.00	1.00	...	2.82	2.82
	- By carrying capacity									
1.11	Up to 249 tonnes	...	9	9	...	1.00	1.00	...	2.82	2.80
1.12	250 - 399 tonnes	...	-	-	...	-	-	...	-	-
1.13	400 - 649 tonnes	...	-	-	...	-	-	...	-	-
1.14	650 - 999 tonnes	...	-	-	...	-	-	...	-	-
1.15	1000 - 1499 tonnes	...	-	-	...	-	-	...	-	-
1.16	1500 - 2999 tonnes	...	-	-	...	-	-	...	-	-
1.17	3000 tonnes and over	...	-	-	...	-	-	...	-	-
	- By year of construction									
1.21	Up to 1949	...	-	-	...	-	-	...	-	-
1.22	1950 - 1969	...	-	-	...	-	-	...	-	-
1.23	1970 - 1979	...	1	1	...	0.00	0.00	...	0.00	0.00
1.24	1980 - 1989	...	6	6	...	0.00	0.00	...	1.32	1.32
1.25	1990 and over	...	2	2	...	0.00	0.00	...	0.93	0.93
2	**Dumb and pushed vessels**	...	-	-	...	-	-	•	•	•
	- By carrying capacity									
2.11	Up to 249 tonnes	...	-	-	...	-	-	•	•	•
2.12	250 - 399 tonnes	...	-	-	...	-	-	•	•	•
2.13	400 - 649 tonnes	...	-	-	...	-	-	•	•	•
2.14	650 - 999 tonnes	...	-	-	...	-	-	•	•	•
2.15	1000 - 1499 tonnes	...	-	-	...	-	-	•	•	•
2.16	1500 - 2999 tonnes	...	-	-	...	-	-	•	•	•
2.17	3000 tonnes and over	...	-	-	...	-	-	•	•	•
	- By year of construction									
2.21	Up to 1949	...	-	-	...	-	-	•	•	•
2.22	1950 - 1969	...	-	-	...	-	-	•	•	•
2.23	1970 - 1979	...	-	-	...	-	-	•	•	•
2.24	1980 - 1989	...	-	-	...	-	-	•	•	•
2.25	1990 and over	...	-	-	...	-	-	•	•	•
3	**Tugs and pushers**	...	-	-	•	•	•	...	-	-
	- By year of construction									
3.21	Up to 1949	...	-	-	•	•	•	...	-	-
3.22	1950 - 1969	...	-	-	•	•	•	...	-	-
3.23	1970 - 1979	...	-	-	•	•	•	...	-	-
3.24	1980 - 1989	...	-	-	•	•	•	...	-	-
3.25	1990 and over	...	-	-	•	•	•	...	-	-

INLAND WATERWAYS - VOIES NAVIGABLES INTERIEURES
ВНУТРЕННИЕ ВОДНЫЕ ПУТИ

15. Inland waterway vessels in service at end of year, by carrying capacity and year of construction

15. Bateaux pour voies navigables intérieures en service à la fin de l'année, selon la capacité de charge et l'année de construction

15. Суда для внутренних водных путей, находящиеся в эксплуатации на конец года, по грузоподъемности грузоподъемности и году выпуска

| | | Austria - Autriche - Австрия | | | | | | | | |
| | | Number Nombre Число | | | Carrying capacity (1000 t.) Capacité de charge (1000 t.) Грузоподъемность (1000 тонн) | | | Power (1000 kW) Puissance (1000 kW) Мощность (1000 кВт) | | |
		1990	1998	1999	1990	1998	1999	1990	1998	1999
1	**Self-propelled vessels**	**39**	**29**	**34**	**45.41**	**32.31**	**40.17**	**31.29**	**25.78**	**31.63**
	- By carrying capacity									
1.11	Up to 249 tonnes	1	7	6	0.06	0.37	0.34	0.16	3.87	3.46
1.12	250 - 399 tonnes	2	1	1	0.63	0.35	0.35	1.01	0.63	0.63
1.13	400 - 649 tonnes	2	2	2	1.00	1.00	1.00	0.56	0.53	0.53
1.14	650 - 999 tonnes	9	2	1	9.29	1.98	0.99	7.53	1.40	0.92
1.15	1000 - 1499 tonnes	19	9	16	22.47	11.37	20.26	14.75	9.48	16.22
1.16	1500 - 2999 tonnes	6	8	8	11.96	17.24	17.24	7.28	9.87	9.87
1.17	3000 tonnes and over	-	-	-	-	-	-	-	-	-
	- By year of construction									
1.21	Up to 1949	-	-	-	-	-	-	-	-	-
1.22	1950 - 1969	15	9	9	16.19	9.84	10.22	...	8.26	8.72
1.23	1970 - 1979	21	14	20	27.88	21.33	28.84	...	14.85	20.81
1.24	1980 - 1989	3	5	4	1.33	1.09	1.06	...	2.55	1.98
1.25	1990 and over	-	1	1	-	0.05	0.05	-	0.12	0.12
2	**Dumb and pushed vessels**	**171**	**141**	**146**	**212.52**	**192.65**	**207.27**	.	.	.
	- By carrying capacity									
2.11	Up to 249 tonnes	10	11	11	1.06	1.14	1.14	.	.	.
2.12	250 - 399 tonnes	16	16	14	5.28	5.67	5.07	.	.	.
2.13	400 - 649 tonnes	2	-	-	0.80	-	-	.	.	.
2.14	650 - 999 tonnes	39	20	14	37.89	19.57	13.73	.	.	.
2.15	1000 - 1499 tonnes	30	16	18	35.89	19.93	22.85	.	.	.
2.16	1500 - 2999 tonnes	74	77	88	131.59	142.93	161.07	.	.	.
2.17	3000 tonnes and over	-	1	1	-	3.41	3.41	.	.	.
	- By year of construction									
2.21	Up to 1949	21	4	1	18.96	2.95	0.06	.	.	.
2.22	1950 - 1969	75	40	38	72.45	32.72	32.03	.	.	.
2.23	1970 - 1979	22	27	38	28.91	35.16	52.17	.	.	.
2.24	1980 - 1989	53	57	58	92.20	99.33	101.13	.	.	.
2.25	1990 and over	(a)	13	11	(a)	22.48	21.88	.	.	.
3	**Tugs and pushers**	**22**	**15**	**17**	.	.	.	**13.12**	**12.73**	**14.12**
	- By year of construction									
3.21	Up to 1949	9	1	1	.	.	.	2.54	0.20	0.20
3.22	1950 - 1969	5	5	6	.	.	.	3.27	3.75	4.62
3.23	1970 - 1979	5	7	7	.	.	.	6.15	7.58	7.58
3.24	1980 - 1989	3	2	3	.	.	.	1.17	1.19	1.71
3.25	1990 and over	(a)	-	-	.	.	.	(a)	-	-

(a) Including under previous item.   (a) Compris sous la rubrique précédente.   (a) Включено в переыдущий показатель.

INLAND WATERWAYS - VOIES NAVIGABLES INTERIEURES
ВНУТРЕННИЕ ВОДНЫЕ ПУТИ

15. Inland waterway vessels in service at end of year, by carrying capacity and year of construction

15. Bateaux pour voies navigables intérieures en service à la fin de l'année, selon la capacité de charge et l'année de construction

15. Суда для внутренних водных путей, находящиеся в эксплуатации на конец года, по грузоподъемности грузоподъемности и году выпуска

		Belgium - Belgique - Бельгия								
		Number Nombre Число			Carrying capacity (1000 t.) Capacité de charge (1000 t.) Грузоподъемность (1000 тонн)			Power (1000 kW) Puissance (1000 kW) Мощность (1000 кВт)		
		1990	1998	1999	1990	1998	1999	1990	1998	1999
1	**Self-propelled vessels**	1 611	...	...	1 144.90	...	...	468.20	...	...
	- By carrying capacity									
1.11	Up to 249 tonnes	36	...	...	3.50	...	...	3.30	...	...
1.12	250 - 399 tonnes	746	...	...	270.10	...	...	117.20	...	...
1.13	400 - 649 tonnes	288	...	...	155.80	...	...	58.20	...	...
1.14	650 - 999 tonnes	199	...	...	165.30	...	...	69.00	...	...
1.15	1000 - 1499 tonnes	219	...	...	270.40	...	...	113.60	...	...
1.16	1500 - 2999 tonnes	104	...	...	214.70	...	...	83.30	...	...
1.17	3000 tonnes and over	19	...	...	65.10	...	...	23.60	...	...
	- By year of construction									
1.21	Up to 1949	...	...	...	...	...	...	...	...	...
1.22	1950 - 1969	...	...	...	...	...	...	...	...	...
1.23	1970 - 1979	...	...	...	...	...	...	...	...	...
1.24	1980 - 1989	...	...	...	...	...	...	...	...	...
1.25	1990 and over	...	...	...	...	...	...	...	...	...
2	**Dumb and pushed vessels**	167	...	...	378.60	...	...	•	•	•
	- By carrying capacity									
2.11	Up to 249 tonnes	3	...	...	0.20	...	...	•	•	•
2.12	250 - 399 tonnes	7	...	...	1.70	...	...	•	•	•
2.13	400 - 649 tonnes	12	...	...	6.70	...	...	•	•	•
2.14	650 - 999 tonnes	3	...	...	2.50	...	...	•	•	•
2.15	1000 - 1499 tonnes	19	...	...	27.10	...	...	•	•	•
2.16	1500 - 2999 tonnes	87	...	...	182.00	...	...	•	•	•
2.17	3000 tonnes and over	36	...	...	158.40	...	...	•	•	•
	- By year of construction									
2.21	Up to 1949	...	...	...	...	...	...	•	•	•
2.22	1950 - 1969	...	...	...	...	...	...	•	•	•
2.23	1970 - 1979	...	...	...	...	...	...	•	•	•
2.24	1980 - 1989	...	...	...	...	...	...	•	•	•
2.25	1990 and over	...	...	...	...	...	...	•	•	•
3	**Tugs and pushers**	260	...	...	•	•	•	77.60	...	...
	- By year of construction									
3.21	Up to 1949	...	...	...	•	•	•	...	...	...
3.22	1950 - 1969	...	...	...	•	•	•	...	...	...
3.23	1970 - 1979	...	...	...	•	•	•	...	...	...
3.24	1980 - 1989	...	...	...	•	•	•	...	...	...
3.25	1990 and over	...	...	...	•	•	•	...	...	...

INLAND WATERWAYS - VOIES NAVIGABLES INTERIEURES
ВНУТРЕННИЕ ВОДНЫЕ ПУТИ

15. Inland waterway vessels in service at end of year, by carrying capacity and year of construction

15. Bateaux pour voies navigables intérieures en service à la fin de l'année, selon la capacité de charge et l'année de construction

15. Суда для внутренних водных путей, находящиеся в эксплуатации на конец года, по грузоподъемности грузоподъемности и году выпуска

		Bulgaria - Bulgarie - Болгария								
		Number Nombre Число			Carrying capacity (1000 t.) Capacité de charge (1000 t.) Грузоподъемность (1000 тонн)			Power (1000 kW) Puissance (1000 kW) Мощность (1000 кВт)		
		1990	1998	1999	1990	1998	1999	1990	1998	1999
1	**Self-propelled vessels**	4	-	...	6.20	-	...	...	-	...
	- By carrying capacity									
1.11	Up to 249 tonnes	-	-	...	-	-	...	-	-	...
1.12	250 - 399 tonnes	-	-	...	-	-	...	-	-	...
1.13	400 - 649 tonnes	-	-	...	-	-	...	-	-	...
1.14	650 - 999 tonnes	-	-	...	-	-	...	-	-	...
1.15	1000 - 1499 tonnes	-	-	...	-	-	...	-	-	...
1.16	1500 - 2999 tonnes	4	-	...	6.20	-	...	...	-	...
1.17	3000 tonnes and over	-	-	...	-	-	...	-	-	...
	- By year of construction									
1.21	Up to 1949	-	-	...	-	-	...	-	-	...
1.22	1950 - 1969	-	-	...	-	-	...	-	-	...
1.23	1970 - 1979	-	-	...	-	-	...	-	-	...
1.24	1980 - 1989	4	-	...	6.20	-	...	...	-	...
1.25	1990 and over	-	-	...	-	-	...	-	-	...
2	**Dumb and pushed vessels**	242	197	183	366.32	290.00	269.00	•	•	•
	- By carrying capacity									
2.11	Up to 249 tonnes	2	-	-	0.40	-	-	•	•	•
2.12	250 - 399 tonnes	-	-	-	-	-	-	•	•	•
2.13	400 - 649 tonnes	-	8	8	-	5.00	5.00	•	•	•
2.14	650 - 999 tonnes	15	18	16	14.50	17.00	15.00	•	•	•
2.15	1000 - 1499 tonnes	59	59	58	64.60	68.00	67.00	•	•	•
2.16	1500 - 2999 tonnes	166	112	101	286.80	201.00	183.00	•	•	•
2.17	3000 tonnes and over	-	-	-	-	-	-	•	•	•
	- By year of construction									
2.21	Up to 1949	-	-	...	-	-	...	•	•	•
2.22	1950 - 1969	93	72	65	110.90	86.27	77.00	•	•	•
2.23	1970 - 1979	92	66	60	149.70	106.43	97.00	•	•	•
2.24	1980 - 1989	57	41	40	105.70	67.44	66.00	•	•	•
2.25	1990 and over	(a)	18	18	(a)	30.12	30.00	•	•	•
3	**Tugs and pushers**	35	33	30	•	•	•	33.46	33.44	31.00
	- By year of construction									
3.21	Up to 1949	2	2	2	•	•	•	0.70	1.03	1.00
3.22	1950 - 1969	15	10	7	•	•	•	11.00	8.43	5.00
3.23	1970 - 1979	11	13	13	•	•	•	11.50	12.31	12.00
3.24	1980 - 1989	7	5	5	•	•	•	10.30	6.09	7.00
3.25	1990 and over	(a)	3	3	•	•	•	(a)	5.59	6.00

(a) Including under previous item.   (a) Compris sous la rubrique précédente.   (a) Включено в переыдущий показатель.

INLAND WATERWAYS - VOIES NAVIGABLES INTERIEURES
ВНУТРЕННИЕ ВОДНЫЕ ПУТИ

15. Inland waterway vessels in service at end of year, by carrying capacity and year of construction

15. Bateaux pour voies navigables intérieures en service à la fin de l'année, selon la capacité de charge et l'année de construction

15. Суда для внутренних водных путей, находящиеся в эксплуатации на конец года, по грузоподъемности грузоподъемности и году выпуска

		Croatia - Croatie - Хорватия								
		Number Nombre Число			Carrying capacity (1000 t.) Capacité de charge (1000 t.) Грузоподъемность (1000 тонн)			Power (1000 kW) Puissance (1000 kW) Мощность (1000 кВт)		
		1990	1998	1999	1990	1998	1999	1990	1998	1999
1	**Self-propelled vessels**	2	1	1	1.65	1.00	1.00	1.88	1.00	1.00
	- By carrying capacity									
1.11	Up to 249 tonnes	-	-	-	-	-	-	-	-	-
1.12	250 - 399 tonnes	-	-	-	-	-	-	-	-	-
1.13	400 - 649 tonnes	-	-	-	-	-	-	-	-	-
1.14	650 - 999 tonnes	2	1	1	1.65	1.00	1.00	1.88	1.00	1.00
1.15	1000 - 1499 tonnes	-	-	-	-	-	-	-	-	-
1.16	1500 - 2999 tonnes	-	-	-	-	-	-	-	-	-
1.17	3000 tonnes and over	-	-	-	-	-	-	-	-	-
	- By year of construction									
1.21	Up to 1949	-	-	-	-	-	-	-	-	-
1.22	1950 - 1969	2	1	1	1.65	1.00	1.00	1.88	1.00	1.00
1.23	1970 - 1979	-	-	-	-	-	-	-	-	-
1.24	1980 - 1989	-	-	-	-	-	-	-	-	-
1.25	1990 and over	-	-	-	-	-	-	-	-	-
2	**Dumb and pushed vessels**	148	136	141	114.46	96.00	99.00	.	.	.
	- By carrying capacity									
2.11	Up to 249 tonnes	17	28	28	2.49	4.00	4.00	.	.	.
2.12	250 - 399 tonnes	9	9	12	2.82	3.00	4.00	.	.	.
2.13	400 - 649 tonnes	30	28	29	14.56	13.00	14.00	.	.	.
2.14	650 - 999 tonnes	51	28	29	44.72	24.00	25.00	.	.	.
2.15	1000 - 1499 tonnes	37	39	39	43.09	45.00	45.00	.	.	.
2.16	1500 - 2999 tonnes	4	4	4	6.78	7.00	7.00	.	.	.
2.17	3000 tonnes and over	-	-	-	-	-	-	.	.	.
	- By year of construction									
2.21	Up to 1949	23	5	5	17.48	4.00	5.00	.	.	.
2.22	1950 - 1969	70	79	83	62.23	56.00	58.00	.	.	.
2.23	1970 - 1979	47	43	43	28.47	28.00	28.00	.	.	.
2.24	1980 - 1989	8	9	10	6.27	8.00	8.00	.	.	.
2.25	1990 and over	-	-	-	-	-	-	.	.	.
3	**Tugs and pushers**	52	40	42	.	.	.	20.68	15.00	15.00
	- By year of construction									
3.21	Up to 1949	9	4	4	.	.	.	1.86	1.00	1.00
3.22	1950 - 1969	26	20	20	.	.	.	11.79	8.00	8.00
3.23	1970 - 1979	11	8	8	.	.	.	5.61	4.00	4.00
3.24	1980 - 1989	6	8	10	.	.	.	1.41	2.00	2.00
3.25	1990 and over	-	-	-	.	.	.	-	-	-

INLAND WATERWAYS - VOIES NAVIGABLES INTERIEURES
ВНУТРЕННИЕ ВОДНЫЕ ПУТИ

15. Inland waterway vessels in service at end of year, by carrying capacity and year of construction

15. Bateaux pour voies navigables intérieures en service à la fin de l'année, selon la capacité de charge et l'année de construction

15. Суда для внутренних водных путей, находящиеся в эксплуатации на конец года, по грузоподъемности грузоподъемности и году выпуска

		Czech Republic - République tchèque - Чешская Республика								
		Number Nombre Число			Carrying capacity (1000 t.) Capacité de charge (1000 t.) Грузоподъемность (1000 тонн)			Power (1000 kW) Puissance (1000 kW) Мощность (1000 кВт)		
		1990	1998	1999	1990	1998	1999	1990	1998	1999
1	**Self-propelled vessels**	...	**79**	**76**	...	**67.97**	**66.39**	...	**32.30**	**31.37**
	- By carrying capacity									
1.11	Up to 249 tonnes	...	...	...	...	...	...	...	...	...
1.12	250 - 399 tonnes	...	...	...	...	...	...	...	...	...
1.13	400 - 649 tonnes	...	...	...	...	...	...	...	...	...
1.14	650 - 999 tonnes	...	...	...	...	...	...	...	...	...
1.15	1000 - 1499 tonnes	...	...	...	...	...	...	...	...	...
1.16	1500 - 2999 tonnes	...	...	...	...	...	...	...	...	...
1.17	3000 tonnes and over	...	...	...	...	...	...	...	...	...
	- By year of construction									
1.21	Up to 1949	...	4	3	...	0.21	0.16	...	0.42	0.34
1.22	1950 - 1969	...	38	37	...	25.12	24.23	...	12.79	12.39
1.23	1970 - 1979	...	28	27	...	32.41	31.77	...	13.02	12.57
1.24	1980 - 1989	...	4	4	...	4.57	4.57	...	2.64	2.64
1.25	1990 and over	...	5	5	...	5.66	5.66	...	3.43	3.43
2	**Dumb and pushed vessels**	...	**294**	**291**	...	**178.29**	**176.73**	.	.	.
	- By carrying capacity									
2.11	Up to 249 tonnes	...	...	...	...	...	...	.	.	.
2.12	250 - 399 tonnes	...	...	...	...	...	...	.	.	.
2.13	400 - 649 tonnes	...	...	...	...	...	...	.	.	.
2.14	650 - 999 tonnes	...	...	...	...	...	...	.	.	.
2.15	1000 - 1499 tonnes	...	...	...	...	...	...	.	.	.
2.16	1500 - 2999 tonnes	...	...	...	...	...	...	.	.	.
2.17	3000 tonnes and over	...	...	...	...	...	...	.	.	.
	- By year of construction									
2.21	Up to 1949	...	1	1	...	0.08	0.08	.	.	.
2.22	1950 - 1969	...	55	54	...	13.93	13.60	.	.	.
2.23	1970 - 1979	...	52	52	...	30.66	30.66	.	.	.
2.24	1980 - 1989	...	168	166	...	122.93	122.45	.	.	.
2.25	1990 and over	...	18	18	...	9.93	9.93	.	.	.
3	**Tugs and pushers**	...	**154**	**151**	.	.	.	...	**52.41**	**51.95**
	- By year of construction									
3.21	Up to 1949	...	2	2	.	.	.	...	0.38	0.38
3.22	1950 - 1969	...	26	28	.	.	.	...	5.39	5.59
3.23	1970 - 1979	...	49	48	.	.	.	...	14.75	14.42
3.24	1980 - 1989	...	68	65	.	.	.	...	28.41	27.61
3.25	1990 and over	...	9	8	.	.	.	...	3.48	3.95

INLAND WATERWAYS - VOIES NAVIGABLES INTERIEURES
ВНУТРЕННИЕ ВОДНЫЕ ПУТИ

15. Inland waterway vessels in service at end of year, by carrying capacity and year of construction

15. Bateaux pour voies navigables intérieures en service à la fin de l'année, selon la capacité de charge et l'année de construction

15. Суда для внутренних водных путей, находящиеся в эксплуатации на конец года, по грузоподъемности грузоподъемности и году выпуска

| | | Estonia - Estonie - Эстония | | | | | | | | |
| | | Number
Nombre
Число | | | Carrying capacity (1000 t.)
Capacité de charge (1000 t.)
Грузоподъемность (1000 тонн) | | | Power (1000 kW)
Puissance (1000 kW)
Мощность (1000 кВт) | | |
		1990	1998	1999	1990	1998	1999	1990	1998	1999
1	**Self-propelled vessels**	3	...	...	0.40	...	...	...	...	...
	- By carrying capacity									
1.11	Up to 249 tonnes	3	...	...	0.40	...	...	...	...	...
1.12	250 - 399 tonnes	-	...	...	-	...	...	-	...	...
1.13	400 - 649 tonnes	-	...	...	-	...	...	-	...	...
1.14	650 - 999 tonnes	-	...	...	-	...	...	-	...	...
1.15	1000 - 1499 tonnes	-	...	...	-	...	...	-	...	...
1.16	1500 - 2999 tonnes	-	...	...	-	...	...	-	...	...
1.17	3000 tonnes and over	-	...	...	-	...	...	-	...	...
	- By year of construction									
1.21	Up to 1949	-	...	...	-	...	...	-	...	...
1.22	1950 - 1969	2	...	...	0.30	...	...	...	...	...
1.23	1970 - 1979	1	...	...	0.10	...	...	...	...	...
1.24	1980 - 1989	-	...	...	-	...	...	...	...	...
1.25	1990 and over	-	...	...	-	...	...	-	...	...
2	**Dumb and pushed vessels**	2	...	...	0.60	...	...	•	•	•
	- By carrying capacity									
2.11	Up to 249 tonnes	-	...	...	-	...	...	•	•	•
2.12	250 - 399 tonnes	2	...	...	0.60	...	...	•	•	•
2.13	400 - 649 tonnes	-	...	...	-	...	...	•	•	•
2.14	650 - 999 tonnes	-	...	...	-	...	...	•	•	•
2.15	1000 - 1499 tonnes	-	...	...	-	...	...	•	•	•
2.16	1500 - 2999 tonnes	-	...	...	-	...	...	•	•	•
2.17	3000 tonnes and over	-	...	...	-	...	...	•	•	•
	- By year of construction									
2.21	Up to 1949	-	...	...	-	...	...	•	•	•
2.22	1950 - 1969	-	...	...	-	...	...	•	•	•
2.23	1970 - 1979	-	...	...	-	...	...	•	•	•
2.24	1980 - 1989	2	...	...	0.60	...	...	•	•	•
2.25	1990 and over	-	...	...	-	...	...	•	•	•
3	**Tugs and pushers**	2	...	...	•	•	•	0.20	...	...
	- By year of construction									
3.21	Up to 1949	-	...	...	•	•	•	-	...	...
3.22	1950 - 1969	-	...	...	•	•	•	-	...	...
3.23	1970 - 1979	-	...	...	•	•	•	-	...	...
3.24	1980 - 1989	2	...	...	•	•	•	0.20	...	...
3.25	1990 and over	-	...	...	•	•	•	-	...	...

INLAND WATERWAYS - VOIES NAVIGABLES INTERIEURES
ВНУТРЕННИЕ ВОДНЫЕ ПУТИ

15. Inland waterway vessels in service at end of year, by carrying capacity and year of construction

15. Bateaux pour voies navigables intérieures en service à la fin de l'année, selon la capacité de charge et l'année de construction

15. Суда для внутренних водных путей, находящиеся в эксплуатации на конец года, по грузоподъемност грузоподъемности и году выпуска

		Finland - Finlande - Финляндия								
		Number Nombre Число			Carrying capacity (1000 t.) Capacité de charge (1000 t.) Грузоподъемность (1000 тонн)			Power (1000 kW) Puissance (1000 kW) Мощность (1000 кВт)		
		1990	1998	1999	1990	1998	1999	1990	1998	1999
1	**Self-propelled vessels**	...	135	138	...	14.00	14.00	...	21.00	21.00
	- By carrying capacity									
1.11	Up to 249 tonnes	...	128	131	...	9.00	9.00	...	18.00	18.00
1.12	250 - 399 tonnes	...	5	5	...	2.00	2.00	...	2.00	2.00
1.13	400 - 649 tonnes	...	-	-	...	-	-	...	-	-
1.14	650 - 999 tonnes	...	1	1	...	1.00	1.00	...	-	-
1.15	1000 - 1499 tonnes	...	-	-	...	-	-	...	-	-
1.16	1500 - 2999 tonnes	...	1	1	...	2.00	2.00	...	1.00	1.00
1.17	3000 tonnes and over	...	-	-	...	-	-	...	-	-
	- By year of construction									
1.21	Up to 1949	...	43	44	...	5.00	5.00	...	5.00	5.00
1.22	1950 - 1969	...	33	32	...	3.00	3.00	...	7.00	7.00
1.23	1970 - 1979	...	10	10	...	1.00	1.00	...	1.00	1.00
1.24	1980 - 1989	...	31	32	...	3.00	3.00	...	5.00	5.00
1.25	1990 and over	...	18	20	...	2.00	2.00	...	3.00	3.00
2	**Dumb and pushed vessels**	23	28	27	...	5.00	4.00	.	.	.
	- By carrying capacity									
2.11	Up to 249 tonnes	21	23	23	...	1.00	1.00	.	.	.
2.12	250 - 399 tonnes	-	-	-	...	-	-	.	.	.
2.13	400 - 649 tonnes	1	2	2	...	1.00	1.00	.	.	.
2.14	650 - 999 tonnes	1	2	2	...	2.00	1.00	.	.	.
2.15	1000 - 1499 tonnes	-	1	1	...	1.00	1.00	.	.	.
2.16	1500 - 2999 tonnes	-	-	-	...	-	-	.	.	.
2.17	3000 tonnes and over	-	-	-	...	-	-	.	.	.
	- By year of construction									
2.21	Up to 1949	14	10	9	...	1.00	1.00	.	.	.
2.22	1950 - 1969	3	2	3	...	0.00	0.00	.	.	.
2.23	1970 - 1979	3	7	6	...	3.00	2.00	.	.	.
2.24	1980 - 1989	3	7	7	...	1.00	1.00	.	.	.
2.25	1990 and over	-	2	2	...	0.00	0.00	.	.	.
3	**Tugs and pushers**	22	33	32	.	.	.	7.60	11.00	11.00
	- By year of construction									
3.21	Up to 1949	14	17	16	.	.	.	3.50	4.00	4.00
3.22	1950 - 1969	3	7	7	.	.	.	1.50	3.00	3.00
3.23	1970 - 1979	2	3	3	.	.	.	0.90	1.00	1.00
3.24	1980 - 1989	3	4	4	.	.	.	1.70	2.00	2.00
3.25	1990 and over	-	2	2	.	.	.	-	1.00	1.00

INLAND WATERWAYS - VOIES NAVIGABLES INTERIEURES
ВНУТРЕННИЕ ВОДНЫЕ ПУТИ

15. Inland waterway vessels in service at end of year, by carrying capacity and year of construction

15. Bateaux pour voies navigables intérieures en service à la fin de l'année, selon la capacité de charge et l'année de construction

15. Суда для внутренних водных путей, находящиеся в эксплуатации на конец года, по грузоподъемности грузоподъемности и году выпуска

		France - France - Франция								
		Number Nombre Число			Carrying capacity (1000 t.) Capacité de charge (1000 t.) Грузоподъемность (1000 тонн)			Power (1000 kW) Puissance (1000 kW) Мощность (1000 кВт)		
		1990	1998	1999	1990	1998	1999	1990	1998	1999
1	**Self-propelled vessels**	**2 111**	**1 246**	**1 211**	**973.60**	**587.00**	**573.00**	**355.80**	**254.00**	**253.00**
	- By carrying capacity									
1.11	Up to 249 tonnes	15	5	5	2.40	1.00	1.00	1.20	1.00	1.00
1.12	250 - 399 tonnes	1 650	941	910	616.00	354.00	343.00	236.30	156.00	154.00
1.13	400 - 649 tonnes	221	152	153	104.10	74.00	74.00	40.30	32.00	32.00
1.14	650 - 999 tonnes	121	93	91	101.00	82.00	76.00	44.10	36.00	35.00
1.15	1000 - 1499 tonnes	30	34	34	35.90	43.00	43.00	14.20	17.00	17.00
1.16	1500 - 2999 tonnes	73	16	18	110.30	33.00	36.00	19.60	12.00	14.00
1.17	3000 tonnes and over	1	-	-	3.90	-	-	0.10	-	-
	- By year of construction									
1.21	Up to 1949	734	305	286	301.80	144.00	136.00	...	59.00	57.00
1.22	1950 - 1969	1 274	902	884	546.80	401.00	395.00	...	175.00	176.00
1.23	1970 - 1979	13	12	13	5.40	13.00	13.00	...	6.00	6.00
1.24	1980 - 1989	90	22	23	119.60	21.00	23.00	...	10.00	11.00
1.25	1990 and over	(a)	5	5	(a)	8.00	7.00	...	4.00	3.00
2	**Dumb and pushed vessels**	**967**	**695**	**679**	**679.00**	**693.00**	**672.00**	•	•	•
	- By carrying capacity									
2.11	Up to 249 tonnes	52	16	13	9.50	4.00	3.00	•	•	•
2.12	250 - 399 tonnes	340	99	97	122.80	34.00	33.00	•	•	•
2.13	400 - 649 tonnes	327	274	278	152.90	132.00	135.00	•	•	•
2.14	650 - 999 tonnes	108	105	99	81.70	80.00	76.00	•	•	•
2.15	1000 - 1499 tonnes	20	27	27	24.20	32.00	32.00	•	•	•
2.16	1500 - 2999 tonnes	116	168	159	275.50	392.00	374.00	•	•	•
2.17	3000 tonnes and over	4	6	6	12.40	19.00	19.00	•	•	•
	- By year of construction									
2.21	Up to 1949	296	116	111	133.30	56.00	53.00	•	•	•
2.22	1950 - 1969	535	376	358	338.70	303.00	278.00	•	•	•
2.23	1970 - 1979	98	105	91	140.30	167.00	137.00	•	•	•
2.24	1980 - 1989	38	29	32	66.70	48.00	59.00	•	•	•
2.25	1990 and over	(a)	69	87	(a)	119.00	145.00	•	•	•
3	**Tugs and pushers**	**214**	**197**	**197**	•	•	•	**110.20**	**85.00**	**90.00**
	- By year of construction									
3.21	Up to 1949	94	89	88	•	•	•	27.60	28.00	29.00
3.22	1950 - 1969	81	77	76	•	•	•	53.30	42.00	42.00
3.23	1970 - 1979	33	24	25	•	•	•	24.30	12.00	15.00
3.24	1980 - 1989	6	2	3	•	•	•	5.00	-	1.00
3.25	1990 and over	-	5	5	•	•	•	-	3.00	3.00

(a) Including under previous item.   (a) Compris sous la rubrique précédente.   (a) Включено в переыдущий показатель.

INLAND WATERWAYS - VOIES NAVIGABLES INTERIEURES
ВНУТРЕННИЕ ВОДНЫЕ ПУТИ

15. Inland waterway vessels in service at end of year, by carrying capacity and year of construction

15. Bateaux pour voies navigables intérieures en service à la fin de l'année, selon la capacité de charge et l'année de construction

15. Суда для внутренних водных путей, находящиеся в эксплуатации на конец года, по грузоподъемности грузоподъемности и году выпуска

		Germany - Allemagne - Германия								
		Number Nombre Число			Carrying capacity (1000 t.) Capacité de charge (1000 t.) Грузоподъемность (1000 тонн)			Power (1000 kW) Puissance (1000 kW) Мощность (1000 кВт)		
		1990	1998	1999	1990	1998	1999	1990	1998	1999
1	**Self-propelled vessels**	...	**2 804**	**2 663**	...	**2 852.00**	**2 753.00**	...	**779.00**	**750.00**
	- By carrying capacity									
1.11	Up to 249 tonnes	...	181	185	...	26.00	26.00	...	9.00	9.00
1.12	250 - 399 tonnes	...	164	143	...	54.00	47.00	...	16.00	15.00
1.13	400 - 649 tonnes	...	718	664	...	328.00	305.00	...	25.00	21.00
1.14	650 - 999 tonnes	...	494	446	...	426.00	386.00	...	122.00	107.00
1.15	1000 - 1499 tonnes	...	715	686	...	872.00	838.00	...	353.00	339.00
1.16	1500 - 2999 tonnes	...	520	529	...	1 107.00	1 119.00	...	248.00	253.00
1.17	3000 tonnes and over	...	12	10	...	39.00	33.00	...	6.00	5.00
	- By year of construction									
1.21	Up to 1949	...	626	566	...	521.00	482.00	...	198.00	184.00
1.22	1950 - 1969	...	893	831	...	858.00	770.00	...	301.00	285.00
1.23	1970 - 1979	...	488	466	...	662.00	634.00	...	170.00	167.00
1.24	1980 - 1989	...	680	676	...	658.00	676.00	...	86.00	87.00
1.25	1990 and over	...	117	124	...	153.00	164.00	...	24.00	27.00
2	**Dumb and pushed vessels**	...	**1 230**	**1 197**	...	**1 056.00**	**1 062.00**	.	.	.
	- By carrying capacity									
2.11	Up to 249 tonnes	...	92	99	...	13.00	14.00	.	.	.
2.12	250 - 399 tonnes	...	75	60	...	25.00	20.00	.	.	.
2.13	400 - 649 tonnes	...	622	587	...	278.00	265.00	.	.	.
2.14	650 - 999 tonnes	...	155	153	...	143.00	141.00	.	.	.
2.15	1000 - 1499 tonnes	...	62	71	...	78.00	87.00	.	.	.
2.16	1500 - 2999 tonnes	...	217	228	...	494.00	511.00	.	.	.
2.17	3000 tonnes and over	...	7	7	...	24.00	24.00	.	.	.
	- By year of construction									
2.21	Up to 1949	...	101	98	...	62.00	60.00	.	.	.
2.22	1950 - 1969	...	210	198	...	141.00	129.00	.	.	.
2.23	1970 - 1979	...	236	224	...	285.00	267.00	.	.	.
2.24	1980 - 1989	...	588	587	...	457.00	476.00	.	.	.
2.25	1990 and over	...	95	97	...	112.00	115.00	.	.	.
3	**Tugs and pushers**	...	**490**	**479**	.	.	.	...	**154.00**	**152.00**
	- By year of construction									
3.21	Up to 1949	...	139	134	.	.	.	...	34.00	32.00
3.22	1950 - 1969	...	180	171	.	.	.	...	43.00	42.00
3.23	1970 - 1979	...	72	72	.	.	.	...	48.00	48.00
3.24	1980 - 1989	...	91	94	.	.	.	...	26.00	27.00
3.25	1990 and over	...	8	8	.	.	.	...	3.00	3.00

INLAND WATERWAYS - VOIES NAVIGABLES INTERIEURES
ВНУТРЕННИЕ ВОДНЫЕ ПУТИ

15. Inland waterway vessels in service at end of year, by carrying capacity and year of construction

15. Bateaux pour voies navigables intérieures en service à la fin de l'année, selon la capacité de charge et l'année de construction

15. Суда для внутренних водных путей, находящиеся в эксплуатации на конец года, по грузоподъемности грузоподъемности и году выпуска

		Hungary - Hongrie - Венгрия								
		Number Nombre Число			Carrying capacity (1000 t.) Capacité de charge (1000 t.) Грузоподъемность (1000 тонн)			Power (1000 kW) Puissance (1000 kW) Мощность (1000 кВт)		
		1990	1998	1999	1990	1998	1999	1990	1998	1999
1	Self-propelled vessels	29	143	143	15.90	18.00	12.00	5.20	...	...
	- By carrying capacity									
1.11	Up to 249 tonnes	...	...	...	...	...	...	...	...	...
1.12	250 - 399 tonnes	...	...	...	...	...	...	...	...	...
1.13	400 - 649 tonnes	...	...	...	...	...	...	...	...	...
1.14	650 - 999 tonnes	...	...	...	...	...	...	...	...	...
1.15	1000 - 1499 tonnes	...	...	...	...	...	...	...	...	...
1.16	1500 - 2999 tonnes	...	...	...	...	...	...	...	...	...
1.17	3000 tonnes and over	...	...	...	...	...	...	...	...	...
	- By year of construction									
1.21	Up to 1949	...	...	...	...	...	...	...	...	...
1.22	1950 - 1969	...	...	...	...	...	...	...	...	...
1.23	1970 - 1979	...	...	...	...	...	...	...	...	...
1.24	1980 - 1989	...	...	...	...	...	...	...	...	...
1.25	1990 and over	...	...	...	...	...	...	...	...	...
2	Dumb and pushed vessels	192	173	182	...	203.00	206.00	•	•	•
	- By carrying capacity									
2.11	Up to 249 tonnes	...	...	...	...	...	...	•	•	•
2.12	250 - 399 tonnes	...	...	...	...	...	...	•	•	•
2.13	400 - 649 tonnes	...	...	...	...	...	...	•	•	•
2.14	650 - 999 tonnes	...	...	...	...	...	...	•	•	•
2.15	1000 - 1499 tonnes	...	...	...	...	...	...	•	•	•
2.16	1500 - 2999 tonnes	...	...	...	...	...	...	•	•	•
2.17	3000 tonnes and over	...	...	...	...	...	...	•	•	•
	- By year of construction									
2.21	Up to 1949	...	...	...	...	...	...	•	•	•
2.22	1950 - 1969	...	...	...	...	...	...	•	•	•
2.23	1970 - 1979	...	...	...	...	...	...	•	•	•
2.24	1980 - 1989	...	...	...	...	...	...	•	•	•
2.25	1990 and over	...	...	...	...	...	...	•	•	•
3	Tugs and pushers	45	45	51	•	•	•	35.30	31.00	35.00
	- By year of construction									
3.21	Up to 1949	...	...	...	•	•	•	...	...	...
3.22	1950 - 1969	...	...	...	•	•	•	...	...	...
3.23	1970 - 1979	...	...	...	•	•	•	...	...	...
3.24	1980 - 1989	...	...	...	•	•	•	...	...	...
3.25	1990 and over	...	...	...	•	•	•	...	...	...

INLAND WATERWAYS - VOIES NAVIGABLES INTERIEURES
ВНУТРЕННИЕ ВОДНЫЕ ПУТИ

15. Inland waterway vessels in service at end of year, by carrying capacity and year of construction

15. Bateaux pour voies navigables intérieures en service à la fin de l'année, selon la capacité de charge et l'année de construction

15. Суда для внутренних водных путей, находящиеся в эксплуатации на конец года, по грузоподъемност грузоподъемности и году выпуска

		Italy - Italie - Италия								
		Number Nombre Число			Carrying capacity (1000 t.) Capacité de charge (1000 t.) Грузоподъемность (1000 тонн)			Power (1000 kW) Puissance (1000 kW) Мощность (1000 кВт)		
		1990	1998	1999	1990	1998	1999	1990	1998	1999
1	**Self-propelled vessels**	**2 665**	**3 089**	**3 101**	...	...	...	...	...	...
	- By carrying capacity									
1.11	Up to 249 tonnes	2 601	3 040	3 051	...	...	...	...	...	...
1.12	250 - 399 tonnes	36	35	36	...	...	...	...	...	...
1.13	400 - 649 tonnes	22	11	12	...	...	...	...	...	...
1.14	650 - 999 tonnes	4	3	2	...	...	...	...	...	...
1.15	1000 - 1499 tonnes	2	-	-	...	...	...	...	...	...
1.16	1500 - 2999 tonnes	...	-	-	...	...	...	...	...	...
1.17	3000 tonnes and over	-	-	-	...	...	...	...	...	...
	- By year of construction									
1.21	Up to 1949	...	...	...	...	...	...	...	...	...
1.22	1950 - 1969	...	...	...	...	...	...	...	...	...
1.23	1970 - 1979	...	...	...	...	...	...	...	...	...
1.24	1980 - 1989	...	...	...	...	...	...	...	...	...
1.25	1990 and over	...	...	...	...	...	...	...	...	...
2	**Dumb and pushed vessels**	**372**	**474**	**437**	...	...	...	·	·	·
	- By carrying capacity									
2.11	Up to 249 tonnes	282	366	330	...	...	...	·	·	·
2.12	250 - 399 tonnes	20	27	27	...	...	...	·	·	·
2.13	400 - 649 tonnes	18	39	38	...	...	...	·	·	·
2.14	650 - 999 tonnes	15	20	20	...	...	...	·	·	·
2.15	1000 - 1499 tonnes	27	...	...	...	...	...	·	·	·
2.16	1500 - 2999 tonnes	...	...	...	...	...	...	·	·	·
2.17	3000 tonnes and over	-	...	...	...	...	...	·	·	·
	- By year of construction									
2.21	Up to 1949	...	...	...	...	...	...	·	·	·
2.22	1950 - 1969	...	...	...	...	...	...	·	·	·
2.23	1970 - 1979	...	...	...	...	...	...	·	·	·
2.24	1980 - 1989	...	...	...	...	...	...	·	·	·
2.25	1990 and over	...	...	...	...	...	...	·	·	·
3	**Tugs and pushers**	**88**	**95**	**96**	·	·	·	...	...	...
	- By year of construction									
3.21	Up to 1949	...	...	...	·	·	·	...	...	...
3.22	1950 - 1969	...	...	...	·	·	·	...	...	...
3.23	1970 - 1979	...	...	...	·	·	·	...	...	...
3.24	1980 - 1989	...	...	...	·	·	·	...	...	...
3.25	1990 and over	...	...	...	·	·	·	...	...	...

INLAND WATERWAYS - VOIES NAVIGABLES INTERIEURES
ВНУТРЕННИЕ ВОДНЫЕ ПУТИ

15. Inland waterway vessels in service at end of year, by carrying capacity and year of construction

15. Bateaux pour voies navigables intérieures en service à la fin de l'année, selon la capacité de charge et l'année de construction

15. Суда для внутренних водных путей, находящиеся в эксплуатации на конец года, по грузоподъемности грузоподъемности и году выпуска

		Kazakhstan - Kazakhstan - Казахстан								
		Number Nombre Число			Carrying capacity (1000 t.) Capacité de charge (1000 t.) Грузоподъемность (1000 тонн)			Power (1000 kW) Puissance (1000 kW) Мощность (1000 кВт)		
		1990	1998	1999	1990	1998	1999	1990	1998	1999
1	Self-propelled vessels	...	3	1	...	5.10	1.70	...	5.10	1.70
	- By carrying capacity									
1.11	Up to 249 tonnes	...	-	-	...	-	-	...	-	-
1.12	250 - 399 tonnes	...	-	-	...	-	-	...	-	-
1.13	400 - 649 tonnes	...	-	-	...	-	-	...	-	-
1.14	650 - 999 tonnes	...	-	-	...	-	-	...	-	-
1.15	1000 - 1499 tonnes	...	-	-	...	-	-	...	-	-
1.16	1500 - 2999 tonnes	...	3	1	...	5.10	1.70	...	5.10	1.70
1.17	3000 tonnes and over	...	-	-	...	-	-	...	-	-
	- By year of construction									
1.21	Up to 1949	...	-	-	...	-	-	...	-	-
1.22	1950 - 1969	...	-	-	...	-	-	...	-	-
1.23	1970 - 1979	...	-	-	...	-	-	...	-	-
1.24	1980 - 1989	...	3	1	...	5.10	1.70	...	5.10	1.70
1.25	1990 and over	...	-	-	...	-	-	...		
2	Dumb and pushed vessels	...	96	81	...	74.60	59.80	.	.	.
	- By carrying capacity									
2.11	Up to 249 tonnes	...	13	13	...	...	...	.	.	.
2.12	250 - 399 tonnes	...	5	5	...	...	...	.	.	.
2.13	400 - 649 tonnes	...	11	10	...	...	...	.	.	.
2.14	650 - 999 tonnes	...	11	11	...	...	...	.	.	.
2.15	1000 - 1499 tonnes	...	56	42	...	...	...	.	.	.
2.16	1500 - 2999 tonnes	...	-	-	...	-	-	.	.	.
2.17	3000 tonnes and over	...	-	-	...	-	-	.	.	.
	- By year of construction									
2.21	Up to 1949	...	-	-	...	-	-	.	.	.
2.22	1950 - 1969	...	17	15	...	10.20	8.20	.	.	.
2.23	1970 - 1979	...	12	9	...	7.60	4.50	.	.	.
2.24	1980 - 1989	...	67	57	...	56.80	47.10	.	.	.
2.25	1990 and over	...	-	-	...	-	-	.	.	.
3	Tugs and pushers	...	62	64	.	.	.	...	20.30	20.60
	- By year of construction									
3.21	Up to 1949	...	-	-	.	.	.	...	-	-
3.22	1950 - 1969	...	2	-	.	.	.	...	0.20	-
3.23	1970 - 1979	...	37	40	.	.	.	...	13.20	13.20
3.24	1980 - 1989	...	23	24	.	.	.	...	6.90	7.40
3.25	1990 and over	...	-	-	.	.	.	...	-	-

INLAND WATERWAYS - VOIES NAVIGABLES INTERIEURES
ВНУТРЕННИЕ ВОДНЫЕ ПУТИ

15. Inland waterway vessels in service at end of year, by carrying capacity and year of construction

15. Bateaux pour voies navigables intérieures en service à la fin de l'année, selon la capacité de charge et l'année de construction

15. Суда для внутренних водных путей, находящиеся в эксплуатации на конец года, по грузоподъемности грузоподъемности и году выпуска

| | | Kyrgyzstan - Kirghizistan - Кыргызстан | | | | | | | | |
| | | Number
Nombre
Число | | | Carrying capacity (1000 t.)
Capacité de charge (1000 t.)
Грузоподъемность (1000 тонн) | | | Power (1000 kW)
Puissance (1000 kW)
Мощность (1000 кВт) | | |
		1990	1998	1999	1990	1998	1999	1990	1998	1999
1	**Self-propelled vessels**	6	5	5	...	...	...	...	...	...
	- By carrying capacity									
1.11	Up to 249 tonnes	...	...	...	...	...	...	...	...	...
1.12	250 - 399 tonnes	...	...	...	...	...	...	...	...	...
1.13	400 - 649 tonnes	...	...	...	...	...	...	...	...	...
1.14	650 - 999 tonnes	...	...	...	...	...	...	...	...	...
1.15	1000 - 1499 tonnes	...	...	...	...	...	...	...	...	...
1.16	1500 - 2999 tonnes	...	...	...	...	...	...	...	...	...
1.17	3000 tonnes and over	...	...	...	...	...	...	...	...	...
	- By year of construction									
1.21	Up to 1949	...	...	...	...	...	...	...	...	...
1.22	1950 - 1969	...	...	...	...	...	...	...	...	...
1.23	1970 - 1979	...	...	...	...	...	...	...	...	...
1.24	1980 - 1989	...	...	...	...	...	...	...	...	...
1.25	1990 and over	...	...	...	...	...	...	...	...	...
2	**Dumb and pushed vessels**	12	9	9	...	...	...	•	•	•
	- By carrying capacity									
2.11	Up to 249 tonnes	...	...	...	...	...	...	•	•	•
2.12	250 - 399 tonnes	...	...	...	...	...	...	•	•	•
2.13	400 - 649 tonnes	...	...	...	...	...	...	•	•	•
2.14	650 - 999 tonnes	...	...	...	...	...	...	•	•	•
2.15	1000 - 1499 tonnes	...	...	...	...	...	...	•	•	•
2.16	1500 - 2999 tonnes	...	...	...	...	...	...	•	•	•
2.17	3000 tonnes and over	...	...	...	...	...	...	•	•	•
	- By year of construction									
2.21	Up to 1949	...	...	...	...	...	...	•	•	•
2.22	1950 - 1969	...	...	...	...	...	...	•	•	•
2.23	1970 - 1979	...	...	...	...	...	...	•	•	•
2.24	1980 - 1989	...	...	...	...	...	...	•	•	•
2.25	1990 and over	...	...	...	...	...	...	•	•	•
3	**Tugs and pushers**	8	6	6	•	•	•	...	...	...
	- By year of construction									
3.21	Up to 1949	...	...	...	•	•	•	...	...	...
3.22	1950 - 1969	...	...	...	•	•	•	...	...	...
3.23	1970 - 1979	...	...	...	•	•	•	...	...	...
3.24	1980 - 1989	...	...	...	•	•	•	...	...	...
3.25	1990 and over	...	...	...	•	•	•	...	...	...

INLAND WATERWAYS - VOIES NAVIGABLES INTERIEURES
ВНУТРЕННИЕ ВОДНЫЕ ПУТИ

15. Inland waterway vessels in service at end of year, by carrying capacity and year of construction

15. Bateaux pour voies navigables intérieures en service à la fin de l'année, selon la capacité de charge et l'année de construction

15. Суда для внутренних водных путей, находящиеся в эксплуатации на конец года, по грузоподъемности грузоподъемности и году выпуска

		Latvia - Lettonie - Латвия								
		Number Nombre Число			Carrying capacity (1000 t.) Capacité de charge (1000 t.) Грузоподъемность (1000 тонн)			Power (1000 kW) Puissance (1000 kW) Мощность (1000 кВт)		
		1990	1998	1999	1990	1998	1999	1990	1998	1999
1	**Self-propelled vessels**	12	-	-	29.10	0.03	0.03	10.90	-	-
	- By carrying capacity									
1.11	Up to 249 tonnes	-	-	-	-	0.03	0.03	-	-	-
1.12	250 - 399 tonnes	-	-	-	-	-	-	-	-	-
1.13	400 - 649 tonnes	-	-	-	-	-	-	-	-	-
1.14	650 - 999 tonnes	2	-	-	2.50	-	-	1.80	-	-
1.15	1000 - 1499 tonnes	6	-	-	13.30	-	-	5.00	-	-
1.16	1500 - 2999 tonnes	4	-	-	13.30	-	-	4.10	-	-
1.17	3000 tonnes and over	-	-	-	-	-	-	-	-	-
	- By year of construction									
1.21	Up to 1949	-	-	-	-	-	-	-	-	-
1.22	1950 - 1969	2	-	-	...	-	-	...	-	-
1.23	1970 - 1979	1	-	-	...	0.03	0.03	...	-	-
1.24	1980 - 1989	9	-	-	...	-	-	...	-	-
1.25	1990 and over	-	-	-	-	-	-	-	-	-
2	**Dumb and pushed vessels**	41	-	-	21.20	-	-	•	•	•
	- By carrying capacity									
2.11	Up to 249 tonnes	-	-	-	-	-	-	•	•	•
2.12	250 - 399 tonnes	7	-	-	2.20	-	-	•	•	•
2.13	400 - 649 tonnes	33	-	-	16.90	-	-	•	•	•
2.14	650 - 999 tonnes	-	-	-	-	-	-	•	•	•
2.15	1000 - 1499 tonnes	-	-	-	-	-	-	•	•	•
2.16	1500 - 2999 tonnes	1	-	-	2.10	-	-	•	•	•
2.17	3000 tonnes and over	-	-	-	-	-	-	•	•	•
	- By year of construction									
2.21	Up to 1949	-	-	-	-	-	-	•	•	•
2.22	1950 - 1969	3	-	-	...	-	-	•	•	•
2.23	1970 - 1979	18	-	-	...	-	-	•	•	•
2.24	1980 - 1989	20	-	-	...	-	-	•	•	•
2.25	1990 and over	-	-	-	-	-	-	•	•	•
3	**Tugs and pushers**	15	-	-	•	•	•	2.80	-	-
	- By year of construction									
3.21	Up to 1949	-	-	-	•	•	•	-	-	-
3.22	1950 - 1969	1	-	-	•	•	•	...	-	-
3.23	1970 - 1979	6	-	-	•	•	•	...	-	-
3.24	1980 - 1989	8	-	-	•	•	•	...	-	-
3.25	1990 and over	-	-	-	•	•	•	-	-	-

15. Inland waterway vessels in service at end of year, by carrying capacity and year of construction

15. Bateaux pour voies navigables intérieures en service à la fin de l'année, selon la capacité de charge et l'année de construction

15. Суда для внутренних водных путей, находящиеся в эксплуатации на конец года, по грузоподъемност грузоподъемности и году выпуска

		Lithuania - Lituanie - Литва								
		Number Nombre Число			Carrying capacity (1000 t.) Capacité de charge (1000 t.) Грузоподъемность (1000 тонн)			Power (1000 kW) Puissance (1000 kW) Мощность (1000 кВт)		
		1990	1998	1999	1990	1998	1999	1990	1998	1999
1	**Self-propelled vessels**	10	11	10	...	3.00	3.00	...	1.00	1.00
	- By carrying capacity									
1.11	Up to 249 tonnes	...	1	1	...	0.00	0.00	...	0.00	0.00
1.12	250 - 399 tonnes	...	10	9	...	3.00	3.00	...	1.00	1.00
1.13	400 - 649 tonnes	...	-	-	...	-	-	...	-	-
1.14	650 - 999 tonnes	...	-	-	...	-	-	...	-	-
1.15	1000 - 1499 tonnes	...	-	-	...	-	-	...	-	-
1.16	1500 - 2999 tonnes	...	-	-	...	-	-	...	-	-
1.17	3000 tonnes and over	...	-	-	...	-	-	...	-	-
	- By year of construction									
1.21	Up to 1949	...	-	-	...	-	-	...	-	-
1.22	1950 - 1969	...	2	2	...	0.00	0.00	...	0.00	0.00
1.23	1970 - 1979	...	9	8	...	3.00	3.00	...	1.00	1.00
1.24	1980 - 1989	...	-	-	...	-	-	...	-	-
1.25	1990 and over	...	-	-	...	-	-	...	-	-
2	**Dumb and pushed vessels**	18	13	11	...	8.00	7.00	.	.	.
	- By carrying capacity									
2.11	Up to 249 tonnes	...	1	1	...	0.00	0.00	.	.	.
2.12	250 - 399 tonnes	...	1	-	...	0.00	-	.	.	.
2.13	400 - 649 tonnes	...	5	4	...	2.00	2.00	.	.	.
2.14	650 - 999 tonnes	...	6	6	...	5.00	5.00	.	.	.
2.15	1000 - 1499 tonnes	...	-	-	...	-	-	.	.	.
2.16	1500 - 2999 tonnes	...	-	-	...	-	-	.	.	.
2.17	3000 tonnes and over	...	-	-	...	-	-	.	.	.
	- By year of construction									
2.21	Up to 1949	...	3	-	...	1.00	-	.	.	.
2.22	1950 - 1969	...	-	1	...	-	0.00	.	.	.
2.23	1970 - 1979	...	3	3	...	1.00	1.00	.	.	.
2.24	1980 - 1989	...	7	7	...	6.00	6.00	.	.	.
2.25	1990 and over	...	-	-	...	-	-	.	.	.
3	**Tugs and pushers**	8	11	11	.	.	.	...	2.00	2.00
	- By year of construction									
3.21	Up to 1949	...	-	-	.	.	.	...	-	-
3.22	1950 - 1969	...	2	2	.	.	.	...	0.00	0.00
3.23	1970 - 1979	...	2	2	.	.	.	...	0.00	0.00
3.24	1980 - 1989	...	7	7	.	.	.	...	1.00	1.00
3.25	1990 and over	...	-	-	.	.	.	...	-	-

INLAND WATERWAYS - VOIES NAVIGABLES INTERIEURES
ВНУТРЕННИЕ ВОДНЫЕ ПУТИ

15. Inland waterway vessels in service at end of year, by carrying capacity and year of construction

15. Bateaux pour voies navigables intérieures en service à la fin de l'année, selon la capacité de charge et l'année de construction

15. Суда для внутренних водных путей, находящиеся в эксплуатации на конец года, по грузоподъемности грузоподъемности и году выпуска

		Luxembourg - Luxembourg - Люксембург								
		Number Nombre Число			Carrying capacity (1000 t.) Capacité de charge (1000 t.) Грузоподъемность (1000 тонн)			Power (1000 kW) Puissance (1000 kW) Мощность (1000 кВт)		
		1990	1998	1999	1990	1998	1999	1990	1998	1999
1	**Self-propelled vessels**	25	...	...	28.60	...	...	14.40	...	...
	- By carrying capacity									
1.11	Up to 249 tonnes	-	...	...	-	...	...	-	...	...
1.12	250 - 399 tonnes	7	...	...	2.70	...	...	1.10	...	...
1.13	400 - 649 tonnes	1	...	...	0.50	...	...	0.40	...	...
1.14	650 - 999 tonnes	4	...	...	3.40	...	...	1.60	...	...
1.15	1000 - 1499 tonnes	9	...	...	11.10	...	...	6.10	...	...
1.16	1500 - 2999 tonnes	2	...	...	3.40	...	...	1.60	...	...
1.17	3000 tonnes and over	2	...	...	7.50	...	...	3.60	...	...
	- By year of construction									
1.21	Up to 1949	8	...	...	7.30	...	...	...	...	...
1.22	1950 - 1969	12	...	...	9.06	...	...	...	...	...
1.23	1970 - 1979	4	...	...	8.23	...	...	...	...	...
1.24	1980 - 1989	1	...	...	4.03	...	...	...	...	...
1.25	1990 and over	-	...	...	-	...	...	...	...	...
2	**Dumb and pushed vessels**	-	...	...	-	...	...	•	•	•
	- By carrying capacity									
2.11	Up to 249 tonnes	-	...	...	-	...	...	•	•	•
2.12	250 - 399 tonnes	-	...	...	-	...	...	•	•	•
2.13	400 - 649 tonnes	-	...	...	-	...	...	•	•	•
2.14	650 - 999 tonnes	-	...	...	-	...	...	•	•	•
2.15	1000 - 1499 tonnes	-	...	...	-	...	...	•	•	•
2.16	1500 - 2999 tonnes	-	...	...	-	...	...	•	•	•
2.17	3000 tonnes and over	-	...	...	-	...	...	•	•	•
	- By year of construction									
2.21	Up to 1949	-	...	...	-	...	...	•	•	•
2.22	1950 - 1969	-	...	...	-	...	...	•	•	•
2.23	1970 - 1979	-	...	...	-	...	...	•	•	•
2.24	1980 - 1989	-	...	...	-	...	...	•	•	•
2.25	1990 and over	-	...	...	-	...	...	•	•	•
3	**Tugs and pushers**	...	...	...	•	•	•	...	...	...
	- By year of construction									
3.21	Up to 1949	...	...	...	•	•	•	...	...	...
3.22	1950 - 1969	...	...	...	•	•	•	...	...	...
3.23	1970 - 1979	...	...	...	•	•	•	...	...	...
3.24	1980 - 1989	...	...	...	•	•	•	...	...	...
3.25	1990 and over	...	...	...	•	•	•	...	...	...

INLAND WATERWAYS - VOIES NAVIGABLES INTERIEURES
ВНУТРЕННИЕ ВОДНЫЕ ПУТИ

15. Inland waterway vessels in service at end of year, by carrying capacity and year of construction

15. Bateaux pour voies navigables intérieures en service à la fin de l'année, selon la capacité de charge et l'année de construction

15. Суда для внутренних водных путей, находящиеся в эксплуатации на конец года, по грузоподъемности грузоподъемности и году выпуска

		Netherlands - Pays-Bas - Нидерланды [1]								
		Number Nombre Число			Carrying capacity (1000 t.) Capacité de charge (1000 t.) Грузоподъемность (1000 тонн)			Power (1000 kW) Puissance (1000 kW) Мощность (1000 кВт)		
		1990	1998	1999	1990	1998	1999	1990	1998	1999
1	**Self-propelled vessels**	5 772	3 768	...	4 474.00	3 743.00	...	1 819.00	1 742.00	...
	- By carrying capacity									
1.11	Up to 249 tonnes	555	149	...	76.00	28.00	...	17.00	19.00	...
1.12	250 - 399 tonnes	985	341	...	329.00	115.00	...	129.00	57.00	...
1.13	400 - 649 tonnes	1 427	759	...	752.00	407.00	...	308.00	197.00	...
1.14	650 - 999 tonnes	1 291	1 002	...	1 045.00	815.00	...	436.00	383.00	...
1.15	1000 - 1499 tonnes	990	911	...	1 185.00	1 105.00	...	498.00	523.00	...
1.16	1500 - 2999 tonnes	469	563	...	905.00	1 130.00	...	366.00	509.00	...
1.17	3000 tonnes and over	55	43	...	182.00	143.00	...	65.00	54.00	...
	- By year of construction									
1.21	Up to 1949	2 514	1 073	...	...	783.00	...	...	355.00	...
1.22	1950 - 1969	2 684	2 002	...	...	1 732.00	...	...	819.00	...
1.23	1970 - 1979	319	347	...	...	557.00	...	...	252.00	...
1.24	1980 - 1989	...	232	...	...	428.00	...	...	192.00	...
1.25	1990 and over	...	114	...	...	243.00	...	...	125.00	...
2	**Dumb and pushed vessels**	3 783	809	...	2 390.00	1 470.00	...			
	- By carrying capacity									
2.11	Up to 249 tonnes	2 146	66	...	190.00	9.00	...			
2.12	250 - 399 tonnes	391	49	...	124.00	16.00	...			
2.13	400 - 649 tonnes	288	57	...	150.00	31.00	...			
2.14	650 - 999 tonnes	163	70	...	135.00	58.00	...			
2.15	1000 - 1499 tonnes	189	102	...	241.00	139.00	...			
2.16	1500 - 2999 tonnes	521	375	...	1 244.00	916.00	...			
2.17	3000 tonnes and over	85	83	...	306.00	301.00	...			
	- By year of construction									
2.21	Up to 1949	...	141	...	...	144.00	...			
2.22	1950 - 1969	...	179	...	...	205.00	...			
2.23	1970 - 1979	...	215	...	...	450.00	...			
2.24	1980 - 1989	...	200	...	...	487.00	...			
2.25	1990 and over	...	74	...	...	184.00	...			
3	**Tugs and pushers**	1 066	318	...				337.00	172.00	...
	- By year of construction									
3.21	Up to 1949	555	141	...				...	52.00	...
3.22	1950 - 1969	355	114	...				...	57.00	...
3.23	1970 - 1979	101	41	...				...	34.00	...
3.24	1980 - 1989	55	21	...				...	25.00	...
3.25	1990 and over	-	1	...				...	4.00	...

1- Power of crafts is given in C.V.　　　1- La puissance des moteurs est donnée en C.V.　　　1- Мощность судов приведена в Л.С.

INLAND WATERWAYS - VOIES NAVIGABLES INTERIEURES
ВНУТРЕННИЕ ВОДНЫЕ ПУТИ

15. Inland waterway vessels in service at end of year, by carrying capacity and year of construction

15. Bateaux pour voies navigables intérieures en service à la fin de l'année, selon la capacité de charge et l'année de construction

15. Суда для внутренних водных путей, находящиеся в эксплуатации на конец года, по грузоподъемности грузоподъемности и году выпуска

		Poland - Pologne - Польша								
		Number Nombre Число			Carrying capacity (1000 t.) Capacité de charge (1000 t.) Грузоподъемность (1000 тонн)			Power (1000 kW) Puissance (1000 kW) Мощность (1000 кВт)		
		1990	1998	1999	1990	1998	1999	1990	1998	1999
1	**Self-propelled vessels**	319	155	113	147.60	72.00	53.00	66.10	37.00	27.00
	- By carrying capacity									
1.11	Up to 249 tonnes	...	-	-	...	-	-	...	-	-
1.12	250 - 399 tonnes	...	2	2	...	1.00	1.00	...	1.00	1.00
1.13	400 - 649 tonnes	...	153	111	...	71.00	52.00	...	36.00	26.00
1.14	650 - 999 tonnes	...	-	-	...	-	-	...	-	-
1.15	1000 - 1499 tonnes	...	-	-	...	-	-	...	-	-
1.16	1500 - 2999 tonnes	...	-	-	...	-	-	...	-	-
1.17	3000 tonnes and over	...	-	-	...	-	-	...	-	-
	- By year of construction									
1.21	Up to 1949	...	-	-	...	-	-	...	-	-
1.22	1950 - 1969	...	146	108	...	68.00	50.00	...	34.00	25.00
1.23	1970 - 1979	...	7	3	...	3.00	2.00	...	2.00	1.00
1.24	1980 - 1989	...	2	2	...	1.00	1.00	...	1.00	1.00
1.25	1990 and over	...	-	-	...	-	-	...	-	-
2	**Dumb and pushed vessels**	1 018	512	443	470.90	264.00	227.00	•	•	•
	- By carrying capacity									
2.11	Up to 249 tonnes	...	20	23	...	2.00	2.00	•	•	•
2.12	250 - 399 tonnes	...	112	93	...	39.00	34.00	•	•	•
2.13	400 - 649 tonnes	...	319	266	...	155.00	130.00	•	•	•
2.14	650 - 999 tonnes	...	40	39	...	32.00	32.00	•	•	•
2.15	1000 - 1499 tonnes	...	10	16	...	12.00	17.00	•	•	•
2.16	1500 - 2999 tonnes	...	11	6	...	24.00	12.00	•	•	•
2.17	3000 tonnes and over	...	-	-	...	-	-	•	•	•
	- By year of construction									
2.21	Up to 1949	...	3	1	...	1.00	1.00	•	•	•
2.22	1950 - 1969	...	40	24	...	18.00	12.00	•	•	•
2.23	1970 - 1979	...	313	264	...	156.00	129.00	•	•	•
2.24	1980 - 1989	...	148	145	...	81.00	79.00	•	•	•
2.25	1990 and over	...	8	9	...	8.00	6.00	•	•	•
3	**Tugs and pushers**	411	303	259	•	•	•	105.76	85.00	74.00
	- By year of construction									
3.21	Up to 1949	...	6	4	•	•	•	...	1.00	1.00
3.22	1950 - 1969	...	67	54	•	•	•	...	18.00	14.00
3.23	1970 - 1979	...	183	158	•	•	•	...	54.00	47.00
3.24	1980 - 1989	...	43	38	•	•	•	...	11.00	11.00
3.25	1990 and over	...	4	5	•	•	•	...	1.00	1.00

INLAND WATERWAYS - VOIES NAVIGABLES INTERIEURES
ВНУТРЕННИЕ ВОДНЫЕ ПУТИ

15. Inland waterway vessels in service at end of year, by carrying capacity and year of construction

15. Bateaux pour voies navigables intérieures en service à la fin de l'année, selon la capacité de charge et l'année de construction

15. Суда для внутренних водных путей, находящиеся в эксплуатации на конец года, по грузоподъемности грузоподъемности и году выпуска

		Republic of Moldova - République de Moldova - Республика Молдова								
		Number Nombre Число			Carrying capacity (1000 t.) Capacité de charge (1000 t.) Грузоподъемность (1000 тонн)			Power (1000 kW) Puissance (1000 kW) Мощность (1000 кВт)		
		1990	1998	1999	1990	1998	1999	1990	1998	1999
1	**Self-propelled vessels**	...	-	-	...	-	-	...	-	-
	- By carrying capacity									
1.11	Up to 249 tonnes	...	-	-	...	-	-	...	-	-
1.12	250 - 399 tonnes	...	-	-	...	-	-	...	-	-
1.13	400 - 649 tonnes	...	-	-	...	-	-	...	-	-
1.14	650 - 999 tonnes	...	-	-	...	-	-	...	-	-
1.15	1000 - 1499 tonnes	...	-	-	...	-	-	...	-	-
1.16	1500 - 2999 tonnes	...	-	-	...	-	-	...	-	-
1.17	3000 tonnes and over	...	-	-	...	-	-	...	-	-
	- By year of construction									
1.21	Up to 1949	...	-	-	...	-	-	...	-	-
1.22	1950 - 1969	...	-	-	...	-	-	...	-	-
1.23	1970 - 1979	...	-	-	...	-	-	...	-	-
1.24	1980 - 1989	...	-	-	...	-	-	...	-	-
1.25	1990 and over	...	-	-	...	-	-	...	-	-
2	**Dumb and pushed vessels**	...	15	15	...	3.60	3.60	•	•	•
	- By carrying capacity									
2.11	Up to 249 tonnes	...	12	12	...	2.40	2.40	•	•	•
2.12	250 - 399 tonnes	...	2	2	...	0.60	0.60	•	•	•
2.13	400 - 649 tonnes	...	1	1	...	0.60	0.60	•	•	•
2.14	650 - 999 tonnes	...	-	-	...	-	-	•	•	•
2.15	1000 - 1499 tonnes	...	-	-	...	-	-	•	•	•
2.16	1500 - 2999 tonnes	...	-	-	...	-	-	•	•	•
2.17	3000 tonnes and over	-	-	-	...	-	-	•	•	•
	- By year of construction									
2.21	Up to 1949	...	-	-	...	-	-	•	•	•
2.22	1950 - 1969	...	-	-	...	-	-	•	•	•
2.23	1970 - 1979	...	-	-	...	-	-	•	•	•
2.24	1980 - 1989	...	12	12	...	2.40	2.40	•	•	•
2.25	1990 and over	...	3	3	...	1.20	1.20	•	•	•
3	**Tugs and pushers**	...	11	11	•	•	•	...	1.21	1.21
	- By year of construction									
3.21	Up to 1949	...	-	-	•	•	•	...	-	-
3.22	1950 - 1969	...	-	-	•	•	•	...	-	-
3.23	1970 - 1979	...	8	8	•	•	•	...	1.00	1.00
3.24	1980 - 1989	...	3	3	•	•	•	...	0.20	0.20
3.25	1990 and over	...			•	•	•	...		

INLAND WATERWAYS - VOIES NAVIGABLES INTERIEURES
ВНУТРЕННИЕ ВОДНЫЕ ПУТИ

15. Inland waterway vessels in service at end of year, by carrying capacity and year of construction

15. Bateaux pour voies navigables intérieures en service à la fin de l'année, selon la capacité de charge et l'année de construction

15. Суда для внутренних водных путей, находящиеся в эксплуатации на конец года, по грузоподъемности грузоподъемности и году выпуска

		Romania - Roumanie - Румыния								
		Number Nombre Число			Carrying capacity (1000 t.) Capacité de charge (1000 t.) Грузоподъемность (1000 тонн)			Power (1000 kW) Puissance (1000 kW) Мощность (1000 кВт)		
		1990	1998	1999	1990	1998	1999	1990	1998	1999
1	**Self-propelled vessels**	...	**1 027**	**1 021**	...	...	...	...	...	...
	- By carrying capacity									
1.11	Up to 249 tonnes	...	...	...	...	...	...	...	...	...
1.12	250 - 399 tonnes	...	...	...	...	...	...	...	...	...
1.13	400 - 649 tonnes	...	...	...	...	...	...	...	...	...
1.14	650 - 999 tonnes	...	...	...	...	...	...	...	...	...
1.15	1000 - 1499 tonnes	...	...	...	...	...	...	...	...	...
1.16	1500 - 2999 tonnes	...	...	...	...	...	...	...	...	...
1.17	3000 tonnes and over	...	...	...	...	...	...	...	...	...
	- By year of construction									
1.21	Up to 1949	...	...	...	...	...	...	...	...	...
1.22	1950 - 1969	...	...	...	...	...	...	...	...	...
1.23	1970 - 1979	...	...	...	...	...	...	...	...	...
1.24	1980 - 1989	...	...	...	...	...	...	...	...	...
1.25	1990 and over	...	...	...	...	...	...	...	...	...
2	**Dumb and pushed vessels**	...	**1 800**	**1 778**	...	**2 271.00**	**2 254.00**	.	.	.
	- By carrying capacity									
2.11	Up to 249 tonnes	...	...	...	...	...	...	.	.	.
2.12	250 - 399 tonnes	...	...	...	...	...	...	.	.	.
2.13	400 - 649 tonnes	...	...	...	...	...	...	.	.	.
2.14	650 - 999 tonnes	...	...	...	...	...	...	.	.	.
2.15	1000 - 1499 tonnes	...	...	...	...	...	...	.	.	.
2.16	1500 - 2999 tonnes	...	...	...	...	...	...	.	.	.
2.17	3000 tonnes and over	...	...	...	...	...	...	.	.	.
	- By year of construction									
2.21	Up to 1949	...	...	...	...	...	...	.	.	.
2.22	1950 - 1969	...	...	...	...	...	...	.	.	.
2.23	1970 - 1979	...	...	...	...	...	...	.	.	.
2.24	1980 - 1989	...	...	...	...	...	...	.	.	.
2.25	1990 and over	...	...	...	...	...	...	.	.	.
3	**Tugs and pushers**	...	**936**	**936**	.	.	.	...	**488.10**	**488.10**
	- By year of construction									
3.21	Up to 1949	...	73	73	.	.	.	...	15.75	15.75
3.22	1950 - 1969	...	373	373	.	.	.	...	78.53	78.53
3.23	1970 - 1979	...	221	221	.	.	.	...	84.77	84.77
3.24	1980 - 1989	...	244	244	.	.	.	...	280.71	280.71
3.25	1990 and over	...	25	25	.	.	.	...	28.34	28.34

INLAND WATERWAYS - VOIES NAVIGABLES INTERIEURES
ВНУТРЕННИЕ ВОДНЫЕ ПУТИ

15. Inland waterway vessels in service at end of year, by carrying capacity and year of construction

15. Bateaux pour voies navigables intérieures en service à la fin de l'année, selon la capacité de charge et l'année de construction

15. Суда для внутренних водных путей, находящиеся в эксплуатации на конец года, по грузоподъемности грузоподъемности и году выпуска

		Russian Federation - Fédération de Russie - Российская Федерация								
		Number Nombre Число			Carrying capacity (1000 t.) Capacité de charge (1000 t.) Грузоподъемность (1000 тонн)			Power (1000 kW) Puissance (1000 kW) Мощность (1000 кВт)		
		1990	1998	1999	1990	1998	1999	1990	1998	1999
1	**Self-propelled vessels**	...	4 231	3 965	...	5 464.50	5 153.40	...	2 306.00	2 978.40
	- By carrying capacity									
1.11	Up to 249 tonnes	...	1 529	1 421	...	...	...	...	...	...
1.12	250 - 399 tonnes	...	234	231	...	...	...	...	...	...
1.13	400 - 649 tonnes	...	405	391	...	...	...	...	...	...
1.14	650 - 999 tonnes	...	185	149	...	...	...	...	...	...
1.15	1000 - 1499 tonnes	...	374	315	...	...	...	...	...	...
1.16	1500 - 2999 tonnes	...	924	861	...	...	...	...	...	...
1.17	3000 tonnes and over	...	580	597	...	...	...	...	...	...
	- By year of construction									
1.21	Up to 1949	...	35	25	...	...	...	...	...	...
1.22	1950 - 1969	...	1 641	1 510	...	...	...	...	...	...
1.23	1970 - 1979	...	1 155	1 073	...	...	...	...	...	...
1.24	1980 - 1989	...	1 111	1 068	...	...	...	...	...	...
1.25	1990 and over	...	289	289	...	...	...	...	...	...
2	**Dumb and pushed vessels**	...	8 109	7 777	...	9 430.70	9 027.10	.	.	.
	- By carrying capacity									
2.11	Up to 249 tonnes	...	2 695	2 570	...	...	...	.	.	.
2.12	250 - 399 tonnes	...	369	337	...	...	...	.	.	.
2.13	400 - 649 tonnes	...	1 001	1 002	...	...	...	.	.	.
2.14	650 - 999 tonnes	...	459	412	...	...	...	.	.	.
2.15	1000 - 1499 tonnes	...	1 457	1 401	...	...	...	.	.	.
2.16	1500 - 2999 tonnes	...	1 261	1 219	...	...	...	.	.	.
2.17	3000 tonnes and over	...	867	836	...	...	...	.	.	.
	- By year of construction									
2.21	Up to 1949	...	65	58	...	...	...	.	.	.
2.22	1950 - 1969	...	1 860	1 702	...	...	...	.	.	.
2.23	1970 - 1979	...	2 532	2 360	...	...	...	.	.	.
2.24	1980 - 1989	...	2 914	2 907	...	...	...	.	.	.
2.25	1990 and over	...	738	750	...	...	...	.	.	.
3	**Tugs and pushers**	...	9 813	9 373	.	.	.	...	2 015.80	1 968.10
	- By year of construction									
3.21	Up to 1949	...	168	157	.	.	.	...	...	...
3.22	1950 - 1969	...	3 420	3 297	.	.	.	...	...	...
3.23	1970 - 1979	...	2 697	2 504	.	.	.	...	...	...
3.24	1980 - 1989	...	3 037	2 914	.	.	.	...	...	...
3.25	1990 and over	...	491	501	.	.	.	...	...	...

INLAND WATERWAYS - VOIES NAVIGABLES INTERIEURES
ВНУТРЕННИЕ ВОДНЫЕ ПУТИ

15. Inland waterway vessels in service at end of year, by carrying capacity and year of construction

15. Bateaux pour voies navigables intérieures en service à la fin de l'année, selon la capacité de charge et l'année de construction

15. Суда для внутренних водных путей, находящиеся в эксплуатации на конец года, по грузоподъемности грузоподъемности и году выпуска

		Slovakia - Slovaquie - Словакия								
		Number Nombre Число			Carrying capacity (1000 t.) Capacité de charge (1000 t.) Грузоподъемность (1000 тонн)			Power (1000 kW) Puissance (1000 kW) Мощность (1000 кВт)		
		1990	1998	1999	1990	1998	1999	1990	1998	1999
1	Self-propelled vessels	8	9	9	13.85	15.00	15.00	7.62	9.00	9.00
	- By carrying capacity									
1.11	Up to 249 tonnes	-	-	-	-	-	-	-	-	-
1.12	250 - 399 tonnes	-	-	-	-	-	-	-	-	-
1.13	400 - 649 tonnes	-	-	-	-	-	-	-	-	-
1.14	650 - 999 tonnes	2	2	2	1.83	2.00	2.00	1.44	2.00	2.00
1.15	1000 - 1499 tonnes	-	4	4	-	-	-	-	4.00	4.00
1.16	1500 - 2999 tonnes	6	3	3	12.02	13.00	13.00	6.18	3.00	3.00
1.17	3000 tonnes and over	-	-	-	-	-	-	-	-	-
	- By year of construction									
1.21	Up to 1949	-	-	-	-	-	-	-	-	-
1.22	1950 - 1969	6	6	6	12.02	12.00	12.00	6.18	6.00	6.00
1.23	1970 - 1979	2	2	2	1.82	2.00	2.00	1.44	2.00	2.00
1.24	1980 - 1989	-	-	-	-	-	-	-	-	-
1.25	1990 and over	-	1	1	-	1.00	1.00	-	1.00	1.00
2	Dumb and pushed vessels	255	226	194	358.49	355.00	301.00	.	.	.
	- By carrying capacity									
2.11	Up to 249 tonnes	...	-	-	...	-	-	.	.	.
2.12	250 - 399 tonnes	...	-	-	...	-	-	.	.	.
2.13	400 - 649 tonnes	...	-	-	...	-	-	.	.	.
2.14	650 - 999 tonnes	...	34	31	...	30.00	27.00	.	.	.
2.15	1000 - 1499 tonnes	...	21	21	...	25.00	26.00	.	.	.
2.16	1500 - 2999 tonnes	...	171	142	...	300.00	248.00	.	.	.
2.17	3000 tonnes and over	...	-	-	...	-	-	.	.	.
	- By year of construction									
2.21	Up to 1949	...	7	7	...	6.00	6.00	.	.	.
2.22	1950 - 1969	...	44	41	...	46.00	43.00	.	.	.
2.23	1970 - 1979	...	31	29	...	53.00	50.00	.	.	.
2.24	1980 - 1989	...	131	104	...	231.00	183.00	.	.	.
2.25	1990 and over	...	13	13	...	19.00	19.00	.	.	.
3	Tugs and pushers	40	42	38	.	.	.	...	46.00	41.00
	- By year of construction									
3.21	Up to 1949	...	1	1	.	.	.	...	0.00	0.00
3.22	1950 - 1969	...	7	5	.	.	.	...	8.00	6.00
3.23	1970 - 1979	...	13	13	.	.	.	...	11.00	11.00
3.24	1980 - 1989	...	17	15	.	.	.	...	20.00	17.00
3.25	1990 and over	...	4	4	.	.	.	...	7.00	7.00

INLAND WATERWAYS - VOIES NAVIGABLES INTERIEURES
ВНУТРЕННИЕ ВОДНЫЕ ПУТИ

15. Inland waterway vessels in service at end of year, by carrying capacity and year of construction

15. Bateaux pour voies navigables intérieures en service à la fin de l'année, selon la capacité de charge et l'année de construction

15. Суда для внутренних водных путей, находящиеся в эксплуатации на конец года, по грузоподъемност грузоподъемности и году выпуска

		Switzerland - Suisse - Швейцария [1]								
		Number Nombre Число			Carrying capacity (1000 t.) Capacité de charge (1000 t.) Грузоподъемность (1000 тонн)			Power (1000 kW) Puissance (1000 kW) Мощность (1000 кВт)		
		1990	1998	1999	1990	1998	1999	1990	1998	1999
1	Self-propelled vessels	130	...	...	230.00	...	...	101.90	...	...
	- By carrying capacity									
1.11	Up to 249 tonnes	-	...	...	-	...	...	-	...	...
1.12	250 - 399 tonnes	4	...	...	1.30	...	...	0.70	...	...
1.13	400 - 649 tonnes	-	...	...	-	...	...	-	...	...
1.14	650 - 999 tonnes	8	...	...	7.40	...	...	3.80	...	...
1.15	1000 - 1499 tonnes	38	...	...	46.90	...	...	21.60	...	...
1.16	1500 - 2999 tonnes	74	...	...	155.50	...	...	69.00	...	...
1.17	3000 tonnes and over	6	...	...	18.90	...	...	6.80	...	...
	- By year of construction									
1.21	Up to 1949	...	...	...	...	...	...	...	...	...
1.22	1950 - 1969	...	...	...	...	...	...	...	...	...
1.23	1970 - 1979	...	...	...	...	...	...	...	...	...
1.24	1980 - 1989	...	...	...	...	...	...	...	...	...
1.25	1990 and over	...	...	...	...	...	...	...	...	...
2	Dumb and pushed vessels							•	•	•
	- By carrying capacity									
2.11	Up to 249 tonnes	-	...	...		...	...	•	•	•
2.12	250 - 399 tonnes	-	...	...		...	...	•	•	•
2.13	400 - 649 tonnes	-	...	...	-	...	...	•	•	•
2.14	650 - 999 tonnes	3	...	...	1.00	...	...	•	•	•
2.15	1000 - 1499 tonnes	4	...	...	5.12	...	...	•	•	•
2.16	1500 - 2999 tonnes	31	...	...	66.00	...	...	•	•	•
2.17	3000 tonnes and over	2	...	...	7.50	...	...	•	•	•
	- By year of construction									
2.21	Up to 1949	...	...	...	...	...	...	•	•	•
2.22	1950 - 1969	...	...	...	...	...	...	•	•	•
2.23	1970 - 1979	...	...	...	...	...	...	•	•	•
2.24	1980 - 1989	...	...	...	...	...	...	•	•	•
2.25	1990 and over	...	...	...	...	...	...	•	•	•
3	Tugs and pushers	17	...	...	•	•	•	...	...	...
	- By year of construction									
3.21	Up to 1949	...	...	...	•	•	•	15.80	...	...
3.22	1950 - 1969	...	...	...	•	•	•	...	...	...
3.23	1970 - 1979	...	...	...	•	•	•	...	...	...
3.24	1980 - 1989	...	...	...	•	•	•	...	...	...
3.25	1990 and over	...	...	...	•	•	•	...	...	...

1- Data refer to crafts navigating on the Rhine.

1- Les données se réfèrent aux bateaux navigant sur le Rhin.

1- Данные отноеятся к флоту плавающему на Рейне.

INLAND WATERWAYS - VOIES NAVIGABLES INTERIEURES
ВНУТРЕННИЕ ВОДНЫЕ ПУТИ

15. Inland waterway vessels in service at end of year, by carrying capacity and year of construction

15. Bateaux pour voies navigables intérieures en service à la fin de l'année, selon la capacité de charge et l'année de construction

15. Суда для внутренних водных путей, находящиеся в эксплуатации на конец года, по грузоподъемности грузоподъемности и году выпуска

		Turkmenistan - Turkménistan - Туркменистан								
		Number Nombre Число			Carrying capacity (1000 t.) Capacité de charge (1000 t.) Грузоподъемность (1000 тонн)			Power (1000 kW) Puissance (1000 kW) Мощность (1000 кВт)		
		1990	1998	1999	1990	1998	1999	1990	1998	1999
1	**Self-propelled vessels**	...	-	...	...	-	...	...	-	...
	- By carrying capacity									
1.11	Up to 249 tonnes	...	-	...	...	-	...	...	-	...
1.12	250 - 399 tonnes	...	-	...	...	-	...	...	-	...
1.13	400 - 649 tonnes	...	-	...	...	-	...	...	-	...
1.14	650 - 999 tonnes	...	-	...	...	-	...	...	-	...
1.15	1000 - 1499 tonnes	...	-	...	...	-	...	...	-	...
1.16	1500 - 2999 tonnes	...	-	...	...	-	...	...	-	...
1.17	3000 tonnes and over	...	-	...	...	-	...	...	-	...
	- By year of construction									
1.21	Up to 1949	...	-	...	...	-	...	...	-	...
1.22	1950 - 1969	...	-	...	...	-	...	...	-	...
1.23	1970 - 1979	...	-	...	...	-	...	...	-	...
1.24	1980 - 1989	...	-	...	...	-	...	...	-	...
1.25	1990 and over	...	-	...	...	-	...	...	-	...
2	**Dumb and pushed vessels**	...	59	...	...	19.70	...	•	•	•
	- By carrying capacity									
2.11	Up to 249 tonnes	...	15	...	...	2.60	...	•	•	•
2.12	250 - 399 tonnes	...	26	...	...	4.60	...	•	•	•
2.13	400 - 649 tonnes	...	3	...	...	12.50	...	•	•	•
2.14	650 - 999 tonnes	...	-	...	...	-	...	•	•	•
2.15	1000 - 1499 tonnes	...	-	...	...	-	...	•	•	•
2.16	1500 - 2999 tonnes	...	-	...	...	-	...	•	•	•
2.17	3000 tonnes and over	...	-	...	...	-	...	•	•	•
	- By year of construction									
2.21	Up to 1949	...	-	...	...	-	...	•	•	•
2.22	1950 - 1969	...	19	...	...	5.30	...	•	•	•
2.23	1970 - 1979	...	5	...	...	1.80	...	•	•	•
2.24	1980 - 1989	...	35	...	...	12.60	...	•	•	•
2.25	1990 and over	...	-	...	...	-	...	•	•	•
3	**Tugs and pushers**	...	38	...	•	•	•	...	9.30	...
	- By year of construction									
3.21	Up to 1949	...	-	...	•	•	•	...	-	...
3.22	1950 - 1969	...	5	...	•	•	•	...	2.40	...
3.23	1970 - 1979	...	7	...	•	•	•	...	1.40	...
3.24	1980 - 1989	...	23	...	•	•	•	...	5.10	...
3.25	1990 and over	...	1	...	•	•	•	...	0.40	...

INLAND WATERWAYS - VOIES NAVIGABLES INTERIEURES
ВНУТРЕННИЕ ВОДНЫЕ ПУТИ

15. Inland waterway vessels in service at end of year, by carrying capacity and year of construction

15. Bateaux pour voies navigables intérieures en service à la fin de l'année, selon la capacité de charge et l'année de construction

15. Суда для внутренних водных путей, находящиеся в эксплуатации на конец года, по грузоподъемности грузоподъемности и году выпуска

		Ukraine - Ukraine - Украина								
		Number Nombre Число			Carrying capacity (1000 t.) Capacité de charge (1000 t.) Грузоподъемность (1000 тонн)			Power (1000 kW) Puissance (1000 kW) Мощность (1000 кВт)		
		1990	1998	1999	1990	1998	1999	1990	1998	1999
1	**Self-propelled vessels**	217	...	...	395.60	...	...	154.10	...	...
	- By carrying capacity									
1.11	Up to 249 tonnes	1	...	...	0.10	...	...	0.20	...	...
1.12	250 - 399 tonnes	-	...	...	-	...	...	-	...	...
1.13	400 - 649 tonnes	45	...	...	27.00	...	...	10.40	...	...
1.14	650 - 999 tonnes	15	...	...	10.50	...	...	5.00	...	...
1.15	1000 - 1499 tonnes	6	...	...	7.90	...	...	5.80	...	...
1.16	1500 - 2999 tonnes	100	...	...	180.20	...	...	76.90	...	...
1.17	3000 tonnes and over	50	...	...	169.90	...	...	55.80	...	...
	- By year of construction									
1.21	Up to 1949	...	...	...	...	...	...	...	...	...
1.22	1950 - 1969	...	...	...	...	...	...	...	...	...
1.23	1970 - 1979	...	...	...	...	...	...	...	...	...
1.24	1980 - 1989	...	...	...	...	...	...	...	...	...
1.25	1990 and over	...	...	...	...	...	...	...	...	...
2	**Dumb and pushed vessels**	399	...	...	355.80	...	...	•	•	•
	- By carrying capacity									
2.11	Up to 249 tonnes	123	...	...	13.50	...	...	•	•	•
2.12	250 - 399 tonnes	20	...	...	6.20	...	...	•	•	•
2.13	400 - 649 tonnes	31	...	...	15.60	...	...	•	•	•
2.14	650 - 999 tonnes	66	...	...	46.20	...	...	•	•	•
2.15	1000 - 1499 tonnes	33	...	...	37.20	...	...	•	•	•
2.16	1500 - 2999 tonnes	120	...	...	213.30	...	...	•	•	•
2.17	3000 tonnes and over	6	...	...	23.80	...	...	•	•	•
	- By year of construction									
2.21	Up to 1949	...	...	...	...	...	...	•	•	•
2.22	1950 - 1969	...	...	...	...	...	...	•	•	•
2.23	1970 - 1979	...	...	...	...	...	...	•	•	•
2.24	1980 - 1989	...	...	...	...	...	...	•	•	•
2.25	1990 and over	...	...	...	...	...	...	•	•	•
3	**Tugs and pushers**	201	...	...	•	•	•	46.60	...	...
	- By year of construction									
3.21	Up to 1949	...	...	...	•	•	•	...	...	...
3.22	1950 - 1969	...	...	...	•	•	•	...	...	...
3.23	1970 - 1979	...	...	...	•	•	•	...	...	...
3.24	1980 - 1989	...	...	...	•	•	•	...	...	...
3.25	1990 and over	...	...	...	•	•	•	...	...	...

INLAND WATERWAYS - VOIES NAVIGABLES INTERIEURES
ВНУТРЕННИЕ ВОДНЫЕ ПУТИ

15. Inland waterway vessels in service at end of year, by carrying capacity and year of construction

15. Bateaux pour voies navigables intérieures en service à la fin de l'année, selon la capacité de charge et l'année de construction

15. Суда для внутренних водных путей, находящиеся в эксплуатации на конец года, по грузоподъемности грузоподъемности и году выпуска

| | | United Kingdom - Royaume-Uni - Соединенное Королевство | | | | | | | | |
| | | Number Nombre Число | | | Carrying capacity (1000 t.) Capacité de charge (1000 t.) Грузоподъемность (1000 тонн) | | | Power (1000 kW) Puissance (1000 kW) Мощность (1000 кВт) | | |
		1990	1998	1999	1990	1998	1999	1990	1998	1999
1	**Self-propelled vessels**	277	186	186	82.80	73.00	73.00	35.20	...	...
	- By carrying capacity									
1.11	Up to 249 tonnes	117	...	...	16.30	...	...	5.60	...	...
1.12	250 - 399 tonnes	89	...	...	25.90	...	...	10.10	...	...
1.13	400 - 649 tonnes	46	...	...	21.80	...	...	9.00	...	...
1.14	650 - 999 tonnes	25	...	...	18.80	...	...	10.50	...	...
1.15	1000 - 1499 tonnes	-	...	...	-	...	...	-	...	...
1.16	1500 - 2999 tonnes	-	...	...	-	...	...	-	...	...
1.17	3000 tonnes and over	-	...	...	-	...	...	-	...	...
	- By year of construction									
1.21	Up to 1949	...	...	...	...	...	...	...	...	...
1.22	1950 - 1969	...	...	...	...	...	...	...	...	...
1.23	1970 - 1979	...	...	...	...	...	...	...	...	...
1.24	1980 - 1989	...	...	...	...	...	...	...	...	...
1.25	1990 and over	...	...	...	...	...	...	...	...	...
2	**Dumb and pushed vessels**	469	361	361	88.70	76.00	76.00	•	•	•
	- By carrying capacity									
2.11	Up to 249 tonnes	160	...	...	28.60	...	...	•	•	•
2.12	250 - 399 tonnes	291	...	...	52.00	...	...	•	•	•
2.13	400 - 649 tonnes	18	...	...	8.10	...	...	•	•	•
2.14	650 - 999 tonnes	-	...	...	-	...	...	•	•	•
2.15	1000 - 1499 tonnes	-	...	...	-	...	...	•	•	•
2.16	1500 - 2999 tonnes	-	...	...	-	...	...	•	•	•
2.17	3000 tonnes and over	-	...	...	-	...	...	•	•	•
	- By year of construction									
2.21	Up to 1949	...	...	...	...	...	...	•	•	•
2.22	1950 - 1969	...	...	...	...	...	...	•	•	•
2.23	1970 - 1979	...	...	...	...	...	...	•	•	•
2.24	1980 - 1989	...	...	...	...	...	...	•	•	•
2.25	1990 and over	...	...	...	...	...	...	•	•	•
3	**Tugs and pushers**	91	91	91	•	•	•	21.90	...	...
	- By year of construction									
3.21	Up to 1949	...	...	...	•	•	•	...	...	...
3.22	1950 - 1969	...	...	...	•	•	•	...	...	...
3.23	1970 - 1979	...	...	...	•	•	•	...	...	...
3.24	1980 - 1989	...	...	...	•	•	•	...	...	...
3.25	1990 and over	...	...	...	•	•	•	...	...	...

INLAND WATERWAYS - VOIES NAVIGABLES INTERIEURES
ВНУТРЕННИЕ ВОДНЫЕ ПУТИ

15. Inland waterway vessels in service at end of year, by carrying capacity and year of construction

15. Bateaux pour voies navigables intérieures en service à la fin de l'année, selon la capacité de charge et l'année de construction

15. Суда для внутренних водных путей, находящиеся в эксплуатации на конец года, по грузоподъемности грузоподъемности и году выпуска

		United States - Etats-Unis - Соединенные Штаты								
		Number Nombre Число			Carrying capacity (1000 t.) Capacité de charge (1000 t.) Грузоподъемность (1000 тонн)			Power (1000 kW) Puissance (1000 kW) Мощность (1000 кВт)		
		1990	1998	1999	1990	1998	1999	1990	1998	1999
1	**Self-propelled vessels**	...	...	...	...	525.10	...	...	...	...
	- By carrying capacity									
1.11	Up to 249 tonnes	...	...	...	...	...	...	...	...	...
1.12	250 - 399 tonnes	...	...	...	...	...	...	...	...	...
1.13	400 - 649 tonnes	...	...	...	...	...	...	...	...	...
1.14	650 - 999 tonnes	...	...	...	...	...	...	...	...	...
1.15	1000 - 1499 tonnes	...	...	...	...	...	...	...	...	...
1.16	1500 - 2999 tonnes	...	...	...	...	...	...	...	...	...
1.17	3000 tonnes and over	...	...	...	...	...	...	...	...	...
	- By year of construction									
1.21	Up to 1949	...	...	...	...	...	...	...	...	...
1.22	1950 - 1969	...	...	...	...	...	...	...	...	...
1.23	1970 - 1979	...	...	...	...	...	...	...	...	...
1.24	1980 - 1989	...	...	...	...	...	...	...	...	...
1.25	1990 and over	...	...	...	...	...	...	...	...	...
2	**Dumb and pushed vessels**	...	29 471	...	...	42 558.90	...	•	•	•
	- By carrying capacity									
2.11	Up to 249 tonnes	...	...	...	...	...	...	•	•	•
2.12	250 - 399 tonnes	...	...	...	...	...	...	•	•	•
2.13	400 - 649 tonnes	...	...	...	...	...	...	•	•	•
2.14	650 - 999 tonnes	...	...	...	...	...	...	•	•	•
2.15	1000 - 1499 tonnes	...	...	...	...	...	...	•	•	•
2.16	1500 - 2999 tonnes	...	...	...	...	...	...	•	•	•
2.17	3000 tonnes and over	...	...	...	...	...	...	•	•	•
	- By year of construction									
2.21	Up to 1949	...	...	...	...	...	...	•	•	•
2.22	1950 - 1969	...	...	...	...	...	...	•	•	•
2.23	1970 - 1979	...	...	...	...	...	...	•	•	•
2.24	1980 - 1989	...	...	...	...	...	...	•	•	•
2.25	1990 and over	...	...	...	...	...	...	•	•	•
3	**Tugs and pushers**	...	3 355	...	•	•	•	...	4 232.60	...
	- By year of construction									
3.21	Up to 1949	...	...	...	•	•	•	...	...	...
3.22	1950 - 1969	...	...	...	•	•	•	...	...	...
3.23	1970 - 1979	...	...	...	•	•	•	...	...	...
3.24	1980 - 1989	...	...	...	•	•	•	...	...	...
3.25	1990 and over	...	...	...	•	•	•	...	...	...

INLAND WATERWAYS - VOIES NAVIGABLES INTERIEURES
ВНУТРЕННИЕ ВОДНЫЕ ПУТИ

15. Inland waterway vessels in service at end of year, by carrying capacity and year of construction

15. Bateaux pour voies navigables intérieures en service à la fin de l'année, selon la capacité de charge et l'année de construction

15. Суда для внутренних водных путей, находящиеся в эксплуатации на конец года, по грузоподъемности грузоподъемности и году выпуска

		Yugoslavia - Yugoslavie - Югославия								
		Number Nombre Число			Carrying capacity (1000 t.) Capacité de charge (1000 t.) Грузоподъемность (1000 тонн)			Power (1000 kW) Puissance (1000 kW) Мощность (1000 кВт)		
		1990	1998	1999	1990	1998	1999	1990	1998	1999
1	**Self-propelled vessels**	...	72	49	...	69.50	44.20	...	24.80	15.40
	- By carrying capacity									
1.11	Up to 249 tonnes	...	5	4	...	0.60	0.50	...	0.70	0.60
1.12	250 - 399 tonnes	...	1	-	...	0.40	-	...	0.20	-
1.13	400 - 649 tonnes	...	-	-	...	-	-	...	-	-
1.14	650 - 999 tonnes	...	45	34	...	36.80	27.60	...	10.60	8.40
1.15	1000 - 1499 tonnes	...	15	8	...	19.00	10.20	...	8.70	4.40
1.16	1500 - 2999 tonnes	...	6	3	...	12.70	5.90	...	4.60	2.00
1.17	3000 tonnes and over	...	-	-	...	-	-	...	-	-
	- By year of construction									
1.21	Up to 1949	...	-	-	...	-	-	...	-	-
1.22	1950 - 1969	...	16	11	...	13.20	9.00	...	4.60	3.10
1.23	1970 - 1979	...	33	22	...	27.70	18.00	...	8.20	6.30
1.24	1980 - 1989	...	23	16	...	28.60	17.20	...	12.00	6.00
1.25	1990 and over	...	-	-	...	-	-	...	-	-
2	**Dumb and pushed vessels**	...	512	91	...	540.90	107.50	•	•	•
	- By carrying capacity									
2.11	Up to 249 tonnes	...	18	1	...	1.70	-	•	•	•
2.12	250 - 399 tonnes	...	11	1	...	3.60	0.30	•	•	•
2.13	400 - 649 tonnes	...	105	20	...	52.00	9.00	•	•	•
2.14	650 - 999 tonnes	...	82	4	...	65.20	3.20	•	•	•
2.15	1000 - 1499 tonnes	...	167	29	...	204.60	36.30	•	•	•
2.16	1500 - 2999 tonnes	...	129	36	...	213.80	58.50	•	•	•
2.17	3000 tonnes and over	...	-	-	...	-	-	•	•	•
	- By year of construction									
2.21	Up to 1949	...	23	1	...	14.50	0.70	•	•	•
2.22	1950 - 1969	...	302	31	...	276.80	29.50	•	•	•
2.23	1970 - 1979	...	130	39	...	159.10	46.70	•	•	•
2.24	1980 - 1989	...	54	18	...	85.40	27.70	•	•	•
2.25	1990 and over	...	3	2	...	5.10	2.90	•	•	•
3	**Tugs and pushers**	...	135	53	•	•	•	...	71.40	23.50
	- By year of construction									
3.21	Up to 1949	...	18	4	•	•	•	...	2.90	0.70
3.22	1950 - 1969	...	70	20	•	•	•	...	28.70	6.80
3.23	1970 - 1979	...	35	21	•	•	•	...	28.50	9.40
3.24	1980 - 1989	...	10	6	•	•	•	...	10.90	6.20
3.25	1990 and over	...	2	2	•	•	•	...	0.40	0.40

INLAND WATERWAYS - VOIES NAVIGABLES INTERIEURES
ВНУТРЕННИЕ ВОДНЫЕ ПУТИ

16. Goods transport by type of transport and vessel on national territory

16. Transport de marchandises par type de transport et de bateaux sur le territoire national

16. Грузовые перевозки по виду транспорта и по судам по национальной территории

Item	Description	Rubrique	Description
1	**Goods carried on national territory (1000 tonnes)**	**1**	**Marchandises transportées sur le territoire national (1000 tonnes)**
	By type of transport		*Par type de transport*
1.1	- National transport	1.1	- Transport national
1.2	- International transport - loaded	1.2	- Transport international - chargements
1.3	- International transport - unloaded	1.3	- Transport international - déchargements
1.4	- Transit by IWT throughout	1.4	- Transit par VNI de bout en bout
	By type of propulsion		*Par type de propulsion*
1.11	- Push / tow	1.11	- Poussé / tiré
1.12	- Self-propelled	1.12	- Automoteur
2	**Goods carried on national territory [1] (million tonne-kilometres)**	**2**	**Marchandises transportées sur le territoire national [1] (million de tonnes-kilomètres)**
	By type of transport		*Par type de transport*
2.1	- National transport	2.1	- Transport national
2.2	- International transport - loaded	2.2	- Transport international - chargements
2.3	- International transport - unloaded	2.3	- Transport international - déchargements
2.4	- Transit by IWT throughout	2.4	- Transit par VNI de bout en bout
	By type of propulsion		*Par type de propulsion*
2.21	- Push / tow	2.21	- Poussé / tiré
2.22	- Self-propelled	2.22	- Automoteur

Статья	Описание
1	**Грузовые перевозки по национальной территоии (1000 тонн)**
	По типу перевозки
1.1	- Национальные перевозки
1.2	- Международные перевозки - загрузка в стране
1.3	- Международные перевозки - разгрузка в стране
1.4	- Сквозные транзитные перевозки судами внутреннего плавания
	По типу тяги
1.11	- Толкание / буксировка
1.12	- Самоходные суда
2	**Грузовые перевозки по национальной территоии (млн. тонн-км) [1]**
	По типу перевозки
2.1	- Национальные перевозки
2.2	- Международные перевозки - загрузка в стране
2.3	- Международные перевозки - разгрузка в стране
2.4	- Сквозные транзитные перевозки судами внутреннего плавания
	По типу тяги
2.21	- Толкание / буксировка
2.22	- Самоходные суда

1 - Kilometres within the territory of the reporting country.

1 - Kilomètres sur le territoire du pays déclarant.

1 - Километраж в пределах территории страны-респондента.

INLAND WATERWAYS - VOIES NAVIGABLES INTERIEURES
ВНУТРЕННИЕ ВОДНЫЕ ПУТИ

16. Goods transport by type of transport and vessel on national territory
16. Transport de marchandises par type de transport et de bateaux sur le territoire national
16. Грузовые перевозки по виду транспорта и по судам по национальной территории

		Austria Autriche Австрия			Belgium Belgique Бельгия			Bulgaria Bulgarie Болгария		
		1990	1998	1999	1990	1998	1999	1990	1998	1999
1	Goods carried (1000 tonnes)	8 140	10 236	9 987	99 976	...	...	2 630	836	439
	By type of transport									
1.11	- National	607	964	774	21 188	...	...	...	7	4
1.12	- International - loaded	1 236	923	1 263	28 739	...	...	...	270	86
1.13	- International - unloaded	4 958	5 309	5 173	46 886	...	...	...	428	248
1.14	- Transit	1 340	3 040	2 777	3 163	...	...	...	131	102
	By type of propulsion									
1.21	- Push/tow	6 418	6 168	5 474	19 271	...	...	...	...	...
1.22	- Self-propelled	1 722	4 069	4 513	80 699	...	...	...	...	...
2	Tonne-km of goods carried (millions) [1]	1 663	11 590	8 639	5 449	...	...	1 606	711	274
	By type of transport									
2.11	- National	101	127	100	1 700	...	...	-	1	1
2.12	- International - loaded	...	970	1 108	1 247	...	...	...	297	73
2.13	- International - unloaded	...	6 753	3 998	2 085	...	...	...	265	113
2.14	- Transit	469	3 740	3 433	417	...	...	135	148	88
	By type of propulsion									
2.21	- Push/tow	1 365	7 142	4 093	...	...	...	...	...	...
2.22	- Self-propelled	298	4 448	4 546	...	...	...	...	...	...

		Canada Canada Канада			Croatia Croatie Хорватия			Czech Republic République tchèque Чешская Республика		
		1990	1998	1999	1990	1998	1999	1990	1998	1999
1	Goods carried (1000 tonnes)	...	321 734	...	2 713	1 297	864	...	1 678	1 877
	By type of transport									
1.11	- National	...	47 928	...	2 424	1 148	747	...	223	407
1.12	- International - loaded	...	178 893	...	113	51	51	...	717	721
1.13	- International - unloaded	...	94 913	...	147	98	66	...	583	574
1.14	- Transit	...	-	...	29	-	-	...	154	174
	By type of propulsion									
1.21	- Push/tow	...	...	...	...	...	...	...	893	1 140
1.22	- Self-propelled	...	...	...	...	...	...	...	784	738
2	Tonne-km of goods carried (millions) [1]	...	...	...	527	53	14	...	915	913
	By type of transport									
2.11	- National	...	...	...	212	7	5	...	15	28
2.12	- International - loaded	...	...	...	112	...	4	...	406	419
2.13	- International - unloaded	...	...	...	158	...	5	...	395	365
2.14	- Transit	...	...	...	46	-	-	...	99	101
	By type of propulsion									
2.21	- Push/tow	...	...	...	...	...	...	...	325	431
2.22	- Self-propelled	...	...	...	...	...	...	...	590	486

1- Kilometres within the territory of the reporting country.

1- Kilomètres sur le territoire du pays déclarant.

1- Километраж в пределах территории страны-респондента.

INLAND WATERWAYS - VOIES NAVIGABLES INTERIEURES
ВНУТРЕННИЕ ВОДНЫЕ ПУТИ

16. Goods transport by type of transport and vessel on national territory
16. Transport de marchandises par type de transport et de bateaux sur le territoire national
16. Грузовые перевозки по виду транспорта и по судам по национальной территории

		Estonia Estonie Эстония			Finland Finlande Финляндия			France France Франция		
		1990	1998	1999	1990	1998	1999	1990	1998	1999
1	**Goods carried (1000 tonnes)**	...	**0**	**0**	**2 054**	**83 859**	**84 135**	**66 086**	**62 060**	**65 509**
	By type of transport									
1.11	- National	...	0	0	399	7 254	6 620	32 871	23 755	26 390
1.12	- International - loaded	...	-	-	711	37 524	39 307	18 538	16 581	16 587
1.13	- International - unloaded	...	-	-	926	39 069	38 196	12 155	10 507	12 014
1.14	- Transit	...	-	-	18	12	12	2 522	11 217	10 518
	By type of propulsion									
1.21	- Push/tow	...	...	...	...	...	...	9 788	7 869	8 711
1.22	- Self-propelled	...	...	...	...	...	...	56 298	54 191	56 798
2	**Tonne-km of goods carried (millions)** [1]	...	**0**	**2**	...	**186 797**	**173 500**	**7 581**	**7 936**	**8 478**
	By type of transport									
2.11	- National	...	0	2	...	2 920	2 830	4 270	3 452	4 106
2.12	- International - loaded	...	-	-	...	110 223	108 199	1 611	1 624	1 534
2.13	- International - unloaded	...	-	-	...	73 654	62 471	1 280	1 131	1 189
2.14	- Transit	...	-	-	...	-	-	420	1 729	1 649
	By type of propulsion									
2.21	- Push/tow	...	...	...	...	...	...	1 442	1 166	1 272
2.22	- Self-propelled	...	...	...	...	...	...	6 139	6 770	7 206

		Germany Allemagne Германия			Hungary Hongrie Венгрия			Italy Italie Италия		
		1990	1998	1999	1990	1998	1999	1990	1998	1999
1	**Goods carried (1000 tonnes)**	...	**236 365**	**229 136**	...	**2 390**	**2 098**	**705**	...	...
	By type of transport									
1.11	- National	...	63 909	62 743	...	747	806	...	1 053	1 355
1.12	- International - loaded	...	42 702	44 741	...	925	866	...	...	...
1.13	- International - unloaded	...	108 738	100 541	...	572	265	...	...	...
1.14	- Transit	...	21 016	21 111	...	146	161	...	...	...
	By type of propulsion									
1.21	- Push/tow	...	45 951	43 219	...	...	...	...	...	...
1.22	- Self-propelled	...	166 956	162 614	...	...	...	...	...	...
2	**Tonne-km of goods carried (millions)** [1]	...	**64 267**	**62 692**	**14 500**	**1 560**	**958**	**117**	...	...
	By type of transport									
2.11	- National	...	14 483	13 973	...	32	30	...	127	173
2.12	- International - loaded	...	11 178	11 640	...	816	633	...	...	...
2.13	- International - unloaded	...	25 497	23 657	...	619	255	...	...	...
2.14	- Transit	...	13 109	13 423	...	93	40	...	...	...
	By type of propulsion									
2.21	- Push/tow	...	...	...	...	...	...	...	...	...
2.22	- Self-propelled	...	...	...	...	...	...	...	...	...

1 - Kilometres within the territory of the reporting country.

1 - Kilomètres sur le territoire du pays déclarant.

1 - Километраж в пределах территории страны-респондента.

INLAND WATERWAYS - VOIES NAVIGABLES INTERIEURES
ВНУТРЕННИЕ ВОДНЫЕ ПУТИ

16. Goods transport by type of transport and vessel on national territory
16. Transport de marchandises par type de transport et de bateaux sur le territoire national
16. Грузовые перевозки по виду транспорта и по судам по национальной территории

		Kazakhstan Kazakhstan Казахстан			Kyrgyzstan Kirghizistan Кыргызстан			Lithuania Lituanie Литва		
		1990	1998	1999	1990	1998	1999	1990	1998	1999
1	**Goods carried (1000 tonnes)**	10 731	447	181	647	31	46	2 400	227	24
	By type of transport									
1.11	- National	...	283	105	647	31	46	2 400	227	24
1.12	- International - loaded	...	53	76	-	-	-	-	-	-
1.13	- International - unloaded	...	111	-	-	-	-	-	-	-
1.14	- Transit	...	-	-	-	-	-	-	-	-
	By type of propulsion									
1.21	- Push/tow	...	...	...	...	...	...	...	171	14
1.22	- Self-propelled	...	...	...	...	...	...	...	55	10
2	**Tonne-km of goods carried (millions)** [1]	3 851	141	25	114	6	8	164	12	3
	By type of transport									
2.11	- National	...	...	...	114	6	8	164	12	3
2.12	- International - loaded	...	...	...	-	-	-	-	-	-
2.13	- International - unloaded	...	...	...	-	-	-	-	-	-
2.14	- Transit	...	...	...	-	-	-	-	-	-
	By type of propulsion									
2.21	- Push/tow	...	...	...	...	...	...	...	10	2
2.22	- Self-propelled	...	...	...	...	...	...	...	2	1

		Luxembourg Luxembourg Люксембург			Netherlands Pays-Bas Нидерланды			Poland Pologne Польша		
		1990	1998	1999	1990	1998	1999	1990	1998	1999
1	**Goods carried (1000 tonnes)**	10 806	...	...	287 399	317 458	...	9 795	9 376	8 382
	By type of transport									
1.11	- National	80	...	...	85 284	97 724	...	8 291	6 046	5 282
1.12	- International - loaded	912	...	...	116 890	131 888	...	1 440	2 220	2 457
1.13	- International - unloaded	1 100	...	...	52 862	52 240	...	62	416	277
1.14	- Transit	8 714	...	...	32 363	35 606	...	2	694	366
	By type of propulsion									
1.21	- Push/tow	-	...	...	65 635	71 625	...	8 374	8 606	7 465
1.22	- Self-propelled	10 806	...	...	221 764	245 833	...	1 421	770	917
2	**Tonne-km of goods carried (millions)** [1]	336	...	...	35 706	40 714	...	1 034	1 100	1 028
	By type of transport									
2.11	- National	...	...	...	6 896	8 877	...	499	387	259
2.12	- International - loaded	...	...	...	15 675	17 439	...	511	431	536
2.13	- International - unloaded	...	...	...	7 119	7 502	...	24	111	93
2.14	- Transit	...	...	...	6 016	6 896	...	-	171	140
	By type of propulsion									
2.21	- Push/tow	-	...	...	7 520	8 299	...	506	875	716
2.22	- Self-propelled	336	...	...	28 186	32 415	...	528	225	312

1- Kilometres within the territory of the reporting country.

1- Kilomètres sur le territoire du pays déclarant.

1- Километраж в пределах территории страны-респондента.

INLAND WATERWAYS - VOIES NAVIGABLES INTERIEURES
ВНУТРЕННИЕ ВОДНЫЕ ПУТИ

16. Goods transport by type of transport and vessel on national territory
16. Transport de marchandises par type de transport et de bateaux sur le territoire national
16. Грузовые перевозки по виду транспорта и по судам по национальной территории

		Republic of Moldova République de Moldova Республика Молдова			Romania Roumanie Румыния			Russian Federation Fédération de Russie Российская Федерация		
		1990	1998	1999	1990	1998	1999	1990	1998	1999
1	Goods carried (1000 tonnes)	2 900	13	16	12 044	14 856	13 976	562 000	94 075	...
	By type of transport									
1.11	- National	...	13	16	...	12 495	12 217	...	75 448	...
1.12	- International - loaded	...	-	-	...	557	527	...	6 264	...
1.13	- International - unloaded	...	-	-	...	56	515	...	1 987	...
1.14	- Transit	...	-	-	166	1 748	717	...	279	...
	By type of propulsion									
1.21	- Push/tow	...	13	16	...	...	...	...	...	...
1.22	- Self-propelled	...	-	-	...	...	...	...	...	...
2	Tonne-km of goods carried (millions)[1]	317	0	0	2 090	4 203	2 802	214 000	65 643	...
	By type of transport									
2.11	- National	...	0	0	...	2 234	2 008	...	33 026	...
2.12	- International - loaded	...	-	-	...	589	271	...	13 378	...
2.13	- International - unloaded	...	-	-	...	19	275	...	156	...
2.14	- Transit	...	-	-	...	1 361	248	...	507	...
	By type of propulsion									
2.21	- Push/tow	...	0	0	...	...	...	...	...	...
2.22	- Self-propelled	...	-	-	...	...	...	...	...	...

		Slovakia Slovaquie Словакия			Switzerland Suisse Швейцария			Turkmenistan Turkménistan Туркменистан		
		1990	1998	1999	1990	1998	1999	1990	1998	1999
1	Goods carried (1000 tonnes)	3 715	1 172	1 507	9 209	...	...	...	1 536	...
	By type of transport									
1.11	- National	1 285	26	-	-	...	...	...	1 536	...
1.12	- International - loaded	...	735	1 095	301	...	...	...	-	...
1.13	- International - unloaded	...	56	51	8 619	...	...	...	-	...
1.14	- Transit	...	355	361	289	...	...	...	-	...
	By type of propulsion									
1.21	- Push/tow	...	...	...	...	...	...	...	...	...
1.22	- Self-propelled	...	...	...	...	...	...	...	...	...
2	Tonne-km of goods carried (millions)[1]	3 017	1 305	1 663	56	...	...	...	8	...
	By type of transport									
2.11	- National	35	5	-	-	...	...	...	8	...
2.12	- International - loaded	...	...	...	...	...	...	...	-	...
2.13	- International - unloaded	...	...	...	...	...	...	...	-	...
2.14	- Transit	...	...	...	2	...	...	...	-	...
	By type of propulsion									
2.21	- Push/tow	...	...	...	...	...	...	...	...	...
2.22	- Self-propelled	...	...	...	...	...	...	...	...	...

1- Kilometres within the territory of the reporting country.

1- Kilomètres sur le territoire du pays déclarant.

1- Километраж в пределах территории страны-респондента.

INLAND WATERWAYS - VOIES NAVIGABLES INTERIEURES
ВНУТРЕННИЕ ВОДНЫЕ ПУТИ

16. Goods transport by type of transport and vessel on national territory
16. Transport de marchandises par type de transport et de bateaux sur le territoire national
16. Грузовые перевозки по виду транспорта и по судам по национальной территории

		Ukraine Ukraine Украина			United Kingdom Royaume-Uni Соединенное Королевство			United States Etats-Unis Соединенные Штаты		
		1990	1998	1999	1990	1998	1999	1990	1998	1999
1	**Goods carried (1000 tonnes)**	65 728	9 045	...	5 993	4	4	...	...	...
	By type of transport									
1.11	- National	...	...	...	5 993	4	4	1 014 068	567 151	...
1.12	- International - loaded	...	...	...	-	-	-	...	...	...
1.13	- International - unloaded	...	...	...	-	-	-	...	...	...
1.14	- Transit	...	...	...	-	-	-	...	...	...
	By type of propulsion									
1.21	- Push/tow	...	...	...	...	...	...	...	...	...
1.22	- Self-propelled	...	...	...	...	...	...	...	...	...
2	**Tonne-km of goods carried (millions)** [1]	11 900	5 800	...	215	150	160	...	...	...
	By type of transport									
2.11	- National	...	...	...	215	150	160	1 216 970	430 570	...
2.12	- International - loaded	...	...	...	-	-	-	...	...	...
2.13	- International - unloaded	...	...	...	-	-	-	...	...	...
2.14	- Transit	...	...	...	-	-	-	...	...	...
	By type of propulsion									
2.21	- Push/tow	...	...	...	...	...	...	...	...	...
2.22	- Self-propelled	...	...	...	...	...	...	...	...	...

		Yugoslavia Yugoslavie Югославия								
		1990	1998	1999						
1	**Goods carried (1000 tonnes)**	...	14 196	5 578						
	By type of transport									
1.11	- National	...	3 975	2 457						
1.12	- International - loaded	...	814	494						
1.13	- International - unloaded	...	3 794	1 564						
1.14	- Transit	...	5 613	1 063						
	By type of propulsion									
1.21	- Push/tow	...	9 549	...						
1.22	- Self-propelled	...	4 647	...						
2	**Tonne-km of goods carried (millions)** [1]	...	13 853	3 787						
	By type of transport									
2.11	- National	...	391	242						
2.12	- International - loaded	...	856	487						
2.13	- International - unloaded	...	3 089	1 272						
2.14	- Transit	...	9 517	1 786						
	By type of propulsion									
2.21	- Push/tow	...	10 679	...						
2.22	- Self-propelled	...	3 174	...						

1- Kilometres within the territory of the reporting country.

1- Kilomètres sur le territoire du pays déclarant.

1- Километраж в пределах территории страны-респондента.

INLAND WATERWAYS - VOIES NAVIGABLES INTERIEURES
ВНУТРЕННИЕ ВОДНЫЕ ПУТИ

17.Total freight transport on the Danube
17. Transport de marchandises sur le Danube
17. Грузовые перевозки по Дунаю

1000 tonnes - 1000 tonnes - 1000 тонн

Country pays Страна	Code Code Шифр	1980	1990	1995	1996	1997	1998	1999
Austria	**A**	830	607	522	539	698	964	774
Autriche	**B**	1 246	1 236	789	812	780	922	1 263
Австрия								
Bulgaria	**A**	8 389	3 060	-	14	11	664	498
Bulgarie	**B**	903	477	222	310	286	241	204
Болгария								
Croatia	**A**	...	...	...	...	...	12	14
Croatie	**B**	...	...	...	...	...	51	51
Хорватия								
Germany	**A**	192	289	...	...	...	55	17
Allemagne	**B**	1 808	1 085	...	...	...	7 075	7 088
Германия								
Hungary	**A**	9 819	4 109	...	...	...	...	...
Hongrie	**B**	1 279	9 114	2 674	2 017	2 414	3 706	2 968
Венгрия								
Romania	**A**	15 003	8 144	4 715	3 686	4 423	3 304	2 934
Roumanie	**B**	3 769	2 120	2 320	3 200	3 353	1 298	1 176
Румыния								
Slovakia	**A**	1 865	3 490	-	11	9	9	11
Slovaquie	**B**	1 885	2 020	1 583	1 495	1 142	1 270	1 087
Словакия								
Ukraine	**A**	7 478	6 776	675	498	561	273	409
Ukraine	**B**	12 029	13 071	5 617	6 360	6 519	5 632	2 881
Украина								
Yugoslavia	**A**	15 156	8 994	...	3 405	3 203	3 705	2 102
Yougoslavie	**B**	612	1 634	...	1 028	586	814	494
Югославия								
Total	**A**	58 731	35 469	5 912	8 153	8 905	8 986	6 759
Total	**B**	23 531	30 757	13 205	15 222	15 080	21 009	17 211
Всего								
Goods entered by sea		8 080	3 345	2 688	2 350	519	572	452
Total transport		**90 342**	**69 571**	**21 805**	**25 725**	**24 504**	**30 567**	**24 422**
Index (1980 = 100)		100	77	24	28	27	34	27

Source: Danube Commission (Budapest), 2001.

Source: Commission du Danube (Budapest), 2001.

Источник: Дунайская Комиссия (Будапешт), 2001.

A = Internal transport; goods carried between the ports of the country.
  Transport interne; marchandises transportées entre les ports du pays.
  Нутренние перевозки; грузы, перевезенные между портами страны.

B = International transport; goods which have been loaded in the country and have left it with a destination, whether Danubian or not.
  Transport international; Marchandises chargées dans le pays et sorties du pays à destination d'un autre pays danubien ou non danubien.
  Международные перевозки; грузы, загруженные в стране и вывезенные из страны и направленные в другие придунайские и непридунайские страны.

a) Excluding goods having passed in transit throughout.

a) A l'exception des marchandises ayant transité de bout en bout.

a) За исключением грузов, следующих сквозным транзитом.

INLAND WATERWAYS - VOIES NAVIGABLES INTERIEURES
ВНУТРЕННИЕ ВОДНЫЕ ПУТИ

18. International freight transport on the Danube [1]
18. Transport international de marchandises sur le Danube [1]
18. Международные грузовые перевозки по Дунаю [1]

1000 tonnes - 1000 tonnes - 1000 тонн

Country of origin / Pays de provenance / Страна происхождения	Year / Année / Год	Austria / Autriche / Австрия	Bulgaria / Bulgarie / Болгария	Croatia / Croatie / Хорватия	Germany / Allemagne / Германия	Hungary / Hongrie / Венгрия	Republic of Moldova / République de Moldova / Республика Молдова	Romania / Roumanie / Румыния	Slovakia / Slovaquie / Словакия	Ukraine / Ukraine / Украина	Yugoslavia / Yougoslavie / Югославия	Other countries / Autres pays / Другие страны	Total exports / Total des exportations / Весь экспорт
Austria	1980		14	...	374	3	...	13	1	617	171	380	1 573
Autriche	1998		...	43	...	102	...	-	1	34	28	500	708
Австрия	1999		...	22	...	133	...	-	1	5	38	505	704
Bulgaria	1980	62		...	112	2	...	-	20	640	44	90	970
Bulgarie	1998	126		-	...	17	...	-	14	85	177	...	419
Болгария	1999	28		-	...	8	14	247	1	85	126	9	517
Croatia	1980	...	...		...	...	...	...	...	...	...	...	...
Croatie	1998	-	-		...	...	...	-	-	-	...	1	1
Хорватия	1999	-	-		...	...	...	-	-	-	...	51	51
Germany	1980	246	3	...		6	...	10	-	69	81	...	415
Allemagne	1998	213	...	19		188	...	-	5	37	163	...	624
Германия	1999	263	12	10		91	...	-	18	9	74	...	476
Hungary	1980	207	5	...	362		...	66	58	422	92	-	1 212
Hongrie	1998	674	...	12	...		...	-	-	574	848	1 236	3 344
Венгрия	1999	1 458	...	33	...		...	-	-	139	290	815	2 735
Republic of Moldova	1980	...	...	...	...	...		...	...	...	...	...	...
République de Moldova	1998	-	-	-	...	-		...	-	-	...	...	...
Республика Молдова	1999	-	-	-	...	-		-	-	-	-	22	22
Romania	1980	72	5	...	156	9	...		259	157	910	2 069	3 637
Roumanie	1998	410	...	9	...	318	...		2	42	1 388	1 841	4 010
Румыния	1999	90	167	-	...	49	2		1	31	750	1 953	3 042
Slovakia	1980	552	160	...	42	62	...	197		429	196	238	1 876
Slovaquie	1998	594	...	1	...	69	...	-		28	162	132	986
Словакия	1999	1 531	3	...	...	49	...	-		4	36	2 272	3 894
Ukraine	1980	1 231	4 671	...	110	1 198	...	14	1 293		1 771	1 110	11 398
Ukraine	1998	2 052	...	15	0	222	...	-	-		1 028	1 629	4 946
Украина	1999	472	158	1	...	40	...	155	-		264	4 542	5 632
Yugoslavia	1980	107	24	...	65	95	...	32	83	291		-	697
Yougoslavie	1998	108	...	-	34	19	...	-	2	120		829	1 112
Югославия	1999	67	12	-	...	5	7	113	2	102		11	318
Other countries	1980	2 034	6	...	-	-	...	6 120	17	741	-		8 918
Autres pays	1998	1 133	...	-	...	450	...	7 830	100	510	-		10 069
Другие страны	1999	1 264	...	0	...	489	...	6 065	116	433	6		8 424
Total imports	1980	13 429	4 888	...	1 221	1 375	...	6 452	1 731	3 366	3 265	3 887	30 696
Total des importations	1998	5 309	2 197	98	3 309	1 385	...	7 830	124	1 431	3 794	6 213	31 691
Весь импорт	1999	5 172	351	66	...	864	22	6 580	139	807	1 584	10 230	25 816

Source: Danube Commission (Budapest), 2001.
Source: Commission du Danube (Budapest), 2001.
Источник: Дунайская Комиссия (Будапешт), 2001.

1- Data for individual countries are based on information from countries of destination, for "Other countries", from countries of origin.
1- Les données pour les pays individuels sont basées sur les informations fournies par les pays de destination, pour les "Autres pays" par les pays de provenance.
1- Данные по отдельным странам основываются на информации, полученной от стран назначения; данные по "Другим странам" - от стран происхождения.

OIL PIPELINE TRANSPORT

TRANSPORT PAR OLEODUCS

НЕФТЕПРОВОДНЫЙ ТРАНСПОРТ

OIL PIPELINE TRANSPORT - TRANSPORT PAR OLEODUCS
НЕФТЕПРОВОДНЫЙ ТРАНСПОРТ

19. Oil pipeline infrastructure and volume of transport
19. Longueur des oléoducs et volume transporté
19. Протяженность трубопроводов и объем транспортировки

Item	Description	Rubrique	Description
1	Total length of pipelines operated (km)	1	Longueur totale des oléoducs exploités (km)
2	Total volume carried (1000 tonnes)	2	Volume total transporté (1000 tonnes)
2.1	- National transport	2.1	- Transport national
2.2	- International transport - loaded	2.2	- Transport international - chargements
2.3	- International transport - unloaded	2.3	- Transport international - déchargements
2.4	- Transit by pipelines throughout	2.4	- Transit par oléoducs de bout en bout
3	Total volume carried (million tonne-kilometres)	3	Volume total transporté (million de tonnes-kilomètres)
3.1	- National transport	3.1	- Transport national
3.2	- International transport - loaded	3.2	- Transport international - chargements
3.3	- International transport - unloaded	3.3	- Transport international - déchargements
3.4	- Transit by pipelines throughout	3.4	- Transit par oléoducs de bout en bout
4	Crude petroleum carried (1000 tonnes)	4	Pétrole brut transporté (1000 tonnes)
4.1	- National transport	4.1	- Transport national
4.2	- International transport - loaded	4.2	- Transport international - chargements
4.3	- International transport - unloaded	4.3	- Transport international - déchargements
4.4	- Transit by pipelines throughout	4.4	- Transit par oléoducs de bout en bout
5	Crude petroleum carried (million tonne-kilometres)	5	Pétrole brut transporté (millions de tonnes-kilomètres)
5.1	- National transport	5.1	- Transport national
5.2	- International transport - loaded	5.2	- Transport international - chargements
5.3	- International transport - unloaded	5.3	- Transport international - déchargements
5.4	- Transit by pipelines throughout	5.4	- Transit par oléoducs de bout en bout

Статья	Описание
1	Протяженность трубопроводов в эксплуатации (км) - всего
2	Весь перевезенный объем (1000 т)
2.1	- Национальные перевозки
2.2	- Международные перевозки - загрузка в стране
2.3	- Международные перевозки - разгрузка в стране
2.4	- Сквозные транзитные перевозки судами внутреннего плавания
3	Весь перевезенный объем (млн. тонн-км)
3.1	- Национальные перевозки
3.2	- Международные перевозки - загрузка в стране
3.3	- Международные перевозки - разгрузка в стране
3.4	- Сквозные транзитные перевозки трубопроводами
4	Перевезенная сырая нефть (1000 т)
4.1	- Национальные перевозки
4.2	- Международные перевозки - загрузка в стране
4.3	- Международные перевозки - разгрузка в стране
4.4	- Сквозные транзитные перевозки трубопроводами
5	Перевезенная сырая нефть (млн. тонн-км)
5.1	- Национальные перевозки
5.2	- Международные перевозки - загрузка в стране
5.3	- Международные перевозки - разгрузка в стране
5.4	- Сквозные транзитные перевозки трубопроводами

OIL PIPELINE TRANSPORT - TRANSPORT PAR OLEODUCS
НЕФТЕПРОВОДНЫЙ ТРАНСПОРТ

19. Oil pipeline infrastructure and volume of transport
19. Longueur des oléoducs et volume transporté
19. Протяженность трубопроводов и объем транспортировки

		Albania Albanie Албания			Austria Autriche Австрия			Azerbaijan Azerbaïdjan Азербайджан		
		1990	1998	1999	1990	1998	1999	1990	1998	1999
1	Total length (km)	...	189	189	777	777	777	...	...	...
2	Goods carried (1000 t.)	...	380	338	35 122	36 889	34 650	...	...	...
2.1	- National	...	380	338	1 486	1 277	1 239	...	...	...
2.2	- International - loaded	-	-	-	-	-	-	...	...	...
2.3	- International - unloaded	-	-	-	6 863	8 378	7 778	...	...	...
2.4	- Transit	-	-	-	26 773	27 234	25 633	...	...	...
3	Tonne-km of goods carried (millions)	...	8.0	7.0	6 370.0	8 165.0	7 631.0	1 252.0	1 378.0	...
3.1	- National	...	8.0	7.0	256.0	220.0	213.0	...	...	...
3.2	- International - loaded	-	-	-	-	-	-	...	...	...
3.3	- International - unloaded	-	-	-	2 929.0	3 571.0	3 301.0	...	...	...
3.4	- Transit	-	-	-	3 185.0	4 374.0	4 117.0	...	...	...
4	Crude petroleum (1000 t.)	...	380	338	35 122	36 889	34 650	...	...	...
4.1	- National	...	380	338	1 486	1 277	1 239	...	...	...
4.2	- International - loaded	-	-	-	-	-	-	...	...	...
4.3	- International - unloaded	-	-	-	6 863	8 378	7 778	...	...	...
4.4	- Transit	-	-	-	26 773	27 234	25 633	...	...	...
5	Tonne-km of crude petroleum carried (millions)	...	8.0	7.0	6 370.0	8 165.0	7 631.0	...	...	...
5.1	- National	...	8.0	7.0	256.0	220.0	213.0	...	...	...
5.2	- International - loaded	-	-	-	-	-	-	...	...	...
5.3	- International - unloaded	-	-	-	2 929.0	3 571.0	3 301.0	...	...	...
5.4	- Transit	-	-	-	3 185.0	4 374.0	4 117.0	...	...	...

		Belgium Belgique Бельгия			Bulgaria Bulgarie Болгария			Croatia Croatie Хорватия		
		1990	1998	1999	1990	1998	1999	1990	1998	1999
1	Total length (km)	301	301	301	578	578	578	865	601	601
2	Goods carried (1000 t.)	21 918	33 482	32 842	14 002	6 492	6 763	8 556	5 735	5 645
2.1	- National	-	...	...	5 068	...	6 763	7 209	3 736	4 456
2.2	- International - loaded	-	...	...	832	...	-	-	-	-
2.3	- International - unloaded	19 596	...	...	8 102	...	...	...	-	-
2.4	- Transit	2 322	...	...	-	...	...	...	1 999	1 189
3	Tonne-km of goods carried (millions)	1 024.0	1 570.3	1 577.0	635.0	244.0	330.0	3 376.0	951.0	623.0
3.1	- National	-	...	...	...	...	330.0	2 981.0	166.0	246.0
3.2	- International - loaded	-	...	...	...	...	-	-	-	-
3.3	- International - unloaded	666.0	...	...	...	...	...	...	-	-
3.4	- Transit	358.0	...	...	...	...	...	-	785.0	377.0
4	Crude petroleum (1000 t.)	19 596	...	...	7 721	...	5 220	8 556	5 735	5 645
4.1	- National	-	...	...	-	...	5 220	7 209	3 736	4 456
4.2	- International - loaded	-	...	...	-	...	...	-	-	-
4.3	- International - unloaded	19 596	...	...	7 721	...	...	-	-	-
4.4	- Transit	-	...	...	-	...	...	...	1 999	1 189
5	Tonne-km of crude petroleum carried (millions)	666.0	...	...	...	...	157.0	3 376.0	951.0	623.0
5.1	- National	-	...	...	...	...	157.0	2 981.0	166.0	246.0
5.2	- International - loaded	-	...	...	...	...	...	-	-	-
5.3	- International - unloaded	666.0	...	...	...	...	...	-	-	-
5.4	- Transit	-	...	...	...	...	...	...	785.0	377.0

OIL PIPELINE TRANSPORT - TRANSPORT PAR OLEODUCS
НЕФТЕПРОВОДНЫЙ ТРАНСПОРТ

19. Oil pipeline infrastructure and volume of transport
19. Longueur des oléoducs et volume transporté
19. Протяженность трубопроводов и объем транспортировки

		Czech Republic République tchèque Чешская Республика			Denmark Danemark Дания			France France Франция		
		1990	1998	1999	1990	1998	1999	1990	1998	1999
1	Total length (km)	...	736	736	444	330	330	4 948	5 746	5 746
2	Goods carried (1000 t.)	...	9 217	8 050	6 037	11 808	12 891	67 975	78 710	76 326
2.1	- National	...	-	-	6 037	...	...	49 238	64 237	61 471
2.2	- International - loaded	...	-	-	-	...	...	17 975	14 473	14 855
2.3	- International - unloaded	...	9 217	8 050	-	...	...	-	-	-
2.4	- Transit	...	-	-	-	...	...	-	-	-
3	Tonne-km of goods carried (millions)	...	2 078.0	1 795.0	1 808.0	3 897.0	4 254.0	19 609.0	21 581.0	21 322.0
3.1	- National	...	-	-	1 808.0	...	...	10 529.0	12 515.0	13 136.0
3.2	- International - loaded	...	-	-	-	...	...	10 785.0	9 066.0	8 186.0
3.3	- International - unloaded	...	2 078.0	1 795.0	-	...	...	-	-	-
3.4	- Transit	...	-	-	-	...	...	-	-	-
4	Crude petroleum (1000 t.)	...	9 217	8 050	5 385	...	...	40 522	41 789	40 776
4.1	- National	...	-	-	5 385	...	...	23 690	28 171	26 643
4.2	- International - loaded	...	-	-	-	...	...	16 612	13 617	14 133
4.3	- International - unloaded	...	9 217	8 050	-	...	...	-	-	-
4.4	- Transit	...	-	-	-	...	...	-	-	-
5	Tonne-km of crude petroleum carried (millions)	...	2 078.0	1 795.0	1 758.0	...	...	13 915.0	14 893.0	14 624.0
5.1	- National	...	-	-	1 758.0	...	...	5 642.0	6 213.0	6 764.0
5.2	- International - loaded	...	-	-	-	...	...	10 035.0	8 680.0	7 860.0
5.3	- International - unloaded	...	2 078.0	1 795.0	-	...	...	-	-	-
5.4	- Transit	...	-	-	-	...	...	-	-	-

		Germany Allemagne Германия			Hungary Hongrie Венгрия			Italy Italie Италия		
		1990	1998	1999	1990	1998	1999	1990	1998	1999
1	Total length (km)	...	2 370	2 370	2 574	2 049	2 049	4 086	4 331	4 364
2	Goods carried (1000 t.)	...	...	...	15 309	13 274	...	70 970	118 216	116 258
2.1	- National	...	...	...	7 143	...	...	39 155	...	...
2.2	- International - loaded	...	...	...	-	...	...	31 815	...	...
2.3	- International - unloaded	...	...	...	7 252	...	...	...	...	...
2.4	- Transit	...	...	...	914	...	...	...	...	...
3	Tonne-km of goods carried (millions)	...	...	...	2 868.0	2 469.5	...	11 098.0	10 624.0	10 411.0
3.1	- National	...	...	...	729.9	...	...	6 045.0	...	...
3.2	- International - loaded	...	...	...	-	...	...	5 053.0	...	...
3.3	- International - unloaded	...	...	...	1 726.2	...	...	-	...	...
3.4	- Transit	...	...	...	411.9	...	...	...	...	...
4	Crude petroleum (1000 t.)	...	90 717	89 296	8 834	7 811	7 360	59 232	...	...
4.1	- National	...	22 042	20 895	1 717	...	...	27 417	...	...
4.2	- International - loaded	...	68 675	68 401	-	...	...	31 815	...	...
4.3	- International - unloaded	...	-	-	6 203	...	...	-	...	...
4.4	- Transit	...	-	-	914	...	...	-	...	...
5	Tonne-km of crude petroleum carried (millions)	...	14 849.0	14 966.0	2 194.8	1 936.5	1 798.0	9 948.0	...	...
5.1	- National	...	4 440.0	4 452.0	177.1	...	...	4 895.0	...	...
5.2	- International - loaded	...	10 409.0	10 515.0	-	...	...	5 053.0	...	...
5.3	- International - unloaded	...	-	-	1 605.8	...	...	-	...	...
5.4	- Transit	...	-	-	411.9	...	...	-	...	...

OIL PIPELINE TRANSPORT - TRANSPORT PAR OLEODUCS
НЕФТЕПРОВОДНЫЙ ТРАНСПОРТ

19. Oil pipeline infrastructure and volume of transport
19. Longueur des oléoducs et volume transporté
19. Протяженность трубопроводов и объем транспортировки

		Kazakhstan / Kazakhstan / Казахстан			Latvia / Lettonie / Латвия			Lithuania / Lituanie / Литва		
		1990	1998	1999	1990	1998	1999	1990	1998	1999
1	Total length (km)	...	6 965	8 060	766	766	766	...	399	500
2	Goods carried (1000 t.)	...	20 379	20 531	...	24 094	21 607	...	24 087	22 249
2.1	- National	...	...	...	...	-	-	...	-	-
2.2	- International - loaded	...	...	...	-	-	-	...	-	-
2.3	- International - unloaded	...	...	...	-	-	-	...	6 295	5 025
2.4	- Transit	...	...	...	...	24 094	21 607	...	17 792	17 224
3	Tonne-km of goods carried (millions)	...	15 365.6	16 922.2	...	6 569.0	6 055.0	...	2 964.0	2 627.0
3.1	- National	...	...	...	...	-	-	...	-	-
3.2	- International - loaded	...	...	...	-	-	-	...	-	-
3.3	- International - unloaded	...	...	...	-	-	-	...	1 416.0	1 120.0
3.4	- Transit	...	...	...	...	6 569.0	6 055.0	...	1 548.0	1 507.0
4	Crude petroleum (1000 t.)	...	20 272	20 272	...	20 888	18 018	...	20 881	18 660
4.1	- National	...	...	...	...	...	...	...	-	-
4.2	- International - loaded	...	...	...	...	...	...	...	-	-
4.3	- International - unloaded	...	...	...	-	-	-	...	6 295	5 025
4.4	- Transit	...	...	...	...	20 888	18 018	...	14 586	13 635
5	Tonne-km of crude petroleum carried (millions)	...	15 336.7	16 811.1	...	5 516.0	4 874.0	...	2 685.0	2 315.0
5.1	- National	...	...	...	...	...	...	...	-	-
5.2	- International - loaded	...	...	...	...	...	...	...	-	-
5.3	- International - unloaded	...	...	...	-	-	-	...	1 416.0	1 120.0
5.4	- Transit	...	...	...	...	5 516.0	4 874.0	...	1 269.0	1 195.0

		Netherlands / Pays-Bas [1] / Нидерланды			Norway / Norvège [2] / Норвегия			Poland / Pologne / Польша		
		1990	1998	1999	1990	1998	1999	1990	1998	1999
1	Total length (km)	391	391	...	521	5 747	6 477	2 039	2 278	2 278
2	Goods carried (1000 t.)	...	...	...	38 610	104 640	...	32 995	40 742	42 849
2.1	- National	...	...	...	17 110	...	...	...	...	...
2.2	- International - loaded	41 146	53 164	...	21 500	...	...	...	...	...
2.3	- International - unloaded	-	-	...	-	...	...	...	...	...
2.4	- Transit	-	-	...	-	...	...	...	...	...
3	Tonne-km of goods carried (millions)	...	...	...	9 508.0	...	...	13 887.0	18 448.0	19 417.0
3.1	- National	...	...	...	1 968.0	...	...	...	4 853.0	...
3.2	- International - loaded	4 873.0	6 043.0	...	7 540.0	...	...	...	...	...
3.3	- International - unloaded	-	-	...	-	...	...	...	...	...
3.4	- Transit	-	-	...	-	...	...	...	...	...
4	Crude petroleum (1000 t.)	...	...	...	38 610	...	...	...	...	...
4.1	- National	...	...	...	17 110	...	...	...	...	...
4.2	- International - loaded	33 912	43 865	...	21 500	...	...	...	...	...
4.3	- International - unloaded	-	-	...	-	...	...	...	...	...
4.4	- Transit	-	-	...	-	...	...	...	...	...
5	Tonne-km of crude petroleum carried (millions)	...	...	...	9 508.0	...	...	...	...	...
5.1	- National	...	...	...	1 968.0	...	...	...	...	...
5.2	- International - loaded	3 766.0	4 620.0	...	7 540.0	...	...	...	...	...
5.3	- International - unloaded	-	-	...	-	...	...	...	...	...
5.4	- Transit	-	-	...	-	...	...	...	...	...

For note see end of table.   Voir note à la fin du tableau.   См. примечания в конце таблицы.

OIL PIPELINE TRANSPORT - TRANSPORT PAR OLEODUCS
НЕФТЕПРОВОДНЫЙ ТРАНСПОРТ

19. Oil pipeline infrastructure and volume of transport
19. Longueur des oléoducs et volume transporté
19. Протяженность трубопроводов и объем транспортировки

		Romania Roumanie Румыния			Russian Federation Fédération de Russie Российская Федерация			Slovakia Slovaquie Словакия		
		1990	1998	1999	1990	1998	1999	1990	1998	1999
1	Total length (km)	3 694	4 629	4 423	...	61 717	60 928	...	...	...
2	Goods carried (1000 t.)	23 487	12 481	9 275	...	302 861	302 990	...	11 136	10 441
2.1	- National	6 314	4 656	6 041	...	...	...	...	1 160	5 488
2.2	- International - loaded	1 940	1 063	...	...	...	...	...	5 576	4 953
2.3	- International - unloaded	15 233	6 762	...	...	...	...	...	11 196	10 440
2.4	- Transit	-	-	...	...	...	...	...	...	...
3	Tonne-km of goods carried (millions)	5 062.0	2 257.0	1 636.0	...	690 808.5	709 526.7	...	...	...
3.1	- National	922.0	699.0	901.0	...	...	...	...	...	...
3.2	- International - loaded	314.0	61.0	...	...	...	...	...	...	...
3.3	- International - unloaded	3 826.0	1 497.0	...	...	...	...	...	...	...
3.4	- Transit	-	-	...	...	...	...	...	...	...
4	Crude petroleum (1000 t.)	19 643	11 154	8 397	...	281 955	282 083	...	...	...
4.1	- National	4 410	4 392	...	...	...	...	...	...	...
4.2	- International - loaded	-	-	-	...	...	...	...	...	...
4.3	- International - unloaded	15 233	6 762	...	...	...	...	...	...	...
4.4	- Transit	-	-	...	...	...	...	...	...	...
5	Tonne-km of crude petroleum carried (millions)	4 540.0	2 151.0	1 470.0	...	669 555.3	685 381.1	...	...	...
5.1	- National	714.0	654.0	...	...	...	...	...	...	...
5.2	- International - loaded	-	-	...	...	...	...	...	...	...
5.3	- International - unloaded	3 826.0	1 497.0	...	...	...	...	...	...	...
5.4	- Transit	-	-	...	...	...	...	...	...	...

		Spain Espagne Испания			Switzerland Suisse Швейцария			Turkey Turquie Турция		
		1990	1998	1999	1990	1998	1999	1990	1998	1999
1	Total length (km)	2 678	3 691	3 698	239	108	...	...	2 112	...
2	Goods carried (1000 t.)	18 858	28 964	29 802	12 483	5 907	...	...	...	...
2.1	- National	18 858	28 964	29 802	-	-	...	...	...	...
2.2	- International - loaded	-	-	-	-	-	...	...	...	...
2.3	- International - unloaded	-	-	-	4 764	5 907	...	...	...	...
2.4	- Transit	-	-	-	7 719	-	...	...	...	...
3	Tonne-km of goods carried (millions)	4 215.0	6 872.0	7 031.0	1 113.0	234.0	...	...	...	...
3.1	- National	4 215.0	6 872.0	7 031.0	-	-	...	...	...	...
3.2	- International - loaded	-	-	-	-	-	...	...	...	...
3.3	- International - unloaded	-	-	-	242.0	234.0	...	...	...	...
3.4	- Transit	-	-	-	871.0	-	...	...	...	...
4	Crude petroleum (1000 t.)	6 758	7 158	7 557	11 016	5 053	...	...	...	...
4.1	- National	6 758	7 158	7 557	-	-	...	...	...	...
4.2	- International - loaded	-	-	-	-	-	...	...	...	...
4.3	- International - unloaded	-	-	-	3 401	5 053	...	...	...	...
4.4	- Transit	-	-	-	7 615	-	...	...	...	...
5	Tonne-km of crude petroleum carried (millions)	1 676.0	1 990.0	2 101.0	1 049.0	222.0	...	...	...	...
5.1	- National	1 676.0	1 990.0	2 101.0	-	-	...	...	...	...
5.2	- International - loaded	-	-	-	-	-	...	...	...	...
5.3	- International - unloaded	-	-	-	191.0	222.0	...	...	...	...
5.4	- Transit	-	-	-	858.0	-	...	...	...	...

OIL PIPELINE TRANSPORT - TRANSPORT PAR OLEODUCS
НЕФТЕПРОВОДНЫЙ ТРАНСПОРТ

19. Oil pipeline infrastructure and volume of transport
19. Longueur des oléoducs et volume transporté
19. Протяженность трубопроводов и объем транспортировки

		Turkmenistan Turkménistan Туркменистан			Ukraine Ukraine Украина			United Kingdom Royaume-Uni [2] Соединенное Королевство		
		1990	1998	1999	1990	1998	1999	1990	1998	1999
1	Total length (km)	...	464	...	5 491	...	...	2 462	3 953	3 603
2	Goods carried (1000 t.)	...	4 403	...	113 875	68 000	68 000	120 890	152 505	155 858
2.1	- National	...	4 403	...	13 335	...	...	120 890	152 505	155 858
2.2	- International - loaded	...	-	...	-	...	...	-	-	-
2.3	- International - unloaded	...	-	...	55 637	...	...	-	-	-
2.4	- Transit	...	-	...	44 903	...	...	-	-	-
3	Tonne-km of goods carried (millions)	...	693.8	...	50 673.0	...	...	11 045.0	11 666.0	11 611.0
3.1	- National	...	693.8	...	2 110.0	...	...	11 045.0	11 666.0	11 611.0
3.2	- International - loaded	...	-	...	-	...	...	-	-	-
3.3	- International - unloaded	...	-	...	30 356.0	...	...	-	-	-
3.4	- Transit	...	-	...	18 356.0	...	...	-	-	-
4	Crude petroleum (1000 t.)	...	4 403	...	...	...	...	66 995	96 219	95 687
4.1	- National	...	4 403	...	...	...	...	66 995	96 219	95 687
4.2	- International - loaded	...	-	...	...	...	...	-	-	-
4.3	- International - unloaded	...	-	...	...	...	...	-	-	-
4.4	- Transit	...	-	...	...	...	...	-	-	-
5	Tonne-km of crude petroleum carried (millions)	...	693.8	...	...	...	...	6 378.0	6 121.0	5 998.0
5.1	- National	...	693.8	...	...	...	...	6 378.0	6 121.0	5 998.0
5.2	- International - loaded	...	-	...	...	...	...	-	-	-
5.3	- International - unloaded	...	-	...	...	...	...	-	-	-
5.4	- Transit	...	-	...	...	...	...	-	-	-

		United States Etats-Unis Соединенные Штаты			Yugoslavia Yugoslavie Югославия					
		1990	1998	1999	1990	1998	1999			
1	Total length (km)	343 651	287 445	...	...	375	376			
2	Goods carried (1000 t.)	...	...	...	...	1 892	918			
2.1	- National	...	...	...	...	686	624			
2.2	- International - loaded	...	...	...	...	-	-			
2.3	- International - unloaded	...	...	...	...	1 206	294			
2.4	- Transit	...	...	...	...	-	-			
3	Tonne-km of goods carried (millions)	852 784.0	904 953.0	...	...	251.0	91.0			
3.1	- National	...	...	...	...	74.0	45.0			
3.2	- International - loaded	...	...	...	...	-	-			
3.3	- International - unloaded	...	...	...	...	177.0	46.0			
3.4	- Transit	...	...	...	...	-	-			
4	Crude petroleum (1000 t.)	...	...	...	...	1 892	918			
4.1	- National	...	...	...	...	686	624			
4.2	- International - loaded	...	...	...	...	-	-			
4.3	- International - unloaded	...	...	...	...	1 206	294			
4.4	- Transit	...	...	...	...	-	-			
5	Tonne-km of crude petroleum carried (millions)	488 807.0	487 810.0	...	...	251.0	91.0			
5.1	- National	...	...	...	...	74.0	45.0			
5.2	- International - loaded	...	...	...	...	-	-			
5.3	- International - unloaded	...	...	...	...	177.0	46.0			
5.4	- Transit	...	...	...	...	-	-			

OIL PIPELINE TRANSPORT - TRANSPORT PAR OLEODUCS
НЕФТЕПРОВОДНЫЙ ТРАНСПОРТ

NOTES TO TABLE 19 - NOTES DU TABLEAU 19 - ПРИМЕЧАНИЯ К ТАБЛИЦЕ 19

Country notes - Notes relatives aux pays - Примечания к данным, представляемым странами

1 - International oil pipelines only.

1 - Oléoducs internationaux uniquement.

1 - Только международные нефтетрубопроводы.

2 - Including pipeline linking Ekofisk with the United Kingdom.

2 - Y compris l'oléoduc reliant Ekofisk au Royaume-Uni.

2 - Включая нефтепровод, соединяющий Экофиск (Норвегия) с Соединенным Королевством.

MARITIME TRANSPORT

TRANSPORT MARITIME

МОРСКОЙ ТРАНСПОРТ

SEA PORTS - PORTS MARITIMES
МОРСКОЙ ТРАНСПОРТ

20. Goods loaded and unloaded at sea ports

20. Marchandises chargées et déchargées dans les ports maritimes

20. Грузы, погруженные и разгруженные в морских портах

Item	Description
1	**International maritime transport in thousand tonnes**
1.11	- Total
1.12	- Goods loaded
1.13	- Goods unloaded
2	**National sea transport in thousand tonnes**
2.11	- Total
2.12	- Goods loaded
2.13	- Goods unloaded

Rubrique	Description
1	**Transport maritime international en milliers de tonnes**
1.11	- Total
1.12	- Marchandises chargées
1.13	- Marchandises déchargées
2	**Transport national par mer en milliers de tonnes**
2.11	- Total
2.12	- Marchandises chargées
2.13	- Marchandises déchargées

Статья	Описание
1	**Международные морские перевозки (1000 тонн)**
1.11	- Всего
1.12	- Погруженные грузы
1.13	- Разгруженные грузы
2	**Национальные морские перевозки (1000 тонн)**
2.11	- Всего
2.12	- Погруженные грузы
2.13	- Разгруженные грузы

20. Goods loaded and unloaded at sea ports
20. Marchandises chargées et déchargées dans les ports maritimes
20. Грузы, погруженные и разгруженные в морских портах

		Albania Albanie Албания			Azerbaijan Azerbaïdjan Азербайджан			Belgium Belgique Бельгия		
		1990	1998	1999	1990	1998	1999	1990	1998	1999
1	International maritime transport in 1000 tonnes									
1.11	- Total	2 819	1 480	1 144	...	8 200	...	159 167	171 559	166 040
1.12	- Goods loaded	...	61	29	...	...	...	55 109	60 430	63 393
1.13	- Goods unloaded	...	1 419	1 115	...	...	...	104 058	111 129	102 647
2	National sea transport in 1000 tonnes									
2.11	- Total	...	-	-	...	...	...	...	...	...
2.12	- Goods loaded	...	-	-	...	...	...	...	...	...
2.13	- Goods unloaded	...	-	-	...	...	...	...	...	...

		Bulgaria Bulgarie Болгария			Canada Canada [1] Канада			Croatia Croatie Хорватия		
		1990	1998	1999	1990	1998	1999	1990	1998	1999
1	International maritime transport in 1000 tonnes									
1.11	- Total	23 175	17 846	16 299	232 337	273 806	...	21 817	12 617	13 147
1.12	- Goods loaded	4 169	6 936	6 602	159 041	178 893	...	4 124	3 586	4 833
1.13	- Goods unloaded	19 006	10 910	9 697	73 296	94 913	...	17 693	9 031	8 314
2	National sea transport in 1000 tonnes									
2.11	- Total	1 702	4	14	120 720	95 856	...	3 473	3 094	3 136
2.12	- Goods loaded	851	...	14	60 360	47 928	...	1 990	1 612	1 577
2.13	- Goods unloaded	851	...	...	60 360	47 928	...	1 483	1 482	1 559

		Cyprus Chypre Кипр			Denmark Danemark Дания			Estonia Estonie Эстония		
		1990	1998	1999	1990	1998	1999	1990	1998	1999
1	International maritime transport in 1000 tonnes									
1.11	- Total	7 170	6 498	6 156	45 614	72 468	72 517	8 030	27 357	34 357
1.12	- Goods loaded	2 757	1 419	1 451	15 596	29 017	30 927	2 860	22 725	28 590
1.13	- Goods unloaded	4 413	5 080	4 706	30 018	43 451	41 590	5 170	4 632	5 767
2	National sea transport in 1000 tonnes									
2.11	- Total	...	-	-	20 220	32 498	24 697	3 750	...	...
2.12	- Goods loaded	...	-	-	11 170	16 796	11 857	1 700	...	...
2.13	- Goods unloaded	...	-	-	9 050	15 702	12 840	2 050	...	...

For note see end of table.   Voir note à la fin du tableau.   См. примечания в конце таблицы.

MARITIME TRANSPORT - TRANSPORT MARITIME
МОРСКОЙ ТРАНСПОРТ

20. Goods loaded and unloaded at sea ports
20. Marchandises chargées et déchargées dans les ports maritimes
20. Грузы, погруженные и разгруженные в морских портах

		Finland Finlande Финляндия			France France Франция			Georgia Georgie Грузия		
		1990	1998	1999	1990	1998	1999	1990	1998	1999
1	**International maritime transport in 1000 tonnes**									
1.11	- Total	58 872	76 594	77 500	297 191	312 670	...	...	600	...
1.12	- Goods loaded	24 047	37 524	39 304	83 978	85 995	...	...	...	...
1.13	- Goods unloaded	34 825	39 070	38 196	213 213	226 675	...	...	...	...
2	**National sea transport in 1000 tonnes**									
2.11	- Total	11 640	14 500	13 240	22 695	23 946	...	...	...	...
2.12	- Goods loaded	5 820	7 250	6 620	10 231	9 993	...	...	...	...
2.13	- Goods unloaded	5 820	7 250	6 620	12 464	13 953	...	...	...	...

		Germany Allemagne Германия			Greece Grèce Греция			Ireland Irlande [2] Ирландия		
		1990	1998	1999	1990	1998	1999	1990	1998	1999
1	**International maritime transport in 1000 tonnes**									
1.11	- Total	...	210 044	211 617	57 410	...	...	23 756	39 954	42 928
1.12	- Goods loaded	...	69 098	73 858	22 260	...	...	6 370	11 260	12 202
1.13	- Goods unloaded	...	140 946	137 759	35 150	...	...	17 386	28 694	30 726
2	**National sea transport in 1000 tonnes**									
2.11	- Total	...	7 444	10 005	40 160	...	...	1 158	1 659	1 696
2.12	- Goods loaded	...	3 378	4 616	20 080	...	...	600	871	915
2.13	- Goods unloaded	...	4 066	5 389	20 080	...	...	558	788	781

		Israel Israël Израиль			Italy Italie Италия			Latvia Lettonie Латвия		
		1990	1998	1999	1990	1998	1999	1990	1998	1999
1	**International maritime transport in 1000 tonnes**									
1.11	- Total	21 676	40 759	41 886	270 780	...	...	36 171	52 292	49 032
1.12	- Goods loaded	7 924	13 488	12 874	42 183	...	...	30 386	48 575	45 145
1.13	- Goods unloaded	13 752	27 271	28 992	228 597	...	...	5 785	3 717	3 887
2	**National sea transport in 1000 tonnes**									
2.11	- Total	...	...	...	134 058	...	...	-	-	-
2.12	- Goods loaded	...	...	...	67 029	...	...	-	-	-
2.13	- Goods unloaded	...	...	...	67 029	...	...	-	-	-

For note see end of table.   Voir note à la fin du tableau.   См. примечания в конце таблицы.

MARITIME TRANSPORT - TRANSPORT MARITIME
МОРСКОЙ ТРАНСПОРТ

20. Goods loaded and unloaded at sea ports

20. Marchandises chargées et déchargées dans les ports maritimes

20. Грузы, погруженные и разгруженные в морских портах

		Lithuania Lituanie Литва			Malta Malte Мальта			Netherlands Pays-Bas [3] Нидерланды		
		1990	1998	1999	1990	1998	1999	1990	1998	1999
1	International maritime transport in 1000 tonnes									
1.11	- Total	16 121	15 016	15 655	2 562	2 506	2 447	373 090	404 821	...
1.12	- Goods loaded	...	12 227	12 864	91	574	610	91 840	85 137	...
1.13	- Goods unloaded	...	2 789	2 791	2 471	1 932	1 837	281 250	319 684	...
2	National sea transport in 1000 tonnes									
2.11	- Total	...	-	-	...	...	...	...	...	...
2.12	- Goods loaded	...	-	-	...	...	...	...	...	...
2.13	- Goods unloaded	...	-	-	...	...	...	...	...	...

		Norway Norvège Норвегия			Poland Pologne Польша			Portugal Portugal Португалия		
		1990	1998	1999	1990	1998	1999	1990	1998	1999
1	International maritime transport in 1000 tonnes									
1.11	- Total	108 870	177 387	175 235	43 227	50 563	49 227	37 650	45 311	38 133
1.12	- Goods loaded	89 300	151 708	150 852	30 729	32 314	33 361	8 600	7 570	5 423
1.13	- Goods unloaded	19 570	25 679	24 383	12 498	18 249	15 866	29 050	37 741	32 710
2	National sea transport in 1000 tonnes									
2.11	- Total	...	59 700	59 600	2 238	866	904	...	12 309	11 598
2.12	- Goods loaded	...	...	...	1 119	433	452	...	6 618	5 891
2.13	- Goods unloaded	...	...	...	1 119	433	452	...	5 691	5 707

		Romania Roumanie Румыния			Russian Federation Fédération de Russie Российская Федерация			Slovenia Slovénie Словения		
		1990	1998	1999	1990	1998	1999	1990	1998	1999
1	International maritime transport in 1000 tonnes									
1.11	- Total	45 805	30 610	23 369	...	89 742	...	5 542	8 446	8 412
1.12	- Goods loaded	12 139	11 673	12 276	...	82 871	82 163	...	2 504	2 461
1.13	- Goods unloaded	33 666	18 937	11 093	...	6 871	9 114	...	5 942	5 951
2	National sea transport in 1000 tonnes									
2.11	- Total	...	29	-	...	8 158	...	...	-	-
2.12	- Goods loaded	...	-	-	...	4 079	7 094	...	-	-
2.13	- Goods unloaded	...	29	-	...	4 079	747	...	-	-

For note see end of table.   Voir note à la fin du tableau.   См. примечания в конце таблицы.

MARITIME TRANSPORT - TRANSPORT MARITIME
МОРСКОЙ ТРАНСПОРТ

20. Goods loaded and unloaded at sea ports
20. Marchandises chargées et déchargées dans les ports maritimes
20. Грузы, погруженные и разгруженные в морских портах

		Spain Espagne Испания			Sweden Suède Швеция			Turkey Turquie [4] Турция		
		1990	1998	1999	1990	1998	1999	1990	1998	1999
1	**International maritime transport in 1000 tonnes**									
1.11	- Total	164 652	...	...	99 690	128 095	130 221	52 280	...	...
1.12	- Goods loaded	40 613	...	...	44 810	56 698	59 775	16 560	...	...
1.13	- Goods unloaded	124 039	...	...	54 880	71 397	70 446	35 720	...	...
2	**National sea transport in 1000 tonnes**									
2.11	- Total	66 096	...	...	28 500	27 627	26 127	...	...	...
2.12	- Goods loaded	33 099	...	...	14 220	13 814	13 223	...	...	...
2.13	- Goods unloaded	32 997	...	...	14 280	13 813	12 904	...	...	...

		Turkmenistan Turkménistan Туркменистан			Ukraine Ukraine Украина			United Kingdom Royaume-Uni [5] Соединенное Королевство		
		1990	1998	1999	1990	1998	1999	1990	1998	1999
1	**International maritime transport in 1000 tonnes**									
1.11	- Total	...	72 802	...	...	70 801	83 251	319 620	371 560	370 735
1.12	- Goods loaded	...	52 695	...	...	...	...	136 160	173 356	177 225
1.13	- Goods unloaded	...	20 113	...	...	...	...	183 460	198 204	193 510
2	**National sea transport in 1000 tonnes**									
2.11	- Total	...	60 404	...	...	1 832	3 140	172 340	158 842	161 785
2.12	- Goods loaded	...	989	...	...	...	...	77 390	74 013	69 648
2.13	- Goods unloaded	...	59 415	...	...	...	...	94 950	84 829	92 137

		United States Etats-Unis [6] Соединенные Штаты			Yugoslavia Yugoslavie Югославия					
		1990	1998	1999	1990	1998	1999			
1	**International maritime transport in 1000 tonnes**									
1.11	- Total	950 371	1 130 115	...	2 308	1 217	943			
1.12	- Goods loaded	408 837	367 248	...	755	480	177			
1.13	- Goods unloaded	541 534	762 868	...	1 553	737	766			
2	**National sea transport in 1000 tonnes**									
2.11	- Total	...	233 076	...	...	7	32			
2.12	- Goods loaded	...	...	...	...	5	15			
2.13	- Goods unloaded	...	...	...	...	2	17			

For note see end of table.   Voir note à la fin du tableau.   См. примечания в конце таблицы.

MARITIME TRANSPORT - TRANSPORT MARITIME
МОРСКОЙ ТРАНСПОРТ

NOTES TO TABLE 20 - NOTES DU TABLEAU 20 - ПРИМЕЧАНИЯ К ТАБЛИЦАМ 20

1 - Including maritime goods traffic of inlands ports.

2 - Excluding livestock.

3 - Including trans-shipments.

4 - Excluding livestock and timber.

5 - Great Britain.

6 - Including international traffic on the Great lakes.

1 - Y compris le transport maritime de marchamdises à destination et en provenance des ports fluviaux.

2 - Non compris le bétail.

3 - Y compris les transbordements.

4 - Non compris le bétail et le bois.

5 - Grande-Bretagne.

6 - Y compris les transports internationaux sur les Grands Lacs.

1 - Включая морскую перевозки внутренних портов.

2 - Исключая скот.

3 - Исключая перегрузки.

4 - Исключая перевозку скота и древесины.

5 - Великобритания.

6 - Включая международные перевозки на Болших Озерах.

INTERMODAL TRANSPORT

TRANSPORT INTERMODAL

ИНТЕРМОДАЛЬНЫЕ ПЕРЕВОЗКИ

INTERMODAL TRANSPORT - TRANSPORT INTERMODAL
ИНТЕРМОДАЛЬНЫЕ ПЕРЕВОЗКИ

21. Intermodal transport including railway transport

21. Transport intermodal par chemin de fer

21. Интермодальные перевозки, в т.ч. по железным дорогам

Item Rubrique Статья	Description	Description	Описание
1	**Number of intermodal transport units forwarded**	**Nombre d'unités de transport intermodal expédiées**	**Число отправленных интермодальных транспортных единиц**
1.1	**Goods Road vehicles**	**Véhicules routiers**	**Дорожные средства**
1.11	- Accompanied	- Accompagnés	- Сопровождаемые
1.12	- Unaccompanied	- Non-accompagnés	- Несопровождаемые
1.2	**Swap bodies**	**Caisses mobiles**	**Съемные кузова**
1.21	- Loaded	- Chargées	- Погружено
1.22	- Unloaded	- Déchargées	- Выгружено
1.3	**Containers**	**Conteneurs**	**Контейнеры**
1.31	- Twenty-foot	- ISO de 20 pieds	- Двадцатифутовые контейнеры
1.32	- Thirty-foot	- ISO de 30 pieds	- Тридцатифутовые контейнеры
1.33	- Forty-foot	- ISO de 40 pieds	- Сорокафутовые контейнеры
2	**Goods carried in intermodal transport unit (1000 tonnes)**	**Marchandises transportées dans les unités de transport intermodal (1000 tonnes)**	**Грузы, перевезенные интермодальными транспортными средствами (1000 тонн)**
2.1	- In goods road vehicles	- En véhicules routiers	- Дорожным транспортным средством
2.2	- In swap bodies	- En caisses mobiles	- Съемным кузовом
2.3	- In containers	- En conteneurs	- Контейнером

INTERMODAL TRANSPORT - TRANSPORT INTERMODAL
ИНТЕРМОДАЛЬНЫЕ ПЕРЕВОЗКИ

21. Intermodal transport including railway transport
21. Transport intermodal par chemin de fer
21. Интермодальные перевозки, в т.ч. по железным дорогам

		Austria Autriche Австрия			Belgium Belgique Бельгия			Bulgaria Bulgarie Болгария		
		1990	1998	1999	1990	1998	1999	1990	1998	1999
1	Number of intermodal transport units forwarded									
1.1	Goods Road vehicles	...	...	...	22 609	...	...	...	...	...
1.11	- Accompanied	...	...	...	...	...	...	...	...	...
1.12	- Unaccompanied	...	...	...	...	...	...	...	...	...
1.2	Swap bodies	...	...	248 232	65 253	...	...	...	...	...
1.21	- Load	...	...	...	...	...	...	...	...	...
1.22	- Unloaded	...	...	...	...	...	...	...	...	...
1.3	Containers	...	355 269	395 402	357 329	...	...	...	79 787	74 225
1.31	- Twenty-foot	...	...	...	...	...	...	...	73 178	72 503
1.32	- Thirty-foot	...	...	...	...	...	...	...	...	...
1.33	- Forty-foot	...	...	...	...	...	...	...	...	...
2	Goods carried in intermodal transport unit (1000 tonnes)									
2.1	- In goods road vehicles	...	...	...	626.0	...	...	...	...	...
2.2	- In swap bodies	...	...	3 554.0	1 102.9	...	...	...	...	...
2.3	- In containers	...	4 654.0	5 294.0	4 919.0	...	...	...	1 486.0	1 181.0

		Croatia Croatie Хорватия			Czech Republic République tchèque Чешская Республика			Finland Finlande Финляндия		
		1990	1998	1999	1990	1998	1999	1990	1998	1999
1	Number of intermodal transport units forwarded									
1.1	Goods Road vehicles	-	-	-	...	99 406	96 342	3 076	12 600	13 600
1.11	- Accompanied	-	-	-	...	99 406	96 342	-	-	-
1.12	- Unaccompanied	-	-	-	...	-	-	3 076	12 600	13 600
1.2	Swap bodies	-	-	-	...	16 002	19 098	...	5 000	5 000
1.21	- Load	-	-	-	...	...	...	...	5 000	5 000
1.22	- Unloaded	-	-	-	...	...	...	...	-	-
1.3	Containers	79 088	...	...	...	...	...	36 705	75 492	69 154
1.31	- Twenty-foot	...	...	...	...	...	...	...	40 413	38 982
1.32	- Thirty-foot	...	...	...	...	...	...	...	815	1 103
1.33	- Forty-foot	...	...	...	...	...	...	...	33 987	29 035
2	Goods carried in intermodal transport unit (1000 tonnes)									
2.1	- In goods road vehicles	-	-	-	...	2 774.0	2 749.0	34.0	278.0	298.0
2.2	- In swap bodies	-	-	-	...	...	...	...	60.0	60.0
2.3	- In containers	769.0	...	...	...	2 227.0	2 449.0	448.0	782.0	833.0

INTERMODAL TRANSPORT - TRANSPORT INTERMODAL
ИНТЕРМОДАЛЬНЫЕ ПЕРЕВОЗКИ

21. Intermodal transport including railway transport
21. Transport intermodal par chemin de fer
21. Интермодальные перевозки, в т.ч. по железным дорогам

		France France Франция			Germany Allemagne Германия			Greece Grèce Греция		
		1990	1998	1999	1990	1998	1999	1990	1998	1999
1	**Number of intermodal transport units forwarded**									
1.1	**Goods Road vehicles**	...	...	...	...	367 000	376 000	...	...	...
1.11	- Accompanied	...	...	...	...	...	...	...	...	...
1.12	- Unaccompanied	...	...	...	...	...	...	...	...	...
1.2	**Swap bodies**	...	...	...	...	2 679 000	2 505 000	...	...	...
1.21	- Load	...	...	...	...	1 925 000	1 843 000	...	...	...
1.22	- Unloaded	...	...	...	...	754 000	662 000	...	...	...
1.3	**Containers**	783 261	...	...	...	...	...	9 968	...	...
1.31	- Twenty-foot	...	...	...	...	...	...	...	...	...
1.32	- Thirty-foot	...	...	...	...	...	...	...	...	...
1.33	- Forty-foot	...	...	...	...	...	...	...	...	...
2	**Goods carried in intermodal transport unit (1000 tonnes)**									
2.1	- In goods road vehicles	...	...	...	...	7 595.0	8 012.0	...	...	...
2.2	- In swap bodies	...	...	...	...	24 055.0	22 848.0	...	...	...
2.3	- In containers	5 670.1	...	...	...	...	...	174.0	...	...

		Hungary Hongrie Венгрия			Kyrgyzstan Kirghizistan Кыргызстан			Latvia Lettonie Латвия		
		1990	1998	1999	1990	1998	1999	1990	1998	1999
1	**Number of intermodal transport units forwarded**									
1.1	**Goods Road vehicles**	...	...	...	...	...	...	...	...	...
1.11	- Accompanied	...	...	...	...	...	...	...	...	...
1.12	- Unaccompanied	...	...	...	...	...	...	...	...	...
1.2	**Swap bodies**	...	...	...	...	...	...	...	...	...
1.21	- Load	...	...	...	...	...	...	...	...	...
1.22	- Unloaded	...	...	...	...	...	...	...	...	...
1.3	**Containers**	382 514	...	...	...	...	...	...	...	10 437
1.31	- Twenty-foot	...	...	...	...	...	...	...	...	...
1.32	- Thirty-foot	...	...	...	...	...	...	...	...	...
1.33	- Forty-foot	...	...	...	...	...	...	...	...	...
2	**Goods carried in intermodal transport unit (1000 tonnes)**									
2.1	- In goods road vehicles	...	...	...	...	...	19.3	...	...	...
2.2	- In swap bodies	...	...	...	26.4	1.7	2.9	...	...	...
2.3	- In containers	2 115.9	...	...	314.5	0.2	0.9	...	112.0	95.0

INTERMODAL TRANSPORT - TRANSPORT INTERMODAL
ИНТЕРМОДАЛЬНЫЕ ПЕРЕВОЗКИ

21. Intermodal transport including railway transport
21. Transport intermodal par chemin de fer
21. Интермодальные перевозки, в т.ч. по железным дорогам

		Luxembourg Luxembourg Люксембург			Netherlands Pays-Bas Нидерланды			Poland Pologne Польша		
		1990	1998	1999	1990	1998	1999	1990	1998	1999
1	Number of intermodal transport units forwarded									
1.1	Goods Road vehicles	...	...	...	...	...	...	...	77	39
1.11	- Accompanied	...	...	...	...	...	...	...	...	...
1.12	- Unaccompanied	...	...	...	...	...	...	...	...	...
1.2	Swap bodies	...	...	...	...	...	...	...	23 746	25 658
1.21	- Load	...	...	...	...	...	...	...	14 020	14 159
1.22	- Unloaded	...	...	...	...	...	...	...	9 726	11 499
1.3	Containers	3 764	...	...	269 640	...	...	...	161 079	124 459
1.31	- Twenty-foot	...	...	...	...	...	...	...	84 816	58 395
1.32	- Thirty-foot	...	...	...	...	...	...	...	1 108	1 895
1.33	- Forty-foot	...	...	...	...	...	...	...	75 155	64 169
2	Goods carried in intermodal transport unit (1000 tonnes)									
2.1	- In goods road vehicles	...	...	...	...	...	...	...	2.0	1.0
2.2	- In swap bodies	...	...	...	...	...	...	...	234.0	224.0
2.3	- In containers	56.0	...	...	3 640.0	...	...	1 454.3	1 790.0	1 521.0

		Portugal Portugal Португалия			Republic of Moldova République de Moldova Республика Молдова			Romania Roumanie Румыния		
		1990	1998	1999	1990	1998	1999	1990	1998	1999
1	Number of intermodal transport units forwarded									
1.1	Goods Road vehicles	...	-	-	...	...	...	...	...	-
1.11	- Accompanied	...	-	-	...	...	...	...	...	...
1.12	- Unaccompanied	...	-	-	...	...	...	...	...	...
1.2	Swap bodies	...	-	-	...	...	...	...	...	...
1.21	- Load	...	-	-	...	...	...	...	...	...
1.22	- Unloaded	...	-	-	...	...	...	...	...	...
1.3	Containers	...	39 397	36 155	...	5 625	4 162	...	91 110	73 018
1.31	- Twenty-foot	...	25 356	22 332	...	2 034	1 296	...	...	70 417
1.32	- Thirty-foot	...	678	645	...	...	...	...	...	...
1.33	- Forty-foot	...	13 363	13 178	...	...	...	...	...	...
2	Goods carried in intermodal transport unit (1000 tonnes)									
2.1	- In goods road vehicles	...	-	-	...	...	...	...	...	-
2.2	- In swap bodies	...	-	-	...	...	...	...	...	-
2.3	- In containers	...	619.0	572.0	...	38.0	28.0	...	1 475.0	1 518.0

INTERMODAL TRANSPORT - TRANSPORT INTERMODAL
ИНТЕРМОДАЛЬНЫЕ ПЕРЕВОЗКИ

21. Intermodal transport including railway transport
21. Transport intermodal par chemin de fer
21. Интермодальные перевозки, в т.ч. по железным дорогам

		Russian Federation Fédération de Russie Российская Федерация			Slovakia Slovaquie Словакия			Slovenia Slovénie Словения		
		1990	1998	1999	1990	1998	1999	1990	1998	1999
1	Number of intermodal transport units forwarded									
1.1	**Goods Road vehicles**	...	...	...	-	38	146	...	15 383	21 824
1.11	- Accompanied	...	...	...	-	38	146	...	15 342	21 790
1.12	- Unaccompanied	...	...	...	-	-	-	...	41	34
1.2	**Swap bodies**	...	...	...	-	-	-	...	14 073	12 860
1.21	- Load	...	...	...				...	12 375	11 346
1.22	- Unloaded	...	...	...	-	-	-	...	1 698	1 514
1.3	**Containers**	...	...	...	...	16 086	12 343	...	49 111	45 401
1.31	- Twenty-foot	...	...	...	...	...	...	...	36 584	31 643
1.32	- Thirty-foot	...	...	...	...	...	...	...	2 334	2 188
1.33	- Forty-foot	...	...	...	...	...	...	...	10 193	11 570
2	Goods carried in intermodal transport unit (1000 tonnes)									
2.1	- In goods road vehicles	...	...	...		-	-	...	410.0	617.0
2.2	- In swap bodies	...	...	...		-	-	...	201.0	184.0
2.3	- In containers	...	6 651.0	8 019.0	...	162.0	114.0	...	695.0	645.0

		Spain Espagne Испания			Sweden Suède Швеция			Switzerland Suisse Швейцария		
		1990	1998	1999	1990	1998	1999	1990	1998	1999
1	Number of intermodal transport units forwarded									
1.1	**Goods Road vehicles**	...	...	...	...	51 641	46 010	...	...	...
1.11	- Accompanied	...	...	...	...	-	-	...	...	...
1.12	- Unaccompanied	...	...	...	...	51 641	46 010	...	...	...
1.2	**Swap bodies**	...	...	...	...	100 771	111 413	...	...	...
1.21	- Load	...	...	...	...	83 403	90 370	...	...	...
1.22	- Unloaded	...	...	...	...	17 368	21 043	...	...	...
1.3	**Containers**	3 865	...	...	...	185 426	182 555	288 937	...	...
1.31	- Twenty-foot	...	...	...	...	56 622	50 517	...	...	...
1.32	- Thirty-foot	...	...	...	...	6 646	6 670	...	...	...
1.33	- Forty-foot	...	...	...	...	122 158	125 368	...	...	...
2	Goods carried in intermodal transport unit (1000 tonnes)									
2.1	- In goods road vehicles	...	...	...	...	1 204.0	1 079.0	...	...	...
2.2	- In swap bodies	...	...	...	...	1 267.0	1 424.0	...	...	...
2.3	- In containers	...	...	...	...	2 055.0	2 082.0	4 187.0	...	...

INTERMODAL TRANSPORT - TRANSPORT INTERMODAL
ИНТЕРМОДАЛЬНЫЕ ПЕРЕВОЗКИ

21. Intermodal transport including railway transport

21. Transport intermodal par chemin de fer

21. Интермодальные перевозки, в т.ч. по железным дорогам

		Ukraine Ukraine Украина			United States Etats-Unis Соединенные Штаты					
		1990	1998	1999	1990	1998	1999			
1	**Number of intermodal transport units forwarded**									
1.1	**Goods Road vehicles**	...	...	...	...	...	...			
1.11	- Accompanied	...	...	...	...	...	...			
1.12	- Unaccompanied	...	...	...	3 451 953	3 353 032	3 298 024			
1.2	**Swap bodies**	...	...	...	...	...	...			
1.21	- Load	...	...	...	...	...	...			
1.22	- Unloaded	...	...	...	...	...	...			
1.3	**Containers**	540 598	...	...	2 754 829	5 419 631	5 743 747			
1.31	- Twenty-foot	...	...	...	...	...	...			
1.32	- Thirty-foot	...	...	...	...	...	...			
1.33	- Forty-foot	...	...	...	...	...	...			
2	**Goods carried in intermodal transport unit (1000 tonnes)**									
2.1	- In goods road vehicles	...	...	...	...	...	...			
2.2	- In swap bodies	...	...	...	...	...	...			
2.3	- In containers	10 050.0	...	...	...	...	...			

INTERMODAL TRANSPORT - TRANSPORT INTERMODAL
ИНТЕРМОДАЛЬНЫЕ ПЕРЕВОЗКИ

22. Intermodal transport including maritime transport
22. Transport intermodal comportant un voyage maritime
22. Интермодальные перевозки, включая морские перевозки

Item Rubrique Статья	Description	Description	Описание
1	Number of intermodal transport units forwarded	Nombre d'unités de transport intermodal expédiées	Число отправленных интермодальных транспортных единиц
1.1	Goods Road vehicles	Véhicules routiers	Грузовые автодорожные транспортные средства
1.11	- Accompanied	- Accompagnés	- Сопровождаемые
1.111	- Loaded on ships	- Chargés sur les navires	- Погружено на суда
1.112	- Unloaded from ships	- Déchargés des navires	- Выгружено с судов
1.12	- Unaccompanied	- Non-accompagnés	- Несопровождаемые
1.121	- Loaded onto ships	- Chargés sur les navires	- Погружено на суда
1.122	- Unloaded from ships	- Déchargés des navires	- Выгружено с судов
1.2	Containers	Conteneurs	Контейнеры
1.21	- Containers with goods	- Conteneurs pleins	- Груженые контейнеры
1.211	- Loaded on ships	- Chargés sur les navires	- Погружено на суда
1.212	- Unloaded from ships	- Déchargés des navires	- Выгружено с судов
1.22	- Empty containers	- Conteneurs vides	- Порожние контейнеры
1.221	- Loaded on ships	- Chargés sur les navires	- Погружено на суда
1.222	- Unloaded from ships	- Déchargés des navires	- Выгружено с судов
2	Goods carried in intermodal transport unit (1000 tonnes)	Marchandises transportées dans les unités de transport intermodal (1000 tonnes)	Грузы, перевезенные грузы интермодальными транспортными средствами (1000 тонн)
2.1	In goods road vehicles	En véhicules routiers	Грузовыми автодорожными транспортными средствами
2.11	- Loaded on ships	- Chargés sur les navires	- Погружено на суда
2.12	- Unloaded from ships	- Déchargés des navires	- Выгружено с судов
2.2	In containers	En conteneurs	В контейнерах
2.21	- Loaded on ships	- Chargés sur les navires	- Погружено на суда
2.22	- Unloaded from ships	- Déchargés des navires	- Выгружено с судов

INTERMODAL TRANSPORT - TRANSPORT INTERMODAL
ИНТЕРМОДАЛЬНЫЕ ПЕРЕВОЗКИ

22. Intermodal transport including maritime transport
22. Transport intermodal comportant un voyage maritime
22. Интермодальные перевозки, включая морские перевозки

		Belgium Belgique Бельгия			Bulgaria Bulgarie Болгария			Canada Canada [1] Канада		
		1990	1998	1999	1990	1998	1999	1990	1998	1999
1	Number of intermodal transport units forwarded									
1.1	**Goods Road vehicles**	...	...	...	...	...	...	-	-	...
1.11	- Accompanied	...	...	...	...	...	...	-	-	...
1.111	- Loaded on ships	...	...	...	...	...	...	-		...
1.112	- Unloaded on ships	...	...	...	...	...	...	-		...
1.12	- Unaccompanied	...	...	...	...	...	...	-		...
1.121	- Loaded on ships	...	...	...	...	...	...	-		...
1.122	- Unloaded on ships	...	...	...	...	...	...	-		...
1.2	**Containers**	**1 405 729**	...	...	...	18 513	10 484	1 102 477	1 954 154	...
1.21	- Containers with goods	1 149 210	...	...	...	15 346	8 584	119 466	167 784	...
1.211	- Loaded on ships	634 407	...	...	...	8 014	5 925	33 604	111 887	...
1.212	- Unloaded on ships	514 803	...	...	...	7 332	2 659	85 862	55 897	...
1.22	- Empty containers	256 519	...	...	...	3 167	1 900	983 011	1 786 370	...
1.221	- Loaded on ships	73 429	...	...	...	1 197	-	565 679	782 954	...
1.222	- Unloaded on ships	183 090	...	...	...	1 970	1 900	417 332	1 003 416	...
2	Goods carried in intermodal transport unit (1000 tonnes)									
2.1	**In goods road vehicles**	**19 969.0**	...	...	...	...	...	-	-	...
2.11	- Loaded on ships	11 174.0	...	...	...	...	...	-	-	...
2.12	- Unloaded on ships	8 795.0	...	...	...	...	...	-	-	...
2.2	**In containers**	...	...	...	...	...	...	**12 257.0**	**20 087.0**	...
2.21	- Loaded on ships	...	...	...	...	...	...	7 063.0	11 680.0	...
2.22	- Unloaded on ships	...	...	...	...	...	...	5 194.0	8 407.0	...

		Croatia Croatie Хорватия			Cyprus Chypre Кипр			Denmark Danemark Дания		
		1990	1998	1999	1990	1998	1999	1990	1998	1999
1	Number of intermodal transport units forwarded									
1.1	**Goods Road vehicles**	-	1 001	1 313	5 848	628	238	...	2 328 707	1 882 369
1.11	- Accompanied	-	...	...	5 848	628	238	...	1 929 492	1 544 657
1.111	- Loaded on ships	-	...	...	3 072	252	85	...	950 578	760 161
1.112	- Unloaded on ships	-	...	...	2 776	376	153	...	978 914	784 496
1.12	- Unaccompanied	-	...	...	-	-	-	...	279 708	204 478
1.121	- Loaded on ships	-	...	...	-	-	-	...	139 340	101 998
1.122	- Unloaded on ships	-	...	...	-	-	-	...	140 368	102 480
1.2	**Containers**	45 828	6 303	7 454	375 608	214 030	239 071	...	270 766	292 219
1.21	- Containers with goods	...	4 227	5 334	241 149	138 430	162 560	...	180 662	201 641
1.211	- Loaded on ships	...	1 656	2 454	104 620	43 471	53 046	...	103 713	118 370
1.212	- Unloaded on ships	...	2 571	2 880	136 529	94 959	109 514	...	76 949	83 271
1.22	- Empty containers	...	2 076	2 120	134 459	75 600	76 511	...	90 104	90 578
1.221	- Loaded on ships	...	959	522	82 944	64 965	64 023	...	37 630	31 638
1.222	- Unloaded on ships	...	1 117	1 598	51 515	10 635	12 488	...	52 474	58 940
2	Goods carried in intermodal transport unit (1000 tonnes)									
2.1	**In goods road vehicles**	-	18.0	16.0	63.8	9.6	2.5	...	30 093.0	24 758.0
2.11	- Loaded on ships	-	5.0	7.0	55.6	4.0	1.0	...	14 631.0	12 049.0
2.12	- Unloaded on ships	-	13.0	9.0	8.2	5.6	1.5	...	15 462.0	12 709.0
2.2	**In containers**	251.0	91.0	92.0	2 459.6	1 272.8	1 649.7	...	2 727.0	3 087.0
2.21	- Loaded on ships	...	31.0	47.0	1 071.8	400.6	624.0	...	1 567.0	1 807.0
2.22	- Unloaded on ships	...	60.0	45.0	1 387.8	872.2	1 025.7	...	1 160.0	1 280.0

For note see end of table.   Voir note à la fin du tableau.   См. примечания в конце таблицы.

INTERMODAL TRANSPORT - TRANSPORT INTERMODAL
ИНТЕРМОДАЛЬНЫЕ ПЕРЕВОЗКИ

22. Intermodal transport including maritime transport
22. Transport intermodal comportant un voyage maritime
22. Интермодальные перевозки, включая морские перевозки

		Finland Finlande Финляндия			France France Франция			Germany Allemagne Германия		
		1990	1998	1999	1990	1998	1999	1990	1998	1999
1	Number of intermodal transport units forwarded									
1.1	**Goods Road vehicles**	**268 951**	**559 701**	**565 470**	...	...	...	...	**1 517 171**	**1 574 180**
1.11	- Accompanied	114 153	254 441	259 166	...	...	...	...	1 074 108	1 148 649
1.111	- Loaded on ships	56 645	125 297	127 060					553 623	586 979
1.112	- Unloaded on ships	57 508	129 144	132 106					520 485	561 670
1.12	- Unaccompanied	154 798	305 260	306 304	...	...	...		443 063	425 531
1.121	- Loaded on ships	77 092	152 546	153 865					220 365	213 608
1.122	- Unloaded on ships	77 706	152 714	152 439					222 698	211 923
1.2	**Containers**	**228 116**	**593 773**	**593 853**	**1 186 917**	...	...	...	**5 402 056**	**5 938 972**
1.21	- Containers with goods	...	484 254	483 283	998 517	...	...	...	4 574 569	5 145 857
1.211	- Loaded on ships	...	238 414	238 281	542 405	...	...	...	2 271 684	2 596 929
1.212	- Unloaded on ships	...	245 840	245 002	456 112	...	...	...	2 302 885	2 548 928
1.22	- Empty containers	...	109 519	110 570	188 400	...	...	...	827 487	793 115
1.221	- Loaded on ships	...	64 543	32 438	45 746	...	...	...	402 437	342 173
1.222	- Unloaded on ships	...	44 976	78 132	142 654	...	...	...	425 050	450 942
2	Goods carried in intermodal transport unit (1000 tonnes)									
2.1	**In goods road vehicles**	**3 962.6**	**8 598.0**	**8 550.0**	...	...	...	...	**18 883.0**	**19 525.0**
2.11	- Loaded on ships	2 063.8	4 491.0	4 577.0	...	...	...	...	9 623.0	9 826.0
2.12	- Unloaded on ships	1 898.8	4 107.0	3 973.0	...	...	...	...	9 260.0	9 699.0
2.2	**In containers**	**2 881.9**	**6 394.0**	**6 714.0**	**15 978.6**	...	...	...	**43 865.0**	**49 763.0**
2.21	- Loaded on ships	1 439.2	3 274.0	3 931.0	8 996.5	...	...	...	22 764.0	26 234.0
2.22	- Unloaded on ships	1 442.7	3 120.0	2 783.0	6 982.0	...	...	...	21 101.0	23 529.0

		Ireland Irlande Ирландия			Latvia Lettonie Латвия			Lithuania Lituanie Литва		
		1990	1998	1999	1990	1998	1999	1990	1998	1999
1	Number of intermodal transport units forwarded									
1.1	**Goods Road vehicles**	...	**538 997**	**598 203**	...	...	...	...	**84 110**	**67 168**
1.11	- Accompanied	...	...	...	...	...	...	...	27 768	28 861
1.111	- Loaded on ships	...	...	...	...	...	...	...	12 625	13 772
1.112	- Unloaded on ships	...	...	...	...	...	...	...	15 143	15 089
1.12	- Unaccompanied	...	...	...	...	...	...	...	56 342	38 307
1.121	- Loaded on ships	...	...	...	...	...	...	...	28 296	18 675
1.122	- Unloaded on ships	...	...	...	...	...	...	...	28 046	19 632
1.2	**Containers**	...	**363 979**	**394 197**	...	**138 293**	**90 272**	...	**22 171**	**18 609**
1.21	- Containers with goods	...	306 106	328 994	...	94 775	66 563	...	13 811	12 496
1.211	- Loaded on ships	...	125 908	134 165	...	35 739	31 101	...	3 944	5 825
1.212	- Unloaded on ships	...	180 198	194 829	...	59 036	35 462	...	9 867	6 671
1.22	- Empty containers	...	57 873	65 203	...	43 518	23 709	...	8 360	6 113
1.221	- Loaded on ships	...	44 389	51 962	...	37 343	11 974	...	7 743	3 783
1.222	- Unloaded on ships	...	13 484	13 241	...	6 175	11 735	...	617	2 330
2	Goods carried in intermodal transport unit (1000 tonnes)									
2.1	**In goods road vehicles**	...	**8.0**	**8.0**	...	...	...	...	**945.0**	**845.0**
2.11	- Loaded on ships	...	3.0	3.0	...	...	...	...	372.0	379.0
2.12	- Unloaded on ships	...	4.0	5.0	...	...	...	...	573.0	466.0
2.2	**In containers**	...	**5.0**	**6.0**	...	**1 168.0**	**856.0**	...	**212.0**	**207.0**
2.21	- Loaded on ships	...	2.0	3.0	...	439.0	404.0	...	69.0	107.0
2.22	- Unloaded on ships	...	3.0	3.0	...	729.0	452.0	...	143.0	100.0

INTERMODAL TRANSPORT - TRANSPORT INTERMODAL
ИНТЕРМОДАЛЬНЫЕ ПЕРЕВОЗКИ

22. Intermodal transport including maritime transport
22. Transport intermodal comportant un voyage maritime
22. Интермодальные перевозки, включая морские перевозки

		Malta Malte Мальта			Netherlands Pays-Bas Нидерланды			Poland Pologne Польша		
		1990	1998	1999	1990	1998	1999	1990	1998	1999
1	Number of intermodal transport units forwarded									
1.1	**Goods Road vehicles**	...	11 877	15 932	...	751 617	...	...	...	109 486
1.11	- Accompanied	...	-	-	...	176 748	...	...	...	101 732
1.111	- Loaded on ships	...	-	-	...	82 198	...	...	...	50 635
1.112	- Unloaded on ships	...	-	-	...	94 550	...	...	...	51 097
1.12	- Unaccompanied	...	11 877	15 932	...	574 869	...	...	...	7 754
1.121	- Loaded on ships	...	5 632	1 193	...	288 823	...	...	...	3 739
1.122	- Unloaded on ships	...	6 245	14 739	...	286 046	...	...	...	4 015
1.2	**Containers**	...	80 071	73 997	2 526 000	3 898 258	...	106 980	187 254	136 809
1.21	- Containers with goods	...	...	...	2 163 000	3 250 264	...	75 157	143 930	102 062
1.211	- Loaded on ships	...	...	...	1 126 000	1 625 955	...	47 529	72 857	47 037
1.212	- Unloaded on ships	...	...	...	1 037 000	1 624 309	...	27 628	71 073	55 025
1.22	- Empty containers	...	...	...	363 000	647 994	...	31 823	43 324	34 747
1.221	- Loaded on ships	...	...	...	126 000	280 525	...	9 566	33 738	23 351
1.222	- Unloaded on ships	...	...	...	237 000	367 469	...	22 257	9 586	11 396
2	Goods carried in intermodal transport unit (1000 tonnes)									
2.1	**In goods road vehicles**	...	...	...	...	17 756.0	...	...	1 331.0	1 430.0
2.11	- Loaded on ships	...	...	...	...	9 348.0	...	...	629.0	673.0
2.12	- Unloaded on ships	...	...	...	...	8 408.0	...	...	702.0	757.0
2.2	**In containers**	...	1 938.0	1 770.0	31 942.0	48 242.0	...	1 198.0	2 096.0	2 055.0
2.21	- Loaded on ships	...	593.0	477.0	17 650.0	26 544.0	...	787.0	934.0	1 025.0
2.22	- Unloaded on ships	...	1 345.0	1 293.0	14 292.0	21 698.0	...	411.0	1 162.0	1 030.0

		Portugal Portugal Португалия			Romania Roumanie Румыния			Russian Federation Fédération de Russie Российская Федерация		
		1990	1998	1999	1990	1998	1999	1990	1998	1999
1	Number of intermodal transport units forwarded									
1.1	**Goods Road vehicles**	...	-	-	...	...	...	...	...	...
1.11	- Accompanied	...	-	-	...	...	...	...	...	...
1.111	- Loaded on ships	...	-	-	...	...	...	...	...	...
1.112	- Unloaded on ships	...	-	-	...	...	...	...	...	...
1.12	- Unaccompanied	...	-	-	...	...	...	...	...	...
1.121	- Loaded on ships	...	-	-	...	...	...	...	...	...
1.122	- Unloaded on ships	...	-	-	...	...	...	...	...	...
1.2	**Containers**	...	409 582	166 249	...	92 212	85 173	...	...	...
1.21	- Containers with goods	...	306 395	127 123	...	65 490	62 290	...	...	...
1.211	- Loaded on ships	...	177 904	67 903	...	21 837	29 719	...	...	...
1.212	- Unloaded on ships	...	128 491	59 220	...	43 653	32 571	...	...	...
1.22	- Empty containers	...	103 187	39 126	...	26 722	22 883	...	...	...
1.221	- Loaded on ships	...	23 623	11 147	...	22 520	16 452	...	...	...
1.222	- Unloaded on ships	...	79 564	27 979	...	4 202	6 431	...	...	...
2	Goods carried in intermodal transport unit (1000 tonnes)									
2.1	**In goods road vehicles**	...	-	-	...	...	...	...	...	...
2.11	- Loaded on ships	...	-	-	...	...	...	...	...	...
2.12	- Unloaded on ships	...	-	-	...	...	...	...	...	...
2.2	**In containers**	...	4 685.0	1 947.0	...	607.0	678.0	...	2 858.5	2 389.3
2.21	- Loaded on ships	...	2 679.0	978.0	...	257.0	309.0	...	...	...
2.22	- Unloaded on ships	...	2 006.0	969.0	...	350.0	369.0	...	...	...

22. Intermodal transport including maritime transport
22. Transport intermodal comportant un voyage maritime
22. Интермодальные перевозки, включая морские перевозки

		Slovenia Slovénie Словения			Sweden Suède Швеция			Turkmenistan Turkménistan Туркменистан		
		1990	1998	1999	1990	1998	1999	1990	1998	1999
1	**Number of intermodal transport units forwarded**									
1.1	**Goods Road vehicles**	...	**217 890**	**297 504**	...	**2 025 731**	**2 104 827**	...	**2 374**	...
1.11	- Accompanied	...	8 382	7 994	...	1 489 566	1 543 630	...	2 374	...
1.111	- Loaded on ships	...	4 610	5 196	...	748 443	770 944	...	1 273	...
1.112	- Unloaded on ships	...	3 772	2 798	...	741 123	772 686	...	1 101	...
1.12	- Unaccompanied	...	209 508	289 510	...	536 165	561 197	...	-	...
1.121	- Loaded on ships	...	70 677	72 312	...	270 302	280 671	...	-	...
1.122	- Unloaded on ships	...	138 831	217 198	...	265 863	280 526	...	-	...
1.2	**Containers**	...	**72 826**	**78 204**	...	**875 589**	**941 094**	...	**51**	...
1.21	- Containers with goods	...	56 283	64 003	...	638 281	697 661	...	7	...
1.211	- Loaded on ships	...	28 950	34 572	...	369 099	412 834	...	-	...
1.212	- Unloaded on ships	...	27 333	29 431	...	269 182	284 827	...	7	...
1.22	- Empty containers	...	16 543	14 201	...	237 308	243 433	...	44	...
1.221	- Loaded on ships	...	7 729	6 851	...	55 343	51 961	...	27	...
1.222	- Unloaded on ships	...	8 814	7 350	...	181 965	191 472	...	17	...
2	**Goods carried in intermodal transport unit (1000 tonnes)**									
2.1	**In goods road vehicles**	...	**292.0**	**432.0**	...	**28 005.0**	**28 597.0**	...	**60.2**	...
2.11	- Loaded on ships	...	136.0	186.0	...	14 528.0	14 731.0	...	30.9	...
2.12	- Unloaded on ships	...	156.0	246.0	...	13 477.0	13 866.0	...	29.3	...
2.2	**In containers**	...	**717.0**	**803.0**	...	**7 546.0**	**7 921.0**	...	**0.9**	...
2.21	- Loaded on ships	...	380.0	437.0	...	4 739.0	5 128.0	...	0.6	...
2.22	- Unloaded on ships	...	337.0	366.0	...	2 807.0	2 793.0	...	0.3	...

NOTES TO TABLE 22 - NOTES DU TABLEAU 22 - ПРИМЕЧАНЯ К ТАБЛИЦЕ 22

Country notes - Notes relatives aux pays - Примечания к данным, представляемым странами

1 - Data related to number of containers are expressed in twenty-foot equivalent units (TEU).

1 - Les données relatives au nombre de conteneurs sont exprimées en unités équivalentes de 20 pieds (TEU).

1 - Данные по чоислу контейнров приводятся в двадцатифутовом эквиваленте (ДФЭ).

ANNEX

ANNEXE

ПРИЛОЖЕНИЕ

SELECTED DEFINITIONS FROM THE GLOSSARY FOR TRANSPORT STATISTICS

INTRODUCTION

In February 1991 an Intersecretariat Group on Transport Statistics (IWG) was set up by the EUROSTAT, ECMT, and UN/ECE secretariats with the aim of harmonizing transport statistics at the international level and ensuring the comparability of data collected by each organization. One of the initial projects of TWG was to establish a list of standard definitions for terms used in transport statistics, based on existing glossaries of statistical terms in transport previously issued by the three organizations. The Glossary for Transport Statistics, which contains common definitions, was intended to be used by Governments, moreover, in filling out the Common Questionnaire for Transport Statistics. The Common Questionnaire was developed by the IWG in an effort to reduce the response burden of member countries when submitting their annual transport statistics to the various organizations.

The First Edition of the Glossary for Transport Statistics was published in 1994 in English, French and Russian, and eventually into all of the languages of the European Union. After consultations among the three secretariats, related international organizations (such as International Union of Railways, International Road Transport Union, International Road Federation, International Union of Public Transport, etc.), and representatives from Central Statistical Offices, the Second Edition of the Glossary was finalized. It now includes terminology in the following areas: infrastructure, transport equipment, transport enterprises, traffic, transport measurement and energy consumption in the fields of Rail, Road, Inland Waterway, Oil Pipeline as well as two new chapters: Maritime and Intermodal transport statistics.

Work will continue in the context of IWG on terminology related to accidents, urban and regional transport, and statistics on the environmental impact of the transport, for possible inclusion in future editions of the Glossary. The Glossary for Transport Statistics is available on the Internet/Word Wide Web (WWW.OECD. ORG/CEM).

Notice:
The explanatory notes in italics, given in some cases below the definitions, were intended to assist countries in filling in questionnaires and are not part of the definitions themselves.

RAILWAY TRANSPORT

ENTERPRISES AND EMPLOYMENT

Principal railway enterprise(s) : Enterprise owning and/or operating the largest network(s) in the country. Urban services operated by principal railway enterprises are included. *The following are considered as principal enterprises:*

Albania: Albanian Railways (HSH
Armenia: Armenian Railways (ARM)
Austria: Austrian Federal Railways (OBB)
Azerbaijan: Azerbaijan Railways (AZ)
Belarus: Belarus Railways (BC)
Belgium: Belgian National Railway Company (SNCB/NMBS)
Bosnia and Herzegovina: Bosnian Railways (ZBH)
Bulgaria: Bulgarian State Railways (BDZ)
Canada: Canadian Pacific (CP)
Croatia: Croatian Railways (HZ)
Czech Republic: Ceske Drahy (CD)
Denmark: Danish State Railways (DSB)
Estonia: Estonian Railway (EVR), South-West Railways Ltd
Finland: Finnish State Railways (VR)
France: French National Railway Company (SNCF)
Georgia: Railways of the Republic of Georgia
Germany: German Federal Railway, German State Railway (DB)
Greece: Hellenic Railways Organization (CH)
Hungary: Hungarian State Railways (GYSEV/ROEE - MAV)
Ireland: Irish Transport Company (CIE)
Israel: Israel State Railways (ISR)
Italy: Italian State Railways (FS)
Kazakhstan: Railways of the Kazakhstan Republic (KSH)
Kyrgyzstan: Kyrgystan Railway (KRG)
Latvia: Latvian State Railways (LDZ)
Lithuania: Lithuanian Railways (LG)
Luxembourg: Luxembourg National Railway Company (CFL)

Netherlands: Netherlands Railways (NS)
Norway: Norwegian State Railways (NSB)
Poland: Polish State Railways (PKP)
Portugal: Portuguese Railways (CP)
Republic of Moldova: Moldova Railways (CFM(E))
Romania: Romanian Railways (CFR)
Russian Federation: Ministry of the Railways of the Russian Federation
Slovakia: Zeleznice Slovenskej Republiky (ZSR)
Slovenia: Slovenian Railways (SZ)
Spain: Spanish National Railway system (RENFE)
Sweden: Swedish State Railays (SJ), and Swedish National Rail Administration (BV)
Switzerland: Swiss Federal Railways (CFF)
Tajikistan: Tajikistan Railway (TZD)
The former Yugoslav Republic of Macedonia: Railways of The former Yugoslav Republic of Macedonia
Turkey: Turkish Republic State Railways (TCDD)
Turkmenistan: State Railway of Turkmenistan (TRK)
Ukraine: Ukrainian Railways (UZ)
United Kingdom: British Railways (BR), and Northern Ireland Railways (NIR)
USA: Association of American Railroads (AAR). All class I line-haul railway enterprises (1)
Uzbekistan: Uzbekistan Railways (UTI)
Yugoslavia: Yugoslav Railways (JZ)

(1) - Class I line-haul railways account for some 83 per cent of total route miles and 97 per cent of freight carryings. The statistics should also take account of the operation and traffic of the National Railroad Passenger Corporation (AMTRAK) and the Auto-Train Corporation. The former is responsible for the greater part of inter-city train service on US railways, while the sole function of the latter is to carry passengers and their motor-cars on a non-stop service between Washington D.C. and Sanford, Florida.

Employment : Average number of persons working during the given period in a railway enterprise, as well as persons working outside the enterprise but who belong to it and are directly paid by it.

Statistics should include the staff employed for performing all principal and ancillary activities of the enterprise (railway operation, renewal, new construction, road and shipping services, electricity, generation, hotels and restaurants etc.).

Types of employment : The main categories of employment being considered are:

General administration - *Includes central and regional management staff (e.g. finance, legal, personnel, etc.) and boards of directors. The management staff of specialist departments (operations and traffic, traction and rolling stock, ways and works) are excluded but are taken into account in the statistics specific to each of these services.*

Operations and traffic - *Station staff, train crews (excluding locomotive crews) and associated central and regional offices. Includes tourism and advertising.*

Traction and rolling stock - *Locomotive crews, workshop, inspection staff and associated central and regional offices.*

Way and works - *Permanent way maintenance and supervision staff.*

Other operation - *Passenger and goods road services, shipping services, electric power plants, hotel staff, etc.*

INFRASTRUCTURE

Railway : Line of communication made up by rail exclusively for the use of railway vehicles. *Line of communication is part of space equipped for the execution of transport.*

Railway network : All railways in a given area.

This does not include stretches of road or water even if rolling stock should be conveyed over such routes, e.g. by wagon-carrying trailers or ferries. Lines solely used for touristic purposes during the season are excluded as are railways constructed solely to serve mines, forests or other industrial or agricultural undertakings and which are not open to public traffic.

Track : A pair of rails over which railway vehicles can run.

Track gauge : Distance between a pair of rails measured between the inside edges of the rail heads. The following track gauges are in use:
- Standard gauge: 1.435 m
- Large gauge: 1.524 m (VR,SZR); 1.600 m (CIE, NIR); 1.668 m (RENFE, CP)
- Narrow gauge: 0.60 m, 0.70 m,0.75 m, 0.76 m, 0.785 m, 0.90 m, 1.00 m.

Electrified track : Track provided with an overhead trolley wire or with conductor rail to permit electric traction.

Sidings : Tracks branching off running tracks. *The length of sidings is included in the length of tracks if the sidings belong to the railway system concerned, private sidings being excluded.*

Line : One or more adjacent running tracks forming a route between two points. Where a section of network comprises two or more lines running alongside one another, there are as many lines as routes to which tracks are allotted exclusively.

Average length of line operated throughout the year : The length of line used for traffic throughout the reported year (including lines operated jointly with other railway enterprises) plus the average length of lines opened or closed during the year (weighted by the number of days they have been operated).

The total length of line operated is the length operated for passenger or goods transport, or both. When a line is operated simultaneously by several enterprises it will be counted only once.

Electrified line : Line with one or more electrified running tracks. Sections of lines adjacent to stations that are electrified only to permit shunting and not electrified as far as the next stations are to be counted as non-electrified lines.

TRANSPORT EQUIPMENT (VEHICLE)

Railway vehicle : Mobile equipment running exclusively on rails, moving either under its own power (locomotives and railcars) or hauled by another vehicle (coaches, railcar trailers, vans and wagons).

The following vehicles are included in the statistics for a principal railway enterprise:
(a) *All railway vehicles belonging to the principal railway enterprise and hired by it and actually at its disposal, including those under or waiting for repair, or stored in working or non-working order, and foreign vehicles at the disposal of the system and vehicles of the enterprise temporarily engaged in the normal course of running abroad, or upon secondary railway enterprises' network.*

(b) *Private owners' wagons, i.e. those not belonging to the principal railway enterprise but registered on it and authorized to run on it under specified conditions, together with wagons hired out by the railway enterprise to private persons and being operated as private owners' wagons.*

Statistics for a principal railway enterprise exclude vehicles not at its disposal, i.e.
(a) *Foreign or secondary railway enterprise vehicles temporarily on railway lines of the principal railway enterprise in the normal course of running.*
(b) *Vehicles which are on hire to, or otherwise at the disposal of, other railway enterprises*
(c) *Vehicles reserved exclusively for service transport, or intended for sale, breaking-up or condemning.*

Tractive vehicle : A vehicle equipped with prime mover and motor, or with motor only, intended solely for hauling other vehicles (a "locomotive") or for both hauling other vehicles and for the carriage of passengers and/or goods (a "railcar").

Locomotive : Railway vehicle equipped with prime mover and motor or with motor only used for hauling railway vehicles.

Only vehicles with a power of 110 kW and above at the draw hook are classed as locomotives; vehicles with less power being described as "light rail motor tractors" are excluded. Light rail motor tractor is low power tractive unit used for shunting or for work trains and short-distance or low-tonnage terminal services. The special non-passenger tractive units for high speed trains are included, even when these vehicles are part of an indivisible set.

Steam locomotive : Locomotive, whether cylinder or turbine driven, in which the source of power is steam irrespective of the type of fuel used.

Electric locomotive : Locomotive with one or more electric motors, deriving current primarily from overhead wires or conductor rails or from accumulators carried on the locomotive. A locomotive so equipped which has also an engine (diesel or other) to supply current to the electric motor when it cannot be obtained from an overhead wire or from a conductor rail is classed as an electric locomotive.

Diesel locomotive : Locomotive, the main source of power of which is a diesel engine, irrespective of the type of transmission installed. However, diesel-electric locomotives equipped to derive power from an overhead wire or from a conductor rail are classed as electric locomotives.

Railcar : Railway vehicle with motor constructed for the conveyance of passengers or goods by rail. The definition of the various categories of locomotives (electric, diesel) apply, mutatis mutandis, to railcars.

In motor vehicle statistics, each railcar in an indivisible set is counted separately; in statistics of passenger vehicles and goods vehicles, each body fitted to carry passengers or goods is counted as a unit.

Passenger railway vehicle : Railway vehicle for the conveyance of passengers, even if it comprises one or more compartments or spaces specially reserved for luggage, parcels, mail, etc.

These vehicles include special vehicles such as sleeping cars, saloon cars, dining cars and ambulance cars. Each separate vehicle of an indivisible set for the conveyance of passengers is counted as a passenger railway vehicle.

Coach : Passenger railway vehicle other than a railcar or a railcar trailer.

Railcar trailer : Passenger railway vehicle coupled to one or more railcars.

Carrying capacity of passenger vehicle : The number of seats and berths and the number of authorized standing places available in a passenger vehicle when performing the service for which it is intended.

Van : Railway vehicle without motor forming part of a passenger or goods train and used by the train crew as well as, if need be, for the conveyance of luggage, parcels, bicycles, etc.

Vehicles possessing one or more passenger compartments must not be counted as vans but as passenger carriages. Mail vans, belonging to railway enterprises, are included under vans when they do not have a passenger compartment.

Wagon : Railway vehicle normally intended for the transport of goods. *Railcars and railcar trailers fitted only for the conveyance of goods are included.*

Covered wagon : Wagon characterized by its closed construction (solid sides all the way up and roof) and by the safety it provides for the goods conveyed in it (possibility of padlocking and sealing).

Wagons with opening roof as well as insulated and refrigerated are included.

High sided wagon : Wagon with no roof and with rigid sides higher than 60 cm.

Flat wagon : Wagon without roof or sides, or wagon without roof but with sides not higher than 60 cm, or swing-bolster wagon, of ordinary or special type.

Wagons designed exclusively to carry containers, swap-bodies or goods vehicles are excluded.

TRAFFIC

Railway traffic : Any movement of a railway vehicle on lines operated.

When a railway vehicle is being carried on another vehicle only the movement of the carrying vehicle (active mode) is considered.

Train : One or more railway vehicles hauled by one or more locomotives or railcars, or by one railcar alone, running under a given number or specific designation from an initial fixed point to a terminal fixed point.

A light engine, i.e. a locomotive travelling on its own, is not considered to be a train.

Types of train : The main categories being considered are:

- Goods train: Train made up of one or more wagons and, possibly, vans moving either empty or under load.
- Passenger train: Train for the carriage of passengers composed of one or more passenger railway vehicles and, possibly, vans moving either empty or under load.
- Mixed train: Train composed of passenger railway vehicles and of wagons.
- Other trains: Trains moving solely for the requirements of the railway enterprise, which involve no commercial traffic.

Train-kilometre : Unit of measure representing the movement of a train over one kilometre.

Tractive vehicle-kilometre : Unit of measure representing any movement of a tractive vehicle over a distance of one kilometre.

Tractive vehicles running light and shunting are included.

Gross tonne-kilometre hauled : Unit of measure representing the movement over a distance of one kilometre of one tonne of vehicle and contents excluding the weight of tractive vehicle. *The weight of railcars is included.*

TRANSPORT MEASUREMENT

Rail transport : Any movement of goods and/or passengers using a railway vehicle on a given railway network.

When a railway vehicle is being carried on another rail vehicle only the movement of the carrying vehicle (active mode) is being considered.

National rail transport : Rail transport between two places (a place of loading/embarkment and a place of unloading/disembarkment) located in the same country irrespective of the country in which the railway vehicles were registered. It may involve transit through a second country.

International rail transport : Rail transport between two places (a place of loading/embarkment and a place of unloading/disembarkment) in two different countries. It may involve transit through one or more additional countries.

Rail passenger : Any person, excluding members of train crew, who makes a journey by railway vehicle.

Passenger making a journey by railway operated ferry or bus services are excluded.

Rail passenger - kilometre : Unit of measure representing the transport of one rail passenger by rail over a distance of one kilometre.

The distance to be taken into consideration should be the distance actually run by the passenger on the concerned network. If it is not available, then the distance charged or estimated should be taken into account.

Goods carried by rail : Any goods moved by rail vehicles.

This includes all packaging and equipment, such as containers, swap-bodies or pallets as well as road goods vehicles carried by rail.

Tonne-kilometre by rail : Unit of measure of goods transport which represents the transport of one tonne of goods by rail over a distance of one kilometre.

Goods loaded : Goods placed on a rail vehicle and dispatched by rail.

Unlike in road and inland waterway transport, transshipments from one rail vehicle to another and change of tractive vehicle are not regarded as loading after unloading.

Goods unloaded : Goods taken off a rail vehicle after transport by rail.

Unlike in road and inland waterway transport, transshipments from one rail vehicle to another and change of tractive vehicle are not regarded as unloading before reloading.

International - loaded
Goods having left the country by rail (other than goods in transit by rail throughout) : Goods loaded on a reporting railway network and transported by rail to be unloaded in a foreign country.

Wagons loaded on a railway network and carried by ferry to a foreign network are included.

International - unloaded
Goods having entered the country by rail (other than goods in transit by rail throughout) : Goods loaded on a foreign railway network and transported by rail on the reporting railway network for unloading in the country of this reporting network.

Wagons loaded on a foreign railway network and carried by ferry to the reporting network are included.

Goods in transit by rail throughout : Goods loaded on a foreign railway network for a destination on a foreign railway network which are transported on the reporting railway network.

Wagons entering and/or leaving the reporting network by ferry are included.

ROAD TRANSPORT

INFRASTRUCTURE

Road : Line of communication (travelled way) using a stabilized base other than rails or air strips open to public traffic, primarily for the use of road motor vehicles running on their own wheels.

Included are bridges, tunnels, supporting structures, junctions, crossings and interchanges. Toll roads are also included. Excluded are dedicated cycle paths.

Category of road (state roads, provincial roads, local roads) : Classification of the road network according to:

(a) administration responsible for its construction maintenance and/or
(b) according to design standards or,
(c) according to the users allowed to have access on the road.

Motorway : Road, specially designed and built for motor traffic, which does not serve properties bordering on it, and which:

(a) is provided, except at special points or temporarily, with separate carriageways for the two directions of traffic, separated from each other, either by a dividing strip not intended for traffic, or exceptionally by other means;
(b) does not cross at level with any road, railway or tramway track, or footpath;
(c) is specially sign-posted as a motorway and is reserved for specific categories of road motor vehicles.

Entry and exit lanes of motorways are included irrespectively of the location of the sign-posts. Urban motorways are also included.

E road : The international "E" network consists of a system of reference roads as laid down in the European Agreement on Main International Arteries, Geneva, 15 November 1975 and its amendments.

TRANSPORT EQUIPMENT (VEHICLES)

Road motor vehicle : A road vehicle fitted with an engine whence it derives its sole means of propulsion, which is normally used for carrying persons or goods or for drawing, on the road, vehicles used for the carriage of persons or goods.

The statistics exclude motor vehicles running on rails.

Stock of road vehicles : Number of road vehicles registered at a given date in a country and licensed to use roads open to public traffic.

This includes road vehicles exempted from annual taxes or license fees; it also includes imported second-hand vehicles and other road vehicles according to national practice. The statistics should exclude military vehicles.

New registration of road vehicle : The registration of a road vehicle for the first time in the reporting country.

This includes both new road vehicles and imported second-hand vehicles registered in the reporting country for the first time.

Age of vehicle : Length of time after the first registration of the road vehicle, irrespective of the registering country.

National road vehicle : A road vehicle registered in the reporting country and bearing registration plates of that country, or having been separately registered (trams, trolleybuses, etc.).

Where registration of a road vehicle does not apply in a specific country, a national road vehicle is a vehicle owned or leased by a company tax resident in that country.

PASSENGER TRANSPORT

Passenger road motor vehicle : A road motor vehicle, exclusively designed or primarily, to carry one or more persons.

Vehicles designed for the transport of both passengers and goods should be classified either among the passenger road vehicles or among the goods road vehicles, depending on their primary purpose, as determined either by their technical characteristics or by their category for tax purposes.

Moped : Two- or three-wheeled road vehicle which is fitted with an engine having a cylinder capacity of less than 50cc (3.05 cu.in) and a maximum authorized design speed in accordance with national regulations.

Motorcycle : Two-wheeled road motor vehicle with or without side-car, including motor scooter, or three-wheeled road motor vehicle not exceeding 400 kg (900 lb) unladen weight. All such vehicles with a cylinder capacity of 50 cc or over are included, as are those under 50 cc which do not meet the definition of moped.

Passenger car : Road motor vehicle, other than a motor cycle, intended for the carriage of passengers and designed to seat no more than nine persons (including the driver).

The term "passenger car" therefore covers microcars (need no permit to be driven), taxis and hired passenger cars, provided that they have fewer than ten seats. This category may also include pick-ups.

Motor-coach or bus : Passenger road motor vehicle designed to seat more than nine persons (including the driver).

Statistics also include mini-buses designed to seat more than 9 persons (including the driver).

Trolleybus : Passenger road vehicle designed to seat more than nine persons (including the driver), which is connected to electric conductors and which is not rail-born.

This term covers vehicles which are sometimes used as trolleybuses and sometimes as buses (since they have an independent motor).

Number of seats/berths in motor coaches, buses and trolleybuses : Number of seats/berths, including the driver's, available in the vehicle when it is performing the service for which it is primarily intended.

In case of doubt, the highest number of seats/berths available should be taken into account.

Tram (street-car) : Passenger road vehicle designed to seat more than nine persons (including the driver), which is connected to electric conductors or powered by diesel engine and which is rail-borne.

GOODS ROAD TRANSPORT

Goods road vehicle : Road vehicle designed, exclusively or primarily, to carry goods.

Vehicles designed for the transport of both passengers and goods should be classified either among the passenger road vehicles or among the goods road vehicles, depending on their primary purpose, as determined either by their technical characteristics or by their category for tax purposes.

Lorry : Rigid road motor vehicle designed, exclusively or primarily, to carry goods.

Includes vans which are rigid road motor vehicles designed exclusively or primarily to carry goods with a gross vehicle weight of not more than 3 500 kg. This category may also include "pick-ups".

Road tractor : Road motor vehicle designed, exclusively or primarily, to haul other road vehicles which are not power-driven (mainly semi-trailers). *Agricultural tractors are excluded.*

Trailer : Goods road vehicle designed to be hauled by a road motor vehicle.

This category exclude agricultural trailers and caravans.

Semi-trailer : Goods road vehicle with no front axle designed in such way that part of the vehicle and a substantial part of its loaded weight rests on the road tractor.

Load capacity : Maximum weight of goods declared permissible by the competent authority of the country of registration of the vehicle.

TRAFFIC AND TRANSPORT

Road traffic : Any movement of a road vehicle on a given network.

When a road vehicle is being carried on another vehicle, only the movement of the carrying vehicle (active mode) is considered.

Road traffic on national territory : Any movement of road vehicles within a national territory irrespective of the country in which these vehicles are registered.

Vehicle-kilometre . Unit of measurement representing the movement of a road motor vehicle over one kilometre.

It includes movements of empty road motor vehicles. Units made up of a tractor and a semi-trailer or a lorry and a trailer are counted as one vehicle.

Road transport : Any movements of goods and/or passengers using a road vehicle on a given road network.

When a road vehicle is being carried on another vehicle, only the movement of the carrying vehicle (active mode) is considered.

National road transport : Road transport between two places (a place of loading/embarkment and a place of unloading/ disembarkment) located in the same country irrespective of the country in which the vehicle is registered. It may involve transit through a second country.

International road transport : Road transport between two places (a place of loading/embarkment and a place of unloading/disembarkment) in two different countries. It may involve transit through one or more additional country or countries.

Road passenger-kilometre : Unit of measure representing the transport of one passenger by road over one kilometre.

A transfer from one road vehicle to another is regarded as disembarkment before re-embarkment.

Goods carried by road : Any goods moved by road goods vehicles

This includes all packaging and equipment such as containers, swap-bodies or pallets.

Tonne-kilometre by road (of goods carried) : Unit of measure of goods transport which represents the transport of one tonne by road over one kilometre.

Goods loaded : Goods placed on a road vehicle and dispatched by road.

Transshipment from one goods road vehicle to another or change of the road tractor are regarded as loading after unloading.

Goods unloaded : Goods taken off a road vehicle after transport by road.

Transshipment from one goods road vehicle to another or change of the road tractor are regarded as unloading before reloading.

International – loaded
Goods having left the country by road (other than goods in transit by road throughout) : Goods which having been loaded on a road vehicle in the country, left the country by road and were unloaded in another country.

International - unloaded
Goods having entered the country by road (other than goods in transit by road throughout) : Goods which, having been loaded on a road vehicle in another country, entered the country by road and were unloaded there.

Road cabotage transport : National road transport performed by a road motor vehicle registered in another country.

Cross trade transport : International road transport performed by a road motor vehicle registered in a third country.

A third country is a country other than the country of loading or than the country of unloading.

Transport for hire or reward : The carriage for remuneration, of persons or goods, on behalf of third parties.

INLAND WATERWAY TRANSPORT

INFRASTRUCTURE

Navigable inland waterway : A stretch of water, not part of the sea, over which vessels of a carrying capacity of not less than 50 tonnes can navigate when normally loaded. This term covers both navigable rivers and lakes and navigable canals.

The length of rivers and canals is measured in mid-channel. The length of lakes and lagoons is measured along the shortest navigable route between the most distant points to and from which transport operations are performed. A waterway forming a common frontier between two countries is reported by both.

Navigable inland waterways regularly used for transport : Waterways over which an amount of transport is performed each year; this amount, expressed as tonne-kilometres per kilometre of waterway, is determined by the authority concerned in the light of conditions prevailing on that country's waterway network.

Navigable river : Natural waterway open for navigation, irrespective of whether it has been improved for that purpose.

Navigable lake : Natural expanse of water open for navigation.

Lagoons (brackish water area separated from the sea by a coastal bank) are included.

Navigable canal : Waterway built primarily for navigation.

TRANSPORT EQUIPMENT (VESSEL)

IWT vessel : Floating craft designed for the carriage of goods or public transport of passengers by navigable inland waterways.

Vessels under repair are included. Vessels suitable for inland navigation but which are authorized to navigate at sea (mixed seagoing and inland waterways vessels) are included. This category excludes: harbour craft, seaport lighters and seaport tugs, ferries, fishery vessels, dredgers, vessels performing hydraulic work and vessels used exclusively for storage, floating workshops, houseboats and pleasure craft.

National IWT vessel : IWT vessel which is registered at a given date in the reporting country.

Where registration of IWT vessels does not apply in a specific country, a national IWT vessel is a vessel owned by a company tax resident in that country.

IWT freight vessel : Vessel with the carrying capacity of not less than 20 tonnes designed for the carriage of freight by navigable inland waterways.

Self-propelled barge : IWT freight vessel having its own means of mechanical propulsion.

Towed barges, pushed barges and pushed-towed barges which have an auxiliary engine only must be regarded as towed barges, pushed barges or pushed-towed barges as the case may be. The fact that a self-propelled barge can be used for towing does not change its nature.

Self-propelled vessel for river-sea navigation : IWT freight vessel having a carrying capacity of at least 20 tonnes also designed for the transport of goods by sea and equipped with their own means of propulsion developing at least 37 Kw.
Dumb barge : IWT freight vessel designed to be towed which does not have its own means of mechanical propulsion.

The act that a dumb barge is fitted with the auxiliary engine does not change its nature.

Pushed barge : IWT freight vessel which is designed to be pushed and does not have its own means of mechanical propulsion.

The fact that a pushed barge is fitted with the auxiliary engine does not change its nature.

Pushed-towed barge : IWT freight vessel which is designed to be either pushed or towed and does not have its own means of mechanical propulsion.

The act that a pushed-towed barge is fitted with an auxiliary engine does not change its nature.

Tug : Powered vessel developing not less than 37 kW and designed for the towing of dumb barges, pushed-towed barges, and rafts, but not for the carriage of goods. *Port and sea tugs are excluded.*

Pusher vessel : Powered vessel developing not less than 37 kW and designed or fitted for the pushing of pushed or pushed-towed barges but not for the carriage of goods. *Port pusher vessels are excluded.*

Pusher tug : Powered vessel developing not less than 37 kW and designed or fitted for the towing of dumb barges, pushed - towed barges, or rafts, and for the pushing of pushed and pushed - towed barges, but not for the carriage of goods.

Carrying capacity : Maximum permissible weight of goods, expressed in tonnes, which a vessel may carry in accordance with its documents.

Power (kW) : Mechanical force developed by the motive power installation in a vessel.

This power should be measured in effective kilowatts (power transmitted to the propeller). 1 kW=36 h.p.; 1 h.p.= 0.735 kW.

Year of construction of vessel : Year of original construction of the hull.

TRANSPORT MEASUREMENT

Inland waterways transport (IWT) : Any movement of goods and/or passengers using an IWT vessel on a given inland waterways network.

When an IWT vessel is being carried on another vehicle, only the movement of the carrying vehicle (active mode) is taken into account.

National inland waterways transport : Inland waterways transport between two places (a place of loading/embarkment and a place of unloading/disembarkment) located in the same country irrespective of the country in which the IWT vessel is registered. It may involve transit through a second country.

International inland waterways transport : Inland waterways transport between two places (a place of loading/embarkment and a place of unloading/disembarkment) located in two different countries. It may involve transit through one or more additional countries.

Goods carried by inland waterways : Any goods moved by IWT freight vessel.

This includes all packaging and equipment such as containers, swap-bodies or pallets.

Tonne-kilometre by inland waterways : Unit of measure of goods transport which represents the transport of one tonne by inland waterways over one kilometre.

Goods loaded : Goods placed on an IWT vessel and dispatched by inland waterways.

Transshipment from one IWT vessel to another is regarded as loading after unloading. The same applies to changes of pusher tugs or tugs.

Goods unloaded : Goods taken of an IWT vessel after transport by inland waterways.

Transshipment from one IWT vessel to another is regarded as unloading before re-loading. The same applies to changes of pusher tugs or tugs.

International - loaded
Goods having left the country by inland waterways (other than goods in transit by inland waterways throughout) : Goods which, having been loaded on an IWT vessel in the country, left the country by inland waterways and were unloaded in another country.

International - unloaded
Goods having entered the country by inland waterways (other than goods in transit by inland waterways throughout) : Goods which, having been loaded on an IWT vessel in another country, entered the country by inland waterways and were unloaded there.

Goods in transit by inland waterways throughout : Goods which entered the country by inland waterways and left the country by inland waterways at a point different from the point of entry, after having been carried across the country solely by inland waterways in the same IWT freight vessel.

Transshipments from one IWT vessel to another and changes of pusher tugs or tugs are regarded as loading/ unloading.

OIL PIPELINE TRANSPORT

INFRASTRUCTURE AND TRANSPORT EQUIPMENT

Oil pipelines : Pipes for the movement of crude or refined liquid petroleum products by pumping.

Branch lines are included as well as oil pipelines between the land and drilling platforms at sea. Excluded are oil pipelines whose total length is less than 50 km or whose inside diameter is less than 15 centimetres and oil pipelines used only for military purposes or located entirely within the site boundaries of an industrial operation, as well as oil pipelines that are entirely off-shore (i.e. located solely out in the open sea). International oil pipelines whose total length is 50 km or more are included even if the section in the reporting country is less than 50 km long. Oil pipelines consisting of two (more) parallel pipelines are to be counted twice (or more).

Only units which actually carry out an activity during the reference period should be considered. "Dormant" units or those not yet having begun their activity are excluded.

TRANSPORT MEASUREMENT

Oil pipeline transport : Any movement of crude or refined liquid petroleum products in a given oil pipeline network.

National oil pipeline transport : Oil pipeline transport between two places (a pumping-in place and a pumping-out place) located in the same country or in that part of the seabed allocated to it. It may involve transit through a second country.

International oil pipeline transport : Oil pipeline transport between two places (a pumping-in place and a pumping-out place) located in two different countries or on those parts of the seabed allocated to them. It may involve transit through one or more additional countries.

Goods transported by oil pipeline : Any crude or refined liquid petroleum products moved by oil pipelines.

Tonne-kilometre by oil pipeline : Unit of measure of transport which represents transport of one tonne of goods by oil pipeline over one kilometre.

International - loaded
Goods having left the country by oil pipeline (other than goods in transit by oil pipeline throughout) : Goods which, having been pumped into an oil pipeline in the country or that part of the seabed allocated to it, left the country by oil pipeline and were pumped out in another country.

International - unloaded
Goods having entered the country by oil pipeline (other than goods in transit by oil pipeline throughout) : Goods which, having been pumped into an oil pipeline in another country or that part of the seabed allocated to it, entered the country by oil pipeline and were pumped out there.

Goods in transit by oil pipeline throughout : Goods which entered the country by oil pipeline and left the country by oil pipeline at a point different from the point of entry, after having been transported across the country solely by oil pipeline.

Goods which entered and/or left the country in question by vessels after pumping into/pumping out of an oil *pipeline at the frontier are included.*

MARITIME TRANSPORT

TRANSPORT MEASUREMENT

International sea transport : Sea transport between two ports (a port of loading/embarkment and a port of unloading/ disembarkment) located in two different countries. *International one port transport is included.*

Cabotage (maritime context) / national sea transport : Sea transport between two ports (a port of loading/embarkment and a port of unloading/disembarkment) located in the same country irrespective of the country in which the seagoing vessel is registered.
Cabotage (maritime context) can be performed by a seagoing vessel registered in the reporting country or in another country. One port transport is included.

Goods carried by sea : Any goods moved by sea. This includes all packaging and equipment such as containers, swap-bodies or pallets.
Mail is included; goods carried on or in wagons, lorries, trailers, semi-trailers or barges are also included.

Conversely, the following items are excluded: road passenger vehicles with drivers, bunkers and stores of vessels, fish landed from fishing vessels and fish processing ships, goods carried internally between different basins or docks of the same port.

Goods loaded : Goods placed on a seagoing vessel and dispatched by sea.

Transshipment from one seagoing vessel to another is regarded as loading after unloading. Goods loaded include national goods, transshipment goods (national or foreign goods arriving in port by sea) and land transit goods (foreign goods arriving in port by road, rail, air or inland waterway).

Goods unloaded : Goods taken off a seagoing vessel after transport by sea.

Transshipment from one seagoing vessel to another is regarded as unloading before re-loading. Goods unloaded include national goods, transshipment goods (national or foreign goods leaving a port by sea) and land transit goods (foreign goods leaving a port by road, rail, air or inland waterway).

INTERMODAL TRANSPORT

Intermodal transport : Movement of goods (in one and the same loading unit or a vehicle) by successive modes of transport without handling of the goods themselves when changing modes.

Vehicle can be a road or rail vehicle or a vessel.

The return movement of empty containers/swap bodies and empty goods road vehicles/trailers are not themselves part of intermodal transport since no goods are being moved. Such movements are associated with intermodal transport and it is desirable that data on empty movements be collected together with data on intermodal transport.

Multimodal Transport :

> ** European Conference of Ministers of Transport (ECMT) defines multimodal transport as the "carriage of goods by at least two different modes of transport". Intermodal transport is therefore a particular type of multimodal transport.*

> ** United Nations Convention on International Multimodal Transport of Goods defines international multimodal transport as "the carriage of goods by at least two different modes of transport on the basis of a multimodal transport contract from a place in one country at which the goods are taken in charge by the multimodal transport operator to a place designated for delivery in a different country;"*

Combined Transport :

> ** UN/ECE used the term combined transport as being identical to the definition for intermodal transport described above, but recently has taken account of the ECMT-definition for combined transport given below.*

> ** According to the rules of application of the ECE/FAL Recommendation No.19 "Code for Modes of Transport" the definition is: "Combined transport: Combination of means of transport where one (passive) transport means is carried by another (active) means which provides traction and consumes energy";*

> ** For transport policy purposes the ECMT restricts the term combined transport to cover: "Intermodal transport where the major part of the European journey is by rail, inland waterways or sea and any initial and/or final leg carried out by road are as short as possible."*

Road accompanied transport : Transport of a complete goods road motor vehicle, accompanied by the driver, by another mode of transport (for example by sea or rail).

Road unaccompanied transport : Transport of goods road motor vehicles or trailers, not accompanied by the driver, by another mode of transport (for example by sea or rail).

EQUIPMENT

Intermodal transport unit (ITU) : Container, swap body or semi-trailer/goods road motor vehicle suitable for intermodal transport.

Container : Special box to carry freight, strengthened and stackable and allowing horizontal or vertical transfers. The technical definition of the container is: "Article of transport equipment which is:

(a) of a permanent character and accordingly strong enough to be suitable for repeated use;
(b) specially designed to facilitate the carriage of goods, by one or more mode of transport, without intermediate reloading;
(c) fitted with devices permitting its ready handling, particularly its transfer from one mode of transport to another;
(d) so designed as to be easy to fill and empty;
(e) stackable; and,
(f) having an internal volume of 1 m^3 or more."

Swap bodies are excluded. Although without internal volume, and therefore not satisfying criterion (f) above, flats used in maritime transport should be considered to be a special type of container and therefore are included here.

Sizes of containers : The main sizes of containers are:

(a) 20 Foot ISO container (length of 20 feet and width of 8 feet);
(b) 40 Foot ISO container (length of 40 feet and width of 8 feet);

(c) Super high cube container (Oversize container); and

(d) Air container (Container conforming to standards laid down for air transportation).

Containers sizes classified under (a) to (c) are referred to as large containers.

Types of containers : The main types of containers, as defined by ISO Standards Handbook on foreign containers are:

1 - General purpose containers;

2 - Specific purpose containers:
   - closed ventilated container;
   - open top container;
   - platform based container open sided;
   - platform based container open sided with complete superstructure;
   - platform based container open sided with incomplete superstructure and fixed ends;
   - platform based container open sided with incomplete superstructure and folding ends;
   - platform (container);

3.- Specific cargo containers:
   - thermal container;
   - insulated container;
   - refrigerated container - (expendable refrigerant);
   - mechanically refrigerated container;
   - heated container;
   - refrigerated and heated container;
   - tank container;
   - dry bulk container;
   - named cargo container (such as automobile, livestock and others); and,
   - air mode container.

TEU (Twenty-foot Equivalent Unit) : Standard unit for counting containers of: various capacities and for describing the capacities of container ships or terminals. One 20 Foot ISO container equals 1 TEU.

One 40 Foot ISO container equals two TEU.

Swap body : Carrying unit strong enough for repeated use, but not enough to be top-lifted or stackable when loaded, designed for intermodal transport of which one leg is road.

Flat : A loadable platform having no superstructure whatever but having the same length and width as the base of a container and equipped with top and bottom corner fittings.

This is an alternative term used for certain types of specific purpose containers - namely platform containers and platform-based containers with incomplete structures.

DEFINITIONS RETENUES DU GLOSSAIRE DES STATISTIQUES DE TRANSPORT

INTRODUCTION

Un Groupe de travail intersecrétariat sur les statistiques de transport (IWG a été constitué en février 1991 par EUROSTAT, la CEMT et la Commission Economique pour l'Europe des Nations Unies (CEE/ONU), dans le but d'harmoniser les statistiques de transport au niveau international et de permettre une meilleure comparabilité des données collectées par chaque organisation. L'un des projets initial de l'IWG.Trans, a été d'établir des définitions communes et normalisées pour les termes utilisés dans les statistiques de transport, sur la base des lexiques déjà utilisés par les trois organisations. Le Glossaire des Statistiques de Transport, qui contient ces définitions communes, est destiné à l'usage des services statistiques nationaux afin de leur permettre de remplir et de compléter le Questionnaire Commun des Statistiques de Transport, également créé par l'IWG dans un souci d'alléger la charge de travail des pays membres.

La première édition du Glossaire des Statistiques de Transport a été publiée en 1994 en Anglais, Français et Russe et, par la suite, également dans la plupart des langues communautaires. Après diverses concertations entre les trois secretariats (tels que l'Union Internationale des Chemins de fer, l'Union Internationale des transports Routiers, la Fédération Routière Internationale, l'Union internationale des Transports Publics...), ainsi que des représentants des offices statistiques nationaux, la seconde édition du Glossaire a été finalisée. Les définitions contenues dans cette édition couvrent les domaines suivants: infrastructures, matériels de transport, entreprises de transport, trafics, mesures du transport et consommation d'énergie. Elles concernent les modes de transports ferroviaires, routiers, par voies navigables intérieures, par oléoducs, ainsi que, innovation par rapport à la précédente édition, deux nouveaux chapitres: maritime et transports intermodaux.

L'IWG prévoit de poursuivre son travail d'harmonisation des définitions dans des domaines tels que les accidentsle transport urbain et régional et l'impact du transport sur l'environnement, afin de les inclure dans les futures éditions du Glossaire. Le Glossaire peut être consulté via le réseau Internet / World Wide Web (WWW.OECD.ORG/CEM).

Avertissement
Les notes explicatives en italiques figurant dans certains cas sous les définitions sont uniquement destinées à aider les pays à remplir les questionnaires et ne font pas partie des définitions elles-mêmes.

TRANSPORTS FERROVIAIRES

ENTREPRISES ET EMPLOI

Entreprise(s) ferroviaire(s) principale(s) : Entreprise possédant et/ou exploitant le ou les réseaux les plus importants dans un pays. Les services urbains effectués par les entreprises ferroviaires principales sont inclus. Les entreprises ferroviaires principales sont les suivantes:

Albanie: Chemins de fer albanais
Allemagne: Chemins de fer fédéraux allemands,Chemins de fer allemands de l'Etat (DB)
Arménie: Chemins de fer arméniens
Autriche: Chemins de fer fédéraux autrichiens (OBB)
Azerbaidjan: Chemins de fer de l'Azerbaijan
Bélarus: Chemins de fer de Belarus (BC)
Belgique: Société nationale des chemins de fer belges (SNCB/NMBS)
Bosnie-Herzégovine: Union des chemins de fer Bosnie-Herzegovine (ZBH)
Bulgarie: Chemins de fer de l'Etat bulgare (BDZ)
Canada: Pacifique canadien (CP)
Croatie: Chemins de fer croates (HZ)
Danemark:: Chemins de fer de l'Etat danois (DSB)
Espagne: Réseau national des chemins de fer espagnols (RENFE)
Estonie: Chemins de fer estoniens (EVR), South -West Railways Ltd
Etats-Unis: Association des chemins de fer américains (AAR) Toutes les entreprises de chemins de fer de classe I (1)
Ex-République yougoslave de Macédoine: Chemins de fer de l'Ex-République yougoslave de Macédoine
Fédération de Russie: Ministère des chemins de fer de la Fédération de Russie
Finlande: Chemins de fer de l'Etat finlandais (VR)
France: Société nationale des chemins de fer français (SNCF)
Géorgie: Chemins de fer de la Republique de Georgie
Grèce: Organisme des chemins de fer hélléniques (CH)
Hongrie: Chemins de fer de l'Etat hongrois (GYSEV/ROEE - MAV)
Irlande: Compagnie des transports irlandais (CIE)

Israël: Chemins de fer de l'Etat israëlien (ISR)
Italie: Chemins de fer de l'Etat italien (FS)
Kazakhstan: Chemins de fer du Kazakhstan
Kirghizistan: Chemins de fer du Kirghizistan
Lettonie: Chemins de fer de l'Etat letton (LDZ)
Lituanie: Chemins de fer lituaniens (LG)
Luxembourg: Société nationale des chemins de fer luxembourgeois (CFL)
Norvège: Chemins de fer de l'Etat norvégien (NSB)
Ouzbékistan: Chemin de fer de la République d'Ouzbékistan
Pays-Bas: Chemins de fer néerlandais (NS)
Pologne: Chemins de fer de l'Etat polonais (PKP)
Portugal: Chemins de fer portugais (CP)
République de Moldova: Chemins de fer de Moldova
République tchèque: Chemins de fer Tchèques (CD)
Roumanie: Chemins de fer roumains (CFR)
Royaume-Uni: Chemins de fer britanniques (BR), Chemins de fer d'Irlande du Nord(NIR)
Slovaquie: Chemins de fer de la République Slovaque (ZSR)
Slovenie: Chemins de fer slovènes (SZ)
Suède: Chemins de fer de l'Etat suédois (SJ) Administration nationale du rail suédois (BV)
Suisse: Chemins de fer fédéraux suisses (CFF)
Tajikistan: Chemin de fer du Tajikistan
Turquie: Chemins de fer d'état de la République turque (TCDD)
Turkménistan: Chemins de fer du Turkmenistan
Ukraine: Chemins de fer ukrainiens (UZ)
Yougoslavie: Communauté des chemins de fer yougoslaves (JZ)

(1) Les réseaux ferroviaires inter-villes de classe I représentent quelque 83% des kilométrages parcourus et 97% des marchandises transportées. Les statistiques devraient aussi tenir compte des opérations et du trafic de la "National Railroad Passenger Corporation - AMTRAK" (Société nationale des transports de voyageurs par chemin de fer) et de la société "Auto-Train". La première de ces deux sociétés assure la plus grande partie du service des trains inter-villes des chemins de fer aux Etats-Unis tandis que le seul but de la seconde est le transport de voyageurs et de leurs automobiles par des trains, sans arrêt commercial en cours de route, entre Washington D.C. et Sandford en Floride.
Emplois : Nombre moyen de personnes travaillant au cours d'une période donnée dans une entreprise ferroviaire, y compris les personnes travaillant à l'extérieur de l'entreprise mais liées à elle par un contrat de travail et rémunérées directement par elle.

Dans les statistiques sont incluses toutes les personnes employées pour les activités principales ou auxiliaires de l'entreprise (exploitation ferroviaire, renouvellement, nouvelles constructions, services routiers et maritimes, production d'électricité, hôtels et restaurants, etc.).

Types d'emploi : Les principaux types d'emploi sont:

Administration générale - *Personnel des services administratifs de la Direction générale et des Directions régionales (i.e. des services des finances, du contentieux, du personnel, etc.) ainsi que l'ensemble des Directeurs. Le personnel administratif des services spécialisés (mouvement et trafic, matériel et traction, installations fixes) est exclu et pris en compte dans les statistiques propres à chacun de ces services.*

Mouvement et trafic - *Personnel des gares, personnel d'accompagnement et de contrôle des trains (à l'exclusion du personnel de conduite) ainsi que le personnel administratif correspondant des services centraux ou régionaux, y compris le personnel des services de tourisme et de publicité.*

Matériel et traction - *Personnel de conduite des véhicules moteurs, personnel des ateliers, personnel d'inspection ainsi que le personnel administratif correspondant des services centraux ou régionaux.*

Installations fixes - *Personnel d'entretien et de surveillance des installations fixes.*

Autres exploitations - *Personnel affecté aux services routiers de voyageurs et de marchandises, aux services de navigation, aux usines électriques, aux services d'hôtellerie, etc.*

INFRASTUCTURES

Chemin de fer : Voie de communication par rail destinée exclusivement à l'usage de véhicules ferroviaires.

Les voies de communication correspondent à la portion d'espace équipé pour la réalisation du transport.

Réseau de chemin de fer : Ensemble des chemins de fer dans une zone considérée.

Les trajets par route ou eau sont exclus quand bien même des véhicules ferroviaires y seraient transportés, par exemple lors de transport de wagons sur remorques ou par transbordeurs (ferries). Les lignes utilisées pour des raisons purement touristiques à des périodes saisonnières sont exclues comme le sont également les chemins de fer construits uniquement pour desservir des mines, des forêts ou d'autres entreprises industrielles ou agricoles, et non ouverts au trafic public.

Voie : Deux rails sur lesquels peuvent circuler des véhicules ferroviaires.

Ecartement de la voie : Distance entre deux rails mesurée entre les bords intérieurs des champignons des rails. Les principaux écartements sont :
- voie normale : 1,435 m
- voie large : 1,524 m (VR, SZR); 1,600 m (CIE, NIR); 1,668 m (RENFE, CP)
- voie étroite : 0,60 m,0,70 m, 0,75 m,0,76 m,0,785 m,0,90 m,1,00 m

Voie électrifiée : Voie pourvue d'un fil de contact aérien ou d'un rail conducteur pour permettre la traction électrique.

Embranchement : Voie bifurquant d'une voie principale.

La longueur des embranchements est comprise dans la longueur des voies si les embranchements font partie du réseau de chemin de fer considéré, les embranchements particuliers étant exclus.

Ligne : Une ou plusieurs voies principales contiguës reliant deux points. Lorsqu'un tronçon de réseau comprend deux ou plusieurs lignes parallèles, on compte autant de lignes qu'il y a d'itinéraires auxquels sont affectées exclusivement les voies.

Longueur moyenne des lignes exploitées au cours de l'année: Longueur de lignes exploitées au cours de l'année considérée (y compris les lignes exploitées en commun avec d'autres entreprises ferroviaires) plus la longueur moyenne des lignes mises en service ou hors service dans le courant de l'année (pondérée en fonction du nombre de jours au cours desquels elles ont été exploitées).

La longueur totale des lignes exploitées est la longueur exploitée pour le transport de voyageurs et/ou de marchandises. Quand une ligne est exploitée simultanément par plusieurs entreprises, elle n'est prise en compte qu'une fois.

Ligne électrifiée : Ligne comportant une ou plusieurs voies principales électrifiées. Les sections de lignes, aux abords des gares, qui sont électrifiées seulement pour permettre des manoeuvres et dont l'électrification ne se continue pas jusqu'à la gare suivante, doivent être comptées dans les lignes non électrifiées.

MATERIEL DE TRANSPORT (véhicules)

Véhicule ferroviaire : Matériel mobile roulant exclusivement sur rails: on distingue les véhicules moteurs (locomotives et automotrices) et les véhicules remorqués/poussés (voitures, remorques d'automotrices, fourgons et wagons).

Dans les statistiques relatives à une entreprise ferroviaire principale sont inclus:

a) Tous les véhicules ferroviaires qui appartiennent à l'entreprise ferroviaire principale, sont pris en location par elle et se trouvent effectivement à sa disposition, y compris les véhicules en cours ou en attente de réparation et les véhicules garés qui sont ou ne sont pas en état de marche, les véhicules étrangers mis à la disposition de l'entreprise et les véhicules de l'entreprise qui, à titre temporaire, circulent normalement à l'étranger ou sur les réseaux d'entreprises secondaires.

b) Les wagons de particuliers, c'est-à-dire les wagons qui n'appartiennent pas à l'entreprise ferroviaire principale, mais sont immatriculés par elle et autorisés à circuler, dans des conditions déterminées, et les wagons donnés en location par l'entreprise ferroviaire principale à des particuliers et exploités sous le régime des wagons de particuliers

Dans les statistiques relatives à une entreprise ferroviaire principale sont exclus les véhicules qui ne se trouvent pas à la disposition de cette entreprise, par exemple :

a) les véhicules étrangers ou les véhicules d'une entreprise ferroviaire secondaire circulant à titre temporaire sur le réseau de l'entreprise ferroviaire principale;

b) les véhicules qui sont donnés en location ou mis d'une autre manière à la disposition d'autres entreprises ferroviaires;

c) les véhicules qui sont réservés exclusivement aux transports de service ou qui sont destinés à la vente, à la démolition ou à la radiation.

Véhicule moteur : Véhicule, soit à force motrice et à moteur, soit à moteur seul, destiné soit à remorquer/pousser d'autres véhicules (locomotive), soit à la fois à remorquer/pousser d'autres véhicules et à transporter des voyageurs et/ou des marchandises (automotrice).

Locomotive : Véhicule ferroviaire, soit à force motrice et à moteur, soit à moteur seul, destiné à remorquer/pousser des véhicules ferroviaires.

Seuls les véhicules d'une puissance égale ou supérieure à 110 kW au crochet sont pris en compte; les véhicules d'une puissance inférieure désignés sous le terme "locotracteurs" sont exclus. Le locotracteur est un engin de traction de faible puissance destiné à des manoeuvres ou à des trains de travaux ainsi qu'à des dessertes terminales de courte distance ou de faible tonnage.
Dans les statistiques de locomotives sont inclus les véhicules moteur spéciaux utilisés pour les trains à grande vitesse et ne transportant pas de voyageurs, même si ces véhicules font partie de rames indéformables.

Locomotive à vapeur : Locomotive à cylindre ou à turbine employant comme force motrice la vapeur, quel que soit le combustible utilisé.

Locomotive électrique : Locomotive pourvue d'un ou plusieurs moteurs électriques actionnés à titre principal par de l'énergie électrique transmise par fil ou par rail, ou provenant d'accumulateurs portés. Les locomotives ainsi équipées qui seraient également pourvues d'une génératrice (diesel ou autre) fournissant du courant au moteur électrique quand celui-ci ne peut s'alimenter à un fil ou à un rail, sont classées comme des locomotives électriques.

Locomotive diesel : Locomotive actionnée à titre principal par un moteur diesel, quel que soit le type de transmission. Toutefois, les locomotives ainsi actionnées qui seraient également équipées pour être actionnées par l'énergie électrique transmise par fil ou par rail, sont classées parmi les locomotives électriques.

Automotrice : Véhicule moteur aménagé pour le transport sur rail de voyageurs ou de marchandises. Les définitions des diverses catégories de locomotives (électriques, diesel) s'appliquent, mutatis mutandis, aux automotrices.

Dans les statistiques des véhicules moteur, chaque automotrice d'une rame indéformable est comptée séparément; dans les statistiques des véhicules de transport de voyageurs ou de marchandises, chaque élément destiné au transport de voyageurs ou de marchandises est compté pour une unité.

Véhicule de transport de voyageurs : Véhicule ferroviaire destiné au transport de voyageurs, même s'il est réservé un ou plusieurs compartiments ou emplacements spéciaux pour les bagages, les colis, la poste, etc.

Sont compris dans ces véhicules, les véhicules spéciaux tels que voitures (wagons)-lits, voitures-salon, voitures-restaurant et voitures sanitaires. Chaque véhicule d'une rame indéformable permettant le transport de voyageurs est compté comme un véhicule de transport de voyageurs.

Voiture : Véhicule ferroviaire de transport de voyageurs autre qu'automotrice et remorque d'automotrice.

Remorque d'automotrice : Véhicule ferroviaire de transport de voyageurs accouplé à une ou plusieurs automotrices.

Capacité de transport d'un véhicule à voyageurs : Nombre de places assises ou couchées et nombre de places debout autorisées dans le véhicule lorsque ce véhicule assure le service auquel il est destiné.

Fourgon : Véhicule ferroviaire sans moteur entrant dans la composition des trains de voyageurs ou de marchandises, et qui est utilisé par le personnel d'accompagnement et pour le transport éventuel de bagages, colis, bicyclettes, etc...

Les véhicules qui comportent un ou plusieurs compartiments pour les voyageurs ne doivent pas être comptés comme fourgons, mais comme voitures. Sont compris dans les fourgons les voitures-poste appartenant aux chemins de fer si elles n'ont pas de compartiment pour les voyageurs.

Wagon : Véhicule ferroviaire normalement destiné au transport de marchandises.

Les automotrices et remorques d'automotrices équipées uniquement pour le transport de marchandises sont incluses.

Wagon couvert : Wagon caractérisé par l'étanchéité de sa construction (parois sur toute la hauteur et toit) et par la sécurité du transport (wagon pouvant être fermé au cadenas ou plombé).

Dans les wagons couverts sont inclus les wagons à toit ouvrant et les wagons isothermes, réfrigérants ou frigorifiques.

Wagon-tombereau : Wagon sans toit fixe et comportant des hausses fixes ayant plus de 60 centimètres.

Wagon plat : Wagon sans toit, sans bords latéraux ou muni de hausses ayant 60 centimètres au maximum, ou wagon à traverses pivotantes. Ces wagons peuvent être de type ordinaire ou spécial.

Les wagons conçus exclusivement pour le transport de conteneurs, de caisses mobiles et de véhicules de transport de marchandises sont exclus.

255

TRAFIC (circulation)

Circulation ferroviaire : Tout mouvement d'un véhicule ferroviaire sur une ligne exploitée.
Lorsqu'un véhicule ferroviaire est transporté par un autre véhicule, seuls les mouvements du véhicule transporteur (mode actif) sont pris en compte.

Train : Un ou plusieurs véhicules ferroviaires remorqués/poussés par une ou plusieurs locomotives ou automotrices, ou bien une automotrice isolée, circulant sous un numéro déterminé ou sous une désignation distincte, d'un point initial fixé à un point terminus fixé. Une locomotive haut le pied, c'est-à-dire circulant seule, n'est pas considérée comme un train.

Types de train : Les principaux types de train sont :
- Train de marchandises : train composé d'un ou plusieurs wagons et éventuellement de fourgons, circulant à vide ou chargés.
- Train de voyageurs : train affecté au transport de voyageurs et composé d'un ou plusieurs véhicules de transport de voyageurs et éventuellement de fourgons, circulant à vide ou chargés.
- Train mixte: train composé de véhicules de transport de voyageurs et de wagons.
- Autres trains : trains circulant exclusivement pour les besoins de l'entreprise ferroviaire, n'assurant aucun trafic commercial.

Train-kilomètre: Unité de mesure correspondant au mouvement d'un train sur un kilomètre.

Véhicule moteur-kilomètre : Unité de mesure correspondant au mouvement d'un véhicule moteur sur une distance d'un kilomètre. Dans les statistiques sont inclus les mouvements haut-le-pied des véhicules moteur ainsi que les mouvements de ces véhicules au cours de manoeuvres.

Tonne-kilomètre brute remorquée: Unité de mesure correspondant au déplacement sur un kilomètre d'une tonne de véhicule ferroviaire et de son contenu, à l'exclusion du poids du véhicule moteur. *Le poids des automotrices est inclus.*

MESURE DU TRANSPORT

Transport ferroviaire : Tout mouvement de marchandises et/ou de voyageurs à bord d'un véhicule ferroviaire sur un réseau ferroviaire donné.
Lorsqu'un véhicule ferroviaire est transporté par un autre véhicule, seuls les mouvements du véhicule transporteur (mode actif) sont pris en compte.

Transport ferroviaire national: Transport ferroviaire entre deux lieux (un lieu de chargement et un lieu de déchargement) situés dans le même pays, quel que soit le pays dans lequel le véhicule ferroviaire est immatriculé; un tel transport peut nécessiter un transit par un second pays.

Transport ferroviaire international: Transport ferroviaire entre deux lieux (un lieu de chargement et un lieu de déchargement) situés dans deux pays différents; un tel transport peut nécessiter un transit par un ou plusieurs autres pays.

Voyageur par chemin de fer : Toute personne, à l'exception du personnel affecté au service du train, qui effectue un parcours dans un véhicule ferroviaire.
Les voyageurs effectuant un parcours par transbordeurs (ferries) ou par autocars exploités par une entreprise ferroviaire sont exclus.

Voyageur-kilomètre par chemin de fer : Unité de mesure correspondant au transport d'un voyageur par chemin de fer sur un kilomètre.
La distance prise en compte est la distance effectivement parcourue par le voyageur sur le réseau considéré. Si ceci n'est pas possible, la distance de taxation ou la distance estimée est prise en compte.

Marchandises transportées par chemin de fer: Toute marchandise déplacée par un véhicule ferroviaire.
Le poids pris en compte inclut la tare des emballages et des conditionnements de transport tels que conteneurs, caisses mobiles et palettes ainsi que les véhicules routiers pour le transport de marchandises transportées par fer.

Tonne-kilomètre par chemin de fer : Unité de mesure correspondant au déplacement par chemin de fer d'une tonne de marchandises sur une distance d'un kilomètre

Marchandises chargées: Marchandises placées sur un véhicule ferroviaire et expédiées par rail.
Les transbordements d'un véhicule ferroviaire à un autre et les changements de véhicules moteurs ne sont pas considérés comme des chargements après déchargement, contrairement à ce qui est retenu pour les transports routiers et les transports par voies navigables intérieures.

Marchandises déchargées : Marchandises débarquées d'un véhicule ferroviaire après avoir été transportées par rail.
Les transbordements d'un véhicule ferroviaire à un autre et les changements de véhicules moteurs ne sont pas considérés comme des déchargements avant rechargement, contrairement à ce qui est retenu pour les transports routiers et les transports par voies navigables intérieures.

Transport international - chargements
Marchandises sorties du pays par rail (autres que les marchandises en transit par rail de bout en bout): Marchandises chargées sur le réseau ferroviaire du pays considéré et transportées par rail pour être déchargées dans un pays étranger.
Les wagons chargés sur un réseau ferroviaire et sortis du pays par transbordeur (ferry) pour être transportés sur un réseau ferroviaire étranger sont inclus.

Transport international - déchargements

Marchandises entrées dans le pays par rail (autres que les marchandises en transit par rail de bout en bout): Marchandises chargées sur un réseau ferroviaire étranger et, après être entrées dans le pays par rail, transportées sur le réseau ferroviaire du pays considéré pour être déchargées dans ce pays.
Les wagons chargés sur un réseau ferroviaire étranger et entrés dans le pays par transbordeur (ferry) pour être transportés sur le réseau ferroviaire du pays considéré sont inclus.

Marchandises en transit par rail de bout en bout : Marchandises chargées sur un réseau ferroviaire étranger et à destination d'un réseau ferroviaire étranger qui sont transportées sur le réseau ferroviaire du pays considéré.
Les wagons entrés et/ou sortis du réseau du pays considéré par transbordeur (ferry) sont pris en compte.

TRANSPORTS ROUTIERS

INFRASTRUCTURES

Route : Voie de communication utilisant une assise stabilisée autre que des rails ou des pistes pour avion, ouverte à la circulation publique et destinée essentiellement à l'usage des véhicules routiers automobiles se déplaçant par leurs propres roues.
Sont inclus les ponts, les tunnels, les autres structures d'appui, les embranchements, les carrefours, les échangeurs. Les routes à péage sont également incluses. Les pistes cyclables spécialisées sont exclues.

Catégories de route : Classification du réseau routier

    a) selon les types définis par l'administration responsable de sa construction, de son entretien et/ou de son exploitation;
    b) selon les normes de construction ou
    c) selon les catégories d'usagers autorisées à l'utiliser.

Autoroute : Route, spécialement conçue et construite pour la circulation automobile, qui ne dessert pas les propriétés riveraines et qui :

    a) sauf en des points singuliers ou à titre temporaire, comporte, pour les deux sens de circulation, des chaussées distinctes séparées l'une de l'autre par une bande de terrain non destinée à la circulation ou, exceptionnellement, par d'autres moyens;
    b) ne croise à niveau ni route, ni voie de chemin de fer ou de tramway, ni chemin pour la circulation de piétons;
    c) est spécialement signalée comme étant une autoroute et est réservée à certaines catégories de véhicules routiers automobiles.
Les voies d'entrée et de sortie des autoroutes sont incluses quel que soit l'emplacement de la signalisation. Les autoroutes urbaines sont également incluses.

Route E : Le réseau international "E" est constitué d'un système de routes repères tel qu'établi par l'Accord européen sur les grandes routes de trafic international, à Genève, en date du 15 novembre 1975, et ses amendements.

MATERIEL DE TRANSPORT (véhicules)

Véhicule routier automobile : Véhicule routier pourvu d'un moteur constituant son seul moyen de propulsion, qui sert normalement au transport de personnes ou de marchandises ou à la traction sur route de véhicules utilisés pour le transport de personnes ou de marchandises.
Les statistiques excluent les véhicules circulant sur rails.

Parc de véhicules routiers : Nombre de véhicules immatriculés à une date donnée dans un pays et autorisés à utiliser les routes ouvertes à la circulation publique. Les véhicules exemptés des taxes annuelles de circulation sont inclus.
Sont inclus également les véhicules d'occasion importés et les autres véhicules routiers selon les pratiques nationales. Les statistiques excluent les véhicules militaires.

Nouvelle immatriculation d'un véhicule routier : Immatriculation d'un véhicule routier pour la première fois dans le pays déclarant.
Les chiffres comprennent à la fois les véhicules routiers neufs et les véhicules d'occasion importés immatriculés pour la première fois dans le pays déclarant.

Age du véhicule routier : Durée écoulée depuis la première immatriculation du véhicule routier, quel que soit le pays d'immatriculation.

Véhicule routier national : Véhicule routier immatriculé dans le pays considéré et portant des plaques d'immatriculation de ce pays, ou ayant fait l'objet d'un enregistrement spécifique (tramway, trolleybus, etc).
Lorsqu'un pays donné n'immatricule pas les véhicules routiers, on entend par véhicule routier national un véhicule appartenant à ou loué par une société ou une personne ayant statut de résident fiscal dans ce pays.

TRANSPORT DES VOYAGEURS

Véhicule routier automobile pour le transport de voyageurs : Véhicule routier conçu exclusivement ou principalement pour le transport d'une ou plusieurs personnes.
Les véhicules conçus pour à la fois le transport de voyageurs et le transport de marchandises sont classés soit parmi les véhicules routiers pour le transport de voyageurs, soit parmi les véhicules routiers pour le transport de marchandises, selon leur destination principale, définie soit par leurs caractéristiques techniques, soit par leur catégorie fiscale.

Cyclomoteur : Véhicule routier à deux ou trois roues qui est pourvu d'un moteur de cylindrée inférieure à 50 cm^3 et dont la vitesse est limitée, par construction, conformément aux réglementations nationales en vigueur.

Motocycle : Véhicule routier automobile à deux roues avec ou sans side-car, y compris les scooters, ou tout véhicule routier automobile à trois roues dont le poids à vide n'excède pas 400 kg. Tous les véhicules de ce genre dont la cylindrée est égale ou supérieure à 50 cm^3 ainsi que ceux dont la cylindrée est inférieure à 50 cm3 mais qui ne relèvent pas de la catégorie des cyclomoteurs sont inclus.

Voiture particulière : Véhicule routier automobile autre qu'un motocycle, destiné au transport de voyageurs et conçu pour un nombre de places assises (y compris celle du conducteur) égal au maximum à neuf.
Le terme "voiture particulière" couvre donc les voiturettes (qui se conduisent sans permis), les taxis et les voitures de location à condition qu'elles aient moins de dix places assises. Cette catégorie peut inclure également les camionnettes "pick-up".

Autocar et autobus : Véhicule routier automobile pour le transport de voyageurs conçu pour un nombre de places assises (y compris celle du conducteur) supérieur à neuf.
Les statistiques incluent aussi les minibus conçus pour plus de 9 places assises (y compris celle du conducteur).

Trolleybus : Véhicule routier pour le transport de voyageurs conçu pour plus de neuf places assises (y compris celle du conducteur), relié à un conducteur électrique et ne circulant pas sur rails.
Ce terme comprend les véhicules utilisés tantôt en trolleybus, tantôt en autobus grâce à un moteur autonome.

Nombre de places assises/couchettes des autocars, autobus et trolleybus : Nombre de places assises ou couchées, y compris la place du conducteur, dans le véhicule lorsqu'il assure le service auquel il est essentiellement destiné.
En cas de doute, le plus grand nombre disponible de places assises ou couchées sera pris en compte.

Tramway : Véhicules routiers pour le transport des voyageurs conçus pour plus de neuf places assises (y compris celle du conducteur), relié à un conducteur électrique ou possédant un moteur diesel et circulant sur rails.

TRANSPORT DES MARCHANDISES

Véhicule routier pour le transport de marchandises : Véhicule routier conçu, exclusivement ou principalement, pour le transport de marchandises.
Les véhicules conçus pour à la fois le transport de voyageurs et le transport de marchandises sont classés soit parmi les véhicules routiers pour le transport de voyageurs, soit parmi les véhicules routiers pour le transport de marchandises, selon leur destination principale, définie soit par leurs caractéristiques techniques, soit par leur catégorie fiscale.

Camion : Véhicule routier automobile rigide conçu, exclusivement ou principalement, pour le transport de marchandises. Cette catégorie inclut les camionnettes, véhicules routiers rigides conçus, exclusivement ou principalement, pour le transport de marchandises, avec un poids maximal autorisé n'excédant pas 3 500 kg. Elle inclut également les camionnettes "pick-up".

Tracteur routier : Véhicule routier automobile conçu, exclusivement ou principalement, pour le remorquage d'autres véhicules routiers non automobiles (essentiellement semi-remorques). *Les tracteurs agricoles ne sont pas inclus dans cette catégorie.*

Remorque : Véhicule routier pour le transport de marchandises conçu pour être remorqué par un véhicule routier automobile.
Les remorques agricoles et les caravanes ne sont pas incluses dans cette catégorie.

Semi-remorque : Véhicule routier pour le transport de marchandises sans essieu avant, conçu de manière à ce qu'une partie du véhicule et une partie importante de son chargement reposent sur le tracteur routier.

Charge utile : Poids maximal de marchandises déclaré admissible par l'autorité compétente du pays d'immatriculation du véhicule.

TRAFIC ET TRANSPORT

Circulation routière : Tout mouvement d'un véhicule routier sur un réseau donné. *Lorsqu'un véhicule routier est transporté par un autre véhicule, seuls les mouvements du véhicule transporteur (mode actif) sont pris en compte.*

Circulation routière sur le territoire national : Tout mouvement d'un véhicule routier à l'intérieur d'un territoire national, quel que soit le pays d'immatriculation de ce véhicule.

Véhicule-kilomètre : Unité de mesure correspondant au mouvement d'un véhicule routier automobile sur un kilomètre.
Les mouvements de véhicules routiers automobiles vides sont inclus. Les ensembles formés par un tracteur et une semi-remorque ou par un camion et une remorque sont comptés comme un seul véhicule.

Transport routier : Tout mouvement de marchandises et/ou de voyageurs à bord d'un véhicule routier sur un réseau routier donné.
Lorsqu'un véhicule routier est transporté par un autre véhicule, seuls les mouvements du véhicule transporteur (mode actif) sont pris en compte.

Transport routier national : Transport routier entre deux lieux (un lieu de chargement/embarquement et un lieu de déchargement/débarquement) situés dans le même pays, quel que soit le pays dans lequel le véhicule routier automobile est immatriculé; un tel transport peut nécessiter un transit par un second pays.

Transport routier international : Transport routier entre deux lieux (un lieu de chargement/embarquement et un lieu de déchargement/débarquement) situés dans deux pays différents; un tel transport peut nécessiter un transit par un ou plusieurs autres pays.

Voyageur-kilomètre par route : Unité de mesure correspondant au transport d'un voyageur par la route sur un kilomètre.

Marchandises transportées par route : Toute marchandise déplacée par un véhicule routier pour le transport des marchandises.
Le poids pris en compte inclut la tare des emballages et des conditionnements de transport tels que conteneurs, caisses mobiles et palettes.

Tonne-kilomètre par route : Unité de mesure correspondant au déplacement par la route d'une tonne de marchandises sur un kilomètre.

Marchandises chargées : Marchandises placées sur un véhicule routier et expédiées par la route.
Les transbordements entre deux véhicules routiers de transport de marchandises ainsi que les changements de tracteurs routiers sont considérés comme des chargements après déchargement.

Marchandises déchargées : Marchandises déchargées d'un véhicule routier après transport par la route.
Les transbordements entre deux véhicules routiers de transport de marchandises ainsi que les changements de tracteurs routiers sont considérés comme des déchargements avant rechargement.

Transport international - chargements
Marchandises sorties du pays par la route (autres que les marchandises en transit par la route de bout en bout) : Marchandises chargées sur un véhicule routier dans le pays, qui ont quitté le pays par la route et ont été déchargées dans un autre pays.

Transport international - déchargements
Marchandises entrées dans le pays par la route (autres que les marchandises en transit par la route de bout en bout) : Marchandises chargées sur un véhicule routier dans un autre pays, qui sont entrées dans le pays par la route et y ont été déchargées.

Cabotage routier.: Transport routier national effectué par un véhicule routier automobile immatriculé dans un autre pays tiers.
Un pays tiers est un pays autre que celui de chargement ou de déchargement.

Transport routier international éffectué par des tiers.: Transport routier international effectué par un véhicule routier automobile immatriculé dans un autre pays.

le compte d'autrui : Transport rénuméré de voyageurs ou de marchandisespour le compte de tiers.

TRANSPORTS PAR VOIES NAVIGABLES INTERIEURES

INFRASTRUCTURES

Voie navigable intérieure : Etendue d'eau ne faisant pas partie de la mer, et sur laquelle des bateaux d'un port en lourd de 50 tonnes au moins peuvent naviguer en charge normale. Le terme s'applique à la fois aux fleuves, rivières et lacs navigables, et aux canaux navigables.
La longueur des fleuves, des rivières et des canaux est mesurée au milieu du chenal. La longueur des lacs ainsi que celle des lagunes correspond à la distance la plus courte séparant les points les plus éloignés l'un de l'autre entre lesquels sont effectués des transports. Une voie navigable constituant une frontière entre deux pays est incluse dans les statistiques de chacun de ces pays.

Voies navigables intérieures régulièrement utilisées pour les transports : Voies d'eau sur lesquelles s'effectue chaque année une quantité minimale de transports; cette quantité, exprimée en tonnes-kilomètres par kilomètre de voie d'eau, est déterminée par l'autorité compétente de chaque pays selon les conditions qui règnent sur le réseau navigable de ce pays.

Fleuve/rivière navigable : Cours d'eau naturel ouvert à la navigation qu'il ait été ou non aménagé à cette fin.

Lac navigable : Etendue d'eau naturelle ouverte à la navigation.
Les lagunes (étendue d'eau saumâtre séparée de la mer par un cordon littoral) sont incluses.

Canal navigable : Cours d'eau construit principalement pour la navigation.

Voies navigables intérieures régulièrement utilisées pour les transports : Voies d'eau sur lesquelles s'effectue chaque année une quantité minimale de transports; cette quantité, exprimée en tonnes-kilomètres par kilomètre de voie d'eau, est déterminée par l'autorité compétente de chaque pays selon les conditions qui règnent sur le réseau navigable de ce pays.

MATERIEL DE TRANSPORT (bateaux)

Bateau pour le transport par voies navigables intérieures : Matériel flottant conçu pour le transport de marchandises ou le transport public de voyageurs par voies navigables intérieures

Sont inclus :
  - *Les bateaux en réparation.*
  - *Les bateaux aptes à la navigation fluviale, mais qui sont autorisés à naviguer sur mer (caboteurs mixtes) sont inclus.*
Sont exclus :
  - *les embarcations de port, les allèges, les remorqueurs des ports maritimes, les bacs, les bateaux utilisés pour la pêche et pour les travaux de dragage ainsi que pour l'exécution de travaux hydrauliques.*
  - *Les bateaux utilisés exclusivement pour l'entreposage, les ateliers flottants, les bateaux d'habitation et les bateaux de plaisance.*

Bateau national pour le transport par voies navigables intérieures : Bateau pour le transport par voies navigables intérieures immatriculé à une date donnée dans le pays considéré.
Lorsqu'un pays donné n'immatricule pas les bateaux utilisés pour le transport par voie navigable intérieure, on entend par bateau national un bateau appartenant à une société ayant statut de résident fiscal dans ce pays.

Bateau pour le transport de marchandises par voies navigables intérieures : Bateau d'un port en lourd minimal de 20 tonnes conçu pour le transport de marchandises par voies navigables intérieures.

Automoteur : Bateau pour le transport de marchandises par voies navigables intérieures pourvu d'un moyen de propulsion mécanique propre.
Les chalands, barges ou chalands-barges n'ayant qu'un moteur auxiliaire sont considérés comme chalands, barges ou chalands-barges, selon les cas. Le fait qu'un automoteur puisse être utilisé pour le remorquage ne change pas sa nature.
Automoteur de navigation fleuve-mer: Bateau pour le transport de marchandises par voies navigables intérieures d'un port en lourd d'au moins 20 tonnes, conçu également pour le transport de marchandise par mer et pourvu d'un moyen de propulsion mécanique propre. d'une puissance d'au moins 37kW

Chaland : Bateau pour le transport de marchandises par voies navigables intérieures destiné à être remorqué et non muni d'un moyen de propulsion mécanique propre. Le fait qu'un chaland soit équipé d'un moteur auxiliaire ne change pas sa nature.

Barge : Bateau pour le transport de marchandises par voies navigables intérieures destiné à être poussé et non muni d'un moyen de propulsion mécanique propre. *Le fait qu'une barge soit équipée d'un moteur auxiliaire ne change pas sa nature.*

Chaland-barge : Bateau pour le transport de marchandises par voies navigables intérieures destiné à être soit poussé, soit remorqué et non muni d'un moyen de propulsion mécanique propre. *Le fait qu'un chaland-barge soit équipé d'un moteur auxiliaire ne change pas sa nature.*

Remorqueur : Bateau pourvu d'une force motrice développant au moins 37 kW et conçu ou aménagé pour la traction de chalands, de chalands-barges ou de radeaux, mais non pour le transport de marchandises. *Les remorqueurs portuaires et maritimes sont exclus.*

Pousseur : Bateau pourvu d'une force motrice développant au moins 37 kW et conçu ou aménagé pour le poussage de barges ou de chalands-barges, mais non pour le transport de marchandises. *Les pousseurs portuaires sont exclus.*

Remorqueur-pousseur : Bateau pourvu d'une force motrice développant au moins 37 kW et conçu ou aménagé pour la traction de chalands, de chalands-barges ou de radeaux, et pour le poussage de barges ou de chalands-barges, mais non pour le transport de marchandises.

Port en lourd : Poids de marchandises maximum autorisé, exprimé en tonnes, qu'un bateau peut transporter d'après les documents de bord.

Puissance (kW) : Puissance mécanique développée par la force motrice de propulsion dont sont pourvus les bateaux.
La puissance est mesurée en kilowatts effectifs (puissance développée à l'hélice) : 1 kW = 1,36 CV; 1 CV = 0,735 kW.

Année de construction du bateau : Année d'achèvement de la construction de la coque d'origine.

MESURE DU TRANSPORT

Transport par voies navigables intérieures : Tout mouvement de marchandises et/ou de voyageurs à bord d'un bateau de navigation intérieure sur un réseau de voies navigables intérieures donné.
Lorsqu'un bateau de navigation intérieure est transporté par un autre véhicule, seuls les mouvements du véhicule transporteur (mode actif) sont pris en compte.

Transport national par voies navigables intérieures : Transport par voies navigables intérieures entre deux lieux (un lieu de chargement/embarquement et un lieu de déchargement/ débarquement) situés dans le même pays, quel que soit le pays d'immatriculation du bateau de navigation intérieure; un tel transport peut nécessiter un transit par un second pays.

Transport international par voies navigables intérieures: Transport par voies navigables intérieures entre deux lieux (un lieu de chargement/embarquement et un lieu de déchargement/ débarquement) situés dans deux pays différents; un tel transport peut nécessiter un transit par un ou plusieurs autres pays.

Marchandise transportée par voies navigables intérieures : Toute marchandise déplacée par un bateau pour le transport de marchandises par voies navigables intérieures.
Le poids pris en compte inclut la tare des emballages et les conditionnements de transport tels que conteneurs, caisses mobiles et palettes.

Tonne-kilomètre par voies navigables intérieures : Unité de mesure correspondant au déplacement par voies navigables d'une tonne de marchandises sur un kilomètre.

Marchandises chargées : Marchandises placées sur un bateau de navigation intérieure et transportées par voies navigables intérieures.
Les transbordements d'un bateau de navigation intérieure à un autre sont considérés comme des chargements après déchargement. Il en est de même des changements de pousseurs ou remorqueurs.

Marchandises déchargées : Marchandises déchargées d'un bateau de navigation intérieure après avoir été transportées par voies navigables intérieures.
Les transbordements d'un bateau de navigation intérieure à un autre sont considérés comme des déchargements avant rechargement. Il en est de même des changements de pousseurs ou remorqueurs.

Transport international - chargements
Marchandises sorties du pays par voies navigables intérieures (autres que les marchandises en transit par voies navigables intérieures de bout en bout) : Marchandises chargées sur un bateau de navigation intérieure dans le pays, qui ont quitté le pays par voies navigables intérieures et ont été déchargées dans un autre pays.

Marchandises entrées dans le pays par voies navigables intérieures (autres que les marchandises en transit par voies navigables intérieures de bout en bout) : Marchandises chargées sur un bateau de navigation intérieures dans un autre pays, qui sont entrées dans le pays par voies navigables intérieures et y ont été déchargées.

Transport international - déchargements
Marchandises en transit par voies navigables intérieures de bout en bout : Marchandises qui entrent dans le pays par voies navigables intérieures et quittent le pays par voies navigables intérieures en un point différent de leur point d'entrée, après avoir été transportées à travers le pays uniquement par voies navigables intérieures, dans le même bateau pour le transport de marchandises par voies navigables intérieures. *Les transbordements entre deux bateaux de navigation intérieure ainsi que les changements de pousseurs ou remorqueurs sont considérés comme des chargements/déchargements.*

TRANSPORT PAR OLEODUCS

INFRASTRUCTURE ET MATERIEL DE TRANSPORT

Oléoducs : Canalisations permettant l'acheminement par pompage de produits pétroliers liquides bruts ou raffinés.

Les embranchements sont inclus ainsi que les oléoducs reliant la terre ferme aux plates-formes de forage en mer.

Sont exclus les oléoducs dont la longueur totale est inférieure à 50 kilomètres ou dont le diamètre intérieur est inférieur à 15 cm. Sont également exclus tous les oléoducs utilisés à des fins uniquement militaires ou entièrement situés dans les limites de sièges d'exploitation industrielle ainsi que les oléoducs purement offshores (c'est-à-dire situés uniquement en haute mer).

Les oléoducs internationaux dont la longueur totale est de 50 km ou plus, sont inclus même si la partie installée dans le pays considéré est inférieure à 50 km.

Les oléoducs se composant de deux canalisations (ou plus) posées en parallèle sont comptés deux fois (ou plus le cas échéant).

Seules doivent être prises en compte les unités réellement actives pendant la période de référence. Les unités "dormantes" ou qui ne sont pas encore entrées en activité ne sont pas concernées

MESURE DU TRANSPORT

Transport par oléoducs : Tout mouvement de produits pétroliers liquides bruts ou raffinés sur un réseau d'oléoducs donné.

Transport national par oléoducs : Transport par oléoducs entre deux lieux (un lieu de chargement et un lieu de déchargement) situés dans le même pays ou sur le secteur du fond marin qui lui a été concédé; un tel transport peut nécessiter un transit par un second pays.

Transport international par oléoducs : Transport par oléoducs entre deux lieux (un lieu de chargement et un lieu de déchargement) situés dans deux pays différents ou sur les secteurs du fond marin qui leur ont été concédés; un tel transport peut nécessiter un transit par un ou plusieurs autres pays.

Marchandise transportée par oléoducs : Tout produit pétrolier liquide brut ou raffiné acheminé par oléoducs.

Tonne-kilomètre par oléoducs : Unité de mesure correspondant au transport par oléoducs d'une tonne de marchandises sur un kilomètre.

Transport international - chargements
Marchandises sorties du pays par oléoducs (autres que les marchandises en transit par oléoducs de bout en bout) : Marchandises chargées dans un oléoduc dans le pays ou le secteur du fond marin qui lui a été concédé, qui ont quitté le pays par oléoducs et ont été déchargées dans un autre pays.

Transport international - déchargements
Marchandises entrées dans le pays par oléoducs (autres que les marchandises en transit par oléoducs de bout en bout) : Marchandises chargées dans un oléoduc dans un autre pays ou sur le secteur du fond marin qui lui a été concédé, qui sont entrées dans le pays par oléoducs et y ont été déchargées.

Marchandises en transit par oléoducs de bout en bout : Marchandises qui entrent dans le pays par oléoducs et quittent le pays par oléoducs en un point différent de leur point d'entrée, après avoir été transportées à travers le pays uniquement par oléoducs.
Les marchandises entrées et/ou sorties du pays considéré par bateaux avec chargement/déchargement dans/d'un oléoduc au point frontière sont incluses.

TRANSPORT MARITIME

MESURE DU TRANSPORT

Transport international par mer: Transport par mer entre deux ports (un port de chargement (ou embarquement) et un port de déchargement (ou débarquement)) situés dans deux pays différents. *Le transport international lié à un seul port est inclus*

Cabotage (maritime)/transport maritime national : Transport par mer entre deux ports (port de chargement (ou embarquement) et port de déchargement (ou débarquement)) situés dans le même pays, quel que soit le pays d'immatriculation du navire.

Le cabotage (maritime) peut être effectué par un navire immatriculé dans le pays déclarant ou dans un autre pays. Le transport lié à un seul port est inclus

175. Marchandise transportée par mer : Toute marchandise déplacée en transport maritime.

Sont inclus :
- Les emballages et les équipements tels que conteneurs, caisses mobiles et palettes
- Les véhicules routiers ou ferroviaires pour le transport de marchandises transportées par mer.

Sont exclus :
- Les véhicules routiers de transport de voyageurs acheminés par transbordeurs (ferries) maritimes lorsque ces véhicules sont accompagnés.
- Les soutes et approvisionnements de navires se déplaçant à la surface de la mer, le poisson déchargé des navires de pêche et des navires de traitement ou de transport de poisson.
- Les marchandises transportées par mouvements internes entre différents bassins ou annexes d'un même port.

Marchandises chargées : Marchandises placées sur un navire et transportées par mer.

Le transbordement d'un navire à un autre est concidéré comme chargement après déchargement.

Les marchandises chargées incluent les marchandises nationales, les marchandises transbordées (marchandises nationales ou étrangères arrivant au port par mer) et les marchandises en transit terrestre (marchandises étrangères arrivant au port par route, par chemin de fer, par voie aérienne ou par voie navigable).

Marchandises déchargées : Marchandises déchargées d'un navire après avoir été transportées par mer.

Le transbordement d'un navire à un autre est concidéré comme déchargement avant chargement.

Les marchandises déchargées incluent les marchandises nationales, les marchandises transbordées (marchandises nationales ou étrangères quittant un port par mer) et les marchandises en transit terrestre (marchandises étrangères quittant un port par route, par chemin de fer, par voie aérienne ou par voie navigable).

TRANSPORT INTERMODAL

Transport intermodal : Mouvement de marchandises (sur une même unité de charge ou sur un même véhicule) par différents modes de transport successifs sans qu'il y ait manutention des marchandises elles-mêmes lors du changement de mode.

Le véhicule peut être un véhicule routier ou ferroviaire, ou un bateau.

Le voyage de retour des conteneurs ou caisses mobiles vides et des véhicules routiers et remorques de transport de marchandises vides ne relève pas du transport intermodal, car il n'est pas alors transporté de marchandises. Ce voyage cependant est lié au transport intermodal, et il est donc souhaitable de rassembler des données sur les mouvements à vide en même temps que des données sur ce dernier.

Transport multimodal :

    *La Conférence européenne des Ministres des transports (CEMT) définit le transport multimodal comme: "transport de marchandises par au moins deux modes de transport différents". Le transport intermodal est donc un type particulier de transport multimodal

    *La Convention des Nations Unies sur le transport multimodal international de marchandises définit le transport multimodal international comme : "transport de marchandises effectué par au moins deux modes de transport différents, en vertu d'un contrat de transport multimodal, à partir d'un lieu situé dans un pays où les marchandises sont prises en charge par l'entrepreneur de transport multimodal jusqu'au lieu désigné pour la livraison dans un pays différent".

Transport combiné :

    *La CEE/ONU utilise le terme "transport combiné" dans un sens identique à celui de transport intermodal (voir plus haut);

    *D'après les règles d'application de la Recommandation No 19 "Code des modes de transport" du Groupe de travail de la facilitation des procédures du commerce international de la CEE, la définition de ce terme est : "transport combiné : combinaison de moyens de transport dans laquelle un moyen de transport (passif) est transporté sur un autre (actif) qui assure la traction et consomme de l'énergie";

    Aux fins de la politique de transport, la CEMT limite la signification du terme "transport combiné" au champ suivant : "Transport intermodal dans lequel la majeure partie du voyage en Europe s'effectue par chemin de fer, par voie navigable intérieure ou par mer et où les trajets de départ et d'arrivée exécutés par route sont aussi courts que possible".

Transport accompagné : Le transport d'un ensemble routier complet, accompagné de son conducteur, par un autre mode de transport (par exemple mer ou chemin de fer).

Transport non accompagné : Transport de véhicules routiers ou de parties de véhicules, sans présence du conducteur, par un autre mode de transport (par exemple mer ou rail).

EQUIPEMENT

Unité de transport intermodal (UTI) : Conteneur, caisse mobile ou semi-remorque/véhicule routier pour le transport de marchandises adapté au transport intermodal.

Conteneur : Caisse conçue pour le transport de marchandises, renforcée, empilable et pouvant être transbordée horizontalement ou verticalement. La définition technique du conteneur est: "elément d'équipement de transport:
    a) de caractère durable et conséquemment assez solide pour supporter des utilisations multiples;

b) conçu de manière à faciliter le transport de biens par un ou plusieurs modes de transport sans rupture de charge;

c) équipé d'accessoires permettant une manutention simple et tout particulièrement le transfert d'un mode de transport à un autre;

d) conçu de manière à être rempli et déchargé;

e) empilable et,

f) ayant un volume intérieur de 1m^3 ou plus".

Les caisses mobiles sont exclues. Quoique sans volume intérieur, et ne satisfaisant donc pas au critère (f) ci-dessus, les "flats", qui sont utilisés en transport maritime, doivent être considérés comme des conteneurs spéciaux, et sont donc inclus ici.

Tailles des conteneurs : Les tailles des conteneurs sont:

a) conteneur ISO de 20 pieds (longueur de 20 pieds et largeur de 8 pieds);

b) conteneur ISO de 40 pieds (longueur de 40 pieds et largeur de 8 pieds);

c) conteneur de très grande capacité (conteneur surdimensionné);

d) conteneur aérien: conteneur adapté aux normes de la navigation aérienne.

les tailles de conteneurs a) à c) sont des "grands conteneurs".

Types de conteneurs : Les principaux types de conteneurs, selon le Recueil de normes ISO "Conteneurs pour le transport de marchandises", sont les suivants :

1. Conteneurs pour usage général;
2. Conteneurs pour usage spécifique
   - conteneur aéré fermé;
   - conteneur à toit ouvert;
   - conteneur type plate-forme à parois latérales ouvertes;
   - conteneur type plate-forme à parois latérales ouvertes et superstructure complète;
   - conteneur type plate-forme à superstructure incomplète et extrémités fixes;
   - conteneur plate-forme à superstructure incomplète et extrémités repliables;
   - conteneur plate-forme.
3. Conteneurs pour marchandises spécifiques
   - conteneur à caractéristiques thermiques;
   - conteneur isotherme;
   - conteneur réfrigéré (à réfrigérant renouvelable);
   - conteneur réfrigéré mécaniquement;
   - conteneur chauffé;
   - conteneur réfrigéré et chauffé;
   - conteneur-citerne;
   - conteneur pour marchandises solides en vrac;
   - conteneur spécialisé;
   - conteneur aérien.

Equivalent 20 pieds (Equivalent Vingt Pieds/Twenty foot Equivalent Unit): Unité pour mesurer un nombre de conteneurs, de différentes longeurs, notamment en fonction de la capacité de logement des navires spécialisés ou des terminaux. Un conteneur ISO de 20 pieds correspond à 1 EVP/TEU. *Un conteneur ISO de 40 pieds correspond à deux EVP/TEU.*

Caisse mobile : Unité conçue pour le transport de marchandises, suffisamment renforcée pour permettre un usage répété, mais trop peu renforcée pour être saisie par le haut, ou empilée lorsqu'elle est chargée. Utilisée généralement en transport rail/route.

"Flat" (Châssis) : Plate-forme chargeable n'ayant aucune superstructure mais de même longeur et largeur qu'un conteneur et équipée au-dessus et en-dessous de pièces de coin

Ceci est un terme alternatif utilisé pour définir certains types de conteneurs à usage spécifique - tels que conteneurs plates-formes et conteneurs avec plate-forme à la base comportant des structures incomplètes.

ОТДЕЛЬНЫЕ ОПРЕДЕЛЕНИЯ ИЗ ГЛОССАРИЯ ПО СТАТИСТИКЕ ТРАНСПОРТА

ВВЕДЕНИЕ

В феврале 1991 года секретариаты ЕВРОСТАТ, ЕКМТ и ЕЭК ООН создали Межсекретариатскую рабочую группу по статистике транспорта. Ее цель заключалась в унификации и, по возможности, стандартизации транспортной статистики на международном уровне для обеспечения сопоставимости данных, публикуемых ЕВРОСТАТ, ЕКМТ и ЕЭК ООН, упорядочения процедур сбора данных на международном уровне и упрощения представления данных национальными статистическими управлениями для этих трех организаций.

В качестве первого шага Межсекретариатская рабочая группа при содействии ряда заинтересованных международных организаций (таких, как Международный союз железных дорог, Международный союз автомобильного транспорта, Международная автомобильная федерация) подготовила глоссарий общих стандартных определений терминов, используемых в международной транспортной статистике, на основе трех существующих глоссариев статистических терминов в области транспорта, выпущенных ЕВРОСТАТ, ЕКМТ и ЕЭК ООН.

Настоящий совместный глоссарий стандартных терминов выпускается в виде брошюры и охватывает тематику инфраструктуры, транспортного оборудования, транспортных предприятий, движения, измерения объема перевозок и потребления энергии в области статистики железнодорожного, автомобильного, внутреннего водного и нефтепроводного транспорта. В результате консультаций со странами - членами упомянутых трех организаций в глоссарий были внесены поправки, после чего он был утвержден Межсекретариатской рабочей группой.

Одной из целей глоссария является представление общих стандартных определений для статистических вопросников упомянутых трех организаций. В тех случаях, когда какая-либо страна представляет данные, не согласующиеся с такими стандартными определениями, в сносках следует указывать характер расхождения. Работа по определениям происшествий, показателей цен и положения на рынке и окружающей среды будет продолжена, и эти определения будут включены в следующие выпуски глоссария. Кроме того, глоссарий будет расширен с охватом других видов транспорта.

На втором, уже начавшемся, этапе работы планируется унифицировать, вопросники, рассылаемые тремя организациями своим странам-членам в целях упрощения процедур сбора данных на национальном и международном уровнях. На завершающем этапе, возможно, будет рассмотрен вопрос о создании в этих трех организациях общей базы данных по статистике транспорта. Конкретные средства создания и использования таких совместных механизмов, а также процедуры распространения данных для такой базы данных должны быть подробно изучены на более позднем этапе.

Примечание:
Подчеркнутые пояснительные замечания, которые приводятся в отдельных случаях под определениями, имеют целью облегчить заполнение вопросника странами и в само определение не входят.

ЖЕЛЕЗНОДОРОЖНЫЙ ТРАНСПОРТ

ПРЕДПРИЯТИЯ, ЭКОНОМИЧЕСКАЯ ДЕЯТЕЛЬНОСТЬ И СФЕРА ЗАНЯТОСТИ

Основном(ых) железнодорожном(ых) предприятии(ях) : Предприятие, владеющее и/или эксплуатирующее самую крупную железнодорожную сеть (сети) в стране. *В эту категорию включаются городские перевозки, осуществляемые основными железнодорожными предприятиями. Следующие железнодорожные предприятия считаются основными:*

Австрия : Федеральные железные дороги Австрии (ФЖДА)
Азербайджан : Азербайджанские государственные железные дороги (АГЖД)
Албания : Железные дороги Албании(ЖДА)
Армения : Армянские железные дороги (АЖД)
Беларусь : Белорусские железные дороги (БЖД)
Бельгия : Национальное общество железных дорог Бельгии (НОЖДБ)
Болгария : Болгарские государственные железные дороги (БГЖД)
Босния и Герцеговина : Железные дороги Боснии (ЖДБ)
Бывшая югославская Республика Македония : Железные дороги Македонии (ЖДМ)
Венгрия : Венгерские государственные железные дороги (ГИСЕВ/РОЕЕ - MAB)
Германия : Германские федеральные железные дороги, Германские государственные железные дороги (ЖДФРГ)
Греция : Греческие железные дороги (ГЖД)
Грузия : Железные дороги Грузии (ЖДГ)
Дания : Датские государственные железные дороги (ДГЖД)
Израиль : Израильские государственные железные дороги (ИГЖД)
Ирландия : Ирландская транспортная компания (ИТК)
Испания : Испанская национальная сеть железных дорог (ИНСЖД)

Италия : Итальянские государственные железные дороги (ИГЖД)
Казахстан : Железные дороги Республики Казахстан (ЖДРК)
Канада : Канадиан пасифик (КП)
Кыргызстан : Кыргызская железная дорога (КЖД)
Латвия : Латвийские государственные железные дороги (ЛГЖД)
Литва : Литовские железные дороги (ЛЖД)
Люксембург : Национальные железные дороги Люксембурга (НЖДЛ)
Нидерланды : Железные дороги Нидерландов (ЖДН)
Норвегия : Государственные железные дороги Норвегии (ГЖДН)
Польша : Польские государственные железные дороги (ПГЖД)
Португалия : Португальские железные дороги (ПЖД)
Республика Молдова : Молдавские железные дороги (МЖД)
Российская Федерация : Министерство путей сообщения Российской Федерации (МПСРФ)
Румыния : Румынские железные дороги (РЖД)
Словакия : Железные дороги Словацкой Республики (ЖДСР)
Словения : Железные дороги Словении (ЖДС)
Соединенное Королевство : Английские железные дороги (АЖД), Северо-ирландские железные дороги (СИЖД)
США : Ассоциация американских железных дорог (ААЖД). Все предприятия железнодорожных перевозок класса I (1)
Таджикистан : Таджикская железная дорога (ТЖД)

Тукменистан : Государственная железная дорога Туркменистана (ГЖДТ)

Турция : Турецкие государственные железные дороги (ТГЖД)

Узбекистан :

Украина : Украинские железные дороги (УЖД)

Финляндия : Государственные железные дороги Финляндии (ГЖДФ)

Франция : Национальное общество железных дорог Франции (НОЖДФ)

Хорватия : Железные дороги Хорватии (ЖДХ)

Чешская Республика : Чешские железные дороги (ЧЖД)

Швейцария : Железные дороги Швейцарской Конфедерации (ЖДШК)

Швеция : Шведские государственные железные дороги (ШГЖД). Шведское национальное железнодорожное управление (ШЖУ)

Эстония : Эстонские железные дороги (ЭЖД), Юго-западные железные дороги Лтд.

Югославия : Югославские железные дороги (ЮЖД)

---

(1) *На железнодорожные перевозки предприятий класса I приходится около 83% общего объема маршрутных перевозок и 97% грузовых перевозок. В этих статистических данных должны также учитываться операции и перевозки, осуществляемые Национальной железнодорожной пассажирской корпорацией (АМТРАК) и Автомобильно-железнодорожной корпорацией. На первую из этих корпораций приходится большая часть междугородних перевозок по железным дорогам США, в то время как единственная функция второй корпорации заключается в экспресс-перевозках пассажиров и их автомобилей между Вашингтоном, округ Колумбия, и Санфордом, Флорида.*

Сфера занятости : Среднее число лиц, работающих в течение данного периода на железнодорожном предприятии, а также лиц, работающих за пределами этого предприятия, однако входящих в его штат и получающих заработную плату непосредственно от этого предприятия.

Эти статистические данные должны включать сотрудников, занятых на выполнении всех основных и вспомогательных видов деятельности предприятия (железнодорожные операции, модернизация, новое строительство, дорожное и экспедиторское обслуживание, производство электроэнергии, гостиницы и рестораны и т.д.).

Виды занятости : К основным категориям занятости относятся:

- общая администрация : *Включается центральный и региональный руководящий персонал (например, по финансовым, правовым, кадровым и т.д. вопросам) и советы директоров. Исключается руководящий персонал специализированных отделов (транспортных операций и управления движением, службы тяги и подвижного состава, дорожно-эксплуатационных и путевых работ), однако учитывается в статистических данных, касающихся каждой из этих служб.*

- транспортные операции и управление движением : *Сотрудники станционных служб, поездные бригады (исключая локомотивные бригады), а также персонал соответствующих центральных и региональных ведомств. Включаются сотрудники туристических и рекламных агентств.*

- службы тяги и подвижного состава : *Локомотивные бригады, персонал мастерских, инспекторы, а также персонал соответствующих центральных и региональных ведомств.*

- дорожно-эксплуатационные и путевые работы : *Постоянный ремонтно-эксплуатационный и контрольный персонал.*

- прочие операции : *Автомобильные пассажирские и грузовые перевозки, экспедиторские услуги, выработка электроэнергии, автотранспортные перевозки, услуги гостиничного персонала и т.д.*

ИНФРАСТРУКТУРА

Железная дорога : Линия сообщения, представляющая собой рельсовый путь и предназначенная исключительно для железнодорожных транспортных средств.

Линия сообщения представляет собой часть пространства, оборудованного для осуществления перевозок.

Железнодорожная сеть : Все железнодорожные линии в данном районе.

В нее не входят участки дорог или водных путей, даже если железнодорожный подвижной состав перевозится по таким маршрутам, например, на прицепах для перевозки вагонов или на железнодорожных паромах. Исключаются железнодорожные линии, используемые только для туристических целей в течение туристического сезона, а также железные дороги, проложенные исключительно для обслуживания шахт, лесоразработок или других промышленных или сельскохозяйственных предприятий и которые закрыты для перевозок общего пользования.

Железнодорожный путь : Пара рельсов, по которым могут передвигаться железнодорожные транспортные средства.

Ширииа колеи : Расстояиие между двумя рельсами измеренное между внутренними краями головок рельыов. В настоящее впемя используется железнодорожная колея следующей ширины

- Нормальная нолея : 1,435 м
- Широкая колея : 1,524 м (ГЖДФ, ЖДСР); 1,600 м (ИТК, СИЖД); 1,668 м (ИНСЖД, ПЖД)
- Узкая колея: 0,60 м,0,70 м, 0,75 м,0,76 м,0,785 м,0,90 м,1,00 м

Электрифицированный путь : Путь, снабженный воздушным контактным проводом или контактным рельсом, чтобы сделать возможной электрическую тягу.

Подъездные железнодорожные пути : Железнодорожные пути, отходящие от главных железнодорожных путей.

Протяженность подъездных железнодорожных путей включается в протяженность железнодорожных путей, если эти подъездные пути входят в соответствующие железнодорожные системы, за исключением подъездных железнодорожных путей, принадлежащих частным владельцам.

Линия : Один или несколько расположенных рядом главных путей, образующих маршрут между двумя пунктами. Если участок сети состоит из двух или нескольких параллельных линий, учитывается столько линий, сколько имеется маршрутов, для исключительного обслуживания которых предназначены пути.

Средняя протяженность линий, эксплуатируемых в течение всего года : Протяженность линии, предназначенной для перевозок в течение всего отчетного года (включая линии, эксплуатируемые совместно с другими железнодорожными предприятиями), плюс средняя протяженность линий, открытых или закрытых в течение года (взвешенная по числу дней, в течение которых они эксплуатировались).

Общей протяженностью эксплуатируемой линии считается протяженность линии, эксплуатируемой для перевозки пассажиров или грузов или совместной перевозки пассажиров и грузов. Если линия эксплуатируется одновременно несколькими предприятиями, она учитывается только один раз.

Электрифицированная линия : Линия с одним или несколькими электрифицированными главными путями. Участки линий, прилегающие к станциям и электрифицированные только для осуществления маневровых операций и неэлектрифицированные на всем их протяжении до следующей станции, учитываются в качестве неэлектрифицированных линий.

ТРАНСПОРТНОЕ ОБОРУДОВАНИЕ (ТРАНСПОРТНЫЕ СРЕДСТВА)

Железнодорожное транспортное средство : Подвижное оборудование, передвигающееся исключительно по рельсам; различают тяговые транспортные средства (локомотивы и автомотрисы) и буксируемые транспортные средства (пассажирские вагоны, прицепные вагоны моторвагонного поезда, багажные и товарные вагоны).

В статистические данные включаются следующие транспортные средства:

(а) Все железнодорожные транспортные средства, принадлежащие основному железнодорожному предприятию, а также средства, взятые этим предприятием внаем и фактически находящиеся в его распоряжении, включая те транспортные средства, которые ремонтируются или ожидают ремонта или хранятся в парке в рабочем или нерабочем состоянии, а также иностранные транспортные средства, находящиеся в распоряжении системы, и транспортные средства предприятия, временно находящиеся в порядке обычной эксплуатации за границей или находящиеся на сети вспомогательных железнодорожных предприятий.

(b) Товарные вагоны, принадлежащие частным владельцам, т.е. товарные вагоны, не принадлежащие основному железнодорожному предприятию, однако зарегистрированные и допущенные к перевозкам этим предприятием при соблюдении специальных условий, а также товарные вагоны, отданные этим железнодорожным предприятием внаем частным владельцам и эксплуатируемые в качестве товарных вагонов, принадлежащих частным владельцам.

Из статистических данных основного железнодорожного предприятия исключаются транспортные средства, которые не находятся в его распоряжении, т.е.:

(а) Транспортные средства иностранных или вспомогательных железнодорожных предприятий, временно находящихся на железнодорожных линиях основного железнодорожного предприятия в порядке обычной эксплуатации.

(b) Транспортные средства, которые отданы внаем или каким-либо иным образом переданные в распоряжение других железнодорожных предприятий.

(с) Транспортные средства, зарезервированные исключительно для технологических перевозок или предназначенные для продажи, на слом или списание.

Тяговое транспортное средство : Транспортное средство, оборудованное первичным двигателем и двигателем или только двигателем и предназначенное исключительно для буксировки других транспортных средств ("локомотив") или для буксировки других транспортных средств и перевозки пассажиров и/или грузов ("автомотриса").

Локомотив : Железнодорожное транспортное средство, оборудованное первичным двигателем и двигателем или только двигателем и используемое только для буксировки железнодорожных транспортных средств.

К локомотивам относятся только те транспортные средства, усилия которых на тяговом крюке составляют 110 кВт и более; транспортные средства с меньшим тяговым усилием, обозначаемые как "легкие мотовозы", из этой категории исключаются. Легкий мотовоз представляет собой тяговую единицу небольшой мощности, предназначенную для маневровой работы или рабочих поездов и для конечных перевозок на небольшие расстояния или с небольшими нагрузками. Специальные непассажирские тяговые единицы для высокоскоростных поездов включаются в эту категорию, даже если эти транспортные средства являются частью неразъемной секции.

Паровоз : Цилиндровый или турбинный локомотив, источником энергии которого является пар, независимо от вида используемого топлива.

Электровоз : Локомотив с одним или несколькими электродвигателями, питаемыми электрическим током, подводимым по контактному проводу или контактному рельсу или поступающим от находящихся на локомотиве аккумуляторов. К категории электровозов относятся оборудованные таким образом локомотивы, снабженные также энергетической установкой (дизельной или иной) для питания током электродвигателя, когда этот ток нельзя получать от контактного провода или контактного рельса.

Тепловоз : Локомотив, основным источником энергии которого является дизельный двигатель, независимо от типа установленной передачи. Однако дизель-электрические локомотивы, оборудованные также для получения электроэнергии, подводимой по контактному проводу или по контактному рельсу, относятся к категории электровозов.

Автомотриса : Моторное железнодорожное транспортное средство, сконструированное для перевозки по железной дороге пассажиров или грузов. Определение различных категорий локомотивов (электровозы, тепловозы) применяются с соответствующими изменениями к автомотрисам.

В статистике механических транспортных средств каждая автомотриса в неразъемной секции учитывается отдельно; в статистике пассажирских транспортных средств и грузовых транспортных средств каждый кузов, оборудованный для перевозки пассажиров или грузов, учитывается в качестве одной единицы.

Пассажирское железнодорожное транспортное средство : Железнодорожное транспортное средство для перевозки пассажиров, даже если в нем имеется одно или несколько специальных отделений или специальных мест для багажа, грузовых мест, почты и т.д.

К этим транспортным средствам относятся такие специальные транспортные средства, как спальные вагоны, вагоны-салоны, вагоны-рестораны и санитарные вагоны. Каждое отдельное транспортное средство неразъемной секции для перевозки пассажиров учитывается в качестве пассажирского железнодорожного транспортного средства.

Пассажирский вагон : Пассажирское железнодорожное транспортное средство за исключением автомотрисы или прицепного вагона моторвагонного поезда.

Вместимость пассажирского транспортного средства : Число сидячих и спальных мест и разрешенное число мест для стоящих пассажиров в пассажирском транспортном средстве, когда оно используется по назначению.

Багажный вагон : Железнодорожное транспортное средство, не имеющее двигателя, входящее в состав пассажирских или грузовых поездов и используемое поездной бригадой в случае необходимости, также для перевозки багажа, грузовых мест, велосипедов и т.д.

Транспортные средства, имеющие одно или несколько купе для пассажиров, должны учитываться не в качестве багажных, а в качестве пассажирских вагонов. Почтовые вагоны, принадлежащие железнодорожному предприятию, считаются багажными вагонами, если они не имеют купе для пассажиров.

Товарный вагон : Железнодорожное транспортное средство, обычно предназначенное для перевозки грузов.

В эту категорию включаются автомотрисы и прицепные вагоны моторвагонного поезда, оборудованные только для перевозки грузов.

Крытый вагон : Товарный вагон, характеризуемый закрытой конструкцией (сплошные стенки до самого верха и крыша) и безопасностью, которую он обеспечивает перевозимым в нем грузам (возможность закрыть вагон на замок и опломбировать).

В эту категорию включаются товарные вагоны с открывающейся крышей, а также изотермические и рефрижераторные вагоны.

Полувагон : Вагон без крыши с неоткидными бортами высотой более 60 см.

Вагон-платформа : Вагон без крыши и бортов или вагон без крыши с бортами высотой не более 60 см или опрокидывающаяся платформа обычного или специального типа.

Вагоны, сконструированные исключительно для перевозки контейнеров, съемных кузовов и грузовых автотранспортных средств в эту категорию не входят.

ДВИЖЕНИЕ

Железнодорожное движение : Любое движение железнодорожного транспортного средства по эксплуатируемым линиям.

Если железнодорожное транспортное средство перевозится на другом транспортном средстве, учитывается движение только перевозящего транспортного средства (активный вид транспорта).

Поезд : Одно или несколько железнодорожных транспортных средств, буксируемых одним или несколькими локомотивами или автомотрисами, или только автомотрисой, двигающихся под определенным номером или под отдельным обозначением между конкретным исходным пунктом и конкретным конечным пунктом.

Одиночный локомотив, т.е. локомотив, осуществляющий самостоятельное движение, в качестве поезда не рассматривается.

Типы поездов : К основным категориям относятся:

- Грузовой поезд: поезд, состоящий из одного или нескольких товарных вагонов и, в случае необходимости, из багажных вагонов, передвигающихся либо порожняком, либо загруженными.

- Пассажирский поезд: поезд, предназначенный для перевозки пассажиров и состоящий из одного или нескольких пассажирских железнодорожных транспортных средств и, в случае необходимости, из багажных вагонов, передвигающихся либо порожняком, либо загруженными.

- Смешанный поезд: поезд, состоящий из пассажирских железнодорожных транспортных средств и товарных вагонов.

- Прочие поезда: поезда, осуществляющие движение только по требованию железнодорожного предприятия и не использующиеся для коммерческих перевозок.

Поездо-километр : Единица измерения, соответствующая передвижению поезда на один километр.

Тяговое транспортное средство-километр : Единица измерения, соответствующая любому передвижению тягового транспортного средства на расстояние в один километр.

В эту категорию включаются одиночные тяговые транспортные средста и тяговые транспортные средства, осуществляющие маневровые операции.

Буксируемая тонна-километр брутто : Единица измерения, соответствующая передвижению на расстояние в один километр одной тонны веса железнодорожного транспортного средства и его груза, исключая вес тягового транспортного средства.

Включается вес автомотрис.

ИЗМЕРЕНИЕ ОБЪЕМА ПЕРЕВОЗОК

Железнодорожная перевозка : Любая перевозка грузов и/или пассажиров на железнодорожном транспортном средстве по данной железнодорожной сети.

Если железнодорожное транспортное средство перевозится на другом железнодорожном транспортном средстве, то учитывается движение только перевозящего транспортного средства (активный вид транспорта).

Национальная железнодорожная перевозка : Железнодорожные перевозки между двумя пунктами (пунктом погрузки и пунктом разгрузки), находящимися в одной и той же стране. Эта перевозка может включать транзитную перевозку через вторую страну.

Международная железнодорожная перевозка : Железнодорожная перевозка между двумя пунктами (пунктом погрузки и пунктом разгрузки) в двух разных странах. Эта перевозка может включать транзитную перевозку через одну или более дополнительных стран.

Пассажир железнодорожного транспорта : Любое лицо, за исключением членов поездной бригады, совершающее поездку на железнодорожном транспортном средстве.

Исключаются пассажиры, совершающие поездку на паромах или автобусах, эксплуатируемых железной дорогой.

Пассажиро - километр на железнодорожном транспорте : Единица измерения, соответствующая перевозке по железной дороге одного пассажира на расстояние в один километр.

Следует учитывать расстояние, которое фактически проехал пассажир. Если это расстояние неизвестно, то в этом случае учитывается расстояние, за которое фактически взимается плата, или оценочное расстояние.

Грузы, перевезенные железнодорожным транспортом : Любые грузы, перевезенные на железнодорожных транспортных средствах.

К этим грузам относятся все грузовые места и оборудование, такое, как контейнеры, съемные кузова или поддоны, а также грузовые автотранспортные средства, перевезенные железнодорожным транспортом.

Тонна-километр на железнодорожном транспорте : Единица измерения грузовых перевозок, соответствующая железнодорожной перевозке одной тонны грузов на расстояние, за которое фактически взимается плата, в один километр.

Погруженный груз : Груз, помещенный на железнодорожное транспортное средство и перевозимый железнодорожным транспортом.

В отличие от автомобильных и внутренних водных перевозок перегрузка с одного железнодорожного транспортного средства на другое и смена тягового транспортного средства не рассматриваются в качестве погрузки после разгрузки.

Выгруженный груз : Груз, снятый с железнодорожного транспортного средства после железнодорожной перевозки.

В отличие от автомобильных и внутренних водных перевозок перегрузка с одного железнодорожного транспортного средства на другое и смена тягового транспортного средства не рассматриваются в качестве разгрузки перед повторной погрузкой.

Международные перевозки - погруженный груз

Грузы, вывозимые из страны железнодорожным транспортом (в отличие от сквозных транзитных грузов, перевозимых железнодорожным транспортом) : Грузы, погруженные на железнодорожной сети, представляющей статистические данные, и перевозимые железнодорожным транспортом с целью их разгрузки в другой стране.

Включаются вагоны, груженые на железнодорожной сети и перевозимые на паромах для последующей перевозки по иностранной сети.

Международные перевозки - выгруженный груз
Грузы, ввозимые в страну железнодорожным транспортом (в отличие от сквозных транзитных грузов, перевозимых железнодорожным транспортом) : Грузы, погруженные на иностранной железнодорожной сети и перевозимые железнодорожным транспортом на железнодорожную сеть, представляющую статистические данные, для разгрузки в стране, где расположена сеть, представляющая статистические данные.

Включаются вагоны, груженые на иностранной железнодорожной сети и ввозимые на паромах для перевозки по сети, представляющей статистические данные.

Сквозные транзитные грузы, перевозимые железнодорожным транспортом : Грузы, погруженные на иностранной железнодорожной сети, следующие в пункт назначения, расположенный на иностранной железнодорожной сети, и перевозимые по железнодорожной сети, представляющей статистичеслие данные.

Включаются вагоны, ввозимые и/или вывозимые с сети, представляющей статистические данные на паромах.

АВТОМОБИЛЬНЫЙ ТРАНСПОРТ

ИНФРАСТРУКТУРА

Дорога : Линия сообщения (проезжий путь), имеющая твердое покрытие, за исключением железных дорог и взлетно-посадочных полос, открытая для общего движения и предназначенная в основном для дорожных механических транспортных средств, передвигающихся на своих собственных колесах.

Включаются мосты, туннели, несущие конструкции, пересечения дорог, перекрестки и развязки. Включаются также платные дороги. Исключаются специальные дорожки для велосипедов.

Категория дороги (государственного, провинциального и местного значения) : Классификация дорожной сети определяется:

 (a) администрацией, несущей ответственность за ее строительство, содержание и/или эксплуатацию;
 (b) в соответствии с конструкционными стандартами, или
 (c) в зависимости от пользователей, имеющих право доступа на дорогу.

Автомагистраль : Дорога, которая специально построена и предназначена для движения автотранспортных средств, не обслуживает придорожных владений ,и :

 (a) за исключением отдельных мест или во временном порядке, имеет для обоих направлений движения отдельные проезжие части, отделенные друг от друга разделительной полосой, не предназначенной для движения или, в исключительных случаях, другими средствами;

 (b) не имеет пересечения на одном уровне ни с дорогами, ни с железнодорожными или трамвайными путями, ни с пешеходными дорожками;

 (c) специально обозначена в качестве автомагистрали и предназначена для использования конкретных категорий дорожных механических транспортных средств.

Полосы для въезда и выезда с автомагистрали включаются независимо от места нахождения дорожного знака. Включаются также городские автомагистрали.

Дорога категории "Е" : Международная сеть дорог категории "Е" состоит из системы дорог, указанных в Европейском соглашении о международных автомагистралях, Женева, 15 ноября 1975 года, и в поправках к нему.
ТРАНСПОРТНОЕ ОБОРУДОВАНИЕ (ТРАНСПОРТНЫЕ СРЕДСТВА)

Дорожное механическое транспортное средство : Дорожное транспортное средство, оборудованное двигателем , который является единственным средством для приведения его в движение, и обычно используемое для перевозки пассажиров или грузов или для буксировки на дорогах транспортных средств, используемых для перевозки пассажиров или грузов.

Из этих статистических данных исключаются механические транспортные средства, осуществляющие движение по рельсам.

Парк дорожных транспортных средств : Количество дорожных транспортных средств, которые зарегистрированы на данную дату в стране и которые можно использовать на дорогах, открытых для общего пользования.

Он включает дорожные транспортные средства, освобожденные от уплаты ежегодных налогов или сборов; он также включает ввезенные подержанные транспортные средства и другие дорожные транспортные средства в соответствии с национальной практикой. Из этих статистических данных следует исключать военные транспортные средства.

Дорожные транспортные средства, впервые зарегистрированные в течение года : Дорожные транспортные средства, впервые зарегистрированные в течение года в стране, представляющей информацию.

Включаются как новые дорожные транспортные средства так и ввезенные подержанные транспортные средства, впервые зарегистрированные в стране, представляющей информацию.

Возраст дорохного транспортного средства : Период времени после первой регистрации дорожного траспортного средстванезависимо от страны регистрации.

Национальные дорожные транспортные средства : Дорожное транспортное средство, зарегистрированное в стране, представляющей информацию, имеющее номерные знаки этой страны, или зарегистрированное отдельно (трамваи, троллейбусы и.т.д.).

Если в какой-либо конкретной стране регистрация дорожных транспортных средств отсутствует, то национальным дорожным транспортным средством является транспортное средство, которым владеет или сдает в наем компания, находящаяся в этой стране и уплачивающая налоги.

ПАССАЖИРСКИЙ ТРАНСПОРТ

Пассажирское дорожное механическое траспортное средство : Дорожное механическое транспортное средство, предназначенное исключительно или преимущественно для перевозки одного или более пассажиров.

Транспортное средство, предназначенное для перевозки как пассажиров ,так и грузов ,следует относить либо к пассажирским дорожным транспортным средствам, либо к грузовым дорожным транспортным средствам в зависимости от их основной цели, что определяется их техническими характеристиками или их категорией для целей налогообложения..

Мопед : Двух- или трехколесное дорожное транспортное средство, оборудованное двигателем с рабочим объемом цилиндров менее 50 см3 (3,05 дюйма3) и максимально разрешаемая конструкционная скорость которых соответствует национальным правилам.

Мотоцикл : Двухколесное дорожное механическое транспортное средство с прицепной коляской или без нее, включая мотороллер или трехколесное дорожное механическое транспортное средство, порожний вес которого не превышает 400 кг (900 фунтов). Включаются все такие транспортные средства с рабочим объемом цилиндров 50 см3 или более, а также транспортные средства, рабочий объем цилиндров которых составляет менее 50 см3 и которые не подпадают под определение мопеда.

Пассажирский автомобиль : Дорожное механическое транспортное средство, иное, чем мотоцикл, предназначенное для перевозки пассажиров и имеющее не более девяти сидячих мест (включая место водителя).

Поэтому термин "пассажирский автомобиль" охватывает микроавтомобили (для вождения которых не требуется водительских удостоверений), такси и взятые напрокат пассажирски еавтомобили при условии, что они имеют менее десяти сидячих мест. В эту категорию могут также входить пикапы.

Автобус дальнего следования или городской автобус : Пассажирское дорожное механическое транспортное средство, предназначенное для перевозки пассажиров и имеющее более девяти сидячих мест (включая место водителя).

В эти статистические данные также включаются мини-автобусы для перевозки пассажиров, имеющие более девяти сидячих мест (включая место водителя).

Троллейбус : Пассажирское дорожное транспортное средство, которое предназначено для перевозки пассажиров, имеет более девяти сидячих мест (включая место водителя), соединено с электрическими проводами и не передвигается по рельсам.

Этот термин охватывает транспортные средства, которые иногда используются в качестве троллейбусов, а иногда - в качестве автобусов, поскольку они имеют отдельный двигатель.

Число сидячих/спальных мест в автобусах дальнего следования, городских автобусах и троллейбусах : Число сидячих/спальных мест, включая место водителя, имеющихся в транспортном средстве при использовании его в целях, для которых оно преимущественно предназначено.

В случае сомнения следует учитывать наибольшее число имеющихся сидячих/спальных мест.

Трамвай : Пассажирское дорожное транспортное средство, ноторое предназначено для перевозки пассажиров, имеет более девяти сидячих мест (внлючая место водителя), соединено с электрическими проводами или приводится в движение с помощью дизельного двигателя и передвигается по реьсам.

ГРУЗОВЫЕ ДОРОЖНЫЕ ПЕРЕВОЗКИ

Грузовое дорожное транспортное средство : Дорожное транспортное средство, предназначенное исключительно или преимущественно для перевозки грузов.

Транспортные средства, предназначенные для перевозки как пассажиров, так и грузов, следует относить либо к пассажирским дорожным транспортным средствам, либо к грузовым дорожным транспортным средствам в зависимости от их основного назначения, что определяется их техническими характеристиками или их категорией для целей налогообложения.

Грузовой автомобиль : Дорожное механическое транспортное средство на жесткой раме, предназначенное исключительно или преимущественно для перевозки грузов.

В эту категорию включаются фургоны, которые представляют собой дорожные механические транспортные средства на жесткой раме, которые предназначены исключительно или преимущественно для перевозки грузов и вес брутто которых составляет менее 3 500 кг. В эту категорию могут также включаться пикапы.

Дорожный тягач : Дорожное механическое транспортное средство, предназначенное исключительно или преимущественно для буксировки других дорожных транспортных средств, которые не имеют механического привода (в основном полуприцепы).

Исключаются сельскохозяйственные тракторы.

Прицеп : Грузовое дорожное транспортное средство, предназначенное для буксировки дорожным механическим транспортным средством.

Из этой категории исключаются сельскохозяйственные прицепы и жилые прицепы.

Полуприцепы : Грузовое дорожное транспортное средство без передней оси, сконструированное таким образом, чтобы часть этого транспортного средства и значительная часть веса находящегося на нем груза опиралась на дорожный тягач.

Грузоподъемность : Максимальный вес грузов, объявленный допустимым компетентным органом страны регистрации транспортного средства.

ДВИЖЕНИЕ И ПЕРЕВОЗКА

Дорожное движение : Любое движение дорожного транспортного средства по данной сети.

Если дорожное транспортное средство перевозится на другом транспортном средстве, учитывается движение только перевозящего транспортного средства (активный вид транспорта).

Дорожное движение по национальной территории : Любое движение дорожных транспортных средств в пределах национальной территории, независимо от страны, в которой это транспортное средство зарегистрировано.

Транспортное средство – километр : Единица измерения, соответствующая передвижению дорожного механического транспортного средства на один километр.

Следует учитывать расстояние фактического пробега. Включается передвижение порожних дорожных механических транспортных средств. Транспортные единицы, состоящие из тягача и полуприцепа или из грузового автомобиля и прицепа, учитываются в качестве одного транспортного средства.

Автодорожная перевозка : Любая перевозка грузов и/или пассажиров на дорожном транспортном средстве по данной дорожной сети.

Если дорожное транспортное средство перевозится на другом транспортном средстве, то учитывается движение только перевозящего транспортного средства (активный вид транспорта).

Национальная автодорожная перевозка : Автодорожная перевозка между двумя пунктами (пунктом погрузки/посадки и пунктом разгрузки/высадки), находящимися в одной и той же стране, независимо от страны, в которой зарегистрировано транспортное средство. Эта перевозка может включать транзитную перевозку через вторую страну.

Международная автодорожная перевозка : Автодорожная перевозка между двумя пунктами (пунктом погрузки/посадки и пунктом разгрузки/высадки) в двух разных странах. Эта перевозка может включать транзитную перевозку через одну или более дополнительных стран.

Пассажиро-километр на автомобильном транспорте : Единица измерения, соответствующая перевозке одного пассажира по автомобильной дороге на расстояние в один километр.

Пересадка с одного дорожного транспортного средства на другое рассматривается в качестве высадки перед повторной посадкой.

Грузы, перевезенные автомобильным транспортом : Любые грузы, перевезенные на грузовых дорожных транспортных средствах.

К этим грузам относятся все грузовые места и оборудование, такое, как контейнеры, съемные кузова или поддоны.

Тонна-километр на автомобильном транспорте : Единица измерения грузовых перевозок, соответствующая автомобильной перевозке одной тонны груза на один километр.

Погруженный груз : Груз, помещенный на дорожное транспортное средство и перевозимый автомобильным транспортом.

Перегрузка с одного грузового дорожного транспортного средства на другое или смена дорожного тягача рассматривается в качестве погрузки после разгрузки.

Выгруженный груз : Груз, снятый с дорожного транспортного средства после автомобильной перевозки.

Перегрузка с одного грузового дорожного транспортного средства на другое или смена дорожного тягача рассматривается в качестве разгрузки перед повторной погрузкой.

Международные перевозки - погруженный груз
Грузы, вывозимые из страны автомобильным транспортом (в отличие от сквозных транзитных грузов, перевозимых автомобильным транспортом) : Грузы, погруженные на дорожное транспортное средство в данной стране, вывезенные из страны автомобильным транспортом и разгруженные в другой стране.

Международные перевозки - выгруженный груз
Грузы, ввозимые в страну автомобильным транспортом (в отличие от сквозных транзитных грузов, перевозимых автомобильным транспортом) : Грузы, погруженные на дорожное транспортное средство в другой стране, ввезенные в страну автомобильным транспортом и разгруженные в этой стране.

Автодорожная каботажная перевозка : Национальая автодорожная перевозка, осуществляемая на механическом транспортном средстве, зарегистрированном в другой стране.

Автодорожная перевозка, осущесвляемая третьей стороной: Международная автодорожная перевозка, осуществляемая на дорожном механическом транспортном средстве, зарегистрированном в треьей стране.

Третьей страной является стана, в которой не производится погрузка, или страна в которой не производится разгрузка.

Перевозка за плату или вознаграждение : Перевозка за плату пассажиров или грузов, производимая за счет третьих лиц.

ВНУТРЕННИЙ ВОДНЫЙ ТРАНСПОРТ

ИНФРАСТРУКТУРА

Судоходный внутренний водный путь : Водное пространство, не являющееся частью моря, по которому могут осуществлять движение нормально груженые суда грузоподъемностью не менее 50 т. Этот термин применяется как в отношении судоходных рек и озер, так и в отношении судоходных каналов.

Длина рек и каналов измеряется по осевой линии фарватера. Длина озер и заливов измеряется по кратчайшему судоходному пути между двумя наиболее удаленными точками, в которые и из которых осуществляются транспортные операции. Водный путь, образующий общую границу между двумя странами, включается в статистические данные обеими странами.

Судоходные внутренние водные пути, регулярно используемые для перевозок : Водные пути, по которым ежегодно производится определенный объем перевозок; этот объем, выраженный в тонно-километрах на километр водного пути, определяется соответствующим компетентным органом с учетом условий на сети водных путей этой страны.

Судоходная река : Природный водный путь, открытый для судоходства, независимо от того, улучшался он для целей судоходства или нет.

Судоходное озеро : Природное водное пространство, открытое для судоходства.

Включаются заливы (водное пространство с содержанием солоноватой воды, отделенное от моря береговой полосой).

Судоходный канал : Водный путь, построенный в основном для судоходства.

ТРАНСПОРТНОЕ ОБОРУДОВАНИЕ (СУДНО)

Суда для перевозок по внутренним водным путям : Находящиеся на плаву суда, предназначенные для перевозки грузов или пассажирских перевозок общего пользования по судоходным внутренним водным путям.

Включаются суда, находящиеся в ремонте. Включаются суда, которые пригодны для внутреннего судоходства, но которые допущены к морским перевозкам (суда смешанного плавания река - море).Из этой категории исключаются: портовые плавучие средства, морские лихтеры и морские буксиры, паромы, рыболовецкие суда, землечерпальные снаряды, суда, осуществляющие гидротехнические работы, и суда, используемые исключительно под складские помещения, плавучие мастерские, плавучие дачи и прогулочные суда.

Национальное судно для перевозок по внутренним водным путям : Судно для перевозок по внутренним водным путям, которое зарегистрировано на данную дату в стране, представляющей информацию.

Если в какой-либо конкретной стране регистрация судов для перевозок по внутренним водным путям отсутствует, то национальным судном для перевозок по внутренним водным путям является судно, которым владеет компания, находящаяся в этой стране и уплачивающая налоги.

Судно для грузовых перевозок по внутренним водным путям : Судно грузоподъемностью не менее 20 тонн, предназначенное для грузовых перевозок по судоходным внутренним водным путям.

Самоходная баржа : Судно для грузовых перевозок по внутренним водным путям, имеющее самостоятельную двигательную установку.

Буксируемые баржи, толкаемые баржи и толкаемые-буксируемые баржи, которые имеют только вспомогательный двигатель, должны рассматриваться в качестве буксируемых барж, толкаемых барж или толкаемых-буксируемых барж в зависимости от случая. Тот факт, что самоходная баржа может быть использована для буксировки, не меняет ее назначения.

Самохоные суда типа река-море : Судно для грузовых перевозок по внутренним водным путям грузоподъемностью не менее 20 т, предназначенное также для перевозки грузов по морю и оборудованное собственной двигательной установкой мощностью не менее 37 кВт.

Несамоходная баржа : Судно для грузовых перевозок по внутренним водным путям, предназначенное для буксировки и не имеющее самостоятельной двигательной установки.

Наличие на несамоходной барже вспомогательного двигателя не меняет ее назначения.

Толкаемая баржа : Судно для грузовых перевозок по внутренним водным путям, предназначенное для толкания и не имеющее самостоятельной двигательной установки.

Наличие на толкаемой барже вспомогательного двигателя не меняет ее назначения.

Толкаемая-буксируемая баржа : Судно для грузовых перевозок по внутренним водным путям, предназначенное для толкания или буксировки и не имеющее самостоятельной двигательной установки.

Наличие на толкаемой-буксируемой барже вспомогательного двигателя не меняет ее назначения.

Буксир : Судно с источником двигательной силы мощностью не менее 37 кВт, предназначенное для буксировки несамоходных барж, толкаемых-буксируемых барж и плотов, но не для перевозки грузов.

Исключаются портовые и морские буксиры.

Толкач : Судно с источником двигательной силы мощностью не менее 37 кВт, предназначенное или приспособленное для толкания толкаемых или толкаемых- буксируемых барж, но не для перевозки грузов.

Исключаются портовые буксиры.

Толкач-буксир : Судно с источником двигательной силы мощностью не менее 37 кВт, предназначенное или приспособленное для буксировки несамоходных барж, толкаемых-буксируемых барж или плотов или для толкания толкаемых и
толкаемых-буксируемых барж, но не для перевозки грузов.

Грузоподъемность : Максимальный выраженный в тоннах разрешенный вес грузов, которые судно может перевозить согласно судовым документам.

Мощность (кВт) : Механическая мощность, развиваемая двигателем, которым оборудовано судно.

Эта мощность измеряется в фактических киловаттах (мощность, передаваемая на гребной винт): 1 кВт =1,36 л.с.; 1 л.с. = 0,735 кВт.

Год постройки судна : Год первоначальной постройки корпуса.

ИЗМЕРЕНИЕ ОБЪЕМА ПЕРЕВОЗОК

Перевозка по внутренним водным путям (ПВВП) : Любая перевозка грузов и/или пассажиров на судне для перевозок по внутренним водным путям по данной сети внутренних водных путей.

Если судно для перевозок по внутренним водным путям перевозится на другом транспортном средстве, то учитывается движение только перевозящего транспортного средства (активный вид транспорта).

Национальная перевозка по внутренним водным путям : Перевозка по внутренним водным путям между двумя пунктами (пунктом погрузки/посадки и пунктом разгрузки/высадки), находящимися в одной и той же стране, независимо от страны, в которой зарегистрировано судно для перевозок по внутренним водным путям. Эта перевозка может включать транзитную перевозку через вторую страну.

Международная перевозка по внутренним водным путям : Перевозка по внутренним водным путям между двумя пунктами (пунктом погрузки/посадки и пунктом разгрузки/высадки), находящимися в двух разных странах. Эта перевозка может включать транзитную перевозку через одну или более дополнительных стран.

Грузы, перевезенные внутренним водным транспортом : Любые грузы, перевезенные на судне для грузовых перевозок по внутренним водным путям.

К этим грузам относятся все грузовые места и оборудование, такое, как контейнеры, съемные кузова или поддоны.

Тонна-километр на внутренних водных путях . Единица измерения грузовых перевозок, соответствующая перевозке одной тонны грузов по внутренним водным путям на один километр.

Погруженный груз . Груз, помещенный на судно для перевозок по внутренним водным путям и перевозимый по внутренним водным путям.

Перегрузка с одного судна для перевозок по внутренним водным путям на другое рассматривается в качестве погрузки после разгрузки. Это также относится к смене толкачей-буксиров или буксиров.

Выгруженный груз : Груз, извлеченный из судна для перевозок по внутренним водным путям после перевозки по внутренним водным путям.

Перегрузка с одного судна для перевозок по внутренним водным путям на другое рассматривается в качестве разгрузки перед повторной погрузкой. Это относится также к смене толкачей-буксиров или буксиров.

Международные перевозки -погруженный груз
Грузы, вывозимые из страны по внутренним водным путям (в отличие от сквозных транзитных грузов, перевозимых по внутренним водным путям) : Грузы, погруженные на судно для перевозок по внутренним водным путям в данной стране, вывезенные из страны по внутренним водным путям и разгруженные в другой стране.

Международные перевозки - выгруженный груз
Грузы, ввозимые в страну по внутренним водным путям (в отличие от сквозных транзитных грузов, перевозимых по внутренним водным путям) : Грузы, погруженные на судно для перевозок по внутренним водным путям в другой стране, ввезенные в страну по внутренним водным путям и разгруженные в этой стране.

Сквозные транзитные грузы, перевозимые по внутренним водным путям сквозным транзитом : Грузы, ввезенные в страну по внутренним водным путям и вывезенные из страны по внутренним водным путям через пункт, иной, чем пункт ввоза, после их перевозки через территорию страны только по внутренним водным путям на одном и том же судне для грузовых перевозок по внутренним водным путям.

Перегрузка с одного судна для перевозок по внутренним водным путям на другое и смена толкачей-буксиров или буксиров рассматривается в качестве погрузки/разгрузки.

НЕФТЕПРОВОДНЫЙ ТРАНСПОРТ

ИНФРАСТРУКТУРА Н ТРАНСПОРТОЕ ОБОРУДОВАННЕ

Нефтепроводы : Трубопроводы для транспортировки сырой нефти или очищенных жидких нефтепродуктов путем их перекачки.

Включаются ответвления, а также нефтепроводы между сушей и буровыми платформами в море. Исключаются нефтепроводы, общая протяженность которых составляет менее 50 км или внутренний диаметр которых составляет менее 15 см, и нефтепроводы, используемые только для военных целей или всецело расположенные в пределах участка промышленного назначения, а также нефтепроводы, всецело расположенные на некотором удалении от берега (т.е. находящиеся только в открытом море). Международные нефтепроводы, общая протяженность которых составляет 50 км или более, включаются, даже если протяженность участка в стране, представляющей информацию, составляет менее 50 км. Нефтепроводы, состоящие из двух (или более) параллельных трубопроводов, следует учитывать дважды (или более).

Следует учитывать только те единицы, которые фактически осуществляют деятельность в течение рассматриваемого периода. Исключаются "спящие" единицы или те единицы, которые не приступили к своей деятельности.

ИЗМЕРЕНИЕ ОБЪЕМА ПЕРЕВОЗОК

Транспортировка по нефтепроводу : Любое перемещение сырой нефти или очищенных жидких нефтепродуктов по данной нефтепроводной сети.

Национальная транспортировка по нефтепроводу : Транспортировка по нефтепроводу между двумя пунктами (пунктом подачи и пунктом приема), находящимися в одной и той же стране или в той части морского дна, которая относится к этой стране. Эта транспортировка может включать транзитную транспортировку через вторую страну.

Международная транспортировка по нефтепроводу : Транспортировка по нефтепроводу между двумя пунктами (пунктом подачи и пунктом приема), находящимися в двух различных странах или на тех частях морского дна, которые относятся к ним. Эта транспортировка может включать транзитную транспортировку через одну или более дополнительных стран.

Грузы, транспортируемые по нефтепроводу : Любая сырая нефть или очищенные жидкие нефтепродукты, транспортируемые по нефтепроводам.

Тонна-километр на нефтепроводном транспорте : Единица измерения транспортировки, соответствующая транспортировке одной тонны грузов по нефтепроводу на один километр.

Международные перевозки -погруженный груз
Грузы, транспортируемые из страны по нефтепроводу (в отличие от сквозных транзитных грузов, транспортируемых по нефтепроводу) : Грузы, поданные в нефтепровод в стране или с той части морского дна, которая относится к этой стране, и
транспортируемые из этой страны по нефтепроводу.

Международные перевозки - выгруженный груз
Грузы, транспортируемые в страну по нефтепроводу (в отличие от сквозных транзитных грузов, транспортируемых по трубопроводу) : Грузы, поданные в нефтепровод в другой стране или с той части морского дна, которая относится к этой стране, и транспортируемые в страну по нефтепроводу и принятые в этой стране.

Сквозные транзитные грузы, транспортируемые по нефтепроводу : Грузы, которые транспортируются в страну по нефтепроводу и транспортируются из страны по нефтепроводу через пункт, иной чем пункт ввоза, после их транспортировки через территорию страны только по нефтепроводу.

Включаются грузы, которые были ввезены и/или вывезены из рассматриваемой страны на судах после их подачи в трубопровод/приемы из трубопровода на границе.

МОРСКОЙ ТРАНСПОРТ

ИЗМЕРЕНИЕ ОБЪЕМА ПЕРЕВОЗОК

Международная морская перевозка : Морская перевозка между двумя портами (портом погрузки/посадки и портом разгрузки/высадки), расположенными в различных странах.
Включается международная перевозка без захода в другой порт.

Каботажная (морская)/национальная морская перевозка : Морская перевозка между двумя портами (портом погрузки/посадки и портом разгрузки/высадки), находящимися в одной и той же стране, независимо от страны, в которой зарегистрировано мореходное судно.

Каботажная перевозка (морская) может осуществляться мореходным судном, зарегистрированным в стране, представляющей информацию, или в другой стране. Включается перевозка без захода в другой порт.

Грузы, перевезенные морским транспортом : Любые грузы, перевезенные по морю. К этим грузам относятся все виды упаковки и такое оборудование, как контейнеры, съемные кузова или поддоны.

Включаются почтовые отправления; включаются также грузы, перевозимые на или в вагонах, грузовых автомобилях, прицепах, полуприцепах или баржах. С другой стороны, включаются следующие виды груза: пассажирские автотранспортные средства с водителем, топливные цистерны и материальные средства на судах, рыба, выгружаемая из рыболовных судов и плавучих рыбообрабатывающих заводов, грузы, перевозимые в рамках одного и того же порта между его различными бассейнами и доками.

Погруженный груз : Груз, помещенный на мореходное судно и перевозимый по морю.

Перегрузка с одного мореходного судна на другое рассматривается в качестве погрузки после разгрузки.
Погруженный груз включает национальный груз, перегруженный груз (национальный или иностранный груз, доставленный в порт по морю) и транзитный груз, доставленный по суше (иностранный груз, доставленный в порт автомобильным, железнодорожным, воздушным или внутренним водным транспортом).

Выгруженный груз : Груз, извлеченный из мореходного судна после перевозки по морю.

Перегрузка с одного мореходного судна на другое рассматривается в качестве разгрузки перед повторной погрузкой.
*Выгруженный груз включает национальный груз, перегруженный груз (национальный **иностранный** груз, вывезенный из порта морем) и транзитный груз, вывезенный по суше (иностранный груз, вывезенный из порта автомобильным, железнодорожным, воздушным или внутренним водным транспортом).*

ИНТЕРМОДАЛЬНЫЕ ПЕРЕВОЗКИ

Интермодальные перевозки : Перевозки грузов (в одной и той же грузовой единице или на одном и том же транспортном средстве) последовательно используемыми видами транспорта без обработки самих грузов при изменении вида транспорта.

Под транспортным средством подразумевается автотранспортное, железнодорожное транспортное средство или судно.

Обратные перевозки пустых контейнеров/съемных кузовов и обратное перемещение порожних грузовых автотранспортных средств/прицепов сами по себе не являются составной частью интермодальных перевозок, поскольку в этом случае не транспортируется никаких грузов. Такие перевозки ассоциируются с интермодальными перевозками, и целесообразно собирать данные о перемещении порожних транспортных средств вместе с данными об интермодальных перевозках.

Смешанные перевозки

* Европейская конференция министров транспорта (ЕКМТ) определяет смешанные перевозки как "перевозки грузов по меньшей мере двумя различными видами транспорта".Следовательно, интермодальные перевозки являются отдельным видом смешанных перевозок.

* В Конвенции Организации Объединенных Наций о международных смешанных перевозках грузов международная смешанная перевозка определяется как "перевозка грузов по меньшей мере двумя разными видами транспорта на основании договора смешанной перевозки из места в одной стране, где грузы поступают в ведение оператора смешанной перевозки, до обусловленного места доставки в другой стране".

Комбинированные перевозки

* Термин "комбинированные перевозки" используется ЕЭК ООН в том же значении, что и вышеприведенное определение интермодальных перевозок.

* В сответствии с правилами применения Рекомендации №19 ЕЭК/ФАЛ "Классификатор видов транспорта" используется следующее определение:"<u>Комбинированные перевозки:</u> Комбинированное использование транспортных средств, когда одно (<u>пассивное</u>) транспортное средство перевозится на другом (<u>активном</u>) транспортном средстве, которое является таковым и потребляет энергию".

* Для целей транспортной политики ЕКМТ ограничивает значение термина "комбинированные перевозки" "интермодальными перевозками, в рамках которых бюльшая часть европейского рейса приходится на железнодорожный, внутренний водный или морской транспорт и любой первоначальный и/или конечный отрезок пути, на котором используется автомобильный транспорт, является максимально коротким".

Перевозка автотранспортного средства с сопровождением : Перевозка всего грузового механического автотранспортного средства в сопровождении водителя другим видом транспорта (например, морским или железнодорожным).

Перевозка автотранспортного средства без сопровождения : Перевозка всего грузового механического автотранспортного средства или прицепа без сопровождения водителя другим видом транспорта (например, морским или железнодорожным)

ОБОРУДОВАНИЕ

Интермодальная транспортная единица (ИТЕ) : Контейнеры, съемные кузова или полуприцепы/грузовые механические автотранспортные средства, пригодные для интермодальных перевозок.

Контейнер : Специальный ящик для перевозки груза, укрепленный, пригодный для штабелирования и горизонтального или вертикального перемещения.

Технически контейнер определяется как: "транспортное оборудование:

(a) имеющее постоянный характер и в силу этого достаточно прочное, чтобы служить для многократного использования;
(b) специально сконструированное для облегчения перевозки грузов одним или несколькими видами транспорта без промежуточной перегрузки грузов;
(c) снабженное приспособлениями, облегчающими его применение, в частности при его перегрузке с одного вида транспорта на другой;
(d) сконструированное таким образом, чтобы его можно было легко наполнять и опорожнять;
(e) пригодное для штабелирования, и
(f) имеющее внутренний объем не менее одного кубического метра".

Исключаются съемные кузова. Несмотря на то, что контейнеры-платформы, используемые в морских перевозках, не характеризуются внутренним объемом и, следовательно, не соответствуют вышеприведенному критерию f), их следует рассматривать в качестве особого вида контейнеров; поэтому они отнесены к данной категории.

Габариты контейнеров : К числу основных относятся следующие габариты контейнеров:

(a) 20-футовый контейнер ИСО: длиной 20 футов и шириной 8 футов;
(b) 40-футовый контейнер ИСО: длиной 40 футов и шириной 8 футов;
(c) суперконтейнер особо большой емкости: (особо крупногабаритный контейнер); и
(d) контейнер авиационный (контейнер, предназначенный для воздушных перевозок)

Контейнеры, указанные в пунктах(a) -(c), относятся к категории крупногабаритных контейнеров.

Виды контейнеров : К числу основных видов контейнеров, определенных в Руководстве по стандартам ИСО, касающимся грузовых контейнеров, относятся:

1 - контейнеры общего назначения;

2 - контейнеры особого назначения:

- контейнер закрытый, вентилируемый;
- контейнер, открытый сверху;
- контейнер на базе платформы (открытый сбоку);
- контейнер на базе платформы (открытый сбоку) с полной верхней рамой;
- контейнер на базе платформы (открытый сбоку) с неполной верхней рамой и жестко закрепленными торцами;
- контейнер на базе платформы (открытый сбоку) с неполной верхней рамой и складными торцами;
- контейнер-платформа;

3 - контейнеры для специальных грузов:

- изотермический контейнер;
- термоизолированный контейнер;
- рефрижераторный контейнер с восполняемым хладагентом;
- рефрижераторный контейнер с машинным охлаждением;
- отапливаемый контейнер;
- рефрижераторный и отапливаемый контейнер;
- контейнер-цистерна;
- контейнер для сыпучих грузов;
- контейнер для других видов грузов (как, например, для перевозки автомобилей, скота и др.)
- контейнеры авиационные.

ДФЭ (двадцатифутовый эквивалент) : Стандартная единица измерения внутреннего объема контейнеров, контейнеровозов и контейнерных терминалов. Единица ДФЭ равняется одному 20-футовому контейнеру ИСО.

Один 40-футовый контейнер ИСО приравнивается к двум единицам ДФЭ.

Съемный кузов : Перевозочная единица, являющаяся достаточно прочной для многократного использования, но не пригодная для захвата сверху или штабелирования при загрузке. Эти единицы используются главным образом в контрэйлерных перевозках.

Контейнер-платформа : Подлежащая загрузке платформа, не имеющая верхней рамы, но обладающая такой же длиной и шириной, что и база контейнера, и оборудованная верхними и нижними угловыми фитингами.

Это альтернативный термин, используемый для определенных типов контейнеров специального назначения, а именно, контейнеров - платформ и контейнеров на базе платформы с неполной верхней рамой.

fine Gardening Design Guides

Creative Ideas from America's Best Gardeners

EXPLORING GARDEN STYLE

EXPLORING
GARDEN STYLE

fine
Gardening Design Guides

EXPLORING GARDEN STYLE

Creative Ideas *from* America's Best Gardeners

The Taunton Press

*Special thanks to the editors, art directors, copy editors,
and other staff members of* Fine Gardening *who contributed
to the development of the articles featured in this book.*

Front cover photographers: Lee Anne White, © The Taunton Press, Inc. (large);
© Allan Mandell (inset)
Back cover photographers: © Allan Mandell (large); author photos
courtesy *Fine Gardening* magazine, © The Taunton Press, Inc.
Publisher: Jim Childs
Acquisitions Editor: Lee Anne White
Editorial Assistant: Meredith DeSousa
Technical Editor: Todd Meier
Copy Editor: Candace Levy
Indexer: Linda Stannard
Art Director: Paula Schlosser
Design Manager: Rosalind Wanke
Cover and Interior Designer: Lori Wendin
Layout Artist: Carol Petro

Taunton
BOOKS & VIDEOS
for fellow enthusiasts

Printed in the United States of America
10 9 8 7 6 5 4 3 2 1

The Taunton Press, Inc., 63 South Main Street, PO Box 5506,
Newtown, CT 06470-5506
e-mail: tp@taunton.com

Distributed by Publishers Group West

Library of Congress Cataloging-in-Publication Data
Exploring garden style : creative ideas from America's best gardeners.
p. cm.—(Fine gardening design guides)
ISBN 1-56158-474-6
1. Gardens—United States. 2. Gardens—United States—Design.
3. Gardens—United States—Styles. I. Fine gardening. II. Series
SB466.U6 E86 2001
712—dc21   00-059935

"Do I just like gardens because they're one more room to furnish? The way I used to think a baby sister or even a baby brother would be another doll to dress?"

—Abbie Zabar,
A Growing Gardener

Contents

PART 3: Specialty Gardens 72

Introduction

Americans have always been adventurous souls. And as a gardening nation, we are finally coming into our own—breaking free from a traditionally European style of gardening and exploring new territory. I believe this is happening for a number of reasons. First, we've finally had time, as a nation, to pursue our interest in gardening. (Remember, we're a young country compared to Great Britain, France, or Italy.) Second, we have a lot of talented gardeners and designers who wish to make their own artistic mark on the landscape. Third, we're letting our diversity—both in culture and growing conditions—drive our style. And finally, I believe that necessity and lifestyle greatly affect the way we garden.

In this book on garden style, you'll see how American-style gardens are evolving. And you'll be delighted by just how diverse these gardens really are. Even among traditional gardens, you'll find some interesting twists—like gardens that were designed to be at their peak beauty and fragrance during the evening hours.

What you'll discover in *Exploring Garden Style* are some of America's most innovative and beautiful private gardens, all of which first appeared on the pages of *Fine Gardening* magazine. Some were professionally designed; others were created entirely by their owners. These aren't estates or public gardens that require upkeep from an army of gardeners. Instead, they are residential gardens maintained by passionate gardeners. And it's these very gardeners who tell the story of their gardens.

TRADITIONAL
GARDENS

1

WHEN WE THINK OF TRADITIONAL gardens in America, images of boxwoods, dog-woods, brick walls, picket fences, and colorful perennial borders come to mind. These gardens may be formal or informal. Often they are a mix of both, with more formal spaces close to the house, and informal areas toward the edges of the property.

Traditional gardens tend to be structured gardens, created around a series of garden rooms or out-door spaces. Contrasting with neatly clipped hedges and carefully mown lawns are masses of spring bulbs and flowering shrubs or brightly colored perennial borders. There is a sense of familiarity in these gardens, something that we cherish from the gardens of our childhood.

While the gardens in this section might be classified as traditional, each has its own sense of spirit and adventure. Some of these gardens were planned in great detail; others evolved over time. Each tells a story and offers ideas for those who desire a traditional garden of their own.

SHARON ABROMS-McHALE

is a landscape designer who specializes in small spaces. She also runs an antique business that sells garden ornaments and other garden-related items.

A Garden Room for Every Mood

A ribbon pathway planted in dwarf mondo grass links outdoor rooms in a garden called love-in-a-mist, named for *Nigella damascena*, a flower the author says has a dual personality.

I CALL MY GARDEN Love-in-a-Mist, which is but one name for *Nigella damascena*. When nigella's wispy blue flowers bloom, the seedpods turn into prickly, horned capsules, and what was once "love-in-a-mist" becomes "devil-in-a-bush." I myself have been called by both names! Like the flower, I've never been of one mind. On my ¾-acre lot, I've chosen to celebrate the vicissitudes of both nature and human nature in four small garden rooms, each with its own personality. The mood of the rooms shifts subtly from peaceful and contemplative to whimsical and untamed. As you walk through my garden on these pages, I hope you'll see what I mean.

Before you begin your tour, I should tell you that I had help planning my gardens. Atlanta garden designer Ryan Gainey divided my grand piano–shaped lot into four distinct areas: the Driveway Garden, the Visitors' Garden, the White Border and the Birdhouse Garden. A narrow garden called the Ribbon Path acts as a hallway to get from one garden room to another. Once we had set up the basic structure of each room, I evoked the different moods through my choice of plants and garden features.

DRIVEWAY GARDEN BALANCES FORMAL WITH INFORMAL

The Driveway Garden has a split personality. I planned it that way because I like formality and neatness in my garden, but I also like the softness of casual plantings. The formal side of the driveway consists of a manicured lawn, a clipped holly hedge (*Ilex crenata* 'Compacta') and a row of shaped littleleaf linden trees (*Tilia cordata*).

The other side of the drive is more easygoing. Here, lush, colorful plantings ease the linear effect of the holly hedge and linden trees across the drive. Old Garden roses, 'Betty Prior' roses, foxgloves (*Digitalis purpurea* 'Foxy'), pinks (*Dianthus* 'Bath's Pink'), worm-

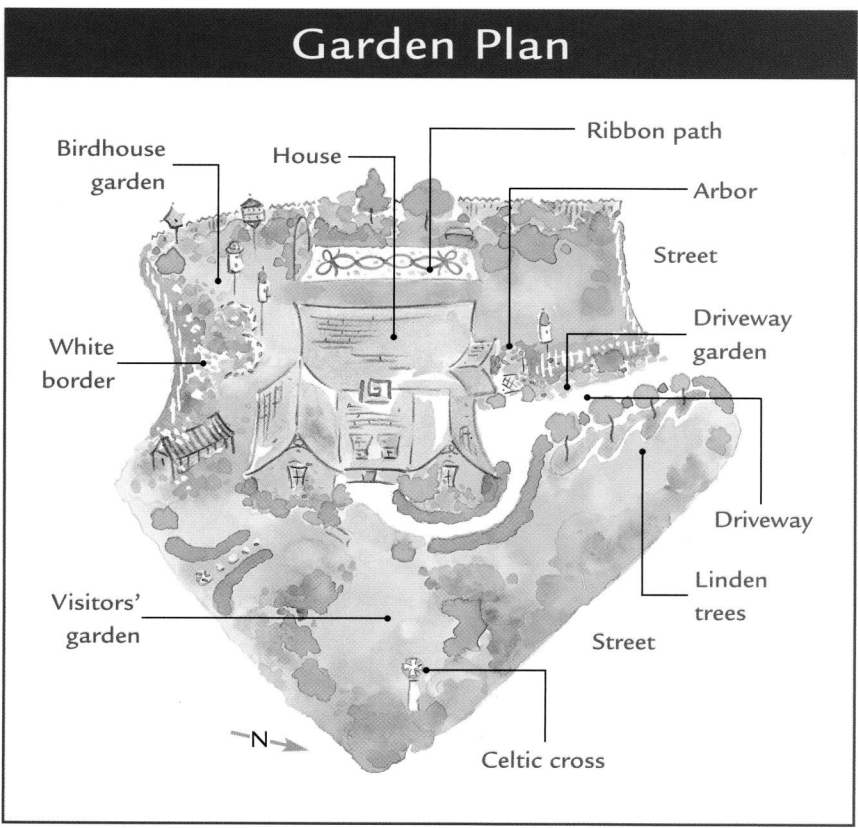

Garden Plan

Birdhouse garden

House

Ribbon path

Arbor

Street

White border

Driveway garden

Visitors' garden

Driveway

Linden trees

Street

N

Celtic cross

Formal faces informal in the Driveway Garden, where shaped lindens (LEFT) contrast a relaxed planting (TOP). Moods collide at the arbor as the linearity of wood yields to a jumble of climbing roses (ABOVE).

(FAR RIGHT) A quiet place for contemplation, the Visitor's Garden features a thought-provoking Celtic cross.

(NEAR RIGHT AND BELOW) A path dotted with hydrangeas leads to the sheltered room.

wood (*Artemisia absinthium* 'Huntington Gardens') and poppies (*Papaver* spp.) all relax in happy abundance across from their manicured neighbors.

VISITORS' GARDEN OFFERS RESPITE

The Visitors' Garden has become a shrine, where visitors leave offerings of flowers or candles. The meditative mood of this garden is enhanced by a reproduction of an ancient Celtic cross. I created this garden after returning from a trip to Ireland, where real Celtic crosses abound.

The Visitors' Garden has a sheltered quality, due to a privacy screen of Leyland cypress (× *Cupressocyparis leylandii*) and Japanese cedar (*Cryptomeria japonica*). A sense of informality is achieved by casual plantings of irises (*Iris* 'Pacific Palisades' and 'Victoria Falls'), 'Bonica' roses, foxgloves and 'New Dawn' climbing roses. The climbing roses cover themselves with creamy pink flowers in spring and repeat their bloom through the season. I have them planted close to the house, where their flower color echoes the color of the walls.

Big-leaf hydrangeas (*H. macrophylla*) and self-seeding begonias (*Begonia grandis*) bloom as summer comes on. Neither flower requires much maintenance, although sometimes the begonias jump out of place, and I find little seedlings popping up among the periwinkle ground cover (*Vinca minor*).

"I like formality and neatness in my garden, but I also like the softness of casual plantings."

"I am always moving things around to suit my mood, experimenting with new plants and different combinations."

A WHITE BORDER FEELS COOLY SERENE

A white garden appealed to me because of the quiet mood I could create with milky flowers, and foliage of silver, gray and green. Varying textures give the white flowers different degrees of light reflection and absorption, challenging the concept of a monochromatic garden.

The White Border varies its look throughout the seasons, but its color scheme is always cool. The spring show includes white false indigo (*Baptisia alba*), white foxgloves (*Digitalis* × 'Emerson'), white 'Iceberg' roses, veronica (*V. spicata* 'Icicle'), poppies, irises (*Iris* 'Skating Party'), wormwood and Southern shield ferns (*Thelypteris normalis* 'Kuentii'). The Southern shield ferns, along with fountain grass (*Pennisetum alopecuroides* 'Moudry'), provide low-maintenance interest throughout the summer, while luminous white roses glow like lamps on summer nights.

BIRDHOUSE GARDEN CONTAINS A TOUCH OF WHIMSY

A sign near the entrance to my birdhouse garden reads: "May all who enter rejoice in the creation of life." The sign sets the tone for what is to come—an exuberant garden that celebrates life, flowers and birds. The birdhouse garden is visible from the street, and passersby just love it.

To enter, one must pass beneath a rustic cedar archway flanked by two large pyramidal hollies (*Ilex latifolia*) underplanted with creep-

ing Jenny (*Lysimachia nummularia*) and *Mazus reptans*, a ground cover with a tiny blue flower.

Within the garden is my collection of birdhouses; the birdhouses look so charming together that I developed a community. There is a school, a church, a general store and even a replica of Tara from *Gone With the Wind*.

RIBBON PATH TIES IT ALL TOGETHER

The Ribbon Path serves as a passageway, connecting the Driveway Garden to the other gardens. To take advantage of the long corridor shape of this area, I designed a dogwood allée with a ribbon pathway. Flanking the pathway are mixed plantings of hydrangeas (*H. paniculata*, *H. quercifolia*, *H. arborescens* 'Annabelle'), hostas, Southern shield ferns, cinnamon ferns

(*Osmunda cinnamomea*) and Japanese painted ferns (*Athyrium niponicum* 'Pictum'). The ribbon itself is made of dwarf mondo grass (*Ophiopogon japonicus* 'Nanus') planted right in the stone "floor."

A SIGN OF APPRECIATION

The one constant of my garden is the pleasure it gives me. I am always moving things around to suit my mood, experimenting with new plants and different combinations. For my efforts, I am rewarded every day by the reactions of visitors and neighbors. One December, someone left a Christmas ornament on my doorstep with a note that read,

"To the Flower Lady,
With thanks for making a lovely garden, which I enjoyed all summer.
You are appreciated.
A Flower Friend."

I will always treasure that simple message. The greatest gift I receive from my garden is the enjoyment other people get from it.

Three faces of one garden. A rustic archway (ABOVE LEFT), a whimsical birdhouse garden (ABOVE RIGHT) and a white border (LEFT) flower together in a garden called "Love-in-a-Mist."

KATHRYN MacDOUGALD

is creator and producer of HGTV's *A Gardener's Diary*. Previously the owner of a garden design business, she still handles several design projects each year.

Planting a Terraced Garden

Plant paths with creepers to make them look aged and noble. Golden creeping thyme covers the central pathway in Kathryn MacDougald's terraced garden.

THE HORRIBLE OLD HOLLIES were dead. Governor Joe Brown's hunting lodge burned to the ground. And my little brother, Stephen, was getting married. I didn't realize it then, but these three incidents were the driving forces behind the creation of my terrace garden.

In 1986, I moved into an 89-year-old log cabin that was nestled into a hillside. On the left, stone steps led to a second-story entrance. But on the right was a weedy slope covered with old, very prickly hollies. For six years, every time I stood and looked up at the cabin, I wondered what to do with the hillside to balance the steps on the left.

Of course, I first had to dig out those deep-rooted hollies. While I was doing all that digging, I decided that terraces carved into the hillside would provide balance and make the hill accessible for gardening. But when Christmas came, with no bulldozer under the tree, I realized that any earth-moving would have to be done by hand.

Container plantings, large and small, are scattered throughout the garden. This rustic planter is filled with foliage rather than flowers.

So rather than dig out the hillside for terraces, I chose to create raised beds with retaining walls and well-amended fill dirt.

USE RETAINING WALLS TO TERRACE A SLOPE

Not far from our cabin stood the 1800s hunting lodge of former Georgia Governor Joe Brown. The abandoned house had been a favorite party spot for local teens over the years, at least until it burned to the ground. After the fire, the owners decided to sell the place, but before they put up the sign, I got their permission to haul away all the stones I could handle. By bribing a neighbor with a reasonable share of the bounty, I enlisted both her and her truck for duty.

Five Ways to Plant a Terrace

1 Shrubs, annuals, and perennials in terraced beds
2 Containers as focal points
3 Large plants or containers at entries
4 Trailing plants hanging over the walls
5 Creepers in the pathways

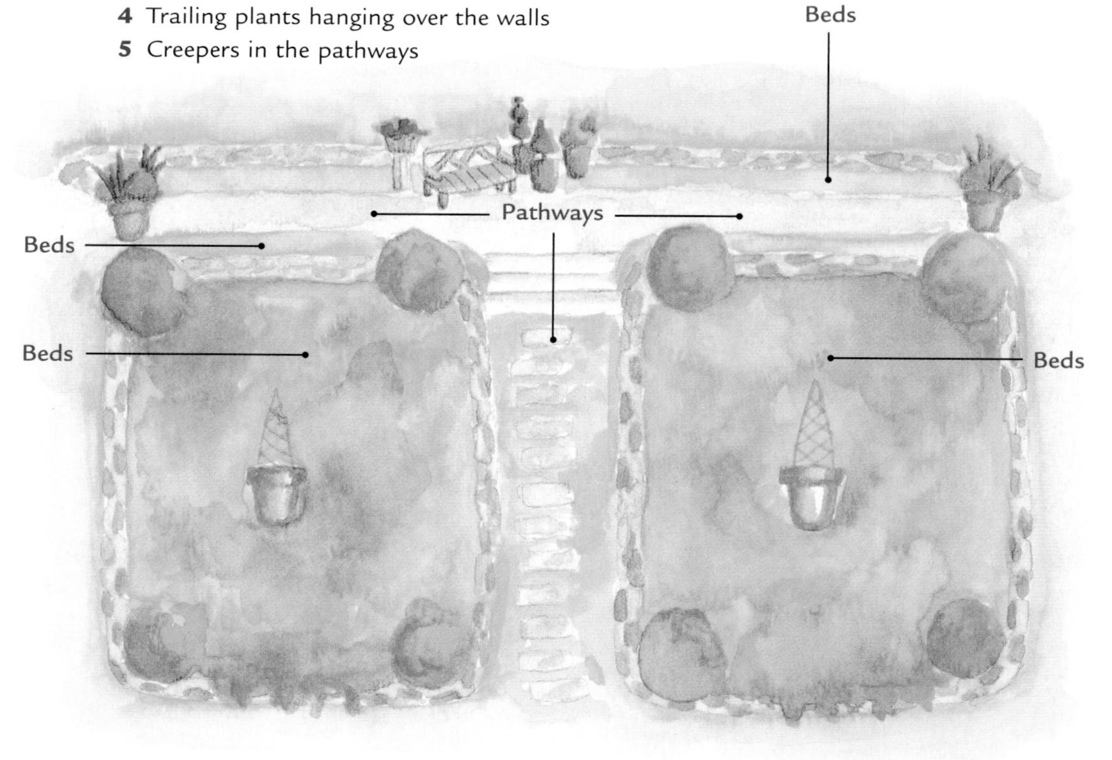

Beds

Beds

Pathways

Beds

Beds

Beds

Container plantings draw the eye through the garden.

A clematis-covered tutuer adds an upright accent to a lower planting bed.

Shrubs and perennials fill the beds.

Stone retaining walls create level terraces for planting.

Trailing plants are allowed to cascade over the stone wall.

Spreading plants with small root systems can be tucked into cracks and crevices.

Within a week, I had completed the first retaining wall. I laid the largest stones at the base and, as the height of the walls grew, laid each layer of stone so the wall angled back. I also wedged lumber against the rocks on the inside of the wall for stability until the fill dirt could be added. To promote good drainage, and to keep my garden soil from washing away, I lined the inside of the wall with crushed gravel from a local quarry. In all, I needed four retaining walls to create two levels with a central path, so I continued to haul stones and build walls for a month. At the end of that time, I had four large garden areas ready for soil and a leisurely planting schedule—or so I thought.

FILL BEHIND WALLS WITH AMENDED SOIL

A few days later, my brother Stephen called to say he was getting married in May, and that, by the way, he would love to have the reception in the field in front of the cabin. Caught up in the excitement of the moment, and not being adept at saying no to my little brother, I began to describe how beautiful the new gardens would look in May. By the next morning,

"Terraces carved into the hillside would provide balance and make the hill accessible for gardening."

Shrubs anchor the planting beds and are surrounded with flowers. Cascading plants are tucked in along the edges, and creepers fill in the cracks and crevices.

I realized not only that it was getting terribly late for planting but also that I didn't even have any soil.

And, oh, how I had taken those "Free Dirt" signs for granted. Now that I needed dirt, there wasn't a sign to be found. How, in a growing city like Atlanta, could there be no dirt? I opted instead for 11 truckloads of composted horse manure, to which I added some leftover crushed gravel, bags of topsoil from the hardware store, and far too many wheelbarrow loads of soil from around my property to count. It wasn't perfect, but it would do.

The gardens—filled at the last minute with foxglove, larkspur, delphinium, roses, rosemary, and thyme—looked lovely for the wed-

ding reception. And since then, I've continued to amend the soil and add favorite plants to the garden.

ESTABLISH PATHWAYS AND PLANT THEM WITH CREEPERS

In a terrace garden, like any other garden, you need to be able to move around. In mine, there is a main path of steps that leads up the center and divides the hillside in half. There is also a second path on the upper terrace that runs from side to side, from the cabin to the barn and the woods.

I had a supply of pavers on hand from the streets of old Atlanta, back when it was named Marthasville, which were perfect for the steps

thyme. On occasion, a moss verbena (*Verbena tenuisecta*)—probably from a long-ago container planting—will volunteer between the pavers and, because of its low-growing habit, I let it be. Violets (*Viola* spp.) that seed themselves in the paths are left to fend the footfalls for themselves. When we first moved into the cabin, impatiens of all colors grew up everywhere. For years, I pulled all but the white ones, and now those white impatiens volunteer in absolutely perfect places.

PLANT BEDS FOR BURSTS OF SEASONAL COLOR

The top terrace, which has the path running through it, is about 6 ft. wide. Here, I've placed a bench against the back wall and scattered container plantings about. And along either side of the path, I created narrow borders. These borders are planted primarily with colorful perennials that don't block the view of the lower gardens. But every 4 ft. or 5 ft. a taller planting screens the view, so that you have to get up and walk around to see what it is hiding.

These top gardens hold geraniums that love to flop over and lay low, such as *Geranium* 'Johnson's Blue', *G.* × *oxonianum* 'Claridge Druce', and *G. sanguineum*. Society garlic (*Tulbaghia fragrans*, also known as *T. simmleri*) stands straight among the geraniums, while *Rosa* 'Clotilde Soupert' droops into a small, everblooming mound. In spring, *Bletilla striata* orchids rise up among the forget-me-nots (*Myosotis sylvatica*), which run rampant through the upper gardens and even into the paths.

and pathways. Embedding them 2 in. to 3 in. apart left plenty of room for creeping plants. And nothing makes a garden look aged and noble like creepers covering a pathway.

I have planted thyme of all varieties, but the golden thyme (*Thymus* × *citriodorus* 'Aureus') settled in so comfortably that I pull it up and give it away freely. For a couple of years, the mat grew so thick that I almost forgot there were stones under the thyme. It is an evergreen ground cover, and if you have a good nose, you can smell the faint, lemony perfume as you walk on it.

Blue star creeper (*Laurentia fluviatilis*) is a much neater creeper between the pavers and appears almost genteel next to the blowzy

"In all, I needed four retaining walls to create two levels with a central path."

There are two squarish, walled garden beds on the bottom terrace with steps up the middle, but I planted them as though they were one big rectangle. I chose small, flowering shrubs to anchor the beds and to serve as focal points, and planted them near the outer walls to balance the center steps. A white, spring-flowering *Deutzia gracilis* graces the left bed, while *Spirea japonica* 'Goldflame' draws your eye to the right. Because each of these shrubs has a solid, mounded shape, I placed taller, loosely shaped plants such as butterfly bush (*Buddleia davidii*), garden phlox (*Phlox paniculata*), and roses nearby.

Plants with rangy, diffuse shapes are placed near companions with clear, strong shapes. The swordlike leaves of Louisiana and Japanese irises along the edges of the gardens lead the eye upward. I keep the colors on the left side in blues and pinks, and on the right I highlight yellows, oranges, and an occasional red. White-flowering plants are used as an accent to make other colors stand out. And purple, my favorite color, is thrown in everywhere possible.

Lamb's ears and cottage pinks drape over the walls, clothing them year-round in evergreen foliage.

MAKE ENTRY POINTS INVITING

At each entrance to the garden I try to create an attention-catching planting. If the eye is immediately challenged, pleased, or excited by an unusual plant or group of plants, then the senses are heightened throughout the rest of the garden. This falls under the old adage that first impressions are important.

One of my favorite combinations is the multicolored *Houttuynia cordata* 'Chameleon' and a green- and white-variegated ivy I purchased at the grocery store. Stuck in one corner of a wall, the ivy cascades and the houttuynia pops up. The combination sounds like it would be too busy, but it is a pleasing sight that causes most people to pause.

Lately, I've taken to planting lemon verbena (*Aloysia triphylla*) at the beginning of the lower path. It spills over into the path and gets so large that it must be pushed out of the way for passage, thus releasing its invigorating perfume. Old iron urns filled with giant candle plant (*Plectranthus forsteri* 'Marginatus') or violets, according to season, sit on the stone wall at the top of the steps, punctuating this central pathway.

TAME TERRACE WALLS WITH TRAILING PLANTS

There are plants that cry out to be draped over walls. At one time, *Verbena* 'Homestead Purple' covered almost all my walls. Now my friends and neighbors, and their friends and neighbors, have this plant in their gardens. There are many cottage pinks (*Dianthus* cvs.) to choose from, and most love hanging over the wall like a great, gray beard.

One fleabane (*Erigeron karvinskianus* 'Profusion') I planted five years ago has seeded all over the garden and especially likes trailing out of the rocks. Variegated ivies planted in crevices, along with cottage pinks, keep the

walls covered in winter. *Nepeta grandiflora* has also proven to be a great wall plant by flowing down over the edge and then flipping back up like a '50s hairstyle.

ACCENT THE GARDEN WITH CONTAINER PLANTINGS

After the gardens grew full and lush, the main path across the top of the hill seemed barren and in need of height. Three-ft.-tall Mexican urns planted with boxwood (*Buxus* spp.) added a new dimension to the garden. Other containers of varying sizes help to close in the open areas and break up the long pathway by creating cozy nooks. I also keep several large terra-cotta pots on hand to fill up spaces that may appear in the middle of the garden as flowers fade in and out of season.

One of my favorite container plantings features a chartreuse sweet potato vine (*Ipomea batatas*) surrounded by *Lantana*, *Scaevola*, and asparagus fern (*Asparagus setaceus*). I love to watch them try to overtake each other and the garden. If I plant them in early summer and put them in a sunny spot, by fall I delight in fantasizing that if a frost did not come, they would be winding their way into the house.

In the center of both rectangular beds, I have matching wrought-iron tuteurs sitting atop iron stands. They serve as focal points year-round, but are at their best when the clematis (*Clematis* 'Henryi', *C.* 'The President', and *C.* Comtesse de Bouchaud') planted at the base wind up them to bloom.

After four more years of standing in the field below my cabin—this time looking at my garden instead of the prickly old hollies—I decided to anchor the terraces by adding a boxwood at each corner. I also added more walls at the top of the slope (behind the upper terrace) to balance the bottom walls. I'm beginning to realize that the terrace gardens may never be complete. But then, isn't that true for any garden?

Large container plantings mark the entrance to the upper path, which runs from the house to the barn and the woods.

A Sanctuary in Every Season

PAT BULLARD is a music publisher and writer in Nashville. She won a Quill and Trowel Award from the Garden Writers' Association of America for this story in *Fine Gardening*.

Limbing up trees opens the garden. Careful pruning turned three overgrown euonymus into stately specimens.

ONE CHILLY NOVEMBER day five years ago, I called my husband, George, to tell him I'd finally found the place we'd been looking for. Something stirred inside me every time I looked out the big bay window in the dining room. I saw a gently sloping backyard and dreamed about filling it with a traditional border overflowing with blossoms.

Little did I know that one day it would be something entirely different, a leafy sanctuary for my soul. After a tragic auto accident, I needed a place to heal and took refuge in the garden. There, I devoted myself to creating a place of understated serenity, where foliage and texture flow like a restful river. Where the gentle fragrance of thyme, lavender, and mint, crushed underfoot, calms my spirit. And where limestone benches soak up sunlight like the ruins of an ancient temple. Who would have guessed that I would learn to see past the fleeting beauty of flowers

Fancy foliage adds color. The mottled leaves of *Pulmonaria* 'Excalibur' shine against a soft, bronzy background of duck-foot coleus.

and to embrace plants for the cool, soothing feel of their foliage? And that, in the process, I would become a gardener?

But first, back to the beginning. We bought the house and moved in. I planted shrubs, filled a bed with white phlox, and cleared honeysuckle. One weekend, I took a break and visited my friend Jo Ann. We were enjoying a drive past fields of late summer wildflowers when a car came around a curve on the wrong side of the road and hit us head-on. I regained consciousness, but Jo Ann never did. I had some fractured bones, but it was my heart that was really broken.

FINDING SOLACE IN THE GARDEN

I returned home, and looked out those same windows. The accident and its aftermath left me feeling disconnected from the rest of the world. I no longer thought of the garden. A

"The overall mood was set by soaring ceilings of hackberry and maple."

couple of months later, my friend Alicia dropped by with a flat of blue and white pansies. I'd just gotten the cast off my right arm and was wearing a removable brace. "These aren't just your ordinary pansies," she announced. "They're thera-pansies, and you're going to plant every single one yourself."

I went obediently to the garden. The soil felt warm from the fall sun. I planted the pansies, marveling at their sweet faces and the white roots threaded through cubes of moist, spongy, earth-scented sphagnum moss. I planted those pansies in pain, and watered them with tears. Then, they began to bloom. Suddenly, I felt alive.

Though my story was too personal to share with most people, the garden seemed to understand; it silently soaked up my sorrow and grief. It gave me solace. I may have been on my hands and knees in the dirt, but I was making progress, physically and spiritually.

FOLIAGE OUTPERFORMS FLOWERS

Once I realized gardening was such a positive tool for me, I put my heart and soul into it, and the effort energized me. I didn't have an overall plan, so I just plunged right in. Back at the window, I planned and plotted for ways to create great views. The courtyard terrace stared back, and I noticed the brown stubble of the white phlox I had planted the summer before. I had initially envisioned the phlox creating a serenely monochromatic color scheme. But when it bloomed, the phlox looked like an eternal wedding. I was tired of it in 15 minutes!

When spring came, I tore out the phlox, and, for the first time, noticed the still-bare bones of dwarf Japanese maple against the green, velvet background of a boxwood's new growth. I saw the similarity between hemlock

needles and the fronds of ferns. I began to realize the importance of foliage: its color, texture,
shape, and structure. Plants aren't flowers
first; they're foliage. Most flowers last a short
time, and then we're left with their foliage for
the rest of the season, so it made sense to
make foliage the first priority in choosing
plants. I recognized, too, that there was something soothing about those many shades of
green. They gave the garden a sense of perma-
nence, a constancy that flowers could never
provide. To me, that sense of continuity is very
calming. As it turned out, I wasn't abandoning
the monochromatic color scheme after all, I
was simply switching to another color—green.
Suddenly, I saw everything differently. It was
as if a magic door had opened.

GARDEN ROOMS NEED TO BE DECORATED

I began to see the garden more clearly. It
would become an outdoor home filled with
rooms. There was a formal courtyard used as
my dining room, a patio area I call the "living
room," a shade garden, and long, curving beds
accented with bright bursts of color. I wanted
a feeling of openness and freedom, so there
would be no fences or gates. Instead, the mood
was set by soaring ceilings of hackberry and
maple, and soft, flowering walls of viburnum
and hydrangea. To that I added furniture of
stone and, of course, plush, leafy carpets of
green. I started looking at plants as if they
were fabric and wallpaper samples, seeing
them as print and floral patterns.

Look out the window
to create harmonious
views inside and out.
The author planned
part of her garden
while gazing out the
dramatic dining-room
picture window that
framed it.

Soaring trees provide a cathedral ceiling overhead. By removing lower limbs, more light was allowed into the garden.

Shades of green provide a soothing setting.

Occasional flowers create a cheerful atmosphere. Used with restraint, even bright colors can be comforting.

The brick terrace needed softening, so I planted several varieties of creeping thyme. Its tiny leaves made a good foil for the hard-edged brick, and they also release a calming fragrance when stepped upon. I filled in an old fish pond nearby and added an assortment of hardy geraniums—their long-lasting, rounded leaves and mounding habit provide a beautiful contrast to the thyme.

Farther out in the yard, I tried to set a spiritual tone at the garden's entry by creating a soothing sweep of foliage, a rich, leafy stream with textures and hues ranging from the round, deep-green, sawtooth-edged leaves of a ligularia to the soft, muted gold of a hosta. I tried to create other compositions using the subtle colors, varied shapes, and different sizes of foliage. I like plant combinations that use leaves of the same shape but in colors and sizes that are very different. One of my favorite groupings contrasts the large, grassy-green, scalloped foliage of an oakleaf hydrangea (*Hydrangea quercifolia*) with the small, lobed, bronze-purple leaves of duckfoot coleus (*Solenostemon scutellarioides*).

To carry that composition into autumn, I rely on color, and pair the burgundy fall color of the oakleaf hydrangea with another type of coleus, any one of the hybrids with the color of red wine.

Elsewhere in the garden, I've added accents of floral color to my leafy palette. In one spot, clumps of bee balm, Jerusalem artichoke, and veronica embrace me like a colorful, cozy, old quilt. Used with restraint, even bright colors can be comforting.

FEEDING THE EARTH NOURISHES THE BODY

I hadn't been much of a gardener before, but I was becoming one, complete with calluses, sore muscles, and dirt under my fingernails. It seemed the more I fed the earth, the more the garden nourished me.

My garden and my sense of well-being grew with each new planting bed. As I prepared new areas, I found some parts of the yard had loose, rich soil, but others were hard clay. So instead of digging down, I built up. I engineered minor drainage systems for some of the wetter areas, and amended the clay with my own "soul food" for the garden. Around our house it's known as "Pat's Soufflé." I make as much of my organic, slow-acting, long-lasting mix as I can afford and use it constantly as a fertilizer, and to prepare new beds. After adding this mixture for the last five years, my trowel easily sinks to my elbow in most of the beds.

A CATHEDRAL CEILING FOR A GARDEN REFUGE

The more time I spent working the beds, the closer I came to realizing the design I envisioned. In my nightgown, with a cup of coffee and bare feet wet with dew, I learned when and where the morning sunlight would show up and, as I lay in the grass and looked up through the smooth, gray hackberry trees, I imagined having tall cathedral ceilings in my outdoor home. With the help of a tree-trimming service, we cut out the lower limbs and, as some areas were too dark, we "lightened" selected branches. Streams of sun suddenly shone like spotlights in the dappled shade.

As my new creations took root, I found myself remembering the gardens from my childhood. I thought about the spirea my sister and I played under, and the dancing dolls we dressed in swirling skirts made from hollyhocks. To heighten the feeling of refuge I wanted my garden to provide, I tried to mirror the peace and innocence of that time. To help recall those bygone days, I planted some passalong plants—including irises and old favorites such as Indian pink (*Spigelia marilandica*)—from my mother-in-law's garden.

Another touchstone to my past came about by chance. A neighbor gave me a block of lime-

Passalong plants bring a piece of the past to the garden. One of the author's favorites is Indian pink, with its red-and-gold blooms. This southeastern native comes from her mother-in-law's garden.

The calming glow of foliage brightens this shade planting of *Ligularia dentata* 'Othello' and *Hosta* 'Zounds' accented by the more delicate leaves of Japanese painted fern, *Astilbe* × *arendsii* 'Federsee', and azaleas.

stone that I used as a bench. Today mosses grow on it, and their sweet scent reminds me of a giant rock down in the woods by the creek where, as children, we spent hours fishing for minnows.

I also began dreaming of all kinds of new plants for my garden. I sat in my lawn chair every morning with a cup of coffee, moving from one location to another, making lists of the things I wanted to try. Then I rediscovered a sign on my refrigerator that says: "The most difficult arithmetic to master is the art of counting your blessings." I used the sign to remind me, during the darkest days of my recovery, of all the good in my life. I realized that idea also applied to the garden and, instead of seeking out new plants, I started evaluating what I already had, wondering which ones might be moved or reshaped. The most obvious candidates were the three huge winged euonymus that had grown into a single, giant mass in part of the garden. I had them pruned into tree forms, and now they reign like royal specimens over the azaleas, astilbes, and ferns in the shade room of the garden.

> *"Instead of seeking out new plants, I started evaluating what I already had, wondering which ones might be moved or reshaped."*

Other plants were moved so often I nearly wore off their roots, but I'm comforted by the many hours of therapy and education they provided. Besides, some actually survived all the abuse I heaped on them!

HIGHLIGHT THE CHANGING SEASONS

Throughout the year, I can see the changes time brings to my garden. Gazing through the picture window, I notice how the pods of Japanese iris (*Iris ensata*) and *Sedum* 'Autumn Joy' take on the look of a photographic negative in winter, and how the green of boxwood looks black against the snow. In spring, the pink flowers of the azaleas and the white blooms of the dogwoods remind me of my grandmother's best Sunday dress. In summer, the walls of the garden, framed by the columns of tree trunks and anchored by smaller flowering shrubs, remind me of a silk wall hanging. And in fall, the carpet of ground covers turns into the lustrous bronze of an oriental carpet.

As my confidence as a gardener grew, my gardens gave me something positive to talk about and to share with others. My friends began to notice. We started having coffee in the courtyard more often, and then they all wanted to walk through the garden. At first, I was self-conscious and apologetic for the rough, unfinished areas and the ragged weeds. But they never saw its faults. Janice loves my peonies and roses. Maureen takes my lilies home for dinner parties, and Randy, a songwriter, loves to walk through it alone, just to clear his mind.

I read somewhere that it takes 10 years for a garden to mature. I've never stayed in one place long enough to find out if that's true, but I'm now over halfway there. My healing garden began with a tragic accident and today, safe within its sanctuary, I see spring's signal, the weeping cherry. Its shining, gray branches now grow nearly to the ground, even though, in my ignorance, I pruned all its weeping tendrils off several years ago. In time it recovered, and grew back with a vengeance. And so have I.

Soul Food for a Garden

RECIPE FOR A SOIL-BUILDING "SOUFFLÉ"

Good garden soils make for bountiful borders. A hearty helping of Pat's Soufflé, the author's concoction of organic nutrients, enriches any soil.

Mix together:
8 shovels mushroom or garden compost
5 lb. greensand
5 shovels fine pine bark
8 shovels potting soil
8 shovels peat moss
4 12-oz. coffee cans of cottonseed meal
   (6 in spring)
4 coffee cans bonemeal
2 coffee cans wood ash
4 coffee cans blood meal
4 coffee cans sheep or chicken manure

Makes a large wheelbarrow load.

PETER LOEWER has written more than 25 gardening books. A member of the Royal Horticultural Society, he serves on the board of the J.C. Raulston Arboretum and is vice president of the Asheville Botanical Gardens.

In the Garden, by the Light of the Moon

Flowers as big as a full moon top a giant hogweed. The author planted this 8-ft.-tall monster along a path.

I'M NOT QUITE SURE when I became enamored with gardening in the evening, but I know that part of the interest arose with being a devotee of horror movies. Oh, not those slasher flicks, but the good, old-fashioned classics, like *Frankenstein*, *Dracula*, and *The Wolf Man*. The plots often included flowers of the night, and scriptwriters actually gave them scientific names just to impress the audience. They must have impressed me, too.

My first evening garden began taking shape almost a decade ago when my wife, Jean, and I lived in the Catskill Mountains of upstate New York. Our backyard patio became a repository for various tropical perennials like the bell-shaped brugmansias (*Brugmansia suaveolens*), a few annuals, pot-grown perennials, and a small pool filled with night-blooming water lilies—all illuminated with six small, low-voltage lights.

Some daylilies prefer night. This night-blooming daylily, *Hemerocallis citrina*, opens its fragrant, lemon-yellow flowers in late afternoon and blooms through the night.

It wasn't long before I saw the value of gardens that bloomed in late afternoon and evening. When other gardeners came home after a hot day of commuting or jockeying the kids back and forth, they found wilting daylilies and parched-looking gardens. I, on the other hand, arrived home to see my nocturnal daylilies just beginning to open and other night-blooming flowers unfurling their blossoms to the evening sky. By 8 o'clock, the garden lights came on, allowing us to enjoy the flowers well into the evening.

"To get a feel for the way things look at night, take a colored comic strip out into the moonlight."

LIGHT COLORS SHINE AT NIGHT

In 1989, we moved to Asheville, North Carolina, where we live on an acre of land overlooking a lake. Our garden meanders down a slope to the water's edge and is divided into four main areas. Two of these—the walled garden at one end of the yard, and the terrace close to the house—were specifically designed to be enjoyed in the evening. That meant doing things differently. To get a feel for the way things look at night, take a colored comic strip out into the moonlight. You will be amazed at what you see. Provided there are no artificial lights nearby, you will discover that there's no color on the page. Instead, you'll just see blacks, whites, and grays.

Though moonlight is usually bright enough for reading a black-and-white newspaper, it is too dim to stimulate the cones of your retina—the part of the eye that responds to color—so colors cease to exist. In a flowering garden at night, the most visible blossoms are those with the lightest colors: white, cream, or shades of yellow. That's why we used white caladiums to line one of our outdoor stairways. On a cloudy summer night, the skies reflect so much of Asheville's light that the white leaves seem to illuminate the steps.

Plants with acid-green foliage are another good choice; they seem to glow at twilight. We marked another of the stairways with a chartreuse coleus named 'Gay's Delight'—it gleams like a beacon at dusk.

Among my favorite light-colored, flowering perennials for the evening garden are the night-blooming daylilies. *Hemerocallis citrina* has lemon-yellow flowers with a lemony fragrance that open around 4 o'clock on a sunny afternoon. For years, *H. citrina* was used in daylily breeding, and, as a result, many of the more common daylily hybrids have nocturnal tendencies. The most famed nocturnal plant is the night-blooming cereus (*Selenicerus grandiflorus*). I grow one in a pot atop a pillar—actually, it's the tall stump of an old dogwood—so visitors can walk beneath the blossoms.

Other night-blooming—or at least night-fragrant—hardy perennials include a fragrant plantain lily (*Hosta plantaginea*), a number of yuccas (*Yucca filamentosa*), white astilbe (*Astilbe × arendsii* 'Snowdrift'), and pink astilbe (*A. simplicifolia* 'Sprite'). In addition to their pale flowers, each of these perennials has a marvelous, sweet smell in the evening.

For light-colored flowers, I like to use annuals like white impatiens (*Impatiens wallerana*), white cosmos (*Cosmos bipinnatus*), white spider flowers (*Cleome hassleriana* 'Helen Campbell'), and both short and tall nicotianas (*Nicotiana* spp.), some of which are very fragrant at night.

Sometimes, though, I've found I can create an effective evening planting without relying on pale or white flowers. In the right situation, bright colors can work. At the edge of one of my evening gardens, a cluster of pink petunias encircling a sundial seems almost luminous in the last moments of twilight.

Bright even in twilight, this cluster of pink petunias seems almost luminous. Some colors, including pinks like these, are most effective at day's end.

Gazing globes glow like earthbound moons. Though the reflective silver finish of this 14-in. gazing globe wore off after a single season, the orb continues to command attention.

BREATHE DEEP, AND INHALE THE HEADY AROMA

The fragrance of an evening garden is different from the fragrance of a daylight garden. Day-blooming flowers usually have light, pleasant odors that, along with their bright colors, attract butterflies, hummingbirds, and day-time insects. Night-bloomers, or those with heightened nighttime fragrance, usually have a heavier scent—honeysuckles (*Lonicera* spp.) and mock oranges (*Philadelphus* spp.) come imme-diately to mind—because the moths or bats

"During a dinner party, guests can watch the flowers open in slow motion."

that pollinate them must find the flowers entirely by their smell. Some nocturnal plants have lemony odors that attract bats and other night creatures. Many night-blooming, tropical trees are even foxy, having a slightly musky odor.

We like to use the annual gourd (*Lagenaria siceraria*), a vine that can grow 25 ft. in one summer, producing hundreds of fragrant, night-blooming flowers of a rare, delicate beauty that eventually turn into bottle gourds. Both evening stocks (*Matthiola longipetala* ssp. *bicornis*) and four o'clocks (*Mirabilis jalapa*) bloom the first year from seed and produce sweet-smelling, nocturnal flowers. And night phlox (*Zaluzianskya capensis*), a half-hardy annual from South Africa, produces beautiful, fragrant, nighttime blossoms of five white petals notched at the tip, which are satiny maroon when closed.

Among perennials, bouncing bet (*Saponaria officinalis*) would be a beloved gar-den plant if her daytime looks matched her nighttime demeanor, for it is in the evening that her tawdry petals perk up and her sweet perfume fills the air. This plant is a stout perennial that spreads by a network of rhi-zomes and is especially valuable in holding on to the earth in a crumbling slope. Some orien-tal lilies such as *Lilium* 'Miss Burma', develop a rich scent when the sun goes down. Along with confederate jasmine (*Trachelospermum jas-minoides*), a tender flowering vine with its own heady bouquet, the lily can be used to create a combination that gets ever more fragrant as dusk deepens.

For an additional touch of white in the gar-den, I like turtlehead (*Chelone glabra*). These moisture-loving plants need full sun in the North and partial shade in the South. They reach a height of 4 ft., performing beautifully along the water's edge. Hanging from a tree at the edge of my main evening garden are pots

Night-blooming cereus
is the most famous of
the plants that flower
at night.

Plants That Perform after Dark

Look for cultivars with white or light-colored flowers or foliage, or those that are especially fragrant in the evening.

Astilbe (*Astilbe* × *arendsii* 'Snowdrift' and *A. simplicifolia* 'Sprite')
Bouncing bet (*Saponaria officinalis*)
Brugmansia (*Brugmansia suaveolens*)
Confederate jasmine (*Trachelospermum jasminoides*)
Cosmos (*Cosmos bipinnatus*)
Cup-and-saucer vine (*Cobaea scandens* 'Alba')
Dahlia (*Dahlia* spp.)
Evening primrose (*Oenothera biennis*)
Evening stock (*Matthiola longipetala* ssp. *bicornis*)
Four o'clocks (*Mirabilis jalapa*)
Foxglove (*Digitalis purpurea* 'Alba')
Gas Plant (*Dictamnus albus*)
Geranium, white (*Pelargonium* × *hortorum* 'Snow White')
Giant hogweed (*Heracleum mantegazzianum*)
Gourd (*Lagenaria siceraria*)
Honeysuckle (*Lonicera* spp.)
Fragrant plantain lily (*Hosta plantaginea*)
Impatiens (*Impatiens wallerana*)
Love-in-a-mist (*Nigella* 'Miss Jekyll Alba')
Mock orange (*Philadelphus* spp.)
Moonflower vine (*Ipomoea alba*)
Nicotiana (*Nicotiana* spp.)
Night phlox (*Zaluzianskya capensis*)
Nocturnal water lilies (*Nymphaea* 'Juno' and 'Sir Galahad')
Nocturnal daylilies (*Hemerocallis citrina* and *H. altissima*)
Oriental lily (*Lilium* 'Miss Burma')
Peacock orchids (*Gladiolus callianthus*)
Pot marigolds, white (*Calendula officinalis*)
Siberian iris (*Iris* 'White Swirl')
Solenostemon 'Gay's Delight' or any other chartreuse-colored coleus cultivar
Spider flower (*Cleome hassleriana* 'Helen Campbell')
Sunflower (*Helianthus annuus* 'Italian White')
Tree mallow (*Lavatera trimestris* 'Mont Blanc')
Turtlehead (*Chelone glabra*)
White poppy (*Papaver orientale* 'Perry's White')
Yucca (*Yucca filamentosa*)

---

filled with white orchids. Other favorites include white Siberian hybrid iris (*Iris* 'White Swirl'), a June-flowering perennial perfect for a moist location, and giant hogweed (*Heracleum mantegazzianum*), an 8-ft.-tall monster with a huge white flower that rises above one of our paths like a full moon. (Note: The sap of this plant can irritate your skin. Giant hogweed is considered invasive in certain areas.)

WATCH WATER SHIMMER AT SUNSET

Our garden overlooks a 12-acre lake, so we have plenty of water. But even if we didn't, I would immediately put in a water feature—perhaps a small pool that could be installed over a weekend—to reflect the moon and stars or shimmer in the setting sun. Then I would plant my pond with a few night-blooming, tropical water lilies. *Nymphaea* 'Juno' has large, white flowers and needs just under five hours of sunlight to bloom. 'Sir Galahad' also has white flowers.

For the first few years in our new garden, we were dismayed by a street light that shone down on our double perennial borders. But in the evening garden, it mimicked the intensity of the moon, and so we have not needed additional lighting. If your local highway department refuses to give you a correctly positioned street light, consider installing one of the many low-voltage night-lighting kits available at garden centers. Low-voltage lighting is safe, easy to install, and comes with a number of well-designed fixtures that no longer look like they belong poolside at a Las Vegas hotel.

And finally, while I'm aghast at the overuse of fairy lights in Christmas displays, a string of white around a small tree or along the edge of a wall will bring a delightful touch of play to the nighttime garden scene.

A PLACE TO GAZE
AT THE MOON AND STARS

A simple concrete stand holds a 14-in., silver gazing globe that serves as a centerpiece of our walled moonlight garden. For a floral centerpiece, I've found the marvelous moonflower vine (*Ipomoea alba*) to be perfect. This tropical perennial blooms the first year from seed and is most often grown as an annual. During a dinner party, guests can watch the flowers open in slow motion, and then observe the hawk moths swooping in on the blossoms.

In our evening garden, you'll also find a cup-and-saucer vine (*Cobaea scandens* 'Alba'); the white form of the popular purple foxglove (*Digitalis purpurea* 'Alba'); and the most perfect sunflower I know, *Helianthus annuus* 'Italian White', with creamy white petals surrounding black centers. Add to this the white form of the annual tree mallow (*Lavatera trimestris* 'Mont Blanc'), with 4-in.-wide flowers that resemble hollyhocks blooming on bushy plants between 2 ft. and 3 ft. high, and the white form of love-in-a-mist (*Nigella* 'Miss Jekyll Alba'), and you have a truly charming place to sit and wonder about the moon.

There's a marvelous painting by Caspar David Friedrich called "Man and Woman Contemplating the Moon" that shows a woman with her arm on a man's shoulder, both of them standing under a very large oak tree at the edge of a forest, gazing at a moon low on the horizon. You can achieve this same feeling by simply using the landscape at hand. Instead of thinking about a sunlit garden, tip your hat to the glowing moon and twinkling stars. Add some fragrant, white-flowering plants, and you'll soon have a romantic painting in your own backyard.

(ABOVE) When the sun goes down, let 'Miss Burma' oriental lilies and confederate jasmine create a heady bouquet.

(LEFT) Chartreuse foliage shines like a beacon in the evening garden. The author marked a landing on one of his outdoor stairways with this coleus named 'Gay's Delight'.

NATURALISTIC
GARDENS

2

AMONG THE MOST SIGNIFICANT TRENDS in American garden design is the move toward naturalistic gardens that capture a sense of nature—even in cities and suburban areas where native vegetation and landforms have been altered dramatically.

A naturalistic garden takes its cues from nature, creating a sense of place that is in keeping with its surroundings. To some, this means using native plants. To others, it means planting in a way that mimics nature at its best. Bed lines tend to be curving, rather than straight. Plants are arranged in a flowing fashion. Foliage is even more important than flowers. And hardscaping materials, like stone and wood, tend to be indigenous to the region.

As a rule, a naturalistic approach to planting creates a lower-maintenance garden. But "low maintenance" doesn't mean "no maintenance." Take a look at these approaches to naturalistic garden design, and decide which lessons you'll apply in your garden.

Gardening in
Harmony
with
Nature

JOSEPH KELLER

is a landscape designer in Ridgefield, Connecticut. He owns a small retail nursery and conducts classes in his own garden, which is open to the public on weekends in season.

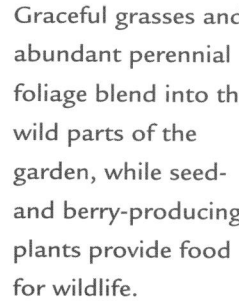

Graceful grasses and abundant perennial foliage blend into the wild parts of the garden, while seed- and berry-producing plants provide food for wildlife.

THE LAND WHERE I WAS RAISED with my brothers held a large vegetable garden and a few flower beds tended by my mother, but mostly it was open lawn, mysterious woods, and swamp. For three boys, it was perfect for an athletic childhood—the lawn was our playing field and the woods camouflaged our tree house. But we dreaded the swamp, home to murderous snapping turtles. It was filled with bottomless ooze we avoided at all costs. Any wayward ball that rolled more than a couple of feet into it we left for dead, and the swamp ate an unfair share of baseballs, golf balls, and footballs.

I returned to this land 11 years ago with a different outlook—not with the eyes of a child looking for open space for a game of catch, but as a gardener looking to add a personal touch to a rich and varied natural landscape. I call the swamp a marsh now (its true name) and delight in its assortment of plant and animal life. The woods, with its high canopy, hosts a wide variety of shade-loving ground covers, shrubs, and trees. The lawn is mostly gone, but what remains serves as a path through the sun-drenched perennial gardens, and I doubt there's enough clear space in the entire garden now for much ball-tossing.

But before I started the garden, I spent a lot of time studying the land, learning what grew here already. An important consideration was how to gracefully tie three very different areas—woods, marsh, and the open field that would become the sunny garden—together. Separately, each area had clearly marked boundary lines, yet my design goal has been to meld each element into the next. I've done this by replicating the feel or look of one area in another, by using cultivated forms of plants already in the landscape, and by blurring the boundaries between each section.

Plans for the garden continue. The author's latest project is this boardwalk across the marsh, which will link the far woods to the garden.

A WOODLAND GARDEN REFLECTS THE NATIVE WOODS

Woods exist on the land in two locations. At the far side of the marsh is dense, wild woodland with a very strong presence. It is the backdrop for most viewing points in the garden. Nearer the house is another woodland area that I've refined into a rich tapestry of plantings. The lush, woodland garden mirrors the wild woods across the marsh, forging a sense of unity between the two spaces and the property as a whole.

Originally, the woods near the house were ash, elm, and sycamore rising out of a hopeless tangle of barberry, poison ivy, and Virginia creeper. I pruned every tree in the woodland garden as high as possible, allowing more light in to sustain understory plantings. Then I cleared out the tangle of undergrowth to make room for other plants. I added a few saplings that will one day take the place of the upper-story ash: a red oak (*Quercus rubra*), several katsura trees (*Cercidiphyllum japonicum*), a few yellowwoods (*Cladrastis lutea*), and a Japanese pagoda tree (*Sophora japonica*). All have performed extremely well as understory trees, and I look forward to the day they fill the sky as the garden's roof.

I then planted smaller trees to fill in the next layer—dogwoods (*Cornus* spp.), silverbells (*Halesia* spp.), Japanese snowbells (*Styrax japonicus*), small maples (*Acer* spp.), and birches (*Betula* spp.). Below these grow mid-sized shrubs such as chokeberry (*Aronia* spp.) and summersweet (*Clethra alnifolia*). Several types of twiggy dogwood and nannyberry (*Viburnum lentago*) grow naturally near the marsh edge and I've added cultivated forms of both shrubs in the woodland garden to reflect their presence.

At ground level are smaller shrubs like Virginia sweetspire (*Itea virginica*) and

In the cultivated woodland, existing trees were limbed up to allow more light in for under-story planting.

Cultivated forms of twiggy dogwood and viburnum are planted to mirror their wild counterparts growing naturally in the garden.

Combining perennials with interesting form and texture adds depth to the woodland floor.

Birdhouses, strategically placed throughout the garden, are always full.

Water features attract birds, frogs, and toads.

Dense planting provides cover and safety for many wild animals.

Man-made arbors offer perches for birds of all kinds.

Hypericum calycinum, and countless woodland perennials and ground covers, including many cultivated geraniums to blend in with the existing wild *Geranium maculatum*. I'm very fond of the combination of *Geranium macrorrhizum* with lady's mantle (*Alchemilla mollis*). They sprawl effortlessly along woodland paths, flower at the same time, and smother all weeds. A few ferns grew in the previous tangle of woods, and I've added many more varieties since, especially intriguing new ones, like the wonderful *Osmunda regalis* 'Purpurascens', a purple-stalked form of royal fern that mixes well with purple-leaved spurges (*Euphorbia* spp.).

Combining perennials with interesting form and texture adds depth to the woodland garden and replicates on a smaller scale the woven intricacy of the woods. Huge hostas like 'Frances Williams' are offset by dwarf mondo grass (*Ophiopogon jaburan* 'Nanus') and tiny barrenworts (*Epimedium* spp.), and *Ligularia dentata* 'Othello' hulks next to dwarf maidenhair fern (*Adiantum aleuticum* var. *subpumilum*). Overhead the woodland forms a dramatic canopy; I try to make it equally memorable down below.

EASE TRANSITIONS BY BLURRING EDGES

The east side of the woodland eases gently into the open, sunny garden because I've worked to blur the line between the two. Woodland plants are gradually replaced by sunny counterparts—the *Geranium macrorrhizum* of the woods becomes *Geranium himalayense* 'Gravetye' in the sunny border. As the woodland recedes, tall trees give way to smaller trees, which then give way to still smaller shrubs. *Magnolia* 'Elizabeth' and *M. virginiana* grow under the last large ash in the woodland, where the chipped bark path gives way to the grassy path of the sunny garden. Smaller trees such as *Stewartia pseudocamellia*, Japanese snowbell, and fringe tree (*Chionanthus virginicus*) grow out in the open; beneath them are barberries (*Berberis* spp.), spireas (*Spiraea* spp.), potentillas (*Potentilla* spp.), and other sunlovers.

This transition from woods to sun is also eased because of the pruning I did to raise the woodland canopy. The resulting shade is light, not dark and dense, so passing from the shade into the sun is gradual instead of shocking.

The line between the marsh and both the woodland and the sunny garden is also blurred. Yellow flag iris (*Iris pseudacorus*) grows naturally in the marsh's water. This 5-ft.-tall giant always grabs the attention of visitors; I suppose it owes its vigor to the constant moisture and seemingly bottomless rich and nutritious muck. I've also planted it and other iris species in a wide zone away from the marsh edge. Similarly, water-loving trees like dawn redwood (*Metasequoia glyptostroboides*) and bald cypress (*Taxodium distichum*) are planted in the water along the marsh edge, and farther away in the garden, to emphasize the idea that the different spaces are interrelated. Cardinal flower (*Lobelia cardinalis*), blue cardinal flower (*L. siphilitica*), several *Eupatorium* species, and ironweed (*Vernonia noveboracensis*) grow well along the marsh edge as well as farther into the garden where the soil is more well drained. Such adaptable plants gracefully interweave the sections of the garden.

"Overhead the woodland forms a dramatic canopy; I try to make it equally memorable down below."

> *"Blurring the boundaries between garden spaces unifies the garden and has given me the freedom to plant creatively."*

CHOOSE CULTIVATED PLANTS TO MIRROR BEAUTIFUL NATIVES

The marsh's wild rice (*Zizania aquatica*) impresses me greatly. Filling the entire 6-acre marsh, it waves stunning tassels throughout the summer, then bursts into seed in early fall. It is a beautiful plant, especially en masse. I've made heavy use of many varieties of ornamental grasses in the sunny garden to replicate the feel created by the wild rice in the marsh. Native grasses like little bluestem (*Schizachyrium scoparium*) and Indian grass (*Sorghastrum avenaceum*), and the exotic giants like *Miscanthus floridulus* and *Saccharum ravennae* (also known as *Erianthus ravennae*) look, feel, and sound like the wild rice in the distant marsh. In fact, from high points in the garden, the line between marsh and garden is nearly invisible. The graceful grasses and abundant perennial foliage of the sunny garden blend seamlessly into the wild.

Blurring the boundaries between garden spaces unifies the garden and has given me the freedom to plant creatively. Sunny garden beds are lushly planted to re-create the luxuriant feel of the marsh. Here, I mix in bold exotics and annuals with common perennials and native plants. So the large, graceful, purple-leaved New Zealand flax (*Phormium tenax*) envelops the silver, succulent leaves of *Rudbeckia maxima*; the 8-ft.-tall bird-of-paradise (*Strelitzia reginae*) is surrounded by coneflowers (*Echinacea spp.*); and variegated bananas (*Musa spp.*) rise from clumps of iris.

I've been pleased that such unusual interlopers look right at home in a setting where all lines curve and blur.

ENCOURAGING WILDLIFE ENRICHES THE GARDEN

My work in the garden has also been driven by another unifying concept—preserving and protecting the wildness of the marsh and the wildlife it supports. The marsh has been undisturbed for many decades. For as long as I can remember, it's been a home to an extravagant number of birds, ducks, geese, beavers, muskrats, frogs, turtles, snakes, and insects. I've tried to identify what these creatures find attractive in the marsh and its edge, and have introduced those conditions into the man-made portion of the garden. I've added small ponds and waterfalls, planted as many berry-producing plants as possible, and created as wild, tangled, and protective a place as I've been able to, while still managing to cultivate and refine the garden.

Aside from their ornamental appeal, man-made structures assist the wildlife, too. Birdhouses are always occupied, and arbors offer perches for birds of all kinds. The water features I've built draw a host of frogs, turtles, and birds.

Of course, I recognize my own place in this natural scheme of things. Several sitting areas—usually partially enclosed or screened with shrubs, trees, or grasses—afford wonderful views of different areas of the garden and the marsh. On hot summer days, the woodland benches offer a cool place to rest. In spring, I always choose a sunny spot to watch the wildlife at work. Since these sitting areas are often hidden from view, they blend in with the garden surroundings.

My efforts to cater to the wildlife seem to be working. In spring, before the garden has been cleaned up, and in fall, after it has reached its peak, a walk through the garden flushes hundreds of birds out from beneath the grasses and shrubs. Out in the marsh, I've recently built the first 80 ft. of boardwalk across to the woodland on the far side. In autumn, early-morning footsteps on the walk prompt the flight of hundreds of waterfowl.

My plans for the garden continue, and there remains much land to cultivate and nurture. All progress, however, still stems from the close observations I first paid to the original landscape, when it was clear that the land seemed to know what was best. When working with a natural landscape, it makes sense to take cues and direction from the land itself. The garden will be the better for it.

Seating areas are scattered throughout the garden, offering wonderful views of the garden and marsh, and of the wildlife at work.

JOHN L. HARPER

is a landscape architect based in Atlanta. His business, Urban Earth, specializes in residential landscape design.

The Pleasures of a No-Lawn Landscape

Fieldstone and native plants are natural companions. Sensitive fern (*Onoclea sensibilis*), soft rush (*Juncus effusus*), golden Japanese sweet flag (*Acorus gramineus* 'Ogon'), white ginger (*Hedychium cornonarium*), and Virginia sweetspire (*Itea virginica* 'Henry's Garnet') surround a sitting area.

IN ATLANTA, as in most of the South, abundant rainfall, high humidity, and a long, hot growing season create a lush, fecund environment that challenges traditional notions of garden design. Most homeowners spend the dog days of summer mowing and watering their lawns, deadheading annuals and roses, and weeding flower beds.

By contrast, the gardens I designed for Dean Bates and Shirl Handly have no prize-winning blossoms, no planting beds, no annual color, no horticultural specimens of note, and, most significant, no lawn. Blame the dappled light of Thompson Mill Forest, the fern glades of Blood Mountain, the sandy shores of the Oconee River. Memories of these enchanted places and other natural ecosystems provided the inspiration for this design: a subtle woodland garden facing the street; an exuberant, grassy wetland garden surrounding a fish pond; and a lush, streamside planting on the steep slope above a stone drainage channel. Each of

Although the pond remained a focal point of the garden, paths were widened and rerouted, and exotic plants were replaced primarily with natives.

BEFORE

IN PROGRESS

these areas features plants from various regions of Georgia and the southeastern United States.

Because we took a more naturalistic approach to garden design, the mower was retired, the weed trimmer was discarded, and birds were invited to dinner, as were friends and family. The elimination of onerous chores enhances the pleasure of walking through a lovely, quietly exciting space.

GOOD CIRCULATION PATTERNS ENCOURAGE EXPLORATION

Although my initial meeting with the clients five years ago was to discuss plants, we really began by reworking circulation in the garden. After all, there wasn't much point in planting a garden if you couldn't get to it. The old deck on the back of the house, with its stairs positioned to create a switchback, was a barrier to entering the garden, so we decided to replace it. This clarified the garden entry and created a central intersection from which you can go to the garage, deck and kitchen, porch and base-ment, or garden. A wide fieldstone path leads directly to the refurbished 1930s fish pond, replacing a narrow path of concrete stepping stones. Now my clients are tempted to enter the garden every time they walk to their cars.

This garden has been articulated with time in mind. Although screened from neighbors with fences, the garden behind the house is open and sunny in winter. Come spring, the

New decks offer a viewing platform.

Native plants, like this oakleaf hydrangea, anchor the garden.

A potting bench doubles as a serving area when entertaining outdoors.

Dry-laid field-stone replaced concrete step-ping stones, creating a more natural setting.

Moisture-loving shade plants were allowed to naturalize near the fish pond.

> *"Those very conditions that kill lawns fuel wildflowers every spring in the forests of northern Georgia."*

⁓

scene changes dramatically as dormant perennials and grasses leap onto the stage, forming undulating walls of color and texture.

Out front, other problems had to be solved. While a path led to the front door, we wanted to walk in the garden, too. The lawn had provided a walking surface, but without a beginning or an end. When we removed tile to resurface the front porch, and discovered a dilapidated foundation, an opportunity emerged. We designed a new porch with a curving granite foundation and iron rail. Then we laid out a garden path that mirrors the curves of the new porch and completes a loop to the front door by way of a gate hidden in the porch rail. Porch materials were repeated in curving waves of granite paving between the sidewalk and street, and in the granite cobblestones used to widen the drive.

NATIVE PLANTS REPLACE LAWN

The practical explanation for the approach taken in this garden is simple: The lawn didn't work. It had no particular function, turned brown and patchy every summer, required frequent fertilization, and had to be reseeded each fall. The combined effect of extreme heat, root competition from large trees, and summer shade was simply too much for it. But those very conditions that kill lawns fuel wildflowers every spring in the forests of northern Georgia. These spring ephemerals—such as cutleaf toothwort (*Cardamine laciniata*), dwarf crested iris (*Iris cristata*), and celandine poppy (*Stylophorum diphyllum*)—take advantage of the

late winter and early spring light that reaches the forest floor, blooming profusely in the moldering leaf litter. Once the trees leaf out, the ephemerals decline, many of them disappearing entirely from view before summer's end. Ferns, well adapted to the low light of summer, emerge to take their place, carpeting the forest in rich, velvety greens. Our plant selection in the front garden reflects this natural cycle that occurs in a mature forest.

Micro-environments in the low woodland garden facing the street provided opportunities to combine woodland plants of upland ravines with those more often found near streams and rivers. Woodvamp (*Decumaria barbara*), Virginia sweetspire (*Itea virginica*), yellowroot (*Xanthorhiza simplicissima*), and Culver's root (*Veronicastrum virginicum*), which often grow near streams or seeps, were planted where ground water collects. Fothergilla (*Fothergilla major*), green-and-gold (*Chrysogonum virginianum*), downy rattlesnake plantain (*Goodyera pubescens*), marginal wood fern (*Dryopteris marginalis*), and crane-fly orchid (*Tipularia discolor*) are more commonly found in rich and often rocky woodlands, and were planted on drier ground near boulders.

Around the backyard fish pond is low, flat ground draining into an old, stone channel. Here we used plants common to floodplains and coastal communities: soft rush (*Juncus effusus*), red hibiscus (*Hibiscus coccineus*), dwarf wax myrtle (*Myrica cerifera* var. *pumila*), spider lily (*Hymenocallis caroliniana*), cinnamon fern (*Osmunda cinnamomea*), royal fern (*Osmunda regalis*), and several species of iris.

The ground rises abruptly behind the fish pond to form an embankment along the drainageway, much as a bank would rise along a river or stream. Here we designed and built footbridges that curve across the stone water channel to meet a stone path halfway up the

BEFORE

IN PROGRESS

bank. On either side of the path thrive bottle-brush buckeye (*Aesculus parviflora*), silver-leaved mountain mint (*Pycnanthemum incanum*), hydrangea (*Hydrangea arborescens* 'Annabelle'), and Solomon's plume (*Smilacina racemosa*).

Long-term stability is improved when you select native plants for the existing conditions and let them naturalize. So when it came to selecting plants for a border in the one truly sunny part of the backyard (and only half a day at that), we opted for river oats (*Chasmanthium latifolium*), beautyberry (*Callicarpa americana*), Joe Pye weed (*Eupatorium purpureum*), turtle-head (*Chelone glabra*), wild azalea (*Rhododendron canescens*), and ironweed (*Vernonia noveboracensis*) over traditional

The front lawn was eliminated and the entry was redesigned. The result was a naturalistic woodland garden that requires little routine maintenance.

Plants from flood-plains and coastal communities inspired the fish pond plantings. Copper iris (*Iris fulva*), pickerelweed (*Pontederia cordata*), sensitive fern (*Onoclea sensibilis*), and bottle-brush buckeye (*Aesculus parviflora*) thrive under moist conditions.

English border perennials. In nature, you'd find these same plants growing in a wet meadow or along streams. Blue-eyed grass (*Sisyrinchium angustifolium*) thrives in this sunny, damp environment, as do sedges (*Carex* spp.) and bee balm (*Monarda didyma* 'Jacob Cline').

Some old rhododendrons that had been languishing on soggy, flat ground for years were moved to the sharply draining slope, where they began to flourish. And because the homeowners were reluctant to toss out plants they already had, room was made for non-natives, too. The placement of non-native camellias, azaleas, astilbes, ajugas, and other plants was determined by cultural requirements, as with the native plants. And now they look almost as wild. In the end, the plants told us where they wanted to be; in fact, they sometimes moved themselves by abandoning unacceptable sites to creep into ecological niches more like their homes.

To create continuity in the garden, we repeated large masses of plants, often overlap-ping the garden divisions. The particular combination of plants in this garden would never occur in nature; rarely, either, would so many species occur in so small a space. By concentrating the experience, however, the garden is made richer.

DOES NO LAWN REALLY MEAN LOW MAINTENANCE?

Lawns are expected to look the same all year, and it takes a great deal of energy to keep things from changing. Our design strategy in this garden has been to link garden maintenance to change, rather than to a static objective.

There is no mowing, of course, and no trimming with power tools. Because native plants are well-adapted to the local climate, watering is necessary only in times of extreme drought. There are no flowering annual beds bordering lawn, so there is no tilling. Nonetheless, flowers bloom year-round. Fertilizing has been reduced so much that to neglect it entirely would not significantly affect the garden for some time, and even then I wonder if the effect would be objectionable. Nutrients are returned to the garden as mulch or compost. The garden is so productive that, occasionally, plants must be dug and removed; these are given to friends or sometimes reluctantly put on the compost heap.

Most pests have been reclassified as bird food or butterflies-in-the-making, and this garden is never without birds. What pests prove persistent can be controlled by manual and biological means, if necessary, or host plants can be removed.

Upkeep is required, but the frequency of chores has been dramatically lessened. Most are done annually rather than consuming valuable weekend time year-round. Hand-weeding is done in cool weather to remove seedlings of trees such as water oak (*Quercus nigra*) and Carolina laurel cherry (*Prunus caroliniana*), and invasive exotics such as Chinese privet (*Ligustrum sinense*). These are easier to see in fall and winter as herbaceous plants decline, and are easier to pull when soil is moist.

Herbaceous perennials are cut back in fall and winter on an as-needed basis. Ornamental grasses and perennials with interesting seedheads are left standing until February. Excess growth is sometimes dug out to preserve the established proportions of the garden. Woody shrubs are pruned in winter, and an arborist is retained to prune large trees every other year.

The work schedule in this garden is flexible and forgiving. If you fail to mow a lawn on schedule, it shows; if you fail to collect organic debris from a garden, it may simply rot before anyone notices, providing fertilizer and a crop of colorful fungi. Weeds not pulled on schedule can be pulled later; they are not immediately recognizable in a garden that is not a monoculture, like a lawn. Some "weeds" overcome

"To create continuity in the garden, we repeated large masses of plants."

the stigma of that unfortunate designation and are allowed to remain as garden plants.

In this garden, the leathery leaves of a large water oak are collected and removed because they have proven too slow to decay. Leaves from a large elm and other trees are gathered from pathways and used to mulch the garden. Storms occur frequently in summer and bring down twigs and branches. Many are left to rot on the ground rather than placed in the trash. An effort is made to remove limbs that might damage or impede the growth of small plants, but they can be tossed among the denser shrub plantings where they rot slowly, providing a rich layer of humus that replenishes the topsoil.

While practical concerns are important, what matters most to my clients is having a beautiful garden. The Bates-Handly garden is quietly radical. It stands out among lawns dotted with crape myrtles and azaleas. But it doesn't shout; it whispers like the woods.

A few well-mannered non-natives blend in almost seamlessly. A 'Blue Angel' hosta and a Japanese maple cohabitate with inkberry (*Ilex glabra* 'Shamrock'), jewel weed (*Impatiens capensis*), astilbe, and Virginia creeper (*Parthenocissus quinquefolia*).

Stroll through the *Seasons* *on a Woodsy Garden* Path

MARGARET DeHAAS van DORSSER

is a garden designer in Portland, Oregon. She is an active member of the Hardy Plant Society of Oregon, as well as a small group in England, The Cottage Gardener.

Four-season interest is no accident. Ensuring visual interest year-round requires more than just flowers. Stark, structural forms help provide winter interest, and foliage colors and shapes carry the other seasons.

A S MARK AND I were walking through our then two-year-old birch path with the former owner of our property and her parents, the mother turned to me and asked if I had ever considered designing gardens for other people. When I told her of my desire to quit teaching junior high school and start my own garden-design business, she asked if she could be my first client. The birch path seems to have a special effect on people who visit, and frequently my clients request a similar feature for their own yards.

When we purchased our acre-and-a-half property in 1990, the landscape consisted predominantly of lawn and pasture. At most, there were two dozen trees scattered about the property. It was a clear canvas on which we could play at will, although landscaping all this space seemed an impossibly large task. As I was reading one of the many lovely gardening books Mark had given me that

Burning bush lights a fire in fall. The brilliant red of *Euonymus alatus* contrasts with the golden leaves of the paper birches.

papyrifera) would be just right to create the effect we had in mind. In winter, their lovely, white, peeling bark would add drama, and in summer, the leaf canopy would create dancing, dappled light beneath. As a bonus, paperbark birches aren't as brittle as many of the other birches.

I pictured the path undulating gently this way and that, creating a feeling of distance as one looks down the path. To get the curves right, I laid garden hoses in place and moved them around until I was happy with the effect.

We bought our first three birches several months after moving in. Within a year, we had planted three clumps and five singles. In the years since, the trees have gained a good bit of height and really started to fill out. We wanted a focal point at the end of the path, a pleasant surprise as one came around the last curve. A Colorado blue spruce (*Picea pungens* f. *glauca*) turned out to be a perfect counterpoint to the birches.

To add to the woodland character of the path, we added nice, flat, irregularly shaped stepping stones. To encourage a slow walk down the path, I spaced the rocks close together, with just 4 in. to 6 in. between them, arranging them so they fit each others' shapes. In the gaps between the stones, I transplanted moss from under one of the handful of mature trees on the property. The moss and the rocks established the informal character of the path, and the close spacing of the stones encourages one to notice the small plants we began to place along the path's edges.

winter, I came across the photo of a winter scene depicting a little meandering stream bordered by coppiced willow trees. It reminded me of a Van Gogh painting of a Flemish countryside. At the same time, Mark was intrigued by another photo, one of a woodland path lined by trees forming a canopy of dappled shade. Those two pictures melded in our minds and hearts, and became the vision toward which we're working still.

We wanted a special location for our path, where we could see and enjoy it often. For that reason, we decided it should start just outside our bedroom window. From there, it meanders off into the distance about 60 ft.

BIRCHES AND STEPPING STONES DEFINE THE PATH

Mark had been reading up on trees, and we decided that paperbark birches (*Betula*

BOLD COLOR AND EVERGREENS BRIGHTEN THE PATH IN WINTER

Right from the start, we wanted the path to be a four-season attraction, a part of our garden we'd want to visit even on the grayest of winter days—so winter interest was a significant consideration when we were choosing plants for the path. Also, because the path is so much more open in the winter, with the deciduous trees and shrubs just skeletal presences, we wanted to give the area surrounding it a greater perceived density. It was important that the shrubs separating and defining the birch path from the rest of the garden contribute to the winter appeal. To accomplish this, on one side I planted two variegated Tatarian dogwoods (*Cornus alba* 'Elegantissima'), using their striking auburn twigs to harmonize with the pink flowers of a *Viburnum × bodnantense* 'Dawn', which starts blooming in November and continues through mid-March. Backing these shrubs, and anchoring them, I placed three Japanese cedars (*Cryptomeria japonica*), which turn a wonderful bronze-green in winter. The effect is stunning.

This same technique—planting winter-flowering trees and shrubs backed by evergreen shrubs—worked well elsewhere along the path. On one side, I planted a witch hazel (*Hamamelis × intermedia* 'Arnold Promise'), its cheery yellow blossoms brightening the path on even the dreariest of rainy days. On the other side, we defined the area with a red-flowered witch hazel (*H. × intermedia* 'Diane') backed by more evergreens—here an unclipped boxwood (*Buxus sempervirens*) and a Berckman's golden arborvitae (*Thuja orientalis* 'Aurea Nana'). These nicely set off the flowers of the witch hazel.

To add yet more contrasting colors and textures in winter, we planted other evergreen shrubs in the area, including another arborvitae (*T. occidentalis* 'Smaragd'), a falsecypress (*Chamaecyparis pisifera* 'Boulevard'), a holly (*Ilex × aquipernyi* 'San Jose'), and two strawberry trees (*Arbutus unedo*).

Several perennials contribute to the winter effect, including *Phlomis russeliana*, which forms large mounds of heart-shaped, evergreen leaves and whose tall, dried flower stems add vertical accents. Another favorite is *Sisyrinchium striatum*, whose fresh, erect, blue-green foliage looks good all winter long. Lenten roses (*Helleborus orientalis*) provide a welcome splash of color with their lovely nodding bells.

SOFT COLORS USHER IN SPRING

Spring arrives with a flourish. A thousand or more daffodils—which have multiplied many times over since we first planted them—line the path. Their cheery white and yellow blooms and the ease with which they naturalize made them an obvious choice when we were establishing the path. Even before they

Plants are at their peak in June, their leaves still fresh and verdant, their blooms bright and beckoning.

Nature, improved. The author's birch path is densely planted, but not overgrown—a careful composition that mimics nature, minus the chaos of vines or invasives run amok.

bloom, their upright foliage against the white bark of the trees establishes a satisfying rhythmic pattern as one's eyes move down the path.

Tucked in front of the daffodils are woodland violets, introduced by us, but by now naturalized, which add to the magic of spring. We appreciate these delicate blossoms for their beauty and their wafting fragrance during warm, sunny spells. In addition to these mass plantings, we also wanted little bits of punctuation at certain places along the path. At one end, we planted a buttercup winter hazel (*Corylopsis pauciflora*), which is aglow with delicate, pale yellow tassels in March. At its foot is a clump of azure blue species crocus (*Crocus chrysanthus* 'Ladykiller'). The species crocuses in soft yellows, purples, and blues delight us with their simplicity.

Serendipity sometimes plays a role in garden design, too. Though I hadn't intended it, one of the pleasures of the path in the spring is a bit of borrowed landscape—our neighbor's ornamental plum, which becomes a cloud of pink for a few weeks each year.

The stars of the spring show, however, are the birches. As they begin to leaf out, soft speckles of spring green unfurling overhead, the play of light in our little woodland starts anew. The dappled light breaking through the birches' new foliage and the clumped brush strokes of color below give the path the look of an impressionist painting. This is our favorite time of the year to visit the path.

BOLD FOLIAGE AND SPLASHES OF COLOR STAR IN SUMMER

Although winter and spring were foremost in our minds when we were designing the path, we wanted it to be lovely in the late spring and summer months as well. Strongly contrasting foliage forms and textures are the main design tools that we used to accomplish this. Towering spires of foxgloves (*Digitalis purpurea*) and spiky verticals of *Sisyrinchium striatum*, *Iris sibirica*, and *I. pallida* contrast with carpets of bloody cranesbills (*Geranium sanguineum*), mounds of velvety, heart-shaped *Phlomis russeliana* leaves, and the feathery leaves of Oriental poppies (*Papaver orientale*).

Foliage alone wouldn't do, though, and there's no shortage of bloom along the path, at least through early summer. The effect that we were looking for in summer, just as in early spring, was that of an impressionist painting—luminescent splashes of color everywhere, yet not so vibrant as to take away from the path's overall tranquility. To accomplish that we stuck with a palette of bloom colors that glow without being bright. The swirls of primrose yellow in *Phlomis russeliana* pick up the gold in the throats of the cream-colored *Sisyrinchium striatum*. Coral-petaled Oriental poppies are splashed here and there alongside purple Siberian irises. Blue bellflowers (*Campanula poscharskyana*) contrast with white foxgloves. Patches of pink are provided by species roses (*Rosa rubrifolia* and *R. rugosa*) and peonies (*Paeonia lactiflora*).

WARM FOLIAGE COLORS ILLUMINATE THE AUTUMN PATH

Fall color was an important consideration when we were choosing plants for foliage interest. As a result, in fall the path is a mosaic of rich, warm colors. Viewed from the far end, and seemingly appearing from nowhere, a hedge of brilliant red burning bush (*Euonymus alatus*) creates a backdrop for the birches, now turning a wonderful pale yellow. The lighting effect is golden and magical. We also placed a lovely coral bark Japanese maple (*Acer palmatum* 'Sango-kaku') so you could just glimpse it from this vantage point, its foliage aglow in soft yellows, oranges, and greens all at once.

Another great fall performer is the previously mentioned, red-flowered 'Diane' witch hazel, whose leaves turn a fiery combination of red, orange, and burgundy just as the birches are starting to lose their leaves. As the birch leaves fall upon the path, it takes on a delicate, lacy look, and the yellow underfoot is set off by the burnished tones of the peony leaves and the red-streaked leaves of the bloody cranesbills. Meanwhile, the monkshoods (*Aconitum × cammarum*) are adding splashes of deep blue, contrasting beautifully with the warm fall colors all around them.

THE PATH PROGRESSES

At barely seven years old, the birch path is still in its youth and continuing to evolve. Mark and I recently extended the path another 20 ft. by planting three more birches. We have yet to place the stepping stones, but we've already planted a dove tree (*Davidia involucrata*) across from the Colorado blue spruce. The dove tree, when it reaches maturity and starts blooming, will look almost as though white handkerchiefs are dangling from its branches. As understory, we have added a number of woodland plants, including native rhododendrons, heavenly bamboo (*Nandina domestica*), Japanese dogwoods (*Cornus kousa*), and more witch hazels.

We're dividing the daffodils still and are planting them further along the path. This year I'm going to plant some Christmas roses (*Helleborus niger*) to provide more winter interest; here in Portland they start blooming in January, even before the Lenten roses, of which I'll be adding more, too. There just can't be too many of them during the late winter months! To provide more late-summer foliage interest, I'm going to add some dramatic, large, blue-leaved hostas.

Through all its glorious seasons, the birch path remains a special place. Even in the dead of winter, dangling birch catkins glisten with crystalline droplets when the sun peeks through the branches. No matter what time of year, no walk in our garden is complete without a stroll through the birches.

"The effect that we were looking for in summer, just as in early spring, was that of an impressionist painting."

Creating a Canyon *from* Scratch

MICHAEL McLAUGHLIN

is a member of the American Rock Garden Society, where he lectures on plants with winter interest. His garden has been featured on numerous tours and HGTV.

Michael McLaughlin reinvented his yard by building a bare-earth berm and then sculpting it with boulders. Plantings complete the scene.

TO ME, ROCKS ARE TIMELESS. Their flecks of color and subtle striations are like messages from the distant past, messages my geologist father was able to read. When I was a boy, he and I used to explore the mountains and plateaus of Colorado. He read the rocks and told me their stories, helping me to see millions of years into the past, back to the days when those mountains were being born.

Years later, when I decided to sculpt a rock outcrop of my own that would mirror my Rocky Mountain surroundings, I brought a certain sense of reverence to the project. Maybe it helped. Now stones anchor my garden to the earth, and bring to it a sense of eternity. They call to mind the enduring nature of the earth, and contrast with the transitory nature of foliage and flowers. The rocks also add texture, color, and year-round interest. And, by creating a

"The stony canyon was also intended to eliminate any hint of the burial-mound look that berms sometimes have."

host of microclimates, they enrich the variety of its plant life.

Our house is built on what was once a hillside, but the lot was flattened when construction began. After we moved in, I decided to re-create part of the hillside by making an earthen berm 50 ft. long and about 4 ft. high. Alongside it, we fashioned a 75-ft. walkway running from the driveway to the front door. To add interest and beauty to the hill and walkway, and to tie them together visually, I decided to build a rock outcrop. The stony canyon was also intended to eliminate any hint of the burial-mound look that berms sometimes have. The rock outcrops—and the undulating hillside they jut from—would be the central feature of my front-yard garden.

I modeled the outcrop on sandstone formations I had seen in the Rockies, and I recalled my father's explanations of how they were formed: Layers of sand deposited at the bottom of a sea were gradually transformed into layers of sandstone, and then, in some geologic cataclysm, pushed back up into the sky to weather for eons. The weathering exposed the layers, called strata, that are the basic building blocks of sandstone. In natural outcrops, the strata protrude from the earth at the same angle, like the pages of a book. They erode layer by layer, so the top of an outcrop is often defined by a harder, erosion-resistant layer of stone. That was the look I wanted to re-create. And though I was working with large boulders, the same principles could be used for a garden on a smaller scale.

My wife, Carrie, and I selected a native, buff-to-red-colored, lichen-covered sandstone from a nearby stoneyard. The biggest stones, which would form the backbone of the outcrop, were as large as 8 ft. across, 6 ft. wide, and up to 2 ft. thick. That thickness seemed about the right size for our 4-ft.-high hill. Since the largest stones weighed about 2 tons, I arranged with the stoneyard to hire a professional who would move and place the rock. I directed him to arrange the more angular stones to form a line along what would be the exposed edge of the outcrop. To make the formation look old, the boulders were placed so their most weathered sides faced up.

I also wanted the biggest stones to be partly buried, and was careful to position them so they would penetrate the hillside with the strata of the different rocks in rough alignment. That would give the impression that the rocks were part of a single vein of sandstone running just beneath the soil's surface.

With custom planting pockets, maintenance is minimal. The author used soil and gravel mixes to enhance microclimates where plants with special needs can thrive.

USE SMALLER STONES TO SOFTEN AND UNIFY THE SCENE

To soften the scene and bring visual unity to the outcrop, I used lots of smaller stones among the larger boulders. Below the brow of the outcrop, I placed 6-in. to 8-in. rocks closely together, like fallen boulders. I filled the space between them with still smaller stones so that it looks like a vein of softer rock that had eroded or been crushed in some seismic upheaval.

We were especially careful in the placement of stones with indentations—we want the holes in the rock to fill with water whenever it rains. In our arid environment, the water and its reflections lend a quality of their own to the garden. On spring mornings we eat breakfast and watch birds bathing themselves in the tiny, sky-reflecting pools.

Rocks on either side of the walkway protrude from the hillside, so the canyon is like a dry, eroded streambed. The embankments allow me to plant flowers closer to eye level so they are easier to see, and each little spot has its own climate where certain plants thrive.

FIND PLANTING POCKETS

Each of the larger rocks in the outcrop creates its own microclimate. The stones collect the sun's heat during the day and radiate it back out at night. This moderates extreme temperatures, which, in our dry, mid-continent climate means daily readings in winter that can range, up and down, by as much as 80 degrees Fahrenheit.

Bulbs planted throughout the area demonstrate the effect of the different microclimates: Crocuses bloom in February in the most southerly, sun-washed areas, but the same crocuses, when planted on the other side of the path in the shade, don't bloom until six weeks later. In the right microclimate, I estimate that we can grow plants normally rated one or two climate zones warmer than our USDA Hardiness Zone 5 site.

The stones also serve as a natural separator for different types of plants. Above the outcrop, it's exposed, dry, and sunny. Below it, planting pockets are generally wetter, more protected, and shadier. Carrie and I tried to enhance specific microclimates by using different types of soil. In cool, shady, moist places, we added peat to retain even more moisture. In sunny, dry areas, we added gravel to ensure fast-draining soil.

PICK AN APPROPRIATE MULCH

Once the outcrop was complete, we began a maintenance program. That mainly meant using different mulches for our various microclimates. I use a mulch of dark compost in places where I want to enrich the soil and to create a lush look, and a mulch of gravel where I want leaner soil.

Over the years, the plants have grown, and in time they seemed to continue the project without any assistance from me. I think the maturing plants have actually strengthened my original design. And there are always those happy mistakes where plant combinations grow into something completely different and more outstanding than I ever imagined. Each season, each day, I love to wander through our garden to see what's coming up or what's newly in bloom. No two trips are ever alike and, to me, each one is an adventure.

Position rocks with large indentations so their depressions catch rainwater. Ephemeral pools of water create pleasing reflections and attract birds to the garden.

Going Native

ANDY WASOWSKI
is a freelance writer and photographer specializing in gardening and environmental issues. He and his wife, Sally, have written eight books on landscaping with native plants, including *The Landscaping Revolution.*

(LEFT) A natural landscape nurtures indigenous wildlife as well as native plants. In the author's Texas garden, anoles dart along branches (TOP INSET), while butterflies enjoy the wildfowers (BOTTOM INSET).

WHEN SALLY AND I PURCHASED our home 15 years ago, we inherited a yard with a conventional assortment of nonnative evergreen shrubs and a St. Augustine lawn. The only indigenous plants were a small bur oak, an ancient *Maclura pomifera*, also known as osage orange, and a young red oak, plus a gorgeous patch of wood violets the previous owner, inexplicably, had tried to kill off. "I poisoned them every year, but they wouldn't go away," she apologized to us. The landscapable areas of the ⅛-acre property, almost all of which are in the front yard, consisted of a few inches of gummy, black clay over limestone and shale.

We moved into the house in June, and realized immediately that keeping its existing vegetation alive and attractive throughout the Texas summer—when temperatures often rise above 100°F—would require daily watering. Then, of course, there was the mowing!

A Garden in Transition

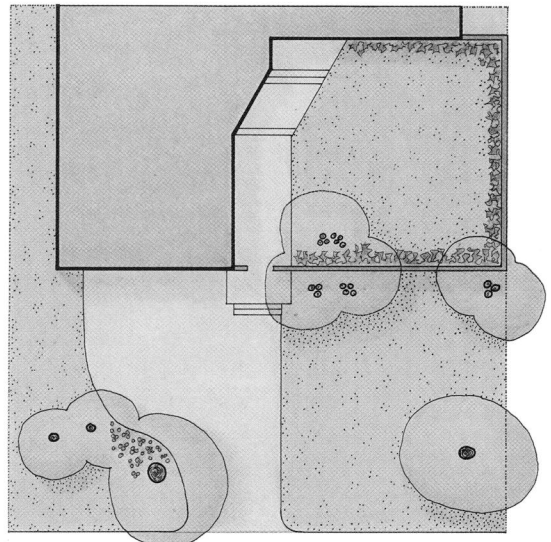

LATE 1970S: A conventional suburban lot. The author's yard consisted of nonnative grass and trees (Japanese maple, crape myrtle) plus a few natives (wood violets, osage orange, bur oak).

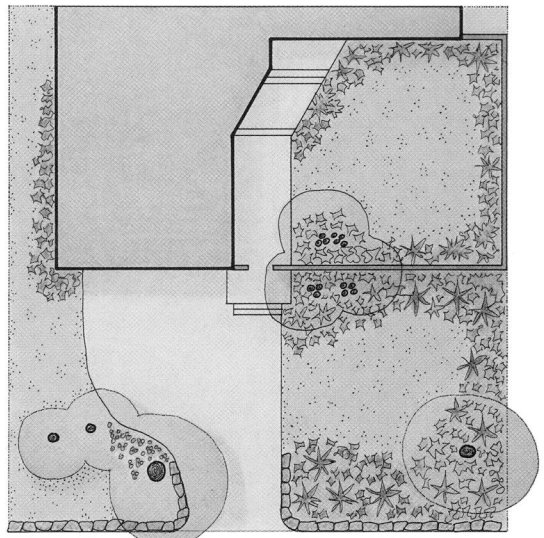

MID-1980S: Eliminating the lawn. The author and his wife ripped up sections of lawn and replaced them with native plants and wildflowers. Like many nonnatives, the Japanese maple succumbed to their minimal watering regimen.

After exactly one month, Sally made a startling decision. We would stop watering altogether. "What survives deserves to be here," she decreed. "What dies didn't belong here in the first place, and good riddance!"

By summer's end, the casualty list included cotoneaster, firethorn, a Japanese maple, and Oregon grape holly—all nonnatives. The St. Augustine lawn, a reputed water-guzzler, was doing just fine. So much for absolutes when you're talking botany. Also among the survivors were a trumpet vine, two yaupon hollies, a crape myrtle, and, of course, the native wood violets.

That fall, Sally attended a seminar on native plants, where she learned of their many virtues: hardiness, drought tolerance, and low-maintenance requirements, not to mention beauty. The seminar was an epiphany. She returned determined to introduce native plants to our own front yard, and to turn our yard from lawn to natural landscape.

ELIMINATING THE LAWN

The transformation was a slow process, undertaken one step at a time. We began with a 15-ft.-square portion of the front yard down by the street. We dug out the turf, mixed in manure to nourish the badly depleted soil, and sowed seeds for native shrubs and wild-

"The transformation was a slow process, undertaken one step at a time."

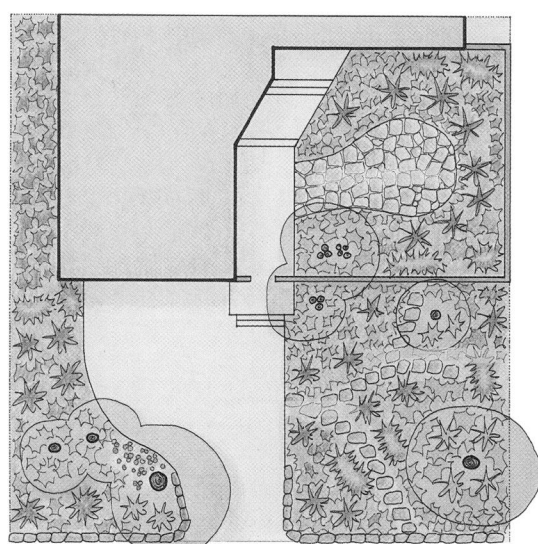

EARLY 1990S: A natural landscape. The entire yard has become a natural ecosystem. Only one of the nonnative crape myrtles has survived. The original natives have thrived, as have the natives the author planted, including an American beautyberry (*Callicarpa americana*).

same plant species. She also planted some naturalized plant seeds. Naturalized plants are those that originated in other parts of the world but have adapted well here because their new home closely resembles their native habitat. Some of them, such as lantana (*Lantana camara*) and yarrow (*Achillea millefolium*), thrived in our yard; others, like chaste tree (*Vitex agnus-castus*) and butterfly bush (*Buddleia alternifolia*), failed to acclimate.

Section by section during the next 10 years, we eliminated all the turf grass from our yard and replaced it with flower beds, a patio, a small wildflower meadow, and walls and walkways made from native limestone. By the second summer, we ended our draconian non-watering regimen and had an automatic irrigation system installed. Still, we were not about to go back to daily watering. Sally waters only in the summer when temperatures are higher

(BELOW LEFT) Nothing but lawn. In 1980, the author's nonnative St. Augustine lawn required daily watering and frequent mowing.

(BELOW RIGHT) A lush mix of natives. After a 10-year conversion, indigenous plants and wildflowers grow where the lawn used to be.

flowers. The following year, we eliminated still more lawn by expanding the plot a full 30 ft. across the front of the yard. Because we were new to this style of gardening, we used these initial lawn-free sections as test plots.

Sally planted seeds that had been collected in Texas, as well as seeds from an out-of-state mail-order company. It was soon obvious that the local seed fared much better than the imports—even when the seeds were for the

BEFORE

AFTER

than 100°F for several days or there has been no rain for a month. Usually, three waterings a summer—along with 35 in. of annual rainfall—keep our landscape green and blooming.

As Sally adds new plants, she gives them extra once-a-week watering during their first summer to get them established—usually with a watering can to keep from overwatering the established inhabitants. The ones that survive must make it through their second summer on the once-a-month watering. Today, only a fraction of the original plantings remain.

Over the years, we have observed a pattern to this do-or-die process: The indigenous plants do best. And, with a few Asian exceptions, such as *Hydrangea macrophylla* and St. John's wort (*Hypericum patulum*), the surviving nonindigenous plants come from neighboring limestone areas such as Arkansas and the Central Texas Hill Country.

THINKING LIKE AN ECOSYSTEM

In creating a more natural landscape in our front yard, we have learned to think of plants not as individuals but as members of an interconnected and harmonious community, or ecosystem, that includes both plants and wildlife. This has been a difficult lesson to learn because it goes against all our previous experience as gardeners. We had gotten used to seeing massed plantings of only one or two species. Now in our yard, as in nature, there is great diversity—dozens of different species in a relatively small area. Compare that to a conventional suburban landscape dominated by lawn grass and a handful of exotics.

A garden composed of only a few plant species is vulnerable to pests or diseases that target these species. On the other hand, a diverse natural landscape like ours, with as many as 40 or 50 different native species, greatly dilutes the impact of any one pest or disease. The predatory insects attracted to a natural landscape also provide pest control. Instead of insecticides, we rely on praying mantises, ladybugs, and lacewings. We even installed a bat house to encourage these voracious and unfairly vilified insectivores to take up residence. Our garden is alive with movement and sounds—butterflies flitting to and fro, bumblebees and hummingbirds drawing

---

In Praise of Native Plants

All the plants in your neighborhood nursery are natives to somewhere, but most of them are not native to where you live. They come from Africa, Asia, South America, and Europe. Called "exotics," they were introduced to this country as long ago as colonial times. Marigolds and mums, azaleas and hostas, Bradford pears and purple-leaf plums, and, well, the list is endless. These exotics are popular for one simple reason: they're pretty. Most survive only because gardeners pamper them with fertilizers, herbicides, pesticides, and, yes, oceans of water. In other words, they survive on artificial life-support systems.

On the other hand, true native plants—trees, shrubs, grasses, wildflowers, ground covers, and vines—need very little attention. They weren't brought here by humans; they've been here for millennia—many since before the last Ice Age—and they've learned to cope nicely with the growing conditions particular to their natural habitat.

Natives are not entirely maintenance-free, but they do require far less maintenance than exotics. How much less depends on your style of gardening. Native plants usually need a little watering during especially hot and rainless periods. Some judicious pruning and deadheading is also a good idea. But that's about it.

This isn't to say that native plants are bulletproof. Too often, someone buys a native plant and then continues to water for the benefit of the exotics. The native drowns, and the gardener says, "Hah! Natives aren't so tough after all!"

Native plants tend to be xeriscapic, that is, they can survive on rainfall alone. A little supplemental watering is fine, just to keep them looking their best. But overwatering is, in many cases, a death sentence.

You don't have to go completely natural to use natives. I've seen them used in English border gardens, in formal landscapes, and in conventional suburban yards. Of course, I admit a bias in favor of natural landscapes.

---

nectar, and an ongoing serenade of songbirds and cicadas.

One other thing that you will see in our garden is caterpillars chewing on leaves. The sight of nibbled leaves has many gardeners reaching for a can of bug spray. But when we see caterpillars, we see a part of nature's life cycle, and we know that soon we'll be rewarded with gorgeous butterflies. Another reason we don't use pesticides is because the insects they kill are a necessary protein source for nesting songbirds. And these birds are better at insect control than the occasional blast of aerosol mist. Instead of using chemical fertilizers, we allow fallen leaves to remain on the ground, where they slowly decompose over the winter and replenish the soil. As a result, our soil is rich in microorganisms and earthworms.

SELL THE LAWN MOWER AND RELAX

Yard work used to be a tedious, seemingly never-ending cycle of mowing, raking, edging, weeding, pruning, and watering. Our naturalistic landscape, on the other hand, has reduced upkeep and maintenance to mere hours per year instead of hours per week.

Sally, who does the bulk of the yard work, spends several hours each spring, usually in early April, pulling out pecan seedlings from nuts planted by squirrels. A month or so later, in mid- to late May, she spends about four hours cutting back the spent blooms from the first early spring show of color.

June to October is the too-hot-to-mess-with period, and we can only look with sympathy at neighbors out in the heat pushing their lawn mowers. While we are looking at them, they are looking at our colorful summer blooms—lantana, summer phlox (*Phlox paniculata*), green-eyes (*Berlandiera texana*), penstemon

sage (*Salvia penstemonoides*), zexmenia (*Wedelia hispida*), and ruellia (*Ruellia ciliosa*).

Following the first frost, usually in November, Sally puts in one last workday preparing the garden for winter. She cuts down frostbitten flowers to 4 in., smoothes out the fallen leaves to form a layer of insulation that will become next year's compost, and calls our tree man to do the annual pruning.

When these tasks are done, the only herbaceous plants left standing are the ornamental grasses—inland seaoats (*Chasmanthium latifolium*), switch grass (*Panicum virgatum*), and seep muhly (*Muhlenbergia rigens*). Their golden foliage remains attractive until February, when we cut it back to make way for new spring growth. Total time spent on the yard—10 hours!

If this sounds like paradise, imagine how a natural landscape would look around your home. Imagine an evolving display of color and texture, changing not just season to season, but year after year. Imagine a landscape that is alive with the sights and sounds of nature. And then imagine never having to mow the lawn again.

Long on beauty, short on upkeep, the author's natural front yard looks good in every season, yet demands a mere 10 hours of maintenance per year. Native plants attract predatory insects, eliminating the need for pest control.

SPECIALTY
GARDENS

3

AVID GARDENERS tend to be passionate gardeners. And many of them are passionate about specific plants or specific styles of gardens. Some are collectors who seek out the latest introductions or rarest plants—whether it's roses, hostas, or ornamental grasses. Others have a particular interest in design—such as creating water gardens or knot gardens. In each case, these gardeners have an interest that permeates all of their gardening activities—from design to planting—and thus tend to create gardens with a theme.

We'll meet a variety of gardeners, and learn how their passions led them to create not only interesting gardens, but beautiful gardens as well. We'll explore a not-so-typical cutting garden that offers materials for arrangements year-round. We'll visit a handful of cottage gardens with a uniquely American twist. And we'll wander through a greenhouse that offers a plant collector a gardening haven through long Boston winters. Take inspiration from these gardeners, and explore your own passions.

VALERIE S. EASTON

is a horticultural librarian at the University of Washington. She reviews garden books for *Pacific Horticulture* and Amazon.com, and is the garden columnist for *The Seattle Times*.

A Cutting Garden
for All Seasons

Planting in layers puts pickings within easy reach and ensures that the garden never looks looted. At left, mophead hydrangea blooms beneath the fuzzy foliage of a *Hydrangea aspera*.

I DELIGHT IN GOING OUT to my garden in winter, spring, summer, or fall and cutting whatever catches my fancy. It keeps me in touch with the passing seasons and lets me appreciate the color, fragrance, and texture of my favorite plants. Once I've filled my basket with fresh-cut flowers, berries, fruit, twigs, and foliage, I bring the outdoors inside to make arrangements—everything from huge, billowy displays to tiny, botanical tableaux. My garden fills every room of the house with the splendor of the season.

It wasn't always this way. When we moved into our 1950s vintage home seven years ago, the garden was little more than a steep, front-yard rockery dominated by a monotonous, monolithic mass of junipers. Leggy rhododendrons, red Hybrid Tea roses, and a ratty expanse of lawn completed the picture. Now, all that is left of that dreary scene is a carefully pruned mugo pine, a couple of the nicest rhododendrons, and a small patch of lawn. My

(ABOVE LEFT) Fiery fall colors look good in garden and vase. The variegated dogwood (*Cornus florida* 'Cherokee Sunset') also bears spring flowers.

(ABOVE RIGHT) Vases filled with cuttings are at home in the garden. A vase of sunflowers shines under a gargoyle's watchful eye.

husband claims that every plant on the property when we bought it has been moved at least once, and he is nearly correct—I think two lilacs and a rugosa rose are still in their original spots.

I've turned the entire landscape into a year-round cutting garden. In spring, bulbs and flowering shrubs provide the high notes; in summer, there's a chorus of perennials and roses; and autumn blazes with a symphony of colorful foliage tamed by the tawny blooms of ornamental grasses. During the winter holidays, conifers and broad-leaved evergreens carry the season, at least until the New Year

steps off with a procession of witch hazel (*Hamamelis* spp.), sweet violets (*Viola* spp.), and hellebores (*Helleborus* spp.).

My first consideration in designing a year-round cutting garden was selecting long-blooming, fragrant treasures that would hold up well in arrangements and would thrive in my garden's organic regimen. My choices were simplified once I decided to base all my design decisions on providing abundant garden bounty for making arrangements in all four seasons. My primary goal was to create a garden that looked good all the time, one that would never show the effects of my plundering shears.

To achieve this, I overplanted shamelessly. Every square foot of my garden is productive, and most areas are planted in five layers. I underplant trees with large shrubs, which, in turn, are skirted with smaller shrubs and perennials. Then I lace the whole mix together with ground covers, vines, annuals, and seasonal bulbs. I've lost plants by ignoring planting-tag guidelines for spacing them a certain distance apart from each other, but those stalwarts that have survived—and even thrived—in these crowded conditions look full and vigorous. And they've crowded out the weeds.

ARRANGE PLANTS IN SEVERAL LAYERS

The idea to plant in layers was born of my compulsion to increase the garden's abundance and inspired, no doubt, by observing nature's planting patterns during family hikes in the Northwest woods. In the forest, there is no careful spacing or rigid formality. No single plant is ever accorded dominance. Instead, it all melds together in a pattern that pleases the eye. That's what I try to emulate in my home garden. That means that I have to prune carefully, move plants when they get too large, and enrich the soil regularly with copious amounts

Site Plan

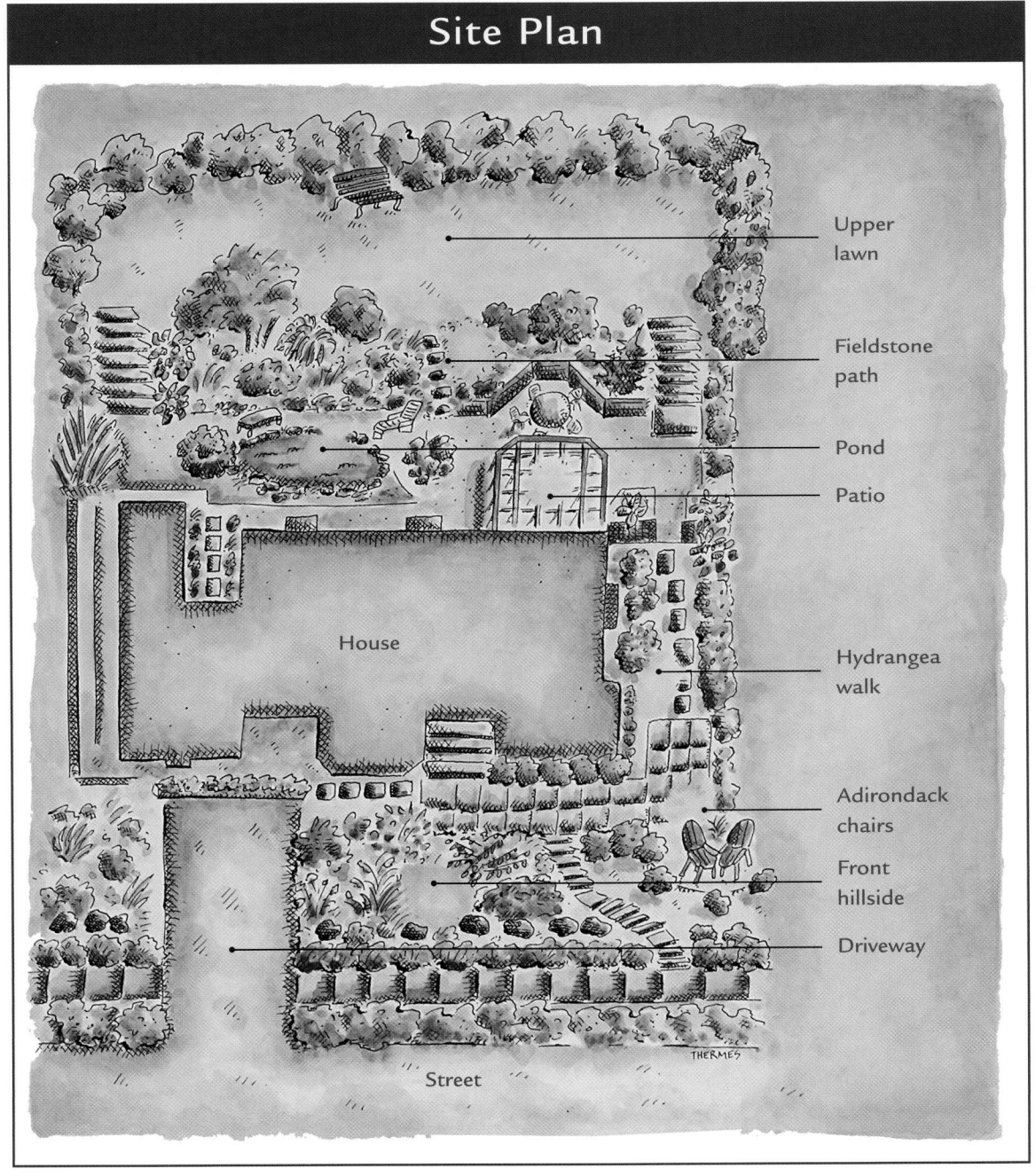

Upper lawn

Fieldstone path

Pond

Patio

House

Hydrangea walk

Adirondack chairs

Front hillside

Driveway

Street

THERMES

These Plants Are Perfect in the Vase and in the Garden

Cutting gardens can be home to everything from trees and grasses to perennials and shrubs. The list of plants included can be as wide as your imagination allows. Over the years, I've discovered a few I wouldn't be without; these now form the backbone of my cutting garden. Each has a long season of interest, and each brings distinctive shape and color to garden and vase.

SMALL TREES

Contorted hazel: *Corylus avellana* 'Contorta' has twining, corkscrew-like branches graced, in spring, with long, yellowish catkins, narrow drips of petalless flowers. It adds drama to arrangements all year round. USDA Hardiness Zone 4.

Strawberry tree: *Arbutus unedo* has a graceful shape, flaky bark, evergreen foliage with red stems, white flowers, and red and yellow fruits in the fall. Zone 7.

Eucalyptus archeri

Alpine cider gum: *Eucalyptus archeri* is my favorite for its disks of blue-green, aromatic leaves. Zone 8.

Magnolia: Small evergreens such as *Magnolia grandiflora* 'Victoria' or 'Little Gem' provide large, shiny leaves with fuzzy, brown undersides for use all year round. In spring and summer, there are huge, ivory-colored, lemon-scented blooms. I like to bring them inside to float in a dish. Zones 7 to 9.

SHRUBS

Artemisias: A wide range of silver and gray foliages makes *Artemisia* species indispensable in the garden and in arrangements. Hardiness varies by species; most thrive over a wide range.

Roses: English rose cultivars developed by David Austin thrive in Zones 5 to 9, provide fragrance, and bloom all summer. Red-leaf rose (*Rosa glauca*) and rugosa roses (*R. rugosa*) have showy foliage and fall fruit. *R. glauca* is hardy in Zones 2 to 8; *R. rugosa* in Zones 2 to 9.

Yellowtwig or redtwig dogwoods: *Cornus stolonifera* 'Flaviramea' and *C. alba* 'Elegantissima' feature variegated leaves for elegant foliage from spring to fall, and colorful branches for winter arrangements. Zones 2 to 8.

Hydrangea macrophylla

Hydrangeas: *Hydrangea macrophylla* or *H. paniculata* has easy-to-dry flowers, with colors ranging from white through all the pinks, wines, and blues to deepest purple. *H. macrophylla* thrives in Zones 6 to 9; *H. paniculata* in Zones 4 to 8.

Hypericums: Shrubby hypericums have attractive foliage and berries. *Hypericum androsaemum* has coral-colored fruit and leaves that turn burgundy in autumn; other cultivars have plum-colored, golden, or variegated foliage. Zones 7 to 8.

BULBS

Allium: *Allium cristophii* and *A. giganteum* provide huge, ball-shaped blooms in lilac and purple that look like spaceships hovering in the garden. They dry on their stalks to form starry, buff-colored heads, and retain their color for months when picked. *A. cristophii* is hardy in Zones 5 to 8; *A. giganteum* in Zones 6 to 10.

VINES/GROUNDCOVERS

Ivy: Small-leaved ivies, such as *Hedera helix* 'Gold Dust' or 'Shamrock' are variegated with splashes of white, yellow, or gold. Zones 5 to 10.

Houttuynia: *Houttuynia cordata* 'Chameleon' features heart-shaped leaves of green, watermelon pink and yellow that blend those disparate colors together beautifully. They can be used as vines trailing down from a vase. Can be aggressive, so grow in a contained area or a pot. Zones 6 to 11.

Clematis tangutica

Clematis: Grow *Clematis tangutica* for its yellow, bell-shaped flowers and fuzzy seed heads colored a ghostly silver. Both add texture and color to arrangements from summer through frost. Zones 6 to 9.

of manure. But my reward is a lush garden that offers an abundant supply of material for cutting.

Many perennials, trees, and shrubs lend themselves to planting in layers but hydrangeas are a particular favorite of mine because their flowers—both fresh and dried—are indispensable for arrangements. I put a ribbon of mophead hydrangeas (*Hydrangea macrophylla*) along the north side of the house and crowned them with a taller, felty-leaved *Hydrangea aspera*. To layer the planting, I added a Japanese snowbell (*Styrax japonicus*), whose delicate form also towers over the mopheads, and a carpet of hostas and bugleweed (*Ajuga reptans*) accented by flowery, early-season spires of monkshood (*Aconitum napellus*) and the midsummer-to-fall flowers of Japanese anemones (*Anemone hupehensis*).

All through the garden, I allow the plants to mingle, to flop a bit, or, in the case of lilies growing through *Brachyglottis greyi*, to hold each other up. I've also used many roses and small trees as living trellises to support clematis and climbing honeysuckles (*Lonicera* spp.); the flowering vines seem to give the roses and woody plants a second season of bloom. All over the garden, plants nudge each other into accommodation, creating patterns and combinations far more interesting than I ever could have planned and engineered myself. The overlapping of textures and the twisting and curling of vines always give me ideas to re-create indoors.

SELECT PLANTS WITH MULTISEASON INTEREST

As I began planting, I learned how quickly a quarter-acre garden fills up. I got more and more choosy—each plant had to have interest in at least two, and preferably three seasons. Of course, I constantly break this rule for the plants I love most, like peonies, irises, and

Water turned an awkward spot into the focal point of the garden. In an area too big for a planting bed and too small for a lawn, an ornamental pond was added.

"*All over the garden, plants nudge each other into accommodation.*"

season. I look at the line and shape of each plant, and concentrate more on its foliage, seed heads, and berries than I do on its flowers. I try to choose plants that will contrast and accent each other, adding bronze, purple, and silver-leaved specimens such as coral bells (*Heuchera* spp.) and artemisia, as well as variegated plants such as white-trimmed ivies and gold-striped ornamental grasses. I never tire of yellow and chartreuse foliage, which brightens the garden on overcast days.

Even in plants where bloom is the main story, I want more than just a pretty flower. The ruby-colored *Knautia macedonia*, for example, looks good in both bud and flower; even when it's past its prime, the spent flower heads, with their flat, button shapes and rays of petals, provide interest in arrangements for months.

One combination that works well in both garden and vase, from June through frost, is a large planting of 'Fireglow' spurge (*Euphorbia griffithii* 'Fireglow'), which begins blooming early in the season. I grow it with *Hypericum androsaemum*, whose bright yellow flowers accent coral berries that fade to black and foliage that turns a striking plum as the weather cools. This is interplanted with *Sedum* 'Autumn Joy' and with 'Rehbraun' switch grass (*Panicum virgatum* 'Rehbraun'), whose delicate brown and red flower spikes mingle with chocolate cosmos (*Cosmos atrosanguineus*) for a touch of drama clear until Thanksgiving.

PATHS AND TRELLISES PULL IT ALL TOGETHER

Deciding what plants to use was only part of my challenge. I also needed to arrange the garden itself in a way that would facilitate cutting. The first step was providing clean, dry

Pathways are perfect for staying dry on collecting trips. All-weather trails make it possible to reach all of the garden without getting wet or muddy.

lilies. To me, they are worth any amount of room, despite, or maybe because of, their fleeting but full-blown moment of glory.

But outside of a few showstoppers, I concentrate most on the chorus line, the stalwarts that hold the garden together from season to

> *"I got more and more choosy—each plant had to have interest in at least two, and preferably three, seasons."*

pathways to circumnavigate the house and to reach into every corner of the garden. Once I had sited (in my mind at least) the major trees and shrubs, I could then figure out how to arrange the hard surfaces around them, making sure that there would be sufficient space for walking, and for placing chairs, tables, and potted plants.

Creating planting beds as generously sized as I wanted meant that nearly all the lawn had to be dug up. That left me a very large and undefined space in back of the house that I didn't want to sacrifice to lawn, even though it was far too big for a planting bed. Adding a patio and pergola helped, but the space still needed distinctness and a focal point. I finally hit upon the idea of a water garden and we spent most of one summer digging an 8-ft. by 14-ft. pond. Once it was filled with water, I immediately recognized it as a central point around which to organize pathways, a little courtyard, and a mounded planting bed.

Now, I can walk out of any door to each part of the garden on a clean, hard surface. With dry, lighted pathways, I often cut flowers early in the morning without drenching my shoes in dew. Paved terraces lead to stepping stones, which lead to gravel pathways, and encourage me to go out to appreciate the garden in any weather.

ENJOY AN ENDLESS ARRAY OF ARRANGEMENTS

One of the most rewarding things about growing my own materials for arrangements is that I'm not confined to the usual assortment of flowers available from the florist or the supermarket. I try to grow a few plants in each season that add a unique and unexpected note to a bouquet. The writhing branches of the contorted hazel (*Corylus avellana* 'Contorta'); the purple, tufted head of a cardoon (*Cynara cardunculus*); or the bold, starry blossoms of Star of Persia (*Allium cristophii*) all warrant a second glance when tucked in among the more usual flowers and foliage.

My garden is now filled and, in some seasons, overflowing. I can cut large arrangements of ornamental grasses, hydrangeas, asters, roses, sweet peas, cardoons, and alliums and not create holes or gaps in the plantings. I am now working on pruning trees and shrubs up to allow more space for bulbs and smaller perennials. I'm also adding more vines to clamber up fences, trees, and large shrubs. There is always room for tall, slender plants, such as lilies, allium, and *Verbena bonariensis* that can poke up through other plantings. And, as for those three plants my husband has not yet dug up and moved...well, there's always next season.

DAVID CULP

is a sales representative for Sunny Border Nurseries, where he also does plant research and development. He teaches at Longwood Gardens and lectures nationally.

A Feast for the Eyes

(LEFT) In spring, peas scramble up tepees while the strong foliage of cabbage anchors a bed. Pink wood betony (*Stachys officinalis*) adds bright color around the birdbath.

(INSET) A perfectly ripe tomato is as beautiful as any flower. Sometimes the author removes leaves just to improve the view.

NO DOUBT ABOUT IT—it was the house that led me to create the vegetable garden. I believe that gardens should look comfortable with their surroundings, rather than appear superimposed on the landscape. We live in an 18th-century Pennsylvania farmhouse. Since farmhouses and vegetable gardens just naturally belong together, this garden was a logical beginning for us.

This isn't a novel idea. Gardening, since its beginning, has largely had a functional intent. Early American settlers brought the concept of the four-square garden with them from Europe. In fact, the four-square style of garden, which we've adopted, is appropriate to the age of our house. It's likely that our home's original inhabitants had a vegetable garden much like ours.

I garden with Mike Alderfer, and with his help and ever-busy hands, the garden has evolved over the years. It seemed right to us from the start that the heart of the garden should be a vegetable garden. Besides that, nothing beats a homegrown tomato or the simple pleasure of dashing out to gather the garden's bounty for dinner—or being able to share its abundance with a friend.

COMBINE STYLE WITH UTILITY

Many vegetable gardens are strictly utilitarian, and though they may possess lots of charm, good looks are usually a secondary consideration. As ornamental gardeners, we tend to demand more from ours, looking at the space with an eye to aesthetics, as much as to taste. A vegetable garden doesn't have to look boring, nor does it need to be a segregated space for production only. We think of this plot as yet another place to experiment with texture and color, both in foliage and flower, combined with the added bonus of fruit. In our minds, there is nothing more beautiful than a garden that melds ornament and style with function and utility.

The importance of structure should never be underestimated. The picket fence around our vegetable garden provides instant structure in an otherwise open field. It creates the feeling of a garden within a garden, separating the vegetable garden from surrounding perennial beds. Thus, the enclosed vegetable garden serves as the nucleus of the larger garden. Within the fenced boundaries, the garden's design is based on simple geometry—it's all about angle and axis. The straight path that runs through the garden from the entrance gate provides structure and formality, as do the angles of simple, clean square beds. These straight lines lead the eye through the garden. As the season progresses, sharp edges are blurred and softened by exuberant plantings.

Several years ago, Mike took the four-square design and divided it into 16 squares. The smaller beds are easier to tend, and crop rotation is simpler with more squares. We treat each square bed as a blank canvas, so with more squares we have more opportunity to experiment with color and texture.

A traditional four-square vegetable garden is at the heart of the larger landscape. It serves as the nucleus of the garden and is surrounded by lush perennial borders.

Four-Square Gardens Offer Design Flexibility

In a four-square garden, each bed can be designed independently. Here, purple, yellow, and red are the colors of choice. Plants vary in height, with pole beans scampering up a tepee in the center, small plants edging the bed, and mid-height flowers and foliage filling the center.

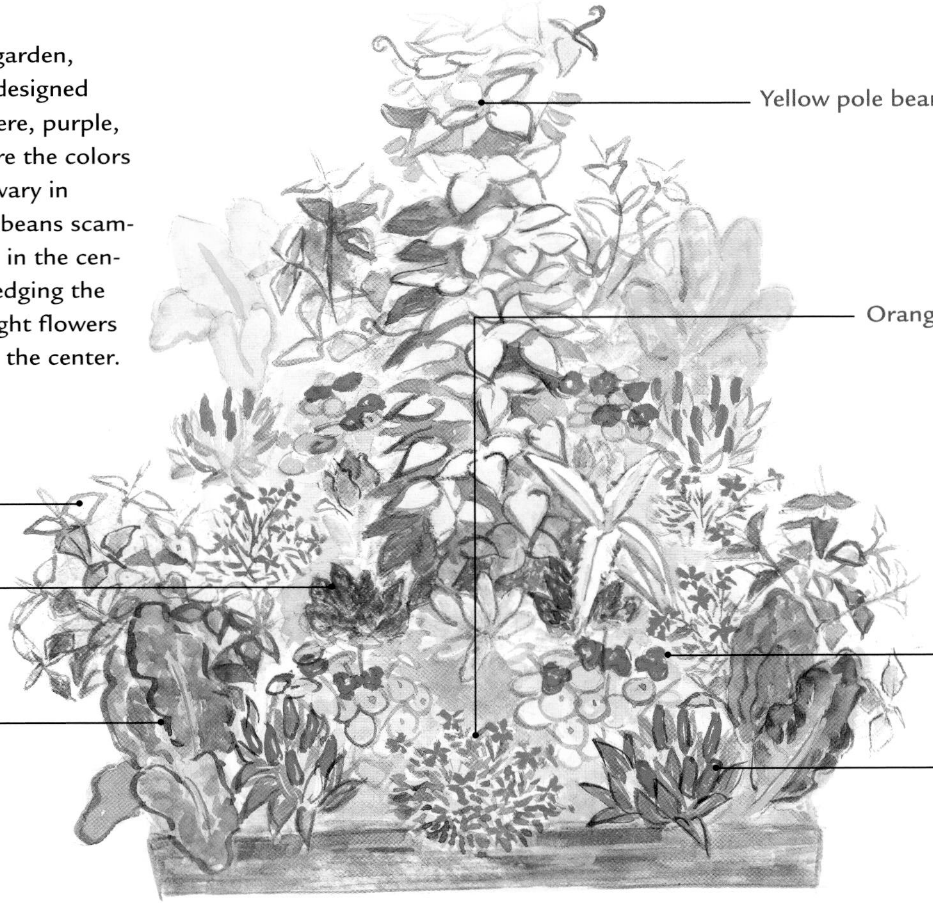

Yellow pole beans

Orange zinnias

Purple shiso

Purple basil

Red nasturtiums

'Bright Lights' Swiss chard

Red peppers

SELECT EDIBLES THAT ARE BEAUTIFUL AND TASTY

Our gardening season begins in early spring, when we plan the layout of the vegetable garden. We select plants based not only on taste, number of days to ripen, or how long they will hold on the pantry shelf, but for ornamental value as well. In early spring we use lettuces like 'Oak Leaf', with delicate, lobed leaves, and 'Red Sails', with ruffled, burgundy leaves, as an edging along the pathways. Parsley, purple basil, other herbs, and flowering plants enliven the beds. We plant the squares in geometric patterns, and the overall effect forms a quilt-like tapestry.

Herbs are a very important part of the vegetable garden. They impart texture to the plantings, and their piquant fragrances refresh the air when visitors brush against them. In season, fresh herbs are indispensable to our cooking, and those we dry provide pleasant winter memories of the garden.

Just as we know that fruits and vegetables feed the body, we know that flowers feed the soul. So we intermingle flowers in all of the squares. Simple annuals like zinnias, with their vibrant colors and easy nature, are often our first choice. Edible flowers like nasturtiums and calendulas receive high accolades from dinner guests, as they make excellent garnishes.

Dazzling Edible Plants

Here's just a sampling of great-looking edible plants. Pictured are (1) the dramatic, silvery leaves of cardoon; (2) a sweet pepper maturing to a golden color near *Zinnia haageana* 'Orange Star'; 3) chile peppers glowing near golden Swiss chard stems; (4) parsley and red-veined sorrel intermingling with chile peppers; (5) the lovely foliage of purple shiso, nasturtiums, and sage; and (6) the deep purple pods of hyacinth beans (*Lablab purpureus*).

ARCHITECTURAL FORM

Angelica
Artichoke
Brussels sprouts
Cardoon
'Red Russian' kale
Rhubarb

ATTRACTIVE FOLIAGE

Red and green cabbage
Bulb fennel
Lettuces:
    'Black-seeded Simpson'
    'Red Sails'
    'Oak Leaf'
    'Deer Tongue'
    'Freckles'
'Ruby Red' Swiss chard
'Bright Lights' Swiss chard
Red shiso

FRAGRANT FOLIAGE

Basil
Purple basil
Cilantro
Dill
Parsley
Rosemary
Sage

EDIBLE FLOWERS

Borage
Calendula
'Gem' marigold
Nasturtium
Scarlet runner bean

COLORFUL FRUIT

Purple:
'Violet Queen' cauliflower
'Machiaw' and 'Rosa Bianca' eggplant
'Caroubyde Maussane' snap peas
'Islander' pepper
'Trionfo' pole beans

Yellow:
'Roc d'Or' bush beans
'Gold Marie' pole beans
'Golden Summer' pepper
'Lillian's Yellow Heirloom',
    'Mandarin Cross', and 'Striped
    German' tomatoes
'Sun Gold' cherry tomato

Orange:
'Valencia' pepper
'Orange Strawberry' and 'Amana
    Orange' tomatoes

Green:
'Green Tiger' eggplant
'Evergreen' and 'Green Zebra'
    tomatoes

Red:
'Apple' pepper
'Thai Dragon' chile pepper
'Brandywine' tomato
'Ruby Pearl' cherry tomato

EXPERIMENT WITH COLOR, TEXTURE, AND FORM

One of the key elements in creating an interesting vegetable garden is a varied use of texture. Bold textures provide drama and accent to the garden. For example, the impressive foliage of cardoon (*Cynara cardunculus*) and rhubarb (*Rheum × hybridum*) serve as focal points, while the broad leaves and stout stems of brassicas like cabbage and broccoli anchor all of the beds. We often contrast these bold textures with fine-foliage plants such as parsley (*Petroselinum crispum*), fennel (*Foeniculum vulgare*), or golden feverfew (*Tanacetum parthenium* 'Aureum').

Since the vegetable garden's interior is largely hidden until you've walked into it, we experiment with colors freely. In early spring, the overall effect is calming as the fresh green of young lettuces and the cool, glaucous foliage of the brassicas dominate. But we often try combinations that just wouldn't work elsewhere in the garden. This is especially true in summer when ripening peppers and tomatoes and hot-colored flowers like zinnias and marigolds abound.

We've found that the repetition of color unites the garden and gives a sense of rhythm to the plantings. For example, we might use the color yellow as a theme for one of the beds by growing a pole bean with long yellow pods up a tepee, then repeating the color with a yellow tomato, a yellow pepper, and edging the bed with golden feverfew or golden oregano (*Origanum vulgare* 'Aureum'). Repeating the color both horizontally and vertically adds depth to the design. The next year the scheme might change to purple beans up the tepee, skirted with dark eggplant, purple peppers, and basil.

Color contrasts also have a vibrant effect in the vegetable garden. Orange zinnias sparkle

"We've found that the repetition of color unites the garden and gives a sense of rhythm to the plantings."

near dark-burgundy leaves of shiso (*Perilla frutescens*), and hot red peppers glow near golden Swiss chard stems.

LEAVE SOME OF THE DESIGN TO CHANCE

We let the garden evolve, leaving some of the work to Mother Nature. Self-sown annuals spring up here and there and help to soften the rigid four-square design. The transformation of the neat, tidy rows of early spring into the abundance and lushness of summer is a cycle I never tire of watching. I'm hopelessly and quite happily hooked. I've even gone as far as to pick off leaves to further expose the wonderful, luminescent beauty of a ripe tomato. It's that sense of profusion, the feeling of ripeness and fullness, that I find so intoxicating.

A simple white picket fence surrounds the garden and provides structure. Inside, lettuces, cabbages, and herbs (like golden feverfew) form a quilt-like tapestry.

MARCIA A. TATROE

has designed commercial, public, and residential gardens, including gardens at the Denver Botanic Gardens. She teaches gardening and is the author of *Perennials for Dummies*.

Defining the New American Cottage Garden

Cottage gardens thrive almost anywhere. Abandoning traditional plants and hardscaping materials of English cottage gardens frees American gardeners to reinvent the theme in regionally appropriate styles. These cottage gardens represent Colorado, Texas, and Georgia.

SEVERAL YEARS AGO, a husband-and-wife team of travel writers from England was touring Colorado and stopped by to see my garden. After walking in the garden and comparing our gardening experiences, successes and failures, we headed indoors to escape the intense July heat. Over cold glasses of lemonade, one of my guests teased, "Well, you've certainly out-cottaged any cottage garden we've ever seen in England."

Up until that point I'd never really thought of my garden as a cottage garden, per se. I certainly had no particular style in mind when I built it. My visitor's remark was offered at least partly tongue-in-cheek, prompted by the unimaginably large number of plants I have stuffed into a very small property.

On reflection, however, I've come to realize that many of the elements of the classical English cottage garden are at work in my garden and the myriad like it popping up all over on this side of the Atlantic.

In America, "cottage garden" has always been a catchall term used to describe a garden that is bursting at the seams and does not otherwise conform to a recognizable style. But these gardens, while highly individualistic, do share a few common characteristics. Typically, they are small, casually informal, residential properties that ignore conventional landscape tenets. Instead of spacious lawns and prim foundation plantings, there are lavishly planted flower gardens accented with rugged, native plants. Front yards, formerly open to

public view, have been enclosed and transformed into intimate spaces. Hardscaping is usually minimal, but most of these cottage gardens are bisected by a path and many include fences, trellises, and patios constructed of natural, indigenous materials. Thanks to the native plants and local building materials, these gardens also capture a flavor distinctive to their region.

COTTAGE GARDENERS IGNORE TRADITIONAL DESIGN ELEMENTS

Cottage gardens are always compact, typically a quarter-acre or less in size. A brisk, two-minute walk will usually take in the entire garden. Because space is at such a premium, the garden inevitably tucks right up against the

Indigenous building materials evoke a sense of place. Throughout the United States, you'll find rustic fences, painted pickets, adobe walls, red brick, weathered stone, and other local building materials, which vary by region. These gardens are located in Washington, New Mexico, and Colorado.

Split-rail fences and stone boulders in this Colorado cottage garden suggest the rugged West.

house, completely embracing it. Invariably, the house is modestly sized as well, but it is still the garden's dominant, central feature. It is the "cottage" of the cottage garden, even though actual cottages are rare in most of America. I suppose we could call our version "house gardens" but then we would lose the romantic connotation.

Whatever we call them, cottage gardens share another trait—they appear to be unstudied, and oblivious to accepted landscape design principles. Formal elements like tidy lawns, sweeping vistas, reflecting ponds, traditional perennial borders, and tree-lined walks simply do not fit. Instead, cottage gardens exhibit a casual, unplanned naivete. Self-sowing annuals may help to create random, but pleasing plant combinations.

Sometimes, their genius stems from the indulgence of personal whims. In a burst of intuition, a gardener may find new life for an old, discarded object. A rusted lawn mower might be put to work as a trellis for morning glory vines, or colorful coffee cups converted

to dangling decorations. Such quirky garden "art" has a spontaneity perfectly suited to a cottage garden.

ABUNDANT PLANTINGS ARE A COTTAGE-GARDEN HALLMARK

Sheer numbers don't often count for much, but a plethora of plants is one of the defining characteristics of the traditional English cottage garden. This is true of both the genuine article—the workingman's humble home surrounded by vegetables, fruits, herbs, and flowers—and of the 19th-century, idealized version, with a storybook cottage adrift in a sea of flowers.

And this abundance is a hallmark of the new cottage gardens blossoming all over this country. In my own yard-turned-garden, every square inch of space is packed with plants, but

"Cottage gardens share another trait— they appear to be unstudied and oblivious to accepted landscape design principles."

While a carefree profusion of plants is a hallmark of cottage gardens, the use of native or regionally identified plants gives American cottage gardens character. These gardens are located in Colorado, Pennslyvania, Arizona, and Oregon.

I'll never admit there's not room for more. In a typical new American cottage garden, walls and fences are lined with trellises groaning under the weight of rambling roses, clematis, and other vines. Porches or patios sport so many containers there's barely room to get through to the door. Conventional foundation plantings composed of masses of matching or sculptural shrubs were torn out long ago, to make room for more roses or a strawberry patch. Lawns are never a major component of the cottage garden; they are either nonexistent or inconsequential.

NATIVE PLANTS PROVIDE A STURDY FRAMEWORK

Within the constraints of climate, American cottage gardens are certain to contain a good number of traditional English cottage garden plants—old-fashioned favorites like peonies, irises, lilacs, roses, and clematis. Traditionally, cottage gardeners have a special fondness for self-sowing annuals and biennials, plants that more sophisticated gardeners might consider weeds. Larkspur (Consolida ajacis), annual poppies (*Papaver* spp.), Canterbury bells (*Campanula medium*), Johnny jump-ups (*Viola tricolor*), and hollyhocks (*Alcea rosea*) pop up each spring to fill every nook and cranny, adding to the garden's overstuffed, comfortable ambience.

But in addition to such standbys, many American cottage gardeners are adding local wildflowers and native plants. In a sense, they are continuing a long tradition—cottage gardeners have always looked to nearby fields and woods for inspiration. In fact, the first cottage flowers were undoubtedly simple wildflowers that caught the fancy of the field worker or housewife gathering firewood for the family's hearth.

Aside from that tradition, however, contemporary American cottage gardeners are making the significant discovery that regional flora will thrive with minimum care in their existing soil and climate. Native plants have had millennia to adapt to local conditions such as rainfall, soil composition, winter cold, and summer heat—conditions that in many parts of the country threaten the very life of plants from more forgiving environments. Growing peonies in Nevada, for example, may be impossible without abundant soil amendments, irrigation, and lots of fussy attention. A Nevada native plant, on the other hand, could just be popped in the ground to thrive with little attention. The native plants' easygoing attitude suits cottage gardening's casual atmosphere as well.

Even more important, native plants have a regionally appropriate look or feel. When used in a garden, native wildflowers, trees, and shrubs provide an echo of the surrounding landscape and help link one to the other. I've used Southwestern natives such as fernbush (*Chamaebatiaria millefolium*), dwarf rabbitbrush (*Chrysothamnus nauseosus*), winecups (*Callirhoe involucrata*), and an assortment of plains and desert cacti and penstemons that relish our harsh climate. Our relatively meager rainfall of 15 in. per year is sufficient for them. These sun- and heat-lovers are a challenge to grow where the weather is wetter and milder, and their success here attests that this is assuredly a Colorado cottage garden.

Elsewhere in the country, different plant palettes are more appropriate. Trilliums and *Hepatica* spp., collectors' rarities in many parts of the country, show up in shady corners of northeastern cottage gardens, highlighting the distinctive character of this area. Tropicals like *Philodendron* and *Bougainvillea* sneak into frost-free California and Gulf Coast gardens to create an entirely different, yet still appropriate, perspective there.

Native plants contribute to a cottagey look even in challenging locations. Palo verde trees (*Cercidium* spp.) are surrounded by prolific and colorful flowers in this Arizona garden.

(COUNTER CLOCKWISE FROM LEFT) Ornaments provide a clue to regional identity and express the personality of the gardener, whether they are cow skulls, a collection of coffee mugs, strands of chili ristras, or a wagon-wheeled cart. Gazing globes, whimsical sculpture, and colorful containers are also common cottage garden ornaments.

USE TOUGH, LOOK-ALIKE PLANTS INSTEAD OF FINICKY FAVORITES

After a decade of living in Holland and England, my family and I moved into our home in Aurora, Colorado, in 1987. I had visions of English cottage gardens and grand estates still dancing in my head and was determined to have a lavish flower garden to rival any I had visited in England. But there are only a few sections of the country with climates similar enough to England's to grow the soaring delphiniums and lupines of stereotypical British cottage gardens. Colorado isn't one of them.

I set out to find a way to have the best of both worlds. That first year I made scale drawings, started visiting area nurseries, and attended xeriscape classes to become familiar with plants that adapt well to this semi-arid region. Our house sits on what was once a shortgrass prairie, so a range of ornamental grasses and plains wildflowers seemed only natural. The foothills and canyonlands to the west provided us with a host of ideas for shrubs and trees.

I soon discovered that even in semi-arid parts of the country, American gardeners can emulate the spirit of the English prototype by trying similar plants with more rugged demeanors. Here in Colorado, I looked for plants with scrappy dispositions. Many of my most reliable plants are far too invasive for gardens in more moderate climates. But ruffians such as yarrow (*Achillea* spp.) and bellflowers (*Campanula* spp.) become nearly tractable when subjected to Colorado's spartan regimen. Roses are essential to the cottage garden but hybrid tea roses seldom survive our bitterly cold winters. I've had better luck with the weather-resistant Canadian Explorer and Parkland series and the hardiest of the old-fashioned roses. Roses will never clamber over our roof as they did in England, but they are undeniably romantic just the same.

USE HARDSCAPE
WITH A REGIONAL FLAVOR

Structure in cottage gardens is of minimum importance and is often limited to walks, trellises and, occasionally, fencing. Materials are simple, even rustic, and not infrequently, recycled. This is where regional peculiarities really stand out. Split rail fences look as if they belong in the west, while picket fences have more of midwestern or northeastern flair.

Historical influences may also play a role in the choice of materials. The cottage gardener is inclined to reap the spoils of urban renewal. Discarded architectural bits and pieces gain new potential in garden construction projects. Well-worn cobblestones rescued from turn-of-the-century streets might be recycled into rustic walkways and walls. In my own garden, my husband and I built a massive arbor of rough-hewn cedar and redwood in a simple, southwestern ramada style. Inspired by local history, we replaced our concrete sidewalk with red flagstone slabs like those we had seen in nearby older neighborhoods. Rock gardens, though not something you would usually find in a cottage garden, further tie us to this region by reflecting the dominating presence of the Rocky Mountains.

More decorative forms of ornamentation offer further clues to regional identity. American cottage gardeners have always drawn on their immediate environs for inspiration and materials. Seaside cottages are often decorated with seashells, driftwood, and nautical geegaws. Southwestern gardeners indulge in such cliches as hanging cow skulls on their fence posts and employ wooden wagon wheels for all manner of uses.

VARIATIONS ON THIS THEME
ARE ENDLESS

I never set out to create a new kind of cottage garden, much less one that would be part of what is emerging as a distinctive, North American garden style. My original design called for conventional lawns surrounded by flower borders, but the garden took on a life of its own. Currently, hundreds of species of flowers, vegetables, fruits, vines, shrubs, and trees share this space in a riot of color and texture.

Our English visitor was right in the end—we have created a variant on the traditional cottage garden. But rather than slavishly imitating a foreign aesthetic, our garden reinterprets the English model with an unmistakable Coloradan accent. The same aesthetic is being replayed in countless dialects throughout America. Midwestern gardens are starting to feature a tallgrass prairie theme. Coastal chaparral plants are making their way into California gardens. Woodland flowers celebrate the northeast. What is developing is a distinctive new style—the new American cottage garden.

"Walls and fences are lined with trellises groaning under the weight of rambling roses, clematis, and other vines."

NANI WADDOUPS

and her husband, Ron Wagner, are working on a new garden in Portland with a tropical influence. Their garden is listed in the Smithsonian Registry of American gardens.

Tropical Garden, Temperate Zone

(LEFT) A hut inspired by Southeast Asian architecture provides a special destination in a part of the garden that might not otherwise be visited.

(INSET) Whimsical touches, such as the ceramic leopard, add to the atmosphere.

THE NEWER PARTS of our garden look a little out of place. Actually, they look a lot out of place. We live in Portland, Oregon, but lately our garden has taken a tilt toward the tropics. Since I'm from Hawaii, visitors often credit me for the tropical influence. They are only part right. My husband, Ron, and I often visit the islands to see my family, and Ron too has come to love the overgrown lushness of the tropics. Together, we've conspired to create our own pseudotropical garden. We may not have Hawaii's year-round warmth, but Portland still gets plenty of rain, and its summer temperatures are high enough to satisfy all kinds of heat-loving tropical plants.

Our gardens are also very much outdoor living areas. Having outside kitchen and dining areas, as well as a few open-air retreats, adds a lot to the tropical ambiance we've tried to create. To make those areas more inviting, we've built a number of Southeast Asian–inspired structures: a clay oven for cooking, a hot-tub enclosure for relaxing, and a hideaway hut where we sometimes spend the night. We also made bamboo fences and added sculptures like those that guard Balinese temples. Against that oriental framework, we use hardy plants in nontraditional ways, primarily for their bold silhouettes, big leaves, and tropical appearance. We also "cheat" by planting tender exotics such as *Brugmansia*, with its foot-long floral trumpets; tart- but sweet-smelling gingers (*Hedychium* spp.); and big-leaved cannas (*Canna* spp.)—which we bring inside when summer disappears. The combined effect gives us a garden filled with dramatic textures, hot colors, wonderful fragrances, and a sense that, if you stopped tending the plants, they'd take over the world.

BIG, BOLD PLANTS INSPIRE A TROPICAL THEME

It all started when we were more or less evicted from a rented apartment. The landlord thought we had too many plants. We bought a home in 1988 with all the land we could afford—it worked out to be just about an acre—and attacked it with the unrivaled energy of first-time homeowners. We soon had more plants than our old landlord could ever have imagined. Our credo was simple: big is better, especially if there's lots of it. By the next summer, the perennial garden we had started in the northeast corner of the yard averaged 8 ft. tall. Hollyhocks, ornamental grasses, butterfly bushes, and sunflowers soared toward the sky.

The immediate gratification we got from the perennial border inspired new efforts. We quickly turned part of our old driveway into a

Site Plan

LEGEND

Tropical motif garden
1 The hut
2 The woods
3 Cooking garden
4 Hot-tub enclosure
5 Plastic-sheathed greenhouse under deck

Temperate garden
6 The farm
7 Perennial garden
8 The pond

15-ft. by 25-ft. water garden and began collecting parrot feather (*Myriophyllum aquaticum*) and water lilies (*Nymphaea* spp.). They grew like, well, weeds. A single clump of pickerel weed (*Pontederia cordata*) grew so quickly we were soon giving away 4-ft.-tall plants to anyone who'd take them. The pond's chaotic lushness gave us our first glimpse at the possibilities of creating a tropical paradise in our temperate, USDA Hardiness Zone 7 garden.

Ron began returning from every outing with big-leafed oddities, rangy bamboos, and billowy grasses. Large tropicals sold as houseplants—like ti plant (*Cordyline furticosa*), with its pink-edged leaves—became our new annuals. The bug had bitten.

TRANSFORMATION BEGINS WITH EXOTIC HOUSEPLANTS AND HOT-COLORED ANNUALS

For our next garden project—screening off the hot tub near our kitchen door—we used both structures and plants to explore the tropical theme. We began with a carved wooden door-

way from Bali, which we got in exchange for restoring an old desk. It made a fine entryway, especially after we finished enclosing the area with wood and reed fencing. Inside, we softened the geometric lines of the walls by adding containers of wispy clumps of bamboo and Japanese aucuba (*Aucuba japonica* 'Gold Strike'), with its gold-splashed, variegated leaves. Japanese aralia (*Fatsia japonica*) added an exotic touch with glossy-green, deeply lobed leaves. We also planted zingy annuals such as orangy-yellow monkey flowers (*Mimulus* spp.) and pink and yellow butterfly flowers (*Schizanthus pinnatus*). A trumpet vine, threatening to cover the enclosure and the house, added to the wild sense of tropical abandon.

(ABOVE RIGHT) The lushness of a water garden inspired the exploration of a tropical theme. The rampant growth of the pond plantings hinted at the possibilities for growing tropical plants.

(ABOVE LEFT) Heady fragrances and bright colors recall the sensual appeal of the tropics. The sweet-scented trumpets of a brugmansia drape over a mound of hardy fuchsia.

(ABOVE) Structures anchor a tropical garden. This carved, wooden Balinese doorway creates an appropriate backdrop for plants with exotic-looking foliage.

(ABOVE RIGHT) The odd-looking leaves of an arisaema add an exotic touch to the edge of a border.

Outside the doorway, we filled oriental water bowls with elephant ears (*Colocasia* spp.), small cannas, and chartreuse Japanese forest grass (*Hakonechloa macra* 'Aureola'). And we posted a sentry: a wooden sculpture of Dawi, the Balinese rice goddess of fertility. Our tropical transformation had begun.

After Dawi's private pleasure palace took shape, we continued the tropical theme on an adjoining landing surrounded by a picket fence. First, we replaced the pickets with tied bamboo sticks. Then, to create a dense, jungly impression, we added luxuriant, billowy plants like northern sea oats (*Chasmanthium latifolium*),

Miscanthus sinensis 'Morning Light', ferns, and tiger lilies (*Liliumlancifolium*). They served as a backdrop for smaller hardy geraniums, sedges (*Carex* spp.), alliums, and bugleweeds (*Ajuga* spp). Clematis vines ramble through everything, and the plants are so intertwined that the whole bed looks like a tangle of wet undergrowth. (Truth be told, it's one of the drier spots on our property, and we have to water it frequently.) For a final touch, we added a mature corkscrew filbert (*Corylus avellana* 'Contorta'), and its unruly curlicues provided yet another measure of out-of-control wildness.

That sense of wildness was just what we were after. Flowers were nice, but it was the contrasting shapes and colors of the foliage that really made the idea work. We wanted a planting that didn't seem too cultivated, and preferred the overgrown, almost unruly look achieved by planting densely. But we also realized our tropical theme wouldn't have been nearly as effective without the accessories—the pots, the Balinese doorway, even a ceramic leopard—that breathed so much life into our illusion.

AN OPEN-AIR KITCHEN ADDS A TASTE OF THE TROPICS

We were so enamored of structures and the way they enhanced our garden that we began a new project. We also wanted more outdoor living areas, since they add so much to the tropi-

> *"We posted a sentry: a wooden sculpture of Dawi, the Balinese rice goddess of fertility."*

cal experience. Our kitchen door is close to the hot-tub enclosure and its nearby garden, so we frequently found ourselves hauling our unaesthetic barbecue grill into this newly picturesque setting. We needed something more fitting for our tropical retreat and decided to build a fireplace with room for chairs around it so that we could sit comfortably. We constructed a simple ring of stones and capped them with flat rocks so we'd have a surface for setting plates. Then we threw the old grill on top of some firebricks inside the ring. Dinners ensued. Ron added to the setting by building a chandelier from driftwood, iron hooks, glass bottles, and some candles. Hanging from a barely visible cable, it seems to float in the air.

Just when I thought this area was complete, we met a resourceful and enthusiastic builder of clay ovens. We organized a workshop and, with his leadership and the help of eight students, we dug up a bunch of clay—our yard is full of it—and, in two days, sculpted a shoulder-high, frog-shaped oven. To its belly, we added swinging iron doors that give us access to a heating chamber where we build fires for roasting and baking. The frog's presence and the outdoor kitchen add yet another life-in-the-open-air element to the tropical ambiance of what we now call The Cooking Garden.

TURNING A TINY FOREST INTO A LUSH, FRAGRANT JUNGLE

As we worked our way around our acre, the garden evolved naturally. We put The Farm—where we grow fruits and vegetables, and raise chickens—far enough from the house so we wouldn't have to see or smell our feathered friends. And there was only one place flat enough to play croquet, so it seemed only natural to plant a lawn there. Then there was The Woods.

Move a Tropical Garden Indoors Each Winter

The tender plants that give our garden its tropical illusion can't survive an Oregon winter. So, in October or November, when nighttime temperatures begin dipping into the 30s, we begin what we call "the fall purge." We dig up all the dracaena, ti plant, cannas, gingers, and brugmansias along with anything else that isn't likely to survive our Zone 7 winter. Then we pot everything in plastic containers and hand cart them to our makeshift greenhouse.

We place the most tender plants in the basement where they benefit from the warmth of the house. The rest go to an area under the deck protected from the elements by "walls" of plastic sheeting draped over evenly spaced 2x4s. Between the two adjoining areas, we have about 300 square ft. of usable space. Last fall, we added four sodium vapor lights and a small heater. We keep the heater on its lowest setting—just enough to prevent temperatures from dropping to freezing. We're not trying to grow the plants during winter; we just want them to survive.

We don't worry about aesthetics either. Everything is crammed together. We don't bother to cut most of the plants back, except for brugmansias, which look like a bare stick by the time we haul them inside.

We've had few problems with disease or insects in our plant refuge. Too much moisture is our primary concern. Once, one of the plastic sheets leaked and a lot of our geraniums got mildew and turned to goo. Now we spray with a fungicide as soon as we see signs of mildew. And, to increase ventilation, we put in a fan.

Sometime in May, as temperatures make their way back to the 60s, we start taking things outside and replanting them. Spring is usually cloudy and rainy here, so we don't worry about sudden changes in brightness harming plants that have been in the basement for several months. By the time we do get sun, it's usually July, and the plants have readapted to being outside. And the tropics touch our gardens again.

A small corner of our acre used to be part of a larger, densely forested area that we planned to leave natural—until our neighbor, on a self-confessed whim, clear-cut his property. Our woodland was suddenly only four firs deep. To make matters worse, we couldn't escape glaring views of his enormous white house. We needed a screen, so we built a cedar fence, planted a row of fast-growing Norway maples, and stopped cutting back the ivy that kept trying to ramble up the bare trunks of the firs. To help fill the area even faster, we added a few stands of fast-spreading bamboo. We didn't care that it was aggressive—that's why we chose it.

The screen turned out to be just the start. We decided to turn The Woods into a backdrop for a sort of fantasy island setting with a tropical-looking retreat and a shallow border of plants selected for their vivid flowers, fragrant scents, or intriguing foliage.

Since we already knew how much structures could add to a garden, we decided a hut would complement the new setting. It would also give us another place to spend time out in the garden, and its horizontal lines would attract the eye away from the looming, vertical lines of the firs.

We researched Indonesian building styles and ended up designing a hideaway on stilts that looks like a cross between an open-sided Balinese hut and a Thai house. We then went to work, relying on hops poles, reed fencing, and Ron's mastery of the saber saw to see the project through.

For a tropical accent, we stapled reed fencing to the hut's roof sheathing so we'd have a decorative ceiling, and "rusted" the tin roofing with paint. To the hut's open sides, we added bamboo blinds, which we can raise or lower whenever the mood strikes. A cushioned, wooden, Thai couch went inside the hut, and a

(ABOVE) Huge leaves give a junglelike look. The giant foliage of an empress tree results from cutting the plant back each spring.

(RIGHT) Frog motifs, embodied by these two amphibians perched on a pier in the water garden, appear throughout the garden.

mosquito net provided an island ambiance. For a crowning touch, we topped the roof with an ornament Ron had carved. The Hut was ready.

At the bottom of the rustic stairway that climbs to The Hut, we made a concession to taming the wild landscape we planted behind it. We dug a trench, poured concrete into it, and studded it with hops poles to create a low wall of edging that we hope will prove an impenetrable barrier for the fast-spreading bamboo.

When we first started work at our new home, we planted with sheer abandon in order to give our blank slate a personality. But once we gave it our imprint, Ron went down the path—I believe it was the path of no return—of the specialty gardener.

The Hut and its surrounds became the focus of Ron's redefined passion: plants with interesting foliage. He nurtured tiny starts of exotic *Arisaema*, hardy fuchsias, and other exotica to planting size, and installed them in the new border flanking the hut. To those, we added treasures like *Sasa palmata*, an evergreen bamboo with purple-streaked stems and rich, green foliage, and a few unusual woody specimens selected for their large or oddly shaped leaves. There was an angelica tree (*Aralia elata*), which we pruned to resemble a palm tree; a fig tree (*Ficus carica*) with huge, deeply lobed foliage; and an empress tree (*Paulownia tomentosa*), which we cut back to the main trunk each spring to encourage the growth of new stalks covered with huge leaves 2 ft. across. We also planted delicacies like daturas (*Brugmansia* spp.), gingers (*Patura* spp.), and dahlias bright with color.

Finally we honored the hut with a pair of ferocious-looking demons. The stone figures seem to smile, perhaps because they know the jungle that surrounds them has only just begun to grow.

FALL PURGES PROTECT A TROPICAL ILLUSION

Until then, we have the task of maintaining our tropical illusion. Our efforts peak in late autumn, when what we call "the fall purge" begins. Protecting the tender "accessories" to our tropical illusion means digging up and potting all the plants that wouldn't survive a Portland winter. We then hand cart them into our makeshift greenhouse and nurse them along until spring returns.

Sometimes I wonder if all the work is worth it. But then, I sit back back on the bench in The Hut, with the mosquito netting tied back. Splinters of sunlight filter through the bamboo blinds. The scent of datura blooms fills the air. From my seat, I can see Dawi, guarding the hot hub and The Cooking Garden, where smoke drifts from the chimneylike mouth of our crouching, clay frog. A few stalks of bamboo create a bright scrim against a leafy backdrop. For a minute, I think I might be in Hawaii, but I'm home, in Oregon. It's worth it.

An unusual, but functional, oven is the centerpiece of an outdoor living area. This sculpted, frog-shaped clay oven, safe beneath its protective roof, presides over the cooking garden. A driftwood, glass, and iron chandelier lights the area at night.

"That sense of wilderness was just what we were after."

English

Roses *Anchor an American Shoreline* Garden

LYNN HUNT

contracted rose fever almost 20 years ago. She is a consulting rosarian and horticultural judge for the American Rose Society, and gives lectures on English Roses.

David Austin roses feature the charm of old garden roses and the vigor and repeat bloom of modern roses. The elegant 'Fair Bianca' blooms almost continuously.

WITH ALL DUE RESPECT to Gertrude Stein, a rose isn't always a rose. I discovered this while living in England in 1991. It seemed that whether it was a tiny patch behind a modest flat or the magnificent collection of old roses at Mottisfont Abbey, British rose gardens looked nothing like the one I'd created in Virginia. There were no boring rectangular beds stocked only with prissy Hybrid Teas. There was no calculated spacing with bushes lined up like dutiful soldiers. No naked, segregated canes to stare at all winter.

Instead, roses were part of the overall landscape. There was an understated accent here, a flashy punctuation point there. And, oh, what wonderful blooms! Some the size of a dinner plate, with a fragrance that took me back to summer days on my grandmother's farm.

I assumed many of these roses I'd come to admire in British cottage gardens were antiques—Comtesse de something or other. But a trip to the Chelsea Flower Show set me straight. There I found not only a collection of the roses that had captured my fancy, but I also met the man behind roses with names like 'Wise Portia', 'Chaucer', 'Gertrude Jekyll', and 'William Shakespeare', the creator of the "English" rose—David Austin.

SELECT ROSES FOR THEIR COLOR AND FRAGRANCE

Imagine being able to wave a magic wand and create the perfect rose. You'd want it to bloom prolifically all summer. You'd make it resistant to disease and hardy in cold climates. You'd give it eye-arresting color. And for the final touches, you'd conjure up a multipetaled form and heady fragrance reminiscent of an era gone by.

With years of hard work, and perhaps a bit of magic, Englishman David Austin has come quite close to creating this vision of perfection. He hybridized a new class of roses by crossing the Gallicas, Damasks, Bourbons, and Portlands of the 18th and 19th centuries with modern Hybrid Teas, Floribundas, and Climbers. As a result, he has captured the appealing features of Old Garden Roses—those introduced prior to 1867—such as cupped or rosette-shaped flowers and strong fragrance in shrubs that have the repeat bloom and vigor of modern roses.

Although he started hybridizing in the '50s, Austin's first big success didn't come until 1961. 'Constance Spry' was a cross between an old Gallica 'Belle Isis' and the Floribunda 'Dainty Maid'. It bloomed only once a year, but the show proved so spectacular that it remains a favorite today. In fact, most gardeners have likely seen the famous photograph of 'Constance Spry' smothering a wall behind an elegant white bench at Mottisfont Abbey.

The first repeat bloomers hit the British market in 1969. However, it was the introduction of 'Mary Rose' and 'Graham Thomas' at Chelsea in 1983 that was Austin's real breakthrough. Word about these new, old-fashioned roses soon spread across the pond, launching another British invasion. The roses quickly became the toast of American gardeners, even those previously leery of the persnickety "Queen of Flowers." For many, their graceful charm was the beginning of a philosophical change in rose gardening.

PLANT ROSES FOR OLD-FASHIONED CHARM

Of course, before David Austin, there was another important Englishman in my life—my husband, Chris. When his career as an officer in the Royal Navy brought us to the British

English Roses

ROSA SPP. (Rō′sa)

- A collection of shrub roses generally noted for their old-fashioned charm, fragrance, and repeat bloom.
- English roses sometimes grow larger in the U.S. than in British gardens—often reaching 8 ft. or 10 ft. in height.
- Grow roses in full sun and provide plenty of water and a balanced fertilizer.
- Although they aren't particular about their soil, roses perform best in loam.
- English roses are more disease-resistant than most modern hybrids, but watch for black spot, mildew, aphids, and Japanese beetles.

Inhale the "Damask" fragrance of 'Gertrude Jekyll' as you admire its full-petaled, pink rosettes. This rose appreciates light pruning throughout the growing season.

Embassy in Washington, D.C., we purchased a small holiday cottage on the Eastern Shore of Maryland. Three years later, when Chris retired from Her Majesty's service, we knocked down the old house and rebuilt.

Sadly, most of my small cottage garden stocked with English roses was lost beneath the piles of construction rubble. Still, I kept a stiff upper lip, realizing that once the house was finished, I'd have room for an even bigger garden. That winter, the plans for my new cottage garden filled with English roses began to take shape.

'Powis Castle' artemisia carpets the ground below the pink 'Cottage Rose'. Its lacy, silver foliage looks great with just about any color rose.

(RIGHT) 'Heritage' ranks among David Austin's personal favorites. Its sweet scent and form are reminiscent of Old Garden Roses.

(FAR RIGHT) Blue flowers complement pink roses. Catnip makes a pleasant garden companion for the English 'Cottage Rose' and the darker Shrub Rose 'Carefree Wonder'.

ENGLISH ROSES OFTEN GROW LARGER IN AMERICAN GARDENS

David Austin recommends planting English roses in groups of two or three of the same variety for an impressive visual impact. To serve as anchors, I selected two bushes each of my favorites: 'Heritage', with its blush-pink blooms; myrrh-scented 'Fair Bianca'; dainty 'Sharifa Asma'; prolific 'Cottage Rose'; and long-lasting, bright crimson 'L.D. Braithwaite'.

My first garden taught me what to expect in size and growth habit. Some of the descriptions coming out of England can be misleading. Bushes here, especially in warmer areas of the country, tend to grow bigger and taller than they do in the cooler U.K. climate.

British books suggest planting these roses 18 in. apart, but I left 3 ft. to 4 ft. between my bushes, which has resulted in a constant parade of bloom without the disease problems that can come with overcrowding. English roses should be planted just as you would any other rose—with the bud union resting just above the soil in warmer areas, and about 2 in. or 3 in. below the soil where winters are severe.

Geography also plays a role in determining how to prune English roses. I've heard from folks in California who must give 'Gertrude Jekyll' quite a harsh haircut to keep her from taking over everything in her path. Here in USDA Hardiness Zone 7, I prune lightly during the blooming season, then take off about one-third of the year's growth in March.

ing soda and 1 tablespoon canola oil mixed well in 1 gallon of water. For insect problems, I also add 1 tablespoon insecticidal soap. This year, frequent sprays of warm, soapy water helped clear up an army of aphids. Last year, during a bad Japanese beetle attack, I used one of the new products made from an extract from the seeds of the neem tree. I sprayed my roses and all my neighbors' roses once a week for three weeks. It appears the stuff really works—only a handful of beetles met their fate under the heel of my shoe this season.

FERTILIZE, BUT LIGHTLY AT FIRST

Before planting the new garden, I had to consider the condition of my soil. First, we cleaned up the rusty nails, broken shingles, and plastic cigarette filters that had been left behind by the carpenters. Then I amended my sandy soil using a recipe I'd heard about in Florida, which called for the following items: 5 shovels peat moss, 4 shovels dehydrated cow manure, 1 cup dolomite lime, 2 cups alfalfa pellets, 2 cups cottonseed meal, 2 cups milorganite, and ½ cup Osmocote. Mixed together in a wheelbarrow, this is about the right amount for eight roses.

The neighbors find it amusing, but before I plant a rose, I mix up a concoction of goodies including banana skins and the sweepings from my haircuts that I bury about 3 in. beneath the planting hole. An old-timer once told me that when the plant roots reach the mix, they have a feast. Also, my grandmother advised me always to place a dead fish underneath a new rose bush. Whether or not these planting rituals help, my roses seem to be very happy with their diet. Just keep in mind that giving new roses too much fertilizer too soon can be deadly. Go easy on feeding until your rosebushes are well established.

EASY CARE, BUT NOT CAREFREE

Many publications, garden catalogs in particular, describe David Austin's English roses as being "carefree." These publications make it sound as if all you have to do is lay back and eat bonbons while these fabulous, fragrant roses flourish effortlessly around you. But the truth is that you will more than likely have to engage in battle with black spot, mildew, and insects from time to time.

Once a week, I try to ward off diseases with a foliar spray consisting of 1½ tablespoons bak-

Fragrance flanks the doorway, providing a welcome greeting to visitors at Lynn Hunt's shoreline cottage garden.

CHOOSE COMPLEMENTARY NEIGHBORS

Selecting the roses was easy. The hard part was deciding on the proper perennials and annuals for neighbors. Fortunately, my preferred palette of pinks, blues, silvers, whites, and lavenders helped narrow the choices. 'Foxy Hybrids' foxgloves (*Digitalis purpurea*), prairie mallows (*Sidalcea malviflora* 'Brilliant'), 'Belladonna' delphiniums (*Delphinium* cvs.), Russian sage (*Perovskia atriplicifolia*), an assortment of lavenders (*Lavandula* spp.), and speedwells (*Veronica spicata* 'Icicle' and *V.* 'Sunny Border Blue') had performed well in my first garden. I found *Verbena bonariensis*, with its 4-ft. stems topped by clusters of small, rosy-lavender flowers, made an eye-catching transition between taller roses. An edging of pink and purple alyssum helped tie all the colors together.

What was missing was something that would spread beneath the roses without competing with them. Something that was beautiful, yet required little care. Something that was unappealing to the billions of bunnies that always seem to be munching on the most expensive plants in my garden. *Artemisia* 'Powis Castle' filled the bill in every way. The silvery filigree of 'Powis Castle' has now spread like a carpet under four roses, while the taller plants come up through the lacy foliage without a problem. This was so successful that I tried southernwood (*Artemisia abrotanum*) beneath the 'Heritage' grouping with the same impressive results. I then sprinkled in some lavenders and valerian (*Centranthus ruber* 'Albus'), with its clusters of white flowers on erect stems, and voila—perfect cottage-garden harmony.

Luck became a factor when I stumbled across anise hyssop (*Agastache foeniculum*). Apparently it isn't an anise or a hyssop, but it grows to about 3 ft. tall with violet flower spikes and has a delightful licorice fragrance. *Achillea ptarmica* 'The Pearl' looks somewhat like baby's breath on steroids, but it has made a perfect underplanting for the weeping standard rose 'Sea Foam'. I'm also sold on the catmints (*Nepeta* × *faassenii* and the taller *N.* 'Six Hills Giant') as excellent companions for lavenders and any color rose.

Gap problems can be easily solved with annuals and herbs. This year, Swan River daisy (*Brachyscome iberidifolia*), spider flower (*Cleome hassleriana* 'Violet Queen'), bronze fennel (*Foeniculum vulgare* 'Purpurascens'), purple sage (*Salvia dorrii*), Mexican sage (*Salvia leucantha*), and African blue bush basil (*Ocimum basilicum* 'African Blue') filled in admirably while waiting for some of my perennials to mature.

Not long ago, my British mother-in-law visited us for the first time since our cottage was rebuilt. As she walked through the yard toward the front door, she turned and proclaimed, "What a lovely English garden!" It suddenly occurred to me that now, even David Austin himself might add an enthusiastic "Hear, hear."

"I mix up a concoction of goodies including banana skins and the sweepings from my haircuts that I bury about 3 in. beneath the planting hole."

An interwoven planting can be enjoyed from ground level or from above.

DENNIS SCHRADER

is co-owner of Landcraft Environments Ltd., and one of the foremost experts in the New York metropolitan area on tropical plants. He is the author of *Hot Plants for Cool Climates*.

Planting a
Knot
Garden

MOST PEOPLE who know my taste in garden styles would be shocked that I'm such a fan of knot gardens. After all, I spend most of my time growing and designing with large-leaved, hot-colored tropical plants. Maybe it's the formal structure of these intricately patterned gardens that grabs my attention. Or perhaps I'm taken in by the illusion of weaving they create. All I know is that I've been hooked on knot gardens for 20-some years.

I'm obviously not alone in my fascination. Ever since ancient times, knotted designs have been prominent in drawings, manuscripts, weavings, tapestries, carvings, and mosaics. The first knot gardens are believed to have been created during the Renaissance period around the mid-1400s, first in Italy and later in France and England. Throughout the 15th, 16th, and 17th centuries, Europeans refined and elaborated on knot garden motifs.

Over the subsequent centuries, the popularity of knot gardens has waxed and waned. Along with many other traditional garden styles, knot gardens are once again popular.

SITE YOUR KNOT GARDEN TO BE VIEWED FROM ABOVE

Among the factors to consider when designing a knot garden, location is critical. It's best to plant the garden where it can be viewed from above—from a porch, terrace, or upper-floor windows. The intricate design and the knots can be better appreciated from a higher vantage point.

My partner, Bill Smith, and I came up with the perfect location for our knot garden. The site had served as a parking area in front of the garage; it was convenient to the house, but somewhat unsightly. We decided to flip the garage doors to the back of the building and replace them with salvaged windows and a passage door, which disguised it as a cottage. Moving the parking area out of view, we ended up with a partially enclosed, rectangular courtyard. Then we planted a yew hedge and

Laying Out the Bed

1 Most traditional knot garden designs rely on geometric shapes. After identifying reference points for a circle or arc, sink a long nail through a washer, attach a string, and stretch it to the specific boundary to be drawn. A nail attached to the far end of the string makes a good drawing tool.

2 Highlight your pattern by marking it with sand or a light powder. The author pours lime through the neck of a plastic bottle, controlling the powder's flow with his finger.

Drawing Circles and Arcs

To draw a circle, start with a square. Measure diagonal lines between opposite corners; the center point (A) is where the lines cross. Stretch a sting from A to a midpoint between two corners of the square (B). To define the circle, rotate the string from that point.

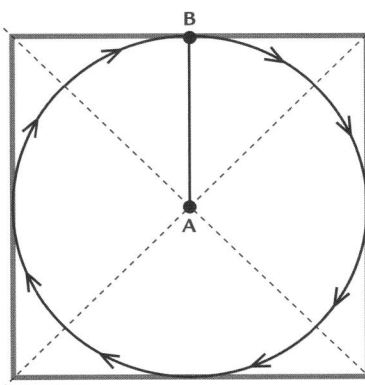

To add arcs to your circle, use any corner (C) of the square as a reference point. Attach a string at C and stretch it outward to the width of the planned arc and rotate the string to the boundaries of the square.

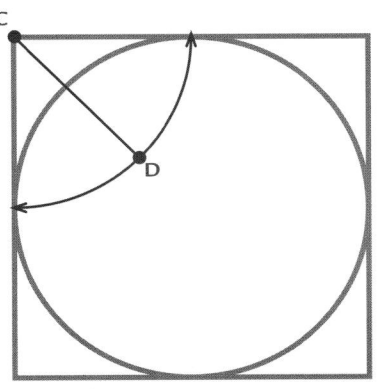

added an entrance gate to delineate the third side. The implied fourth side opens to a wide lawn. Our oval-shaped knot garden fits comfortably in this courtyard and can be viewed from our back porch, as well as from upstairs windows.

DESIGN TO SCALE ON PAPER

With the garden space defined, I could begin to design on paper. The shape and size of an area will dictate the overall design of a knot garden. Traditional shapes include squares, circles, triangles, rectangles, and diamonds. The garden's layout can be based on a classic design, such as the lover's knot, or can be a reproduction of one of the designs in the 16th-century garden book *The Gardener's Labyrinth*. The design can also be inspired by surrounding architecture, nearby garden beds, other decorative patterns, or just sheer whimsy.

Since a knot garden is tightly structured, the design must be accurately drawn to scale. Before committing to a final design, I often doodle freehand sketches. Then, using graph paper, a ruler, and a compass, I work on a ¼-in. or ½-in. scale, and draw in pencil, keeping an eraser handy. One aspect of designing a knot garden is deciding how the knots will inter-

sect. Usually one line of plants is designed to appear as if it's weaving over another.

USE SLOW-GROWING, COMPACT PLANTS

After drawing your design to scale on paper, it's time to select the type and quantity of plants. Depending on your design, you may want to use just one species of plant or a combination of three or more. Plants best suited to permanent knot gardens have a few basic characteristics. They should be slow-growing, have a compact nature, and reach an ultimate height of no more than 18 in. to 24 in. Successful knot gardens can be evergreen or deciduous, or a combination of both. (See the sidebar on p. 116 for suggestions.)

In addition to a plant's shape and growth habit, consider its leaf color and texture, cultural needs, what the plant looks like in different seasons, and whether it flowers. One style of knot garden, referred to as closed knots, includes plantings within the open spaces. These spaces can be planted with herbs, peren-

"It's best to plant the garden where it can be viewed from above."

Good Plants for Knot Gardens

The author recommends the following plants for creating knot garden hedges. An asterisk denotes plants that traditionally have been used.

SLOW-GROWING DWARF SHRUBS

Abelia (*Abelia* × *grandiflora* 'Compacta')

Azaleas (*Rhododendron* spp. and cvs.)

Barberry* (*Berberis thunbergii* 'Aurea Nana' and 'Royal Burgundy')

Blue mist shrub (*Caryopteris* × *clandonensis* 'Blue Mist')

Boxwood (*Buxus sempervirens* 'Northland' and 'Suffruticosa' and *B. microphylla* 'Wintergreen')

Cinquefoil (*Potentilla fruticosa*)

Cotoneaster* (*Cotoneaster congesta*, *C. dammeri* 'Lowfast' and 'Coral Beauty', *C. horizontalis**, *C. linearfolius*, and *C. microphyllus*)

Cypress (*Chamaecyparis obtusa* 'Nana' and 'Nana Gracilis', *C. pisifera* 'Nana Albovariegata' and 'Sungold')

Daphne (*Daphne* × *burkwoodii* and *D. cneorum*)

Deutzia (*Deutzia* 'Nikko')

Heaths (*Erica* spp. and cvs.)

Heathers (*Calluna vulgaris* cvs.)

Holly (*Ilex crenata* 'Compacta', 'Dwarf Pagoda', 'Helleri', 'Kingsville Green Cushion', 'Microphylla', and 'Northern Beauty')

Honeysuckle (*Lonicera nitida* 'Baggesen's Gold')

Juniper (*Juniperus horizontalis* 'Bar Harbor', 'Blue Horizon', 'Compacta', and 'Plumosa' and *J. procumbens* 'Nana')

Skimmia (*Skimmia japonica*)

Spirea* (*Spiraea japonica* 'Alpina', 'Crispa', 'Firelight', and 'Gold Mound')

Sweet box (*Sarcococca hookeriana*)

Willow (*Salix purpurea* 'Nana')

Wintercreeper (*Euonymus fortunei* 'Emerald Gaiety')

Yew (*Taxus cuspidata* 'Intermedia' and 'Nana')

PERENNIALS

Catmint (*Nepeta* × *faassenii*)

English ivy (*Hedera helix*)

Germander* (*Teucrium chamaedrys*)

Hyssop* (*Hyssopus officinalis*)

Lavenders* (*Lavandula* spp.)

Lavender cotton* (*Santolina chamaecyparissus*)

Lilyturf (*Liriope muscari*)

Mondo grass (*Ophiopogon planiscapus*)

Rue (*Ruta graveolens*)

Rosemary* (*Rosmarinus officinalis*)

Sages (*Salvia* spp.)

Thymes* (*Thymus* spp.)

ANNUALS

Blood leaf (*Alternanthera ficoidea*)

Blue daisy (*Felicia amelloides*)

Bush violet (*Browallia speciosa*)

Coleus (*Solenostemon scutellarioides* cvs.)

Dusty miller (*Senecio cineraria*)

Floss flower (*Ageratum houstonianum*)

Fuchsias (*Fuchsia* cvs.)

Heliotrope (*Heliotropium arborescens*)

Impatiens (*Impatiens* cvs.)

Licorice plant (*Helichrysum petiolare*)

Lobelia (*Lobelia erinus*)

Marigold (*Tagetes* cvs.)

Shrub verbena (*Lantana camara* cvs.)

Sweet alyssum (*Alyssum maritimum*)

---

nials, annuals, vegetables, spring bulbs, and other seasonal plants. The height and spread of the filler plants should not overpower the low hedges that form the knot design.

By combining plants with contrasting leaf colors, the geometric shapes and entwining knots are easily distinguished. With this in mind, I selected plants that echo some of the colors throughout our garden. The golden-yellow and deep-burgundy leaves of two barberry cultivars, *Berberis thunbergii* 'Aurea Nana' and *B. t.* 'Royal Burgundy', contrast nicely. As an evergreen component, I used a compact-growing boxwood (*Buxus microphylla* 'Wintergreen'). Finally, I planted germander (*Teucrium chamaedrys*) for its dark-green leaf surface and silver-gray underside and new growth.

I also enjoy designing seasonal knot gardens with annuals and tender perennials. Most tender plants are fast-growing, allowing them to mesh and grow together more rapidly. Since designs with tender plants are not permanent, I can be more unbridled in my configurations.

PREPARE THE SOIL AND DEFINE THE GARDEN'S PERIMETERS

Preparing the site for a knot garden is crucial to its success. First, create a blank canvas by removing existing turf and other vegetation. If necessary, amend the soil to meet the needs of the plants. In general, average, well-draining garden soil will do just fine. Excessively irrigated or overly fertile soil will result in rapid plant growth, which will increase the need for maintenance.

Before laying out the design in the soil, rake the area to make it as smooth as possible. Following your graph-paper design, define the outside perimeters of the garden. The outside edges or borders of the design help define the garden's dimensions and are best made of a permanent material, such as brick, stone, or metal.

Once the edges are defined, it's possible to locate a few key reference points for the design. I mark these locations with a large nail or a stake. I also use one of these implements to draw out the design on the soil surface.

To delineate circles and arcs, tie a string to a large washer that a nail or stake can slip into. This lets the string rotate easily around the marker. To make a straight line, locate two end points and tie a string between them as a guide to mark the line.

Most knot designs are balanced and symmetrical, so once the initial drawing process is figured out, it's just a matter of reproducing these shapes in different sections of the garden. When the entire design has been laid out on the soil, step back, take a look, and decide if any changes are necessary.

After drawing my original design on the ground, I decided it looked unbalanced. So I added part of another design I'd been toying with: a diamond shape connecting two circles. This element pulled it all together and made the knot design more complex and intriguing.

To distinguish the pattern outline from the surrounding soil, it's best to highlight it with sand, powdered lime, chalk, or sawdust. The pattern will hold up better once you start planting and the lines get a little smudged. To mark the lines, I cut the bottom out of a plastic soda bottle to create a funnel for the powder.

PLACE THE PLANTS AND DIG TRENCHES OR HOLES FOR THEM

Once the lines are all highlighted, the plants can be positioned. Pay close attention to your design at this point, making sure not to mix up the plants; otherwise, you will end up with a knot that will take quite a while to untangle.

Putting In the Plants

1 (ABOVE) Lay out all the plants. The spacing of plants depends on their size and how long you want to wait for them to merge.

2 (LEFT) Some initial pruning will help define the design. All knot gardens need periodic trimming.

3 (RIGHT) Mulch helps reduce a knot garden's maintenance. A dark-colored mulch also accentuates the garden's design.

Plants in mature knot gardens appear seamlessly woven together. Pruning defines the hedge shapes and the relationship between the knots.

To plant, start at one point of the design with one type of plant and follow along that line, digging as you go. When a line of plants intersects another, refer to the design to determine whether the plant will appear to be growing over or under its neighbor to form the knot.

Rooted cuttings are an inexpensive way to start a knot garden, but they will take longer to fill in. Established plants grown in quart-size or larger pots will give you a head start, but will also cost more. The number of plants you'll need will depend on how long you're willing to wait for your knot design to mature.

A basic rule for cuttings is to plant them 6 in. apart. When using larger plants and if you want quicker results, the plants can be positioned so they are almost touching.

When planting small plants or rooted cuttings, dig individual holes. With larger plants, it's easier to dig a trench and place the plants in it. Backfill the soil only after all the individual plants of one type are in their proper trenches or holes. Repeat the process of planting and backfilling with each type of plant. Installing the plants in stages helps you avoid mix-ups.

> *"Maintaining a knot garden is an ongoing task.
> Besides regular watering and weeding, pruning is critical."*

When all the plants are in the ground, water them in thoroughly and keep them watered until they're established. Lastly, do some initial pruning to define the fledgling hedges and accentuate the knot shapes.

KEEP AN EYE ON MAINTENANCE

Maintaining a knot garden is an ongoing task. Besides regular watering and weeding, pruning is critical. Depending on the plants used, pruning will be necessary anywhere from every few weeks to just a few times a year.

When pruning these little hedges, pay particular attention to the crossover areas of the knots. The plants that are growing over the others should be allowed to grow taller to emphasize and accentuate the illusion of interweaving.

Mulch will keep down weeds, protect and insulate the soil, and improve the garden's appearance. A dark-colored mulch like leaf mold, compost, buckwheat hulls, cocoa fiber, or fine bark chips will highlight the plants.

It's also a good idea to grow a few back-up plants elsewhere in the garden. Then, if a misguided soccer ball or an overexcited pet runs amok in the garden, it will be possible to replace afflicted plants with understudies.

Even just after our knot garden was planted, I marveled at the feeling of harmony it gave to our courtyard. Now I look forward to watching it mature.

Play with annuals to grow a seasonal knot garden. The author used burgundy and chartreuse blood leaf edged by tropical plants.

GARY KEIM

is a garden designer in Media, Pennsylvania. He has worked in both public and private sectors, including Longwood Gardens, and frequently writes for gardening publications.

Weave a Garden of Self-Sown Splendor

(INSET) In spring, foliage fills the author's front yard.

(LEFT) By summer, the view from the porch is flower-filled, with evening primroses and snow daisies undulating through the garden.

BELIEVE IT OR NOT, though I've earned my living as a gardener and horticulturist for most of my adult life, it wasn't until a few years ago that I began to plan the first garden I could call my own. My gardens had always been shared with my parents or clients. This time around, though, I had the chance to transform the forlorn front lawn of a quaint bungalow I'd just moved into.

I decided on a relaxed style for my new garden to reflect the bungalow's informality. It would also allow me to grow a variety of plants cheek-by-jowl—designing fantastic combinations and reveling in those resulting from sheer luck.

I knew it would take years for perennials to mature, so I filled in gaps with annuals and scattered the seed of self-sowing plants. It's these self-sowers that have transformed my yard into a lush, ever-changing kaleidoscope of flowers, foliage, and garden drama.

Self-sowers may be annuals, biennials, or short-lived perennials. The trait they share is an eagerness to procreate in the garden without coddling or hassle on the part of the gardener. Their seeds germinate readily from one season to the next. I always sow them directly into garden soil, whether I'm introducing a new plant or replenishing an old favorite. From there, Mother Nature takes over, and the seeds sprout and grow when garden conditions are right for them.

Annuals, and some of the perennials, bloom the first year; biennials grow foliage the first year and bloom the next spring. So, in the relatively short time frame of two years, these plants fill beds with attractive foliage and beautiful flowers. I've come to rely on them as workhorses of the garden; self-sowers are at the heart of my garden's design.

UNITY THROUGH REPETITION

Self-sowers provide strength in numbers—many seeds germinate and quickly develop into masses of bloom. Their repetitive appearance in beds unifies the garden and ties color schemes together. For example, big-flowered evening primroses (*Oenothera glazioviana*) undulate through my beds in waves, providing cohesiveness with their buttery-yellow flowers and strong, upright form. Likewise, billowing masses of tiny snow daisies (*Tanacetum niveum*) punctuate the beds at regular intervals, their cool-white flowers and sage-green foliage a wonderful contrast to larger, color-saturated blooms.

"Self-sowers provide strength in numbers— many seeds germinate and quickly develop into masses of bloom."

Some self-sowers have terrific foliage. One of my favorites, red orache (*Atriplex hortensis* var. *rubra*), has tiny seedlings emerging in early spring in a deep purple color. As the vigorous plants grow, the foliage color softens to reddish purple. Then by midsummer, at a height of 5 ft., this wonderful plant adds a vertical accent. Its insignificant flowers mature into beautiful seed stalks by autumn. I like to leave some for winter interest and find the birds like them, too.

With self-sowers, seedlings spring up where you least expect them. Not only do they fill gaps in borders, they also provide fantastic plant combinations. One self-sower that blooms early in my garden, bronze-leaved corydalis (*Corydalis ophiocarpa*), appeared last spring amid dusky, dark-purple 'Queen of Night' tulips. Its soft, maroon-tinged, yellow flowers contrasted wonderfully with the tulips. A patch of bronze fennel (*Foeniculum vulgare* 'Purpureum') also grew nearby; its purple-hued foliage provided a rich backdrop for the velvety tulip blooms.

Other self-sowers give exclamation points to the garden. In its second year, biennial clary sage (*Salvia sclarea* var. *turkestanica*) sends up stately spikes with lovely pinkish-white flowers. Similarly, spiny plume thistle (*Cirsium spinosissimum*) emerges from a tight, variegated rosette into bold stalks topped with spiny, purple blossoms. Both add drama and excitement to beds.

SOW SEEDS DIRECTLY IN THE GARDEN

I acquire the seeds of self-sowers from a variety of sources. I order some from gardening catalogs or from organizations like The Hardy Plant Society. I've also been lucky to have generous gardening friends who give me seeds. One of the great things about these plants is

(RIGHT) In late April, thin seedlings to avoid crowding existing perennials.

(BELOW) About three weeks later, thin again. Think about interesting contrasts in foliage and how much space each mature plant will need.

they usually produce more seed than one gardener could possibly want. If you time your visit well to a garden of self-sowers, its owner may gladly send you off with small packets of seed to grow in your own garden.

I like to spread seeds quite early in the year—late February to early March in my Pennsylvania (USDA Hardiness Zone 6) garden. I simply sprinkle the seeds in the area where I want to establish plants. This early sowing ensures a chilling period for seeds requiring a cool spell for germination. It's a good idea to stick a label in the soil to mark the spot, especially if the plant is new to you and your garden. After a while, you'll recognize the seedlings of your self-sowers as quickly as you recognize the seedlings of common weeds in your yard.

Once the seeds are sprinkled, I stand back and let Mother Nature take over. The seeds find their way into little niches in the earth, and rain washes them into contact with the soil. Although there are some plants I have to fuss over, these self-sowers are not among them. A completely relaxed approach has always worked for me with self-sowers.

(ABOVE) By early summer, carefully thinned plants fill in and flower. Clary sage becomes an exclamation point in the garden, and snow daisies by the hundreds form a cloudlike effect around perennials like purple spiderwort (*Tradescantia* 'Concord Grape').

A Sampler of Dazzling Self-Sowers

ANNUALS

Red orache (*Atriplex hortensis* var. *rubra***)**
Grown for its marvelous, deep-wine-colored foliage, this leafy plant provides a tremendous foil for many other flowers and leaves. Early to appear in spring, the seedlings quickly mature to reach 4 ft. to 5 ft. by mid-summer. Keep some seed stalks for late summer interest. Does not transplant well.

Thorow-wax (*Bupleurum rotundifolium***)**
Often mistaken for a euphorbia, this parsley-family member has chartreuse flowers set among light-green bracts. Plants grow 18 in. to 30 in. tall and provide color for several weeks in June and July. A good cut flower, its lively blooms combine well with all other colors. Very young plants transplant well.

Bachelor's buttons (*Centaurea cyanus***)**
This self-sower may germinate in late fall. Overwintered plants will bloom early; those that germinate in early spring will bloom through summer. Colors come in shades of blue, pink, white, and deep maroon. Dead-heading prolongs the bloom period. Great for cutting. Seedlings transplant well.

Opium poppy (*Papaver somniferum***)**
From late-winter-germinated seeds, plants grow rapidly to 3 ft. or 4 ft. Foliage is glaucous, gray-green in color. Pendant flower buds open to large, frilly flowers in June and July. Colors include red, pink, white, deep-purple, lavender, or salmon in single, semi-double, or double flower forms. Seed pods are excellent for drying. Cold temperatures enhance germination. Does not transplant well.

Bupleurum rotundifolium

Papaver somniferum

BIENNIALS

Spiny plume thistle (*Cirsium spinosissimum***)**
Extremely spiny, variegated leaves form rosettes the first season. The second year, plants shoot upward, producing reddish-purple flowers in spiky heads atop white, woolly, 2-ft. stems. After flowering, seed heads burst into fluffy clusters which attract finches. Do not grow in areas where people could step barefoot onto plants. Does not transplant well.

Bronze-leaved corydalis (*Corydalis ophiocarpa***)**
Pale yellow flowers appear in spikes in early spring, a delicate accompaniment to the olive-green, fern-like foliage which rises to 12 in. Plants bloom longer in shady conditions. Associates well with spring bulbs. Seedlings transplant well.

Corydalis ophiocarpa

Rose campion (*Lychnis coronaria***)**
Rosettes of fuzzy, gray leaves expand in their second spring to 2 ft. tall. Stems are topped by intense magenta, pale-pink, or cool-white five-petaled flowers from June through July. Deadheading will prolong flowering, but plants eventually die. Seeds require cold treatment for germination. Seedlings transplant well.

Big-flowered evening primrose (*Oenothera glazioviana***)**
Flat rosettes shoot skyward in their second spring, reaching 3 ft. to 4 ft. by July. Sweetly scented, clear yellow flowers top stems. At nightfall, they burst into bloom in front of your very eyes like time-lapse photography, attracting moths, friends, and neighbors. Seed stalks are attractive in winter. Seedlings transplant well.

Clary sage (*Salvia sclarea* var. *turkestanica*)
In the first year, large, furrowed leaves form a rosette. In the second year, plants grow to 4 ft. Strong, square stems support small flowers held in big, white-flushed, pink bracts from June through July. Leaves and stems are sticky to the touch. Mixes well with taller perennials. Seedlings transplant well.

PERENNIALS

Bronze fennel
(*Foeniculum vulgare* 'Purpureum')
Ferny, smoky-maroon foliage emerges in early spring. Wonderful accompaniment to tulips and alliums. Plants eventually reach 5 ft. to 6 ft. in height, with stems topped by golden yellow flowers in mid-summer. If plants are cut back hard when 3 ft. tall, height can be controlled and flowering delayed until late summer. This plant self-sows prolifically, so allow only a couple of stalks to ripen seed. Seedlings transplant well.

Snow daisy (*Tanacetum niveum*)
Sage-green, finely cut, fernlike leaves expand in spring to 1-ft.-wide clumps. Hundreds of white daisies form a cloudlike effect over the foliage. Combines well with many perennials. Wonderful underplanting for lilies. Seedlings transplant well.

Lychnis coronaria **and** *Tanacetum niveum*

Don't worry about seedlings appearing too early. The seeds will germinate when conditions are right for their growth. Young self-sowers are a hardy lot, and freezing temperatures won't harm them. Those seeds requiring warmer conditions to germinate will lie on the ground until the soil and air are suitable for them. Plants that germinate early get a jump on the season, growing and thriving in the cool weather and ample moisture of early spring. As the weeks slide into the spring season, temperatures moderate and the sun intensifies, and you'll notice the profound growth rate of these robust, young plants.

THIN SEEDLINGS TO GIVE THEM GROWING ROOM

Emotionally, thinning may be one of the hardest things you do in the garden, but you must remove some of your seedlings for those remaining to flourish. I like to think of this as creative "editing" in the garden. I get around to my first thinning of self-sowers in late April to early May—about the time late-season tulips are blooming. First I remove those seedlings that have come up in or near the crowns of perennials. Be warned: You may be tearing out seedlings by the handful. But, chin up, it's all for the best. Toss the unwanted seedlings on the compost pile, or pot some up to give away. With care, you can transplant seedlings just before rainfall to fill in gaps; some self-sowers, however, resent transplanting.

I like to allow about 6 in. to 8 in. of open space around plants. This way, the self-sowers have the breathing room they need, and the spacing also ensures that existing young perennials won't be smothered by fast-growing neighbors. The self-sowers that remain will thrive and grow rapidly.

Three weeks later, it's time for the second thinning. This may be even more painful than the first thinning because now you must pull out perfectly well-grown plants. My goal is to allow each self-sower the space to develop into a full-grown specimen. With this thinning I may remove seedlings I missed the first time around, or decide one plant or another needs additional space to reach its full potential. In the end, it's better to help one plant thrive than leave three or four to struggle and compete for limited resources.

A GOOD ORGANIC MULCH HELPS SELF-SOWERS THRIVE

It's common practice to apply mulch to beds in early spring as perennials are emerging. But in a garden filled with self-sowers, you'll need to modify your mulching methods. Spreading mulch in early spring is likely to smother tiny, emerging seedlings. So, I wait until after my second thinning to put down mulch. This is also about the time I add frost-tender annuals to the garden.

Any organic mulch such as shredded leaves, compost, or finely ground bark will work. Your goal is not only to protect the garden from weeds and summer dry spells, but also to ensure a friable, porous soil surface upon which seeds will fall at the end of the season. That's why it's important to mulch with an organic material that will decompose over the course of the season. Never use heavy bark chips or black plastic in a garden of self-sowers.

First year foliage, second year flowers. Spiny plume thistle forms a rosette of variegated leaves its first year, then attractive, spiny, purplish-red flowers appear the next.

> *"Don't worry about seedlings appearing too early.*
> *The seeds will germinate when conditions are*
> *right for their growth."*

I spread the mulch to a depth of 1 in. to 2 in., erring on the thin side rather than spreading it too thick. It takes a bit more finesse to deliver mulch around all your seedlings, and a little more time as well. Rather than pouring mulch around plants by the bagful, or tossing it on beds by the shovelful, you'll need to spread your mulch around self-sowers by the handful. It's a slower process, but well worth the effort.

LEAVE SOME SEED HEADS TO SELF-SOW

As the season comes to an end, don't rush to remove all the spent plants. In a garden of self-sowers, it's vital to leave some in place, allowing seeds to mature and fully ripen to provide plants for the subsequent year. If you want to keep plants in approximately the same area they're presently growing, simply knock the ripe seed heads about before pulling out spent stalks. This will scatter the seed in a random pattern, much as nature would if stalks were left standing through the winter. Rain will work the seeds into a secure niche in the ground.

It's a good idea to collect and save some extra seed at this time. Keep an eye on your plants as seedpods mature and ripen, so you'll catch the seed at the right time, hopefully before the pods burst and the seeds scatter. Give some to friends, and set aside a packet for yourself in case one of your favorites doesn't return in spring.

Remember that, once they're established, what self-sowers do best is return on their own each year. They are likely to spring up in new places from season to season, with the help of birds, the wind, and the rain. This only adds to their charm, as plant combinations happen unintentionally rather than by our own plotting. Every time I pass through my crowded walkway, I marvel at the lavish growth and the bounty of blooms, all from a handful of seed.

Site the greenhouse
with a southern
exposure, where
plants can soak up
the most winter sun.

KEVIN J. DOYLE

is a garden designer and lecturer in Dover, Massachusetts. His garden, Cairn Croft, has been featured on the Garden Conservancy Tour and *The Victory Garden.*

Design *a* Greenhouse

from the Ground Up

D URING THE COURSE of my odysseylike adventure in gardening, fellow gardeners who had a sixth sense about my garden dreams led me to a greenhouse on the grounds of an old country estate. The owners of the property were not interested in using the greenhouse themselves but were eager to see it in use. Not one to pass up a golden opportunity, I decided to move in.

I spent hours there tending my eclectic collection of plants during the frosty months. A breath of greenhouse air on cold, snowy days provided sustenance to this winter-weary gardener. Winter bloomers like camellias and orchids made their homes there, as well as specimen plants such as palms and oleander that I placed outdoors during the summer. I realized that I never wanted to be without a greenhouse and began making plans for owning my own.

It was also about this time that we were planning to remodel our home. It seemed only natural for my greenhouse to become part of this substantial renovation. It would be placed across the south-facing rear of the house, where my plants would soak up the rays of the winter sun.

A GREENHOUSE IS FOR PLANTS, A SUN SPACE IS FOR PEOPLE

The search for the perfect greenhouse lasted for a solid year, as there were many models to choose from. I sifted through and separated the greenhouse vendors from the sun-space vendors. The Oriental carpets and upholstered furniture often found in sun spaces don't hold up in the garden and won't hold up in a greenhouse. I wanted a greenhouse that was horticulturally sound, addressing plant needs before human comfort. Also, being a landscape designer by profession, I placed a lot of importance on the aesthetics of the greenhouse, inside and out. I wanted it to look like a botanical conservatory. Issues like ventilation, humidity, temperature control, and shading were equally paramount.

Finding a structure that addressed all these criteria while still being affordable became the challenge. The one I selected was a compromise between finances that dictated a modest choice and dreams that nudged me toward extravagance. Knowing that custom work tends to take on a life—and a budget—of its own, the best solution for me was to order a factory-engineered, lean-to style greenhouse.

A WELL-INSULATED STRUCTURE SAVES HEATING COSTS

I chose a 16-ft. by 30-ft. greenhouse with a thermally broken aluminum frame. This means that insulating rubber gaskets between the glass and the aluminum help block the transfer of heat from inside the greenhouse to outdoors, which saves on heating costs.

Manufacturers offer a variety of glazing types with various sun-filter treatments. I chose double-paned, clear glazing. Cloths simply draped over bamboo rods horizontally hung down the length of the greenhouse create shade quite fashionably.

For ventilation, thermostatically controlled ridge vents run the length of the roof. These skylightlike windows open to 8 in., depending on how great the need is to expel hot air. Also, awning-type windows run just above ground level on two sides of the structure to allow the inflow of cool air. These awning-type windows can be kept open in all sorts of weather. I also installed screens in the windows, doors, and ridge vents to keep out pests.

ELECTRIC FANS CIRCULATE COOL AND WARM AIR

Electric fans were installed at strategic locations to keep air circulating around the plants during the heating season. I was sure to include GFCI (ground fault circuit interrupter) receptacles in strategic locations for convenient power sources for the fans. I also added plenty of hose bibs for irrigation. For

Personalize your space. The reassuring coo of ring-necked doves in a cage complement this dreamlike interior garden setting.

Fashion a casual, welcoming look by clustering plants in pots to echo the design of an informal garden border.

> *"The mechanical aspects keep the greenhouse functioning, while the aesthetic qualities keep me functioning."*

me, the ability to walk about my plant collection, misting with a hose as opposed to a watering can, is a true joy.

Since compromising on a heating system could seriously threaten the well being of plants, I chose carefully, opting for an oil-fired, forced-hot-water greenhouse heating system separate from my residential system. The radiator is a 2-in. copper pipe with 4-in. aluminum fins that runs around the entire perimeter of the greenhouse just above floor level. This allows heat to rise on the cold, outside-facing windows and walls.

USE ARCHITECTURAL ELEMENTS TO PERSONALIZE YOUR SPACE

The mechanical aspects keep the greenhouse functioning, while the aesthetic qualities keep me functioning. To achieve a courtyard effect and a sense of enclosure and warmth, the northeast side of the greenhouse is a traditional wood frame wall with a door and two windows. The reason for this is twofold: little light

comes from that direction and the solid facade is mysterious. When approaching the greenhouse from the east, no hint of a greenhouse is given. Only when you step up to the door is the secret revealed.

The interior walls of the greenhouse are sheathed in cement stucco with a fine sand texture and a soft buff color. The stucco holds heat well, is waterproof, and creates a superlative background for plants. The flooring is bare earth topped with a 2-in.-thick layer of ⅜-in., brown pea stone. This arrangement absorbs heat by day and radiates it at night. Wetting the stone with a hose on hot, dry days is an effective way to humidify the greenhouse. The pea stone allows drainage and makes a soft, soothing crunching sound when tread upon. Also, plants can be easily grown right in the ground.

MULTIPLE LEVELS ADD DIMENSION TO AN INDOOR GARDEN

Three levels add depth and dimension to the space. The highest level is a deck with a commanding bird's-eye view of the greenhouse. Two doors—one from inside the house and one from outside the greenhouse—provide access from this deck. From there, three steps lead down to the next level, where a pool emerges from beneath the deck. Two more steps—nestled into a dry fieldstone wall spanning the length of the greenhouse—lead to the lowest level.

These awning-type windows keep out rain and snow and can be left open in any season for ventilation.

I did not install plant benches but chose instead to display the plants as if they were on a terrace or in a garden border, with some hanging from rafters and others clustered in ornamental pots.

Viewing a greenhouse from the outside in on a cold, winter night is a mystical sight. Blushes of green behind heavily frosted glass beckon you to come inside. To heighten this effect, I mounted small halogen spotlights directly to the overhead frame. These lights are controlled by dimmers and can be directed to highlight particular areas. They also give off enough light to enable thorough examination of plants for signs of insects or disease.

A pair of ring-necked doves in a cage, a few fish in the sunken pool, and a very personable, free-flying cockatiel complete the environment by adding the elements of sound and movement to the experience. The greenhouse allows me to enjoy this garden setting all winter.

CATHERINE TAYLOR

a former landscape designer, currently devotes her time to raising funds and friends for Hoyt Arboretum. She has a special interest in trees and shrubs, and has taught classes on this subject.

An Inspired Alpine Garden

Steps make for easy climbing through the author's alpine garden. Here, in "the rockery," ferns and other ground covers flourish in the company of mountain wildflowers like *Penstemon cardwellii.*

I LOVE TO WALK in the alpine wilderness of the Oregon Cascade mountains. A welcome reclusion from my sometimes hectic professional life, my hikes take me through jagged-rock ravines and into serene grassy valleys. The plant life is as varied as the terrain; many different dwarf and hardy plants grow among the rocks and through the grasses.

When we bought our new house, I decided that I would try my hand at alpine gardening. I have always loved being in the mountains and looking at all the plants that grow there, but I had never had an opportunity to experiment with alpine gardening.

Why alpine? The site and climate are ideal. An existing tumble of rocks at the steep north end of the yard seemed an obvious home for alpine plants. Our house sits on a ridge, west of downtown Portland, at an elevation of 1,200 ft. A wicked east wind that blows for days several times each winter brings temperatures in the teens or below—an exception to our mild Pacific Northwest climate. Snow cover is infrequent. The alpine heritage of most rock-garden plants would allow them to withstand our winter winds.

Also, I thought a wide range of alpine plants, with their habits and different-colored flowers, would provide year-round interest in my garden, which runs between the driveway and the front of the house. While not a traditional front yard—it is not visible from the street—I wanted the area to be attractive both from the house and to arriving visitors. And alpine plants are generally low-growing, so they would leave distant views of mountains and rivers unimpeded.

START WITH RELIABLE ROCK GARDEN PLANTS

When I started my alpine garden, a good friend, who is an experienced rock gardener, gave me a list of a dozen of the best plants for Portland gardens. I purchased my plants by mail and at local plant-society sales. Dwarf rhododendrons came from a favorite Portland nursery; dwarf conifers and small deciduous shrubs came from specialty growers nearby.

After a few years of growing various plants, reading about alpine and rock gardening, and attending rock-garden meetings and conferences, I learned that I was far from a purist. While true alpine enthusiasts gravitate toward the most varied, rare and demanding plants, my preferences lie with those that are reliable, tough and attractive all year.

"Alpine plants are generally low-growing, so they would leave distant views unimpeded."

Tiny starts of bellflowers (*Campanula* spp.), rockfoils (*Saxifraga* spp.), stone cress (*Aethionema* grandiflorum), rock cresses (*Arabis* spp.), hardy geraniums (*Geranium* spp.), speedwells (*Veronica* spp.) and sedums (*Sedum* spp.) have grown to form handsome mats and provide great displays of bloom. Western natives—rock-loving penstemons, lewisia (*Lewisia cotyledon*), and Pacific Coast irises (*Iris* spp. and cvs.)—have been star performers and require so little care that I sometimes forget to value them.

Dwarf conifers and rhododendrons have grown slowly and now provide some welcome height and variety to the rock plantings. Grasses and smaller flower bulbs have extended the season. They share the same ground because the bulbs, planted at the base of the grasses, bloom in early spring when the grasses have been cut back and then hide under the grass foliage and seed heads that persist into the winter months.

TALLER PLANTS MIMIC AN ALPINE MEADOW

In the middle of the garden, where the ground is nearly level, I wanted to grow plants that were taller—up to knee high—to give the area the feel of an alpine meadow. I chose a range of hardy perennials and ornamental grasses, and interspersed them with dwarf conifers and shrubs.

Many of the perennials grew too tall and lush during our long Oregon spring, and then fell over. Gradually, I am replacing droopy perennials with ones that grow lean, mean, and upright. I am especially eager to find perennials whose seed heads will offer fall and winter interest. Taller sedums fill this bill, as do hardy lavender cotton (*Santolina chamaecyparissus*), globe thistle (*Echinops ritro*) and threadleaf coreopsis (*Coreopsis verticillata*

Volcanic boulders create suitable planting pockets for alpine plants.

Yellow Pacific Coast irises are trouble-free and provide a bright spot of color.

By using mostly low-growing plants, the garden can be seen from the house and by arriving guests.

Dwarf rhododendrons add height and an evergreen presence in the garden.

'Zagreb'). I also added taller plants—mulleins (*Verbascum* spp.), Russian sage (*Perovskia atriplicifolia*) and *Gaura lindheimeri*—to give some variety and romance to the meadow.

EVERGREENS OFFER YEAR-ROUND INTEREST

Because this is the first part of the garden seen by people climbing out of their cars, I needed some good year-round performers. Another hiking trip to the Oregon Cascades inspired me to plant a mixture of low, woody shrubs, like heathers (*Calluna vulgaris*): the heathers

themselves, dwarf rhododendrons, bearberry (*Arctostaphylos uva-ursi*) and mountain laurel (*Kalmia latifolia*).

PLANTS SHIFT TO FAVORED SPACES

I was casual about color combinations when I began planting; I thought I would just move those that clashed. I found that many classic alpine mat-forming plants bloomed from white to pink to rose, and these I had luckily placed together in the steeper rocks. Gradually, I removed the hotter colors to the mid-

A Sampling of Alpines

Erinus alpinus

ALPINE LIVERWORT (*Erinus alpinus*)—Tiny plant with small, toothed leaves in a small tuft, and purplish rose flowers in spring. Happiest in rock crevices. Will self-sow in a favorable environment. Zone 4.

BASKET OF GOLD (*Aurinia saxatilis*)—Sulfur-yellow flowers in early spring cover silvery green foliage. Easy and reliable. Zone 3.

DWARF NORWAY SPRUCE (*Picea abies* 'Little Gem')—Dwarf conifer with lime-green new foliage and a handsome texture year-round. Zone 3 (-40°F).

EVERGREEN CANDYTUFT (*Iberis sempervirens*)—Great show of white flowers in spring. Evergreen, long-lived mats of foliage. Cut it back hard after flowering. Zone 5.

GLOBE DAISY (*Globularia cordifolia*)—Green leaves with purple or red cast. Flowers look like blue pompoms in early summer. Likes full sun. Zone 5.

Globularia cordifolia

LEWISIA (*Lewisia cotyledon*)—Long-lasting pink, white and yellow flowers. Evergreen, nearly succulent leaves. Plant in well-drained soil. Zone 6.

Lewisia cotyledon

Aubrieta deltoidea

PASQUE FLOWER (*Pulsatilla vulgaris*)—Small plant with low, vivid flowers in early spring in shades of purple, rose and white. Silvery green foliage. Increases slowly over the years to make great displays. Zone 5.

Pulsatilla vulgaris

CARDWELL'S PENSTEMON—Pink flowers cover the plant in late spring. Robust, small evergreen shrub. Zone 6.

STONE CRESS (*Aethionema* 'Warley Rose')—Evergreen, needlelike foliage and rose-pink flowers in spring; looks like a tiny conifer. Hardy to USDA Hardiness Zone 7.

PURPLE AUBRIETA (*Aubrieta deltoidea*)—Reliable rock-garden carpet, with sheets of purple, rosy red and white in spring. Best where roots are protected by rocks. Zone 5.

ROCK CRESS (*Arabis caucasica*)—Makes a small clump of evergreen leaves and white flowers in spring. Inconspicuous but impeccable. Zone 4.

SEA THRIFT (*Armeria maritima*)—Leaves make a grassy hummock. Rounded pink flowers in late spring. Some continue flowering through summer. Zone 3.

SNOW-IN-SUMMER (*Cerastium tomentosum*)—Among the easiest of rockery plants, sporting in late spring a snowbank of white flowers with evergreen silvery foliage. Zone 3.

SUN ROSE (*Helianthemum nummularium*)—Hardy, reliable low, evergreen foliage. Blooms in many colors: white, pink, yellow and apricot. Trim back to a compact, bushy form. Zone 6.

dle area of the garden, grouping them with silvery-leaved plants. The taller perennials that have been successful in the alpine meadow have blooms of yellow, blue, or purple, and I let this be the organizing color scheme. The heathers and rhododendrons have a wide range of bloom colors, but the cast of the evergreen foliage is often tinged with reds or browns; to these areas I added brown and silvery grasses.

Some of the delicate alpines began their garden tenure carefully placed in soil pockets but have gradually relocated to adjacent cracks and crevices. Others, like alpine lady's mantle (*Alche-milla alpina*) and the blue-flowering navelwort (*Omphalodes cappadocica*), have colonized in shady spots. Bronze sedge (*Carex aenea*) and silvery leaved pussytoes (*Antennaria dioica*) have jumped clear across the garden; some small cinquefoils (*Potentilla* spp.) and sea thrifts (*Armeria maritima*) have moved only short distances but, curiously, always downhill.

> *"Some small cinquefoils and sea thrifts have moved only short distances but, curiously, always downhill."*

LESSONS LEARNED AND RELEARNED

This garden has been a source of pleasure and learning. Over the past six years, I have tried more than 150 plant varieties, and about two-thirds still grow in the garden, although not necessarily where first placed.

The garden has also taught me to be a better student of nature. I am always reminded that the rational gardener is never really in charge—rather, irrational nature and the impulses of the heart rule in the garden.

Changing seasons, changing colors. In late summer, *Sedum* 'Autumn Joy' is surrounded by a sea of blue catmint (*Nepeta* × *faassenii* 'Blue Wonder') and Russian sage (*Perovskia atriplicifolia*). As fall approaches, the blue flowers subside. The sedum turns a deep rose amid fountain grass (*Pennisetum alopecuroides*) and a low mat of silvery lamb's ears (*Stachys byzantina* 'Silver Carpet').

Designing
Water
Gardens

RUDY PERKINS

was the gardener, researcher, and associate producer for public television's weekly program *The Victory Garden*. He is now an attorney specializing in environmental and land use laws.

Ease transitions. A water garden looks more natural when the edge between it and the surrounding landscape is hidden. One method for hiding the edge is to extend a deck over the water.

A LBERT EINSTEIN characterized our age as one of "perfection of means, but confusion of goals." This confusion applies no less to gardeners than to the world at large. We rush off to build our gardens without first clarifying what we want to accomplish.

The first step in successfully designing a water garden is simply to decide what you want from it. These overall goals will then shape your design. Do you want to create a restful sitting area beside a tranquil pond? Do you want to shape a liquid mirror to reflect your garden? Perhaps you need a setting for fish or water lilies. Is attracting wildlife your goal? Maybe you just want bring a little piece of nature into your own backyard.

As one of the staff members who waded through more than a thousand entries in a water-garden design contest sponsored by public television's weekly program *The Victory Garden*, I saw firsthand what makes a pleasing

EASE TRANSITIONS, OBSCURE BOUNDARIES

Most gardeners hope to duplicate a little piece of nature with their water gardens—a small mountain stream or a pond, perhaps. But most of our yards are extremely man-made in appearance, with rectangular grids of closely cropped grass and sudden walls of fencing along straight property perimeters. Yet many water features are naturalistic and informal in their style, and without careful attention to the transition from the artificial zones of the yard to the naturalistic, curving lines of the water feature, a water garden can look uncomfortably inappropriate.

The best water gardens ease transitions and obscure boundaries. A neighbor's fence can be hidden by a hemlock hedge or even a row of bamboo, for example. A waterfall can be tucked under the arching branches of a Japanese maple so that its source, though artificial, appears to be a natural stream emerging from the woods.

One effective method for obscuring the edges of a water garden is to extend a deck over one side of it. If you don't see the entire pond, the mind assumes that the water continues under the whole deck, and perhaps beyond, psychologically expanding its size. Simple decking now takes on the feel of a bridge or dock, creating a vantage point and living area from which to enjoy the water garden close-up.

BUILD A BRIDGE TO SOMEWHERE

A bridge is a natural addition to a water feature, yet it is frequently one of the most unnatural-looking elements in water gardens. To look as though it belongs, a bridge must have a reason to exist. A bridge's reason for being is to go somewhere; merely connecting two disparate bits of lawn isn't enough.

Obscure boundaries. The boundaries of this water garden and a perennial garden beyond are hidden by a graceful screen of bamboo.

design. The successful water-garden designs I observed were the product of clear goals and six basic design practices:

- fashioning a smooth transition from the landscape to the water garden,

- finding a natural position for bridges,

- deciding early in the process whether to build in a naturalistic or formal style,

- forming the right habitat for the fish and plants desired,

- creating a shaded vantage point from which to view the water garden, and

- manipulating the water to produce reflection, movement or sound.

This design problem can be solved in a number of ways. The water garden can be positioned next to a currently existing pathway—the approach to the back door, for example. Or, you can create a real destination, such as a garden pavilion, on the other side of a stream. If there is no real destination, hide the end of the path from the bridge by curving the path around a stand of trees or the corner of the house. The mind assumes that a path going "off-camera" is heading somewhere and creates a sense of destination even where one doesn't actually exist.

Choosing the right style for a bridge also can add to its effect. A log span may reinforce the wild, woodland nature of a garden. A wisteria-shrouded bridge, done in the style made famous by French Impressionist painter Claude Monet, can convey the romantic, light-filled feeling of an earlier age.

Stepping stones are the most engaging of bridges. They engage us because they require more attention when we cross a pond. They fascinate because water courses visibly between each step, not hidden beneath our feet as it would be beneath a solid bridge.

Water lilies prefer shallow ponds in sunny sites.

Stepping stones appear to float in the pond.

Keep artifice with artifice: the materials of the patio are reflected around the pond.

Formal pools highlight geometric designs and are clearly manmade.

Stone is an appropriate edging for naturalistic ponds.

This shady setting is appropriate for fish, which prefer deeper and cooler water.

Naturalistic ponds have soft curves and hidden edges.

Loose plantings add to the naturalistic look of this pond.

KEEP NATURE WITH NATURE AND ARTIFICE WITH ARTIFICE

Early on, make a clear-cut decision on whether you want a water garden that will imitate natural forms or one that will be clearly artificial, a style sometimes referred to as "formal" or "architectural." Some of the most skilled garden designers create dramatic water features by contrasting the straight lines of obviously artificial waterworks with the wild, cascading foliage of a naturalistic planting. In most cases, however, water gardens that mix naturalistic and formal elements, though sometimes charming in detail, tend to look confused in overview.

From the many examples I saw, I believe the majority of American gardeners are interested in creating naturalistic water gardens. Their most pleasing designs stuck closely to this natural approach, keeping nature with nature and leaving obvious artifice to other sections of the landscape.

Naturalistic and formal water gardens call for different approaches. Irregular curves and natural stone are typical design elements and materials used in naturalistic water gardens. Straight lines, regular curves, cut stone or concrete are common design features and building materials used in formal water gardens.

A naturalistic water garden depends not just on its stonework, but also on its plantings. Surprisingly, some gardeners take great pains to arrange stones in a natural stream course and then plant bright blocks of bedding annuals next to them, a practice bound to undermine the naturalistic effect. Nature provides a good guide to a plant palette, and using wetland plants and unhybridized species is one straightforward approach to a naturalistic planting. You can also achieve a naturalistic effect with garden cultivars, however, if you choose them carefully. Look for plants with soft colors and a small flower form, and plant them in blended plant communities instead of segregated blocks.

The intrusive appearance of a pond's shiny plastic liner is another common flaw in otherwise naturalistic water features. Letting plants cascade over the edge of a pond is one means of hiding its lining. Stones can also be used to hide the liner, but beware of encircling your pond with a single ring of stones, a practice that usually emphasizes the artificial nature of the water body. One alternative is to extend the stones out into the surrounding landscape; another is to carry the rock work well down into the water, where stones can rest on a submerged ledge. Using gravel or natural stone on adjoining paths will help make the stone at the pond margin into a natural extension of the surroundings.

Soil can also be brought over the liner and down into the water, as long as sensitive water-filtration systems are not involved. The soil is blended into pebbles and sand on the pond bottom. This soil disguises the liner and creates a habitat for marsh plants.

A formal style represents a different approach to water gardening. Ornately tiled Moorish courtyards and pool gardens, Italian cascading-water courses and the geometric basins of classical French gardens all prove that a water garden does not have to take a natural form to be restful and beautiful.

If your tastes run toward statuary fountains or sharp-edged concrete, my suggestion would be to create an obviously artificial design for your water garden. Such man-made features will not jar when the pond is also obviously

"To look as though it belongs, a bridge must have a reason to exist."

"Perhaps even more satisfying than the sight of sparkling water is its relaxing, refreshing sound."

man-made. Rectangular or straight-edged forms leave no doubt that the water feature is in no sense meant to mimic a natural pond—keeping artifice with artifice.

Formal water gardens are also more tolerant of obviously human-created plantings. Geometric bedding displays, tightly clipped hedges and formal topiary sit more comfortably next to architectural water features.

WATER LILIES NEED SUN, FISH NEED COOL SHADE

Fish and water plants add to the charm of a water garden, but they need the right conditions to thrive. Water lilies and many other aquatic plants need full sun to be at their best.

The healthiest water plants I've seen have been in ponds sited away from shade cast by overhanging trees or the walls of buildings. These water gardens get strong sunlight most of the day and aren't littered with leaves, which can cause water-filtration problems.

Relentless sun can cause problems for fish, however, especially if the pond is not deep enough to maintain cool temperatures. Fish need ponds deeper than those that are optimal for water lilies or for attracting wildlife. For water lilies, 24 in. deep or less is recommended, depending on the type of lily. To attract small birds, build sections of the pool at very shallow depths. But to keep larger fish like koi, the iridescent show fish bred in Asia from carp, you need pools of 36 in. or deeper.

The oxygen-holding capacity of water diminishes as the water heats up. Several large fish in a shallow pond on a hot day can use up the available oxygen faster than it can be replenished by oxygenating plants, waterfalls or aerators. That's why koi fanciers usually

Reflection, movement and sound. This waterfall cools and oxygenates the water for plants and wildlife while providing a visual focal point. In a formal garden such as this one, a straight overhang produces a brilliant sheet of water.

pick shaded sites for their ponds or construct some type of lath work to shade the ponds.

Mix fish and water plants with care. Koi tend to eat and dig up many aquatic plants, so if you have koi, you must screen off the part of the pond where you want to grow water plants. Goldfish, which are less aggressive, can be substituted for koi.

CREATE A SHADED VANTAGE POINT

The sight of water is cooling in the withering heat of summer, but it's most pleasant if you can appreciate it from a shady sitting area. One approach is to place the water garden near the house, framed by a picture window or by the railings of a shady porch. You won't have to make a special trip to see the water garden, so you are more likely to view it year-round, in gray weather as well as on clear blue July days. You may, in fact, appreciate it most when raindrops dimple the water, or when snow-laden branches stand in quiet contrast to the darkened mirror of water in winter. If you need to stroll to reach your pond, create a waterside viewing area, such as a gazebo, sheltered from the sun and rain.

USE WATER FOR REFLECTION, MOVEMENT OR SOUND

Some of the most beautiful images of water are due to the reflective qualities of a still pond. On the other hand, watching the churning, ever-changing sparkle of a cascade of water is as soothing and hypnotically restful as watching a fire. It's hard to have both. Your preference for plants or fish can be a determining factor—water lilies prefer still water; fish relish the oxygenating qualities of moving water.

If your pond is large, you can have a fountain or waterfall at one end and relatively still water at the other end. You can also incorpo-

rate a stream into your landscape, and by diminishing the grade, you can create a wide, tranquil reflecting pool at one end.

Perhaps even more satisfying than the sight of sparkling water is its relaxing, refreshing sound. Here naturalistic cascades seem to have a distinct advantage over artificial fountains. In fountains, where the water's motion is fairly constant and predictable, its sound is less satisfying. But in the tumble and hop of water dancing down a mountain streambed, the sound is random and ever-changing, qualities that seem, paradoxically, more restful. The richness of the sound seems directly connected to the volume of water moved—the more, the better.

With these design principles as a starting point, you can get the best insights for creating a natural style of water gardening by taking the time to study natural watercourses and ponds. Gardening is never the mere duplication of nature, though. Even in naturalistic gardens, nature is intensified, concentrated and rearranged. But by studying the natural forms of stone, water and wetland plant communities, the astute water gardener can soften or even hide completely the artifice involved in a water garden.

Water lilies need sun. Hardy water lilies (*Nymphaea* cvs.) and parrot feathers (*Myriophyllum aquaticum*), which aid in oxygenating the water, thrive in a shallow, sunny pond. A curious frog pokes his head out from under a water lily.

Welsh Mts.

Pond

drainage ditch

Larkspur

Apple Trees

Spring
Cement
drain
cellar

Barn
Garden

Central Garden

Fевr   Square

Gar   den

Sundial
Patio

Pear Trees

Barn

House

Site Plan

Driveway

Scharr

Herbs
in the
Ornamental
Garden

YVONNE ENGLAND runs England's Herb Farm in Chester County, Pennsylvania. She lectures and teaches on a variety of gardening topics and has also written articles for several gardening publications.

Herbs and flowers create a colorful quilt. White yarrow, golden lovage and red bee balm stand out against silver-leaved artemisia in the author's garden.

I ONCE THOUGHT herbs were the dried, bottled plants stored in the pantry. But later in life I learned that an herb is any plant that has ever been grown for its usefulness or its ability to delight the senses. Because many herbs are as pleasing to the eye as to the palate, they have a rightful place in ornamental gardens. Celebrated by artists and poets and biblical psalmists, herbs can bring the richness of tradition to your garden. But best of all, herbs can greatly increase your palette of colors and textures when designing an ornamental landscape.

About 20 years ago, I planted a small garden here in Honey Brook, Pennsylvania (USDA Hardiness Zone 6), which I have expanded over the past two decades. The design I worked out for my garden is composed of about 85% herbs. Trees, shrubs and colorful, flowering plants typically planted in perennial gardens make up the remain-

> *"The design I worked out for my garden is composed of about 85% herbs."*

ing 15% of the plants. I have also become a landscape designer who incorporates any number of herbs into the gardens I design for my clients.

CONCEIVING THE DESIGN

My garden's design was inspired by traditional quilt patterns. It features a neutral-colored background of silver-leaved herbs, white-flowered herbs and green, ground-hugging conifers. Displayed against this background are flowering plants that I choose simply because I find their colors beautiful.

Just as the variously colored patches of cloth in a quilt are edged with a band of cloth, my garden has borders. Two sides are anchored by buildings, and the third side is edged by a line of trees. The fourth side is framed by a glorious view of the distant, blue-hazed Welsh Mountains.

I designed my garden to be viewed from the house, which is at the highest point on the property. Because you look down on the garden from this point, you can see all of the plants and the pattern of their layout. This unusual perspective allowed me to disregard height as I arranged the plants in clumps according to their color alone. The effect is just what I'd hoped for—a garden that looks like a fluffy patchwork comforter.

Even the paths in my garden contribute to its overall design. They focus attention on beautiful details, direct a visitor's eye to views

A path directs the eye to a patch of filmy, blue-flowered larkspur, which echoes the misty blue of the mountains.

of the mountains beyond, and set off the colorful plants that grow along their edges.

The paths also serve utilitarian functions in the garden. They separate borders and provide access to them. And I solved a critical drainage problem when I laid them—I lowered my paths a few inches and used the soil that I removed from them to build up the beds. The paths now act as drainage ditches, channeling rainwater away from the beds.

Aesthetically and practically, these paths stitch together the sections of my patchwork garden into a pleasing herbal whole.

THE GARDEN LAYOUT

The first part of my garden was a 53-ft. by 80-ft. vegetable plot. I separated it into four sections with two grass paths that intersect at the center, creating what I call the four-square garden.

This garden is backed by a row of conifers along the eastern border. The trees are quite tall, so I planted flowering perennials and herbs that grow shoulder high in front of them to visually bring them down to earth. I also clustered slightly shorter plants around the tall specimens and filled in spaces with low-growing plants to form a tapestry of color and texture.

Just west of the four-square garden is a series of borders that I designed around two apple and two pear trees that remained from an old orchard. First, I pruned the trees into tidy gumdrop shapes about 6 ft. tall so they wouldn't block my view of the mountains. Then I planted ribbons of low-growing and medium-sized perennials and low-growing shrubs around the trees, mingling the cool blues, bright pinks and warm yellows of their flowers with the green foliage of dwarf conifers. I added more and more clumps of these plants until I had gradually created two

Colorful Herbs

HERBS FOR BACKGROUND FOLIAGE COLOR

Green-leaved
Mint (*Mentha* spp.)—(Zone 7, many hardier)
Lemon balm (*Melissa officinalis*)—(Zones 3–7)
Yellow archangel (*Lamium galeobdolon* 'Variegatum')—(Zones 4–8)
Bishop's hat (*Epimedium* × *versicolor* 'Sulphureum')—(Zones 5–9)

Silver-leaved
Lavender cotton (*Santolina chamaecyparissus* spp.)—(Zones 6–9)
Artemisias (*Artemisia* spp.)—(Zones 5–8, many hardier)
Lambs' ears (*Stachys byzantina*)—(Zones 4–8)

HERBS VALUED FOR THEIR FLOWERS

Blue flowers
Flowering onions (*Allium schoenoprasum*)—(Zones 3–9)
Lavender (*Lavandula angustifolia* 'Hidcote')—(Zones 5–8)

Multicolored flowers
Columbine (*Aquilegia canadensis*)—(Zones 3–8)
Thymes (*Thymus* spp.)—(Zones 6–9, some hardier)
Culver's root (*Veronicastrum virginicum*)—(Zones 3–8)

Dark red flowers
Bee balm (*Monarda* 'Mahogany')—(Zones 4–9)

Yellow flowers
Angelica (*Angelica archangelica*)—(Zones 4–9)
Lady's mantle (*Alchemilla mollis*)—(Zones 4–7)
Rue (*Ruta graveolens*)—(Zones 5–9)
Yarrow (*Achillea* 'Taygetea')—(Zones 3–8)

White or near-white flowers
Colewort (*Crambe cordifolia*)—(Zones 6–9)
Hardy geranium (*Geranium macrorrhizum* 'Album')—(Zones 4–8)
Statice (*Goniolimon tataricum*)—(Zones 4–10)
Sweet woodruff (*Galium odoratum*)—(Zones 5–8)

9-ft. by 60-ft. borders and one 14-ft. by 60-ft. border.

West of the central beds is a 77-ft. long border that I designed to be seen from the barn where I have a shop and sell herbs. In this border a background of herbs with soft-colored flowers is punctuated by spikes of the brilliant red-flowered *Crocosmia* 'Lucifer'.

Choosing plants for my garden seemed simple at first, because I knew so little. But as I read about more plants and became a better gardener, my plant palette increased. Here I am, 20 years later—still creating an ever-changing patchwork of color.

(ABOVE) Pruning trees into tidy balls leaves room to underplant them with silvery-leaved artemisia, blue-flowered lavender and yellow-flowered lady's mantle. The foreground of the scene is warmed by *Achillea millefolium* 'Paprika'.

(RIGHT) Heathery-hued herbs form a living potpourri. In the foreground are clumps of white-flowered German statice, *Salvianemorosa* 'East Friesland' and *Achillea* 'Moonshine'. The far end of the border, which was flooded by a natural spring, awaits replanting.

∼ Reclaiming a Flooded Herb Bed ∼

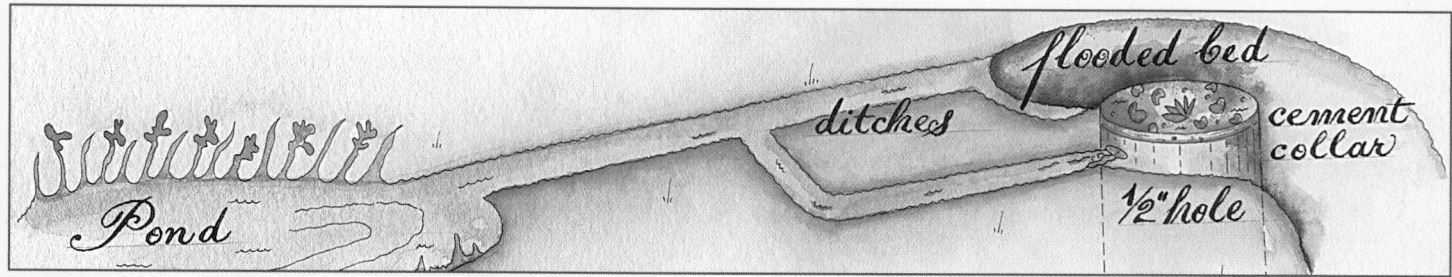

Poorly drained garden soil can mean death to many herbs. Luckily, poor drainage can be improved dramatically. Incorporating organic matter into the soil raises the beds above grade and improves friability; digging ditches creates a means to carry away excess surface water. I used both methods to reclaim a flooded herb border in my garden.

At the back of one of my borders is an area with poorly drained, compacted soil. It is part of what I call my barn border. I tried to grow herbs here, but many of them need well-drained soil. Over the years, however, I improved the drainage and friability of the soil by working in grass clippings, wood chips, aged sawdust and spoiled hay. The herbs thrived, even though the area is often wet during the winter and spring rains. Two winters ago a spring erupted at the edge of my barn border, flooding it for several months. The herbs that grew there could not survive in the soggy soil.

I had to drain away excess water from the border before I could consider planting more herbs. As soon as the soil thawed, I dug a hole where the spring emerged. Then I contained it within a 24-in.-diameter, 18-in.-tall concrete collar fitting for a water main, which I found at a roadside construction site about 15 years ago. (You could substitute a clay drain tile, of the type that are sold at home supply stores.) I drilled a ½-in. hole through one side of the buried collar, about an inch from the top, to serve as an overflow drain.

Next, I dug two shallow ditches. One begins at the overflow hole in the collar and ends at the shore of a

nearby pond, and the other runs from the edge of the border to the pond. The ditches channel water as it gurgles out of the hole from the spring and from the flooded bed to the pond. I covered the muddy ground in the border with a mulch of wood chips so that I could walk on it. By May the area had dried out enough in places to allow me to begin planting. As the surrounding lawn began to dry out, I could once again mow the grass. Now the garden looks better than ever.

To contain the rising waters of a spring, the author sunk a concrete collar into the ground, then beautified the spring with water lilies.

Thriving in the runoff of a drainage ditch, blue-flowered pickerel weed grows at pond's edge.

(TOP) Prairie gardens can be an attractive alternative to large expanses of lawn. This Minneapolis backyard has been transformed with native plantings into a haven for butterflies and birds.

C. COLSTON BURRELL

is the author of *Perennials for Today's Gardens* and *A Gardener's Encyclopedia of Wildflowers*. He recently traded in his prairie for a meadow and woodland in Virginia.

Plant a Prairie Garden

(BOTTOM) Open prairies once covered most of the Midwest and Great Plains. This tall-grass prairie in Wisconsin is home to many colorful wild-flowers. Here, the purple spikes of prairie blazing star (*Liatris pycnostachya*) stand out in a sea of oxeye (*Heliopsis helianthoides*).

NATIVE PRAIRIES once formed a verdant carpet across the Midwest and Great Plains, offering unobstructed views for miles. Now, less than a tenth of 1 percent of that once-vast sea of grass and flowers remains.

The first prairie gardens were large-scale restorations in nature centers and public gardens. In recent years, many gardeners have chosen to design and plant prairies as intentional gardens. Living in Minnesota for 12 years, I created prairie gardens for all types of sites, from small city lots to large open areas.

A prairie garden offers many advantages. It can renew our connection to the natural landscape and bring us into daily contact with the cooing of a quail, the bubbling of a bobolink, and the bright sails of drifting butterflies. Although a prairie garden can take a few years to become established, it offers a low-maintenance alternative to traditional gardens. Prairie plants are both beautiful and resilient. Many of them, such as blazing star (*Liatris spicata*) and coneflower (*Echinacea purpurea*), have become mainstays in perennial borders.

A PRAIRIE GARDEN IS A SELF-SUFFICIENT ECOSYSTEM

Because it's filled with colorful flowering plants and elegant grasses, a prairie garden is every bit as attractive as a perennial border. Planting a prairie is much like creating a perennial garden. But, since you're developing an ecosystem, an established prairie garden becomes more self-sufficient. Best of all, even small prairie gardens attract butterflies, songbirds, and other wildlife.

Ideally, prairies should be planted with locally native plants. As with any garden, the plants must be carefully chosen to match the growing conditions of the site.

PRAIRIES VARY IN THEIR SOIL AND MOISTURE PATTERNS

There's not just one kind of prairie, but rather a continuum of types, which support different plants. They range from the moist, tall-grass prairies of Ohio and Indiana to the short-grass prairies in the rain shadow of the Rocky Mountains. Ecologists classify prairies into three broad categories based on soil and moisture patterns. There are xeric, or dry, prairies; mesic, or moist, prairies; and hydric, or wet, prairies. In general, dry prairies are at the highest elevations and on gravely or sandy soils. Moist prairies occur at intermediate elevations on loamy soils composed of silt and clay. Wet prairies are often covered with water in winter and spring, and have either heavy clay or highly organic soils called peat.

Prairies are dominated by herbaceous wildflowers, also called forbs, and by grasses. The word "prairie" comes from the French word for meadow, but prairies, unlike meadows, are stable ecosystems. In contrast, today's meadows are transitional ecosystems created primarily where forest was cleared for agriculture and then crop land was allowed to lie fallow. Common in the eastern United States, these old-field meadows consist of both native and nonnative, naturalized grasses and wildflowers, such as Kentucky blue grass (*Poa pratensis*) and Queen Anne's lace (*Daucus carota*). Over time, such meadows usually revert to woodlands.

The Midwest and Great Plains regions were once dominated by prairies, due to their specific climate and conditions. High summer heat, persistent winds, and low precipitation mean that during the growing season, more moisture is lost through plant foliage than is accumulated in the soil from precipitation. This makes it difficult for most trees to thrive. Grasses and wildflowers flourish because their roots probe deeply for moisture. Since most of the growth of prairie plants takes place underground, these plants were protected from the periodic fires that once swept the region.

SUCCESSFUL PRAIRIE DESIGNS ARE WELL PLANNED

For a prairie to be successful in a residential neighborhood, it should be designed like a traditional garden, with a cohesive layout and planting scheme. The design must indicate that it's an intentional, albeit nontraditional, garden.

In cities and suburbs, where well-maintained turf, trimmed shrubs, and blooming flowers are considered signs of good citizenship, it's wise to honor these conventions, as well as any local lawn-and-garden ordinances. Design elements can include turf borders or mowing strips that set the prairie garden back from property lines, especially in the front and on sides viewed or shared by neighbors.

Although grasses form the backdrop and support for wildflowers, a prairie garden should have a high ratio of flowers and a succession of bloom to keep it attractive all season. In the front yard, it's best to include only plants under 3 feet tall, such as butterfly weed (*Asclepias tuberosa*) and prairie phlox (*Phlox pilosa*). Use taller plants in the rear of a bed as a backdrop.

The size of a prairie garden will also influence its design and planting. Small gardens can be designed like perennial beds, and are usually planted with small starter plants. Larger gardens are usually planted with seeds, and the plants grow in more natural patterns.

Choose Prairie Plants to Suit Your Soil

PLANTS FOR DRY SOIL

Wildflowers
Antennaria neglecta (pussy toes)
Artemisia ludoviciana (prairie sage)
Asclepias tuberosa (butterfly weed)
Aster oolentangiensis (sky blue aster)
Baptisia bracteata (creamy wild indigo)
Echinacea angustifolia (narrow purple coneflower)
Geum triflorum (prairie smoke)
Heuchera richardsonii (alumroot)
Liatris aspera (rough blazing star)
Liatris punctata (dotted blazing star)
Penstemon gracilis (slender penstemon)
Pulsatilla patens (pasque flower)
Sisyrinchium campestre (blue-eyed grass)
Solidago nemoralis (gray goldenrod)
Solidago speciosa (showy goldenrod)
Tradescantia ohiensis (spiderwort)

Grasses
Bouteloua curtipendula (side oats grama)
Schizachyrium scoparium (little bluestem)
Sporobolis heterolepis (prairie dropseed)
Stipa spartea (porcupine grass)

PLANTS FOR MOIST SOIL

Wildflowers
Aster laevis (smooth aster)
Baptisia alba (white wild indigo)
Dalea purpurea (purple prairie clover)
Echinacea pallida (pale purple coneflower)
Eryngium yuccifolium (rattlesnake master)
Euphorbia corollata (flowering spurge)
Heliopsis helianthoides (oxeye)
Liatris pycnostachya (prairie blazing star)
Monarda fistulosa (wild bergamot)
Phlox pilosa (prairie phlox)
Pycnanthemum virginianum (mountain mint)
Rudbeckia hirta and *R. subtomentosa* (black-eyed Susan)
Silphium laciniatum (compass plant)
Solidago rigida (stiff goldenrod)
Zizia aptera (golden Alexander)

Grasses
Andropogon gerardii (big bluestem)
Schizachyrium scoparium (little bluestem)
Sorghastrum nutans (Indian grass)
Sporobolis heterolepis (prairie dropseed)

PLANTS FOR WET SOIL

Wildflowers
Anemone canadensis (Canada May flower)
Asclepias incarnata (swamp milkweed)
Aster novae-angliae (New England aster)
Carex crinita (fringed sedge)
Chelone glabra (white turtlehead)
Eupatorium maculatum (spotted Joe Pye weed)
Filipendula rubra (queen of the prairie)
Gentiana andrewsii (bottle gentian)
Helianthus maximiliani (Maximillian sunflower)
Iris versicolor (blue flag iris)
Liatris pycnostachya (prairie blazing star)
Lobelia siphilitica (great blue lobelia)
Silphium terebinthinaceum (prairie dock)
Verbena hastata (blue vervain)
Vernonia gigantea (tall ironweed)
Veronicastrum virginicum (Culver's root)
Zigadenus elegans (death camass)
Zizia aptera (heartleaf golden Alexander)

Grasses
Calamagrostis canadensis (Canada bluejoint)
Panicum virgatum (switch grass)
Spartina pectinata (prairie cordgrass)

Tradescantia ohiensis

Phlox pilosa

Asclepias incarnata

It's essential to create a plant list based on soil type, soil depth, and available moisture. To function as an ecosystem, a prairie garden must mimic the diversity of species found in native prairies. A prairie may have as many as 300 species but is usually dominated by three to four grasses and about 20 wildflowers. To approximate this diversity, your plant list or seed mix should have at least 25 to 30 reliable species of wildflowers and grasses. On a limited budget, start with a small area and expand it later, rather than using fewer species.

The proportion of grasses to wildflowers in a native prairie varies, but the average is 80 to 90 percent grasses to 10 to 20 percent wildflowers. The mix you choose is a matter of personal preference. Small-scale gardens are usually planted with a higher proportion of flowers. I often plant 50 percent grasses and 50 percent wildflowers. This makes a showy garden, but with enough grasses to make it feel like a prairie rather than a traditional perennial bed. Small gardens may be nearly all flowers, with a few grasses for accent. The more flowers there are, the less wild the garden will appear.

To keep a prairie garden visually exciting throughout the growing season, I pay careful attention to flowering sequences. The more different wildflowers there are, the greater the likelihood of having something in bloom all season.

It pays to be picky about the source of plants and seed used for prairie gardens. The genetic makeup of certain prairie plants influences their ability to survive in a particular location. Although there's little conclusive research on most species, I recommend taking a conservative approach. I try to order prairie plants from nurseries within a 50- to 250-mile radius of where I live. If this isn't possible, order as close to home as you can.

PREPARE YOUR SITE WITH CARE

Thorough site preparation is critical to the success of prairie gardens. To eliminate competition for water, nutrients, and space, all existing weeds and sod must be removed before planting. This can be the biggest challenge in starting a prairie garden, so consider carefully how you want to approach this task.

You can get rid of turf either manually or with herbicide. Sod stripping is great exercise, but a lot of work. It's practical only for small gardens. The disadvantage of cutting sod is that you lose your topsoil with the turf roots. You can also smother grass and weeds with newspaper or black plastic, but it takes a full growing season to be effective.

For easier removal of turf, I spray the entire area with a contact glyphosate herbicide like Roundup. A light application according to label directions is an efficient way to kill most lawn grasses. Stubborn perennial weeds may require several applications or removal by hand. If you're planting seedlings, the site is ready after weeds are eliminated. For seeded areas, till the site to prepare for planting. After the soil is sufficiently loosened, rake it to break up the large clods and smooth out the seed bed. Additional herbicide or light tilling may be required to control weeds that resprout.

Small prairies can be planted with starter plants, either as seedlings, called plugs, or as bare-root transplants. I use mostly plugs, especially for the wildflowers, and I sometimes overseed the planting with grasses. I usually plant one seedling per square foot. The advantage of seedlings is that they grow fast and may even bloom the first year. They can be planted anytime throughout the growing season. Bare-root transplants can be planted in spring or fall before the soil freezes. Mulch helps to keep the soil moist and weed-free and can prevent fall-planted seedlings or transplants from frost heaving.

On the scale of a half-acre or more, seeding is the least expensive alternative. When choosing a seed mix, include as many species as you can, since it's often difficult to add plants once the garden is established. The popular meadow-in-a-can products are not a viable option. Many of these mass-market products are composed of nonnative, even invasive, species.

The best times to seed are between April and June and from mid-September to freeze-up. The ideal time for your region will vary according to temperature and rainfall patterns. In spring, the moisture is high and temperatures are cool, giving seedlings a chance to get established before summer heat or drought. Fall seeding provides a natural cold treatment that can help spur germination. Small seeding projects can be planted by hand broadcasting or with a fertilizer spreader. Rake in broadcast seed. After seeding, mulch with clean, weed-free straw to a depth of 2 in. Water seeded areas and seedlings regularly until they become established.

EARLY MAINTENANCE HELPS TO ENSURE SUCCESSFUL PRAIRIES

Prairie gardens must be diligently maintained for the first several years, after which they require less attention.

Even established prairie gardens require hand weeding and, if possible, periodic mowing. Pull familiar weeds and leave those you don't know. Since seeded prairies take several years to mature, you can mow weeds the first year or two without harming the wildflowers and grasses. Set the mower blade high to cut back the weeds without removing the growing point of desirable plants. In the third year and beyond, the grasses and forbs will begin to outcompete or shade the weeds, cutting down on maintenance.

Mature prairie plants are usually left standing at the end of the growing season for winter interest and to provide food and habitat for wildlife. Mow in early spring to make way for the new growth. If you can get a permit to burn your prairie, which will renew it, do so in the third or fourth year and on a similar cycle thereafter. By then, your prairie garden will have taken on a life of its own.

Paths help to establish prairies as intentional gardens. Walkways can be made from permanent materials such as gravel or mulch, or simply by keeping part of a prairie mowed.

RICHARD McPHERSON

is a landscape architect
with more than 16 years
of experience designing
residential gardens. He
is also a landscape
instructor for the
University of California
Extension Service.

Grasses
Grace a
Garden

Ornamental grasses
are the main attraction
in this dry-climate
garden. Their billowing
form and striking flow-
ers enliven the garden
in every season.

WHEN I FIRST placed one gallon
pots containing what appeared to
be lifeless tufts of plants around
my client's property in Saratoga,
California, they gazed at me in a sort
of blank bewilderment. "Just wait," I said. I could see the
future. Indeed, these small sprigs soon exploded into giant,
grassy life forms with a fascinating array of foliage and
flowers. Their dramatic development, coupled with their
soft, billowy textures, was awe inspiring.

Over the past six years, this once-bare, one-acre lot has
been transformed into a rugged, natural strolling garden.
It has provided the perfect setting for more than 30 varieties of ornamental grasses, along with an array of flowering perennials. Grasses were used extensively for their dry
landscape ambiance, ability to quickly cover large areas,
and ease of maintenance.

Select Grasses Based on Their Role in the Landscape

Most ornamental grasses can be used in any number of ways. Here are a few of the author's top recommendations for designing with grasses.

ACCENT PLANTINGS

'Cabaret' Japanese silver grass (*Miscanthus sinensis* 'Cabaret')
Drooping sedge (*Carex pendula*)
Dwarf pampas grass (*Cortaderia selloana* 'Pumila')
Evergreen silver grass (*Miscanthus transmorrisonensis*)
Feather reed grass (*Calamagrostis* × *acutiflora* 'Stricta')
Giant Chinese silver grass (*Miscanthus floridulus*)
Giant feather grass (*Stipa gigantea*)
'Gold Band' pampas grass (*Cortaderia selloana* 'Gold Band', male variety)
Mexican feather grass (*Stipa tenuissima*)*
Mosquito grass (*Bouteloua gracilis*)
'Overdam' reed grass (*Calamagrostis* × *acutiflora* 'Overdam')

EROSION CONTROL

Buffalo grass (*Buchloe dactyloides*)
Deer grass (*Muhlenbergia rigens*)
Mexican feather grass (*Stipa tenuissima*)*

LAWN SUBSTITUTES

Foothill sedge (*Carex tumulicola*)
Buffalo grass (*Buchloe dactyloides*)
Mosquito grass (*Bouteloua gracilis*)

MASS PLANTINGS

Foothill sedge (*Carex tumulicola*)
California black-flowering sedge (*Carex nudata*)
Deer grass (*Muhlenbergia rigens*)
Drooping sedge (*Carex pendula*)
Dwarf silver grass (*Miscanthus sinensis* 'Yaku Jima')
Evergreen silver grass (*Miscanthus transmorrisonensis*)
Feather reed grass (*Calamagrostis* × *acutiflora* 'Stricta')
Mexican feather grass (*Stipa tenuissima*)*
Mosquito grass (*Bouteloua gracilis*)
'Overdam' reed grass (*Calamagrostis* × *acutiflora* 'Overdam')
Oriental fountain grass (*Pennisetum orientale*)
Silver variegated Japanese sedge (*Carex morrowii* 'Variegata')

MEADOW

Foothill sedge (*Carex tumulicola*)
Buffalo grass (*Buchloe dactyloides*)
Idaho fescue (*Festuca idahoensis*)
Mosquito grass (*Bouteloua gracilis*)
Perennial quaking grass (*Briza media*)
Red molate fescue (*Fetuca rubra* 'Molate')

MIXED OR ALL GRASS BORDERS

Dwarf silver grass (*Miscanthus sinensis* 'Yaku Jima')
Feather reed grass (*Calamagrostis* × *acutiflora* 'Stricta')
Giant feather grass (*Stipa gigantea*)
Maiden grass (*Miscanthus sinensis* 'Gracillimus')
'Overdam' reed grass (*Calamagrostis* × *acutiflora* 'Overdam')
Oriental fountain grass (*Pennisetum orientale*)
Silver variegated Japanese sedge (*Carex morrowii* 'Variegata')

POND EDGE (MOIST SITE)

Foothill sedge (*Carex tumulicola*)
California black-flowering sedge (*Carex nudata*)
Drooping sedge (*Carex pendula*)
Dwarf pampas grass (*Cortaderia silloana* 'Pumila')
'Gold Band' pampas grass (*Cortaderia selloana* 'Gold Band', male variety)
Maiden grass (*Miscanthus sinensis* Gracillimus')
Silver variegated Japanese sedge (*Carex morrowii* 'Variegata')

SCREEN OR HEDGE

Giant Chinese silver grass (*Miscanthus floridulus*)
Maiden grass (*Miscanthus sinensis* 'Gracillimus')
Giant Chinese silver grass (*Miscanthus floridulus*)
Maiden grass (*Miscanthus sinensis* 'Gracillimus')

* Notes: Buffalo grass is the only non-clumping grass listed.
  Mexican feather grass will reseed itself.

In this case, that means cutting winter-dormant grasses to the ground in early spring and removing the flowers of evergreen grasses and sedges when they begin to look tattered. Almost all of the grasses used in this garden have a clumping growth habit and do not reseed themselves. (Spreading and reseeding grasses can be difficult to contain; use with caution.)

While designing this garden I found all manner of uses for grasses—as ground covers and lawn substitutes, in mixed borders, as focal points, and in all-grass borders. Grasses announce the changing seasons better than any other plants I know. From the fresh growth of spring and lush foliage of summer, come stunning flowers that fade to tan in the fall, and straw-colored foliage that often lasts through winter. As in any garden, I believe the key to designing with grasses is to contrast the shape, size, texture, and color of plants.

MASS ORNAMENTAL GRASSES AS GROUND COVERS

When covering large areas, grasses offer a viable alternative to lawns and traditional ground covers. Though I had only seen evergreen silver grass (*Miscanthus transmorrisonensis*) grown as a single specimen, I thought it would make a fun ground cover for a sloping area next to the house. Its bronze, spidery flowers contrast nicely with the large, bold leaves of *Gunnera manicata*, creating a striking show in the garden.

Oriental fountain grass (*Pennisetum orientale*) also makes a great ground cover. Topping out at 2½ ft., including its season-long display of soft, pinkish flowers, each clump reaches a width of 3 ft. or more. Several fountain grasses are on the market; oriental fountain grass is my favorite because of its smaller form and overall superior appearance.

Mass grasses to create eye-catching ground covers. These oriental fountain grasses flaunt soft, billowy flowers. The fine-leaved maiden grass and the broad-leaved giant Chinese silver grass provide a bold backdrop.

In areas where erosion was a problem, buffalo grass (*Buchloe dactyloides*, male variety) proved to be the solution. At only 4 in. tall, it has a ground-hugging habit that makes it especially suitable to steeper sites. It grows rapidly, covering planting areas in only a few months. An annual mowing keeps it fresh looking.

Mosquito grass, also known as blue grama (*Bouteloua gracilis*), when mowed, makes a great lawn substitute, though in this garden we let it grow to its full 12-in. height. The charm of this grass is its 10-in. flower stems that, as the name implies, have the appearance of mosquitoes hovering above the grass.

One corner of the dry pond is edged by a mound of soil covered with Mexican feather grass (*Stipa tenuissima*), which has proved to be one of the most satisfying areas in the garden. Swaying in the slightest breeze, this fine-textured grass brings a welcome coolness to this hot summer garden. An evergreen grass, it produces lush green new growth that, as the

Grasses and perennials make great companions. In a front-yard bed, 'Nippon' Japanese silver grass and oriental fountain grass mix with sea lavender, wall germander, and society garlic.

Mix grasses with different forms, textures, and colors. Oriental fountain grass (front), evergreen silver grass (left), and maiden grass (far right) create an imaginative combination.

season progresses, gradually turns to shades of tan. It can be cut back two or three times a season to produce a fresh crop of lush, feathery foliage. Its only drawback is that it reseeds profusely, and the seedlings must be pulled by hand, but this planting is so dramatic that it is worth the extra effort.

When using clumping grasses as ground covers there is always the question of spacing. I tend to spot plants so that the side growth touches in a year or two. Closer spacing supplies a quicker effect, but plants may tend to crowd their neighbors and their graceful form is lost. Since clumping grasses slowly increase their diameter over the years, there may come a time when the clump just feels too large or out-of-scale for the space. When this happens, you'll want to lift, divide, and replant your grasses.

Along one side of the property, we seeded red molate fescue (*Festuca rubra* 'Molate') and Idaho fescue (*F. idahoensis*), a common blend in this area. Standing 7 in. to 10 in. tall, these grasses create the wild look of a meadow.

ADD GRASSES TO MIXED BORDERS

For me, the fine texture of ornamental grasses is the perfect complement to perennials and roses. Perennials, in a garden of grasses, offer bright flower colors and variety in leaf shape.

> *"For me, the fine texture of ornamental grasses is the perfect complement to perennials and roses."*

In a garden bed backed by a stucco wall, I used the semi-dwarf 'Nippon' Japanese silver grass (*Miscanthus sinensis* 'Nippon') fronted by a mass of oriental fountain grass. White Meidiland roses (*Rosa* 'The Pearl') are mixed with the cool blue, lavender, and magenta flowers of sea lavender (*Limonium perezii*), wall germander (*Teucrium chamaedrys*), society garlic (*Tulbaghia violacea*), bearded iris (*Iris* cvs.), and ground morning glory (*Convolvulvus sabatius*). The effect in this hot climate is cool and welcoming.

Behind a rear patio, on a slight slope above a flagstone wall, Mexican feather grass complements Meidiland pink roses (*Rosa* 'Royal Bonica'), society garlic, sea lavender, twinspur (*Diascia barberae* 'Blackthorn Apricot'), *Stokesia laevis* 'Blue Danube', and ground morning glory. Pink, apricot, blue, and lavender were the color choices for this area.

For creating a dramatic view from the street, the two front lawn areas are ringed with the low-maintenance, pink Flower Carpet roses (*Rosa* × Flower Carpet 'Noatraum'). To the roses, I added deer grass (*Muhlenbergia rigens*), maiden grass (*Miscanthus sinensis* 'Gracillimus'), and a row of flax (*Phormium* 'Sunset').

CREATE AN ALL-GRASS BORDER

Grasses offer such variety in color, height, and texture that an all-grass border can be dramatic. Along the sunny dry-creek bed, Oriental fountain grass, maiden grass, and evergreen silver grass are towered over by the 10-ft.-tall giant Chinese silver grass (*Miscanthus floridulus*), with its wide, tropical-looking leaves. The visual effect with the contrasting textures is striking.

In a shadier part of the garden, another grass combination offers a more refined look: 'Overdam' reed grass (*Calamagrostis* × *acutiflora* 'Overdam') has cream, variegated foliage and a 3-ft. mounding habit with long-stem flowers, while foothill sedge (*Carex tumulicola*) contrasts with its dark-green, low, arching form and thin blades tipped with small flowers.

This northern California garden features more than 30 different grasses, illustrating just how much variety there is in grass shape, size, and texture.

Strolling Garden Site Plan

Since 1994, this once-bare, one-acre lot in USDA Hardiness Zone 9 has been transformed into a rugged, natural strolling garden of winding paths, dry-creek beds, and bridges, accented by a pergola, flagstone patio, water cascade, and pond.

1 Flagstone patio
2 Water cascade
3 Pond
4 Dry pond
5 Dry stream bed
6 Seating area
7 Pergola
8 Meadow
9 Bridge
10 Path
11 Front lawn
12 Mixed border
13 Grass border

UNIQUE GRASSES MAKE GOOD SPECIMEN PLANTINGS

Accent or specimen grasses were some of my favorites to utilize in this garden. Knowing that the eye would be drawn toward them, I located each where I felt it would be most appealing—coming suddenly into view as one rounded corner or ascended some steps.

My favorite accent grass is feather reed grass (*Calamagrostis* × *acutiflora* 'Stricta'), which displays a narrow, vertical appearance in its foliage and flowering habit. It grows 3 ft. or 4 ft. high, then sends up wispy flower spikes of equal height above the foliage that emerge green, but later turn straw-colored.

'Gold Band' pampas grass (*Cortederia selloana* 'Gold Band') is an elegant, variegated version of the common pampas grass. Reaching 7 ft. in height, it has green leaves striped yellow-gold. In late summer, the stately flowers are creamy white and very showy when viewed from the nearby meadow area.

"I tend to spot plants so that the side growth touches in a year or two."

Place especially striking grasses in prominent places to serve as focal points. This feather reed grass touts its tall, narrowly upright flower stalks.

My favorite variegated grass is the stunning 'Cabaret' Japanese silver grass (*Miscanthus sinensis* 'Cabaret'). A 6-ft.-tall, billowy grass with broad, ivory-colored stripes running the length of the wide, ribbon-like leaves, it is a true focal point in the garden even before its copper-colored flowers emerge in fall. Like most silver grasses, it displays a straw-colored silhouette in winter.

Giant feather grass (*Stipa gigantea*) is a specimen that I feel is most appreciated when viewed up close, so I placed one beside each of the two arching bridges. It has a low, mounding form of gray green foliage with very tall, thin flower stalks rising 4 ft. to 5 ft. above the foliage throughout the summer.

As a hopeless grass aficionado I am constantly finding spots to try out unfamiliar species, so the numbers and varieties of grasses in this garden keep growing. In fact, there are now so many varieties that it has evolved into a demonstration garden where I have been able to share my passion for grasses with other landscapers.

Just beyond the back door is a flagstone patio, water cascade, and pond. A mix of grasses, perennials, and roses soften the stone edges.

Credits

PHOTOS

Front matter

Steve Silk, © The Taunton Press, Inc.—p. ii
© Allan Mandell—p. iii
Steve Silk, © The Taunton Press, Inc.; © Allan Mandell; Steve Silk, © The Taunton Press, Inc.; © Charles Mann (top); Lee Anne White, © The Taunton Press, Inc. (bottom)—Contents (from left)
Lee Anne White, © The Taunton Press, Inc.—p. 2

Part I: Traditional Gardens

© Peter Loewer—p. 4
Delilah Smittle, © The Taunton Press, Inc.—pp. 5, 6–13
Lee Anne White, © The Taunton Press, Inc.—pp. 14, 16–21, 48, 50 (top), 51, 53, 54, 55
© J. Paul Moore—pp. 22, 24-28
Steve Silk, © The Taunton Press, Inc.—pp. 30, 33, 34, 37
© Peter Loewer—pp. 32, 35

Part II: Naturalistic Gardens

© Allan Mandell—pp. 38, 56, 58–60
Steve Silk, © The Taunton Press, Inc.—pp. 39–41, 43, 44, 47, 62 (large photo), 64
Amy Rapaport, © The Taunton Press, Inc.—p. 42
© Dean Bates—pp. 50 (bottom), 53 (bottom)
© Michael McLaughlin—pp. 62 (inset), 65
© Andy Wasowski—pp. 66–67, 69–71

Part III: Specialty Gardens

© Allan Mandell—pp. 72, 96, 97, 99–103, 134, 137–139
© Susan A. Roth—pp. 73, 119
Steve Silk, © The Taunton Press, Inc.—pp. 74, 75, 76 (left), 78–80, 83, 84, 86, 92 (top right and bottom left), 120, 123–127
© Joan Lockhart—p. 76 (right)
© David McDonald—p. 82, 87
Lee Anne White, © The Taunton Press, Inc.—pp. 88 (bottom), 104, 107–110, 128, 130–133, 160, 162–165, 167
© Charles Mann—pp. 88 (top photos), 90, 91, 92 (top left and bottom right), 93, 94
Virginia Small, © The Taunton Press, Inc.—pp. 112, 114, 117, 118 (Bridge Gardens Trust, Bridgehampton, N.Y.)
Delilah Smittle, © The Taunton Press, Inc.—pp. 140, 142–144, 146–148, 150–153
© Eric Blasco—p. 141 (author photo)
© C. Colston Burrell—p. 154 (top)
© Ken Druse—pp. 154 (bottom), 155 (bottom), 159
© David Dvorak—p. 157

ILLUSTRATIONS

Lainé Roundy—p. 9
Jodie Delohery—pp. 16, 113, 115
Vince Babak—pp. 68, 69
Jennifer Thermes—p. 77
Julia Brine—p. 85
Rodica Prato—p. 98
Katie Lee—p. 106
Grace Scharr—pp. 148, 153
Mary Ellen Didion—p. 166

Index

Note: page references in bold indicate a drawing; page references in italics indicate a photograph.